CITIZENS
ELECTIONS
PARTIES

 *Comparative Studies of Political Life*

Series Editor MARTIN O. HEISLER

CITIZENS
ELECTIONS
PARTIES

Approaches to the Comparative Study of the Processes of
Development

by STEIN ROKKAN
with Angus Campbell, Per Torsvik,
and Henry Valen

New York
David McKay Company, Inc.

Oslo
Universitetsforlaget

UNIVERSITETSFORLAGET

Distribution Offices:
Norway: Blindern, Oslo 3
United Kingdom: Cannon House, Park Farm Road, Folkestone, Kent

Published in The United States of America by
DAVID McKAY COMPANY, INC.

Distribution Office:
USA: 750 Third Avenue, New York 10017

Library of Congress Catalogue Card Number 7097493

Printed in Denmark by P. J. Schmidt A/S, Vojens

Preface

This collection of synthesizing essays and analytical reports centres on three dominant themes in my work as a sociologist and a political scientist:

– first the search for *models for the explanation of variations in processes of national political development;*

– secondly the endeavour to test such models through *comparative statistical analyses* of data on mobilization, activation and integration;

– and thirdly the emphasis on *international co-operation and co-ordination* in the advancement of comparative research across the countries and the cultures of the Western world.

These have been central themes in my work ever since I joined my friend and mentor Professor Arne Naess in the UNESCO project on "Democracy" in 1948: my work on the volume *Democracy in a World of Tensions*[1] whetted my appetite for comparative research on the development of mass politics, and my early experiences in UNESCO and such satellite organizations as the International Sociological Association and the International Social Science Council made me a lifelong enthusiast for international co-operation.

The fourteen papers offered in this collection have hitherto led a scattered existence in a variety of journals, symposia and joint publications: they have been assembled in one volume for the convenience of students and colleagues. The publication history of each of these papers is given in a footnote on the first page of the chapter. To simplify the footnote apparatus all the original bibliographies have been merged into one: references to this unified bibliography are by author and year only. This reorganization at the same time allowed me to update the references in several of the chapters. I have otherwise made no attempt at serious revision: I have deleted a number of superfluous (or erroneous) references to forthcoming publications but have otherwise not tried to bring in later data or later findings into my presentation. Most of the chapters *are* dated in this sense, but I saw no point in bringing them further up to the present

[1] Richard McKeon with the assistance of Stein Rokkan, *Democracy in a World of Tensions* (Chicago: University of Chicago Press, and Paris: UNESCO, 1951).

for this volume: any serious attempt in that direction would have produced a new volume and not a record of past endeavours.

These fourteen chapters were produced in a great variety of institutional settings and reflect a wide range of organizational experiences.

Several of the chapters grew out of my work within the Department of Social Sciences in UNESCO: I was first introduced to that environment in 1948 and I have kept up close contact ever since. I am very much indebted to Alva Myrdal, Thomas Marshall, Samy Friedman and Marie-Anne de Franz for their help and encouragement over many years.

Two Norwegian institutions gave me decisive support during my career as a political sociologist: the Institute for Social Research in Oslo and the Chr. Michelsen Institute in Bergen. Most of the analytical work for the chapters in this volume was carried out at these institutes. The Oslo Institute gave me a chance to immerse myself in the methodology of comparative survey research (Chapters 8, 9 and 10) and offered the initial base for the Norwegian programme of electoral research (Chapters 11–14). The Michelsen Institute offered generous support for a joint programme of research on elections and politics and gave me freedom to broaden the scope of my studies, both back in time and across a wider range of European political systems. My work on models of nation-building and mass mobilization was initiated at the Michelsen Institute: I am lastingly indebted to my colleagues and helpers there for years of patient encouragement.

The Norwegian programme of electoral research has generated a large number of publications:[2] only a small portion of them are reproduced in this volume. Two of the chapters growing out of this programme were originally written in collaboration with close friends: Henry Valen did much of the analysis work for Chapter 6 and Per Torsvik gathered an important share of the information for Chapter 13. The three of us have enjoyed some twelve years of close co-operation in the programme and can hardly tell any more who wrote what with whom. But these two chapters seem largely to have been given their final form by my pen.

Two American institutions have also had a decisive impact on the work reported on in these chapters. Originally trained in philosophy, I learnt my trade as a sociologist and a political scientist from the extraordinary group of survey enthusiasts at Michigan: our initial work at the Oslo Institute was largely inspired by visitors from Ann Arbor and a number of us were intensively trained, if not indoctrinated, at the Mecca of empirical research, the Survey Research Center. One of the chapters in this volume (Ch. 12) was originally co-authored by the grand old man of electoral analysis at Ann Arbor, Angus Campbell, but this, as any reader can judge, is only one of the many signs of a pervasive influence on

[2] See reports in (Stammer, 1960; Rokkan, 1966: 7).

my work. Another American institution gave me heartening support during two periods: the Center for Advanced Study at Stanford. Three of the chapters presented in this volume (Chapters 1, 3 and 12) were completed at that great institution: I am most grateful for all the help and the gentle encouragement I was given during 1959–60 and 1967.

This volume is part of a series of publications sponsored by the Committee on Political Sociology of the International Sociological Association. I have given an account on the history of this body elsewhere.[3] My work as a Secretary of this Committee gave me access to a great deal of information and opened up a wide range of contacts: much of the knowledge of European political systems reflected in these chapters grew out of the numerous encounters and exchanges organized under the Committee. I am grateful to Seymour Martin Lipset for his wise leadership and to Erik Allardt for years of effective collaboration within the Committee: without the encouragement of these two friends this volume would not have seen the light of day.

I would finally like to thank all those who helped me so efficiently in the final production of this volume: Hjørdis Storetvedt at the Michelsen Institute, Kirsti Sælen, Esther Nilsen and Mairi McNeil Lande at the Institute of Sociology at the University of Bergen, Elina Almasy at the International Social Science Council in Paris (Ch. 8), and, last but not least, my family who bore with me in spite of an excessive amount of absentmindedness and an excessive number of evenings at the desk.

[3] Stein Rokkan, "International Co-operation in Political Sociology" in E. Allardt and S. Rokkan (eds.) *Mass Politics* (New York: Free Press, 1969).

Bergen, June 1969.

Stein Rokkan

Contents

I

Nation-Building, Citizenship and Political Mobilization: Approaches and Models

ONE

The Comparative Study of
Political Participation

I. *The Emergence of Micropolitics*

However academic, the discipline of politics has not escaped the impact of changes in the conditions and the contexts of governmental decision-making. New tasks for inquiry and interpretation have come to the fore as new developments have brought about new inflows of data.

In the first phases of the growth of nation-states the emphasis was on the analysis of data produced at the upper levels of each hierarchy and at the centres of decision-making: the outputs of commands, regulations and laws from monarchs, cabinets, courts, administrative agencies, parliaments and councils, and the records of deliberations and bargains within and between such bodies as well as within parties, clubs and associations of *notables* and other prominent power-holders.

With the gradual extension of the suffrage and the growth of mass parties in the Western polities during the nineteenth and the twentieth centuries the conditions for scholarly work on politics underwent change: the entry into politics of the underprivileged strata of the national com-

Origin: Prepared at the Center for Advanced Study, Stanford, Calif. for presentation at the IPSA Conference at the University of Michigan, Sept. 1960. First published in its entirety in A. Ranney (ed.) *Essays on the Behavioral Study of Politics*. University of Illinois Press, 1962.

munities and the organization of standardized 'one citizen, one vote' elections not only set new tasks for research but called for new approaches and new techniques of study. The expansion of the representative bases of each regime and the mobilization of all accountable citizens into direct confrontation with the issues of politics brought about an extraordinary increase and diversification in the data for research: not just statistics on turnout and party support but also information on the memberships of the parties, the attendance at their meetings and demonstrations, the circulation of their newspapers and their campaign literature, the growth of support from voluntary associations, the results of canvasses and polls. These data did not easily lend themselves to treatment by the traditional methods of historiography nor could they be dealt with through the established procedures of institutional description: they could only be systematically exploited through the use of techniques of statistical analysis and they could only be meaningfully interpreted within the broader framework of the concepts and models of the generalizing sciences of society.

It took some time before the potentialities of these new bodies of data were fully realized by Western students of politics, but from the 'thirties' onwards there was unmistakable evidence of academic recognition of statistical studies of parties, popular movements and mass reactions to politics. The spectacular expansion of empirical research in the social sciences stimulated the development of new techniques and new approaches to the study of what came to be called *micropolitics:* the analysis of the individual citizens' reactions to the political events and alternatives in their communities.

Three fundamental technical and methodological developments accelerated the growth of this branch of politics: first the development of *statistical machinery* for the handling of the often overwhelming masses of individual or aggregated data; secondly, the development of probabilistic procedures for *sampling* in the handling of existing data as well as in the collection of new data; and thirdly, the establishment in one country after another *of organizations for the conduct of interview surveys* of mass reactions to politics.

II. *The Challenge of Comparative Microanalysis*

Vast bodies of data on micropolitical behaviours have been accumulated in the democracies of the West over recent decades and increasing numbers of studies have been undertaken to establish distributions, to trace trends and to account for differences in such data. The bulk of these studies have limited themselves to *one national setting:* they may have compared data for different local communities, constituencies, regions, but they have stayed within the overall structure of the national political system. Only very few studies have ventured beyond the one national setting and sought to account for consistencies and differences across several systems.

The early comparative studies of turnout and party vote hardly went beyond the collation of parallel series of aggregate figures. Herbert Tingsten was the first to see the potentialities of comparative microanalysis in the exploration of general propositions about factors in political behaviour: he was particularly concerned with the reactions of the *newest entrants into the national mass electorates, the workers and the women,* and he assembled statistics for a variety of elections and referenda in the countries of the West to test hypotheses about conditions likely to affect their actions in this new institutional setting (Tingsten, 1937).

With the growth of organized interview research in the countries of the West after World War II came a scattering of attempts at comparisons of data on voters and the background and motivation of their decisions, but only a handful of these studies went beyond the collation of independently produced tabulations to a detailed consideration of the *system contexts* of the reactions reported on in the interviews.[1] There is much to be mined from the rapidly growing archives of the private, academic and governmental survey organizations in the different countries:[2] much the same questions about socioeconomic origins and current status have been asked in extensive series of election surveys for each country and some of these surveys have gone far beyond the obvious questions about turnout and party choice and inquired into motivations for the vote, party images, exposure to party campaign efforts, interest and level of information, participation in politics and community life. The collation of comparative tables from independently designed and organized surveys will invariably prove tricky and the interpretation of findings from such 'secondary analysis' will often be fraught with hazards, but this is clearly an essential step in the development of systematic research on the dynamics of mass reactions to politics in systems of differing structure.[3] So far, we have records of only an odd dozen attempts to go further in this direction to design and carry out cross-nationally coordinated survey operations in a series of countries to ensure a basis for systematic comparisons: the most extensive programme of this kind is probably the one initiated by Gabriel Almond (Almond, 1963) [4] and carried forward by Sidney Verba (Verba, 1965 : 2). Such programmes of coordinated cross-national research are costly and confront social scientists with complex but challenging problems of design and organization: it not only becomes possible to ensure better coverage of items and variables across the countries to be compared, it also becomes possible to standardize field procedures, question sequences and response classifications, to evaluate with greater precision the comparability of the data, and, what is crucial in this line of analysis, to explore, in much more detail than through secondary analysis of independently conducted surveys, the *structural contexts of the individual reactions to politics.*

In analyses of one-nation records of elections and other consultations of the general citizenry the structural contexts of such micro-behaviours are regularly overlooked or deliberately disregarded. The electoral codes are assumed to be uniformly enforced throughout the system, the alternatives facing the citizen are taken to be roughly equivalent in all communities, and the instituted procedures for registering and aggregating his decisions are assumed to make the data comparable across the entire nation-state: the analysis, consequently, will focus on the variations in the individual reactions to these uniform sets of stimuli, not on the possible effects of variations in the local settings of the electoral decisions. Such assumptions will generally prove justifiable in analyses of citizen reactions in referenda and plebiscites within unitary nation-states, but will rarely hold for analyses of sequences of elections between parties. Even in highly centralized systems, there will be marked local differences in the range and character of the alternatives presented to the citizens on polling day, not just because of the variations in the group appeals of the party candidates but even more because of the variations in *the extent of local resistance to partisan conflict:* even highly disciplined national party organizations are not able to present the same alternatives to the citizens in all constituencies, let alone at elections at all levels of government. Such variations in the range and character of the alternatives facing the citizen, whether from one national election to another or from one level of government to another, are bound to affect in various ways not only his behaviour on successive polling days but also his basic sense of identification with one contesting party rather than another. In our ecological analysis of commune data for turnout in Norway, we have found telling evidence of the importance of variations between national and local elections: if *fewer* parties present themselves at local than at national elections in the given commune, turnout will be *low,* also at the national elections, but if the *same* range of party alternatives is presented at local as at national elections, turnout will be *average or high.* This raises intriguing problems of macro-micro analysis of the sequences of steps in the electoral decision-making process: the national party organizations set alternatives for the actual or potential leaders in each constituency, the constituency parties set alternatives for the actual or potential party officials in each unit of local administration, and only the local party organizations are in a position to ensure that the same broad alternatives of choice are put before the general citizenry in every election.[5] The behaviour of the citizen at the polls represents his decisions between institutionally set alternatives and reflects in one way or another experiences flowing from decisions among alternatives in earlier elections: even in a system of completely 'nationalized' politics, therefore, any analysis of electoral behaviour will be incomplete as long as it has not traced the effects of differences between communities and changes over time in the ranges and characteristics of the alternatives presented to the electorate.

This goes *a fortiori* for analyses within *federations of states* differing not only in their party systems but in their electoral provisions and procedures. Within the United States, V. O. Key has urged the importance of comparative community studies for an understanding of the 'macro-contexts' of individual political decisions: such studies 'might shed light on the questions of the relation between the extent and nature of citizen participation and the character of political systems in the large.' (Key, 1959: p. 638.) So far, however, the vast majority of political behaviour studies in the United States have either concentrated on single communities or dealt with samples of the entire national electorate. There are indications, however, of a trend toward increasing investments in comparative data gathering across communities differing in the formal and institutional settings of their politics as well as in their party traditions and their leadership. The controversy over methodology and theory in the study of 'community power elites' has stimulated a great deal of interest in the comparison of local political systems,[6] but the comparative studies so far undertaken have concentrated on top decision-makers and influentials rather than on the general citizenry and its reactions.[7] The most promising designs for detailed quantitative analysis of the impact of macro-forces on micro-behaviours have so far been developed within metropolitan and other large urban areas: the Rossi-Cutright (Cutright, 1958; Rossi, 1960: 1) and the Eldersveld-Katz (Katz, 1961: 2) studies of precinct and ward variations in the efficacy of party organizations. Similar explorations of the effects of structural contexts on citizen decisions at the polls have been attempted at the county and the state levels. The regional panel surveys organized by the Bureau of Applied Social Research at Columbia University were motivated by such concerns (McPhee, 1962). The Survey Research Center at the University of Michigan has endeavoured to strengthen the tie-in between studies of national cross-sections and studies of local communities and has shown, in the analysis of the nation-wide sample data for the 1956 election, that it is possible to find meaningful ways of analyzing within this research design the effects of differences in the 'macro' contexts of the electoral act. Angus Campbell and his co-workers have shown how the state-to-state differences in suffrage requirements affect the life-time frequency of turnout at elections both in the North and the South and have documented the importance of the formal rules of registration as well as of the form of the ballot for the actual voting of citizens differing in the strength of their partisanship and their concern for politics (Campbell, 1957; Campbell, 1960: Ch. 11). Warren Miller has gone further to an exploration of the effects on individual political orientations and decisions of county-to-county differences in the character of the party system (Miller, 1956) and has taken an important step toward bridging the 'micro-macro' gap through the design of a nation-wide study of the interrelations between party candidates for Congress and the citizens in their constituencies.

These developments in the design and organization of cross-community and cross-constituency studies *within* national systems cannot fail to influence the continuing efforts to advance comparative micro-analyses *across* different nations: they force us to differentiate our comparisons by levels in each system, they alert us to new sources of variations, and they add further perspective in our interpretations of similarities and differences.

With the accumulation of attempts to assemble parallel micro-tabulations across differing political systems has come an increasing concern with the underlying logic of such comparisons, with the 'grammar' of cross-national research. So far, no single scholar has ventured a frontal attack on these problems: what we find in the literature are varieties of hints and suggestions but hardly a single attempt at a systematic treatment. This goes for comparisons in most fields of the social sciences: [8] it is eminently true of comparative politics.[9] This is a challenge to all scholars concerned to advance the codification of the procedures of observation, analysis and inference in the study of politics. What I can do toward this end in this chapter is very little: I shall suggest some distinctions I have found of importance in my current work on electoral and other forms of political behaviour, I shall present a chart for the location of major variables in the comparative study of such microdata, and I shall try to formulate and discuss in historical and comparative terms three central problems in the study of citizen participation in public affairs.

III. *Paradigms and Models for Comparisons of Microdata*
Comparisons of micropolitical data lead to analyses in two distinct directions:

1) in the direction of the *structurally set restraints* on the decisions recorded – the rules of procedure and the enforcement practices, the number of alternatives and the difference between them, the methods used in aggregating the choices and determining the outcomes, the probabilities of 'pay-off' for choices for each of the given alternatives:
2) in the direction of the *personal background* of the choice between the given alternatives, the experiences and expectations, the group pressures and the individual motivations prompting the choice for one alternative rather than another.

In the language of David Easton's model of the political process (Easton, 1957; cf. Almond, 1960: pp. 12–25), the restraints on the micro-decisions constitute *outputs* from the system: they regulate and set conditions for the *feedback flow of inputs* into the system from the general territorial population. In any such system changes in the outputs will occur whenever the variations in the inputs exceed critical limits. With the rapid changes in the socio-economic bases of politics in the Western systems during the nineteenth and the early twentieth century went a series of crucial changes in the outputs of restraints on micro-decisions: political citizenship rights were extended to vast numbers of hitherto unrecognized members of the national community, the formal equality of all citizens was recognized through the institution of 'one citizen, one vote' rules, procedures were introduced to ensure the compulsory anonymity of each vote. Since the end of the First World War these basic restraints have been maintained without much change in the majority of Western systems despite marked variations in the outcomes of elections and other consultations. The rules for the aggregation of votes into mandates have proved much less stable and have been modified again and again under the impact of changing constellations of micro-decisions. The restraints on the number and the range of alternatives facing the individual citizen will, within flexible limits, vary with the results of successive consultations of the given constituency: this goes without saying for the 'pay-off' probabilities for each of the choices open to him. A party may lose so many votes at time t_1 that it will prove unable to present itself as an alternative at time t_2. Two parties may compete so hard to reach the majority point that they become indistinguishable in their appeals and their policy commitments and provoke the development of splinter movements presenting new alternatives to the citizens.[10] Changes in the alignments of socio-economic groupings behind the parties in a system may bring about greater dissensus or increasing consensus across party lines and as a result make for changes in the ranges of alternatives open to the citizenry at election time.[11]

These macro-micro interdependencies have been recognized again and again in analyses of electoral and other political behaviour data, but the implications have nowhere been spelled out in any detail in a comparative framework.

The studies we find in the literature may roughly be grouped in four classes according to the direction of the analysis:

micro-micro studies focusing on relationships between individual background characteristics, roles, cognitions and motivations on the one hand and political dispositions and decisions on the other;

macro-micro studies exploring the effects of variations and changes in the structural contexts on the rates of given political decisions and on the strength and direction of micro-micro relationships;

micro-macro studies concerned with the effects of the attitudes and decisions of the general citizenry on the policies, strategies and tactics of the parties and on the operation of the established systems of structural restraints on decision-making;

and finally, *macro-macro* studies concerned with the functions of given structural restraints in the maintenance, legitimation and stabilization of the overall political system.

A conscientious classification of all the categories of variables taken

Fig. 1. A Typology of 'Orders' of Comparisons: Micro-Comparisons of Lower Complexity

| Order | Alternatives set for citizen | | Collectivities significant for citizen | Citizen's | | Examples of propositions derived or derivable from the given order of comparison: For references to sources for examples see p. 21. |
	National level (N)	Local level (L)	(C)	Regular Roles (R)	Political Behaviour (B)	
First:					*micro*	
Second: N	macro				micro	1) Turnout rates (B) for national electorates higher in W. Europe than in the U.S.
L		macro			micro	2) Turnout rates (B) higher in systems with official registration and short ballots (N) than in systems with voluntary registration and complex ballots.
C			macro		micro	3) Turnout rates (B) for localities increase with the proportions of votes cast for dominant party (L).
R				micro	micro	4) Turnout rates (B) for localities increase with increasing socio-economic or cultural homogeneity (C).
						5) Turnout rate (B) higher for men and married citizens than for women and single citizens (R).
Third: NL	macro	macro			micro	6) Turnout rates (B) for localities increase with one party dominance (L) in PR systems (N), not in plurality systems.
NC	macro		macro		micro	7) Turnout rates (B) for localities more likely to increase with increasing socio-economic homogeneity (C) within markedly status-polarized party systems (N).
NR	macro			micro	micro	8) Educational differential in political participation (R–B) smaller the more marked the status polarization of the national party system (N).
LC		macro	macro		micro	9) Turnout rates (B) not so likely to increase with increasing socio-economic homogeneity (C) in nonpartisan local elections (L).
LR		macro		micro	micro	10) Educational differential in political participation (R–B) will be more marked the less partisan the politics of the locality (L).
CR			macro	macro	micro	11) Status differential in turnout (R–B) decreases with increasing residential segregation of workers vs. others (C).

into account in studies of each of these types would require a great deal of space. Suffice it here to point to a series of distinctions of possible *'orders of comparison'* in the exploration of micro-micro and macro-micro propositions: this is done in *Figure 1*.

This typology starts out from direct comparisons of the aggregated rates of given political behaviours within territorial units: comparisons of such familiar statistics as those for relative turnout and party strength or of such less accessible data as the proportions of dues-paying party members, of attendants at party meetings, of subscribers to party journals, of listeners to party broadcasts, of active 'opinion leaders'. These are all examples of 'dependent' variables: it is the task of comparative analysis to account for variations in such rates through breakdowns at successive levels of the political system. In the schematic typology presented here only four such levels have been distinguished:

– the level of the *roles and statuses* of the individual actor in the collectivities and the organizations he is part of;

– the level of the macro-characteristics of such *collectivities or organizations,* whether aggregated across their members or determined by their structure, their leadership or their position in the established conflict alignments in the political system;

– the structural restraints on micro-decisions at the *local level,* the level of the most immediate unit of elective government in the actor's regular environment;

– the structural restraints on micro-decisions at the *national level,* the level of the total territorial system within which the actor is a political subject.

Notes to Figure 1.
1) (Gosnell, 1930: Ch. VIII; cf. Rokkan, 1960: 2).
2) (Gosnell, 1930: pp. 185–87).
3) (Allardt, 1956: 2, pp. 30–33). The alternative proposition, that turnout will be highest in closely contested districts was documented by Gosnell (Gosnell, 1930). Tables II (Britain), V (France), VII (German *Reich*), and pp. 199–201 (U. S. A.). Tabulations for Britain indicate that the highest turnouts will be found *either* in closely contested constituencies *or* in heavily labour-dominated ones, cf. (Nicholas, 1951: p. 318).
4) (Allardt, 1956: pp. 56–59).
5) (Tingsten, 1937; Dogan, 1955: Ch. VI; Allardt, 1956: pp. 124–30).
6) (Rokkan, 1960: 5, pp. 36–37).
7) Implications of findings in (Rokkan, 1960: 2), not documented.
8) (Rokkan, 1960: 2, pp. 84–89, 93–96).
9) Not documented.
10) Not documented: derivable from (Rossi, 1960: 4, pp. 37–42).
11) This is Tingsten's 'law of the social centre of gravity', (Tingsten, 1937: pp. 170–72; Allardt, 1956: 1, pp. 55–76; Lipset, 1960: pp. 205–07).

Several further levels could no doubt be distinguished but these are the ones most likely to prove useful in comparisons across unitary nation-states: federations add further complexity to any scheme of comparison.

Only three orders of comparison are identified and exemplified in the chart: only very few comparisons so far attempted go any further, although this is logically perfectly possible.

The 'second order' comparisons most frequently found in the research literature are of the *'micro-micro'* variety: such comparisons are essentially replications of the same analytical breakdowns within a variety of localities and national systems to test the generality of differences in political behaviour between individuals in different roles. Most of Tingsten's analyses were of this order: he studied differences in turnout and 'left-right' voting by sex, age, marital status, education and occupation. His most important analyses, however, went beyond this stage: in these he concerned himself with the broader social settings most likely to bring about such 'micro-micro' relationships. He showed for several localities that the socio-economic homogeneity of the residential area affected the differences in turnout between workers and middle class citizens and, what was sociologically of even greater interest, that this curve for 'residence-sensitivity' was markedly steeper for women than for men (Tingsten, 1937: pp. 126–27; 170–72; cf. Lane, 1959). These were clearly 'third order' comparisons: localities and areas were ranked on given unit characteristics to determine the impact of the residential environment on the political behaviours of citizens differing in their role positions within the community. This type of comparison has since become a major analytical device in political sociology: the much-discussed theories about the stabilizing impact of increasing cross-class communication and the radicalizing effects of working class isolation clearly prompt continued replication of such 'third order' comparisons (Lipset, 1956: Ch. VII; Kornhauser, 1959, Ch. 12). In these comparisons, the structural restraints set by the electoral procedures and the party systems are deliberately disregarded, at least in the first rounds of analysis: the comparisons aim at the establishment *across* a variety of political systems of generalizations about political reactions in residential environments differing in their socio-cultural homogeneity. The rationale for cross-national studies of this kind is twofold: by going beyond the one nation the *number of cases* that can be tested is vastly increased and *the range of variability* in the cases is extended. The between-community variability *within* the given nation may be very small and produce only minor variations in the dependent behaviours: to get data on cases farther apart on the given collectivity variable it will then be essential to go to a number of different national settings. This, of course, goes for any group or collectivity of potential political relevance for the citizen who is part of it: families, work organizations, unions, churches, sects, voluntary associations, parties. I have myself suggested as a possible task for comparative political research the collection of data on the degree of 'status distinctiveness' of the major parties of the West and the testing of hypotheses about the effects of within-party homogeneity vs. heterogeneity on the recruitment of active participants (Rokkan,1960: 1). What is important here is perhaps not so much the establishment of invariant relationships as the identification and analysis of *deviant cases:* this may give us new cues to the historical study of particular developments and alert us to sources of variations at *higher levels* within each system. 'Third order' comparisons of the recruitment channels within different parties could in this way lead on to 'fourth order' comparisons of the local settings of these processes and to 'fifth order' comparisons of the over-all national decision-making structures and the limits they set for the parties and their active participants.

Our tentative typology of comparisons implies a 'model' of the complex processes leading to individual political decisions: the typology singles out as crucially important in the flow of influences on the given political act the *roles* the individual has in his life environments, the *collectivities* he identifies with, the *choices open to him* within his *immediate local community* and the choices open to him as a *subject of a national political system.* These have been the basic categories of variables in research on electoral statistics since the early pioneers and they are still the ones that account for the greatest number of tabulations in the literature. The development of survey research has made it possible to go much further in the differentiation of variables within each of these categories and, what is even more important, to enrich the analysis through the addition of information on other phases in the process: on the exposure to influences from the mass media and the immediate role environment, on reactions to conditions within these environments, on identifications with politically relevant collectivities, on images of ideologies, parties and alternatives for action, on the interest manifested in political affairs and the manifold forms of private or public participation in conflicts over policies and between parties. This extraordinary wealth and diversity of data cannot easily be fitted into a coherent theory of the processes at work in such differing structural contexts. In planning our programme of electoral studies in Norway we did not attempt to construct anything like a 'conceptual model' for such research, but we did find it helpful to work out in some detail a 'location chart' for the principal variables to be taken into account either in the design of the actual data gathering instruments or in the analyses and interpretations of the information assembled. In confronting our Norwegian data with evidence from studies in other countries we have found this a useful framework for the discussion of similarities and differences: it is therefore reproduced here, after some revision, as *Figure 2.*

This chart represents essentially an attempt at a codification, within the

Fig. 2. Location Chart for Variables in Election Research

Citizen's Life Cycle

State of System	External circumstances Central decision-making Cleavage bases Conflict alignments		Changes		Current state
Alternatives for Citizen	Suffrage requirements; Electoral procedures, barriers; Party organizations, differences on policy *Nationally:* Range of party choice, chances to gain mandates, power *Locally:* Non-partisan traditions		Changes		Current alternatives
Message Flows — Sources	Governmental, official; Parties, movements, organizations; Publicists, ideologues		Changes in volume content, lines of argumentation		Current campaign
Message Flows — Channels	*Mass* channels: mass media, party literature, rallies *Role* channels: local party workers, opinion leaders		Changes in channels		Current campaign
Message Flows — Exposure	*Mass:* Accessibility, nearness to urban centers. *Role:* Nearness to activists; political divisions within/between role environments		Changes in accessibility		Current campaign
Roles in Regular Environments	*Parents' Roles/Activities in:* Community Kin, friendship circles Household Work milieu Associations Church, sect	*Own entrance* Socialization, Formal education Apprenticeship	Mobility Residential Social Marital Occupational Economic Religious		*Curr. roles/ activities in:* Community Kin, friends Household Work milieu Associations Church, sect
Orientations — Identifications	*Parents' orientations to/ identifications with:* – own community, kin, ethnicity; – paternal authority; – economic conditions, prospects; – workmates, unions; – church, sect; – parties	*Own on entering adulthood* Conformity – revolt			Own current orientations/ identifications
Perceived Alternatives	*Parents' perceptions/images of:* – *Local* political alternatives, diff. in policies, leaders, support, chances to gain mandates, majority; – *National* political alternatives	*Own early perceptions/ images:* Changes in local context Changes nationally			Own current perceptions/ images
Political Behaviour — Private	*Parents' behaviours:* Interest in, knowledge of politics; Information seeking; Articulateness on issues; Commitments on issues; Party preference	*Own on entering electorate:* "Socialization" to political activity/inactivity			*Own current:* Level of private participation
Political Behaviour — Public	Open advocacy of policies; Activity in policy-influencing organizations; Party membership, subscriptions; Elections { Active campaign work / Turnout / Party vote	Recruitment to active participation First votes			Public/or- ganizational activity Curr. turnout Curr. party vote

Macro — System Dimension — Micro

Citizen's Life Cycle

limits of a two-dimensional schema, of the designs of data gathering and analysis now in use in research on elections and other forms of mass participation in politics. The 'locations of politically relevant variability' are ordered along two axes:

one '*macro-micro*' axis running from the conditions in the total political system down through the influences on the citizen in his every day roles to his actual decisions during the campaign and on polling day:

one *time* axis running from the situation in the citizen's family of origin through the changes in his environments during the formative years of early adulthood to his current situation.

In its basic structure this two-dimensional schema will be seen to be closely akin to the notion of a '*funnel of causality*' so suggestively set out by Angus Campbell and his co-workers in their discussion of strategies of research in their volume on the 1956 Presidential election (Campbell, 1960: pp. 24–32). The focus is on the terminal acts of choice at the election under study: in our chart these are located in the lower right corner, in the funnel model they are at the end of the narrowing stem. In both models *time* is a central ordering dimension: the final political act is traced back to states and events in the life history of the citizen and the system he is part of. In the Michigan model the conditions at each cross-section in time are ordered from a central core of politically relevant and personally experienced events toward a periphery of politically irrelevant events beyond the actor's ken. In the chart we used in designing our Norwegian studies, we focused on what we considered to be the analytically relevant conditions at each cross-section in time and ordered these by *levels in the political system:*

— at the first level, nearest to the terminal acts under study, the citizens' *behaviours in other political contexts,* his privately expressed concerns with public issues as well as his public participation in policy-influencing organizations or in political parties;

— at the second level, his *images and judgements of the political alternatives* open to him;

— at the third, the *orientations and attitudes* to critical issues in his regular environments and his *identifications* with collectivities engaged on one side or the other in given conflicts;

— at the fourth, his *roles and activities in his regular environments,* the collectivities he spends the bulk of his time on;

— at the fifth, his *exposure to political influences* in these environments, through majority pressure, through active opinion leaders, through the mass media;

— at the sixth, and this is the first *macro* level, the *messages, the information, the arguments and the appeals* sent to him from the organizations and the corporate units active in the contests for support within the system;

– at the seventh, the *actual alternatives* set by the system for the ordinary citizen, locally as well as nationally;

– and finally, the eighth level, the given *state of the system,* the external pressures on it, the cleavages within it and the alignments of forces among the full-time decision-makers, whether political, administrative, economic or cultural.

A chart such as this is not a substitute for a rigorous design: it simply serves as a guide to remind us of sources of variation to be taken into account, whether data on the sources can be assembled or not. What is important here is that it underscores the need to take *contexts* into account in comparing data on political behaviour, whether *within* one national system or *across* several systems.

IV. *Contrasting Contexts of Citizen Participation in Decision-making: the Electoral vs. the Traditional and the Organizational*

The lines of influence set out in our chart converge on the terminal acts of choice on election day: the choice between turning out and staying home, the choice between the *n* lists or the *n* candidates.

These acts constitute *inputs* into the process of decision-making for the territorial community but they make up only one of a great variety of categories of such inputs. Individual acts of disobedience or resistance, spontaneous demonstrations, public articulations of opinion, mass media campaigns, demands, appeals and threats from organized movements and interest groups, offers and counteroffers in bargains between corporate units, reactions and suggestions flowing back from administrative agencies: there are so many examples of inputs to be taken into account in any analysis of the processes of decision-making in the nation-state. How do the electoral inputs fit into this broader framework of articulations of demands and aggregations of pressure? [12] This is a problem of central importance in the integration of approaches to the study of political processes: important in the analysis of the functional unity of systems, and important in the study of the motivations and manifestations of individual participation in the affairs of the community and the nation.

This problem has a crucial *historical* dimension. The processes of centralization and democratization during the nineteenth and the early twentieth century brought about a more and more marked contrast between the electoral and the other channels of participation in decision-making: the seemingly irresistible trend toward the formal standardization of procedures and enforcement practices gradually set the electoral mode of aggregation distinctly apart from other modes, both from the traditional influences of locally dominant families and from the emerging influences of functionally differentiated national organizations.

In fully-fledged political democracies, electoral acts of participation will differ from other acts on three crucial counts:

first the *universality of access* – all accountable adults without severe criminal records are given the vote, however peripheral their concern for politics and public affairs, however dependent and subordinate their roles in their community or their organizations;

secondly the *equality of influence* – each vote cast counts as one anonymous unit of influence and is completely divorced from the person and the roles of the participating citizen;

and thirdly *the privacy and the 'irresponsibility' of the participant act* – the vote is given the status of a 'privileged communication' to the territorial authorities, there is no feedback to the citizen's other roles in his community and it is consequently up to each voter to decide whether or not to reveal his act and take responsibility for it in his day-to-day environment.

The history of the movement toward formal democracy in the West could appropriately be written as an analysis of the sequences of decisions that led to the adoption and enforcement of these three institutional solutions to the problem of the legitimacy of representation. What was central in this development was the growing acceptance of the concept of the *unit citizen* of the nation-state acting in abstraction from his particular roles in the organizational and institutional structure of society. It is tempting to see the development of these channels for mass participation in politics as one element in the complex series of processes that led to the growth and integration of territorially defined nation-states. The extension of political citizenship rights to all accountable adults and the equalization of all votes within a standardized system of electoral decision-making was one of several important facets of an overall process of *political mobilization* within the national territory: a process bringing about a steady increase in the proportion of the territorial population standing in direct, unmediated communication with the central authorities.[13] It is not difficult to trace this process in the history of the consolidation and integration of the nation-states of the West in the nineteenth century and there are important parallels in the current developments in the new states in Africa and Asia.[14] Essentially what we find is a process of institutional innovation leading to the imposition of formally equal obligations and the granting of formally equal rights to all accountable adults independently of differences in their established influence through roles in the kinship system, the local community or other corporate bodies. Direct taxation, military conscription and compulsory education would be major examples of formally universalized obligations to the nation-state, while equality before the courts, social security provisions and universal suffrage would be the principal examples of national citizen rights.[15] We rarely find any straight progression toward the universalization of all these obligations and all these rights: what we find is a series of temporary compromises in a complex bargaining process between major power groups in each polity.

What needs to be emphasized in this context is that this process of nation-building brought with it almost as a matter of necessity the enfranchisement of vast masses of politically inarticulate citizens and at the same time made it formally possible for them to cut off traditional allegiances to the local communities and their hierarchies of influence. Edmund Burke was probably the first to see the growth of formal equality in this perspective: he denounced the French revolution for instituting an abstract equality of citizenship in order to ensure greater centralization under the national government.

Alexis de Tocqueville went further in this analysis of the parallel movements toward national integration and universal suffrage. He saw in the growth of *démocratie* a part-process in the total mobilization of all adult subjects into direct, unmediated relationship to the nation-state: *démocratie* implied more than an extension of political citizenship rights to the bourgeoisie and the lower classes, it stood for a trend toward the disintegration of all intermediate authorities between the government and the mass of legally equal citizens. In fact for Tocqueville the levelling of all differences in legal and political status among the subjects of the régime was at the heart of the overall trend toward a centralization of territorial authority in the nation-state: the demands of the subjects for greater equality strengthened the claims of the centralized state and the central power-holders reinforced these same demands in order to undercut all interference from intermediary powers, whether feudal, local or associational. Tocqueville prophesied that this dialectical process would be accelerated through the growth of manufacturing industries and the decline of local power based on agriculture: industrialization would not only bring with it changes in the social structure and intensify the demands for equality of status, it would also create conflicts that would increase the need for regulations of local affairs by the central government.

How did these projections into the future fit the actual facts of the political developments in the Western nation-states during the hundred years that followed? Tocqueville proved remarkably prophetic at one level: at the level of the development of *formal* political institutions and regulations. The continued growth of the manufacturing industries *did* bring about increased centralization of the national decision-making systems and *did* lead to the equalization of citizenship rights and obligations: by the end of World War I practically all nations of the West had introduced universal manhood suffrage and a majority of them also extended these rights to women. What Tocqueville was less ready to see was that *this development toward formal equalization could proceed pari passu with the steady growth of a pluralist network of associations and corporate bodies:* the systems of 'one citizen, one vote' decision-making were gradually balanced off, so to speak, against systems of bargaining, consultation and representation among growing numbers of interest organizations, voluntary associations and public bodies. Tocqueville saw this coming in his description of the political and civil associations in the United States but somehow these insights did little to change his central vision of the growth of mass democracy. He did not see that the institutionalization of formal equality would not only allow, but sometimes even encourage the persistence of traditional loyalties to local notables and trusted spokesmen in guilds and associations and, what was to become even more important, set the stage for the growth of new organizations.

V. *Three Central Problems for Comparative Research on Citizen Participation*

Gabriel Almond has argued persuasively for the development of 'dualistic models' in the comparison of political systems at different stages of growth: a system may be 'modern', 'universalistic' and 'achievement-oriented' at one level and in one of its channels of decision-making, and still remain 'traditional', 'particularistic' and 'ascriptive' at other levels and in other channels of decision-making (Almond, 1960: pp. 20–25). National political systems are 'multistructural': the growing complexity of the economy may bring about a variety of differentiated rational-legal systems of decision-making, but the traditional local structures will invariably persist in one form or another and decisively affect the actual functioning of the new institutions.

Almond urges the importance of this perspective in functional comparisons of total systems: the perspective is of equal importance in the study of the structural contexts of individual participation in decision-making. Almond's primary example highlights the contrast between the opportunities for formal participation opened up by the extension of the suffrage and the persistence of earlier structures of dependence on local spokesmen: the contrast between the assumptions of equality, anonymity and individual choice underlying the institutions of mass democracy and the discovery in *The People's Choice* (Lazarsfeld, 1944; Anderson, B., 1959; Himmelstand, 1960: sect. 2. 5. 5.) and a long series of other empirical studies of the importance of face-to-face communication with opinion leaders in the immediate environments of the enfranchised citizen.

Students of political behaviour have again and again been struck by this contrast between the 'one citizen, one vote' provisions of political democracy and the persistent inequalities in the actual processes of decision-making. Study after study has underscored the contrast between the high proportion of voters and the very low proportion of politically concerned and alert citizens within the mass electorate:

– on the one hand a large majority of *'only-voters'*, of citizens who turn up at their polling stations but show very little of articulate concern about the issues of politics, only rudimentary knowledge of the alternatives and no willingness to take an active part in the conflict between the parties;

– on the other hand a small minority of *active participants* in the political system, of articulate and informed citizens motivated to act and to take a stand.

These inequalities have persisted in all mass democracies: they invariably became even more marked with the extension of the suffrage to women. The improvement of educational standards, the spread of the mass media of communication, the organizational work of the mass parties may have helped to raise the 'political literacy' levels in most systems, but the basic inequalities in participation have remained. The persistence of these inequalities raises a series of questions about the *implications of the introduction of universal suffrage* for the functioning of modern political systems. So far, such questions of functional relationships have mainly been raised in discussions of evidence from single countries (Berelson, 1952; Berelson, 1954: pp. 314–17; Milne, 1958, Ch. 13; Lane, 1959; pp. 340–48; Campbell, 1960: Ch. 20). To gain a *comparative perspective* on such 'macro-macro' consequences we shall clearly have to do much more to collate data from countries differing in their characteristic sequences of developments towards fully-fledged democracy and differing in the political alignments of the masses of citizens enfranchised through these developments:

– we need *historical* comparisons of the processes of decision-making which led to the expansion of the electorate and the standardization of registration and voting procedures;

– we need *statistical* comparisons of trends in political reactions of the masses of lower class citizens and of women after their entry into the electorate;

– and we need *institutional and structural* comparisons of the different ways in which the pressures of the mass electorate, the parties and the elective bodies are dovetailed into a broader system of decision-making among interest organizations and private and public corporate units.

These are the three sets of problems I consider crucial in any systematic study of the structural contexts of political participation:

– first, the series of decisions which *set the formal conditions* for the political mobilization of the masses of inarticulate subjects within each territory;

– secondly, the actual *rates of mobilization* to political activity and the conditions making for higher or lower rates;

– thirdly, the conditions for given types of *tie-ins between party-political activities and participation in other policy-influencing groups, collectivities and organizations.*

This is not the place for a detailed discussion of the current status of research on each of these problems: I shall limit myself to a few suggestions of promising lines of analysis.

1) *The Institutional Settings and the Structural Restraints*

Discussing the progress of democracy in the U. S., Alexis de Tocqueville pointed to an 'invariable rule in the history of society': once the first step had been taken to reduce the qualifications for the vote it would be impossible to halt the movement at any point short of universal suffrage. (Tocqueville, 1835: Vol. I, Ch. IV). It is extraordinary to see how Tocqueville's projections turned out to fit the actual developments toward fully-fledged formal democracy in nation-state after nation-state: the decision to extend the vote was not uniformly a response to pressures from below, it was as often the results of contests for influence at the top and of deliberate moves to broaden the bases for an integrated national power structure. The French Revolution had sown its plebiscitarian seeds and the success of Napoleon III had a distinct impact on political minds in W. Europe (cf. Gollwitzer, 1952). By a much-debated historical coincidence, the two great Conservative leaders Disraeli and Bismarck proceeded in 1867 within months of each other to extend the suffrage further than their Liberal antagonists had wanted.[16] In both cases these 'leaps in the dark' were motivated by a profound belief that the entry of the working classes into the electorate would strengthen the unity and stability of the nation-state. Disraeli expressed great faith in the working class and saw a major source of strength for the Conservative party in these new entrants into the electorate. In the words of a *Times* obituary 16 years later, Disraeli discerned the Conservative working man *'in the inarticulate mass of the English populace'* just as 'the sculptor perceived the angel in a block of marble'.[17] Bismarck also saw a major ally against the Liberals in the working class and was clearly very much influenced in his decision by his secret conversations with Ferdinand Lasalle: the Junker and the Socialist found a common ground in their belief in the integrating and centralizing impact of the introduction of universal manhood suffrage (Augst, 1916; Mayer 1929). The motive for extending the suffrage to the workers was patently not to create a channel for the articulation of the interests of the economically dependent strata: the objective was to strengthen the policies of centralization by enlisting the support of the least articulate classes in German society. Bismarck even toyed with the possibility of introducing a system for ensuring numerical support through the tacit acquiescence of the inarticulate masses: the votes of those who did not turn out were to be counted in favour of the governmental candidates (Mayer, 1929: p. 36; Eyck, 1945: Vol. I, p. 601). Lasalle developed the idea, he called it his *Zauberrezepte,*[18] of ensuring results in the same direction by a system of *obligatory voting.* This idea was not taken up in the debate over the constitution of the North German Federation, but was later to become a standard strategy in efforts to ensure an equilibrium of power in mass suffrage systems.[19]

At the heart of the bitter debates over the extension of the suffrage were conflicting expectations concerning the repercussions of the entry of the 'politically illiterate' into the electoral arena: conflicting views of the *allegiances and probable reactions* of these masses once enfranchised, and conflicting evaluations of the possibilities of *controlling and channelling* these new forces. Liberals tended to express fear of an irresponsible and disruptive radicalization of politics, Conservative and Christian party leaders were more likely to see in the enfranchisement of the lower classes and of all women a major strategic move in the stabilization of the national system against the attacks from the Socialist Left. An extraordinary variety of institutional compromises was tried out in response to these conflicting pressures. The history of these innovations is not of merely antiquarian interest: these developments set the stage for the organization of mass politics in each country and the particular solutions reached at each stage helped to determine the conditions for the integration of the lower classes into the national community.

In a systematic comparison of the sequences of decisions that led to the introduction of fully-fledged formal democracy a great number of *dimensions of institutional change* would have to be considered. For the present purposes a simplified schematic chart has been prepared *(Fig. 3)* to set in relief some of the salient differences between Western European countries in the developments that led to the enfranchisement of the politically least articulate strata of each population.[20] This chart takes into account only three dimensions of variation: the steps in the *extension of the suffrage,* the decisions on the *weighting of the votes,* and the steps toward the *privatization of electoral preferences.*

A comparison of these sequences of decisions reveals some marked contrasts: not just in the number of years and the number of steps it took to reach universal suffrage but even more in the decisions taken at the entry into politics of the hitherto unrecognized strata of the population.

It would be difficult to devise an electoral measure more calculated to alienate the lower classes from the national political system than the one promulgated in Prussia in 1849: all adult men were given the vote but the workers and the lower middle class were given only a token chance to influence the elections because of the three-class division of the electorate. What is even more remarkable about the Prussian case is that it was possible to maintain for more than two generations a system of universal manhood suffrage with *oral voting at public sessions.* Of other countries only Denmark kept up provisions for public voting for any length of time after the introduction of near-universal manhood suffrage. In France the provisions for secrecy were largely nominal far into the era of the Third Republic: mayors and other officials had little difficulty in controlling the votes of the less articulate. In most other countries of Western Europe provisions for the secrecy of the vote either preceded or were developed *pari passu* with the extension of the suffrage to the lower classes.

Fig. 3. Comparative Chronology of Decisions on Suffrage Extensions
and Voting Procedures:
Selected W. European countries

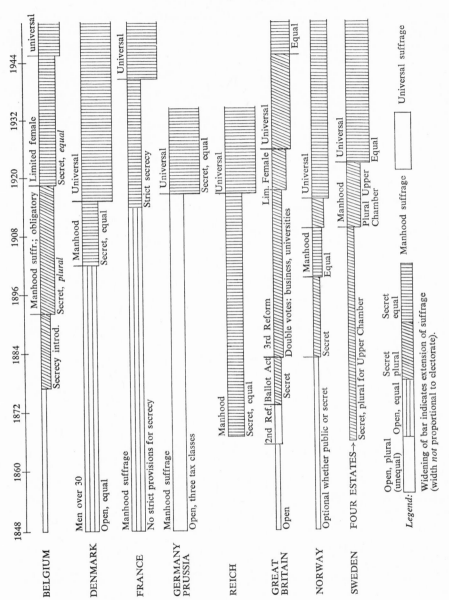

The extraordinary contrast between the electoral systems of Prussia and the Reich from 1870 to 1918 has given rise to a great deal of discussion among historians and political theorists: in Prussia a system of extremely unequal, open and indirect elections, in the Reich a system of equal, secret and direct voting, but for a Diet without decisive influence in the affairs of the nation. There is a wealth of evidence to show that this constellation of institutions was highly dysfunctional: the extension of the suffrage appeared to encourage the participation of the lower classes but the contrast between the two systems of elections made for widespread resentment and helped to isolate the workers in permanent opposition to the régime.

Ernst Fraenkel has recently suggested that the introduction of *secret voting* in the Reich contributed decisively to the isolation of the urban working class in *eine soziale Ghettopartei* (Fraenkel, 1958: p. 178): what he has in mind is that the deep resentments caused by the Prussian system of unequal and open voting could find secret and safe expression in votes for the Reichstag without any pressure on the ordinary voter to articulate his feelings openly in his community. In the deeply divided German society, the introduction of secret voting in fact tended to keep the newly enfranchised citizens in isolation outside the national political system and clearly did not contribute to the integration of the polity.

Interestingly enough, the evidence for the developments in other countries, particularly in Britain, suggest the opposite. The Ballot Act was passed five years after the decisive extension of the suffrage in 1867 and coincided with the great efforts of the Conservative party to organize clubs of workingmen for political action. The Ballot Act reduced drastically the opportunities for local influence on the worker vote through bribery and chicanery but at the same time made it possible for the 'deferent working man' to vote with his superiors without making this an issue in his day-to-day life with his fellow workers. The decisive difference between the developments in Britain and in Germany after the extension of the suffrage in 1867 was no doubt due to the action of the parties: in Britain both the Conservatives and the Liberals developed mass organizations aimed at the new entrants into the electorate; in Germany the parties on the right remained *Honoratiorenparteien* and left it to the Social Democrats to develop a network of political, social and cultural organizations for the workers which kept them clearly apart from the rest of the body politic. The introduction of secret voting in both countries accentuated these differences in development.

This contrast raises a series of intriguing questions about the functions for political systems of the introduction of institutions for the safeguarding of the *privacy of the voting act*. It is remarkable how little attention has been given in the literature to the effects of these profound changes in electoral procedures.[21] What can be said at this stage will of necessity be based on speculation and only scattered and unsystematic evidence.

Tocqueville would clearly have seen in the provisions for secrecy a further extension of the tendency for the centralizing nation state to enter into direct communication with each individual subject and to undermine all intermediary powers: the essential effect of the secrecy institution is to accentuate the equality of each voter by isolating him from the hierarchical influences in the local community. Through the secrecy provisions the power of the local aristocracy, the notables and the clergy is further reduced and, to follow the Tocqueville model, the tendencies toward centralization correspondingly strengthened.

In sociological terms we might say that in the situation of secret voting the individual adult is cut off from all his roles in the subordinate systems of the household, the neighbourhood, the work organization, the church and the civil association and set to act exclusively in the abstract role of a citizen of the over-all political system: there will be no feedback from what he does in this anonymous role to what he does in the other roles and therefore no need for him to take responsibility for the act of voting in his everyday interaction in his regular environment.

The obvious manifest reasons for introducing the secrecy provisions were the numerous public scandals over attempts at intimidation and bribery.

The primary motive for the introduction of the ballot system was to make it possible to escape sanctions from superiors: this was the essence of the Chartists' early demands and has also been a basic concern of working class movements.

What has been less emphasized in histories of electoral institutions is that the provisions for secrecy could cut the voter off from his *peers* as well as his *superiors*. It is often overlooked that there are two distinct elements in the secrecy provisions: the first is to make it *possible* for the voter to keep his decision private and avoid sanctions from those he *does not* want to know; the second is to make it *impossible* for the voter to prove how he voted to those he *does* want to know. The very rigorous rules set up in country after country for the invalidation of all irregularly marked ballots was directed to this second point: they were devised to ensure that the citizen could no longer treat his vote as a commodity for sale. He might well be bribed but the price per vote would clearly decrease as soon as it proved impossible to check whether it was actually delivered.[22] The salient point here is that by ensuring the complete anonymity of the ballots it became possible not only to reduce bribery of the economically dependent by their superiors but also to reduce the pressures towards conformity and solidarity within the working class.

The secrecy provisions clearly constituted an important mechanism of escape for the politically inarticulate entrants to the electorate. The actual political affects of this privatization of the vote varied enormously, however, with the organizational environments of these citizens.[23] In Germany, the Social Democrat party was able, at least in the major cities, to create a highly homogeneous working class environment through the development of a wide variety of secondary organizations: it became what Sigmund Neumann has called *eine integrale Partei*, a party that could claim the allegiance of its voters in all their social roles and therefore isolated them from disturbing cross-pressures. In this case, the introduction of secret voting for the Reichstag contributed further to the isolation of this sub-system since it reduced to a minimum the need for community interaction about political differences. In Britain the mass-directed efforts of the Conservative and the Liberal parties subjected the new entrants into the electorate to conflicting pressures: in this situation the institution of secrecy became an important device for the stabilization of the system since it allowed legitimate withdrawal from open political strife, not just by abstaining from the vote, but also by keeping preferences private and without consequence in everyday life. With increasing social mobility and the cross-cutting influences brought about by expanding associations in the community and the nation, more and more workers must have come under conflicting political pressures and must have felt the need for such provisions for the privatization of the act of voting.

What is crucial here is that this need for privatization tends to be much more marked among the politically inarticulate than among those who for one reason or another have become motivated to concern themselves with public issues. Under regulations for secret voting there is an important *asymmetry* in the system-voter relationship: the 'system' is pledged to the safeguarding of the secrecy of the vote but the voter is under no legal obligations to keep his preferences private, however little he can do to provide direct proof of his actual behaviour at the poll. The institution of secret voting in this way places every citizen before another set of alternative decisions: should he keep his vote completely to himself as is his right, or should he make his preference known to others within his primary groups only, within the organizations and associations he is part of, or to the general public?

This in fact brings about a *stratification* of the electorate on a 'privacy-publicity' dimension: from those who never reveal their vote to anyone to those who publicly take their stand on the alternatives set and openly proclaim how they will vote or have voted. The *active* and the *militant* in the political parties clearly cannot make much use of the secrecy provisions: they may be important for them in the choice of particular *candidates* but it is part of their community role to commit themselves publicly between the major alternatives.

2) *The Political Mobilization of the 'Inarticulate' Strata*
The effects of the secrecy provisions on the behaviour of the masses of workers and later of women enfranchised through the final universalization

of the suffrage have neven been systematically studied. The marked contrasts in the turnout proportions between parallel elections in Prussia and in the Reich have frequently been documented, but no detailed ecological comparisons of results in open and results in secret elections have, as far as I have been able to ascertain, ever been attempted. Erik Högh has under way a fascinating analysis of the electoral registers for a sample of Danish constituencies from the period of open elections: here it will be of the greatest interest to analyze the extent of participation and the political preferences of the various categories of manual workers.

Comparative research on the processes of *entry into politics* is indeed still in its infancy. Tingsten was probably the first to give serious attention to the study of the electoral records for the last to be enfranchised, the workers and the women.[24] His actual analyses, however, did not go beyond the *first step* in this process: the *use of the vote*. Statistics on the turnout of the latest entrants into the electorate were available for some countries: statistics on their *further advances* into the political arena have generally proved much more difficult to assemble and, what is crucial here, much more difficult to break down by categories of the electorate.

Maurice Duverger assembled an important body of comparative information on *party memberships* and established trends in the member-voter ratios for mass parties in W. Europe (Duverger, 1951: Ch. II): these, however, were all derived from aggregate figures for entire parties, without any breakdowns by the occupation or the sex of the member. Historical statistics on the recruitment of party members from the ranks of the latest entrants into the electorate may still be assembled for the better-documented parties but the data are often fragmentary and hard to evaluate. The outlook for historical comparisons is markedly better for the *ultimate steps* in participation in each system: for competitive participation in *candidacies* and for actual participation in decision-making in formally established *elective offices*. For such studies there will generally prove to be an abundance of documentary materials available for coding and counting, but so far hardly anything has been done in any country to assemble such statistics for the *lower rungs* of political systems: there is a growing body of literature on the recruitment of participants in *central, national* decision-making (cf. Lasswell, 1952; Marwick, 1960), but to reach fuller understanding of the 'entry-into-politics' process we shall clearly have to collect data on candidates and officers in samples of *local* administrative districts.[25]

Data on the socio-economic backgrounds of party members, candidates and elected officials can to a large extent be assembled from regularly maintained 'book-keeping' records. Sources of this kind will only rarely, however, offer detailed data for analyses of the *paths of recruitment* and the *over-all patterns of participation in community life, in policy-influencing organization and in the flow of public and private communication* about the polity and its affairs. To ensure a basis for such analyses we will normally have to proceed to *direct data gathering,* either through local inquiries and the use of informants, or through personal interviews. Two distinct strategies of data gathering have been developed in such studies: the one starts out from rosters of *organizationally visible participants* (e.g., party members (Rantala, 1956; Mayntz, 1959), party officials (Valen, 1961), candidates (Valen, 1966), elected officials), the other is to select *cross-sectional samples from the electorate-at-large* and to rely on break-downs by levels of activity within the samples. Each procedure has its drawbacks as well as its advantages: the ideal solution is a design that combines the two (Katz, 1961; Valen, 1961). Studies focusing ex-clusively on the visible participants will only allow very few comparisons with the rest of the electorate. Cross-sectional studies will allow a wide range of direct comparisons but will in most cases have to be prohibitively large to permit analyses of upper-échelon participants.[26] The basic diffi-culty, however, lies in the *time* dimension: in most Western countries it took years after the final extension of the suffrage before adequate survey data started to get accumulated. Any time series that can be established for the recruitment of active participants among the lower strata and among women will be very short indeed. Something can be done through breakdowns by age within the samples, even more through the systematic use of recall questions about the activity levels in the family of origin and through analyses of social and political mobility, but serious gaps in our knowledge of the time sequences in the 'entry-into-politics' processes will remain whatever we do in this direction.

However limited the possibilities of historical comparisons, cross-nation-al analyses of survey data are clearly essential in any attempt to reach some understanding of the implications of mass suffrage for the function-ing of Western-type political systems. Comparisons of the extent and scope of participation within the lower-socio-economic strata can help us to gain insight into the functional importance of the right to the vote: what does the suffrage mean for citizens in these strata? is voting a peripheral activity of little consequence or does it fit in with a wider range of participant activities in the community, in associations, in politics? Sample surveys can give us data on these wider contexts of participation and comparisons of such data across communities and across national systems can give us clues to an understanding of the importance of the structural settings and the alternatives in the system for the recruitment of active participants from the lower strata within each society.

Our recent attempt at comparing data on participation from two systems differing as much from each other as Norway and the United States (Rokkan, 1960: 2) points to a possible line of research in this direction. Our principal concern here was with the extent of political participation within the lower strata of the two electorates: the workers as contrasted with the salaried employees, the professional people and the businessmen, the primary-educated as contrasted with the secondary-educated and the college-educated. We found for both countries the usual differences in turnout between the strata and we found consistent differences in the same direction for the extent of *attention to the mass media* during the campaign: here we simply dealt with replications of 'micro-micro' breakdowns. What changed the character of the analysis was the finding that there was no such uniform differences between the strata for *organizational activity in politics:* using a simple index of participation based on party membership, attendance at meetings and electoral work, we found *no consistent differences between strata in the Norwegian sample but a marked and consistent one in the U. S.* We interpreted this to reflect the contrast between the two regimes in the *alternatives set for the citizens,* both as voters and as potential recruits to party activity: in the one case a markedly class-distinct, 'status-polarized' party system, in the other much less correspondence between the lines of socio-economic cleavage and the lines of political conflict.[27] To explore this further we proceeded to a 'third-order' 'macro-micro-micro' comparison (CR-B in the typology suggested in *Fig. 1*). We rank-ordered the parties in the two systems according to the proportions of manual workers among their voters and we found that the class character of the parties made a decisive difference in the recruitment of active participants in political work. In the Norwegian Labour party we found manual workers more likely to be active than middle class voters. In the more heterogeneous Democratic party in the U. S. we found a tendency in the opposite direction: the level of participation was slightly lower for workers than for middle class voters. The most marked status differentials in participation were found within the parties with the lowest proportions of working class voters: the opposition parties in Norway and the Republican party in the U. S. This, of course, cannot be taken to be conclusive evidence: the differences were found within *nation-wide* cross-sections and will need to be tested by *categories of communities.* However, the findings do suggest important hypotheses for continued comparative research: they accentuate the importance of assembling data on the character of the *political choices confronting the worker,* on the opportunities open to him for *experience and training in organizational skills,* and on the *channels of recruitment* from class-distinct associations such as unions to membership and activity in political parties.

Perhaps the most important set of factors to be taken into account in any comparative study of participation bear on the *organizational bases* for the recruitment of active supporters in party-political work: how open, direct, stable are the channels of recruitment from the given economic, cultural or religious organization to the given party? what are the alternative 'policy pay-offs' of other affiliations, other modes of influence, for the given organization? what are the alternative prospects of achievement and advancement for the active participants in the given organization?

Questions along these lines may be raised for any association or organization and for any party. They are of particular importance in comparative studies of the socio-economic bases for party conflict. In pushing further our tentative comparisons between Norway and the United States, these are exactly the questions we shall want to explore in detail: the character of the tie-ins between the different labour unions and the parties, the distinctiveness of the union votes, the extent of recruitment from union activity to political activity, the relationships between union activity and participation in other organizations and associations in the community and the nation.[28]

3) *Party-political Activity, Community Influence and Organizational Power*

With these questions we are already at the heart of another important area for comparative research: the study of factors making for differences between systems and changes within systems in the importance of party politics and elections in the overall process of decision-making for the territorial population.

In an attempt to clarify issues in the current debate over method and theory in the study of community power structures, Peter Rossi recently suggested a typology and a set of hypotheses of general importance in comparative research on participation (Rossi, 1960: 4).

Rossi's basic concern is with community conditions making for *separation between the political elite and the economic elite:* in terms of our discussion the focus of his analysis is on conditions for the development of two distinct channels of decision-making, one based on mass suffrage and party organization, the other based on professional status, managerial position and the control of wealth.

Rossi specifies three sets of conditions for the development of such separate channels.

First the *size* of the community: this determines the extent to which local government offices will be full-time roles segregated from any other roles of the incumbents;

secondly, the *strength of partisan traditions in local government:* the stability and competitive character of the local party system;

and thirdly, the extent of *'political crystallization':* [29] the extent to which the social structure of the community is reflected in the divisions of the electorate at the polls.

Rossi sees a 'natural strain' in community life toward overlap and congruence between economic and political dominance. This is the normal situation in small communities, whether run by the Democrats in the South or the Republicans in the North. There is a tendency in the same direction in larger communities with strong traditions of *non-partisan, 'managerial'* government: such traditions generally tend to strengthen the position of the local economic elite and prevents the growth of 'countervailing powers' deriving their strength from the mass suffrage.

A marked separation between political and economic elites will generally be found in Northern cities governed by Democratic politicians deriving their power from socio-economically and ethnically distinctive electorates. In such communities the level of status polarization will regularly be found to be as high as in countries with clearly class-divided party systems throughout their territory: [30] if we compared just these U. S. cities with cities in a country with a major Labour party such as Norway we should *not* find differences of the magnitude we reported for nationwide samples. It is important to note that in the United States a high level of status polarization in the division of local votes does not appear to increase appreciably the recruitment of *working class citizens* to public positions. Comparative evidence from communities differing in the level of status polarization should not be very difficult to assemble, but the scattered local studies at hand are not always easy to compare for rates of recruitment. Reviewing such evidence as is at hand, Rossi finds that the cleavage between the political and the occupational elites will largely tend to be a cleavage *within* the world of business and the professions: the leaders in the 'public' sectors of such communities are most likely to be recruited from the ranks of small businessmen and lawyers at the hearts of extensive networks of local face-to-face acquaintanceships while the leaders in the 'private', economic and professional, sectors are more likely to derive their power from positions in large-scale territory-wide organizations cutting across a variety of localities.[31]

Here we touch on an important theme in the analysis of the implications of mass suffrage for the functioning of pluralist political systems: what changes will occur in the over-all processes of decision-making with the mobilization of the less articulate electorates for political action and with the consequent growth of independent centers of electoral power?

Rossi hypothesizes that the three basic strategies used by economic elites in countering the effects of this growth of electoral power will be these:

1) the promotion of non-partisan electoral systems and of technically neutral administrative agencies;

2) the intensified proliferation of privately controlled community institutions and voluntary civic associations serving as instruments of influence and pressure in conflicts over local policies; and

3) the development of state-wide or nation-wide interest organizations to influence policies beyond the control of the local political elite.

Hypotheses of this kind may be tested either *diachronically* or *synchronically*. Several attempts have been made to establish *trends toward a withdrawal of the economic elites from local politics* in the U. S. over the last decades (Schultze, 1958; Schultze, 1961), but the factors accounting for such trends are complex: they certainly cannot be attributed solely to the growth of independent electoral power centers. *Synchronic* comparisons of the extent of private policy-influencing activity through community institutions and voluntary associations have, to my knowledge, never been attempted in the United States: Rossi's hypothesis is that such activities would be more extensive the more marked the separation of the economic from the political elite in the community. The basic task here would be to find some meaningful measure of the 'importance' of the private institutions and the voluntary associations in each community: mere statistics on size of memberships and the economic roles of the active participants would not be likely to take us very far in this direction.

Whatever the technical difficulties of testing the hypotheses suggested by Rossi, the underlying reasoning about the processes of decision-making in mass-suffrage systems will clearly prove important in future attempts at cross-national comparisons.

The most straightforward of the tasks to be taken up in comparative research on these wider contexts of participation is the collation of national statistics on the recruitment of *members and officers* in different categories of *voluntary associations*. Studies of the linkages between association memberships and political activity have been undertaken in several countries over the last years [32] and evidence on the character of such linkages can now be assembled for a wide range of structurally different systems. The studies so far undertaken have focused on social activities in the community and in wider organizations as sets of *conditioning variables* in explaining levels of political partisanship and participation: the simplest way of establishing the linkages have been by direct counts of the total number of non-political memberships and offices held by each respondent and by analyses of the correlations with indices of political activity. In moving toward comparative analyses of channels of influence on community policy-making it will clearly be essential to go beyond such crude correlations: voluntary associations and private organizations will have to be differentiated not only according to their substantive goals and their membership criteria (cf. Rose, 1954: Ch. 3), but also in terms of the socio-economic background and political partisanship of their clientele and their leaders and, what is of particular importance here, in terms of the *'pay-off' probabilities of action through parties vs. action directly on policy makers and administrative agencies*. Detailed studies along these lines would require the co-ordination of institutional analyses with surveys of samples of community leaders as well as of the rank-and-file electorate. Attempts in this direction have been made in some countries but research in this area is still at a very early stage of development.

Comparative research along these lines may help us to gain further insight into the implications of the processes of political change in systems undergoing economic growth. With the early phases of industrialization went a variety of tendencies towards greater integration of the national decision-making machinery and a widening of the representative bases of each régime. The introduction of mass suffrage made it possible to mobilize the lower strata of economically dependent citizens into distinctive political parties and set the stage for the development of new channels of influence on the processes of decision at local and national levels. At the same time, and partly in reaction to these developments, most systems of the West witnessed an extraordinary growth in the scope and activity of voluntary associations and interest organizations. With the continued growth and diversification of each national economy, these networks of organizations have tended to cut across the earlier party-political divisions and create cross-pressures making for a lowering of the polarization in the system.[33]If Rossi is right in his conjectures, we are faced here with an intriguing process of historical dialectics: the extension of the suffrage increased the chances for a status polarization of national politics, but this very polarization brought about a proliferation of sectional and functional organizations which in turn tended to soften the overall strains in the system and reduce the level of polarization.[34] What we tend to find is a cumulation of forces making for a narrowing of the alternatives for national politics, a fragmentation of the networks of policy-influencing organizations, and a consequent decline in the importance of the decisions of the electorate-at-large. This may tend to lower the level of general political participation and to alienate from politics sizable sections of the once enfranchised citizenry, leaving the basic decisions to a bargaining process between interest organizations, parties and agencies and departments of the national bureaucracy. We see tendencies in these directions in many countries of the West: the developments toward *Entideologisierung* and 'all party governments' are cases in point (Kirchheimer, 1957; Vulpius, 1957). We know far too little about the dynamics of these developments and we need to do much more to facilitate co-operation and co-ordination of studies of these problems in different countries.

NOTES

[1] Large numbers of tables for the social and religious backgrounds of voting in W. Europe have been assembled in (de Jong, 1956) and (Fogarty, 1957: Ch. XXII). Mattei Dogan has compared Western European survey data on the electoral behaviour of women (Dogan, 1956: 147–86), and on the party allegiances of *workers* (Dogan, 1960: 25–44). S. M. Lipset has assembled an extensive file of tabulations and IBM cards from a wide variety of surveys of a number of Western Countries (Lipset & Linz, 1956) and has reported on some of his findings in (Lipset, 1960: esp. Ch. VI and VII). For further information see (Rokkan, 1969: 3).

[2] On the possibility of developing an *international archive* of raw data from interview surveys, see a report to the Ford Foundation (Lucci & Rokkan, 1957). For further development, see (Merritt, 1966: 1) and (Rokkan, 1966: 3).

[3] On the problem of 'levels' in comparative studies see (Duijker & Rokkan, 1954) and (Rokkan, 1956: 2).

[4] Earlier attempts: the nine-nation UNESCO survey of national stereotypes, only peripherally concerned with political behaviour (Buchanan, 1953); the OCSR surveys of teachers' politics in seven countries of W. Europe (Rokkan, 1955: 3); the Columbia University surveys of opinions in six Middle Eastern countries (Lerner, 1958); the comparative 'elite' interviews conducted in Britain, France and W. Germany under the direction of Daniel Lerner and currently under analysis at the Center for International Studies at M.I.T.; the studies conducted in a number of countries by the Institute for International Social Research on 'protest voting' (Cantril, 1958) and the foreign policy views of legislators (Free, 1959). For further discussion see Chapter 8.

[5] For details on the Norwegian programme of electoral studies, see (Rokkan, 1960: 5, pp. 120–25, with bibl. at pp. 237–49). An analysis of the effects of differences in the degree of 'politicization' of local elections is given in (Rokkan, 1962: 2) and in (Hjellum, 1967: 1 and 2): see Ch. 6 below.

[6] The simple technique of 'elite sociometry' used in (Hunter, 1953), was taken up in a wide variety of local studies but has lately come under vigorous attack from Robert A. Dahl and his co-workers at Yale University: see (Dahl, 1958), and the detailed discussion of studies of this type in (Polsby, 1963).

[7] Peter H. Rossi has suggested a typology of local political systems and a set of hypotheses about the socio-cultural bases of community politics which can only be put to a test through such 'macro-micro' studies: see (Rossi, 1960: 2) and (Rossi, 1960: 4).

[8] Social anthropologists have, for obvious reasons, paid more attention to these problems than other social scientists, cf. (Whiting, 1954) & (Lewis, 1956).

[9] None of the discussions of the methodology of comparative politics published over the last decades deal in any detail with microcomparisons. G. Heckscher's account of the IPSA symposium (Heckscher, 1957), has hardly more than one page about cross-national analyses of electoral statistics. The most important contribution to theory development and model construction in comparative politics is the 'Introduction' to (Almond, 1960). This, however, is only indirectly concerned with microcomparisons.

[10] For formalizations of such micro-macro interpendencies, see particularly (Downs, 1957: Ch. 8).

[11] The possibility that the realignment of voters brought about by continued economic growth will push further toward between-party consensus is discussed in (Rokkan, 1960: 3 and 1966: 5 and 1967).

[12] The concepts of 'interest articulation' and 'interest aggregation' are discussed in detail by (Almond, 1960: pp. 33–45).

[13] For an attempt to develop this concept in detail, see (Deutsch, 1953: pp. 100–101). For a fascinating analysis of the role of the mass media in such processes of political mobilization, see (Lerner, 1958).

[14] The term 'political mobilization' is discussed by (Rustow, 1956: pp. 16–18). Comparative studies of the impact of mass suffrage in underdeveloped countries are essential for an understanding of factors making for integration or dissensus, cf. (MacKenzie, 1960; Smith, 1960). A fascinating account of the effects of the introduction of a system of mass elections in a traditional, highly stratified society is (Maquet, 1959).

[15] The most remarkable single-nation study of such processes of change is (Marshall, 1950).

[16] For the developments leading to the Second Reform Act, see particularly (Seymour, 1915); for the decision of the North German Federation, see (Oncken, 1914, Vol. II, pp. 157–92; Gagel, 1959).

[17] *The Times*, 18 April, 1883, quoted in R. T. MacKenzie, *British Political Parties*. London, Macmillan, 1955, p. 147. The most recent discussion of the Conservative

belief in the principle of 'one man, one vote, one value' is in (Jennings, 1960: pp. 18–28).

[18] Letter to Bismarck, 13 Jan. 1864, (Mayer, 1929: p. 81).

[19] For a general review of these developments, see (Braunias, 1932: Vol. II, pp. 35–45).

[20] Secondary sources: (Seymour, 1918; Braunias, 1932: Vol. II).

[21] The formal history of the Anglo-Saxon systems is well covered in (Wigmore, 1889; Evans, 1917). On other systems, see (Braunias, 1932: Vol. II, pp. 168–74) and (Mayer, 1903: pp. 528–65).

[22] See (Seymour, 1915: pp. 434–35), and for details on the effect on the 'vote market' (Hanham, 1959: Ch. 13).

[23] This, of course, is the theme of Ostrogorski's volumes. For a detailed account of developments in England, Scotland, Wales and Ireland, see (Hanham, 1959). For developments in Germany, see particularly (Ritter, 1959; Nipperdey, 1961).

[24] Tingsten's work on the behaviour of recently enfranchised groups needs to be completed and systematized on a variety of points. Quite particularly, it would be of great theoretical interest to undertake comparative analyses of the rate of 'politicization' in the peripheral areas of each nation-state, the remote, less 'modernized' areas of the national territory. This is a central concern in our current studies of electoral participation in Norway. We find clear evidence that women are least prone to vote in the less accessible, least politicized areas along the coast: see chapter 6 below. It is of interest to note that similar differences in the votes for women appeared in German statistics just after the introduction of female suffrage (Bremme, 1956: p. 45), but have tended to disappear in post war elections. This has been interpreted in terms of a process of 'mobilization' by E. Faul (Faul, 1960).

[25] Our Norwegian programme of research on parties, elections and political behaviour includes a study of the recruitment to local elective offices, but so far only for elections after World War II. (cf. Rokkan, 1960: pp. 81–84).

[26] This, of course, will vary with the administrative structure and the population density of the country: figures for Finland and Norway indicate that up to 2 % of any nationwide sample will be candidates for offices in local elections, see the articles on 'Finland' and 'Norway and the United States of America' in S. Rokkan, ed., 'Citizen participation in political life', *Int. Soc. Sci. J.* (12) 1, 1960: particularly pp. 31–32 and 81–84 (the second of these articles will be found below, Ch. 12).

[27] For a general discussion of concepts of 'status-polarization', see (Campbell, 1960: Ch. 13).

[28] A report on a comparison of union-party tie-ins is in progress.

[29] This is the term introduced by G. E. Lenski (Lenski, 1954), in this context it is synonymous with the term 'status polarization' used elsewhere in this chapter.

[30] Correlations by precinct between economic/ethnic indices and the Democratic vote have been found to be very high in such cities: see (Rossi, 1960: 1; Katz, 1961: 2).

[31] This contrast is discussed in some detail by Rossi in a thought-provoking paper prepared for The Fund for the Advancement of Education (Rossi, 1960: 3).

[32] For the U. S., see the secondary analyses of NORC data (Wright, 1958). For Finland (Allardt, 1958), for Germany (Reigzrotzki, 1956), for Norway (Rokkan, 1959: 1), for Sweden (Zetterberg, 1960).

[33] This point of view has been developed in further detail for Sweden (Zetterberg, 1960).

[34] N. W. Polsby has suggested such a cyclical pattern for developments in U. S. cities since the peak inflows of ethnically distinct lower class citizens (Polsby, 1963: Ch. VII).

TWO

Methods and Models in the Comparative Study of Nation-Building

The extraordinary growth in the number of legally independent units of government during the 1950s and '60s has prompted a wide variety of scholarly efforts toward description, analysis and theorizing. The literature generated through these efforts is voluminous and dispersed and has so far never been subject to systematic codification.[35] In this brief chapter there can be no question of doing justice to the entire range of approaches to the comparative study of state formation and national development. Only a few lines of attack will be singled out for discussion and

Origin: An early version of this paper was prepared at the Center for Advanced Study at Stanford, Calif. in July, 1967. This version was expanded for presentation at the UNESCO Symposium on Nation-Building at Aspenäs Studiegård near Gothenburg in August, 1968. It has subsequently been printed in *Acta sociologica* vol. 12 (2), 1969.

even these will not be evaluated in any great detail: the purpose is not to review the past literature but to define priority tasks for future cooperative data processing and interpretation.

Imbalances in Current Research

There are curious discontinuities in the history of the comparative study of national development. Karl Deutsch published his pioneering study of *Nationalism and Social Communication* in 1953 and focused all but one of his quantitative analyses of rates of assimilation and mobilization on European nations. Two of these were post-World War I nations: Czechoslovakia and Finland. The third was a nation but not a sovereign state: Scotland. And only the fourth was a new nation of the under-developed world: India. These analyses appeared just a few years before the great onrush of new state formations in Africa and Asia: the UN added some fifty new states to its roster of members from 1953 to the end of 1966.

This extraordinarily rapid wave of decolonization and state formation deeply affected the priorities within the social science community from the mid-fifties onward: vast investments were made in research on the political and the economic developments in this 'third world' and a great phalanx of scholars were able to familiarize themselves with the intricacies of these many cases of state formation and initial nation-building. These efforts went beyond mere fact-finding: the great wave of 'third world' studies also triggered impressive efforts of theory construction.

Perhaps the most influential of the these efforts of conceptualization and theorizing was the series of studies of political development organized by the Almond-Pye Committee of the American Social Science Research Council:[36] these studies represented a persistent and systematic endeavour to identify crucial variables in a generic process of change from the traditional tribal polity to the modern 'bureaucratic-participant' state and have exerted a great deal of influence on the structure and the style of current research on the politics of the developing countries.

But the very success of these efforts of research on the developing areas of the world threatened to disrupt the continuity of scholarly concern with processes of state formation and nation-building: the theories of the late 'fifties and the early 'sixties tended to concentrate exclusively on the experiences and the potentialities of the polities just emerging from colonial status and showed only minimal concern with the early histories of nation-building in Europe and in the European-settled territories. The idea of the participant nation-state was European in origin and had been exported to the developing world through colonization and ideological diffusion: yet there was a great deal of reluctance to draw directly on the rich European experience in developing models for the explanation of the processes of change inherent in the growth of national polities. There were many reasons for this reluctance: the great complexity of the European developments, the linguistic difficulties, the low level of communication between historians and generalizing social scientists. It was easier to deal in comparative terms with the less history-burdened, less documented and less scrutinized countries of the developing world: the working languages were fewer because of the colonial inheritance, and there were fewer professional historians around to question the interpretations and the classifications of the social scientists.

There are many signs of uneasiness about this gap. A number of comparisons across the developed and the developing polities have been published in recent years and still more are under way and will help to pave the way for a *rapprochement* (LaPalombara, 1968 : 2) The Committee on Comparative Politics has itself given increasing attention to the peculiarities of the developments in Europe and has encouraged attempts to incorporate the variations within Europe in a broader model of political modernization.[37] A number of attempts have been at comparisons across pairs or multiples of contrasting polities in the West and the East: among the most important of these are Reinhard Bendix's work on aspects of nation-building in Germany, Russia, Japan and India (Bendix, 1964 : 2), Robert Holt and John Turner's paired comparisons of England and Japan, France and China (Holt, 1966), Barrington Moore's analysis of the economic basis of political development in England, France, the United States and Germany, Russia, China, India and Japan (Moore, 1966) Seymour Martin Lipset's attempt at a comparison of the early stages of nation-building in the United States with the current efforts of integration and consolidation in the newest states of Africa and Asia (Lipset, 1963) points in the same direction and so does Samuel Huntington's current work on contrasts in the timing of social and political modernization (Huntington, 1965, 1966, 1968). Karl Deutsch and his team at Yale, since 1966 at Harvard, have extended the programme of research implicit in the 1953 volume: Deutsch has not only deepened his analysis of conditions and varieties of nation-building through his work on the Swiss case (Deutsch, 1965 : 2; Deutsch forthc.) but he has also built up, with his colleagues, an important computer archive of data on the new as well as the old units of the expanding international system (Russett, 1964; cf. Merritt & Rokkan, 1966).

These varied attempts at bridge-building across the great gap in the comparative study of political development have helped to clarify the priorities of further research but have barely scratched the surface of the vast masses of data to be processed in any serious and systematic effort to test alternative models and hypotheses.

There are still marked imbalances in the ranges of cases and variables covered in comparative analysis of processes of political development:

1) *The large-nation bias*
   – most comparisons, whether within the West or with developing polities, have limited themselves to the larger and more influential
   units[38] and have tended to neglect the richly varied experiences of the
   smaller polities, particularly the many European 'secession states' after 1814, 1830 and 1918 and their histories of nationbuilding: these
   are, after all, the units most immediately comparable to the recently
   formed states of the 'third world'.
2) *The 'whole-nation' bias*
   – most comparisons have been limited to institutional or aggregate
   statistical data for each nation as a unit and have tended to neglect
   highly significant variations in the rates of growth among competing
   economic, political or cultural centres and between such centres and
   the rural peripheries.[39]
3) *The 'economic growth' bias*
   – most comparisons have limited themselves to the most easily accessible time series data from censuses and economic bookkeeping
   statistics and have neglected a wide range of less complete data series
   for levels and rates of social, educational and cultural mobilization, all
   processes of crucial importance in the study of nation-building.

This chapter will discuss alternative strategies in coping with these defi-
ciencies in the data bases for comparative developmental analysis:
   – it will first review salient features of recently advanced *models of
   nation-building,*
   – it will pass on to a listing of *priority variables* for comparative data
   collation and analysis
   – and it will wind up with some suggestions for *international action* to
   accelerate the development and testing of different models through a
   series of encounters between historians and social scientists.

A Sample of Models
Models of political development vary along a variety of dimensions: in their
logical structure and their openness to direct empirical testing, in the
number and precision of the variables and in the possibilities of adequate
matching with actual or potential data sources, in the ranges of historically
given variations they seek to explain.
   Let us, to simplify the mapping of variations in the organization of
models, try to locate a few of best-known ones within a two-dimensional
diagram inspired by Talcott Parsons on page 50.
   Karl Deutsch focuses on the centre-periphery axis: his model is primarily
designed to predict variations in the extent of territorial-cultural integration
through the joint, but not necessarily parallel, processes of national standardization and social mobilization: his dependent variables bear on
nation-building and his model simply assumes some initial level of state
formation through inter-elite coalitions.

4. Citizens

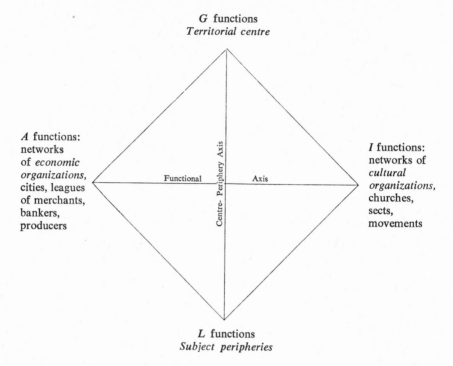

The Deutsch model is particularly appropriate in the study of the actual or potential breakup of multi-lingual empires: it is no accident that his four examples of quantitative analysis bear on such linguistically divided territories as Finland (Finnish vs. Swedish), Bohemia-Moravia-Silesia (Czech vs. German), Scotland (Gaelic vs. English) and India-Pakistan (Hindi vs. other vernaculars vs. English).

The model posits a *centre* and a *leading group of active 'nation-builders'* and seeks to specify the conditions for the development, within the territory controlled from this centre or reached by this group, of a *culturally cohesive, or at least complementary, community* clearly distinct from the surrounding populations (Deutsch, 1968: pp. 101–104).

The core of the model explores the interrelations between two rates of change in the process of nation-building or nation-fragmentation:

> – the rate of *assimilation,* defined as an increase or decrease from t_1 to t_2 in the subset (A) of the territorial population (P) who have become speakers of the predominant ('nation-building') language;
> – the rate of *mobilization,* defined as an increase or decrease from t_1 to t_2 in the subset (M) of P who are no longer exclusively tied to the traditional, locally-bounded communication environments and have in some sense entered the broader, urban, if not nation-wide, system of social communication.[41]

At any one point in time t_i after the initial drive the extent of unification or integration may be measured by the sizes of the four cross-products of these two dichotomies:

the *mobilized and assimilated* (M_A)
the *mobilized but still differentiated* (M_D)
the *underlying but assimilated* (U_A)
the *underlying and differentiated* (U_D)

The rise and fall in these shares of the territorial population from one point in time to another will obviously be affected by the interaction between the two processes of change but the character of this interaction will vary over time and as a function of the levels already reached on each variable. A number of extraneous variables will also affect the inter-relations of assimilation and mobilization: differential fertility and mortality, the economic or military strength of alternative centres or clusters of nation-builders, the extent of exogenous mobilization through economic, ecclesiastical or other cultural networks.

There is no attempt in *Nationalism and Social Communication* to spell out in any formal detail the consequences of this simple model: there is a brief mathematical appendix on the relationships between the principal rates of change distinguished (Deutsch, 1968: App. V) but there are no explicit formulations of functional relationships between the rates of assimilation and mobilization and the finally generated national structure. There is a series of illuminating applications to concrete historical developments but no easily identifiable generalizations for empirical testing across a broad range of nations. Karl Deutsch's model is essentially heuristic: it suggests a priority in comparative data collation and then simply exhorts us to develop generalizations inductively through the processing of such materials.

The Deutsch model fired the imagination of a number of scholars: it was a first attempt to apply notions from information theory and cybernetics to the study of political development and it pointed to exciting possibilities of empirical testing through the construction of quantitative indicators from historical statistical data. But the core of the model limited itself to *mass effects*: the focus was primarily on the incorporation of peripheral populations within some form of national community, much less on the actual political or administrative measures of nation-building at the territorial centres or on the conflicts among competing elites and organizations over such policies.

A variety of difficulties, terminological, conceptual, empirical, confront the student of processes of centre formation. In this quick review we shall focus on attempts to cut across the historically inherited confusions of national terminologies through the identification of discriminating variables and through the development of models for the cross-classification of cases and the establishment of distinctive syndromes and configurations.

Much of the literature in this field focuses on single cases of centre formation and nation-building and offers only *ad hoc* comparisons: outstanding examples are Lipset's interpretation of the United States as *The First New Nation* and Ralf Dahrendorf's *Gesellschaft und Demokratie in Deutschland*.[42] Conceptually and empirically much more taxing, but of greater potential value in the development of systematic macro-theory, is the strategy of *paired comparisons* attempted in a number of recent writings. Such confrontations of pairs of contrasting cases of centre formation and nation-building may not only offer opportunities for a deepening of insights into the dynamics of each system but also offer springboards for further model building across a broader range of cases.

This strategy is well-known in comparative economic history: consider Clapham's classic study of the French and the German economies (Clapham, 1921), Habakkuk's path-breaking study of technological developments in Britain and the United States (Habakkuk, 1962), Kindleberger's attempt at a systematic confrontation of data on society and economy in Britain and France (Kindleberger, 1964). Students of comparative political development have found the method of paired contrasts of great value, both as a device in the ordering and evaluation of data, and as a procedure in the generation of hypotheses and insights. Possibly the best example of a collective effort of this type is the symposium organized by the Almond-Pye Committee on contrasts in the development of the Japanese and the Turkish political system (Ward, 1964). Excellent examples of the use of this strategy in a broader context of theory development are Reinhard Bendix's work on the development of territorial systems of public authority in Prussia/Germany and Russia and in India and Japan (Bendix, 1964: 2) and Robert Holt and John Turner's (Holt, 1966) paired comparisons of two early industrializers, England and Japan, with two late industrializers, France and China. Both these works focus on variations in the distinctiveness, the strength and the cohesion of the centre-forming collectivities in each territory: the aim is to pinpoint contrasts in the characteristics of the agencies of territorial decision-making and control and to develop models for the explanation of such contrasts. Bendix's analysis focuses on the tactics of centre-forming collectivities, dynastic bureaucracies and military organizations in breaking down local solidarities and creating direct links between the territorial nation and its individual subjects through the development of universalistic criteria of citizen rights and citizen obligations. The study by Holt and Turner is organized around a distinctive hypothetico-deductive model : it seeks to test a set of propositions about the likelihood of economic innovations under different conditions of administrative centralization.

These studies help to underscore the importance of the 'centre' variables

for an understanding of contrasts in nation-building processes. Nationalization processes in the territorial peripheries are clearly conditioned by
circumstances of cultural as well as physical distance and by the possibilities of concerted mobilization of local resources against the standardizing
agencies but the *contents* of the communications spread through the actual
or potential national territory are primarily determined by the centre-
forming collectivities. No typology of nation-building processes can be
developed without an analysis of variations in the structures and the functions of the territorial centres. Among recent attempts at classifications of
such structures two deserve particular attention: Samuel Huntington's
analysis of the contrast between the United States and what he calls
'Europe', in fact primarily England, France, Prussia and Sweden, and
Peter Nettl's effort to identify dimensions of 'stateness'. Huntington's
much-discussed article focuses on the origins of the marked differences in
the speed of political modernization between England and France on the
one hand, the United States on the other. This dependent variable is a
composite of several indicators of organizational complexity: the extent to
which traditional, familial, religious and ethnic authorities have been
replaced by a single, secular, nation-centered political authority, the extent
of differentiation within the political and the bureaucratic machinery, and
the extent of the development of parties and interest associations for the
channelling and mobilization of popular participation (Huntington, 1966).
His explanatory variables are essentially social-structural: the higher levels
of centralization and administrative differentiation characteristic of a
number of European polities can only be understood against the background of long histories of feudal resistance and of secular-religious conflicts; the 'fusion of functions' and the 'division of power' characteristic of
the United States could only emerge in a settler society freed from any
legacy of feudalism and unencumbered by entanglements with a dominant
supranational Church (Huntington, 1966). Peter Nettl goes one step further: relying heavily on Weber's analysis of the growth of bureaucratic
organizations, he suggests a scheme for the rank ordering of historically
given political systems on a number of dimensions of 'stateness' (Nettl,
1968: 2). He does not attempt any detailed ordering of a wide range of
polities along such dimensions but concentrates his attention on four
particularly significant cases: Prussia/Germany, France, Britain and the
United States. The Continental polities were built up around increasingly autonomous bodies of territorial administrators, the British polity around coalitions of elite 'establishments' embodied in parties, while the American polity
stuck to what Huntington calls the 'Tudor constitution' in its heavier
emphasis on the integrative role of the courts and the legal profession.
Schemes of this type clearly have to be spelled out in greater detail before
they can subjected to tests against empirical indicators: among the most
obvious ones would be time series data on the growth of full-time ad-

ministrative personnel in each territory, on the economic resource bases of each category of administrators, their family and kin links to local power-holders, the distinctiveness of their education, the standardization of criteria of entry and promotion. The marked variations in administrative structures within the 'developed' world have never been adequately mapped: Huntington and Nettl tend to group together in their 'European – Continental' category markedly different cases of centre-formation. Clearly, we cannot expect much progress in the empirical testing of models of political development without some concerted action to organize confrontations between generalizing social scientists and students steeped in the administrative histories of pairs or triples of developed systems, smaller as well as larger.

The great merit of Nettl's analysis in this context is his systematic insistence on the logical and empirical independence of the variables 'state-ness' and 'nation-ness': there have been many examples of non-national states and there are a great number of national polities without any 'intrasocietal' state apparatus. A territorial nation need not be built around an autonomous state in the Weberian sense. 'What constitutes nations is surely the organized diffusion of common experience, and this may be structured and experienced by a King, leader, church, party, army *or* state – or all of them.' [43] In this style of conceptualization the term 'nation-state' is an unfortunately misnomer: 'If the entry of the third world onto the stage of modern socioscientific consciousness have had one immediate result (or should have had), it is *the snapping of the link between state and nation*'. [44] In the language of our Parsonian diagram the national centre can be organized around collectivities and coalitions varying markedly in power resources and styles of legitimation: the national centre need not constitute a 'state' except in the elementary sense that it is the locus of external representation.

This is the great thrust of Barrington Moore's path-breaking analysis of the centre-forming coalitions of the leading powers of the modern world (Moore, 1966): he proposes a model of 'polity-building' options and seeks to substantiate a set of propositions about the consequences of such options for the structuring of the central institutions in each territory.

Moore's model posits four sets of actors in the historical process of change from traditional to modern society: the central dynasty and its bureaucracy, the trading and manufacturing bourgeoisie in the cities, the lords of the land, and the peasantry. None of these four sets of actors is strong enough to constitute a centre-forming collectivity on its own: the model forces them to enter into coalitions by pairs or triples and at least one set of actors will be left outside to form an opposition front against this 'nation-building alliance'.

Moore does not attempt any formalization of his model but the underlying combinatorics are easily spelled out. The system mathematically allows six two-against-two and four three-against-one coalitions. Four of these are highly unlikely to occur in any historical situation: the likelihood of any form of bourgeois-peasant co-operation is very small and so is a direct landowner-peasant front against the others. Of the remaining six coalitions Moore singles out four for detailed study: these are the ones he uses in his attempts to explain the variations among seven of his eight leading polities and at the same time constitutes the alternatives he finds it most fruitful to concentrate on in his analysis of the one deviant case, India.

The four alliance options and their consequences in the seven empirical cases may be set out schematically as follows:

Type of coalition	*Cases*	*Decisive modernizing revolution*	*Consequences for structure of polity*
Urban with *Landed* interests	Britain	Puritan Rev. 1640–1660: subordination of dynastic bureaucracy.	Weak, elite-dominated bureaucracy, rule through alternation of parties.
Urban with *Landed* interests	U.S.	Civil War 1860–1865: defeat of Southern 'Junkers'.	Weak, dispersed bureaucracy; rule through pluralist bargaining between courts and established interests.
Urban with *Landed* interests *and* with *Bureaucracy*	France	Great Rev. 1789–1815: abolition of feudal privileges, but increased openings for bourgeois land ownership and strengthened peasantry.	Strongly centralized egalitarian-competitive bureaucracy; oscillation between plebiscitarian rule and fragmented multiparty bargaining.
Landed interests with *Bureaucracy*	Prussia/ German Reich	No 'bourgeois' revolution: failure in 1848. Modernization from above: alliance of bureaucracy, armed forces and Junker landowners.	Strong, elite-dominated bureaucracy, autocratic rule leading to mass dictatorship.
	Japan	No revolution: Imperial Restoration in 1868 through action of modernizing landowners.	Feudalized bureaucracy, autocratic rule leading to period of fascist-military domination.

Type of coalition	Cases	Decisive modernizing revolution	Consequences for structure of polity
Bureaucracy with peasantry	Russia	October Rev. 1917: temporary coalition of peasantry with party bureaucracy against the old 'agrarian bureaucracy', the landowners and the (weak) bourgeoisie.	Strong centralizing bureaucracy, single-party rule.
	China	Long March 1934: party-peasantry coalition against traditional gentry-scholar bureaucracy.	Single-party rule.

This schema obviously cannot do full justice to Moore's richly faceted comparative analysis but it does help to bring out the structure of the argument. In the language of our Parsonian diagram the Moore model concentrates on variables on the *G–A–L* side: on options on the economic front. Linguistic and religious variations enter only marginally into the discussion. True enough, Moore does analyze the weight of religious traditions in the structuring of elite coalitions and peasant reactions in his comparison of India, Japan and China, but he quickly comes to the conclusion that the inherited system of beliefs and ritual was less important than the style of centre-formation: in India continuous segmentation through the operation of caste codes, in Japan fragmentation of peasant oppositions through the feudal control system, in China a much higher level of vulnerability to peasant mobilization because of the heavy concentration of power in the 'agrarian bureaucracy'. Moore is anxious to keep his model free of redundancies: the merit of his analysis lies exactly in the parsimony of his selection of explanatory variables. But this leaves the question of the *range of variations to be accounted for* in any such model of centre-formation and nation-building. Moore argues strongly for a concentration of attention on leading nations: his model focuses on the variations among the eight economically and politically most powerful polities of the modern world and explicitly leaves out of consideration all the smaller and less influential units of the international system. He even goes so far as to question the possibility of any general model of political development: '. . . a general statement about the historical preconditions of democracy or authoritarianism covering small countries as well as large would very likely be so broad as to be abstractly platitudinous' (Moore, 1966: p. XIII).

Moore is probably right in questioning the possibility of constructing empirically models for cross-polity variations at all levels of size *across all cultural regions of the world:* this may work, as he so ably shows, for large and powerful units, but the smaller political systems tend to be so heavily dependent on their cultural contexts that there is likely to be very small payoffs in attempts at indiscriminate comparisons across distinctive cultural regions. This still leaves one important strategy open: the development of *region-specific models* for the explanation of variations in centre-formation and national-building. Such regionally focused models cannot fruitfully be restricted to the large and powerful leader polities, on the contrary the purpose is to account for variations among *all* the distinctive polities in the region and this requires direct attention to the possible consequences of such factors as size, economic resource potential and location in the international power system.

A model of this type has been sketched out for one cultural region of the world: it differs markedly from Moore in its dependent variable but is astoundingly similar in its logical structure. Seymour Martin Lipset and I presented a first version of this model in our Introduction to the volume *Party Systems and Voter Alignments* (Lipset & Rokkan, 1967: 1): we developed a scheme of successive 'option points' in each nation-building history to account for variations in the party systems which emerged in Western Europe with the extension of the suffrage to all adult men. In my further work on 'the politics of the smaller European democracies',[45] I have tried to extend the model to account for variations in the entire process of mass mobilization: differences in the sequences and the timing of measures of democratization as well as differences in the aggregation of party fronts across historically given cleavage lines.

By contrast to Moore's schema, this model posits initial variations on both sides of the Parsonian diagram: the G–I–L side as well as the G–A–L side. The model proceeds in two steps: at the first step it maps variations in the *preconditions* for actual or potential nation-building in the period *before* the decisive thrusts towards mass mobilization in the wake of the French Revolution, at the second it traces options at a number of choice points in the early histories of mass politics in each country.

Again very schematically, the determining variable of the model can be set out as shown on pages 58–59.

These variations in nation-building history serve in the next round as parameters in propositions about steps in the democratization process and about the generation of party systems. The 'precondition' variables help to predict variations in the timing of decisions on democratization, the 'system option' variables to account for variations in party systems. In a fuller statement of the model the linkages between the early preconditions and the later system options will be spelt out in greater detail: in this context our primary concern is to bring out the similarities and the differences in

I. *Precondition variables.*	*Location in diagram:*	*Alternative states of system:*
1. Territorial	*G–L*	Timing of territorial consolidation/secession: – before 1648 – after Napoleonic wars
2. Cultural	*L–I*	Cultural dependence on outside metropolitan centre: – high (same language) – divided – low
	G–I	State-Church settlement: – All Protestant – Catholic minority – Independent Catholic (France) – Counter-Reformation State-Church alliance.
3. Economic	*G–A*	Centralization of urban network: – monocephalic – polycephalic
4. Political	*G*	Structure of central decision-making organs: – continuous history of corporate participation/ representation (city councils, estate assemblies) – significant period of absolute monarchic rule

II. *System options:*	*Location in diagram:*	*Critical juncture:*	*Alternatives:*
1. Cultural	*L–I*	'Reformation': identification of culture and territory.	– one standard national language, suppression of alternatives – one or more minor (subject) languages tolerated – two standard languages
	G–I	National Revolution: control of educational agencies	– national Church allied to secular State – supranational Church (Roman Catholic Church) allied to national State – secular State opposed to supranational Church.

II. *System options:*	*Location in diagram:*	*Critical juncture:*	*Alternatives:*
2. Economic	L–A	Industrial Revolution: agricultural versus commercial-industrial interests	– State allied to agricultural interests (high corn tariff) – State allied to commercial-industrial interests (low tariff).
	G–A	Industrial Revolution: owner versus worker interests	– protect rights of owners/ employers – protect rights of workers/ propertyless.

structure between the Moore model for the eight world powers and this model for eleven smaller and five larger polities of Western Europe.

Moore's model focuses on the *L–A* option but at a different stage in the development of each system: he seeks to characterize the conditions for alliances between rural and urban interests in the centuries before the National and the Industrial Revolutions and tries to generate propositions about the chances for competitive pluralist democracy or authoritarian monolithic rule given the variations in such initial conditions. In our model these early alliance conditions were not brought in to explain variations in the stages and the timing of the decisions on democratization: the *L–A* alternatives were not included among the 'preconditions' variables, only at the level of elite options accounting for the structuring of the national party systems (II.2 above). This difference in the strategy of explanation has obvious consequences for the classification of empirical cases. Moore contrasts the English and the Prussian developments on the basis of the alliance choice of the landowners while our party systems model group the two together because they constitute a configuration unlikely to lead to distinctive agrarian party formations (Lipset & Rokkan, 1967: 1, pp. 44-46). All this finally comes down to a decision about the ranges of dependent variables to be accounted for in the model. Our eleven plus five country scheme restricts itself rigorously to the tasks of predicting variations in the steps taken towards full-suffrage democracy and in the character of the national party systems by the 1920s. Such a model does not necessarily generate propositions about the *stability* or the *vulnerability* of such full-suffrage system.[46] This is a different task: Moore has pointed to a possible scheme of explanation for the larger powers but has made no effort to account for variations among polities at varying levels of size and economic strength; in fact he rejects this task as unworthy of his intellectual efforts. To students of comparative nation-building this constitutes a real challenge: the small nations have developed their own distinctive strategies of consolidation and survival, they have accumulated a wealth of experiences of conflict resolutions and institution-building, and there are enough of them to tempt the ingenuities of all manner of generalizers and model-builders.

We are, it is true, still far from any sort of general consensus on procedures in such comparative studies of nation-building. A number of enthusiasts have tried to develop schemes for world-wide comparisons of nation-building process. Karl Deutsch's data bank was organized for this purpose, Arthur Banks and Robert Textor included all UN members in their *Cross-Polity Survey* (Banks, 1963), Gabriel Almond, Lucian Pye and their colleagues have proposed paradigms for the comparison of nation-building processes wherever they might occur.[47] Our objectives in constructing a model for the eleven smaller and the five larger countries of W. Europe were much more restricted: our model is confined to the territories of Europe affected by the drive toward state-formation and the struggle with the supranational church in the 16th and the 17th centuries and serves to identify only the minimum of elements in the histories of these countries which help to predict the later variations in electoral arrangements and party systems. These are deliberate and programmatic restrictions: they serve to increase the possibilities of operationalization and empirical testing but for that very reason do not claim validity for polities developed from other initial conditions, or for other ranges of dependent variables. It is hoped, of course, that this is a case of *reculer pour mieux sauter:* similarly region-specific models are under construction for Latin America (cf. Cornblit, 1968) and could certainly be developed for other parts of the world. Whether in the end it will be possible to validate universal, world-wide models of political development must still remain an open question: a great deal of hard work will have to be done, not only on the internal logic of each effort of model-building, but even more on the systematic coding of information country by country to test the alternative derivations of the models already advanced.

Priority Variables for Comparative Developmental Research
However controversial the models, however imprecise the concepts, there is already a great deal of implicit consensus on the ranges of data required for the testing of alternative derivations. There may be significant differences in the *strategy of data assembly and processing:* some of us find it easier to work with the extant series of book-keeping data and simply want to transfer a maximum of the already coded information on to cards or tape for computer processing, while others among us are willing and anxious to take on the much more laborious, but possibly more rewarding, task of imposing their own classification schemes on the wealth of 'process produced' material they find at hand country by country, be they biographical records, legislative or ministerial documents, or literary products. Some division of labour is clearly essential: no single centre can work on

all countries and on all variables with any hope of intellectual payoff. But there *is* a need for cross-communication and a minimum of co-ordination. The 'archival revolution' will soon catch up with the vast masses of book-keeping data for the 19th and early 20th centuries: these efforts will clearly help forward the work on each of the *national* sequences of development, but if they are also to advance *comparative* analysis, facilities will have to be set up for regular consultations on the definition of the variables, the coding schemes, data management practices and analysis tools.

Gabriel Almond, Lucian Pye and their associates have suggested a paradigm which may offer a convenient grid for the ordering of variables in such comparative research.

This paradigm is organized around six 'crises of development': these constitute challenges, issues, policy options, to be faced in the course of *any* process of nation-building.

Very schematically these six critical junctures can be described as follows: [48]

Crises, challenges, problems	Institutional solutions: examples	Corresponding locations in A–G–I–L diagram.[49]
Penetration	Establishment of a rational field administration for resource mobilization (taxes, manpower), creation of public order, and the coordination of collective efforts (infrastructure development, emergency action, defense).	G–L (extension of centre control over periphery)
Integration	Establishment of allocation rules equalizing the shares of offices, benefits, resources among all culturally and/or politically distinct sectors of the national community.	G–I (sharing of control powers across elites, segments, strata)
Participation	Extension of suffrage to hitherto under-privileged strata of population. Protection of the rights of organized opposition.	I–L (equalization of opportunities in mobilization markets)
Identity	Development of media and agencies for the socialization of future citizens into the national community: schools, literary media, institutionalized rituals and symbols (myths, flags, songs).	L–G (acceptance/support of territorial agencies)
Legitimacy	Any effort to create loyalty to and confidence in the established structure of political institutions in the given system and to ensure regular conformity to rules and regulations issued by the agencies authorized within the system.	I–G (acceptance/support of distribution of control powers)

Crises, challenges, problems	Institutional solutions: examples	Corresponding locations in A–G–I–L diagram.[49]
Distribution	Establishment of social services and social security measures, income equalization through progressive taxation and transfer between poorer and richer localities.	G–A–L (central control of labour-commodity markets)

The sequences of such critical challenges will of course vary markedly from case to case. In the older European polities the challenges of state-building had to be faced long before the crises of identity and legitimacy triggered by the spread of the ideas of the French Revolution. In the later secession states and for the states emerging from the colonial empires in the 'third world' the time order of crises differed markedly from the earlier sequences and tended to cumulate one upon the other without much let-up. Lucian Pye's ordering and description of the six crises essentially fits the ideal-typical inchoate state emerging from colonial dependence (Pye, 1968):

The Identity Crisis. The first and most fundamental crisis is that of achieving a common sense of identity. The people in a new state must come to recognize their national territory as being their true homeland, and they must feel as individuals that their own personal identities are in part defined by their identification with their territorially delimited country. In most of the new states traditional forms of identity ranging from tribe or caste to ethnic and linguistic groups compete with the sense of larger national identity.

The identity crisis also involves the resolution of the problem of traditional heritage and modern practices, the dilemma of parochial sentiments and cosmopolitan practices. . . . As long as people feel pulled between two worlds and are without roots in any society they cannot have the firm sense of identity necessary for building a stable, modern nation-state.

The Legitimacy Crisis. Closely related to the identity crisis is the problem of achieving agreement about the legitimate nature of authority and the proper responsibilities of government. In many new states the crisis of legitimacy is a straightforward constitutional problem: what should be the relationship between central and local authorities? What are the proper limits of the bureaucracy, or of the army, in the nation's political life? Or possibly the conflict is over how much of the colonial structure of government should be preserved in an independent state.

In other new states the question of legitimacy is more diffuse, and it involves sentiments about what should be the underlying spirit of government and the primary goals of national effort. For example, in some Moslem lands there is a deep desire that the state should in some fashion reflect the spirit of Islam. In other societies the issue of legitimacy involves questions about how far the governmental authorities should directly push economic development as compared with other possible goals. Above all, in traditional societies there can be a deep crisis of authority because all attempts at ruling are challenged by different people for different reasons, and no leaders are able to gain a full command of legitimate authority.

The Penetration Crisis. The critical problems of administration in the new states give rise to the penetration crisis, which involves the problems of government in reaching down into the society and effecting basic policies. . . . In traditional societies government had limited demands to make on the society, and in most transitional systems the governments are far more ambitious. This is particularly true if the rulers seek to accelerate the pace of economic development and social change. To carry out significant developmental policies a government must be able to reach down to the village level and touch the daily lives of people.

Yet . . . a dominant characteristic of transitional societies is the gap between the world of the ruling elite and that of the masses of the people who are still oriented toward their parochial ways. The penetration problem is that of building up the effectiveness of the formal institutions of government and of establishing confidence and rapport between rulers and subjects. Initially governments often find it difficult to motivate the population or to change its values and habits in order to bring support to programs of national development. On the other hand, at times the effectiveness of the government in breaking down old patterns of control can unleash widespread demands for a greater influence on governmental policies. When this occurs the result is another crisis, that of participation.

The Participation Crisis. . . . The participation crisis occurs when there is uncertainty over the appropriate rate of expansion and when the influx of new participants creates serious strains on the existing institutions. As new segments of the population are brought into the political process, new interests and new issues begin to arise so that the continuity of the old polity is broken and there is the need to re-establish the entire structure of political relations.

In a sense the participation crisis arises out of the emergence of interest groups and the formation of a party system. The question in many new states is whether the expansion in participation is likely to be effectively organized into specific interest groups or whether the pressures will lead only to mass demands and widespread feelings of anomie. It should also be noted that the appearance of a participation crisis does not necessarily signal pressures for democratic processes. The participation crisis can be organized as in totalitarian states to provide the basis for manipulated mass organizations and demonstrational politics.

Integration Crisis. This crisis covers the problems of relating popular politics to governmental performance and thus it represents the effective and compatible solution of both the penetration and the participation crisis. The problem of integration therefore deals with the extent to which the entire polity is organized as a system of interacting relationships, first among the officers and agencies of government, and then among the various groups and interests seeking to make demands upon the system, and finally in the relationships between officials and articulating citizens.

In many of the transitional systems there may be many different group-ings of interests, but they hardly interact with each other, and at best each seeks to make its separate demands upon the government. The government must seek to cope with all these demands simultaneously. Yet at the same time the government itself may not be well integrated. The result is a low level of general performance throughout the political system.

The Distribution Crisis. The final crisis in the development process in-volves questions about how governmental powers are to be used to in-fluence the distribution of goods, services, and values throughout the society. Who is to benefit from government, and what should the govern-ment be doing to bring greater benefits to different segments of the society?

Much of the stress on economic development and the popularity of socialist slogans in the new states is a reflection of the basic crisis. In some cases governments seek to meet the problem by directly intervening in the distribution of wealth; in other cases the approach is to strengthen the op-portunities and potentialities of the disadvantaged groups.

There are obvious difficulties of operationalization in this scheme: what are the criteria for recognizing a particular set of differences over strategy or policy as an element in a deeper crisis? What if there are elements of two, three or all these challenges at a given critical juncture? What indi-cators can be constructed for measuring a) the severity of the crisis on one or more of the six dimensions, b) the effects of the measures taken to solve it?

Very little work has as yet been done on the development of such opera-tional criteria or indices and very little has been done in the way of systematic coding of extant cases of political change within this framework. Sidney Verba has prepared a hardheaded analysis of the problems of cumulation and compounding in the handling of critical challenges and has tried to work out criteria for the differentiation of long-run system management problems from short-run crisis of imperative structural change:

A crisis of development may be defined as a short-run development cycle that involves
— a shift in the relationship between *environmental pressures* and *level of politicization* on the one hand, and *governmental output and institu-tionalizations* on the other,
— such that the *institutionalization of a new level of governmental output* is required
— if the pressures resulting from the environment and/or the shift in poli-

ticization are to be prevented from leading to *the overthrow of the elite structure of the society* or to the changing of the societal boundaries.[50]

The obvious implication is that far from all such problems of system development need lead to threatening situations of 'either – or' option. Each of the six sets of challenges may be handled through long series of adjustments and need not increase in severity to the point where the choice is a brutal yes or no: quick changes in the output of commands and in the structure of institutions, or else revolution or invasion from outside. It is not difficult to identify for each of the six sets of challenges a set of crucial governmental decisions, but many if not most of these decisions were not taken in the face of severe internal or external threats but simply to gain strategic advantages in struggles between competing elites. In fact it would be possible to pinpoint, for any of the nation-states formed up to World War II or thereabouts (much more difficult for later states because of the compounding of challenges), the most significant legislative or ministerial decisions on each dimension of development and to classify each such decision on some index for the severity of the actually evidenced threat to the system:

– for the *'penetration'* challenge one would look for decisions on the reform of the administration (the equivalent of the Northcote-Trevelyan Act);
– for the *'integration'* challenge one would check decisions on criteria of recruitment, the equalization of opportunities and obligations, etc.;
– for the *'identity'* challenge there would be decisions on language and religion in the schools, on the protection of national symbols, on the handling of minorities;
– for the *'legitimacy'* challenge one could count the number and the severity of the changes in the constitution, and check all decisions on the handling of anti-system movements, treasonable activities and subversion;
– for the *'participation'* challenge it is easy to list the laws on the extension and equalization of the suffrage and the protection of the rights of communication, assembly and association;
– and for the *'distribution'* challenge it is again easy to list the sequences of decisions on taxation, social services, pensions and other measures of income and opportunity equalization.

It is in fact tempting to go further in the reinterpretation of this paradigm: to treat it essentially as a series of *headings in a classification of time series data and composite indicators* of potential utility in comparative analysis of nation-building processes.

A first sketch of such a listing follows:

1. *Penetration*

Time series data for *growth of public sector:*

1.1 central personnel
1.2 field personnel by region and type of locality
1.3 recruitment criteria: family and local ties vs. education, cf. 2.1 for recruitment by cultural/political *divisions*
1.4 governmental share of GNP: central, intermediary and local
1.5 bases of resource extraction: the change from external (customs duties) to internal control (property, income taxation)
1.6 government investments in centre-forming infrastructure (build-up of capital, periphery to capital communications)
1.7 levels of public debt and dependence on foreign finance
1.8 levels of military preparedness and the extent of mobilization for armed service.

2. *Integration*

Time series data for

2.1 the recruitment of elite personnel (appointed officials, elected representatives, intellectual leaders) for each major regional cultural/political division of the country (e.g., per cent Protestants/Catholics in bureaucracy, per cent from minority language groups, from peripheral provinces)
2.2 shares of infrastructure investments (roads, railways, schools, etc.) by region and distance from centre(s)
2.3 in religiously mixed nations, government contributions per pupil for schooling
2.4 income differentials by region and type of locality (use of 'peripherality' scores).

3. *Identity*

Time series data for

3.1 development of mass literacy by region and type of locality
3.2 development of secondary education: school places by region, type of locality, and affiliation of school
3.3 types of teacher education: numbers trained for each category of school (denominational vs. secular, elite vs. minority language)
3.4 religious affiliation and, for the years available, religious participation (no. of *messalisants)* by region and type of locality
3.5 linguistic divisions by region and type of locality.

4. *Legitimacy*

Time series data, if any, for

4.1 numbers involved in strikes or lockouts, demonstrations, riots
4.2 votes for 'anti-system' parties in regular elections.

5. *Participation*

Time series data for

5.1 per cent enfranchised by region and type of locality, whenever possible (Sweden) also by occupational stratum
5.2 per cent electoral turnout by region, by locality and for the two sexes
5.3 organizational participation: memberships in parties, popular movements, unions and other interest associations
5.4 cultural participation: readership of newspapers, popular magazines, books, exposure to films, radio, TV.

6. *Distribution*
Time series data on
6.1 shares of governmental revenue allocated for education, social services, pensions
6.2 categories, memberships and coverage of social services
6.3 central and local tax burdens by levels of income and, if possible, by major occupational groups (farmers, employers and employees).

Each of these variables bears in one way or another on governmental actions and will have to be studied against the background of a broader array of 'benchmark' data on demographic development, settlement structure and class divisions.

Karl Deutsch's ideal measure of mobilization cuts across the two fields of variations: some of the criteria refer to movements at a high level of independence from governmental actions, others reflect governmental interventions very directly.

In his *Nationalism,* Deutsch lists *fourteen* possible 'yardsticks of measurement' (Deutsch, 1968, p. 126; cf. Deutsch, 1961). Nine of these are already covered in our list under Penetration, Identity, Participation or Distribution. The five others are:

– the proportion of the territorial population in *urban settlements,*
– the proportion in the *secondary and tertiary* sectors of the economy,
– the proportion *working for money wages in units of five or more employees,*
– the proportion *attending markets* regularly,
– the proportion *sending or receiving a letter* at least once a month.

Useful time series for *all these* variables are obviously very hard to come by even for a *single* country: there is no hope of acquiring such extensive batteries for *comparative* analysis. In fact in his four country analyses, Deutsch used only *one* criterion of mobilization each time: urbanization in Finland and India, the proportion in the secondary or tertiary sectors in Czechoslovakia and Scotland. With the accumulation of time series data in computer archives it should clearly be possible to develop much more elaborate analyses of the relationships among the indicators and establish empirical typologies through such techniques as principal components analysis. An example of what can soon be done cross-nationally is Paavo Seppänen's analysis of overall social change in Finland from 1911 to 1961: this is based on over 100 time series variables and proceeds by factor analysis to establish basic dimensions as well as critical phases in the process of change (Seppänen, 1965). Once the Yale Data Program [51] has been extended to cover time series country by country it should be possible to carry out comparative studies of rates and time phases of change for a broad range of countries, at least within Europe and the West. Wolfgang Zapf's work on comparative indicators of development shows how it is possible to proceed on the basis of careful library searches (Zapf, 1969). Once such analyses get under way there will clearly be pressures to go beyond the national aggregate to assemble data on the extent of variations among regions and provinces and between central and peripheral localities in each National territory. Ecological archives have by now been established for over a dozen countries and the time span of some of the variables, especially census and election data, will soon be stretched to cover most of the bookkeeping histories of each country (Rokkan, 1966: 3; Dogan, 1969). The same goes for the developing archives of information from *elite biographies:* statistics of the background characteristics and careers of parliamentarians have been assembled for computer processing in a number of countries and will offer a basis for comparative studies of processes of social change.[52] The pioneering work of a group of Uppsala historians on the spread of *voluntary associations* throughout Sweden in the 19th century will no doubt lead to similar efforts in other countries (Andrae, 1968). The spread of computing facilities to more and more universities is bound to bring about a fundamental change in the conditions for comparative research within a foreseeable future: to forestall useless divergencies in the design of coding schemes and in data management procedures it will clearly be imperative to develop facilities for close cooperation among the active builders and users of such data archives.

The International Social Science Council has taken important steps in this direction through the establishment of a *Standing Committee on Social Science Data Archives:* this will help to spread technical and substantive information about archives at different stages of development and will facilitate exchanges of data for purposes of comparative analysis (Bisco, 1967). UNESCO has taken a further step in this direction through its plans to launch a series of computer-aided *data confrontation seminars:* the first of these was organized in 1969 by the Inter-University Consortium at Ann Arbor, Michigan.

The idea of these seminars is deceptively simple but seems to hold great potentialities for the future of cross-national research: experts on quantitative analysis from *n* countries are invited to join in a two-to-three week seminar of comparative analysis but are not asked to contribute papers in advance in the usual style of international scholarship; instead they are asked to send *data decks* covering an agreed set of units and an agreed range of variables to the seminar site for reformatting and advance analysis on the local computer; the task of the actual seminar is then to work out the details of the comparisons through joint interpretations of the initial output and through regular interaction with the computer through the introduction of further controls and through the testing of alternative analysis procedures.

This procedure seems to hold a great deal of promise in the analysis of data readily at hand in established archives, whether they are data from sample surveys or polls, data from ecological files for recent censuses, elections and other official statistics, or data from bibliographical files for given elite categories. Data such as these require very little recoding and can be prepared for uniform analysis without too great investments of time and personnel. The situation is quite different for longer-term developmental data of the type discussed in this chapter: the planning of cross-national analysis seminars for 19th-century and early 20th-century materials will clearly require much more intensive interaction among the experts on each country's history and statistics and cannot be achieved in one single step. For such data the best procedure seems to be to persuade small groups of collaborating research centres to concentrate their efforts on the establishment of time series for their countries for some limited range of variables. This is in fact what has occurred, without much formal prodding, in the field of economic history and development economics. Similar working arrangements have been discussed for other sets of data: [53] there is a thriving international movement in demographic history,[54] and some initial spadework has been done to prepare for international comparisons of data on political mobilization and the growth of mass organizations (Rokkan, 1962: 2; Rokkan, 1966: 4; Lipset & Rokkan, 1967; Rokkan, 1969: 4). The international team currently at work on the politics of eleven smaller European democracies (Rokkan, 1968: 3 and Ch. 3 below; Dahl, 1967) have collected a considerable number of time series tables for indicators of political development and there is good hope that this work will be followed up in the future through further data collation and analysis. Within the four Scandinavian countries a collective study of differences and similarities in social structure is currently under discussion (Dahlström, 1968): in this study it is hoped that it will be possible to enlist statistically oriented historians for collaboration with sociologists and political scientists in comparative analysis of the initial conditions at some arbitrary 'year zero' (say, 1850) and of the subsequent variations in the rates of change.

For UNESCO such efforts of intensive comparative analysis of factors affecting the success or failure of nation-building would appear to be particularly fruitful. UNESCO has taken on important responsibilities for the advancement of literacy and culture in the developing world and is highly dependent on research on earlier experiences of mass education and cultural mobilization: this goes for the dominant countries and their histories of nation-building but it is of even greater importance to foster detailed comparative studies of *19th- and early 20th-century developments in the units most comparable to the new states of the 1950s and 1960s, the smaller and the more marginal of the European and the European-settled polities.* UNESCO has already taken steps to carry out comparative studies of the relationships between economic growth, mass education and the spread of the mass media (UNESCO, 1961; Schramm, 1964; United Nations, 1968), but these have been limited to very short time series or very few countries and have not considered the broader context of nation-building. Within an expanded programme of comparative research on nation-building it should be possible both to extend the time series and to enrich the analysis through the addition of further contextual variables. It is not likely that this can be done for more than a few countries at a time but this may in itself be an advantage: 'third world' social scientists invited to attend seminars on such intensive comparative analysis may in fact carry home with them much more realistic notions of the strategies and costs of development and acquire deeper insight into the alternatives facing their own countries.

NOTES

[35] These are probably the most complete bibliographical listings: (Pinson, 1935; Deutsch, 1956; Deutsch, 1968). For a useful review of major writings from 1953 through 1965, see (Deutsch, 1953; 2nd ed. 1966: pp. 1–14).

[36] The initial formulations appeared in (Almond, 1960). The Committee on Comparative Politics has so far published six volumes in the series *Studies in Political Development:* (Pye, 1963; La Palombara, 1963; Ward, 1964; Coleman, 1965: 2; Pye, 1965: 3; La Palombara, 1966).

[37] Several of the publications flowing from the Committee or its individual members evidence interest in the theoretical implications of the variations within Europe and the West, see esp. (Almond, 1963; Almond, 1966).

[38] Cf. a typical remark by Barrington Moore (Moore, 1966: pp. XII–XIII): 'This study concentrates on certain important stages in a prolonged social process which has worked itself out in several countries. As a part of this process new social arrangements have grown up by violence or in other ways which have made certain countries political leaders at different points in time during the first half of the twentieth century. The focus of interest is on innovation that has led to political power, not only the spread and reception of institutions that have been hammered out elsewhere, except where they have led to significant power in world politics. *The fact that the smaller countries depend economically and politically on big and powerful ones means that the decisive causes of their politics lie outside their own boundaries. It also means that their political problems are not really comparable to those of larger countries. Therefore a general statement about the historical preconditions of democracy or authoritarianism covering smaller countries as well as large would very likely be so broad as to be abstractly platitudinous'* (our italics). Clearly there are as good intellectual reasons for studying diffusion and reception as for analyzing conflict and innovation in major centres: after all most of the units open to comparative

research are 'follower' nations rather than leaders. But this surely is not always and exclusively a matter of size: Greece and Israel produced the greatest innovations of the ancient world and Sweden, the Netherlands and Switzerland can hardly be fruitfully studied as passive victims of exogenous pressures.

[39] For discussion of the 'whole nation' bias in the draft version of (Russett, 1964), see (Merritt, 1966: 1, Part III; Berry, 1966).

[40] This 'hierarchization' of the Parsonian *A–G–I–L* scheme of functional differentiation was first presented in the Introduction to (Lipset & Rokkan, 1967: 2). For a further utilization of this imagery in the study of the *inter*-national system see (Nettl, 1968: 1, pp. 162–68).

[41] See the definitions in (Deutsch, 1968: Ch. 6). For a further elaboration of the concept of mobilization see (Deutsch, 1961). A similar listing of variables is discussed in Chapter 7 below.

[42] (Dahrendorf, 1965). Cf. the parallel analysis of central political institutions in (Bracher, 1968).

[43] (Nettl, 1968: 2, pp. 565–66). Nettl's italics.

[44] (Nettl, 1968: 2, p. 560). Our italics.

[45] On this project see (Lorwin, 1968). A first report on an attempt at a systematization of data on electoral arrangements and party systems in these eleven countries (the five Nordic countries, the three BE-NE-LUX ones, Ireland, Switzerland and Austria) will be found in (Rokkan, 1968: 4): part of this article has been reproduced in Ch. 3 of this volume.

[46] Cf. the discussion of the conditions for the breakdown of European multiparty systems in (Lipset & Rokkan, 1967: 1, pp. 50–56) and Ch. 3 below.

[47] See the volumes listed in footnote 36 and especially (Pye, 1965: 1) and (Pye, 1968).

[48] This schematic presentation reflects a reading of *early* drafts of chapters for the prospective volume on *Crises of political development*. These drafts were given restricted circulation by the Committee in 1967: (Coleman, 1965: 1; Pye, 1965: 2; Weiner, 1965; Verba, 1965: 1).

[49] These interpretations have not been checked with members of the SSRC Committee.

[50] (Verba, 1965: 1, p. 30), our emphases and paragraph structure.

[51] The second edition of (Russett, 1964) will include a number of shorter, mainly post-1945, time series: this edition is due in 1970.

[52] Archives of biographical statistics for parliamentary personnel have been built up in Britain, Finland, France, Germany, Italy, Norway and Switzerland, and will be built up in the Netherlands, Sweden and several other countries in the near future. Among descriptive or analytical reports based on such files these appear particularly important: (Guttsman, 1963; Sartori, 1963; Zapf, 1965; Gruner, 1966; Valen, 1966; Pedersen, 1968; Rokkan, 1968).

[53] An important vehicle for communication on computerization projects in history is *Historical Methods Newsletter,* Univ. of Pittsburgh, Dept. of History: this was first issued in Dec. 1967.

[54] See (Glass, 1965; Wrigley, 1966). These works are heavily influenced by the French school of historical demography and suggest possibilities of comparative research on pre-censal populations on the basis of the Henry-Fleury method of family reconstitution from samples of parish registers. The rationale for work of the Cambridge group for the History of Population and Sociology is set out with great enthusiasm in (Laslett, 1965), cf. the progress report on pre-censal ecology in (Laslett, 1969).

THREE

Nation-Building, Cleavage Formation and the Structuring of Mass Politics

Typologies of Political Systems

There is a curious awkwardness about discussions of 'types' in comparative politics. Aristotle and Montesquieu taught us to proceed by classifications of regimes and the current generation of computer enthusiasts have offered us more and more powerful tools for the handling of wide ranges of attributes of political entities and for the establishment of complex multi-dimensional typologies. Yet as soon as we are confronted with a concrete table of alternative types and look over the lists of cases assigned to each cell, our first reaction is almost immediately to add further distinctions, to reject the imposition of similarities across historically distinct units. The student of politics is torn between two sets of superego demands: he feels an obligation to reduce the welter of empirical facts to a body of parsimoniously organized general propositions but he also feels under pressure to treat each case *sui generis,* as a unique configuration worthy of an effort of understanding all on its own. This is of course a dilemma common to all social sciences but is particularly difficult to handle in the study of

Origin: This chapter merges elements from two earlier publications: (Lipset & Rokkan, 1967: 1) Free Press, New York, 1967, and (Rokkan, 1968: 3) *Comparative Studies in Society and History,* Cambridge University Press, 1968. This amalgam was originally produced at the behest of Samuel Eisenstadt: I am most grateful to him for his encouragement.

such highly visible, amply documented macro-units as historical polities. Students of census records, elections and survey data have an enormous analytical advantage: they deal with large numbers of anonymous units and can therefore proceed with the analysis of their data with a minimum of interference from exogeneous 'noise'. The student of comparative politics is roughly in the position of a social scientist asked to analyze the census records or the survey responses of a set of close friends: he cannot prevent himself from bringing into his analysis of the coded data on the punched cards a wide range of uncoded 'surplus' information acquired through years of acquaintance with the subjects. The standardized sample survey derives great methodological strength from its programmatic insistence on equality, anonymity and distance in the treatment of the information collected: the data are given once and for all in the protocols or on the IBM cards and there is no allowance for fuzzy interaction with the subjects outside that framework. The student of comparative politics has not developed any similar device for screening off 'background noise' in his attempts at analyzing similarities and differences among regimes and in testing out generalizations: he has been exposed to messages from or communications about many of these units since his early childhood and he tends to be heavily burdened with such random *ad hoc* surplus information whenever he judges a particular scheme of coding or a table of compound types. It is probably significant that the great 'leap forward' in comparative politics came with a mushrooming of new macro-units on the world arena in the 'fifties: the increase in numbers and the decrease in the average level of familiarity made it psychologically easier to treat the units as if they were the anonymous subjects of a census or a survey rather than multi-faceted, multi-layered historical configurations. It is probably no less significant that the early enthusiasm for global generalization has been on the wane in the last two or three years: the massive inflow of scattered information has caught up with the theory-builders and the greater familiarity with configurational details has increased the resistance to the simplifying typologies of the pioneers.

Hopefully, this does not mean that the discipline has come full circle; that we are back to the production of idiosyncratic monographs on unique constellations of institutions and processes. The phase of global generalization-mongering has taught us to look for the significant communalities in the operation of political systems and to concentrate on a series of critical choice-points in their historical development. What we have to learn is to develop *multi-dimensional typologies for configurational complexes:* typologies which tap significant elements of each historical-political context and yet allow wide-ranging comparative analysis, dimension by dimension. Any attempt to develop a scheme of codes or to construct a typology implies a series of choices and a series of rejections within a vast mass of actually assembled or potentially 'collectable' information: to assign units to types means to leave out large chunks of information in an effort to establish knowledge of invariances across them. It is easy enough to develop typologies in ignorance of the information lost through the choice of attributes and the assignment of codes: our task is to develop and test alternative typologies *in full awareness* of the information lost through each such effort.

A Model in Two Steps
This chapter explores one possible line of progress in this direction: it represents an effort to formulate a model for the generation of one set of such configurational typologies.

The model I shall propose focuses on a limited range of institutions within a limited range of polities: it represents an effort to arrive at a parsimonious description of the *critical steps in the development and structuring of competitive mass politics* in the countries of Western Europe.

This concentration on one set of institutions and one set of countries does not imply an outright rejection of the efforts made to construct universal models of political development: some elements of the region-specific model I shall propose may be built into models for other regions of the world but the basic structure of the model reflects a uniquely European experience.[56]

The model grows out of work on the comparative sociology of elections and electoral behaviour: in fact, the first version was worked out in response to the call for a broader theoretical framework for a series of cross-national analyses of sociocultural factors affecting the behaviour of voters.

Countless tables have been prepared for country after country of the electoral choices of the two sexes, for the different age groups, for the various occupational strata, denominations, ethnic and linguistic divisions. There are wellknown difficulties of comparison on the side of the *independent* variables in such analyses but these are vastly easier to handle than the difficulties on the *dependent* side: the variations in the actual political choices of the different citizenries. The twin processes of urbanization and industrialization have tended to increase the comparability of occupational structures across the nations but have not produced anything approaching uniformity in the *structures of political alternatives* confronting the citizens of the different polities. These cross-national variations in the character of the categories of political choice present a major challenge to students of comparative politics. In some initial comparative analyses attempts were made to reduce the multi-dimensional variations of party choice to some form of 'left-right' dichotomy or 'left-center-right' trichotomy (Lipset, 1954): this worked for some, but not all, of the Anglo-American democracies (Alford, 1963) but clearly entailed significant losses of information in comparative analyses of Continental and Scandinavian data. To make any headway in cross-national research on electoral behaviour we shall clearly have to devote much more detailed study to the character of the electoral options facing the citizens in the different systems and seek to identify the crucial dimensions of variation among the sets of alternatives.

There are many ways of proceeding in such comparative analyses of the choices before different national electorates.

One can proceed *synchronically* and map out the differences among the electoral alternatives country by country during a given period of time, e.g., the years since World War II:

– one possibility is to start at the *micro* level of the voter and inquire into the sources of variations in the *subjective rank ordering of the different parties* on different dimensions of identification, ideology, candidate characteristics or policy expectations;[57]

– another is to focus on the *candidates presented* and work out indexes of distinctiveness among the parties;[58]

– a third is to look at the themes of the campaigns, the programmes and the public expressions of party ideologies and identify the dimensions of differentiation;[59]

– and a fourth is to check the *legislative behaviour* of the party representatives, their votes and their stands on electorally significant issues.[60]

One can also proceed *diachronically* and try to pin down the crucial differences from country to country in *the sequences in the establishment of the rules of the electoral game and in the formation of party alternatives:* this is the historical-developmental approach chosen in this chapter.

In future work it will be essential to link up such diachronic approaches with the several synchronic procedures: in fact it will not be possible to check through all the predictions from the developmental model without a sequence of such synchronic analyses at a number of time points before and after the 'freezing' of each national system of alternatives.

The developmental model to be explored posits clear-cut time limits to its operation:

its *terminus a quo* is the conflict over the cultural-religious identity of the emerging nation-state in the sixteenth century;

its *terminus ad quem* is the establishment of universal and equal electoral democracy and the 'freezing' of party alternatives, in most countries during the 1920s and the 1930s, at any rate before World War II.

This limitation in time span obviously also defines the geographical focus of the model: it only applies to the territories and the polities which were immediately affected by the clashes between the Reformers and the Roman Church and the consequent strains between secular and religious powers.

In fact we shall concentrate our analysis even further: we shall focus on the still competitive polities of the West and shall, within this orbit, give particular attention to the *smaller* of the surviving units.[61]

The eleven 'smaller European democracies' to be dealt with are the five Nordic countries, the three BE-NE-LUX countries, the Republic of Ireland, the Swiss Confederation, and Austria.

These eleven units will not only be compared among themselves but on a number of points contrasted with one or the other of the five larger polities: Britain, France, Prussia/Germany, Italy, and in a few cases, Spain.

These countries can all point to long, if checkered, histories of competitive parliamentary politics. By the early 1920s they had all *extended the rights of political citizenship* to all adults: in Switzerland, France and Italy exclusively to the men, in Belgium to a few war-qualified women (mothers and widows of fallen soldiers) in addition to the men, in Britain to the upper stratum of women only, in the other ten countries to women on a par with men. But there were important differences in the character of electoral competition in the fifteen countries: the conflicts over representation had been increasingly nationalized through the development of mass parties but the stakes of the electoral struggles differed fundamentally between *majoritarian* countries and *proportionalist* countries. This is a point of crucial importance in any discussion of differences between the smaller and the larger of the units in the Western European system: the smaller democracies have been much more prone to accept the principle of proportionality, the larger ones have either rejected it or been riven by controversies over its maintenance.

The *Proporz* is indeed a highly significant common denominator across the eleven smaller countries: they all left the plurality principle, some of the Swiss cantons already in the early 1890s, Belgium in 1899, Finland in 1906, Sweden in 1909, the other countries from 1915 to 1922. The one late-comer to the PR league was Iceland. The smallest of our smaller democracies did not go all the way when the electoral law was changed in 1920: the traditional system was kept up in the rural districts and was not replaced by PR in all constituencies until 1959. This is perhaps the one characteristic which sets the clearest contrast between the political structures of the smaller and the larger polities in Western Europe. Britain stuck steadfastly to the plurality system, France suffered only brief lapses into proportionalism while Germany and Italy experienced protracted difficulties and controversies over their electoral arrangements ever since PR was introduced in the wake of World War I. There was obviously a great deal of discussion on the pros and cons of electoral systems in the smaller countries as well but once the party systems had accommodated themselves to the new rules of the game there were few serious, sustained campaigns for a return to plurality-type elections: there was a great deal of debate over the threshold levels and districting,[62] but few direct challenges to the principle of proportionality as such until the mid-sixties.[63] This contrast between the larger and the smaller polities is doubly significant in the light of the analyses offered in the polemical literature against PR. Again and again we come across attempts to reconcile the theorizing with the empirical evidence by emphasizing the differences in the consequences of electoral decisions for the smaller as against the larger countries: PR is tolerable in the smaller units because they face lesser loads of decision-making, it is disastrous for the larger countries because of their heavier burdens of responsibility (Friedrich, 1941: p. XXXV; Unkelbach, 1956: pp. 59–65).

These elements add up to a good prima facie case for a comparative analysis of the structuring of mass politics just in these smaller countries: the similarities of the electoral institutions make it easier to pin down the effects of differences in historical circumstances and sociocultural structure. Indeed, the very fact that these are the PR countries par excellence invites such attempts at comparison: PR helps to 'freeze' the early structures of articulation and aggregation and for that very reason makes it easier to pinpoint variations in the socio-cultural basis of support for the different political alternatives.[64]

With all the similarities they developed in their formal institutions the eleven smaller countries do indeed offer an extraordinary range of variations in the structuring of their political life: not only did they proceed along very different paths towards their present systems of competitive mass democracy but they still offer strikingly different electoral alternatives to their citizenries. To understand the similarities and the differences in the behaviours of the voters in these eleven countries we shall clearly have to go back into history and consider the steps in the setting of these widely differing alternatives for electoral choice: we shall have to resort to developmental analysis to pin down the sources of variations in the 'macro' conditions for 'micro' behaviours.[65]

Through an intriguing process of dialectics this 'return to history' has been strongly stimulated by the programmatically *a*historical analyses of the psychology of partisanship pursued with such vigour by the great team of electoral analysts at the University of Michigan:[66] the concentration on variations in the intensity of identifications with such historically given entities as political parties must of necessity arouse curiosity about the origins, the age and the continuity of these objects in the political landscape.

'Parties do not simply present themselves *de novo* to the citizen at each election: they each have a history and so have the constellations of alternatives they present to the electorate. In single-nation studies we need not always take this history into account in analyzing current alignments: we assume that the parties are equally visible 'givens' to all the citizens within the nation. But as soon as we move into comparative analysis we have to add a historical dimension: we simply cannot make sense of variations in current alignments without detailed data on differences in the sequences of party formation and in the character of the alternatives presented to the electorates before and after the extension of the suffrage. We have to carry out our comparative analyses in several steps: we first have to consider the initial developments toward competitive politics and the institutionalization of mass elections, we next have to disentangle the constellation of cleavages and oppositions which produced the national system of mass organizations for electoral action, and then, and only then, can we make headway toward some understanding of the forces producing the current alignments of voters behind the historically given alternatives. In our Western democracies the voters are only rarely called upon to express their stands on single issues: they are faced with choices among historically given 'packages' of programmes, commitments, outlooks, and, sometimes, *Weltanschauungen,* and we cannot understand their current behaviours without some knowledge of the sequences of events and the combinations of forces which produced these 'packages'. Our task is to develop realistic models to explain the formation of different systems of such 'packages' under different conditions of national politics and socioeconomic development and to fit information on these variations in the character of the alternatives into our schemes for the analysis of current electoral behaviour' (Lipset & Rokkan, 1967: 1, pp. 2–3).

This is a task I shall try to tackle, first for the eleven smaller polities, later for all the fifteen competitive systems in Western Europe: I shall suggest, in crude outline, a model for the explanation of variations in the sequences of democratization and in the structuring of the party systems in these countries, and shall discuss, by way of conclusion, some of the implications for comparative research on electoral behaviour.

The task is to generate hypotheses about invariances in the bewildering wealth of data about the course of political change: to bring some intellectual order into the study of processes of democratization and partisan mobilization for electoral competition.

The questions asked about such processes can, without great conceptual violence, be grouped under two headings:

questions about variations and changes in the institutional *'rules of the game'* in the given polity;

questions about variations and changes in the *culturally, socially and economically given opportunities for the articulation of protest, the aggregation of demands, the mobilization of support.*

The first set of questions focuses on *system response:* the outputs of institutional rearrangements in the face of pressures from below or from outside.

The second set of questions focuses on variations in the *sources of inputs:* in the markets for the mobilization of support for particular demands, for broadly aggregated or narrowly articulated pressures on the decision-making system.

The ultimate goal is to account for the processes of interaction between outputs and inputs: to pin down the consequences of new outputs for later inputs, the impact of new inputs on the ranges of options for the decision-makers and on the generation of new outputs.

To make any sort of progress towards this goal we clearly have to concentrate our initial efforts on the construction of two distinct typologies of sequences: one for institutional outputs, another for socio-cultural inputs. Once such typologies have been worked out and tested against the extant evidence it may prove fruitful to move on to the next step: the comparative analysis of sequences of interaction in the development of competitive democratic politics.

The Four Institutional Thresholds
Sir Lewis Namier once likened elections to locks in a canal: they allow the rising socio-cultural forces to flow further through the established channels of the system but also make it possible to stem the tide, to keep back the flood. This simile is possibly even more appropriate in describing the typical sequences in processes of democratization and mass mobilization: any rising political movement has to pass through a series of locks on its way inwards towards the core of the political system, upwards towards the central arena of decision-making.

In our current attempt to pin down sources of variations among our eleven countries we have focused on four such critical points: we might have stuck to the hydraulic imagery and called them 'locks', but we prefer the statistically more appealing term *threshold*.

The first is the threshold of *legitimation:* from which point in the history of state formation and nation-building was there effective recognition of the right of petition, criticism, demonstration against the regime? from which year or decade will historians judge that there was regular protection of the rights of assembly, expression and publication, and within what limits?

The second is the threshold of *incorporation:* how long did it take before the potential supporters of rising movements of opposition were given formal rights of participation in the choice of representatives on a par with the established strata?

The third is the threshold of *representation:* how high were the original barriers against the representation of new movements and when and in what ways were the barriers lowered to make it easier to gain seats in the legislature:

And the fourth is the threshold of *executive power:* how immune were the executive organs against legislative pressures and how long did it take before parliamentary strength could be translated into direct influence on executive decision-making, whether under some form of *Proporz* rule of access for minority parties or through the institutionalization of cabinet responsibility to legislative majorities?

The first two thresholds control the development of competitive mass politics. Once the threshold of legitimation is lowered there is a significant change in the character of politics: conspirational elite conflicts and repres-

Table 1. A Developmental Typology of Conditions for the Growth of Mass Democracy in Europe

Medieval consolidation	Continuity of representative organs	Seniority	Status in international system Power rating: for old established units its own rating; for later units the rating of the territorial centre	Polities in given category
1. Separate dynasty	11. High: minimal periods of absolute rule	111. Old-established	1111. Major	Britain
			1112. Lesser	Sweden
		112. Late independence	1121. Major	Ireland (under Britain to 1922)
			1122. Lesser	Finland (under Sweden to 1809, Russia to 1917)
	12. Low: protracted periods of absolute rule	121. Old-established	1211. Major	Spain France Prussia Austria: Empire
			1212. Lesser	Denmark
		122. Late independence	1221. Major	Austria: Republic
			1222. Lesser	Norway (under Denmark to 1814, Sweden to 1905) Iceland (Denmark to 1940)

2. Cities, principalities and provinces within successive Continental Empires	21. Minor external disruptions: strong traditions of local democracy, minimal efforts of centralization	211. Old-established	2111. Major	No case
			2112. Lesser	Switzerland
	22. Strong traditions of estate representation but brief periods of near-absolutist centralization	212. Late independence		No case
		221. Old-established	2211. Major	No case
			2212. Lesser	Netherlands
		222. Late independence	2221. Major	Belgium (under Austria to 1794, France to 1815, Netherlands to 1830).
			2222. Lesser	Luxembourg (Netherlands, 1815–1839, part of German *Bund* to 1866)
	23. Oligarchic-absolutist heritage: violent centralization	232. Late independence	2321. Major	Italy (unified 1860–70)

sive measures against dissidents tend to give way to public debate and open competition for support. Once the suffrage threshold is lowered the potential audience for such debate and the potential market for such competitive efforts increases by leaps and bounds: the result will almost invariably be a rush to develop organizations for the recruitment of support and for the consolidation of political identities.

Empirically changes in the one threshold sooner or later generated pressures for change in the other but the timing of such decisions varied significantly from polity to polity.

To gain some understanding of the sources of such variations we clearly have to analyze the sequences of state formation and institution-building in each polity. The starting points for the processes of democratization varied markedly from case to case: to take only two extremes within the range of our fifteen democracies, the Swiss could build further on well-established traditions of representative city government and even of direct popular consultations in some rural cantons, while the Danes had lived under absolute monarchic rule from 1660 to 1831.

Four dimensions of variation seem particularly important in accounting for the timing of decisions on the two first thresholds:

– first, the extent of territorial consolidation during the Middle Ages – the early national dynasties *vs.* the loosely federated provinces and cities within the successive Continental empires;

– second, the continuity in the operation of the medieval organs of representation – the countries maintaining some forms of representation by territory and/or estates throughout the period from the Reformation to the French Revolution *vs.* the countries subjected to protracted periods of absolutist rule;

– third, the differentiation between old-established and newly-independent after the French Revolution – the older polities established up to 1648 *vs.* the newer ones generated through territorial separation and secession from 1814 onwards;

– and fourth, the size and strength of the dominant polity before secession – the British-Irish case *vs.* the Danish-Norwegian.

These four criteria generate a typology for the ordering of the current West European polities by the initial conditions of democratic development. This is set out in *Table 1*.

The consequences of these marked differences can be traced from one point to the other in the process of democratization. Four generalizations about such effects seem worthy of detailed consideration:

First, the stronger the inherited traditions of representative rule, whether within estates, territorial assemblies or city councils, the greater the chances of early legitimation of opposition.

Secondly, the higher the international status of the dominant country the higher the barrier of legitimation in the dependent territory and the greater, consequently, the risk of violence in the internal politics of the seceding nation-state.

Thirdly, the stronger the inherited traditions of representative rule, the slower, and the less likely to be reversed, the process of enfranchisement and equalization.

And fourthly, whatever the traditions of representation, the greater the threat to the aspirations of national independence the fewer the steps in the process of democratization.

There are no simple ways of testing the two first hypotheses: there are few incontrovertible measures of the severity of sanctions against opponents and competitors. It is certainly possible to pin down the sequences of legislative and ministerial decisions on the freedom of expression and the right of association, but it is much more difficult to map the regularity of enforcement. Statistics of political violence, illegal demonstrations, secret organizations may be obtainable for a number of countries, but so far no serious attempts have been made at comparative analysis.[67] Whatever the difficulties of precise measurement there is no dearth of qualitative evidence of the importance of the factors singled out in the two first hypotheses. There is little doubt that the absolutist heritage tended to keep the barrier of legitimation at a high level: the checkered record of censorship, repression and alienation in Spain, France, Prussia, Austria and Italy cannot easily be matched in the other countries of Western Europe. But the size of the polity and its experiences in acquiring independence will temper this generalization. Denmark remained an absolute monarchy until 1831 but was very quick to open up channels for competitive mass politics after the wave of revolutions in 1848:[68] nevertheless the strength of the absolutist heritage found reflection in a protracted struggle between the forces of democracy in Parliament and the forces of bureaucracy under the Cabinet all the way up to 1901. The Irish benefited enormously from their experiences of parliamentary politics in Dublin and at Westminster but the overwhelming dominance of the English created deep divisions within the movement for independence and fostered a variety of conspiratorial underground oppositions which proved difficult to reconcile even after years of national independence.[69] This is a point of great importance in the discussion of the consequences of the size of national resources for the structure of domestic politics. Three of the new European nation-states of the twentieth century have had particularly unhappy histories of civil strife: Finland, Ireland and Austria. It is tempting to look for common features in their location in the international system: in all the three cases a small national unit was divided under the impact of the presence of a dominant and threatening neighbour. If we compare these three with the other cases of late accession to independence we find the threatening neighbours either to be much smaller in national resources (Norway vis-à-vis Denmark and Sweden, Iceland vis-à-vis Denmark) or to be much more evenly balanced

Table 2. *Variations in Extensions of Suffrage in Europe: By Type of Inherited Traditions of Rule*

Type of State Formation:	Medieval dynasties:				Territories within continental empires:			
	Continuous organs of representation				City oligarchies and provincial estates			
Inherited Style of Rule	Britain	Ireland	Sweden	Finland	Netherlands	Belgium	Luxembourg	Switzerland
Older Nation-states / Newer 'Secession States'	*(Older)*	*(Newer)*	*(Older)*	*(Newer)*	*(Older)*	*(Newer)*	*(Newer)*	
Initial Organ of Representation	House of Commons	Grattan's Parliament to 1801	Four-Estate Riksdag	Four-Estate Diet 1809	Estates-General: Two houses 1815	Provincial Estates	Estate Assembly 1841	City Councils, Cantonal Assemblies
Major Post-Revolutionary Reorganization		British Parliament 1801–1918 Dail 1918	Two-Chamber Riksdag 1866	Unicameral Diet 1906	Direct El. 1848	Parliament 1831	Direct El. 1848, 1868 Reversal 1856	Nationalrat 1848
Percent of Population Enfranchised under Old Rules	1830: 2.3 %	1830: 0.2 %	1865: 4.8 1866: 5.7		1851: 2.4	1831: 1%	1848: 2 %	
First Extension: Lower houses only	1832	1832	1909		1887	1848	1848	
Later Extensions	1867 1884	1867 1884			1896	1893	1868, 1892, 1901	
Formally Instituted Electoral Inequalities – Character	Business, University votes	Business, University votes	Weighted tax vote			Plural votes		
– Terminated	1948	1923	1920			1919		
Manhood Suffrage – Minor Qualifications	1918	1918	→1920	→1906	→1917	1919	→1919	→1848 Cantonal Citizenship
– Removed								
Universal Suffrage: – Women as well as Men	1929	1923			1919	1949		

Table 2. *Variations in Extensions of Suffrage in Europe: By Type of Inherited Traditions of Rule*

Type of State Formation:	Territories within continental empires:			Medieval dynasties:		Protracted absolutist rule	
Inherited Style of Rule	Absolutist heritage		Austria: Empire Republic	Iceland	Norway	Denmark	France
Older Nation-states / Newer 'Secession States'	Italy	Prussia → Reich					
Initial Organ of Representation	Sardinian Parliament 1848	Bundestag 1815, Provincial Estates, Landtage	Provincial Estates, Indirectly el. Reichsrat 1861	Althing: Consultative 1843–74	Storting 1814	Provincial Estates 1831–1849	Estates-General 1789
Major Post-Revolutionary Reorganization	Italian Parliament 1860	*Prussia* Landtag 1849 / *Bund/Reich* 1848	Four-Curiae Reichsrat 1873	Legislature 1874		Two-Chamber Parliament 1849	National Assembly 1789 Convention 1792, etc.
Percent of Population Enfranchised under Old Rules	1871: 2.3 %		1873: 6 %	1903: 9.8	1814: 10 %	1849: 14–15 %	1815: 0.25 %
First Extension: Lower houses only / Later Extensions	1882: 7 % / 1912		1882 / 1897 Fifth Curia	1903 / 1915	1885	Reversal for Upper House 1866	Reversals: 1795, 1814, 1852 Extension 1830
Formally Instituted Electoral Inequalities – Character		Three Class Electorate 1919	Marked Inter-Curia Inequality 1907				
– Terminated	→ 1919	1919			→ 1898	→ 1849	→ 1793, 1848, 1875
Manhood Suffrage	1919	1849	1867	1907	1920	1898	1849 (30 years)	1793, 1848, 1875
– Minor Qualifications Removed				Paupers 1934	Paupers 1913–19	Servants 1901	
Universal Suffrage: – Women as well as Men	1945	1919	1919	1920	1915	1915	1945

among each other (Belgium between Britain, Germany and France, Luxembourg between France and Germany). It is possible, but does not seem likely that the timing of the accession to independence was as important as the location in geopolitical space: Norway, Belgium and Luxembourg reached at least domestic sovereignty *before* the great waves of democratization while Finland and Ireland seceded with fully enfranchised citizenries and the Austrian Republic emerged out of the debris of the Habsburg Empire at the end of a process of accelerating democratization. But this does not fit the Icelandic case: the latest of our nation-states was quick to lower the barrier of legitimation and proceeded slowly and quietly to democratize its political life. It is tempting to try out the generalization that the weaker or the more evenly equilibriated the pressures from the international environment, the greater the drive to legitimize oppositions within the body politic and the more persistent the efforts to accommodate conflicting forces within an overarching system of pluralist decision-making.[70]

The two hypotheses about the process of enfranchisement and equalization are easier to test: the succession of electoral laws can be coded on the different dimensions without great violence, and the accelerating production of electoral statistics allows detailed quantitative controls for levels of participation and rates of mobilization (Rokkan, 1966: 4; Rokkan, 1969).

Table 2 allows quick inspection of the characteristic variations in sequences of democratization. The sequences for the eleven smaller countries have been located between two extremes: the English model of slow, step-by-step enfranchisement without reversals but with long periods of formal recognition of inequalities; and the French model of early and sudden universalization and equalization of political citizenship but with frequent reversals and with tendencies towards plebiscitarian exploitation of mass support.

Of the polities with strong traditions of representative government, Sweden, the Netherlands, Belgium, Luxembourg came closest to the English: Ireland, of course, followed willy-nilly under British rule. The exceptions fall at each extreme of the series. The Swiss cantons, the units with the longest experience of democratic or representative rule, followed the French model and agreed to introduce universal manhood suffrage as early as 1848. What is important in their case, however, is that there were no reversals and that the process was not pushed further to the ultimate goal of suffrage for women as well as men. At the other extreme, the Finns had the most explosive of all histories of democratization: the country moved in one single step from estate representation to universal suffrage for women and men in 1906.

Of the polities with histories of absolute rule, Denmark and Prussia/Germany came closest to the French model. The Danes experienced sudden universalization and equalization in the wake of the February Revolution, but like the French, had to suffer a serious reversal: the Upper House was returned to oligarchic control in 1866. The development in Norway differed on one important point: a wide suffrage introduced as early as in 1814, was extended in three steps from 1884 to 1913 without any of the transitional inequalities characteristic of the English model, but there were *no reversals*. The schizophrenic developments in the Prussian-German territories have been extensively analyzed in the literature on suffrage extensions: on the one hand the medieval traditions of the *Standesstaat,* on the other the plebiscitarian influences from Paris. The Prussian King promulgated universal male suffrage in 1849 but maintained an element of estate representation in the 'three-class' system: the votes of the richest citizens counted vastly heavier than the votes of the poor. Bismarck went one step further in 1867 and introduced *universal, equal and secret* suffrage for all men of age, but this was still a plebiscitarian device: the people might elect representatives to the *Reichstag* but these representatives had only minimal influence on the German Executive. The two remaining countries do not fit any of these patterns. The multinational Habsburg Empire was caught in a difficult dilemma: democratization was functional for the mobilization of support within the Cisleithian German territory but potentially explosive within the subject territories. The result was a complex series of compromises from 1848 to 1907. At the other extreme, the smallest of the pluralist polities at the periphery of Europe could look back on a strong if disrupted tradition of democratic rule and was not driven by external pressures to mobilize its population to a maximum: as a result, the Icelanders did not rush into full democracy after the re-establishment of the Althing but moved cautiously step by step, in fact almost *pari passu* with the very gradual process of liberation from the Danes.

The first two thresholds set the stage for the emergence of competitive mass politics: once a system has moved across these first two barriers, it enters the era of mass electioneering and mass organization. But this does not necessarily make for any uniformity in the structure of electoral politics: the stakes of the game will vary with the rules of representation and the rules of access to executive power.

The *threshold of representation* came under heavy pressure once the rights of political participation had been extended to most or all male citizens: the rising parties of the hitherto disfranchised protested against the numerical injustices of the plurality systems; the smaller of the already entrenched *régime censitaire* parties feared for their survival and found it easier to lower the barrier than to merge with the dominant party in defense against the new claimants for power.

This is a fascinating field of comparative analysis: what were the socio-cultural conditions and the organizational constellations that made decisions in one direction more likely than decisions in the other? what considerations of alternative pay-offs and costs produced enough consensus to maintain the barriers or to yield to the pressure for some form of PR? Unfortunately, much of the scholarly literature on electoral systems has been bogged down in questions of morality and long-term functionality for the survival of each regime: this has led to a great deal of speculation about hypothetical developments but very little concrete analysis of decision-making situations.

The eleven smaller European democracies offer an interesting array of cases for comparison: they all yielded to the pressures for a lowering of the threshold but at different times and for very different reasons. The ethnically and religiously most divided of the polities were the first to break with the old tradition of 'winner-take-all' representation: Denmark in the 1850s already to accommodate the Schleswig minority, five of the Swiss cantons in the early 1890s, Belgium in 1899, Finland in 1906. In the other smaller countries the rapid growth of the working-class parties immediately before or in the wake of the extension of the suffrage threatened the survival of at least one of the older parties and produced constellations where PR was the 'saddle-point' solution in the game of opposition forces. This was true for Belgium in 1899, for Sweden in 1909, for the Danish Lower House in 1915, for the Netherlands, Luxembourg, Norway, Austria and the entire Swiss Confederation at the end of or just after World War I. Only one of the eleven countries lagged behind in this movement: Iceland introduced PR in its economically and politically differentiated capital in 1920 but kept up the plurality system in some of the rural districts all the way up to 1959.

In most of the smaller countries the pressures for a lowering of the threshold took longer to make themselves felt in the rural peripheries than in the centres of economic and administrative development, but once the pressures mounted in the centres, there was little over-all resistance to the PR solution. In the larger countries of Europe the extension of the suffrage and the continuing processes of urbanization and industrialization generated heavy pressures for a lowering of the traditional thresholds. But the central establishments could muster greater resources against these movements and did not yield as easily: the English survived even the 1931 crisis without succumbing to the lures of PR or the alternative vote; the French gave in for brief periods only after each World War and the Germans after the collapse in 1918.

It is tempting to generalize from these contrasts:

1) The pressures for PR will increase with the ethnic and/or religious heterogeneity of the citizenry and, even in ethnically/religiously homogeneous electorates, with the increased economic differentiation generated through urbanization and the monetization of transactions;

2) PR is more likely to prove the line of least resistance in differentiated democracies with smaller governmental resources, while plurality systems

are more likely to be effectively defended in larger polities with stronger governmental establishments.

There is a great deal of evidence for the effects of urbanization and economic growth on partisan competition and mobilization (Rokkan, 1966: 4). The lower the density, the smaller the communities, the less developed and differentiated the economy, the more personal and territorial the style of representation and the less developed the organizations for local electoral competition. This has been shown across a number of countries in studies of partisanship at the *local* level,[71] but there can be little doubt that similar processes are at work at higher-level units of government. In Switzerland five cantons and two half-cantons still retain the traditional style of plurality voting: these are among the geographically most isolated and economically most backward within the Confederation.[72] The Icelandic and the Irish cases also fit in very well in this schema. The Icelanders compromised by allowing one electoral law for each sector of a still dual economy. In Ireland the system of the Single Transferable Vote represented a happy compromise for a small and heavily agricultural country: it broke away from the 'all-or-none' tradition of plurality voting identified with British rule and at the same time allowed the backward communities in the hinterland to enjoy the benefits of direct personal representation.

It is much more difficult to fit the second of the two empirical generalizations into any body of established social science theorizing: why should the smaller democracies on the whole tend to yield so much more readily, and with much less regret, to the pressures for PR than the larger ones? Clearly not just because there were deeper cleavages and more parties to accommodate already and therefore greater concern at the outset to protect the stakes of each of the established organizations. This fits many of the cases but only raises further questions about differences in the conditions for cross-cleavage aggregation in smaller versus larger systems. To put it in abstract game-theoretical terms: is it theoretically plausible to assume that party leaders in smaller polities are more likely to depart from the zero-sum model of political competition than their opposite numbers in larger systems?

Coalition theorists such as William Riker admit that zero-sum reasoning tends to break down in small groups.[73] The strict principle of coalition up to the 'majority +1' point but no further simply will not work in collectivities below given sizes. The difficulty is that there is hardly a trace of systematic research on the effects of variations in size above the typical small-group level: will there still be meaningful differences at the 100 vs. 200 level, the 200 vs. 400? All we can do at this stage is to suggest a few hypotheses for further evaluation and, whenever possible, empirical testing.

The greater ease of communication in the smaller system: The smaller the total number of legislators the greater the frequency of interaction among party leaders and the greater their reluctance to force one set of established bargaining partners to merge with one larger set through the maintenance of a polarizing plurality system.

The smaller resources for side-payments for prospective coalition partners: The smaller the democratic polity, the more limited the resources to be gained through straight majority victories, the less the total amount of 'side payments' available and the greater the cost of bargains with prospective coalition partners; the greater, consequently, the temptation to leave such potential coalition partners to their electoral fates under some form of PR.[74]

The greater dependence on the stability of the international system: The smaller the polity, the less the leeway for independent action and the greater the concern to maintain national unity across party lines; the greater the pressure to maintain solidarity, the less the emphasis on zero-sum plurality competition and the greater, therefore, the tendency to accept PR as a safeguard against the uncertainties of a polarized 'all-or-none' constellation.[75]

In line with Giovanni Sartori's classification of electoral systems the option for PR may be characterized as a 'strategy of the weak': the leaders of the smaller democracies were so much more willing to yield to the pressures for a lowering of the threshold of representation because they tended to prefer the safety of their established positions of control in minority parties to the uncertainties of mergers and 'winner-take-all' plurality elections. This is a point of critical importance in the comparative study of party systems. The introduction of PR in the final phase of mass mobilization helped to stabilize, if not ossify, the structure of partisan alternatives in the central, more differentiated regions of each country. The party systems of 1960s still

'. . . reflect, with few but significant exceptions, the cleavage structures of the 1920s. This is a crucial characteristic of Western competitive politics in the age of 'high mass consumption': *the party alternatives, and in remarkably many cases the party organizations are older than the majorities of the national electorates.* To most of the citizens of the West the currently active parties have been part of the political landscape since their childhood or at least since they were first faced with the choice between alternative 'packages' on election day (Lipset & Rokkan, 1967: 1, p. 50).'

This 'organizational lag' has rarely been given the attention it deserves in comparative work on contemporary electoral data: to understand the current trends in each country and in each type of locality we have to bring in information not only about processes of socio-economic change but also about the *age and stability* of the *party alternatives.*

'This joining of diachronic and synchronic analysis strategies is of particular importance for an understanding of the mass politics of the organizationally saturated 'high mass consumption' societies of the sixties: decades of structural change and economic growth have made the old-stablished alternatives increasingly irrelevant but the high level of organizational mobilization of most sectors of the community has left very little leeway for a decisive breakthrough of new party alternatives. It is not an accident that situations of this type generate a great deal of frustration, alienation and protestation within the organizationally least committed sections of the community: the *young* and, quite particularly the *students* (Lipset & Rokkan, 1967: 1, p. 54).'

Nor, it would seem, is it an accident that these waves of dissatisfaction with the established party alternatives started out in the central areas and the cities: in many of the rural peripheries the old parties are still eagerly mobilizing further support and have not reached the same degree of structural ossification as at the centres.

Such variations in the lag between the process of socio-economic change and the process of political development cannot be studied without detailed consideration of the role of the parties in *executive decision-making:* the *fourth* and the final threshold in our abstract model.

Let us, to rub in the structure of our argument, again follow the fate of our typical movement of opposition to established privileges, whether based on Orthodox Protestant rejection of the State Church, Catholic protest against secular control of education, or working-class claims against owners and employers.

It has crossed the *first* threshold: it is given the right to communicate its views, to organize, to take part in elections. It has also crossed the *second* threshold: it is not only free to recruit support but each supporter is given rights to influence the choice of representatives on a par with the supporters of the established régime. It has even crossed the *third* threshold: it has not only collected votes but had them translated into seats in the legislature at the same rate as any of the earlier, and possibly larger, parties. This leaves the *final* threshold, the threshold of executive power: how many votes, how many seats are needed before the party is given a chance to exert effective influence on central decisions for the polity?

Leon D. Epstein has argued the critical importance of this last threshold for the formation of disciplined and coherent mass parties: his brilliant analysis of the contrasts between the American and the Canadian party systems is bound to inspire further comparisons across the total range of competitive polities (Epstein, 1964).

Our European polities varied significantly in the timing of decisions on the threshold of executive power: some of them followed the British example and introduced the principle of Cabinet responsibility to Parliamentary majorities well before the decisive extensions of the suffrage, some lowered the two thresholds roughly at the same time, while others stuck to the separation-of-powers doctrine for decades after the broadening of the suffrage. Belgium and the Netherlands came closest to the English model of *régime censitaire* parliamentarism. The Belgians introduced responsible government from the very beginning of 1831; the Dutch from 1848 onwards. Norway reached the same stage later but the victory of Parliament over the Executive came on top of a major wave of partisan mobilization and was soon to lead on to full manhood suffrage. Denmark, Sweden and the Austrian Empire came close to what we might call the German model: manhood suffrage came before the introduction of Parliamentary rule. The German case is well known: all Prussian men were given the vote in 1848, all citizens of the *Bund* and *Reich* in 1867, but parliamentary rule was not established until after the defeat in 1918. The lag was also marked in Denmark: the wide suffrage introduced in 1849 had allowed the anti-establishment movements to mobilize broad support and to gain a parliamentary majority long before the Executive finally gave way in 1901. The lag was not that critical in Sweden: manhood suffrage came in 1909 and the final victory over the Executive came in 1920. In Austria, as in Germany, the threshold fell with the military defeat of the old regime in 1918. In two of the youngest of our eleven polities, Finland and Ireland, the power of Parliament was tempered by the authority of the President. Both Finland and Ireland experienced great difficulties in establishing a balance between the elected representatives and the Executive in the early phase of independent government, but the *principle* of Cabinet responsibility to the majority of the elected representatives was never seriously challenged.

In all these cases the threshold of executive power was formally lowered to the 50 per cent point only: a party or a block could only gain access to Cabinet positions by securing majority support in the Legislature. The Swiss went one step further: they gave minority parties regular access to the cantonal and the federal executives and established the principle of *Proporz* representation not only at the level of the elected assemblies, but even in the designation of members of the Cabinet. This system of 'two-tier PR' was approximated in other deeply segmented polities in Europe: the long series of coalition governments in the Netherlands allowed parties in the 10–15 percent range frequent if not automatic access to the Executive and the three-cornered struggle among the *familles spirituelles* in Belgium and Luxembourg and the *Lager* in Austria often lowered the threshold of executive power well below the 50 percent mark. In general, the likelihood of minority participation in the Executive appears to be increased a) with the distance of the largest party from the majority point, b) with the closeness and 'bargainability' of the policy alternatives represented by the potential coalition partners, c) with the severity of the pressures from the international environment. Our eleven countries have differed markedly on each of these scores, both over time, from phase to phase since the introduction of parliamentary rule, and among each other. Any attempt to account for the variations in electoral behaviour across all these countries must take this into account: in some countries elections have had the character of an effective choice among alternative teams of governors, in others they have simply served to express segmental loyalties and to ensure the right of each segment to *some* representation, even if only a single portfolio, in a coalition cabinet.

The salient differences in the structure of electoral alternatives can be brought out through a crude classification by type of contest: this is attempted for the smaller democracies in *Table 3*.

None of our eleven democracies have experienced extended periods of straight alternation between two major parties: the typical 'ins-outs' politics characteristic of Britain, the United States and some of the white Commonwealth countries. Austria and Ireland, and during some periods Belgium, have come closest to what German commentators have called the two-and-a-half party system: two large parties running neck and neck for the majority point but generally thwarted in their endeavours by the persistence of one small above-threshold party. This was the situation in Austria practically from the first republican election: the Nationalist camp was just strong enough to prevent one of the two large parties from gaining a safe majority. The Irish party system came close to this model in the late twenties but the Republican *Fianna Fail* party was soon to take the lead and left the pro-Treaty *Fine Gael* well behind in election after election. In fact, the Irish constellations of the fifties and sixties are almost halfway between the German-Austrian system and the Scandinavian: one large party near the majority point and several middle-sized parties competing for the next places. Belgium enjoyed a two-party system during the *régime censitaire* but has since oscillated between the Austrian-Irish constellation and what we shall call the 'segmented pluralism' model.

In Sweden, Denmark and Norway the first elections after the introduction of PR produced very even distribution among three to four parties, but the Social Democrats soon moved up to the majority point and left the other contenders competing for the other half of the votes. This process went furthest in Sweden and in Norway: the Swedish Social Democrats entered the Executive as early as in 1917 and have managed to stay in power on majorities or near-majorities for over thirty years; the Norwegian Labour party had its first taste of ministerial Socialism in 1927 and stayed in power for thirty years from 1935 to 1965. The Danish Social Democrats never reached clear majorities: they have enjoyed long periods of Cabinet power but have either relied on *ad hoc* aggregations of support in Parliament or entered into coalition with minor partners. With

Table 3. A Classification of the Party Systems of the Smaller European Democracies after World War I:
By the Likelihood of Single-Party Majorities and the Distribution of Minority Party Strengths

Country		Period	Total seats (lower house)	Largest party: distance from majority point		Two next parties: seats below first party				Other parties: total seats	
						Second party		Third party			
				Min.	Max.	Min.	Max.	Min.	Max.	Min.	Max.
I. The British-German '1 vs. 1 + 1' System											
	AUSTRIA	I. Rep.	159–183	− 1	−11	2	16	45	67	0	3
	IRELAND	II. Rep.	165	+ 2	− 9	1	11	60	(none)	0	5
		1922–32	128, 153	− 5	−30	3	23	25	65	17	40
		1933–44	153, 138	+ 8	− 2	21	46	50	68	7	24
		1944–65	147, 144	+ 4	− 9	15	38	46	66	3	34
II. The Scandinavian '1 vs. 3 − 4' System											
	SWEDEN	1921–32	230	−11	−25	17	46	58	76	28	39
		1936–44	230	+19	− 3	68	92	76	106	26	41
		1948–64	230, 233	− 2	−10	48	74	64	82	25	45
	DENMARK	1920–29	139, 148	−13	−23	3	18	20	37	19	22
		1932–57	148, 175	− 6	−26	8	40	22	44	21	36
		1960–66	175	−12	−19	34	38	35	44	25	37
	NORWAY	1921–30	150	−16	−28	6	29	14	30	27	38
		1933–57	150	+10	− 6	34	62	45	64	21	31
		1961–65	150	− 1	− 7	37	45	50	58	31	33
III. Even Multiparty Systems: '1 vs. 1 vs. 1 + 2 − 3'											
1. Scandinavian 'Split Working Class' systems											
	FINLAND	1919–39	200	−15	−47	1	38	18	62	33	67
		1945–66	200	−44	−50	1	6	1	18	50	62
	ICELAND	1923–37	42, 49	+ 2	− 6	2	8	10	19	0	5
		1942–63	49, 60	− 5	− 7	1	7	10	15	6	9
2. 'Segmented Pluralism'	NETHERLANDS	1918–37	100	−18	−22	6	12	14	18	29	36
		1946–56	100	−16	−20	0	5	18	24	23	28
		1959–67	150	−25	−33	1	7	25	35	34	54
	BELGIUM	1919–39	186, 202	−15	−31	1	9	39	55	9	48
		1946–65	202, 212	+ 2	−29	9	39	29	88	3	23
	LUXEMBOURG	1945–59	51, 52	0	− 5	2	14	10	20	3	6
	SWITZERLAND	1919–39	187–198	−37	−44	2	17	8	17	42	53
		1943–63	194–200	−41	−47	0	9	3	13	46	50

the spectacular gain of the Left Socialists in 1966, the Danish system in fact moved closer to the other Scandinavian model: the type of structure produced in Finland and Iceland through the split between Communists and Social Democrats.

The Finnish constellation was quite similar to the Danish until the Second World War: one large Social Democrat party, one middle-sized Agrarian party, and a couple of parties (Finland: 3, Denmark: 2) in the 10–15 percent range. With the legalization of the Communist party in 1944 the working class Left was split down the middle: the result was a '1 *vs.* 1 *vs.* 1 + 3' system doomed to some form of coalition government or, when coalitions could not be kept together, transitional admixtures of technocrats or even direct trade union representatives. There was a similar development in Iceland: before the war a period of majorities or near-majorities for the Conservative-Liberal and later the Independence party, later an even split among 3 to 4 parties.

This, of course, had been the typical constellation in the religiously and ethnically split countries along the Protestant-Catholic border belt across the Continent. In the Netherlands and in Switzerland no party was ever within shooting range of the majority point after the end of World War I. In Belgium the situation was very similar before World War II, but changed for a couple of periods after World War II. From 1949 to 1954 and again in 1958 the Catholics hovered close to the majority point and the system approached the '1 *vs.* 1 + 1' constellation we identified as Austrian-Irish: this, of course, came to an abrupt end with the politicization of the linguistic cleavages in the 1960s and the resurgence of the Liberals and the Flemish Nationalists.

This typology of party constellations is purely numerical: the decisive criteria of differentiation are the proximity to the majority and the evenness of the contests for the top position.

In our comments on the table, we have slipped into concrete interpretations of particular national cleavage structures, but the trust of our argument is that the abstract numerical constellation is of critical importance in the comparative study of electoral behaviour: there is good reason to believe that is makes a difference, both in the style of party activity and in the behaviour of potential supporters, how close the system is to straight majority dominance and how much responsibility each competing party has had for central executive decision-making. This is an important field for detailed research across countries and across parties. There has been a great deal of excited speculation about the 'domestication' effects of proximity to national power (e.g. Rokkan, 1966: 6) but no one has as yet tried to assemble even very simple arrays of information on party structure, party personnel and party ideology across countries differing in their sequences of decisions on the fourth and final threshold. To make any headway in this direction it would be essential to seek out socio-culturally similar parties at roughly the same levels of national strength and study their structures and their ideological outpourings at three distinct stages of development:

as a force of pure opposition outside and/or inside the Legislature, as a partner in a coalition, as the sole governing party. But the effects of such changes in proximity to the national power resources cannot be studied *in abstracto:* the institutional rules of the game set a variety of constraints on the actions of party personnel and party representatives once they approach power, but their actual options within these limits can only be understood against the history of cleavage articulation and interest aggregation in each country. This is an equally important, equally challenging field of variation among our countries: the second 'ladder' of our model seeks to bring some semblance of order into the mapping of these variations.

The Four Poles of Conflict

Our aim is to reduce to the smallest possible number the range of explanatory variables required to account for the variations in electoral alternatives in the eleven countries:

Why did some polities develop party oppositions over issues of ethnic-cultural identity while others left such issues to be settled *within* broader party fronts?

Why did some polities develop strong parties for the defense of the rights of organized churches and religious movements, while some developed only small or short-lived parties of this type, and others were able to keep religious divisions completely out of politics?

Why did the peasantry organize their own parties in some countries or regions while in others they never found this necessary?

Why did the working classes develop strong and unified political movements in some countries, much weaker ones in other countries, and deeply divided organizations in still others?

It is easy enough to spin out strings of explanations for one country at a time: the task is to develop a unified scheme of accounting that will hold up across a maximum of empirically extant cases.

In our attempt at accounting for the marked variations in the timing, the speed and the scope of the measures taken to institutionalize competitive mass politics we started out from a typology of the *initial conditions of nation-building:* the character of the medieval organization of the given territory, the exposure to absolutist centralization, the final definition of the territorial nation-state through the processes of secession and consolidation after the Napoleonic upheavals, and, finally, the size of each resultant polity and its position in the international interaction system.

In our attempt at an explanation of the variations in the structuring of partisan polities we have found it fruitful to proceed through a parallel series of steps:

− we first identify 'critical junctures' in the sequences of nation building;

− we next identify the principal *cleavage lines* generated by the decision taken at each critical juncture;

− and we finally generate from each of the possible cleavage structures *core systems of full-suffrage parties* and test these predictions against the historically given cases.

Our analysis starts out from a reinterpretation of the Parsonian *A–G–I–L* schema for the differentiation of societal subsystems.[76]

We have focused on his *I* quadrant and interpret it as the locus for the development of cross-household, cross-local 'fronts of political aggregation'. Within this quadrant we have proposed a two-dimensional schema for the ordering of the territorial-cultural and socio-economic cleavages in each national polity: the crucial fronts of political opposition are located at or between the poles of this Cartesian space. What we suggest is that the crucial cleavages and their political expressions can be ordered within the two-dimensional space generated by the two diagonals of the Parsonian double dichotomy:

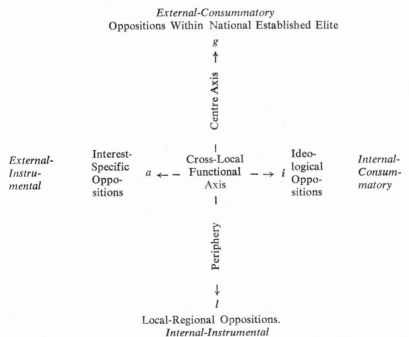

Figure 1. *A Possible Interpretation of the Internal Structure of the I Quadrant*

In this model the Parsonian dichotomies have been transformed into continuous coordinates: the *l–g* line represents a *territorial* dimension of the national cleavage structure and the *a–i* line a *functional* dimension.[77]

At the *l* end of the territorial axis we would find strictly local oppositions to encroachments of the aspiring or the dominant national elites and their bureaucracies: the typical reactions of peripheral regions, linguistic minorities, and culturally threatened populations to the pressures of the centralizing, standardizing, and 'rationalizing' machinery of the nation-state. At the *g* end of the axis we would find conflict not between territorial units *within* the system but over the control, the organization, the goals, and the policy options of the system *as a whole*. These might be nothing more than direct struggles among competing elites for central power, but they might also reflect deeper differences in conceptions of nationhood, over domestic priorities and over external strategies.

Conflicts along the *a–i* axis *cut across* the territorial units of the nation. They produce alliances of similarly situated or similarly oriented subjects and households over wide ranges of localities and tend to undermine the inherited solidarity of the established territorial communities. At the *a* end of this dimension we would find the typical conflict over short-term or long-term allocations of resources, products, and benefits in the economy: conflicts between producers and buyers, between workers and employers, between borrowers and lenders, between tenants and owners, between contributors and beneficiaries. At this end the alignments are specific and the conflicts tend to be solved through rational bargaining and the establishment of universalistic rules of allocation. The farther we move toward the *i* end of the axis, the more diffuse the criteria of alignment, the more intensive the identification with the 'we' group, and the more uncompromising the rejection of the 'they' group. At the *i* end of the dimension we find the typical 'friend-foe' oppositions of tight-knit religious or ideological movements to the surrounding community. The conflict is no longer over specific gains or losses but over conceptions of moral right and over the interpretation of history and human destiny: membership is no longer a matter of multiple affiliation in many directions, but a diffuse '24-hour' commitment incompatible with other ties within the community; and communication is no longer kept flowing freely over the cleavage lines but restricted and regulated to protect the movement against impurities and the seeds of compromise.

Historically documented cleavages rarely fall at the poles of the two axes: a concrete conflict is rarely exclusively territorial or exclusively functional but will feed on strains in both directions. The model essentially serves as a *grid* in the comparative analysis of political systems: the task is to locate the alliances behind given parties at given times within this two-dimensional space. The axes are not easily quantifiable, and they may not satisfy any criteria of strict scalability; nevertheless, they seem heuristically useful in attempts such as ours at linking up empirical variations in political structures with current conceptualizations in sociological theory.

A few concrete illustrations of party developments may help to clarify the distinctions in our model.

In Britain, the first nation-state to recognize the legitimacy of party oppositions, the initial conflicts were essentially of the types we have located at the *l* end of the vertical axis. The heads of independent landed families in the counties opposed the powers and the decisions of the government and the administration in London. The opposition between the 'Country party' of knights and squires and the 'Court and Treasury party' of the Whig magnates and the 'placemen' was primarily territorial. The animosities of the Tories were not necessarily directed against the predominance of London in the affairs of the nation, but they were certainly aroused by the highhanded manipulations of the influential officeholders in the administration and their powerful allies in the boroughs. The conflict was not over general policies but over patronage and places. The gentry did not get their share of the *quid pro quo* exchanges of local influence against governmental offices and never established a clear-cut common front against the central power-holders. 'Toryism about 1750 was primarily the opposition of the local rulers to central authority and vanished wherever members of that class entered the orbit of Government.' [78]

Such particularistic, kin-centred, 'ins-outs' oppositions are common in the early phases of nation-building: the electoral clienteles are small, undifferentiated, and easily controlled, and the stakes to be gained or lost in public life tend to be personal and concrete rather than collective and general.

Purely territorial oppositions rarely survive extensions of the suffrage. Much will depend, of course, on the timing of the crucial steps in the building of the nation: territorial unification, the establishment of legitimate government and the monopolization of the agencies of violence, the takeoff toward industrialization and economic growth, the development of popular education, and the entry of the lower classes into organized politics. Early democratization will not necessarily generate clear-cut divisions on functional lines. The initial result of a widening of the suffrage will often be an accentuation of the contrasts between the countryside and the urban centres and between the orthodox-fundamentalist beliefs of the peasantry and the small-town citizens and the secularism fostered in the larger cities and the metropolis. In the United States, the cleavages were typically cultural and religious. The struggles between the Jeffersonians and the Federalists, the Jacksonians and the Whigs, the Democrats and the Republicans centred on contrasting conceptions of public morality and pitted Puritans and other Protestants against Deists, Freemasons, and immigrant Catholics and Jews.[79] The accelerating influx of lower-class immigrants into the metropolitan areas and the centres of industry accentuated the contrasts between the rural and the urban cultural environments and between the backward and the advanced states of the Union. Such cumulations of territorial and cultural cleavages in the early phases of democratization can be documented for country after country. In Norway, all freehold and most leasehold peasants were given the vote as early as in 1814, but took several decades to mobilize in opposition to the King's officials and the dominance of the cities in the national economy. The crucial cleavages brought out into the open in the seventies were essentially territorial and cultural: the provinces were pitted against the capital; the increasingly estate-conscious peasants defended their traditions and their culture against the standards forced on them by the bureaucracy and the urban bourgeoisie. Interestingly, the extension of the suffrage to the landless labourers in the countryside and the propertyless workers in the cities did not bring about an immediate polarization of the polity on class lines. Issues of language, religion, and morality kept up the territorial oppositions in the system and cut across issues between the poorer and the better-off strata of the population. There were significant variations, however, between localities and between religions: the initial 'politics of cultural defense' survived the extension of the suffrage in the egalitarian communities of the South and the West, but lost to straight class politics in the economically backward, hierarchically organized communities of the North (Rokkan, 1964: 2; Rokkan, 1967). The developments in the South and West of Norway find interesting parallels in the 'Celtic fringe' of Britain. In these areas, particularly in Wales, opposition to the territorial, cultural, and economic dominance of the English offered a basis for communitywide support for the Liberals and retarded the development of straight class politics, even in the coalfields.[80] The sudden upsurge of Socialist strength in the northern periphery of Norway parallels the spectacular victory of the Finnish working-class party at the first election under universal suffrage: the fishermen and the crofters of the Norwegian North backed a distinct lower-class party as soon as they got the vote, and so did the Finnish rural proletariat.[81] In terms of our abstract model the politics of the western peripheries of Norway and Britain has its focus at the lower end of the $l–g$ axis, whereas the politics of the backward districts of Finland and the Norwegian North represent alliance formations closer to g and at varying points of the $a–i$ axis. In the one case the decisive criterion of alignment is *commitment to the locality and its dominant culture:* you vote with your community and its leaders irrespective of your economic position. In the other the criterion is *commitment to a class and its collective interests:* you vote with others in the same position as yourself whatever their localities, and you are willing to do so even if this brings you into opposition with members of your community. We rarely find one criterion of alignment completely dominant. There will be deviants from straight territorial voting just as often as from straight class voting. But we often find marked differences between regions in the *weight* of the one or the other criterion of alignment. Here ecological analyses of electoral records and census data for the early phases of mobilization may help us to map such variations in greater detail and to pinpoint factors strengthening the dominance of territorial politics and factors accelerating the process of class polarization (cf. Chapter 6 and 7 below).

The Two Revolutions: The National and the Industrial
Territorial oppositions set limits to the process of nation-building; pushed to their extreme they lead to war, secession, possibly even population transfers. Functional oppositions can only develop after some initial consolidation of the national territory. They emerge with increasing interaction and communication across the localities and the regions, and they spread through a process of 'social mobilization.' [82] The growing nation-state developed a wide range of agencies of unification and standardization and gradually penetrated the bastions of 'primordial' local culture.[83] So did the organizations of the Church, sometimes in close co-operation with the secular administrators, often in opposition to and competition with the officers of the state. And so did the many autonomous agencies of economic development and growth, the networks of traders and merchants, of bankers and financiers, of artisans and industrial entrepreneurs.

The early growth of the national bureaucracy tended to produce essentially territorial oppositions, but the subsequent widening of the scope of governmental activities and the acceleration of cross-local interactions gradually made for much more complex systems of alignments, some of them *between* localities, and others *across* and *within* localities.

The early waves of countermobilization often threatened the territorial unity of the nation, the federation, or the empire. The mobilization of the peasantry in Norway and in Sweden made it gradually impossible to keep up the union; the mobilization of the subject peoples of the Hapsburg territories broke up the empire; the mobilization of the Irish Catholics led to civil war and secession. The current strains of nation-building in the new states of Africa and Asia reflect similar conflicts between dominant and subject cultures; the recent histories of the Congo, India, Indonesia, Malaysia, Nigeria, and the Sudan can all be written in such terms. In some cases the early waves of mobilization may not have brought the territorial system to the brink of disruption but left an intractable heritage of territorial-cultural conflict: the Catalan-Basque-Castilian oppositions in Spain, the conflict between Flemings and Walloons in Belgium, and the English-French cleavages in Canada. The conditions for the softening or hardening of such cleavage lines in fully mobilized polities have been poorly studied. The multiple ethnic-religious cleavages of Switzerland and the language conflicts in Finland and Norway have proved much more manageable than the recently aggravated conflict between Netherlands-speakers and francophones in Belgium and between Quebec and the English-speaking provinces of Canada.

To account for such variations we clearly cannot proceed cleavage by cleavage but must analyze *constellations* of conflict lines within each polity.

To account for the variations in such constellations we have found it illuminating to distinguish *four critical lines of cleavage:*

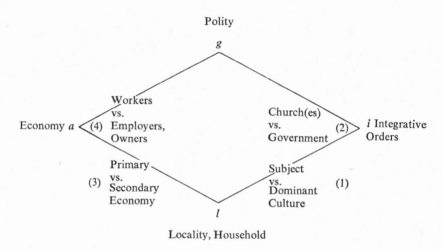

Figure 2. *Suggested Locations of Four Critical Cleavages in the a–g–i–l Paradigm*

Two of these cleavages are direct products of what we might call the *National* Revolution: the conflict between *the central nation-building culture* and the increasing resistance of the ethnically, linguistically, or religiously distinct *subject populations* in the provinces and the peripheries (1 in Fig. 2); the conflict between the centralizing, standardizing, and mobilizing *Nation-State* and the historically established corporate privileges of the *Church* (2).

Two of them are products of the *Industrial* Revolution: the conflict between the *landed interests* and the rising class of *industrial entrepreneurs* (3); the conflict between *owners and employers* on the one side and *tenants, labourers, and workers* on the other (4).

Much of the history of Europe since the beginning of the nineteenth century can be described in terms of the interaction between these two processes of revolutionary change: the one triggered in France and the other originating in Britain. Both had consequences for the cleavage structure of each nation, but the French Revolution produced the deepest and bitterest oppositions. The decisive battle came to stand between *the aspirations of the mobilizing nation-state and the corporate claims of the churches.* This was far more than a matter of economics. It is true that the status of church properties and the financing of religious activities were the subjects of violent controversy, but the fundamental issue was one of morals, of the control of community norms. This found reflection in fights over such matters as the solemnization of marriage and the granting of divorces, the organization of charities and the handling of deviants, the functions of medical versus religious officers, and the arrangements for funerals. However, the fundamental issue between Church and State focused on the *control of education.*

The Church, whether Roman Catholic, Lutheran, or Reformed, had for centuries claimed the right to represent man's 'spiritual estate' and to control the education of children in the right faith. In the Lutheran countries, steps were taken as early as in the seventeenth century to enforce elementary education in the vernacular for all children. The established national churches simply became agents of the state and had no reason to oppose such measures. In the religiously mixed countries and in purely Catholic ones, however, the ideas of the French Revolution proved highly divisive. The development of compulsory education under centralized secular control for all children of the nation came into direct conflict with the established rights of the religious *pouvoirs intermédiaires* and triggered waves of mass mobilization into nationwide parties of protest. To the radicals and liberals inspired by the French Revolution, the introduction of compulsory education was only one among several measures in a systematic effort to create direct links of influence and control between the nation-state and the individual citizen, but their attempt to penetrate directly to the children without consulting the parents and their spiritual authorities aroused widespread opposition and bitter fights.[84]

The parties of religious defense generated through this process grew into broad mass movements after the introduction of manhood suffrage and were able to claim the loyalties of remarkably high proportions of the church-goers in the working class. These proportions increased even more, of course, as the franchise was extended to women on a par with men. Through a process very similar to the one to be described for the Socialist parties, these church movements tended to isolate their supporters from outside influence through the development of a wide variety of parallel organizations and agencies: they did not only build up schools and youth movements of their own, but also developed confessionally distinct trade unions, sports clubs, leisure associations, publishing houses, magazines, newspapers, in one or two cases even radio and television stations.[85]

Perhaps the best example of institutionalized segmentation is found in the Netherlands; in fact, the Dutch word *Verzuiling* has recently become a standard term for tendencies to develop vertical networks (*zuilen,* columns or pillars) of associations and institutions to ensure maximum loyalty to each church and to protect the supporters from cross-cutting communications and pressures. Dutch society has for close to a century been divided into three distinct subcultures: the national-liberal-secular, frequently referred to as the *algemene,* the 'general' sector; the orthodox Protestant column; and the Roman Catholic column.[86]

The orthodox Protestant column developed through a series of violent conflicts over doctrinal issues within the established National Church. The *Nederlands Hervormde Kerk* came under heavy pressure in the decades after the French Revolution and the Napoleonic upheavals. With the spread of secularism and rationalism, the fundamentalists were increasingly pushed into a minority position, both within the Church and in the field of education. Originally, the orthodox protests against these developments restricted themselves to intellectual evangelical movements within the Establishment and to an isolationist walkout of pietistic lower-class elements in the separation *(Afscheiding)* of 1843. But from the 1860's onward, the movement achieved massive momentum under the organizational inspiration of Abraham Kuyper. This fundamentalist clergyman organized an Anti-School-Law League in 1872 and in 1879 succeeded in bringing together a variety of orthodox groups in a party explicitly directed against the ideas of the French Revolution, the *Anti-Revolutionary* party. This vigorous mass movement soon split up, however, over issues of doctrine and of cultural identification. Kuyper led his followers out of the Mother Church in 1886 and defended the rights of the *Kerkvolk,* the committed Calvinist Christians, to establish their own cultural community, free of any ties to the state and the nation. The very extremism of this anti-establishment posture produced several countermovements within the *Hervormde Kerk.* Important groups of orthodox Calvinists did *not* want to leave the Mother Church but wanted to reform it from within; they wanted a broad *Volkskerk* rather than an isolated *Kerkvolk.* The conflict between these two conceptions of the Christian community led to the breakup of the Anti-Revolutionary party in 1894 and the gradual formation of a second Calvinist party, the *Christian Historical Union,* formally consolidated in 1908. These two parties became the core organizations of the two wings of the orthodox Protestant front in Dutch society: the Anti-Revolutionaries deriving their essential strength from *Gereformeerden,* whether in separate dissenter churches or in *Hervormde* congregations controlled by clergymen of the same persuasion; the Christian Historicals deriving practically all their support from other orthodox segments *within* the Mother Church.

The Roman Catholic minority had at first found it to their advantage to work with the Liberal majority, but from the sixties onward took steps to form distinct political and social organizations. This was a slow process, however; the first federation of Catholic voters' associations was not formed until 1904 and a formally organized national party was not established until the twenties.[87]

Both the Protestant and the Catholic movements eventually developed large networks of associations and institutions for their members and were able to establish remarkably stable bases of support even within the working class. Evidence from sample surveys shows that the segmentation is most complete within the active and intransigent minority movements: *the Gereformeerden,* the religiously active *Hervormden,* and the Catholics. The passive members of the traditional National Church and the *onkerkelijken* tend to be aligned by class rather than by religious commitment: this was for long the only segment in which there was effective crosscutting of influences in the Dutch electorate.

In terms of our paradigm the orthodox Protestant and the Catholics form political fronts near the i pole of the cross-local axis. If all *three* of the subcultures had developed such strong barriers against each other, the system might conceivably have exploded, much in the way the Austrian polity did in 1934. The lower level of *Verzuiling* in the 'national' sector and the greater possibilities of compromise and accommodation in a triangular system of oppositions may go far to explain the successful operation of corporate pluralism in the Dutch polity.

Analysts of the Dutch data on the three subcultures have tried to establish a variety of indicators of *changes over time* in the degree of insulation of each of the vertical segments: they use the term *Ontzuiling* for reductions in the distinctiveness of each segment and *Verzuiling* for increases (Kruijt, 1962). In our paradigm these correspond to movements along the $a-i$ axis: the more *ontzuild* a given opposition, the more crisscrossing of multiple memberships in the system and, in general, the less intolerance and distrust of citizens on the 'other' side; the more *verzuild* the opposition, the fewer the crosspressures and the rarer the memberships across the cleavages. In a highly *ontzuild* system there is *low membership crystallization;* most of the participants tend to be tied to organizations and environments exposing them to *divergent* political pressures. By contrast in a highly *verzuild* system there is *high* membership crystallization; most of the participants tend to be exposed to messages and persuasive efforts in the *same* general direction in *all* their '24-hour, 7-day' environments.[88]

This dimension cuts across the whole range of functional cleavages in our paradigm, whether economic, social, or religious. The symmetric representation of the four basic cleavage lines in Fig. 2 refers to *average tendencies* only and does not exclude wide variations in location along the $a-i$ axis. Conflicts over the civic integration of recalcitrant regional cultures (1) or religious organizations (2) need not always lead to *Verzuiling*. An analysis of the contrasts between Switzerland and the Netherlands would tell us a great deal about differences in the conditions for the development of pluralist insulation. Conflicts between primary producers and the urban-industrial interests have *normally* tended towards the *a* pole of the axis, but there are many examples of highly ideologized peasant oppositions to officials and burghers. Conflicts between workers and employers have always contained elements of economic bargaining, but there have also often been strong elements of cultural opposition and ideological insulation. Working-class parties in opposition and without power have tended to be more *verzuild,* more wrapped up in their own distinct mythology, more insulated against the rest of the society. By contrast the victorious Labour parties have tended to become *ontzuild,* domesticated, more open to influence from all segments within the national society.

Similar variations will occur at a wide range of points on the *territorial* axis of our schema. In our initial discussion of the *l* pole we gave examples of *cultural* and *religious* resistances to the domination of the central national elite, but such oppositions are not always *purely* territorial. The movements may be completely dominant in their provincial strongholds but may also find allies in the central areas and thus contribute to the development of *cross-local* and *cross-regional* fronts.

The opposition of the Old Left in Norway was essentially of this character. It was from the outset a movement of territorial protest against the dominance of the central elite of officials and patricians but gradually broadened into a mass movement of cultural opposition to the dominant urban strata. As the suffrage was extended and the mobilization efforts proceeded it was also able to entrench itself in the central cities and even gain control in some of them (Torgersen, 1964). This very broadening of the movement made the Old Left increasingly vulnerable to fragmentation. One wing moved toward the *a* pole and set itself up as an *Agrarian* party (3 in Fig. 2), another wing moved toward the *i* pole and established a distinctive *Christian* party (1). The Scandinavian countries have seen the formation of several such moralist-evangelist parties opposed to the tolerant pragmatism of the Established Lutheran Church.[89] They differ from the Christian parties on the Continent: they have not opposed national education as such and have not built up extensive networks of functional organizations around their followers; they have been primarily concerned to defend the traditions of orthodox evangelism against the onslaught of urban secularism and to use the legislative and the executive machinery of the state to protect the young against the evils of modern life. In their rejection of the lukewarm latitudinarianism of the national Mother Church they resemble the nonconformists in Great Britain and the Anti-Revolutionaries in the Netherlands, but the contexts of their efforts have been very different. In the British case the religious activists could work *within* the Liberal Party (later, of course, also within Labour) and found it possible to advance their views without establishing a party of their own. In the Dutch case, the orthodox dissidents not only set up their own party but built up a strong column of vertical organizations around it.

The National Revolution forced ever-widening circles of the territorial population to choose sides in conflicts over *values* and *cultural identities.* The Industrial Revolution also triggered a variety of cultural counter-movements, but in the longer run tended to cut across the value communities within the nation and to force the enfranchised citizenry to choose sides in terms of their *economic interests,* their shares in the increased wealth generated through the spread of the new technologies and the widening markets.

In our *a–g–i–l* paradigm we have distinguished two types of such interest cleavages: cleavages between rural and urban interests (3) and cleavages between worker and employer interests (4).

The spectacular growth of world trade and industrial production generated increasing strains between the primary producers in the countryside and the merchants and the entrepreneurs in the towns and the cities. On the continent, the conflicting interests of the rural and urban areas had been recognized since the Middle Ages in the separate representation of the estates: the nobility and, in exceptional cases, the freehold peasants spoke for the land, and the burghers spoke for the cities. The Industrial Revolution deepened these conflicts and in country after country produced distinct rural-urban alignments in the national legislatures. Often the old divisions between estates were simply carried over into the unified parliaments and found expression in oppositions between Conservative-Agrarian and Liberal-Radical parties. The conflicts between rural and urban interests had been much less marked in Great Britain than on the continent. The House of Commons was not an assembly of the burgher estate but a body of legislators representing the constituent localities of the realm, the counties and the boroughs.[90] Yet even there the Industrial Revolution produced deep and bitter cleavages between the landed interests and the urban; in England, if not in Wales and Scotland, the opposition between Conservatives and Liberals fed largely on these strains until the 1880's.[91]

There was a hard core of economic conflict in these oppositions, but what made them so deep and bitter was the struggle for the maintenance of acquired status and the recognition of achievement. In England, the landed elite ruled the country, and the rising class of industrial entrepreneurs, many of them religiously at odds with the established church, for decades aligned themselves in opposition both to defend their economic interests and to assert their claims to status. It would be a misunderstanding, says the historian George Kitson Clark,[92] to think of agriculture 'as an industry organized like any other industry – primarily for the purpose of efficient production. *It was . . . rather organized to ensure the survival intact of a caste.* The proprietors of the great estates were not just very rich men whose capital happened to be invested in land, they were rather the life tenants of very considerable positions which it was their duty to leave intact to their successors. In a way it was the estate that mattered and not the holder of the estate . . .' The conflict between Conservatives and Liberals reflected an opposition between two value orientations: the recognition of status through *ascription and kin connections* versus the claims for status through *achievement and enterprise*.

These are typical strains in all transitional societies; they tend to be most intensive in the early phases of industrialization and to soften as the rising elite establishes itself in the community. In England, this process of reconciliation proceeded quite rapidly. In a society open to extensive mobility and intermarriage, urban and industrial wealth could gradually be translated into full recognition within the traditional hierarchy of the landed families. More and more mergers took place between the agricultural and the business interests, and this consolidation of the national elite soon changed the character of the Conservative-Liberal conflict. As James Cornford has shown through his detailed ecological studies, the movement of the business owners into the countryside and the suburbs divorced them from their workers and brought them into close relations with the landed gentry. The result was a softening of the rural-urban conflict in the system and a rapidly increasing class polarization of the widened electorate (Cornford, 1963).

A similar *rapprochement* took place between the east Elbian agricultural interests and the western business bourgeoisie in Germany, but there, significantly, the bulk of the Liberals sided with the Conservatives and did not try to rally the working-class electorate on their side in the way the British party did during the period up to World War I. The result was a deepening of the chasm between burghers and workers and a variety of desperate attempts to bridge it through appeals to national and military values.[93]

In other countries of the European continent the rural-urban cleavage continued to assert itself in national politics far into the twentieth century, but the political expressions of the cleavage varied widely. Much depended on the concentrations of wealth and political control in the cities and on the ownership structure in the rural economy. In the Low Countries, France, Italy, and Spain, rural-urban cleavages rarely found direct expression in the development of party oppositions. Other cleavages, particularly between the state and the churches and between owners and tenants, had greater impact on the alignments of the electorates. By contrast, in the five Nordic countries the cities had traditionally dominated national political life, and the struggle for democracy and parliamentary rule was triggered off through a broad process of mobilization within the peasantry (Hovde, 1948: partic. Chs. VIII–IV, XIII). This was essentially an expression of protest against the central elite of officials and patricians (a cleavage on the *l–g* axis in our model), but there were also elements of economic opposition in the movement: the peasants felt exploited in their dealings with city folk and wanted to shift the tax burdens to the expanding urban economies. These economic cleavages became more and more pronounced as the primary-producing communities entered into the national money and market economy. The result was the formation of a broad front of interest organizations and cooperatives and the development of distinctive Agrarian parties. Even after the rise of the working-class parties to national dominance, these Agrarian parties did not find it possible to establish common fronts with the Conservative defenders of the business community. The cultural contrasts between the countryside and the cities were still strong, and the strict market controls favoured by the Agrarians could not easily be reconciled with the philosophy of free competition espoused by many conservatives.

The conflict between landed and urban interests was centred in the *commodity* market. The peasants wanted to sell their wares at the best possible prices and to buy what they needed from the industrial and urban producers at low cost. Such conflicts did not invariably prove party-forming. They could be dealt with within broad party fronts or could be channelled through interest organizations into narrower arenas of functional representation and bargaining. Distinctly agrarian parties have only emerged where strong cultural oppositions have deepened and embittered the strictly economic conflicts.

Conflicts in the *labour* market proved much more uniformly divisive. Working-class parties emerged in every country of Europe in the wake of the early waves of industrialization. The rising masses of wage earners, whether in large-scale farming, in forestry, or in industry, resented their conditions of work and the insecurity of their contracts, and many of them felt socially and culturally alienated from the owners and the employers. The result was the formation of a variety of labour unions and the development of nationwide Socialist parties. The success of such movements depended on a variety of factors: the strength of the paternalist traditions of ascriptive recognition of the worker status, the size of the work unit and the local ties of the workers, the level of prosperity and the stability of employment in the given industry, and the chances of improvements and promotion through loyal devotion or through education and achievement.

A crucial factor in the development of distinct working-class movements was the *openness* of the given society: Was the worker status a lifetime predicament or were there openings for advancement? How easy was it to get an education qualifying for a change in status? What prospects were there for striking out on one's own, for establishing independent work units? The contrasts between American and European developments must clearly be analyzed in these terms; the American workers were not only given the vote much earlier than their comrades in Europe; but they also found their way into the national system so much more easily because of the greater stress on equality and achievement, because of the many openings to better education, and, last but not least, because the established workers could advance to better positions as new waves of immigrants took over the lower-status jobs (Lipset, 1963: Chs. 5, 6, 7). A similar process is currently under way in the advanced countries of Western Europe. The immigrant proletariats from the Mediterranean countries and from the West Indies allow the children of the established national working class to move into the middle class, and these new waves of mobility tend to drain off traditional sources of resentment.

In nineteenth and early twentieth century Europe the status barriers were markedly higher. The traditions from the estate-divided society kept the workers in their place, and the narrowness of the educational channels of mobility also made it difficult for sons and daughters to rise above their fathers. There were, however, important variations among the countries of Europe in the attitudes of the established and the rising elites to the claims of the workers, and these differences clearly affected the development of the unions and the Socialist parties. In Britain and the Scandinavian countries the attitudes of the elites tended to be open and pragmatic. As in all other countries there was active resistance to the claims of the workers, but little or no direct repression. These are today the countries with the largest and the most domesticated Labour parties in Europe. In Germany and Austria, France, Italy, and Spain the cleavages went much deeper. A number of attempts were made to repress the unions and the Socialists, and the working-class organizations consequently tended to isolate themselves from the national culture and to develop *soziale Ghettoparteien*,[94] strongly ideological movements seeking to isolate their members and their supporters from influences from the encompassing social environments. In terms of our paradigm, these parties were just as close to the *i* pole as their opponents in the religious camp. This 'anti-system' orientation of large sections of the European working class was brought to a climax in the aftermath of the Russian Revolution. The Communist movement did not just speak for an alienated stratum of the territorial community but came to be seen as an external conspiracy against the nation. These developments brought a number of European countries to the point of civil war in the twenties and the thirties. The greater the number of citizens caught in such direct 'friend-foe' oppositions to each other the greater the danger of total disruption of the body politic.

Developments since World War II have pointed toward a reduction of such pitched oppositions and some softening of ideological tensions: a movement from the *i* toward the *a* pole in our paradigm.[95] A variety of factors contributed to this development: the experience of national cooperation during the war, the improvements in the standard of living in the fifties, the rapid growth of a 'new middle class' bridging the gaps between the traditional working class and the bourgeoisie. But the most important factor was possibly the *entrenchment of the working-class parties in local and national governmental structures* and their consequent 'domestication' within the established system. The developments in Austria offer a particularly revealing example. The extreme opposition between Socialists and Catholics had ended in civil war in 1934, but after the experience of National Socialist domination, war, and occupation, the two parties settled down to share government responsibilities under a *Proporz* system, a settlement still based on mutual distrust between the two camps but at least one that recognized the necessity for coexistence (Vodopivec, 1961; Engelmann, 1966). Comparisons of positions taken by two leading Communist parties in Western Europe, the Italian and the French, also point to the importance of entrenchments in the national system of government. The French party has been much less involved in the running of local communities and has remained much more isolated within the national system, while the Italian party has responded much more dynamically to the exigencies of community decision-making (Laqueur, 1962; Labedz, 1962; Lipset, 1964: 1). Erik Allardt has implicitly demonstrated the importance of similar factors in a comparison of levels of class polarization in the Nordic countries. He points out that while the percentage of working-class voters siding with the Left (Communists and Social Democrats) is roughly the same in Finland as in Norway and Sweden, the percentage of middle-class leftists used to be much lower in Finland than in the two other countries. This difference appears to be related to a contrast in the chances of upward mobility from the working class: very low in Finland, markedly higher in the other countries (Allardt, 1964). The continued isolation of the Finnish working-class parties may reflect a lower level of participation in responsible decision-making in the local communities and in the nation. This has not yet been investigated in detail, but studies of working class mobility and political changes carried out in Norway (Rokkan, 1967; Fivelsdal, 1964) suggest that the principal channels of advancement were in the public sector and that the decisive wave of 'bourgeoisification' came in the wake of the accession of the Labour party to a position of dominance in the system. In Finland the protracted period of underground Communism until 1944 and the deep split in the working-class movement during the next decades tended to keep the two parties from decisive influence on the public sector and maintained the old barriers against mobility; in the other Scandinavian countries the victories of the Social Democrat Labour parties had opened up new channels of mobility and helped to break down the isolation of the working class.

This, of course, applies to the situation during the 1950s only. The disruption of the working class leadership and the increasing strains between the radical leftist youth and the established party apparatuses in the 1960s cannot be analyzed within this framework. But these are many indications that these developments can be best understood as a reaction to the 'clogging' of all channels of influence in a situation of intensified international awareness triggered by the educational explosion of the late 1950s and early 1960s.

Four 'Critical Junctures'

Our abstract schema distinguishes four decisive dimensions of opposition in Western politics:

two of them were steps in a *National* Revolution (1 and 2);

and two were generated through the *Industrial* Revolution (3 and 4).

In their basic characteristics the party systems that emerged in the Western European politics during the early phase of competition and mobilization can be interpreted as products of *sequential interactions between these two fundamental processes of change.*

Differences in the timing and character of the *National* Revolution set the stage for striking divergencies in the European party system. In the Protestant countries the conflicts between the claims of the State and the Church had been temporarily settled by royal *fiats* at the time of the Reformation, and the processes of centralization and standardization triggered off after 1789 did not immediately bring about a conflict between the two. The temporal and the spiritual establishments were at one in the defence of the central nation-building culture but came increasingly under attack by the leaders and ideologists of counter-movements in the provinces, in the peripheries and within the underprivileged strata of peasants, craftsmen and workers. The other countries of Western Europe were all split to the core in the wake of the secularizing French Revolution and without exception developed strong parties for the defence of the Church, either explicitly as in Germany, the Low Countries, Switzerland, Austria, Italy, and Spain or implicitly as in the case of the Right in France.

Differences in the timing and character of the *Industrial* Revolution also made for contrasts among the national party systems in Europe.

Conflicts in the *commodity* market tended to produce highly divergent party alliances in Europe. In some countries the majority of the market farmers found it possible to join with the owner interests in the secondary sector of the economy; in others the two remained in opposition to each other and developed parties of their own. Conflicts in the *labour* market, by contrast, proved much more uniformly divisive: all countries of Western Europe developed lower-class mass parties at some point or other before World War I. These were rarely unified into single working-class parties. In Latin Europe the lower-class movements were sharply divided among revolutionary anarchists, anarchosyndicalists and Marxist factions on the one hand and revisionist socialists on the other. The Russian Revolution of 1917 split the working-class organizations throughout Europe. Today we find in practically all countries of the West divisions between Communists, left Socialist splinters, and revisionist Social Democrat parties.

Our task, however, is not just to account for the emergence of single parties but to analyze the processes of alliance formation that led to the development of stable *systems* of political organizations in country after country. To approach some understanding of these alliance formations, we have to study the *interactions* between the two revolutionary processes of change in each polity: How far had the National Revolution proceeded at the point of the industrial 'takeoff' and how did the two processes of mobilization, the cultural and the economic, affect each other, positively by producing common fronts or negatively by maintaining divisions?

The decisive contrasts among the Western party systems clearly reflect differences in the *national histories of conflict and compromise across the first three of the four cleavage lines* distinguished in our analytical schema: the 'centre-periphery,' the state-church, and the land-industry cleavages generated national developments in *divergent* directions, while the owner-worker cleavage tended to bring the party systems *closer to each other* in their basic structure. The crucial differences among the party systems emerged in the early phases of competitive politics, before the final phase of mass mobilization. They reflected basic contrasts in the conditions and sequences of nation-building and in the structure of the economy at the point of takeoff toward sustained growth. This, to be sure, does not mean that the systems vary exclusively on the 'Right' and at the centre, but are much more alike on the 'Left' of the political spectrum. There are working-class movements throughout the West, but they differ conspicuously in size, in cohesion, in ideological orientation, and in the extent of their integration into, or alienation from, the historically given national policy. Our point is simply that the factors generating these differences on the left are *secondary*. The decisive contrasts among the systems had emerged before the entry of the working-class parties into the political arena, and the character of these mass parties was heavily influenced by the con-stellations of ideologies, movements, and organizations they had to con-front in that arena.

To understand the differences among the Western party systems we have to start out from an analysis of the *situation of the active nation-building elite on the eve of the breakthrough to democratization and mass mobilization:* What had they achieved and where had they met most resistance? What were their resources, who were their nearest allies, and where could they hope to find further support? Who were their enemies, what were their resources, and where could they recruit allies and rally reinforcement?

Any attempt at comparative analysis across so many divergent national histories is fraught with grave risks. It is easy to get lost in the wealth of fascinating detail, and it is equally easy to succumb to facile generalities and irresponsible abstractions. Scholarly prudence prompts us to proceed case by case, but intellectual impatience urges us to go beyond the analysis of concrete contrasts and try out alternative schemes of systematization across the known cases.

To clarify the logic of our approach to the comparative analysis of party systems, we have developed a *model of alternative alliances and oppositions*. We have posited several sets of actors, have set up a series of rules of alliance and opposition among these, and have tested the resultant typology of potential party systems against a range of empirically known cases.

Our model bears on relationships of alliance, neutrality or opposition among seven sets of actors. To underscore the abstract character of our exercise we shall refer to each set by a shorthand symbol:

N – a central core of cooperating 'nation-builders' controlling major elements of the machinery of the 'state';

C – an ecclesiastical body established within the national territory and given a large measure of control over education;

R – the supranationally established ecclesiastical body organized under the Roman Curia and the Pope;

D – a dissident, nonconformist body of religious activists opposed to C and R;

L – a cooperating body of established landowners controlling a substantial share of the total primary production of the national territory;

U – a cooperating body of urban commercial and industrial entrepreneurs controlling the advancing secondary sectors of the national economy;

P – a movement of resistance in the subject periphery against central national control.

The model sets these *restrictions on alliance formation:*

1) N and D and N and P will invariably be opposed, never in any joint alliance;

2) N must decide on alliances on two fronts: the *religious* and the *economic;*

3) on the religious front, N is faced with three options:
– alliance with C,
– a secular posture S,
– alliance with R;

4) on the economic front, N is restricted to two alliance options:
– with L,
– with U;

5) N's alliances determine P's choice of alliances but with these restrictions: (a) if N is allied to C, the model allows two contingent outcomes: (aa) if C is dominant, the only P option on the religious front is D, (bb) if R still constitutes a strong minority, P will be split in two alliance-groups: the response to N–C–L will be P_1–S–U and P_2–R, the response to N–C–U will be P_1–D–L and P_2–R–L: (b) if N chooses S or R, the only

possible P alliances are P–S–U and P–R–L or simply P–U and P–L; P–R–U and P–S–L do not occur.

These various elements and restrictions combine to produce an eightfold typology of basic political oppositions:

Type	N's commitments — Religious front: Option	N's commitments — Religious front: Conditions	Economic front	P's response	Country	Closest empirical examples — 'N' party (parties)	Closest empirical examples — 'P' parties
I	C	C dominant	L	P–D–U	Britain	CONS. vs.	LIB: {Celtic Fringe, Dissenters, Industry}
II	C	C dominant	U	P–D–L	Scandinavia	CONS. vs.	'LEFT' {AGRARIANS, CHRISTIANS, RADICALS}
III	C	R strong minority	L	P_1–S–U / P_2–R	Prussia/ Reich	CONS. vs.	{BAVARIANS, LIB., ZENTRUM}
IV	C	R strong minority	U	P_1–D–L / P_2–R–L	Netherlands	LIB. vs.	Calvinists: CHU, AR {Catholics: KVP}
V	S		L	P_1–U / P_2–R	Spain	LIB. vs.	{Catalan LLIGA, Carlists}
VI	S		U	P–R–L	France Italy	LIB./RAD. vs.	CONS.-CATH.-CHR.
VII	R		L	P–S–U	Austria	CHR. vs. LIB.	{Pan-Germans, Industry}
VIII	R		U	P–L	Belgium	CHR./LIB. vs.	Flemish separatists

This typological exercise may appear excessively abstract and unneces-sarily mechanical. To us the gains in analytical perspective outweigh the loss in historic immediacy: the model not only offers a grid for the mapping of parallels and contrasts among national developments, it also represents an attempt to establish an explanatory paradigm of the simplest possible structure to account for a wide range of empirical variations. The literature on democratic politics is replete with examples of isolated discussions of parallels and contrasts among national party systems: ours, we believe, is the first attempt to develop a general typology of such variations from a unified set of postulates and hypotheses.

Our model seeks to reduce the bewildering variety of empirical party systems *to a set of ordered consequences of decisions and developments at three crucial junctures in the history of each nation:*

first, during the *Reformation* – the struggle for the control of the ecclesiastical organizations within the national territory;

second, in the wake of the *'Democratic Revolution'* after 1789 – the conflict over the control of the vast machineries of mass education to be built up by the mobilizing nation-states;

finally, during the early phases of the *Industrial Revolution* – the opposition between landed interests and the claims of the rising com-mercial and industrial leadership in cities and towns.

Our eight types of alliance-opposition structure are in fact the simple combinatorial products of three successive dichotomies:

First Dichotomy: The Reformation

I–IV	V–VIII
State Controls National Church	State Allied to Roman Catholic Church

Second Dichotomy: The 'Democratic Revolution'

I–II	III–IV	V–VI	VII–VIII
National Church Dominant	Strong Roman Minority	Secularizing Revolution	State Allied to Roman Church

Third Dichotomy: The Industrial Revolution

Commitment to		Commitment to		Commitment to		Commitment to	
Landed Interests	Urban	Landed Interests	Urban	Landed Interests	Urban	Landed Interests	Urban
Type: I	II	III	IV	V	VI	VII	VIII

The model spells out the consequences of the fateful division of Europe brought about through Reformation and the Counter-Reformation. The outcomes of the early struggles between State and Church determined the structure of national politics in the era of democratization and mass mobilization three hundred years later. In Southern and Central Europe the Counter-Reformation had consolidated the position of the Church and tied its fate to the privileged bodies of the *ancien régime*. The result was a polarization of politics between a national-radical-secular movement and a Catholic-traditionalist one. In Northwest Europe, in Britain and in Scandinavia, the settlement of the sixteenth century gave a very different structure to the cleavages of the nineteenth. The established churches did not stand in opposition to the nation-builders in the way the Roman Catholic Church did on the continent, and the 'Left' movements opposed to the religious establishment found most of their support among newly enfranchised dissenters, nonconformists, and fundamentalists in the peripheries and within the rising urban strata. In Southern and Central Europe the bourgeois opposition to the *ancien régime* tended to be indifferent if not hostile to the teachings of the Church: the cultural integration of the nation came first and the Church had to find whatever place it could within the new political order. In Northwest Europe the opposition to the *ancien régime* was far from indifferent to religious values. The broad 'Left' coalitions against the established powers recruited decisive support among orthodox Protestants in a variety of sectarian movements outside and inside the national churches.

The distinction between these two types of 'Left' alliances against the inherited political structure is fundamental for an understanding of European political developments in the age of mass elections. It is of particular importance in the analysis of the religiously most divided of the European polities: types III and IV in our $2 \times 2 \times 2$ schema. The religious frontiers of Europe went straight through the territories of the Low Countries, the old German *Reich,* and Switzerland; in each of these the clash between the nation-builders and the strong Roman Catholic minorities produced lasting divisions of the bodies politic and determined the structure of their party systems. The Dutch system came closest to a direct merger of the South-Central type (VI–VIII) and the Northwestern: on the one hand a nation-building party of increasingly secularized Liberals, on the other hand a Protestant 'Left' recruited from orthodox milieus of the same type as those behind the old opposition parties in England and Scandinavia.

The difference between England and the Netherlands is indeed instructive. Both countries had their strong peripheral concentrations of Catholic opposed to central authority: the English in Ireland, the Dutch in the south. In Ireland, the cumulation of ethnic, social, and religious conflicts could not be resolved within the old system; the result was a history of intermittent violence and finally territorial separation. In the Netherlands the secession of the Belgians still left a sizable Catholic minority, but the inherited tradition of corporate pluralism helped to ease them into the system. The Catholics established their own broad column of association and a strong political party and gradually found acceptance within a markedly segmented but still cohesive national polity.

A comparison of the Dutch and the Swiss case would add further depth to this analysis of the conditions for the differentiation of parties within national systems. Both countries come close to our type IV: Protestant national leadership, strong Catholic minorities, predominance of the cities in the national economy. In setting the assumption of our model we predicted a split in the peripheral opposition to the nation-builders: one orthodox Protestant opposition (P–D–L) and one Roman Catholic (P–R–L). This clearly fits the Dutch case but not so well the Swiss. How is this to be accounted for? Contrasts of this type open up fascinating possibilities of comparative historical analysis; all we can do here is to suggest a simple hypothesis. Our model not only simplifies complex historical developments through its strict selection of conditioning variables, it also reduces empirical continuities to crude dichotomies. The difference between the Dutch and the Swiss cases can possibly be accounted for through further differentiation in the centre-periphery axis. The drive for national centralization was stronger in the Netherlands and had been slowed down in Switzerland through the experiences of the war between the Protestant cantons and the Catholic *Sonderbund*. In the Netherlands the Liberal drive for centralization produced resistance both among the Protestants and the Catholics. In Switzerland the Radicals had few difficulties on the Protestant side and needed support in their opposition to the Catholics. The result was a party system of essentially the same structure as in the typical Southern-Central cases (types VI and VII in the typology).

Further differentiations of the 'N–P' axis in our model will also make it easier to fit the extraordinary case of *France* into this system of controlled dimension-by-dimension comparisons.

In our model we have placed France with Italy as an example of an alliance-opposition system of type VI: Catholic dominance through the Counter-Reformation, secularization and religious conflict during the next phase of nation-building in the nineteenth century, clear predominance of the cities in national politics. But this is an analytical juxtaposition of polities with diametrically opposed histories of development and consolidation – France one of the oldest and most centralized nation-states in Europe, Italy a territory unified long after the French revolutions had paved the way for the 'participant nation,' the integrated political structure committing the entire territorial population to the same historical destiny. To us this is not a weakness in our model, however. The party systems of the countries *are* curiously similar, and any scheme of comparative analysis must somehow or other bring this out. The point is that our distinction between 'nation-builder' alliances and 'periphery' alliances must take on very different meanings in the two contexts. In France the distinction between 'centre' and 'periphery' was far more than a matter of geography; it reflected long-standing historical commitments for or against the Revolution. As spelt out in detail in Siegfried's classic *Tableau,* the *Droite* had its strongholds in the districts which had most stubbornly resisted the revolutionary drive for centralization and equalization,[96] but it was far more than a movement of peripheral protest – it was a broad alliance of alienated elite groups, of frustrated nation-builders who felt that their rightful powers had been usurped by men without faith and without roots. In Italy there was no basis for such a broad alliance against the secular nation-builders, since the established local elites offered little resistance to the lures of *trasformismo,* and the Church kept its faithful followers out of national politics for nearly two generations.

These contrasts during the initial phases of mass mobilization had far-reaching consequences for each party system. With the broadening of the electorates and the strengthening of the working-class parties, the Church felt impelled to defend its position through its own resources. In France, the result was an attempt to divorce the defence of the Catholic schools from the defence of the established rural hierarchy. This trend had first found expression through the establishment of Christian trade unions and in 1944 finally led to the formation of the MRP. The burden of historic commitments was too strong, however; the young party was unable to establish itself as a broad mass party defending the principles of Christian democracy. By contrast, in Italy, history had left the Church with only insignificant rivals to the right of the working class parties. The result was the formation of a broad alliance of a variety of interests and movements, frequently at loggerheads with each other, but united in their defence of the rights of the central institution of the fragmented *ancien régime,* the Roman Catholic Church. In both cases there was a clear-cut tendency toward religious polarization, but differences in the histories of nation-building made for differences in the resultant systems of party alliances and oppositions.

We could go into further detail on every one of the eight types distinguished in our model, but this would take us too far into single-country histories. We are less concerned with the specifics of the degrees of fit in each national case than with the overall structure of the model. There is clearly nothing final about any such scheme; it simply sets a series of themes for detailed comparisons and suggests ways of organizing the results within a manageable conceptual framework. The model is a tool and its utility can be tested only through continuous development: through the addition of further variables to account for observed differences as well as through refinements in the definition and grading of the variables already included.

Two developments from the model require immediate detailed consideration:

1) What variables have to be added to account for the formation of *distinctly territorial* parties?

2) What criteria should count in differentiating between N–L and N–U

alliances, and what conditional variables can be entered into the model to account for the emergence of *explicitly agrarian parties?*

Developments and Deviations: Parties for Territorial Defence

Nation-building invariably generates territorial resistances and cultural strains. There will be competition between potential centres of political control; there may be conflict between the capital and the areas of growth in the provinces; and there will be unavoidable tension between the culturally and economically advanced areas and the backward periphery.[97] Some of these territorial-cultural conflicts were solved through secession or boundary changes, but others were intensified through unification movements. To take one obvious example, the dismemberment of the Hapsburg Empire certainly settled a great number of hopelessly entangled conflicts, but it also led to the political unification of such culturally and economically heterogeneous entities as Italy, Yugoslavia, and Czechoslovakia. Territorial-cultural conflicts do not just find political expression in secessionist and irredentist movements, however; they feed into the overall cleavage structure in the national community and help to condition the development not only of each nationwide party organization but even more of the entire system of party oppositions and alignments.

The contrast between the British and the Scandinavian party systems stands out with great clarity in our step-by-step accounting scheme. The countries of Northwest Europe had all opted for national religious solutions at the time of the Reformation, but they nevertheless developed markedly different party systems during the early phases of democratization and mobilization. This contrast in political development clearly did not reflect a difference in the salience of any *single* line of cleavage but a difference in the *joint* operation of two sets of cleavages: the opposition between the central nation-building culture and the traditions of the periphery, and the opposition between the primary and the secondary sectors of the economy. In Britain the central culture was upheld and reinforced by a vast network of *landed* families, in the Nordic countries by an essentially *urban* elite of officials and patricians. In Britain the two cleavage lines *cut across* each other; in Scandinavia they *reinforced* each other. The British structure encouraged a gradual merger of urban and rural interests, while the Scandinavian made for division and opposition (Rokkan, 1966: 4). The British Conservative Party was able to establish a joint front of landed and industrial owner interests, while the Scandinavian 'Right' remained essentially urban and proved unable to establish any durable alliance with the Agrarians and the peripheral 'Left.'

Similar processes of interaction can be observed at work in the development of the continental party system. Conflicts between mobilizing elites and peripheral cultures have in some cases been reinforced, in some cases dampened, by conflicts between the State and the Church and by oppositions between urban and rural interests. Belgium offers a striking example of cleavage reinforcement. The 'Union of Oppositions' of the early years of nation-building broke up over the schools issue, but this was only the first step in a gradual deepening of cleavages. The continuing processes of economic, social and cultural mobilization brought the country closer to a polarization between French-speaking, secular and industrial Wallonia and *Nederlands*-speaking, Catholic and agricultural Flanders.[98] This polarizing cleavage structure contrasts dramatically with the criss-crossing of religious and linguistic oppositions in Switzerland. Of the five French-speaking cantons three are Protestant and two Catholic, and of the nineteen Alemannic cantons or half-cantons ten are Protestant and nine Catholic: 'this creates loyalties and affinities which counterbalance the linguistic interrelationships' (Luethy, 1962: p. 25).

Conditions for the emergence and consolidation of territorial counter-cultures have varied significantly within Europe. Organized resistance against the centralizing apparatus of the mobilizing nation-state appears to have been most likely to develop in three sets of situations:

– heavy concentration of the counter-culture within one clear-cut territory;

– few ties of communication, alliance, and bargaining experience toward the national centre and more toward external centres of cultural or economic influence;

– minimal economic dependence on the political metropolis.

Federalist, autonomist, and separatist movements and parties are most likely to occur through a cumulation of such conditions. A comparison of Spain and Italy tells us a great deal about such processes of cleavage cumulation. Both countries have for centuries been heavily dominated by the Catholic Church. Both were caught in a violent conflict between secular power and ecclesiastical privileges in the wake of the National Revolution, and both have remained highly heterogeneous in their ethnic structure, in cultural traditions, and in historical commitments. Yet they differed markedly in the character of the party systems they developed in the phase of initial mass mobilization. Spanish politics was dominated by territorial oppositions; Italy developed a national party system, fragmented but with irredentist-separatist parties only in such extreme cases as the South Tyrol and the Val d'Aosta.

In Spain, the opposition of the Pyrennean periphery to the centralizing Castilian regime first found expression in the mobilization of the Carlist peasantry in defence of the Church and their local liberties against the Liberals and the Freemasons in the army and government bureaucracy during the second half of the nineteenth century. Around 1900, the Catalan industrial bourgeoisie and significant parts of the Basque middle classes and peasantry turned to regionalist and separatist parties to fight the parasitic central administration identified with the economically backward centre of the nation. In the Basque areas, strong religious loyalties contributed to increase the hostility toward an anticlerical central government. In Catalonia, separatist sentiments could not repress cleavages along class lines. The conflicts between businessmen and workers, landowners and tenant-farmers divided the regionalist forces into a right (the *Lliga*) and a left (the *Esquerra*).[99]

In Italy, the thrust of national mobilization came from the economically advanced North. The impoverished provinces to the South and on the islands resisted the new administrators as alien usurpers but did not develop parties of regional resistance: the prefects ruled through varying mixtures of *combinazione* and force and proved as efficient instruments of centralization in the backward areas of Italy as the *caciques* in the regions of Spain controlled from Madrid.[100] There was an obvious element of territorial protest in the papal repudiation of the new nation-state, but it took several decades before this conflict found expression in the formation of a distinctly Catholic party. The loyal Catholics did not just oppose the Piedmontese administration as a threat to the established privileges of the Church; Rome fought the Liberal nation-builders as the conquerors of the Papal territories. But these resentments were not channelled into national politics. The intransigeant policy of *non expedit* kept the Catholics out of the give and take of electoral bargaining and discouraged the eager advocates of a mass party for the defence of the Church. This policy of isolation divided the communities throughout the Italian territory. When the Pope finally gave in on the eve of the introduction of mass suffrage, these cross-local cleavages produced a nationwide system of oppositions among Liberals, Catholics, and Socialists. There were marked regional variations in the strength of each camp. Dogan's work on regional variations in the stratification of the Italian vote tells us a great deal about the factors at work (Dogan, 1963; Dogan, 1967). But in contrast to the development in Spain, the territorial conflict within Italy found no direct expression in the party system. This was not a sign of national integration, however; the country was torn by irreconcilable conflicts among ideologically distinct camps, but the conflict cut across the communities and the regions. There were still unsettled and unsettling territorial problems, but these were at the frontiers. The irredentist claims against France and the Hapsburgs generated a nationalist-imperialist ideology and prepared the ground for the rise of Fascism (Webster, 1960).

Such comparisons can be multiplied throughout Europe. In the multi-centred German Reich the contrast between East and West, North and South generated a variety of territorial tensions. The conflict between the Hamburg Liberals and the East Elbian Conservatives went far beyond the tariff issue – it reflected an important cultural opposition. The Bavarian particularists again and again set up parties of their own and have to this day found it difficult to fit into a nationwide system of party oppositions.[101]

By contrast, in hydrocephalic France conflicts between the capital and the provincial 'desert' [102] had been endemic since the sixteenth century but did *not* generate distinct regional parties. Paris was without serious competitors for political, economic, and cultural power – there was no basis for durable alliances against the centre. 'Paris was not only comparable to New York and Washington, as was London, but also to Chicago in transport, Detroit and Cincinnati in manufacturing, and Boston in letters and education' (Kindleberger, 1964: p. 255).

So far our attention has focused on the *larger* units of the European system. The weight of the centre-periphery cleavage is even greater in the *smaller* countries. This is not at all surprising. With two possible exceptions, Sweden and the Netherlands, our eleven smaller democracies have all been marginal in the European structure, all highly dependent on the inflow of political, economic and cultural resources from outside. Such situations of dependence tend to produce deep cleavages. With the spread of literacy, urbanization and economic growth, the elites closest to the external centre come under increasing pressures from nationalist-separatist counter-elites. Depending on the geopolitical situation, such cleavages may generate elite factions or opposed mass parties, or lead on to a fight for territorial secession. A critical consideration in all such sequences of 'nation-accentuating' politics is the extent of metropolitan settlement within the peripheral territory: had there been a history of colonization from the dominant centre? how large, how strong, how concentrated was this settlement? how closely was its elite tied in with the fate of the metropolis?

Let us try out a classification of our cases in these terms and see whether we can detect any regularity in the resulting party divisions: *Table 4* represents a first attempt in this direction.

The Table excludes the oldest and the ethnically most homogeneous of our eleven polities: Sweden, Denmark, the Netherlands and Luxembourg. Of these three, Sweden has been least afflicted by ethnic-territorial cleavages (the Danish territories to the South and the Norwegian ones to the West were incorporated well before mass literacy and therefore proved much less resistant to the national standardization process). Denmark has had a long history of border disputes with the Germans and its politics were for decades dominated by this issue: it has not, however, produced any major party division (apart, of course, from the persistence until recently of the minor German party in Schleswig). The Netherlands solved its major ethnic-territorial problem through the secessions of Belgium and Luxembourg in 1831–39: the remaining South-North opposition was contained within the Church-State cleavage. Luxembourg, finally, requires no separate discussion in this context. Territorial-cultural conflicts never counted within this small border polity: it was caught between pressures from two major powers but the issues of foreign policy were continuously kept out of party politics.

Table 4. *The Political Consequences of Liberation/Secession Struggles:*
Dimensions of Territorial Conflict in Seven Smaller European Nations

Status of settlement	Dependence on metropolis	Case	Situation	Expression in party system
Total core area 'Metropolitan' part of larger area of ethnic/cultural identity	Competitive metropolis, later dependent on larger unit	AUSTRIA	Dominant within old Empire, dependent after rise of Prussian Reich (defeat in 1866)	Pan-Germans *vs.* Catholics
Territorially concentrated settlement from metropolis	Highly dependent	IRELAND	English/Scottish settlement in East, North.	Secession of six Northern counties; party division over acceptance/rejection of secession: *Fine Gael* pro-Commonwealth solution, *Fianna Fáil* pro-total separation from metropolis
Same	Once dependent, later disrupted	FINLAND	Double front: Swedish settlement in Southwest; struggle for independence from Russia	No secession of Swedish areas (problem of Åland Islands). Separate Swedish party. Early Finnish party division over external strategy: Constitutionalists (Young Finns) *vs.* Compliants (Old Finns)
Weak concentration	Slow disruption of cultural ties	NORWAY	Danish cultural influence in East and in cities	Left-Right opposition over culture, language, religion
No territorial concentration	Distant, weak	ICELAND	Diffuse Danish impact on bureaucracy, patriciate	Original division over speed of liberation were soon overcome; functional party system emerged during 1920
Cultural/ethnic division of national territory	Divided dependence: one major centre outside, one minor	BELGIUM	French-speaking elite, Flemish-speaking subject population	No direct expression of territorial cleavage in party system before 1920s: Flemish separatists, *Volksunie*
Same	Divided dependence: two major centres outside	SWITZER-LAND	Major language groups: German, French	No direct expression of territorial cleavage in party system (except Jura area of Berne in 1950s–60s)

The other seven polities all had to face potentially disruptive conflicts over issues of ethnic-cultural dominance. Of these seven, the Swiss Confederation stands out as most successful in integrating so many historically distinct ethnicities and cultures. The contrast between Switzerland and Belgium has given rise to much speculation. The differences in geopolitical location and in religious structure stand out as immediately relevant: in Switzerland the two leading languages both enjoyed high international prestige; in Belgium the one was distinctly an elite language, the other not. In Switzerland the upper and the lower strata of each territory spoke the same language but the linguistic cleavage was cross-cut by two powerful Churches. In Belgium the established elite identified with the French language throughout the country and the Flemish opposition expressed a class cleavage as much as a territorial-cultural cleavage: the Liberal associations and the Catholic hierarchy were for a long time able to maintain channels of communication between the two cultures but could not prevent the foundation of regionalist-federalist parties after World War I.

It is indeed impossible to analyze the translation of territorial-cultural cleavages into party oppositions without considering the religious context of nation-building: the *Church-State* cleavage. The prudent federalism of the Swiss can only be understood against the experiences of the war against the Catholic *Sonderbund:* the legitimation of the Catholic opposition and the later incorporation of Catholic representatives in the Federal Executive were an essential response to pressures of territorial fragmentation. By contrast to the Swiss *Sonderbund,* Belgium and the Catholic counties of Ireland did manage to secede from a dominant Protestant power. Why, then, such remarkable differences between the two party systems? In some ways the *Fianna Fail* opposition in Ireland corresponded to the Flemish movement against the predominance of French culture: as Rumpf has shown through his historical cartography, the early strength of the Anti-Treaty Republicans increased along a Northeast-Southwest gradient, while the Pro-Treaty Conservatives were stronger in the English Pale and the old 'Land of Peace' counties (Rumpf, 1959: Ch. II). What distinguishes the Irish from the Belgian, and, for that matter, all the other Catholic cases in Europe, is the absence of any party-political expression of a Church-State opposition.

It is easy to say that the Irish Catholic Church did not need any party to defend it: the state-builders and the Church were natural allies and the secession of the Northern counties had made the territorial population nearly completely Catholic. But this does not explain the absence of a strong secular-religious cleavage of the type that generated party divisions in all the other Catholic countries. Two factors seem important here: first, the very low level of urbanization in Ireland; secondly, the very close ties between the Church and the peasantry and the absence of opposition over Church lands. As the historian J. G. A. Pocock has put it:

Being a hierarchical and bureaucratic organization more or less coter-minous with the geographic nation, (the Church) exerted a structurally unifying influence, and historical circumstances ensured that it was identical neither with the legal sovereign (the Crown of England) nor with the governing . . . aristocracy (the Anglo-Irish settlers). An accidental but very important benefit of English rule to Ireland was that the Church never became a major landowner; and in this and other ways it differed from the Counter-Reformation norm. Growing up in the very adverse circumstances of the 17th and 18th centuries . . . it emerged as a bureaucratic and popular structure nowhere organically linked with a ruling aristocracy (Pocock, 1966).

In these terms the Irish deviation does not disconfirm the prediction of the model but simply helps to specify the conditions for the emergence of a significant Church-State conflict and the articulation of Church interests in an explicit party front. Irish politics remained at the level of territorial-cultural polarization typical of the Protestant secession state: there are remarkable parallels between the early party divisions for and against the Treaty of 1922 and the split in Norway over the acceptance of the cultural dominance of the East (Rokkan, 1967), and there is an equally intriguing similarity with the conflict in Finland over liberation strategies in the double front between the Swedish settlement and the Russian political supremacy.[103] The East-West gradient brought out for Ireland by Rumpf has its counterpart in the contrast between Eastern centre and South-Western counter-culture in Norway and in the clear-cut demarcation in Finland between the conservative Finnish nationalism of the West and the radical democratic independence movement of the East.

Developments and Deviations: Parties for Agrarian Defence
We distinguish in our initial paradigm (Fig. 2) between two 'typical' cleavages at the *l* end of the territorial-cultural axis: on the *i* side the opposition of ethnic-linguistic minorities against the upholders of the dominant national culture (1), on the *a* side the opposition of the peasantry against economic exploitation by the financial, commercial, and industrial interests in the cities (3).

Our discussion of the 'party formation' model brought out a few hy-potheses about the transformation of cleavages of type 1 into distinct parties for territorial defence. We shall now proceed to a parallel discussion for cleavages of type 3 in Fig. 2.

Our model predicts that agrarian interests are most likely to find direct political expression in systems of close alliance between nation-builders and the urban economic leadership – the four N–U cases in our eightfold typology. But in three of the four cases the opposition of the peasantry to the dominance of the cities tended to be closely linked up with a rejection of the moral and religious standards of the nation-builders. This produced

D–L alliances in Scandinavia (type II) and the Netherlands (type IV) and R–L alliances in the secularizing southern countries (type VI). In the fourth N–U case (type VIII) there was no basis for explicit mergers of agrarian with religious opposition movements: the Belgian Roman Catholics were strong both in the urban 'establishment' and among the farmers but, as it happened, were themselves torn between the *l* and the *g* poles over issues of ethnic-linguistic identity between Flemings and Walloons.

In only one of these four cases did distinctly agrarian parties emerge as stable elements of the national systems of electoral constellations – in the five countries of the North. A peasant party also established itself in the Protestant cantons of Switzerland. In the other countries of the West there may have been peasants lists at a few elections, but the interests of agriculture were generally aggregated into broader party fronts: the Conservative parties in Britain, in Prussia, and in France, the Christian parties elsewhere.

Why these differences? This raises a number of difficult questions about the economics of nation-building. In our three-step model we brutally reduced the options of the central elite to a choice between an alliance with the *landed* interests and an alliance with the *urban-financial-commercial-industrial*. This, of course, was never a matter of either/or but of continuing adjustment to changes in the overall equilibrium of forces in each territory. Our dichotomy does not help the description of any single case but simply serves to bring out contrasts among systems in the *relative* openness to alliances in the one direction or the other at the decisive stages of partisan mobilization.

To understand the conditions for alliance options in the one direction or the other it is essential to go into details of the *organization of rural society* at the time of the extensions of the suffrage. What counted more than anything else was the *concentration of resources for the control of the process of mobilization,* and in the countryside the *size of the units of production* and the *hierarchies of dependence* expressed in the tenure systems counted more than any other factors: the greater the concentration of economic power and social prestige the easier it was to control the rural votes and the greater the political payoffs of alliances with landowners. It was no accident that Conservative leaders such as Bismarck and Disraeli took a lead in the extension of the suffrage; they counted on the loyalty and obedience of the dependent tenants and the agricultural workers (Rokkan, 1961). To measure the political potentialities of the landowning classes it would be essential to assemble comparative statistics on the proportions of the arable land and the agricultural manpower under the control of the large estate owners in each country. Unfortunately there are many lacunae in the historical statistics and comparisons are fraught with many hazards. The data at hand suggest that the countries we identified as typical 'N–L cases' (types I, III, V, and VII in our eightfold model) all tended to be dominated by large estates, at least in their central territories. This was the case in most of England and Scotland, in Prussia east of the Elbe, in the *Reconquista* provinces of Spain, and in lowland Austria.[104] There were, to be sure, large estates in many of the countries we have identified as 'N–U cases' (types II, IV, VI and VIII), but such alliances as there were between urban and rural elites still left large groups of self-owning peasants free to join counter-alliances on their own. In Belgium and the Netherlands the holdings tended to be small and closely tied in with the urban economy. In France and Italy there were always marked regional variations in the size of holdings and the systems of land tenure, and the peasantry was deeply divided over cultural, religious, and economic issues. There were large estates in Jutland, in southern Sweden, and in southwestern Finland, and the owners of these helped to consolidate the conservative establishments in the early phases of competitive politics, but the broad masses of the Nordic peasantry could not be brought into any such alliances with the established urban elites. The traditions of independent peasant representation were strong and there was widespread rejection of the cultural influences from the encroaching cities. In Denmark, Norway, and Sweden the decisive 'Left' fronts against the old regime were coalitions of urban radicals and increasingly estate-conscious peasants, but these coalitions broke up as soon as the new parties entered government. In Denmark the urban Radicals left the agrarian *Venstre;* in Norway and Sweden the old 'Left' was split in several directions on moralist-religious as well as on economic lines. Distinctly agrarian parties also emerged in the two still 'colonial' countries of the North, Finland and Iceland. In these predominantly primary-producing countries the struggle for external independence dominated political life in the decades after the introduction of universal suffrage, and there was not the same need for broad opposition fronts against the establishments *within* each nation.

Typically, agrarian parties appear to have emerged in countries or provinces

1) where the cities and the industrial centres were still numerically weak at the time of the decisive extensions of the suffrage;

2) where the bulk of the agricultural populations were active in family-size farming and either owned their farms themselves or were legally protected lease-holders largely independent of socially superior landowners;

3) where there were important cultural barriers between the countryside and the cities and much resistance to the incorporation of farm production in the capitalist economy of the cities; and

4) where the Catholic Church was without significant influence.

These criteria fit not only the Nordic countries but also the Protestant cantons of Switzerland and even some areas of German Austria. A *Bauern, Gewerbe- und Bürgerpartei* emerged in Berne, Zurich, and other heavily Alemannic-Protestant cantons after the introduction of PR in Switzerland in 1919. This was essentially a splinter from the old Radical-Liberal Party and recruited most of its support in the countryside. In the Catholic cantons the peasants remained loyal to their old party even after PR. Similarly in the Austrian First Republic the Nationalist *Lager* was split in a middle-class *Grossdeutsche Volkspartei* and a *Landbund* recruited among the anti-clerical peasants in Carinthia and Styria. The Christian Social Party recruited the bulk of its support among the Catholic peasantry but was able to keep the rural-urban tensions within bounds through elaborate organizational differentiations within the party.

We can clearly identify three major agencies of rural mobilization before the breakthrough of the Socialist parties in the wake of the decisive extensions of the suffrage: the large-scale estate, the cultural and the economic organizations of freehold family farmers, the Catholic Church. The Roman Catholic movements have throughout continental Europe proved able to cross-cut the cleavage between rural and urban economic interests generated by the Industrial Revolution: distinctly Agrarian parties have rarely if ever emerged in countries or regions with strong Catholic parties. Ireland is a very interesting case just from this point of view: in the only Catholic country *without* a distinctive Catholic party, sizeable groups of farmers *have* found it to their advantage to put up their own candidates and organize for separate political action (the Farmer's party won 15 seats in 1923, 11 in 1927 but disappeared and was followed by a Centre party and the *Clann na Talmhan* which won 14 seats in 1943, 11 in 1944 but petered out by 1961).

The Fourth Step: Variations in the Strength and Structure of the Working-Class Movements

Our stree-step model stops short at a point before the decisive thrust toward universal suffrage. It pinpoints sources of variations in the systems of division within the 'independent' strata of the European national electorates, among the owners of property and the holders of professional or educational privileges qualifying them for the vote during the *régime censitaire*.

But this is hardly more than half the story. The extension of the suffrage to the lower classes changed the character of each national political system, generated new cleavages, and brought about a restructuring of the old alignments.

Why did we not bring these important developments into our model of European party systems? Clearly not because the three first cleavage lines were more important than the fourth in the explanation of *any one national party system*. On the contrary, in sheer statistical terms the fourth cleavage lines will in at least half of the cases under consideration explain much more of the variance in the distributions of full-suffrage votes than any one of the others.[105] We focused on the three first cleavage lines because these were the ones that appeared to account for most of the variance *among systems:* the interactions of the 'centre-periphery,' state-church, and land-industry cleavages tended to produce much more marked, and apparently much more stubborn, differences among the national party systems than any of the cleavages brought about through the rise of the working-class movements.

We could of course have gone on to present a four-step model immediately, but this proved very cumbersome and produced a variety of uncomfortable redundancies. Clearly what had to be explained was not the emergence of a distinctive working-class movement at some point or other before or after the extension of the suffrage but the *strength and solidarity* of any such movement, its capacity to mobilize the underprivileged classes for action and its ability to maintain unity in the face of the many forces making for division and fragmentation. All the European polities developed some sort of working-class movement at some point between the first extensions of the suffrage and the various 'post-democratic' attempts at the repression of partisan pluralism. To predict the *presence* of such movements was simple; to predict which ones would be strong and which ones weak, which ones unified and which ones split down the middle, required much more knowledge of national conditions and developments and a much more elaborate model of the historical interaction process. Our three-step model does not go this far for *any* party; it predicts the presence of such-and-such parties in polities characterized by such-and-such cleavages, but it does not give any formula for accounting for the strength or the cohesion of any one party. This *could* be built into the model through the introduction of various population parameters (percent speaking each language or dialect, percent committed to each of the churches or dissenting bodies, ratios of concentrations of wealth and dependent labour in industry versus landed estates), and possibly of some indicators of the cleavage 'distance' (differences in the chances of interaction across the cleavage line, whether physically determined or normatively regulated), but any attempt in this direction would take us much too far in this all-too-long introductory essay. At this point we limit ourselves to an elementary discussion of the between-system variations which would have to be explained through such an extension of our model. We shall suggest a 'fourth step' and point to a possible scheme for the explanation of differences in the formation of national party systems under the impact of universal suffrage.

Our initial scheme of analysis posited four decisive dimensions of cleavage in Western polities. Our model for the generation of party systems pinpointed three crucial junctures in national history corresponding to the first three of these dimensions:

Critical juncture	Cleavage	Issues
Reformation-Counter-Reformation: 16th–17th centuries	Centre-Periphery	National vs. supranational religion National language vs. Latin
Democratic Revolution: 1789 and after	State-Church	Secular vs. religious control of mass education
Industrial Revolution: 19th century	Land-Industry	Tariff levels for agricultural products: control vs. freedom for industrial enterprise

It is tempting to add to this a fourth dimension and a fourth juncture:

Critical juncture	Cleavage	Issues
The Russian Revolution: 1917 and after	Owner-Worker	Integration into national polity vs. commitment to international revolutionary movement

Table 5 adds this fourth dichotomy to the typology already presented and seeks to locate six larger and eleven smaller European polities within the resulting $2 \times 2 \times 2 \times 2$ attribute space. *Table 6* spells out the steps in the argument in further details and presents 'predictions' of the weight of each cleavage in the formation of national party systems. *Table 7* presents the cleavage structures to be expected for five of the sixteen initial types and identifies the 'core' party systems generated for each structure through a set of uniform assumptions about probabilities of coalition and aggregation: these 'generated' systems are finally tested against the historically extant cases and the principal deviations are listed.

There is an intriguing cyclical movement in this scheme. The process gets under way with the breakdown of one supranational order and the establishment of strong territorial bureaucracies legitimizing themselves through the standardizing of nationally distinct religions and languages, and it ends with a conflict over national versus international loyalties within the last of the strata to be formally integrated into the nation-state, the rural and the industrial workers.

The conditions for the development of distinctive working-class parties varied markedly from country to country within Europe. These differences emerged well before World War I. The Russian Revolution did not generate new cleavages but simply accentuated long-established lines of division within the working-class elite.

Our three-step model does not produce clear-cut predictions of these developments. True enough, the most unified and the most 'domesticable' working-class movements emerged in the Protestant-dominated countries with the smoothest histories of nation-building: Britain, Denmark, and

Table 5. *A 2 × 2 × 2 × 2 Typology of Cleavage Structures and its Fit with the Empirical Cases in Western Europe*

	1. National State Church								2. State(s) Allied With RC Church							
	11. Strong Prot. Dissent				12. Strong RC Dissent				21. Secularizing Revolution				22. State-RC Alliance			
	111. State Close to Landed Int.		112. State Close to Urban Int.		121. Landed Int.		122. Urban Int.		211. Landed Int.		212. Urban Int.		221. Landed Int.		222. Urban Int.	
	1111. Minor	1112. Major	1121. Minor	1122. Major	1211. Minor	1212. Major	1221. Minor	1222. Major	2111. Minor	2112. Major	2121. Minor	2122. Major	2211. Minor	2212. Major	2221. Minor	2222. Major
I. *Reformation*																
II. *National Revolution*																
III. *Industrial Revolution*																
IV. *International Revolution*	Split	Split														
Nearest Empirical Examples:																
Large Early	G. B. Prussia (Excl. Irel.)				G. B. (Incl. Irel.) *Reich*				Spain		France		Hapsb. Empire			
Late											Italy					
Smaller Early			Denm. Swed.				Neth. Switz.									
Late			Nor. Finl. Icel.										Austria Ireland		Belg. Lux.	
Type (p. 115)	I		II		III		IV		V		VI		VII		VIII	

Table 6. *A Schema of Developmental Linkages: Revolutions, Issues, Cleavages, and Party Systems in Western Europe*

Critical juncture	Crucial issue	Resultant cleavages	Weight of each cleavage in the formation of the national party system: * — Smaller European democracies only					
			Protestant		**Mixed**		**Catholic**	
			Early Consolidation	Late Independence	Unitary	Federal	Early Consolidation	Late Independence
I. *Reformation:* the 1648 settlement and the 19th-20th century secessions	Consolidation of territorial state	1. Peripheries vs. centre: subject ethnicities/language groups against central dominance	x	xxx	x	x	x	xxx
		2. Moralist/religious rejection of central culture	xx	—	xxx	xxx	xxx	x
II. *National Revolution:* post-Napoleonic nation-building	Control of territorial standardization media: primarily mass education	Church vs. Secular State	—	xxx	xxx	xxx	xxx	xxx
III. *Industrial Revolution:* 1850's onwards	1. The primary economy: protection vs. modernization (tariff issue)	1. Rural/agricultural vs. urban/industrial interests	xxx	xxx	xx	xx	x	x
	2. The secondary economy: freedom of enterprise vs. state control; rights of owners/employers vs. rights of workers/employees	2. Worker-owner cleavage	xxx	xxx	xxx	xxx	xxx	xxx
IV. *International Revolution:* Russian Revolution and after	Integration of under-privileged strata in national community	1. Communism vs. Socialism	x	xxx	x	x	x	xxx
		2. Pacifism neutralism vs. commitment to nation/larger alliance	No direct predictions					

* The predicted weight of the given cleavage in the process of partisan aggregation is indicated by the number of x's: three x's indicate direct translation of one of the cleavage fronts into a *lasting* national party alternative, two x's a translation into a shorter-lived or regionally specific party, one x that the cleavage enters as a significant element in a broader process of aggregation.

Table 7. *Cleavage Structures and Party Systems:*
The Eleven Smaller European Democracies

Type in Table 5	Characteristic cleavages					Generated 'core' system of parties		Deviant cases
	Periphery-Centre	Church-State	Urban-Rural	Worker-Owner	International-National	Early	Late	
1121	xx					Cons. 'Left'	Radical Prohibitionist	DENMARK: a) No Prohibitionist split b) Georgist party
			xx				Agrarian	SWEDEN: Split Radical-Prohibitionist party 12 years (1922–1934). Minor Christian party 1964.
				xxx	x		Soc. Dem. CP (weak)	
1122	xxx					Cons.		FINLAND: Old Finns vs. Young Finns (Independence struggle); Swedish party ICELAND: Merger Cons./Lib. Independence party
						Left	Radical; Christian Prohibitionist Agrarian	
		xxx						*Only in Norway*
				xxx	xxx		Soc. Dem. CP (strong)	NORWAY: Labour with Comintern party 20s, CP weak except 1945.
1221	xxx					Lib./Rad. Orthodox Prot. Cath.		NETH.: Lib. CHU, Anti-Rev. Cath. Minor SWITZ.: Rad. Lib.-Dem. (regional) Cath.-Cons. Regional
		xxx						
			xx	xxx	x		Agr. (weak) Soc. Dem. CP (weak)	
2211	xxx					Pro-larger unit Cath.		AUSTRIA: Pan-Germans vs. Cath.-Cons. *Landbund* (regional I. Rep.) IRELAND: *Fine Gael* vs. *Fianna Fail* *No church party.* Minor
		xxx						
			xx				Agr. (weak)	
				xxx	x		Soc. CP (weak)	Strong Weak Weak Weak
2221	xxx						Regionalists	BELGIUM: Flemish party, *Volksunie* LUXEMB.: None
		xxx				Lib. Cath.		
				xxx	x		Soc. CP (weak)	

Sweden (types I and II in our model). Equally true, the Catholic-dominated countries with difficult or very recent histories of nation-building also produced deeply divided, largely alienated working-class movements – France – Italy, Spain (types V and VI). But other variables clearly have to be brought into account for variations in the intermediary zone between the Protestant Northwest and the Latin South (types III and IV, VII and VIII). Both the Austrian and the German working-class movements developed their distinctive counter-cultures against the dominant national elites. The Austrian Socialist *Lager,* heavily concentrated as it was in Vienna, was able to maintain its unity in the face of the clerical-conservatives and the pan-German nationalists after the dissolution of the Hapsburg Empire.[106] By contrast, the German working-class movement was deeply divided after the defeat in 1918. Sharply contrasted conceptions of the rules of the political game stood opposed to each other and were to prove fatal in the fight against the wave of mass nationalism of the early thirties (Bracher, 1960: Chs. III–IV; Matthias, 1960: pp. 154–58, 655–739). In Switzerland and the Netherlands (both type IV in our scheme), the Russian and the German revolutions produced a few disturbances, but the leftward split-offs from the main working class by parties were of little significance. The marked cultural and religious cleavages reduced the potentials for the Socialist parties, but the traditions of pluralism were gradually to help their entry into national politics.

Of all the intermediary countries Belgium (type VIII in our model) presents perhaps the most interesting case. By our overall rule, the Belgian working class should be deeply divided: a thoroughly Catholic country with a particularly difficult history of nation-building across two distinct language communities. In this case the smallness and the international dependence of the nation may well have created restraints on the internal forces of division and fragmentation. Val Lorwin has pointed to such factors in his analysis of Belgian-French contrasts (Lorwin, 1958).

The reconciliation of the Belgian working class to the political and social order, divided though the workers are by language and religion and the Flemish-Walloon question, makes a vivid contrast with the experience of France. The differences did not arise from the material fruits of economic growth, for both long were rather low-wage countries, and Belgian wages were the lower. In some ways the two countries had similar economic development. But Belgium's industrialization began earlier; it was more dependent on international commerce, both for markets and for its transit trade; it had a faster growing population; and it became much more urbanized than France. The small new nation, 'the cockpit of Europe,' could not permit itself social and political conflict to the breaking point. Perhaps France could not either, but it was harder for the bigger nation to realize it.

The contrast between France, Italy, and Spain on the one hand and

Austria and Belgium on the other suggests a possible generalization: the working-class movement tended to be much more divided in the countries where the 'nation-builders' and the Church were openly or latently opposed to each other during the crucial phases of educational development and mass mobilization (our 'S' cases, types V and VI) than in the countries where the Church had, at least initially, sided with the nation-builders against some common enemy outside (our 'R' cases, an alliance against Protestant Prussia and the dependent Hapsburg peoples in the case of Austria; against the Calvinist Dutch in the case of Belgium). This fits the Irish case as well. The Catholic Church was no less hostile to the English than the secular nationalists, and the union of the two forces not only reduced the possibilities of a polarization of Irish politics on class lines but made the likelihood of a Communist splinter of any importance very small indeed.

It is tempting to apply a similar generalization to the Protestant North: the greater the internal division during the struggle for nationhood, the greater the impact of the Russian Revolution on the divisions within the working class. We have already pointed to the profound split within the German working class. The German Reich was a late-comer among European nations, and none of the territorial and religious conflicts within the nation was anywhere near settlement by the time the working-class parties entered the political arena. Among the northern countries the two oldest nations, Denmark and Sweden, were least affected by the Communist-Socialist division. The three countries emerging from colonial status were much more directly affected: Norway (domestically independent from 1814, a sovereign state from 1905) for only a brief period in the early 1920's; Finland (independent in 1917) and Iceland (domestically independent in 1916 and a sovereign state from 1944) for a much longer period. These differences among the northern countries have been frequently commented on in the literature of comparative politics. The radicalization of the Norwegian Labour Party has been interpreted within several alternative models, one emphasizing the alliance options of the party leaders, another the grass-roots reactions to sudden industrialization in the peripheral country-side, and a third the openness of the party structure and the possibilities of quick feedback from the mobilized voters. There is no doubt that the early mobilization of the peasantry and the quick victory over the old regime of the officials had left the emerging Norwegian working-class party much more isolated, much less important as a coalition partner, than its Danish and Swedish counterparts.[107] There is also a great deal of evidence to support the old Bull hypothesis of the radicalizing effects of sudden industrialization, but recent research suggests that this was only one element in a broad process of political change. The Labour Party recruited many more of its voters in the established cities and in the forestry and fisheries districts, but the openness of the party structure allowed the radicals to establish themselves very quickly and to take over the majority wing of the party during the crucial years just after the Russian Revolution (Torgersen, 1966: pp. 39–46, 73–98). This very openness to rank-and-file influences made the alliance with Moscow very short-lived; the Communists split off in 1924 and the old majority party 'joined the nation' step by step until it took power in 1935 (Roset, 1964; Rokkan, 1966: 5).

Only two of the Scandinavian countries retained strong Communist parties after World War II – Finland and Iceland. Superficially these countries have two features in common: prolonged struggles for cultural and political independence, and late industrialization. In fact the two countries went through very different processes of political change from the initial phase of nationalist mobilization to the final formation of the full-suffrage party system. One obvious source of variation was the distance from Russia. The sudden upsurge of the Socialist Party in Finland in 1906 (the party gained 37 per cent of the votes cast at the first election under universal suffrage) was part of a general wave of mobilization against the Tsarist regime. The Russian Revolution of 1917 split Finland down the middle; the working-class voters were torn between their loyalty to their national culture and its social hierarchy and their solidarity with their class and its revolutionary defenders (Hodgson, 1966). The victory of the 'Whites' and the subsequent suppression of the Communist Party (1919–21, 1923–25, 1930–44) left deep scars; the upsurge of the leftist SKDL after the Soviet victory in 1945 reflected deep-seated resentments not only against the 'lords' and the employers of labour but generally against the upholders of the central national culture. The split in the Icelandic labour movement was much less dramatic; in the oldest and smallest of the European democracies there was little basis for mass conflicts, and the oppositions between Communist sympathizers and Socialists appeared to reflect essentially personal antagonisms among groups of activists (Olmsted, 1958; Nuechterlein, 1961: Ch. I).

Our analysis of the 'fourth-revolution' splits in the Western European party systems may be schematically summarized in the table on p. 138.

In the Protestant and the Mixed countries the differentiating criterion appears to be the *recency of the nation-building process:* the less settled the issues of national identity and the deeper the ongoing conflicts over cultural standardization, the greater the chances of radicalization and fragmentation within the working class.

In the Catholic countries a similar process seems to have been at work but in different terms: the deeper and more persistent the Church-State conflicts, the greater the fragmentation of the working class; the closer the historical ties between the ecclesiastical hierarchy and the secular 'nation-builders,' the less the chances of left-wing split-offs.

	Unified 'domesticable' labour movements			Deep splits in labour movements (strong CP wings)		
Protestant countries	*Early consolidation*			*Late independence, unification*		
	Smaller		Larger	Smaller		Larger
	DENMARK		BRITAIN	NORWAY (1920s)		
	SWEDEN			FINLAND		
				ICELAND		
Mixed countries	NETHERLANDS					REICH
	SWITZERLAND					
Catholic countries	*Initial Church-State Alliance*			*Marked State-Church Cleavage*		
	AUSTRIA					FRANCE
	BELGIUM					ITALY
	LUXEMBOURG					SPAIN
	IRELAND					

The Empirical Testing of the Model

Space will not allow me to pursue in further detail this review of parallels and contrasts in the development of cleavage structures and party systems in Western Europe. I hope that I have gone far enough in my presentation of the model to give an impression of the rich opportunities for detailed developmental comparisons across these countries. My work with the eleven smaller democracies has made me more and more convinced that further efforts of formalization and testing of models of the type I have sketched may not only help us build better theories of comparative political development at the macro-level but also prove directly useful in our continued efforts to make sense of the similarities and the differences found in comparative analyses at the micro-level.

In fact the model I have suggested seeks to specify invariances at four different levels:

– at the level of critical options for each territorial system as a whole – the four 'Revolutions';

– at the level of solidarities and conflicts within the territorial population – the five 'Cleavage lines';

– at the level of the system of electoral alternatives presented by organized parties;

– and finally and not least important, at the level of *the individual citizen and his behaviour* within the limits set by the past and the present configurations of his polity.

I believe we shall find in the future testing of models of this type that the hypotheses generated at the higher levels will have very direct consequences for our priorities in developmental analyses of statistics at the micro-level (this would include analyses of recall data from surveys as well as the typical ecological analyses of time series by locality): the five cleavage lines differentiated in *Tables 6 and 7* constitute as many top-priority variables in the developmental study of partisan strength in our European countries.

To get closer to an understanding of the processes at work in the translation of socio-cultural cleavages into party systems, we shall have to start out with multivariate analyses of the weight of our five core variables in the determination of the strength of each party:

1. We need to know how heavily *territorial, ethnic* or *linguistic* divisions counted in the production of given distributions of votes;

2. we need to know how strongly the distributions were influenced by variations in *church membership* and in *religious activity;*

3. we need information about the differences by *rates and levels of urbanization* and by the character of the *primary economy* (land tenure systems, strength of forestry, fisheries sectors);

4. we need more details about the variations, from locality to locality and from period to period, in the *class basis* of the vote, and

5. we shall have to pin down in the same detail the factors making for *splits within the working-class vote,* particularly in the early 1920s and during the period of peak CP strength after World War II.

Work along these lines is far advanced in some countries and has hardly begun in others. We can safely predict that a great deal of further effort will be made in this direction during the next few years. A major accelerating factor will be the development in country after country of *data archives* for computer processing of early election and census records (Rokkan, 1966: 3; Rokkan, 1966: 4). There is every reason for us to push ahead with such work, but it is very important that we do this within the broader perspective of comparative development, of comparative nation-building. We clearly shall not be assembling such sets of analyses just to test hypotheses about individual behaviour. We shall also do so to establish important benchmark data for a typology of the macro-contexts of political behaviour: in fact any such analysis of the weight of the core variables in the production of votes for each party will help us to characterize the differences among the historically given 'packages' still facing these different national citizenries. Our 'ultra-generalist' friends will say that this is outright surrender to abject 'configurationism': my reply is that we have to live with comparisons of unique configurations but can still make headway in comparative electoral research by resolutely tackling the tasks of identifying the critical dimensions of variation across the historically given systems of political interaction.

NOTES

[56] A vastly more complex model has been developed to map out the sources of variations among *Latin American* polities at the di Tella Institute in Buenos Aires: see (Cornblit, 1968).

[57] A pioneering effort along these lines is (Converse, 1966: 2).

[58] Data archives for parliamentary personnel are under development in a number of countries and will soon allow detailed comparisons of variations in the socio-economic distinctiveness of the parties at this level, see e. g. (Valen, 1966).

[59] For an example of a possible approach, see (Borg, 1966).

[60] Here again a number of national studies of party cohesion and party distinctiveness will offer possibilities of cross-country comparisons, see e. g. (Pedersen, 1967).

[61] This chapter in fact represents a report on one facet of the work carried out within the collaborative international project 'The Politics of the Smaller European Democracies'. This project has been supported by the Ford Foundation and is directed by four 'editors': Hans Daalder, Robert Dahl, Val Lorwin and Stein Rokkan.

[62] For details on PR thresholds see (Rokkan, 1968: 2).

[63] A proposal to go back to the British system of single-member plurality was defeated in Ireland in 1959 and again in 1968. The breakup of the rigidities of the Dutch party system after 1965 has produced a variety of proposals for a return to some form of majoritarianism, possibly through the institution of plebiscitarian elections of prime ministers, see (Gruijters, 1967). In Belgium, Switzerland and the Nordic countries there are no signs of any serious attempts at a reversal to majoritarian principles.

[64] This point has been brought out with great force in Giovanni Sartori's analysis of the aggregating effects of 'strong' electoral systems such as the single-member plurality, the absolute majority run-off or the high-threshold small constituency PR as against 'weak' systems such as the low-threshold, large-constituency PR: see (Sartori, 1969: Ch. 21).

[65] For a first attempt at a clarification of the issues of 'macro' – 'micro' logic, see (Rokkan, 1962: 1, are printed as Chapter 1 above).

[66] The original designs were heavily influenced by Lewinian field psychology, see esp. the theoretical introduction to (Campbell, 1960). The Michigan analysts were themselves among the leaders in the movement to develop the historical dimensions of electoral analysis and have pioneered the organization of a large-scale computer archive for time series data for elections and censuses, see (Campbell, 1966).

[67] For Britain, see (Taylor, 1962). For Ireland, see the maps for the frequencies of British-Irish aggression in (Rumpf, 1959: pp. 62–63, 73–74, 81).

[68] For evidence of the openness of the Danish absolutist regime to pressures from dissident publics see the remarkable analysis by J. A. Seip (Seip, 1958).

[69] For a penetrating analysis of sequences in the legitimation of opposition politics in the Republic see (Munger, 1966).

[70] This argument has been elaborated in further detail in (Lehmbruch, 1967). He stresses the functions of pluralist segmentation and *Proporz* executives for the stabilization of the national polity against disruptive pressures from the international environment; his main examples are Switzerland, Austria, the Lebanon and Cyprus.

[71] For France see (Kesselman, 1966). For details on Norway see Chapter 6 below and (Hjellum, 1967: 2). An analysis of the spread of national parties in *Iceland* confirms the findings of the Norwegian studies:

	Turnout and Partisan Voting in Local Elections		
	Turnout	Percent of valid votes in contested elections cast for:	
		'non-core' parties, local party alliances	non-partisan lists
1950 Towns	86.2	1.1	0.0
Villages	81.4	19.5	24.4
Other rural	56.0	8.0	69.2
1962 Towns	88.4	4.0	3.6
Villages	83.3	0.0	35.7
Other rural	68.3	5.8	64.9

[72] In order of precedence: Uri, Obwalden, Nidwalden, Appenzell Inner Rhodes, Appenzell Outer Rhodes, Grisons. For details see (Girod, 1964).

[73] 'Especially in small groups making genuine decisions rather than playing what they know is a game, considerations of maintaining the solidarity of the group and the loyalty of members to it probably dominate considerations of maximum victory on particular decisions' (Riker, 1962: p. 51).

[74] For a classification of such coalition costs see (Riker, 1962: pp. 115–20).

[75] Similar arguments have been advanced for the Netherlands by Arend Lijphart (Lijphart, 1968; Lijphart, 1969). All the eleven smaller democracies are markedly more dependent on international trade than any of the larger ones. See (Russett, 1964: Tab. 46; Dahl, 1967).

[76] The first extensive development of the schema is found in (Parsons, 1956). A simplified restatement is found in (Parsons, 1959: 1). Extensive revisions in the schema were adumbrated in (Parsons, 1960) and have been presented in further detail in (Parsons, 1963). For an attempt to use the Parsonian schema in political analysis see (Mitchell, 1962; Mitchell, 1967). For applications to the analysis of *electoral* developments see (Parsons, 1959: 2; Rokkan, 1961; Parsons, 1964: particularly pp. 354–56).

[77] In conformity with Parsonian conventions we use *lower-case* symbols for the parts of *sub*systems and *capitals* for the parts of total systems.

[78] (Namier, 1930), quoted from second ed. (1961) p. 183.

[79] For a detailed discussion of the linkage between religious cleavages and political alliances in the United States see (Lipset, 1963: Ch. 4; Lipset, 1964: 2).

[80] See (Morgan, 1963: pp. 245–55). For a detailed analysis of vote distributions in Wales 1861–1951 see (Cox, 1966). Cox explains the strength of the liberals in Wales in much the same terms as Rokkan and Valen explain the strength of the Left 'counter-culture' in the south and west of Norway, the predominance of small farms, the egalitarian class structure, linguistic opposition and religious nonconformity.

[81] For Norway see the writings of S. Rokkan already cited. For Finland see (Rommi, 1964; Allardt, 1964; Allardt, 1965).

[82] For a definition of this concept and a specification of possible indicators, see (Deutsch, 1961).

[83] The contrast between 'primordial attachment' to the 'givens' of social existence (contiguity, kinship, local languages, and religious customs – all at our l pole) and 'national identification' (our g pole) has been described with great acumen by Clifford Geertz (Geertz, 1963), see also (Shils, 1957).

[84] For an analysis of steps in the extension of citizenship rights and duties to all accountable adults, see (Rokkan, 1961; Bendix & Rokkan, 1964). For a review of the politics of educational developments see (Ulich, 1961).

[85] This of course was not a peculiarity of Catholic-Calvinist countries, it can be

observed in a number of politics with geographically dispersed if locally segregated ethnic minorities. For an insightful discussion of a similar development in Russia, see (Woodhouse, 1966).

[86] For detailed statistics see (Kruijt, 1959; Kruijt, 1962). For an attempt at a broader interpretation of *Verzuiling* and its consequences for the theory of democracy, see (Lijphart, 1968). For comparative interpretations of data on religious segmentation, see (Moberg, 1961; Lenski, 1963: pp. 359–66; Mathes, 1965).

[87] For general accounts of the development of party oppositions and segmented politics in the Netherlands, see (Daalder, 1955; Daalder, 1966). Detailed party chronologies and 'pedigrees' are given in (Daalder, 1958).

[88] The concept of 'membership crystallization' has been formulated by analogy with the concept *status* crystallization developed in (Lenski, 1956), see (Allardt, 1962; Himmelstrand, 1962).

[89] The Swedish liberals split into two parties over alchohol policies in 1923 but these merged again in 1934. A new party, the Christian Democrat Union, was set up by Free Church leaders in 1964, but failed in the election that year.

[90] For a comparative analysis of differences in the organization of estate assemblies, see esp. (Hintze, 1930; Hartung, 1965; Palmer, 1959: Ch. II).

[91] The critical issues between the two sectors of the economy concerned foreign trade: Should domestic agriculture be protected against the cheaper grain produced overseas or should the manufacturing industry be supported through the supply of cheaper food for their workers? For a comparative review of the politics of the grain tariffs see (Gerschenkron, 1943).

[92] (Clark, 1962), our italics. For a broader treatment see (Thompson, 1963).

[93] On the unsuccessful attempts of the Progressive Liberals to broaden their working-class base, see esp. (Nipperdey, 1961: pp. 187–92; Link, 1964). On the 'plebiscitarian nationalism' of Friedrich Naumann and Max Weber, see (Heuss, 1957; Mommsen, 1959) and the discussion at the Weber centenary conference at Heidelberg reported in (Stammer, 1965).

[94] This is the phrase used by Ernest Fraenkel (Fraenkel, 1958: p. 178). For further details on German development, see (Roth, 1963: Chs. VII–X).

[95] One of the first political analysts to call attention to these developments was Herbert Tingsten, then editor-in-chief of the leading Swedish newspaper *Dagens Nyheter*, see his autobiography (Tingsten, 1963: pp. 224–31). For further details, see (Lipset, 1964: 1).

[96] For an illuminating analysis of the socio-cultural characteristics of the classic region of counter-revolutionary resistance, see (Tilly, 1965).

[97] For an interesting approach to the analysis of the political consequences of 'monocephality' vs. 'polycephality' see (Linz, 1966).

[98] For an analysis of the three decisive cleavage lines in Belgian politics, the language conflict, the church-school issue, and the owner-worker opposition, see (Lorwin, 1966). It is interesting to note that the same factors disrupted Belgian Fascism during the 1930s and made it impossible to build a single major nationalist-Fascist party, see (Stengers, 1966).

[99] For sociological analyses of the system of cleavages in Spanish society after 1815, see (Brenan, 1943; Rama, 1962; Linz, 1966; Linz, 1964). See also the analysis of the elections of 1931, 1933, 1936 in (Becarud, 1962).

[100] On the function of the *cacique* as the controller or rural support in the initial phase of mass mobilization, see (Brenan, 1943: pp. 5–8; Carr, 1966: pp. 366–79) and the classic analyses in (Costa, 1902).

[101] On the origin of the particularist movements in Germany, see esp. (Conze, 1962).

[102] The vivid expression coined by Jean-François Gravier (Gravier, 1958).

[103] See esp. (Jutikkala, 1960), particularly at p. 175 ('one of the most striking ex-

amples of a geographic division of public opinion in any European country in modern time'), also (Rantala, 1967). Erik Allardt has based a number of his ecological factor analyses on the regional demarcation originally established on the basis of the votes for Old Finns vs. Young Finns.

[104] For a detailed evaluation of the comparative statistics of agricultural holdings see (Dovring, 1960: Ch. 3 and Appendices). The standard source of nineteenth century statistics of landholdings in Britain is (Bateman, 1883), see (Thompson, 1963: Ch. V). On *latifundia* and *minifundia* in Spain, see (Brenan, 1943: Ch. 6).

[105] Recent advances in the techniques of electoral analysis make it possible to test such statements about the weight of the different cleavage dimensions in conditioning the alignments of voters. For data from *sample surveys* the development of *'tree analysis'* procedures opens up interesting possibilities of comparison. A 'tree analysis' of data for the *Bundesrepublik* for 1957, 1961, and 1965 gives interesting evidence of the interaction of two major cleavage dimensions in that setting:

Owner-worker cleavage: status of head of household	Church-state: commitment of respondent	Percent voting SPD in total electorate		
		1957	1961	1965
Worker, unionized	None	56	61	64
Worker, not unionized	None	37	41	43
Worker, middle-class aspirations	–	18	28	28
Worker, unionized	Committed Catholic	14	24	33
Worker, not unionized	Committed Catholic	15	10	15
Middle class, of working class origins	–	27	24	41
Salaried, civil servants, unionized	–	25	39	52
Middle class	Committed Catholic	6	5	9

Source: K. Liepelt, 'Wählerbewegungen in der Bundesrepublik,' Paper, Arbeitstagung 21. Juli 1966, Institut für angewandte Sozialforschung, Bad Godesberg. For periods before the advent of the sample survey similar analyses can be produced through ecological regression analysis. So far very few statistically sophisticated analyses have been carried out for European electoral time series before the 1950's: an exception is (Cox, 1966); this includes a factor analysis of the rural vote in Wales from 1861 to 1921. For an illuminating example of a possible procedure, see the analysis of the French rural cantons by Mattei Dogan (Dogan, 1966). His Tables 11 and 13 give these correlation coefficients for the electoral strengths of the two left parties in 1956:

	PCF				*SFIO*			
	Rural France	West	Centre	North	Rural France	West	Centre	North
Percent industrial workers:								
– direct correlation	.28	.26	.16	.55	.33	.19	.05	.03
– partial correlation	.25	.12	.08	.39	.01	.09	.03	.19
Percent attending mass								
– direct correlation	−.60	−.62	−.48	−.67	−.21	−.39	−.10	−.30
– partial correlation	−.59	−.59	−.47	−.58	−.21	−.36	−.09	.35
Multiple correlation	.64	.62	.49	.73	.21	.40	.10	.35

Within rural France the traditions of anticlericalism clearly count heavier than class in the generation of votes for the Left. If the Parisian suburbs and the other urban areas had been included in the analysis class would obviously have weighed much heavier in the equation; see (Dogan, 1967). To test the implications of our model, analyses along the lines suggested by Cox and Dogan ought to be carried out for the elections just before and just after the extensions of the suffrage in a number of different countries; see the contrasted maps for 1849 and 1936 in (Dupeux, 1959), pp. 169–70 and discussion pp. 157–71.

[106] For an insightful analysis of the conditions for the development of these three *Lager,* see (Wandruszka, 1952: pp. 298–485, 618–21).

[107] This was a major point in the classic article by the elder Edvard Bull (Bull, 1922.)

II

Suffrage Extensions and Waves of Mobilization: Empirical and Statistical Studies

Electoral Systems

Elections are institutionalized procedures for the choosing of officeholders by some or all of the recognized members of an organization. Whether the organization is a club, a company, a party, or a territorial polity, an electoral institution can be described in a series of dimensions: the scope and structure of the organizational unit; the tasks and the authority of the offices to be filled; the types and levels of membership in the organization and the qualifications for participation in the choice of officers; the criteria, if any, used in differentiating the numerical weight of the choice of each qualified member; the extent and character of the subdivisions instituted within the organizations for purposes of such choice; the procedures for the setting of the alternatives of choice; the procedures used in eliciting and registering choices among these alternatives; and the methods used in translating the aggregated choices of members into authoritative collective decisions on the attribution of the given offices.

A club might recognize as qualified electors only a few senior members and require these to vote by a show of hands or by acclamation. This practice would contrast on a number of dimensions with the elaborate procedures of some joint-stock companies: all shareholders have the right to participate, but the weight of their votes is a function of the number of shares they hold; their preferences are expressed under elaborate provisions of secrecy, and their votes are aggregated through strict rules of accountability. A systematic discussion of all such dimensions of variation, even for just the major types of organizations, would take us far afield. In this chapter the discussion will centre on one distinct type of organization: the territorially defined units of the nation-state – the self-governing local community and the overarching unitary or federal body politic.

The histories of the known political systems present a bewildering

Origin: This is a revised version of an article published in the *International Encyclopedia of the Social Sciences* edited by David Sills, Volume 5, pp. 6–21. Copyright © 1968 by Crowell Collier and Macmillan, Inc. Reproduced by permission of the Publisher.

variety of electoral arrangements (Meyer, 1903; Braunias, 1932). Any attempt to account for these variations through the construction of a basic model of strategic options and structural restraints must start out from an analysis of the histories of changes in each of six dimensions of the local and the national electoral system:

1) The qualifications for franchise: how does a subject of the territory acquire political citizenship rights?

2) The weighting of influence: how many votes are formally attributed to each elector and on what grounds? what is done to ensure differentiation or equality in the actual influence of each vote?

3) The standardization of the voting procedures and the protection of the freedom to choose: what is done to ensure uniform and accountable practices of electoral administration, and what provisions are made to equalize the immediate cost of all alternatives for the elector?

4) The territorial levels of choice: how is the territory divided for purposes of election, and how many levels of electoral aggregation are distinguished?

5) The stages of electoral choice: how are the alternatives set for the electors? to what extent are the alternatives set in advance, and to what extent is the range still open for the electors?

6) The procedures of calculation: how are the votes aggregated, and how are the aggregated distributions translated into authoritative collective decisions on territorial representation?

One Man, One Vote, One Value
The Western development toward equalitarian electoral democracy may conveniently be analyzed against an 'ideal-type' model of five successive phases.

1) An early, prerevolutionary phase was characterized by marked provincial and local variations in franchise practices but implicit or explicit recognition of membership in some corporate estate (the nobility, the clergy, the city corporations of merchants and artisans, or, in some cases, the freehold peasantry) as a condition of political citizenship (Hintze, 1962; Lousse, 1943; Palmer, 1959).

2) In the wake of the American and French revolutions, there was a period of increasing standardization of franchise rules; the strict regulation of access to the political arena under a *régime censitaire* was accompanied by formal equality of influence among the citizens allowed to vote under the given property or income criteria (Meyer, 1903; Williamson, 1960).

3) In the first phase of mass mobilization the suffrage was greatly extended, but formal inequalities of influence persisted, under arrangements for multiple votes or for differential ratios of votes to representatives.

4) In the next phase, manhood suffrage, all significant social and economic criteria of qualification for men over a given age were abolished.

Although there were now no formal inequalities of voting rights within constituency electorates, marked differences in the weight of votes across the constituencies still existed (Zwager, 1958).

5) Finally, in the current phase, one of continued democratization, steps were taken toward the maximization of universal and equal citizenship rights by *(a)* extension of the suffrage to women, to younger age groups (down to 21 or even 18), and to short-term residents (reductions in 'quarantine' periods) and *(b)* further equalization of voter-representative ratios throughout the national or federal territory.

Only three of the nation-states of the West passed through these five stages in anything like a regular sequence: England, Belgium, and Sweden. The step-by-step evolution characteristic of these countries contrasts violently with the abrupt and revolutionary changes in France (Bendix & Rokkan, 1964; Rokkan, 1961).

In England (Seymour, 1915) the process took more than one hundred years, from the Reform Act of 1832 to the abolition of multiple votes in 1948. In Sweden (Verney, 1957) the system of estate representation was abolished in 1866, but the extreme inequalities of electoral influence were maintained until 1921. The Belgians (Gilissen, 1958) passed from the phase of estate representation into a *régime censitaire* as soon as they had achieved independence in 1831 and went through an intriguing phase of multiple voting from 1893 to 1917: all men over 25 were enfranchised, but additional votes were granted not only on *censitaire* criteria but also in recognition of educational achievement *(principe capacitaire)* and of responsibility for the maintenance of a family.

By contrast, in France (Bastid, 1948; Charnay, 1965) the transition from the first to the fourth stage took a mere four years: the Law of January 1789 maintained a system of indirect elections within the recognized corporations of nobles, clergy, and the *tiers état;* the constitution of 1791 stipulated a tax-paying criterion and introduced the concept of the *citoyen actif;* and the constitution of 1793 went straight to the stage of manhood suffrage, the only remaining qualification being a six-month minimum residence in the canton. This sudden thrust toward maximal mass democracy proved very short-lived: the Terror intervened, and for decades France was torn between traditionalist attempts to restrict the suffrage to a narrow stratum of owners and high officials and radical-plebiscitarian pressures for universal and equal elections. The period from 1815 to 1848 was one of classic *régime censitaire:* the property qualifications limited the franchise to less than 100,000 out of 7 million adult males before 1830 and to roughly 240,000 in 1848. The Revolution of 1848 brought on the next sudden thrust toward maximal democracy: the first modern mass election took place on Easter day that year, and 84 per cent of the 9,360,000 electors went to the polling stations.

The electoral histories of the rest of Europe fall at various points between these two models. In northwest Europe the Dutch went through the same sequence as the British and the Swedes, while Denmark and Norway came closer to the French model. The Dutch passed from estate representation to *régime censitaire* in 1848 but did not go through any phase of plural voting before they opted for manhood suffrage during World War I (Geismann, 1964). Denmark, the most absolutist of the Nordic polities, went through a brief period of estate representation after 1831 and then moved straight into a system of nationwide elections under a very extensive manhood suffrage in 1849: the result, again as in France, was a half century of constitutional struggle between an oligarchic elite and a coalition of urban radicals and the mobilizing peasantry. Under the impact of the struggle for independence, the dependent 'colonial' territories of the north all proceeded rapidly to maximal suffrage. Norway gave the vote to close to half her adult males on establishing her own parliament in 1814 and proceeded to full manhood suffrage during the conflict over union with Sweden in the 1890s. Finland stuck to the inherited Swedish system of four estates until 1906 and then all of a sudden passed from the first to the fifth phase of the model: not only all men but also all women were given the vote, and the process of mass mobilization had gone so far under the restrictive estate system that the turnout at the first election under universal suffrage reached the record height of 70.7 per cent. Developments in the third of the Nordic 'colonies' were less spectacular: Iceland saw the re-establishment of its parliament in 1874 and then passed through two successive phases of *régime censitaire* before the stage of near-universal suffrage for men and women was reached in 1915 (as in most other countries of the north, paupers receiving public assistance were kept out in the first round; the Icelanders did not admit them until 1934).

The German territories were torn among several competing models of the representative polity: the traditional notions of election through established estates; the *altliberale* ideology of unified national representation under a property or income suffrage; the Napoleonic ideas of plebiscitarian mass democracy; and the Roman Catholic models of functional representation within the corporate state, the *Ständestaat*. This electoral schizophrenia found a number of intriguing expressions. In Prussia and the Bismarckian Reich, two sharply contrasted systems of elections coexisted for half a century. In Prussia the 'lower orders' had been given the right to vote in the wake of the Revolution of 1848, but the weight of their votes was infinitesimal in the three-class system introduced to protect the interests of the landowners and the officials. By contrast, the Reichstag was elected on strict criteria of equal suffrage for all men: this principle had been laid down, after much debate, by the German National Assembly in Frankfurt in 1848 but was not enforced until 1867, when Bismarck saw the importance of general elections as a source of legitimacy for the new Reich. The Hapsburg empire went through a much longer and more tortuous process of democratization: first, estate representation; from 1861, corporate-interest representation under a system of four *curiae;* in 1896, an extraordinary attempt to stave off equalitarian democracy by adding a fifth *curia* for the citizens so far without representation; and finally, in 1907, a unified system of national representation and enforcement of 'one man, one vote, one value.'

By the end of World War I the great majority of European and European-settled polities had opted for manhood suffrage, many of them even for universal suffrage for women as well. Suffrage for women (Kraditor, 1965) came first in the settler nations (Wyoming, 1890, all of the United States, 1920; New Zealand, 1893; South Australia, 1895) and in Scandinavia (Finland, 1906; Norway, 1910 to 1913; Denmark, 1915; Sweden, 1918 to 1921). The British proceeded by steps: restricted suffrage for women in 1918; full suffrage, on a par with men, in 1928. The 'Roman' countries took longer to recognize the rights of women: France, Belgium, and Italy waited until the end of World War II before they admitted all women to political citizenship, and Switzerland has still, after 120 years of smoothly functioning manhood democracy, to reach agreement on the enfranchisement of her women.

With the victory over the Axis powers in World War II and the subsequent dismantling of colonial empires, the principle of 'one man, one vote' gained ground throughout the world, even in countries at the lowest level of literacy and without a trace of the traditions of pluralist competition, which had been essential for the growth of effective party oppositions in the West. In an increasing number of newly independent states the enforcement of equal and universal rights of political citizenship was no longer seen as a means for the channelling of legitimate claims against the power holders but was regarded simply as an element in a strategy of national unification and the control of dissidence. Really serious struggles over the old cry of 'one man, one vote, one value' only occurred in the ethnically most divided polities, in South Africa, Rhodesia, and the United States.

Resistance to electoral equalitarianism has generally tended to be stronger at the level of local government than at the national or federal level. Payment of local property taxes remained in many cases a criterion of local franchise long after the abolition of *régime censitaire* at the national level. Residence requirements, too, were retained much longer for local than for national elections. In fact, in recent years the increased flow of labour from the backward to the economically advanced countries is bringing about extensive disfranchisement even at the national level. In the earlier phase the migrant workers within the one national territory were kept locally disfranchised; today vast numbers of immigrants are denied political rights in their host countries because of the high barriers against citizenship. 'One man, one vote, one value' may be upheld as a principle within a population of settled territorial citizens, but it breaks down at the cross-national level.

Standardization of Electoral Practices

The extension of the franchise to the economically and culturally dependent strata of each national society increased the pressures for a standardization of electoral practices. Before elections could be established as essential instruments of legitimation, local variations in the arrangements for the elicitation and recording of choices had to be minimized. The electoral returns constituted claims to legitimate representation that had to be established through procedures acceptable to all, or at least to the dominant, competitors for office and power. The history of the democratization of the suffrage was paralleled in country after country by a history of increasing standardization of administrative procedures in all phases of the electoral process: the establishment of registers; the determination of voting rights; the maintenance of order at the polling stations; the casting of the vote; the recording of the act in the register; the counting of choices; the calculation of outcomes.

Of all the issues facing the national administrations in the early phases of suffrage extension, one was of particular importance for the functioning of the electoral system: the measures taken to ensure the independence of the individual electoral decision (Rokkan, 1961).

The defenders of the estate traditions and the *régime censitaire* had argued that economically and culturally dependent subjects could not be expected to form independent political judgements: therefore the vote should be given only to citizens likely to withstand social or economic pressures and able to take public responsibility for their choices on election day.

Liberal advocates of an extended suffrage, such as John Stuart Mill, were placed in a dilemma. They knew that the new voters could easily be swayed by their social superiors or their economic masters, yet they were convinced that the vote ought to be open, that each voter ought to be prepared to defend his decision in his day-to-day environments. This moralist argument for the old tradition of open voting soon had to yield to another imperative: the safeguarding of the integrative and legitimizing functions of the electoral ritual. To generate legitimacy, elections had to be dignified and without any tinge of violence. The maintenance of the system of open voting under the conditions of mass elections could lead only to alienation, corruption, and disrespect for the institutions of the nation.

The result was a widespread movement to ensure the secrecy of the act of voting. To qualify as 'democratic,' elections had to be not only universal and equal but also secret. The French were the first to introduce this principle. The electoral law establishing the States General in 1789 retained open oral voting at the level of the general electorate but called for secret ballots in the colleges of delegates. The electoral law establishing the first legislative assembly in 1791 introduced secrecy at all levels of the electorate, but very little was done to ensure regular enforcement. There was a great deal of opposition to the principle; the Jacobins, in particular, wanted open voting to control dissidence. The constitution of 1793 left it to the voters themselves to decide whether to vote openly or in secret. Subsequent laws reintroduced the principle of secrecy for all voters, but electoral administration remained at a low level of standardization through-out the nineteenth century. The *isoloir* and the standard envelope for the ballot were introduced by law in 1913, but even these highly detailed provisions left leeway for a variety of abuses and manipulations, particularly in the south, in Corsica, and in the overseas *départements* (Charnay, 1965).

The extension of the suffrage to vast numbers of illiterates made it impossible to stick to a strict rule of secrecy. In the economically and culturally backward areas of the national hinterland, it proved particularly easy to control the votes of the lower classes even under strict rules of secrecy. The secret ballot expressed an essential feature of literate urban society: it introduced an element of anonymity, specificity, and abstraction in the system of political interchange.

Significantly, the countries that retained the old tradition of open and oral voting longest were all heavily dominated by landed interests: Denmark did not abolish it until 1901; Iceland, until 1906; Prussia, until the collapse of the Reich in 1918; and Hungary retained it even into the 1930s. By contrast, Belgium, Switzerland, and Sweden had opted for secrecy even under the *régime censitaire,* and the English had only waited five years after the Reform Act of 1867 to introduce the Ballot Act, which ensured the freedom of the voters from intimidation and bribery. In the settler nations overseas, the principle of secrecy was recognized quite early but there were marked local variations in enforcement. One of the Australian states developed an effective procedure of secret voting as early as 1856, and this innovation, the 'Australian ballot,' (Wigmore 1889) spread very rapidly through the United States during the 1880s and 1890s. The open recognition of legitimate partisanship made secrecy less important in the United States than in Europe. Most states allow primary elections within each party, and participation in these cannot easily be hidden from the public.

In all these countries the underlying purpose of the introduction of the ballot system was to take the act of voting out of the regular give and take of day-to-day life and enhance its dignity and ritual significance by isolating it from the sordid pressures and temptations of an unequal and divided society. Most histories of electoral arrangements emphasize the importance of secrecy as a device to protect the economically dependent from the sanctions of their superiors. This was the essence of the Chartists' early demands in England, and it has traditionally been a basic concern of working-class movements. What has often been overlooked is that the provisions for secrecy could as easily cut the voter off from his peers as from his superiors. In fact, the secrecy provisions fulfil two distinct functions: first, they make it possible for the voter to keep his decision private and avoid sanctions from those he does not want to know; second, they make it impossible for the voter to prove how he voted to those he does want to know. The very rigorous rules set up in country after country for the invalidation of all irregularly marked ballots was directed to this second point. They were devised to ensure that the citizen could no longer treat his vote as a commodity for sale. He might well be bribed, but the price per vote clearly would decrease as soon as it proved impossible to check whether it was actually delivered. The salient point here is that by ensuring the complete anonymity of the ballots it became possible not only to reduce bribery of the economically dependent by their superiors but also to reduce the pressures toward conformity and solidarity within the working class.

With the secret ballot, a personal choice was placed before the worker that made him, at least temporarily, independent of his immediate environment: was he primarily a worker or primarily a citizen of the broader local or national community? Secret voting made it possible for the inarticulate rank and file to escape the pressures of their organizations, and at the same time it put the onus of political visibility on the activists within the working-class movement. The established national 'system' opened up channels for the expression of secret loyalties, while forcing 'deviants' to declare themselves openly. Some socialist parties tried to turn the tables by establishing intimate organizational ties with the trade unions and imposing political levies on their members, irrespective of their actual preferences. The controversy over 'contracting in' versus 'contracting out' in the British labour movement can be interpreted as the counterpart of the controversy over open versus secret voting in the total system. The Labour party wanted to put the onus of visibility on its own 'deviants,' the trade union members who did not want to vote for the party (contracting out), while the Conservatives and Liberals wanted the inarticulate masses to stay out of political commitments and to put the onus of visibility on the socialist militants (contracting in).

The introduction of mass elections in the developing countries of Africa and Asia during the final phases of decolonization raised a number of technical issues (Mackenzie, 1960; Maquet, 1959; Smith, 1960). In some British territories a system of separate ballot boxes for each candidate or party was introduced. These were marked by distinguishing symbols (a lion, an elephant, etc.) and the illiterate voters were asked to drop their ballot paper into the box of their choice. There were elaborate rules for the stamping of official identification marks on the ballot papers and for the screening of the ballot boxes from the eyes of the officials, but this procedure still left a wide margin for interference with the choice of individual voters. In other British colonies with high rates of illiteracy the voters had to mark off on the ballot the candidates of their choice. This often made it essential to allow election officials to accept 'whispering votes' from voters who could not read the names on the ballot. The French colonies and their successor states adopted the system of separate party ballots and the *isoloir* for the placing of the chosen list in the official envelope. This simplified procedures (although it wasted a lot of paper) but still left a great deal of leeway for the exertion of social pressure. Even if the village chieftains or the political agents could not see what the voter did inside the *isoloir,* they could either observe him when he chose his party ballot from the separate piles placed at the polling station or, what was more common, prevail upon him to show them afterward the ballots he had not used, as proof that he had voted as instructed. There was nothing new about this, of course. The experiences in the developing countries simply confirmed what had been known about voting in the backward rural areas of Europe for decades. Any attempt to uphold strict rules of secrecy in societies at low levels of economic differentiation is bound to run into difficulties. Relationships are too diffuse and the possibilities of observation too many to allow individuals to escape from control through the isolation of particular acts from their daily contexts.

From Votes to Seats

The emergence of mass electorates produced a great literature of political engineering, not just on the organization of party work and the waging of campaigns but also on the territorial structuring of constituencies and on the strategic pros and cons of alternative procedures of translating the registered distributions of votes into legitimate decisions on representation. Of the extraordinary tangle of issues debated in this literature, only two interconnected questions will be discussed here: the delimitation of units of aggregation, and the procedures for the allocation of seats within each unit. Basically, the bitter debates over the two issues reflect fears and resentments generated through changes in the equilibrium of political power under the impact of mass democracy: the influx of new voters altered the character of the system and a great variety of stratagems were tried out to bring it back into equilibrium.

Varieties of majority systems. The early systems of electoral representation all rested on some kind of majority principle. The will of a part of the electorate was taken to express the will of the whole, and all the participants were taken to be bound in law and conscience by the decision reached through this procedure.

Three distinct varieties of majoritarian decision-making procedure established themselves during the early phases of electoral development. The first of these stipulated *one* round of election, with decisions by simple plurality. The second and the third both stipulated *several* rounds and required absolute majorities in the first round. They differed, however, in their requirements for the final and decisive round. The second allowed an open field of candidacies and simple plurality; the third restricted the competition to the two foremost candidates and retained the absolute-majority requirement to the very end.

The first of the three procedures had been established in England since the Middle Ages and had been used to ensure the election of 'two knights from every shire and two burgesses from every borough' to the House of Commons. It also became the standard method in the United States and soon spread to the other English-settled nations overseas. The method was originally used in two-member constituencies, but it met with general acceptance even when applied in single-member units.

The method of repeated ballots had a long tradition in the Roman Catholic church (Moulin, 1953) and was formally instituted in the French *ordonnance* calling for elections to the States General in 1789. This stipulated three successive ballots – the first two open, the final one restricted to just twice as many candidates as there were seats left to fill. Three-ballot systems of this type prevailed throughout the *régime censitaire*. This method was clearly best suited to elections restricted to the economically independent classes, with leisure enough to travel to electoral sessions and spend the day or more required to get through all the balloting. The Revolution of 1848 swept away this system and introduced single-ballot mass elections. The old habit of repeated ballots persisted, however. Only four years after the revolution, Napoleon III devised a system of two-ballot elections suited to the new situation of manhood suffrage. He broke with the old tradition on a point of fundamental importance: he allowed an open field of candidacies even at the second ballot and required simple plurality only. This was an astute strategic move; in the half-free elections of the Empire, it allowed the officials maximal freedom of manoeuvre against the opposition. Interestingly, there was no return to the principle of second-ballot absolute majority in the Third, Fourth, or Fifth Republic: none of the parties or *groupements* wanted to be faced with the cruel yes-or-no alternatives of the two-way fight.

Other polities on the European continent stuck to the old rule of absolute majority and restricted last-ballot candidacies. This was the system upheld in the German Reich down to its defeat in 1918; it was, also, used in Switzerland until 1900 and in Austria, Italy, and the Netherlands until the end of World War I.

These majoritarian electoral methods came under heavy attack in the later phases of democratization. The extension of the suffrage made possible the organization of strong lower-class parties but the electoral systems, inherited from the ages of estate representation and *régime censitaire,* set high barriers against the entry of such parties into national politics. The German rule of absolute majority set the highest barrier. A lower-class party had to reach the 50 per cent mark or go without representation. The French and the Anglo-American systems also set high barriers against rising movements of the hitherto disfranchised, but the initial levels were not frozen at 50 per cent; the height of the barriers varied with the strategies of established, *censitaire,* parties. The essential difference between the French and the Anglo-American systems was that the one made for much greater local variations in such counterstrategies than the other: the first-ballot results offered a basis for bargaining among the established parties, and the coalition strategies would of necessity vary from constituency to constituency. The height of the barrier against new entrants depended essentially on the willingness of the established parties to enter into alliances. This was not always exclusively a matter of immediate payoffs but of trust and the openness of communication channels.

Origins of proportional representation. Karl Braunias (Braunias, 1932) distinguished two phases in the spread of proportional representation: the 'minority protection' phase, before World War I; and the 'antisocialist' phase, in the years immediately after the armistice. It was no accident that the earliest moves toward proportional representation (PR) came in the ethnically most heterogeneous European countries: Denmark in 1855; the Swiss cantons in 1891; Belgium in 1899; Moravia in 1905; Finland in 1906. In linguistically and religiously divided societies majority elections could clearly threaten the continued existence of the political system. The introduction of some element of minority representation came to be seen as an essential step in a strategy of territorial consolidation.

As the pressures mounted for extensions of the suffrage, demands for proportionality were also heard in the culturally more homogeneous nation-states. In most cases the victory of the new principle of representation came about through a convergence of pressures from below and from above. The rising working class wanted to lower the thresholds of representation in order to gain access to the legislatures, and the most threatened of the old-established parties demanded PR to protect their position against the new waves of mobilized voters created by universal suffrage. In Belgium the introduction of graduated manhood suffrage in 1893 brought about an increasing polarization between the Labour party and the Catholics and threatened the continued existence of the Liberals. The introduction of PR restored some equilibrium to the system (Gilissen, 1958).

The history of the struggles over electoral procedures in Sweden and Norway tells us a great deal about the consequences of the lowering of one threshold for the bargaining over the level of the next. In Sweden, Liberals and Social Democrats fought a long fight for universal and equal suffrage and at first also advocated PR, to ensure easier access to the legislature.

The remarkable success of their mobilization efforts made them change their strategy, however, and from 1904 onward they advocated majority elections in single-member constituencies (Verney, 1957). This aroused fears among the farmers and the urban conservatives, who, to protect their own interests, made the introduction of PR a condition for acceptance of manhood suffrage. Accordingly, the two barriers fell together. It became easier to enter the electorate and easier to gain representation. In Norway (Rokkan, 1966: 5 and 1967) there was a longer lag between waves of mobilization. The franchise was much wider from the outset, and the first wave of peasant mobilization brought down the old regime as early as 1884. As a result, the suffrage had been extended well before the final mobilization of the rural proletariat and the industrial workers under the impact of rapid economic change. The victorious radical-agrarian 'Left' felt no need to lower the threshold of representation and, in fact, helped to raise it through the introduction of a two-ballot system of the French type in 1906. There is little doubt that this contributed greatly to the radicalization and alienation of the Norwegian Labour party, which in 1915 gained 32 per cent of all the votes cast but which was given barely 15 per cent of the seats. The 'Left' did not agree to lower the threshold until 1921; the decisive motive was clearly not just a sense of equalitarian justice but the fear of rapid decline with further Labour advances across the majority threshold.

In all these cases the high threshold might have been maintained if the parties of the property-owning classes had been able to make common cause against the rising working-class movements. But the inheritance of hostility and distrust was too strong. The Belgian Liberals could not face the possibility of a merger with the Catholics, and the cleavages between the rural and the urban interests went too deep in the Nordic countries to make it possible to build up any joint antisocialist front. By contrast, the higher level of industrialization and the progressive merger of rural and urban interests in Britain made it possible to withstand the demand for a change in the system of representation: the Labour party was seriously under-represented only during a brief initial period, and the Conservatives were able to establish broad enough alliances in the counties and the suburbs to keep their votes well above the critical point.

Threshold strategies under PR. PR systems differ markedly in their threshold levels, however, and the struggles over these details of electoral engineering tell us a great deal about the dynamics of multiparty systems.

The variant most frequently introduced in continental Europe was the one invented by the Belgian professor Victor d'Hondt (d'Hondt, 1878; d'Hondt, 1882): the method of the 'largest average.' This method favours the largest party and, in fact, lowers the threshold very little in constituencies electing few members and choosing among few competing party lists. If the total number of votes cast is designated as V, the total number of mandates as M, and the total number of parties as P, the threshold formula for the d'Hondt procedure will read

$$T = \frac{V-1}{M+P-1}.$$

This means that the smallest number of votes (T) required for representation will be a function not only of the size of the constituency and its share of seats but also of the number of parties. A fragmented party system lowers the threshold but, by implication, also increases the over-representation of the largest of the parties (particularly if $P > M$, since the votes for a number of the small parties must of necessity go unrepresented).

Thus, the debates and bargains over electoral arrangements in a great number of PR countries have centred on the questions: Should there be some gentle over-representation of the largest party? and Should the threshold for the first seat be set high enough to discourage new parties and splinter movements? These concerns have been particularly prominent in the Scandinavian countries: the typical constellation there has been one party, Labour, in the range just below the 50 per cent mark; three or four parties, all nonsocialist, in the 5–20 per cent range; and one or two very small parties, with only minimal chances of representation. In such constellations the d'Hondt procedure would give the largest party more seats than its votes justified. In fact it often gave the Labour parties clear majorities in parliament without majorities among the voters. This over-representation was essentially achieved at the expense of the very smallest of the parties, such as the Communist, but often hurt the efforts of the one-seat parties to gain additional representation. A variety of remedies were suggested. The Danes retained the high d'Hondt threshold but ensured greater proportionality among the already represented parties through a two-level procedure: any under-representation produced at the constituency level was corrected through the allocation of additional seats at the regional level. In Sweden and in Norway the non-socialist parties opted for another strategy: they found it impossible to join forces under one single list, but they were anxious to increase their representation through provisions for electoral cartels. In Sweden such cartels were allowed after 1921 and cost the Social Democrats a substantial number of seats. The system placed the Agrarians in a very difficult position. To avoid under-representation, they were tempted to join in cartels with the other non-socialist parties; but to advance the interests of the farmers they found it best to support the Social Democratic government. In the end the provisions for cartels were abolished and the Sainte-Laguë method (Sainte-Laguë 1910) of calculation was introduced.

By a curious coincidence this alternative was adopted in all the three Scandinavian countries during 1952 and 1953. The Norwegian Labour party had gained a majority in parliament in 1945 and by 1947 had abolished the cartels. As a result, the party received 45.7 per cent of the votes but 56.7 per cent of the seats in the 1949 election. This caused a great deal of recrimination, and the party finally accepted the new method of allocation in 1952. A similar lowering of threshold was also brought about in Denmark, through provisions in the constitution of 1953.

The Sainte-Laguë method was once described as a 'miracle formula' by the leader of the Swedish Agrarian party. In the typical Scandinavian situation it had a threefold effect: it strengthened the middle-sized nonsocialist parties by reducing the over-representation of the Social Democrats; it was nevertheless of strategic advantage to the governing parties because it reduced the pay-offs of mergers within the opposition; and finally, it helped all the established parties by discouraging splinters and new parties. How could all this be achieved in one formula? To explain this, we have to go into some technicalities of electoral mathematics (Janson, 1961; Rokkan, 1966: 6).

Two procedures were frequently suggested as alternatives to d'Hondt in the discussions in the Scandinavian countries: the method of the 'greatest remainder' and the Sainte-Laguë system of successive division by odd integers.

The method of the 'greatest remainder' lowers the threshold of representation to a minimum: the threshold formula is $T = V/(MP)$. This is a direct invitation to party fragmentation, since the threshold decreases rapidly with increases in the number of parties. The simple Sainte-Laguë formula does not go quite that far. The threshold formula is $(V - 1)/(2M + P - 2)$. Its crucial contribution is the progressive increase in the cost of new seats. The greater the number of seats already won by a party in a given constituency, the more votes it will take to add yet another. The d'Hondt formula makes no distinction between first and later seats. The total votes cast for each party are divided successively by 1, 2, 3, $\cdots$. The Sainte-Laguë method is to divide by 1, 3, 5, $\cdots$. Thus, if the first seat costs each party 1,000 votes, the second seat will cost the party $(1,000 \cdot 3)/2 = 1,500$ votes and the third seat $(1,000 \cdot 5)/3 = 1,667$ votes, and so on. This is definitely the optimal formula for small parties: it is easy to gain representation but hard to reach a majority in parliament. At the same time, it discourages mergers and cartels. Two parties polling just beyond the threshold for their first seats will, in fact, lose out if they merge.

This procedure appealed both to the nonsocialist parties, typically at the one-seat level in most constituencies, and to the governing Social Democrats. The nonsocialists were anxious to reduce the 'government bonus' built into the d'Hondt procedure, and the Social Democrats wanted to make sure that their opponents did not find it profitable to merge into one broad competitive party.

But this was not all. The electoral strategists went even further to ensure the perpetuation of the established party constellations. They wanted lower thresholds, but they wanted them set just below the typical voting levels of the smallest of the established parties. If the threshold were to be set much lower, it would increase the chances of even smaller, 'antisystem' parties and encourage splinter movements. The solution proved very simple: the first divisor was set, not at 1, but at 1.4. In the example already used, this would mean that the first seat would cost 1,400 votes as against 1,500 for the second and 1,667 for the third. It cost more to gain entry, but once a party was in, the steps toward further representation were no longer so steep.

This formula fitted the established power constellations as closely as any procedure at this level of simplicity could ever be expected to. It had all the appearance of a universal rule, but in fact it was essentially designed to stabilize the party system at the point of equilibrium reached by the early 1950s.

Developments in the late 1950s and the early 1960s showed that even this formula would not protect the system against change. The Social Democrats began to regret that they had given up so much of their 'government bonus.' Their parliamentary majorities had become very small and highly vulnerable, and they were reluctant to contemplate long-term alliances with one of the opposition parties. In Sweden the Royal Commission on Constitutional Reform proposed in 1963 a two-tier system of representation. They wanted to use the Sainte-Laguë procedure at the level of the old constituencies and the d'Hondt procedure to elect regional members at large. This was a deliberate attempt to bring back into the system some measure of over-representation for the largest party. The motive was explicitly stated to be the need for some stabilization of the majority basis for the cabinet. In the ensuing bargaining, the 'high-threshold' spokesmen lost out: the party leaders agreed to stick to Sainte-Laguë even for the second tier allocation. Similar discussions got under way in Norway in the wake of the defeat of the Labour party in the election of 1961. Some Labour strategists have guardedly suggested a return to d'Hondt or even a switch to simple majority elections of the British type, while some of their rivals in the nonsocialist camp have put forth a diametrically opposed solution: the lowering of the Sainte-Laguë threshold to 1.3 or even 1.2. Paradoxically, the old Labour party, once the champion of PR, now wants to increase the threshold of representation, while at least some of their opponents, once the defenders of the old majority threshold, now advocate a radical lowering. Their aim is clearly to encourage the Left Socialist splinters from Labour, but this gain can be bought only at the cost of all future mergers of the nonsocialist parties (Rokkan, 1966: 6).

PR without party lists. By 1920 PR systems of one sort or another had won out throughout Europe. Even the French gave up their two-ballot, single-member procedure from 1917 to 1927 and introduced a curious mixture of d'Hondt proportionality and majoritarianism. These systems all required the voter to elect several representatives at the same time and to choose among a number of lists of candidates. These lists were normally set up by competing political parties. The voters might have some influence on the fate of individual candidates on such lists, but it was nearly impossible to elect anyone not appearing on the initial lists. The Continental PR was a product of party bargaining. The parties wanted to survive and saw that they rated the best chances under a system that would allow them not only to control nominations but also to gain representation even when in minority.

In the Anglo-Saxon countries this type of PR never caught on. There were strong party organizations, but there was also a strong tradition of direct territorial representation through individual representatives. The early English advocates of proportionality were profoundly indifferent to the survival of organized parties; they wanted to equalize the influence of individual voters. The great innovation of these electoral reformers was the introduction of a procedure for the aggregation of individual rank-order choices. The election was not to be decided through the counting of so many choices for X and so many for Y but through the comparison of schedules of preference. The possibilities of such aggregations of rank orders had been analyzed with great ingenuity by Charles de Borda and the Marquis de Condorcet in the eighteenth century (Black, 1958; Ross, 1955), but these theoretical discussions had been confined to decision-making in committees and assemblies. The French method of repeated ballots, in fact, developed out of decision-making situations in assemblies and entailed a rank ordering of preferences; the voters for the candidates at the bottom had to decide on their next-order preferences. The Australian system of the 'alternative vote' is another approximation; the voter indicates his second and third choices, as well as his first, and knows that these lower preferences will be brought into the count if his first preference should not receive enough support. These methods, however, aim at the maximizing of support behind each candidate. First preferences count to the end, even when there are many more than needed to elect the given candidate. The great strength of the movement for the 'single transferable vote' lay precisely in the insistence on the effective use of all the preference schedules, not only the ones given to the candidates with the smallest followings but also of those 'wasted' through over-concentration on a single candidate.

This required the setting of a quota – the smallest number of preferences required for election. The inventors of the system, a Dane, Andrae (1855), and an Englishman, Hare (1857), set it at Votes ÷ Seats, but this was quickly shown to be too high. H. R. Droop (1868) had no difficulty in demonstrating that the correct quota would be [Votes/(Seats + 1)] + 1. This would be just enough to beat competitors for the last of the seats.

Once the quota had been set, the procedure was in itself straightforward, if time consuming. The wasted first preferences at the top of the poll were treated just like the wasted ones at the bottom – the lower preferences were entered when the first ones could no longer help. There was one difference. At the bottom all the first preferences were wasted and had to be examined for lower preferences, while at the top it was impossible to say which ones were wasted – which ones were in the quota and which ones were beyond. The solution was to work out proportional shares of lower preferences. If an elected candidate had received 10,000 first preferences but needed only 9,000, the below-quota candidates would get $(10,000 - 9,000) \div 10,000 = \frac{1}{10}$ of the second preferences given each of them by those 10,000 voters (Lakeman & Lambert 1955).

The Andrae variant of this system was used in the election of some of the members of the Danish Rigsraad from 1855 to 1866 and in the electoral colleges for the Upper House from 1866 to 1915, but the method has otherwise found acceptance only in Britain and the British-settled areas: Tasmania since 1907, the two Irelands since 1920 (quickly abolished in Northern Ireland), Malta since 1921, New South Wales since 1932, and the Australian Senate since 1949. The 'single transferable vote' was ardently advocated by British Liberals but never gained much of a foothold in England. Most Conservatives were against it, and the Labour party found it less and less interesting as they grew in strength. There was a strong move toward proportionalism in 1931. Labour promoted an 'alternative-vote' bill and was supported by the Liberals in the House of Commons, but the government fell and the law was never enacted (Butler, 1953).

On the European continent there has always been a great deal of resistance to the dominance of the organized parties in the determination of the lists of candidates, and a variety of devices has been invented to ensure some measure of voter influence on the fate of individual candidates. Denmark was the only country on the Continent to go as far as to opt for PR without party lists. The current Danish system provides for three levels of electoral aggregation. At the level of the nomination district the voters choose among individual candidates; at the level of the constituency their votes are aggregated by party to determine the allocation of direct seats; while at the level of the region there is a further round of aggregation to decide the attribution of additional seats designed to maximize proportionality (Pedersen, 1966). Another multilevel solution has been devised in the German Federal Republic. There the voters are allowed two votes, one for a simple plurality election in single-member constituencies, the other for a PR election among party lists. A high degree of candidate orientation can also be achieved in a single-level PR system. The Finnish system provides the most interesting example. The parties do not present multicandidate lists or indicate a preferred order among them but submit a number of separate candidacies. The voters then choose individual candidates only, but the votes are aggregated by party within each constituency to determine the allocation of seats.

Single-member versus multimember constituencies. On the Continent the conflict between the majority principle and the proportionality principle was, at the same time, a conflict over conceptions of the territoriality of elections. Majority elections were typically tied to single-member constituencies and posited close interaction between the elected representative and the entire local electorate. Proportional elections were held in larger constituencies and posited interaction between organized parties and functionally defined core sectors of the population. The Single Transferable Vote made little sense in single-member constituencies but offered an alternative to party dominance in multi-member units. The voter was free to establish his own list of candidates and did not have to abide by any party nominations. Thomas Hare (1857) and John Stuart Mill went so far as to propose that all of Britain be turned into one single constituency, but this clearly would make for enormously laborious computations of transfers. The Government of Ireland Act of 1920 stipulated constituencies of three to eight members each, and most advocates of the Hare system now give five seats as the ideal (O'Leary, 1961; Ross, 1959).

PR list systems have allowed wide variations in the size of constituencies. Several countries have, in fact, made the entire national territory one constituency. This was the system of the Weimar Republic, and it is still the system in use in the Netherlands; it has also been used in Israel since 1949. This does not necessarily mean that the same set of candidates is presented throughout the national territory. There may be primary constituencies for the presentation of local party lists, but the fate of these lists is not determined within that constituency alone but by the success of the party in the total national territory. The electoral arrangements in Denmark and in the German Federal Republic are of this type. Some of the seats are allocated directly by constituency (in Denmark by the Sainte-Laguë formula, in Germany by plurality); others are allocated on the basis of the nationwide result to ensure proportionality.

Such large constituencies obviously favour the formation of splinter parties: direct PR thresholds are functions of both the number of seats and the number of parties. To guard against party fragmentation, many systems have introduced higher barriers, either on the basis of the percentage share of the total national vote or on the basis of the number of direct seats already won. Danish law requires as a condition for the allocation of 'proportionalized seats' that the party has (*a*) gained one direct seat or (*b*) received 2 per cent or more of the vote across the nation or (*c*) received in two of the three regions a total number of votes higher than the average regional cost of direct seats. The German threshold is 5 per cent of the federal vote or three direct seats.

Cross-constituency equality. The demand for equality of representation was at first met at the constituency level only. 'One man, one vote, one value' was enforced within the local unit of aggregation but not throughout the national territory. There were everywhere highly vocal movements for the equalization of electoral districts, but these demands met with greater resistance than the claims for equality of influence within each unit. Under the inherited systems of estate representation, elections were taken to express the will, not of individual citizens, but of the corporate units of the nation. A shire or borough might have declined in population or in number of enfranchised citizens, but it still constituted a unit of government worthy of representation on a par with larger units. Even after the Reform Act of 1832 in England, differences between the lowest and the highest numbers of constituents per representative were of the order of 1 to 60. The radical redistribution carried out in 1885 brought the ratio down to 1 to 7, but further progress was slow. Even after the reorganization of 1948 there are still constituencies with electorates only one-third the size of the largest in the country.

Great variations in the ratios of representatives to electorates was the rule throughout Europe and the West until well into the twentieth century. On the European continent the early systems of representation generally gave great advantages to the cities; the centres of commerce and industry were still small in population but had major stakes in the building of the nations. The continuing growth of the national economies brought about changes in this urban-rural balance. As the populations of the cities grew and the franchise was widened, the rural areas gradually gained in their electorate – representative ratios and became heavily over-represented. This inequality of representation proved highly resistant to protest movements. The more conservative voters in the cities had found important allies in the countryside and preferred to stay under-represented at home as long as their allies could help them in their fight against urban radicals (Cotteret, 1960; David, 1961–62; De Grazia, 1963).

In some countries this urban-rural conflict was reinforced through conflicts between the central districts and the peripheries. The constituencies farthest away from the capital and the economically most advanced areas of the nation claimed a right to numerical over-representation to offset the difficulties of communication with the decision makers and the officials at the centre. In Denmark the constitution of 1953 even goes so far as to stipulate that constituencies be allotted seats based not only on their population but also on the size of their territories. A representative speaks not just for a given number of citizens but also for a unit of physical territory. Even in the most 'proportionalized' of democracies, the electoral arrangements still reflect tensions between three conceptions of representation: the numerical, the functional, and the territorial.

Priorities for Comparative Research

The development in so many countries of standardized arrangements for the conduct of elections at several levels of the polity sets a wide variety of challenging tasks for comparative social research. The comparative studies carried out thus far leave great gaps in our knowledge. It is, in fact, much easier to pinpoint lacunae and lost opportunities than to describe positive achievements.

Given the crucial importance of the organization of legitimate elections in the development of the mass democracies of the twentieth century, it is indeed astounding to discover how little serious effort has been invested in the comparative study of the wealth of information available. There is no dearth of literature, but exceedingly little of it stands up to scrutiny in the light of current standards of social science methodology. The great bulk of the items bear on technicalities and controversies within a single national or regional tradition, and the few wider-ranging ones tend to take the form of vehement polemics against competing systems, even when couched in the terms of academic discourse.

The polemical writers tend to fall into two categories: the violent majoritarians or the impassioned single-vote proportionalists. It is hard to trace any distinctive school of list-system proportionalists. The party lists have certainly had their defenders, but these have tended to be pragmatic and contextual in their argumentation and have not been inclined to advertise their solutions as panaceas for all countries of the world.

The majoritarians have been particularly articulate in the three European countries with the unhappiest records of mass politics: Germany, Italy, and France. In all these deeply divided countries there has been widespread nostalgia for the simplicity of the Anglo-Saxon system of plurality elections. A great number of publicists had hoped for the development of unified national political cultures that would foster the kind of trust in territorial representatives they could observe in England and had somehow come to the conclusion that this could be brought about through straightforward electoral engineering.

In its academic guise this argument was developed into a scheme of purportedly universal propositions about the consequences of electoral systems for the health of the body politic (Hermens, 1941; 1951). This proved a very difficult enterprise. A great deal of information for a wide range of countries was processed, but the results were meagre. The universal propositions gave way to complex statements about concrete sequences of change, and a bewildering multiplicity of conditioning variables had to be brought into the analysis. It turned out to be simply impossible to formulate any single-variable statements about the political consequences of plurality as opposed to those of PR. A variety of contextual conditions had to be brought into the analysis: the character of the national cleavage system; the cultural conditions for the legitimation of representatives; the burdens of government and the leeway for legislative versus executive action (Duverger, 1950; 1951; Epstein, 1964; Grumm, 1958).

This did not reduce appreciably the ardour of the majoritarians. They stuck to their guns in discussing the three major countries of the western European continent, but they admitted that PR might not hurt the functioning of democracy in the smaller nations (Unkelbach, 1956). A broad phalanx of arguments, some *a priori,* some empirical, some strategic, were advanced during the 1960s for majority elections in West Germany,(Sternberger, 1964; Scheuch, 1965), but the academic enterprise broke down as soon as attempts were made to argue this move for all full-suffrage democracies, whatever their structure and whatever their experiences in consensus building.

In Anglo-Saxon circles the polemics *against* plurality elections have not been quite as vehement. Advocates of PR could not blame the inherited electoral system for major national disasters, such as Fascism in Italy, National Socialism in Germany, the 1940 debacle in France. The single-vote proportionalists (Lakeman, 1955; Ross, 1955) do have something in common with the majoritarians. They tend to express the same naive belief in the possibilities of electoral engineering, and they show little awareness of the cultural and the organizational conditions for the acceptance of different systems of representation.

The majoritarian-proportionalist polemic has recently been given a new dimension through the discussion of the consequences of electoral arrangements for the achievement and/or survival of democracy in the developing countries. A leading analyst of the conditions of economic growth, W. Arthur Lewis, has formulated a strong indictment of the Anglo-French majority systems which the new African states inherited from their colonial masters. He argues that the Anglo-French systems had been developed and had found widespread acceptance in 'class societies' and cannot work in the same way in the African 'plural' societies – territorial polities seeking to integrate within their boundaries populations historically hostile to each other.

The surest way to kill the idea of democracy in a plural society is to adopt the Anglo-American electoral system of first-past-the-post. . . . First-past-the-post does not even require 51 per cent of the votes in each constituency to give one party all the votes. If there are three parties it can be done theoretically, with only 34 per cent; or if there are four parties, with only 26 per cent. Governments can get away with this in secure democracies without destroying faith. But if you belong to a minority in a new state, and are being asked to accept parliamentary democracy, you can hardly build much faith in the system if you win 30 per cent of those votes and get only 20 per cent of the seats, or even no seats at all. If minorities are to accept Parliament, they must be adequately represented in Parliament. (Lewis, 1965: pp. 71–72.)

These, of course, are exactly the arguments used in the 'plural societies' of Europe for the introduction of PR. The entrenched linguistic, religious, or ethnic minorities had no faith in the majority representatives and threatened to disrupt the system. The introduction of PR was essentially part of a strategy of national integration – an alternative to monopolization of influence or civil war. But the extent of minority entrenchment varied greatly from country to country, and the pressures for proportionalization were nowhere exactly the same. This is a high-priority area for comparative research. To bring about some understanding of the great variations in electoral arrangements both in the West and in the postcolonial polities, it will be essential to study the crucial decisions on the suffrage, on privacy versus secrecy, on plurality versus PR, in the context of the process of nation-building (Bendix, 1964; Rokkan, 1961; Rokkan, 1966: 4).

Electoral systems have not changed *in vacuo*. They function within culturally given contexts of legitimacy, and they are changed under the strains of critical 'growing pains' in the development of the over-all constellations of national institutions. The comparative study of electoral developments can contribute a great deal to the understanding of processes and strategies of national integration, but the contributions will be meagre and unreliable as long as the principal motivation for new research is a concern with the pros and cons of different schemes of electoral engineering.

The conditions for a real advance in comparative electoral research are present. An increasing number of dispassionate analyses of national electoral histories have been forthcoming in recent years, and steps are being taken to facilitate the conduct of statistical investigations through the development of 'data archives' for computer analyses of time-series records (Rokkan, 1966: 2; Rokkan, 1969: 2). What has been lacking so far has been an international forum for the advancement of detailed comparative studies. A beginning has been made, however, and it is hoped that the next decades will see a breakthrough in the comparative study of electoral systems.

FIVE

The Comparative Study of Electoral Statistics

Early Developments

The regular production, dissemination and scrutiny of mass statistics is a hall-mark of the nation-state: the consolidation of the European administrative structures during the mercantilist era generated a series of efforts to standardize the collection and presentation of numerical information about each subject population and gave rise to the academic discipline of *statistica,* literally the *science of the state.*[108]

The earliest efforts of nation-wide data gathering grew out of the eminently practical needs for information about military and economic potentials: the census was an essential tool in the establishment of national policies. Equally pragmatic considerations prompted the development of other bodies of statistics: registrations of marriages and births, divorce, disease, crime, mortality. All these statistics underwent a great deal of change during the first century of regular official bookkeeping: changes in data-gathering procedures, in definitions and classifications, in modes of presentation and publication. But there was an unmistakable trend toward routinization and standardization over time: the gathering of such statistics was recognized as an administrative necessity and the utility of the data was enhanced through the emphasis on comparability over long spans of time.

Eminently pragmatic motives also prompted the development of another branch of national statistics: the statistics of elections, popular consultations and organs of representation. But the need for such statistics varied much more with the internal structure of the polity: censuses became part and parcel of the process of national administration but political enumera-

Origin: This chapter was originally written as the Introduction to the first volume of the *International Guide to Electoral Statistics,* (The Hague; Mouton, 1969) (Rokkan, 1969: 2).

tions only made sense in representative régimes and even within these only after the spread of partisan contests and the standardization of electoral practices. The counting of votes was the administrative alternative to conflict and intrigue: the organization of electoral statistics was a direct product of the efforts to routinize the resolution of conflicts within the body politic through the holding of regular elections under the control of formally neutral bodies of officials. To achieve legitimacy the decisions of the electorate had to be documented and made available for scrutiny from all sides: the organization of regular electoral bookkeeping was a response to the widespread questioning of the electoral verdicts. The electoral records were essentially judicial documents: they were there to uphold claims on legitimate representation. The production of political statistics could not be divorced from the process of politics itself: the structure of local and national politics determined the character of the electoral record-keeping.

This meant that the statistics of elections were essentially *national* in character: they differed from country to country in their degree of centralization, in the amount of detail given, in the style of presentation and analysis. A strong international movement for the standardization of censuses and the registration of marriages, births, diseases and deaths got under way in the middle of the 19th century: there was no question of any parallel movement for political statistics.

The decades after the upheavals of 1848 saw a remarkable increase in the production of literature on the franchise, on the organization of elections and on the behaviour of the electorates but the great majority of these writings stayed within the confines of the one nation. The controversies over the extension of the franchise inspired a few attempts at comparative tabulations but none of them went very far in analytical detail:[109] it took a long time before anyone even thought of subjecting electoral data to the sort of systematic comparison tried out on suicide statistics by Durkheim.

A few solid works of comparative scholarship saw the light but these were less concerned with statistical analysis than with the philosophical and the ideological justifications of alternative electoral systems and with accounts of sequences of development nation by nation. The great work of Georg Meyer (Meyer, 1903) is still an invaluable source of information for early European developments. The later compilation by Seymour and Frary (Seymour, 1918) adds an important Western perspective but does not maintain the same level of scholarship. The classical treatise on comparative electoral law came much later still. Karl Braunias's two-volume work *Das parlamentarische Wahlrecht* (Braunias, 1932) was brought out in 1932 and reflected quite a different stage in the history of mass politics: it gave less attention than Meyer to the early developments up to the universalization of the suffrage but concentrated its efforts of systematization on the great varieties of arrangements in the mobilized full suffrage democracies of the decade after the First World War. No work of such scope has been attempted after World War II: this is one of the great lacunae of contemporary scholarship.[110]

The early discussions of the pros and cons of different electoral systems suggested a number of challenging tasks of comparative statistical analysis but the technical difficulties of data access and data processing tended to discourage even the most assiduous of scholars. There was a scattering of discussions of methods and procedures of political statistics but these generally failed to tackle any of the challenging issues of comparative analysis.[111] Curiously, the breakthrough toward a comparative perspective did not come in the wake of the many parallel movements towards universal manhood suffrage: it came as soon as the *women* had been given the vote in a wide variety of countries just before or just after the First World War. The emerging mass democracy had inspired a number of great treatises of comparative politics (Ostrogorski, 1902; Michels, 1911; Bryce, 1921), but these gave only passing attention to numerical evidence. The decisive breakthrough toward systematic statistical comparisons came in the 1930s: the American political scientist Harold Gosnell, one of the pioneers of the Chicago school, brought together a vast body of information about European elections and tried to pinpoint a few regularities (Gosnell, 1930) and his Swedish colleague Herbert Tingsten followed this up through a series of much more detailed analyses of geographical, social and economic determinants of the behaviours of the enfranchised citizenry (Tingsten, 1937). Both of them focused attention on the latest entrants into the electoral arena: the *workers* and, quite particularly, the *women*. In fact, the extension of the suffrage to women triggered off a series of new developments in electoral statistics: a great deal of public interest centred on the behaviour of the women at the polls and efforts were made in country after country to ensure the collection of the necessary data for detailed analyses of differences between the two sexes. Only two leading countries kept outside this movement: Great Britain and the United States. In the countries of the European Continent (equally in Australia and New Zealand) the electoral registers were set up to allow analyses of variations in *turnout* between the sexes and in a few countries, notably in Weimar Germany and in the First Austrian Republic, arrangements were even made for separate counts of *party votes* by sex (Tingsten, 1937: Ch. I; Dogan, 1956). These developments in official book-keeping offered a tempting platform for comparative analysis. Tingsten based most of his comparisons on the tabulations already published by local or national statistical bureaux but in a couple of cases managed to get behind the screen of published tabulations to the raw data on the electoral registers. His concerns were essentially *developmental:* he was concerned with the analysis of the *processes of change* triggered off by the extension of the suffrage to all adults and he wanted to pinpoint the *geographical* spread of these changes.[112] For technical reasons the bulk of his analyses focused on the *women,* the latest category of subjects granted rights of participation in the political system. But he was equally concerned with the behaviours of the *workers:* their entrance contributed much more decisively to the restructuring of national politics and their willingness to be mobilized in one direction or another offered a challenging theme of comparative research.

A number of attempts had been made in different countries to identify conditions making for rapid mobilization of the enfranchised working class.[113] What distinguished Tingsten's contribution was not just the attempt at a systematization of findings across so many countries but even more his persistent search for regularities in *variations by type of localities within each country:* he did not content himself with the establishment of similarities or differences in national *averages* for each category of citizens but concentrated much more energy on the analysis of variations *among localities* within each nation.

Whenever the sources made it possible he grouped the data on electoral behaviour by *types of locality:* by voting districts in the larger cities and by commune or other units of local administration in the countryside. Tingsten became the father of *comparative political ecology:* he was the first to attempt the formulation of a general regularity in the contextual conditioning of electoral behaviour. His suggestion of a general 'law of the social centre of gravity' inspired a variety of further analyses: the notion that socially homogeneous environments offered the best conditions for political mobilization was not in any sense novel, but his demonstration of the possibilities of detailed testing of such hypotheses through the processing of mass data caught the imagination of a number of leading methodologists in the sociological profession and inspired a variety of further analyses.

An intriguing merger of research traditions took place in the wake of Tingsten's pioneering efforts. The story is complex and cannot be summarized in a few paragraphs.[114] In this quick introduction we cannot enter into details: we shall offer a simple scheme of alternative strategies and discuss trends towards a convergence of concerns in the comparative study of elections.

The Central Challenge: the Secrecy of Individual Decisions
To the social scientist elections represent mass experiments of unprecedented scope:

- you define a given population through strict rules of inclusion and exclusion;
- you force all the members of the population to choose among the same basic alternatives: vote for party A, party B . . . , or abstain;

– you register each individual decision and you collect in the same run a variety of other data about each actor.

But there is one decisive limitation: the individual decisions are conscientiously *registered* but they are *counted as anonymous acts cut off from their origins*. The experiment produces vast masses of statistics for the social scientist but the rules of secrecy set barriers to his analyses: at least for the decisions between the parties he must confine himself to the aggregate counts by locality or constituency and is cut off from the data at the level of the individual citizen.

This contrast sets the central challenge of electoral statistics: vast masses of well-established data in the aggregate, legal barriers against direct analysis at the individual level.

This contrast was in itself a product of the process of democratic development: the introduction of strict rules of secrecy was part and parcel of a general process of administrative standardization triggered off through the widening of the suffrage and the consequent efforts of mass mobilization (Rokkan, 1961). In the *régime censitaire* the vote was a publicly visible act: the citizen was accountable for his choice of candidate or party and had to be prepared to defend it in his dealings with his fellow men. In some cases voting was entirely oral and there was no record of individual votes. In other cases detailed registers of all the eligible voters were maintained for the recording of their votes: this source of data on early divisions in the body politic has only recently been opened up by historians and holds great promise for systematic research.[115] With the extension of the suffrage to the dependent strata of the population this onus of choice produced strains in the body politic and tended to defeat the purposes of election: the peaceful resolution of conflicts over representation. There were marked differences in the reactions to these strains. Countries heavily dominated by landowners tended to maintain open voting even after the enfranchisement of the dependent strata: thus Denmark, Hungary and Prussia. Other countries introduced formal secrecy at an early stage but encountered great difficulties in the standardization of electoral practices.[116] But whatever the details of application the rule of secrecy determined the character of the statistical product of the elections: the act of voting was severed from the enfranchised citizen and was only registered and counted as a contribution toward a territorial total. There were often no difficulties in establishing lists of individual voters for each party in the *rural* districts but this was vastly more difficult in the anonymous and multi-faceted *urban* communities (Siegfried, 1913: p. X). Whatever the actual possibilities of obtaining such information the rule of secrecy made it impossible to establish authentic statistics of candidate or party choice at the individual level: it was administratively possible to carry out analyses of individual variations in *turnout* but the *actual votes cast* were only reported by aggregates and could no longer be officially tabulated at the level of individuals on the registers.

This set a challenging task of statistical analysis: the aggregate results were known but the unknowns of the generating equations could only be solved through a variety of indirect procedures of estimation.

The history of electoral research is essentially the history of the strategies chosen in the search for such estimates.

Four such strategies can conveniently be distinguished:

– the Siegfried strategy of *electoral cartography;* the production of detailed maps of variations in territorial aggregates and the analysis of similarities and differences through the scrutiny of local evidence;

– the Tönnies – Rice – Heberle strategy of *political ecology,* the calculation of the correlations of the social, economic and cultural characteristics of each locality with the aggregate results of elections;

– the Lazarsfeld strategy of *community surveys,* the organization of direct interview inquiries with samples of local electorates and the analysis of the social, economic and cultural backgrounds of the voting decisions on the basis of such individual data;

– the Campbell strategy of *nation-wide surveys,* the conduct of interview inquiries with samples representative of entire national electorates and the analysis of average statistical associations and correlations across wide ranges of communities and constituencies, whether grouped by geographical regions or by type of locality.

The first two of these approaches were fully developed before the Second World War. André Siegfried's classic treatise on the West of France was published as early as in 1913 and is still a model of regional research. There was nothing new about the use of maps in political analysis:[117] the novelty of Siegfried's enterprise was the systematic collation of evidence, geographic, economic, cultural, historical, to account for contrasting local traditions of politics. He did not just compare one map with another: he ordered many of the data statistically and came very near to the type of correlational analysis favoured by Tönnies and Heberle [118] in Germany, Rice and his followers in the United States (Rice, 1924; Rice, 1928; Rossi, 1959; Diederich, 1965: Ch. III). The distance between the two strategies was particularly marked in the years after World War II: the French school of *géographie électorale* continued to produce maps by the hundreds while social science methodologists in other countries tended to concentrate much more attention on the logic of reasoning in studies of ecological variations. In recent years there have been many signs of a merging of the two traditions. Electoral geographers such as Alain Lancelot and Jean Ranger have shown great interest in alternative procedures of analysis (Lancelot, 1964) and the political sociologist Mattei Dogan has demonstrated the great possibilities of simple statistical models for the calculation of the distributions at the origins of the aggregate results

(Dogan, 1965; Dogan, 1967). The work of French statisticians such as Joseph Klatzmann, Jacques Desabie and G. Vangrevelinghe have added further strength to this movement: they have suggested ways of getting beyond the timeworn methods of multiple regression analysis towards solutions through matrix analysis of systems of equations (Klatzmann, 1957; Klatzmann, 1958; Desabie, 1959; Vangrevelinghe, 1961).

A parallel merger of traditions can be observed in the United States. The breakthrough in the mathematics of sampling and the growth of academic interest in standardized field operations set the stage for a remarkable innovation in the study of politics: the analyst was no longer content to order and collate the evidence produced by the political process itself but went out to elicit and collect data directly from the population he wanted to know about. The technique of the sample survey opened up a wide range of new avenues of analysis and called attention to new dimensions of the political process. In the early years there were important differences of strategy in the use of this technique: Lazarsfeld and the Columbia group wanted to reduce the range of political variability within the population under study and wanted to test out their hypotheses through sample surveys in *single communities* while Campbell and his team at Michigan wanted to study the whole range of variations, political or otherwise, across the entire national electorate.[119] During the last years there have been a number of signs of a merging of these two traditions: a number of analyses have brought out the importance of local political contexts for electoral behaviour and more and more attempts have been made to map out the dimensions of variability in such contexts and to pin down the typical behavioural consequences of such variations (Campbell, 1960: Ch. 11; Miller, 1966: 2).

What is even more important is that there has been persistent signs of a *rapprochement* between the essentially European tradition of political ecology and the typically American tradition of the sample survey. It is deeply significant that a great archive of electoral ecology is currently under development at Ann Arbor, the Mecca of survey research: the Inter-University Consortium set up to service the growing number of graduate schools of political science is no longer confining its holdings of data for reanalysis to past academic surveys but is building up a vast file of electoral records and census data for practically all counties of the U. S. since the 1820s (Bisco, 1966; Miller, 1966: 1).

The rationale of this development is twofold

– first of all electoral analysts have become increasingly impressed by the stubborn *historical continuities* in local electoral behaviour and have become interested in pinning down the sources of these traditions through long-term time series analysis;

– and secondly, the analysis of aggregate records is no longer seen as 'the poor man's alternative' to sample surveys but as a great intellectual challenge, as an incentive to the construction and testing of developmental models at a high level of theoretical articulation (Dogan & Rokkan, 1969).

The contrast between the two traditions was at its peak in the early 'fifties: this was the heyday of pronouncements about the 'ecological fallacy' and the pitfalls of official statistics.[120] During the last decade, these over-heated debates have given way to a variety of serious efforts to analyze the logical structure of inference from one level of description to another and to compare systematically the available strategies in the uses of aggregate data.[121] There is a great deal of intellectual excitement about these issues in the logic of research and some of the best brains in the profession have been at work on them in recent years. One important source of stimulation has been the *econometric* movement: there is the same emphasis on the use of the products of official statistical bookkeeping, the same concern with problems of aggregation and disaggregation, the same interest in processes of change over time. It is indeed not inconceivable that we shall see before long the development of '*politometrics*' as a parallel to econometrics.

The Need for Cross-national Stock-taking of the Data Resources for Political Analysis: the Rationale for the International Guide

These developments have so far taken place in single-nation settings: there has been a great deal of interchange at the level of models and methods but no concerted efforts to make systematic use of the great wealth of historical electoral data in cross-national comparisons: no one has as yet dared to 'do a Tingsten' for the era of the computer and the data bank. A movement is under way, however, and there is every reason to expect important initiatives in this direction within the next decade. The success of the Inter-University Consortium has stimulated a number of parallel efforts in Europe: given the long traditions of centralized electoral book-keeping the jobs of data assembly and data preparation will in many cases be found easier than in the States.[122] The increasing interest in the quantitative study of processes of nation-building is bound to lead to pro-posals for cross-national analyses of historical election statistics. Karl Deutsch has called for concerted efforts to establish a broad basis for comparative analyses of rates and patterns of 'social mobilization':[123] in any such scheme the statistics of elections, parties and political personnel is bound to be given high priority. Gabriel Almond, Lucian Pye and Sidney Verba have tried to formulate a body of general propositions about steps in the development of nations and have identified seven decisive 'crises' in the development of modern policies: the crises of identity, of legitimacy, of territorial penetration, of participation, of integration and of distribu-tion.[124] For all these critical periods time series data of some sort *can* be established for most modern nations but the conditions for the production of such data have varied a great deal and the strategy of analysis cannot be the same in all cases. To get beyond the impressionistic summaries so characteristic of much of the literature of comparative politics it will be essential to get down to such detailed studies of the available time series data, preferably through the establishment of data banks and the exploration of possibilities of computer processing.

But there are many difficulties to be tackled before any such programme of comparative developmental analysis can be got off the ground. The essential first step would seem to be to take stock of the data resources nation by nation and to review the analyses already carried out within each of them: this is what we hoped to achieve in launching our *International Guide to Electoral Statistics* and this is how we want our effort to be judged.

We are well aware that efforts are under way in several countries to ensure much more detailed stocktaking than could be contemplated within this international context: the easier access to large-scale computer facilities for political analysts has prompted parallel initiatives in a number of countries already [125] and is bound to stimulate further entrepreneurship. Our concern has been to increase international cross-discussions of such developments and to give all the potential participants a chance to acquaint themselves with the peculiarities of the data resources of the other countries. We have not succeeded equally well on all points but we hope we have at least been able to add significantly to the small arsenal of tools at the disposal of the student of comparative politics.

There is one particular point on which, in retrospect, we wish we had taken a stronger line: this concerns the statistics on the recruitment of candidates and parliamentary personnel. Some of our chapters go very far towards covering the available literature in this field, others have left it out entirely. We regret this very much. This is an important field of research: a number of pathbreaking studies have been completed during recent years [126] and efforts are under way in several countries to establish *computer-formated archives of bibliographical data for political personnel.* [127] This is a development of great potential interest in comparative research and we hope to remedy the lacunae of this first effort through another volume currently under consideration within our series of *Guides to Data for Comparative Research:* an *International Guide to Biographical Statistics.*

With all its shortcomings this first volume must essentially be judged as one step in a long-term process of stocktaking for comparative cross-national research. It is our hope that this effort will stimulate further initiatives within and across a number of countries and that by the time we shall consider a follow-up volume for the fifteen countries of Western Europe, we shall be able to report on a mushrooming of archives for computer analyses of historical electoral statistics.

NOTES

[108] See (John, 1884; Westergaard, 1932). For an illuminating account of the contrast between the English tradition of 'political arithmetic' and the German *Statistik-Staatenkunde* see (Lazarsfeld, 1961).

[109] Examples of early compilations: (Villey, 1895; Benoist, 1896; LeFèvre-Pontalis, 1902; Pyfferoen, 1903).

[110] Given the immediate political interests of the European organizations in questions of electoral standardization this is indeed an astounding lacuna. Among the few attempts to fill this gap in the literature these deserve mention:

F. A. Hermens. *Democracy or Anarchy?* (Notre Dame: University of Notre Dame Press, 1941), new ed. *Europe between Democracy and Anarchy* (Notre Dame: University of Notre Dame Press, 1951) and *The Representative Republic* (Notre Dame: University of Notre Dame Press, 1958): the great defender of the Anglo-American system of single-member constituencies and plurality decisions, adamantly biased against PR systems;

M. Duverger *et al. L'influence des systèmes electoraux sur la vie politique* (Paris: Colin, 1950): a general discussion mainly concerned with analyses of developments before 1939, in need of detailed revision and updating.

Enid Lakeman and J. D. Lambert. *Voting in Democracies* (London: Faber, 1955): a passionate plea for the Hare system, offers a detailed classification of electoral systems with much solid information, less informed about PR list systems.

Giovanni Schepis. *I sistemi elettorali* (Empoli: Ed. Caparrini, 1955): details of calculation procedures, uneven accounts of positive legislation without any attempt at historical explanation.

H. Unkelbach. *Grundlagen der Wahlsystematik.* (Göttingen: Vandenhoeck, 1956): refinements on the Hermens arguments, no detailed analyses of the actual workings of systems.

W. J. M. Mackenzie. *Free Elections.* (London: Allen & Union, 1958): a standard work on electoral organization at a high level of theoretical articulation, no country-by-country treatment.

Institute of Electoral Research. *A Review of Elections 1954–1958, ... 1959, ... 1960, ... 1961–62.* (London: the Institute, 1960 et sqq.)

Parliaments and Electoral Systems. A World Handbook (London: the Institute, 1962, 128 pp.): useful compendia, but leaves out important details and gives very little background information.

W. Birke. *European Elections by Direct Suffrage* (Leyden: Sijthoff, 1961, 124 pp.): covers 16 countries of W. Europe, very superficial, without theoretical perspective.

U. Kitzinger. *Britain, Europe and Beyond. Essays in European Politics.* (Leiden, Sijthoff, 1964), 222 pp. Part III and Appendix.: details of electoral systems in Germany, Austria, Switzerland, Belgium and Luxembourg, post-war election results tabulated for 16 W. European countries, percentages only.

For details of the discussion of the unification of electoral law in Europe see (Birke, 1961) and *Les élections européennes au suffrage universel direct.* Brussels, Institut de Sociologie Solvay, 1960, 317 pp.

[111] The voluminous treatise on statistics by Georg von Mayr, (Mayr, 1895–1917) was to have included a volume on political statistics, but this does not seem to have been published. A couple of German dissertations give useful details on early analyses of electoral data, particularly (Bock, 1919; Herz, 1932).

[112] A general rationale for this developmental approach to the study of electoral records is given in Chapter 7 below.

[113] Among the earliest examples: (Braun, 1903; Blank, 1904–5; Michels, 1906; Tynell, 1910; Olsson, 1923).

[114] For accounts of the history of electoral research see (Eldersveld, 1951; Heberle, 1951: pp. 206–65; Dupeux, 1954–55; Bendix, 1957; Butler, 1958; Stammer, 1960: esp. the article by S. Rokkan & H. Valen; Ranney, 1962: esp. articles by Campbell, Rokkan, Ranney, Butler & Personen; Diederich, 1965).

[115] The most important work of this type has been done by J. R. Vincent at Cambridge, see (Vincent, 1966). Similar work has been done by E. Høgh for the Danish elections up to 1901 (Høgh, 1968) and by T. Solhaug for a local election in early 19th century Norway.

[116] On the complex history of electoral administration in France see (Charnay, 1965: esp. pp. 179–334, 583–636; Charnay, 1964: Ch. III–IV).

[117] Among early efforts of political cartography the curious work of the Norwegian geologist Amund Hansen deserves particular attention: in (Hansen, 1899) he presented maps of the division between 'Left' and 'Right' in Norway and tried to relate the differences in local voting to differences in ethnic origins as measured by skull indexes and hair colour.

[118] (Tönnies, 1924), cf. the discussion of the 'sociographic' school in (Oberschall, 1965: Ch. III). Tönnies's work was followed up by Rudolf Heberle in *From Democracy to Nazism* (Heberle, 1945), a work originally carried out in 1932–34 but not published in German until 1963: *Landbevölkerung und Nationalsozialismus.*

[119] The literature of these movements is voluminous and need not be accounted for here: the classical texts of the two traditions are (Lazarsfeld, 1944; Campbell, 1960).

[120] The initial statement on the ecological fallacy is due to W. S. Robinson (Robinson, 1950).

[121] Major contributions to this literature are (Goodman, 1959; Boudon, 1963; Stokes, 1965). These issues have been placed in a broader methodological context by Erik Allardt and Erwin Scheuch (Allardt, 1966: 2; Scheuch, 1966) and have been fitted into an interesting general classification of types of 'fallacies' by Hayward R. Alker (Alker, 1965: Ch. 5), cf. also (Dogan & Rokkan, 1969).

[122] See articles by E. Allardt and O. Riihinen and S. Rokkan and H. Valen in (Rokkan, 1966: 3) and the information on the Datum archive at Bad Godesberg in (Bisco, 1966). Mattei Dogan has established a *Bureau d'Analyses Quantitatives Internationales* in Paris for the accumulation of ecological data for France, Belgium and Italy. For further detail on the growth ecological archives see the last section of (Dogan & Rokkan, 1969) and (Rokkan, 1969: 2).

[123] (Deutsch, 1961). The case for the use of electoral data in developmental analysis has been made Chapters 1 above and 7 below.

[124] Initial statements of this theory of successive 'crises' can be found in the Introduction and the Conclusion of (Pye, 1965: 3), and in (Pye, 1968). A fuller statement will be presented in the forthcoming volume by Leonard Binder *et al.* (Binder, forthc).

[125] Among recent, partly computer produced, collections of electoral documents and data these deserve particular attention: (Sänger & Liepelt, 1965), a 2500-page compendium giving not only all post-war election results but also social structure data on each *Wahlkreis* and a similar four-volume collection for Austria (Stiefbold, 1966). Such collections have even been prepared for a 'developing' country such as Argentina, see D. Canton. *Materiales.*

[126] Among the most important recent efforts of large-scale processing of data on political personnel these deserve particular attention: (Guttsman, 1963; Ranney, 1965; Zapf, 1965; Sartori, 1963; Gruner, 1966; Valen, 1966).

[127] The idea of such archives was first launched by Harold Lasswell *et al.* (Lasswell, 1952). A number of such archives are currently under development. Information on archives in the U.S.A. is given in (Glaser, 1966). In France, an extensive file of biographical data on the parties of the Third and Fourth Republics has been established by Mattei Dogan. In Norway, an archive of data on members of the professions since the 18th century has been established by Vilhelm Aubert, Ulf Torgersen, and Tore Lindbekk, see (Aubert, 1960; Lindbekk, 1967). Within the Norwegian programme of electoral research an archive of parliamentary nominees has been set up by Henry Valen (Valen, 1966); this has recently been extended by S. Rokkan and associates to cover the entire parliamentary personnel since 1814, see (Rokkan, 1966: 7; 1968: 4).

SIX

The Mobilization of the Periphery:
Data on Turnout, Party Membership and
Candidate Recruitment in Norway

Introduction

We shall present and discuss in this chapter a set of data on turnout, party membership and candidate recruitment in Norway.

Our approach is essentially *ecological:* we shall present our statistics by local administrative units and will be particularly concerned to highlight differences between the central, urbanized districts and the peripheral, sparsely populated districts.

Our data were assembled within a programme of research on *elections after World War II:* the bulk of them came from the *punched-card archives of commune data and candidate data* set up jointly by the Chr. Michelsen Institute and the Institute for Social Research.[128]

Our perspective on these data is not limited to the post-war period, however. Our analysis experience soon prompted us to look back over a longer period of time and to interpret our findings in a developmental perspective.

We chose as our points of departure the first elections after the introduction of universal suffrage: for elections for the *Storting* this was in 1900 for the men and in 1915 for the women, for local elections the crucial years were 1901 and 1910. These were indeed decisive events in the history of the nation: large sections of the adult population were for the first time given formal rights to take part in political decision-making and

Origin: This chapter was originally published in the collection *Approaches to the Study of Political Participation*, Acta Sociologica, 1962.

allowed to make their preferences count in moulding local and national politics. Our concern is to gain insight into *the implications for the polity* of the entry of these new masses of citizens into the electoral contests. The first prerequisite in any such study is detailed information on the *reactions of the last enfranchised:* how much difference did suffrage make to them? how easily could they be persuaded to make use of their rights, to mobilize for joint action, to take a direct part in organizational work?

The focus in our analysis is on *time-lags* in these processes of mobilization and activation: we are concerned with the *length of time* it takes before the bulk of the 'new' citizens make effective use of their rights.

We have asked questions about such time-lags at three levels:

(1) for *turnout* – how many elections had to pass before the new categories of the electorate got used to the vote and took part at the polls in the same proportion as the older categories?

(2) *for party memberships* – how quickly were the parties able to recruit members within the new categories of voters and how did the parties differ in their rates of organizational growth?

(3) *for candidate recruitment* – how long did it take before citizens from these new categories were nominated as candidates for public office and how have the recruitment ratios from the 'new' vs. the 'old' categories changed over time?

Such questions about processes of change over time may be asked for the total political system and they may be asked for each of the smallest administrative units in the territory. Our concern is not primarily with the aggregate rates of mobilization and activation for the entire national electorate: we focus on *differences in time-lags between local units* and are particularly concerned to explore possible processes of spread from the central, highly commercialized and industrialized areas, to the peripheral, economically less developed areas. Our concern is not only with a process in *time* but also with a process in *space*.

Our data differ very much in coverage from period to period. For the period from 1900 to 1936 we have to rely almost exclusively on crude aggregate statistics in official publications: if we were to undertake detailed commune-by-commune analyses of the time-lags in this early period we would not only have to carry out a great number of computational adjustments because of the many boundary changes and split-offs, but we would also be faced with much laborious sifting of information from scattered archives and newspapers. We have drawn up plans for such work, but in this paper we limit our detailed ecological analysis to data for the *latest phase* in the process: the period since 1945.

We shall in fact be concerned with the *end-phase* in a continuous movement toward a 'politicization' of the total territory, a maximal mobilization of the total adult population. Our analysis will focus on the characteristics of the rapidly dwindling pockets of communities in the 'prepolitical' phase:

the last of the communes to be brought under the sway of the national party system. It is paradoxical that it is just in this period of belated 'politicization' in the peripheral areas that we find a number of indications of increasing 'depoliticization' in the major cities: on this development at the centre we refer to Ulf Torgersen's article on 'The Trend toward Political Consensus (Torgersen, 1962).

I. *Turnout Levels in Central vs. Peripheral Communes*
The differences between cities and the countryside constituted a central theme in the early analyses of the repercussions of manhood suffrage: evidence from a number of countries showed that it was easier to mobilize the newly enfranchised workers in the densely populated, economically segregated areas of the cities than in villages and farm communities.[129]

The urban-rural differences were as marked in Norway as in any Western country. The statistics do not make it possible to establish this through direct breakdowns of the electorate according to the categories of the franchise provisions, but the aggregate counts before and after the suffrage extensions tell a very clear story even so.

The Constitution of 1814 restricted the franchise to officials, freeholders and leaseholders in the countryside, owners of real estate and holders of merchant's and artisan's licences in the cities. The total electorate in 1815 is estimated at less than 100,000, probably about 10 % of the total population. Only about 59,000 of these were actually on the electoral rolls, however: citizens had to put in personal requests for registration and were only given the right to vote if they swore allegiance to the Constitution. There was little change in the effective electorate until 1884: then the franchise was extended to residents qualifying as taxpayers on the basis of their assessed income. The total number of qualified citizens rose from 146,000 in 1882 to 182,000 in 1885. Of the new entrants to the electorate, estimates indicated that 48 % were manual workers: this class now made up about 14 % of the electorate as against 23 % from the upper and middle classes and 62 % farmers and fishermen.[130] With the emergence of the first party organizations came a variety of efforts to mobilize the potential electorate for action: from 1876, the last election before the direct party contests, to 1897, the registration figures rose from 57 % to 85 % in the cities and from 63 % to 81 % in the rural communes, and the turnout among those qualifying for the franchise rose from 31 % to 78 % in the cities and 26 % to 68 % in the countryside.

The pressures for an extension of the suffrage to all adult men became increasingly insistent in the nineties and the Storting passed the decisive legislation in 1898. All accountable men over 25 were now given the vote: their rights might, however, be suspended as long as they received public assistance as paupers or as long as they were in bankruptcy proceedings. The electorate now suddenly increased from 238,000 qualified and 196,000 registered in 1897 to 440,000 qualified and registered in 1900. The proportion of manual workers increased to 37 % as against 39 % self-employed farmers and fishermen and 24 % independent artisans, business men, officials and salaried employees.[131] The provisions for voluntary registration also disappeared and it became decisively easier to mobilize new masses of citizens at the polls. It took some time, however, before the new entrants made use of their rights: *Table 1.1.* shows that there was an over-all drop in turnout by about 16 % at the first national election after the introduction of manhood suffrage and that it took more than twenty years, in fact until 1924, before the percentage level for men reached the pre-1900 level.

There were similar drops in aggregate turnout with the extension of the franchise to all *women* on a par with the men. Women were at first given the vote under an income franchise: they qualified if they themselves or their spouse had an assessed income above a given minimum. It is interesting to note that during this period of limited franchise the aggregate turnout was *higher* for women than for men in the cities: see the entries for 1909 and 1912 in *Table 1.1*. With the extension of the suffrage to all women aged 25 and over there was a marked drop in the turnout: in the national elections the percentage for women fell from 72.8 % in 1912 to 65.5 % in 1915 in the cities and from 49.8 % to 43.6 % in the rural communes, while for the men there was an increase of 2.7 in the cities and a drop of less than one per cent in the countryside. This initial discrepancy between the rates for men and women was gradually to become less pronounced, however. By 1930 it had practically disappeared in national elections in the cities. In the countryside it has taken much longer to mobilize the women to the same extent as the men: the gap has been narrowing steadily, but it is still there.

The tendencies are roughly the same for local elections, but the over-all turnout has been several percentage points lower. There has clearly been less pressure to mobilize a maximum of the electorate in local contests. The difference between local and national elections has, however, been less pronounced in the cities than in the countryside. The turnout among *women* has tended to vary most with the electoral contest; the gap between the rates for men and the rates for women has tended to be largest in local contests in the rural communes, least in national contests in the cities. The over-all tendency, however, has been towards a levelling out of differences in rates of mobilization: in 1901 the 9.5 % who voted among rural women could be contrasted with the 59.9 % who had voted among men in the cities, but by 1955 this gap had dwindled to as little as 9.7 percentage points: 68.0 % vs. 77.7 %

Such processes of mobilization can no doubt be documented for a great variety of countries. The geographical fragmentation of the Norwegian territory made it a slow and sometimes irregular process. In other countries

Table 1.1. *Electoral Turnout in Norway 1897–1957 – Differences between Rates for Men and Women*

Storting elections

Year	Total electorate in 1000s Cities M	W	Rural M	W	Over-all turnout Cities	Rural	Difference M-W rates Cities	Rural
1897	59	–	180	–	77.7	67.8	–	–
1900	104	–	336	–	62.8	51.6	–	–
1903	111	–	346	–	64.7	48.7	–	–
1906	116	–	354	–	70.7	58.7	–	–
1909	122	96	363	199	72.9	59.0	– 0.5	+ 19.0
1912	130	106	372	219	72.8	61.1	– 1.8	+ 17.9
1915	142	190	390	412	69.4	54.9	+ 9.2	+ 23.3
1918	152	202	411	437	71.3	54.9	+ 9.1	+ 24.9
1921	175	229	462	487	76.9	64.0	+ 7.8	+ 20.7
1924	181	240	483	510	80.1	65.4	+ 4.3	+ 16.8
1927	190	251	508	537	76.9	64.3	+ 5.3	+ 18.2
1930	198	263	532	558	81.6	75.7	+ 2.1	+ 9.9
1933	213	278	568	586	81.8	73.9	+ 5.0	+ 13.5
1936	229	294	605	616	87.5	82.4	+ 3.0	+ 9.0
1945	258	320	715	708	80.6	72.6	+ 2.5	+ 9.2
1949	320	395	733	724	86.4	79.2	+ 2.6	+ 8.6
1953	336	408	767	748	84.0	76.9	+ 1.7	+ 7.7
1957	340	411	786	762	82.5	76.3	+ 1.2	+ 6.0

Local elections

Year	Total electorate in 1000s Urban M	W	Rural M	W	Over-all turnout Urban	Rural	Difference M-W rates Urban	Rural
1898	53	–	156	–	Information incomplete			
1901	107	70	317	163	53.3	30.1	+ 8.9	+ 31.7
1904	Information incomplete				Information incomplete			
1907	115	91	331	179	67.1	38.3	+ 8.2	+ 29.8
1910	121	164	344	356	66.7	40.4	+ 11.7	+ 28.9
1913	127	175	351	369	69.0	43.7	+ 9.8	+ 27.7
1916	139	187	366	391	63.8	42.4	+ 7.4	+ 24.2
1919	147	196	382	408	62.6	48.1	+ 10.1	+ 22.4
1922	173	224	437	457	70.9	51.4	+ 7.4	+ 22.1
1925	179	235	457	477	77.6	56.0	+ 5.5	+ 18.8
1928	186	245	482	502	79.6	59.4	+ 4.1	+ 18.1
1931	197	257	507	523	77.0	61.1	+ 6.2	+ 17.8
1934	212	217	542	549	79.8	66.6	+ 4.5	+ 15.9
1937	237	300	591	596	79.5	67.8	+ 3.1	+ 13.3
1945	276	337	728	720	70.1	63.5	+ 6.6	+ 13.6
1947	323	397	692	676	79.0	67.6	+ 3.4	+ 10.9
1951	338	412	723	704	80.2	68.8	+ 1.5	+ 8.7
1955	353	426	759	735	77.2	68.6	+ 0.4	+ 6.6

NOTE: Turnout has been calculated on the basis of the total *qualified* to vote, inclusive of those temporarily suspended. For 1897, when registration was still voluntary, the turnout rate is based on the estimated totals of citizens having the stated qualifications for the franchise, *not* the total registered (on the latter basis, the rate would have been 90.7 and 83.4).

of Western Europe we find evidence of rapid mobilization over short spans of elections.

Suffice it here to call attention to a set of data on changes in mobilization rates in *Germany* since the early elections under universal suffrage for both sexes in the Weimar era: [132]

	Urban		Rural	
	(Gemeinden	50.000 and over)	(under	2000)
	M	W	M	W
1922 Sachsen	84.0	79.3	79.8	58.1
1928 Hessen	75.5	64.7	72.8	52.1
	(Gemeinden	5.000 and over)	(under	3000)
1953 Bundesgebiet	85.9	83.4	89.7	85.3

The figures from elections in the 1920's give a pattern similar to the Norwegian, but in the postwar *Bundestag* elections the level of mobilization tends to be higher in the small rural communities than in the cities and the differences between the rates for men and women have practically disappeared.

Erwin Faul has recently interpreted the data as evidence of the rapid 'nationalization' of political life in Germany: 'Es gibt seither keine politisch unberührten Flecke in Deutschland mehr' (Faul, 1960, p. 159). It will be an interesting task for comparative research to assemble data for a number of countries on the rapidity of this process of mobilization and national political integration and to analyze the resulting differences in a broader context of information on the conditions for party work in peripheral vs. central areas.[133]

The official breakdown in *Table 1.1* gives a very crude picture of the process of change over time. The 'rural' category in these statistics covers a great variety of territorial units: it includes the small market towns as well as a wide range of administratively equal, but structurally very disparate *herreder,* from high-density suburban and industrialized communes to sparsely populated tracts of land without commercial or industrial agglomerations of any size. We have not yet been able to establish any corresponding time series for each of the principal categories of communes, but our analyses of differences among communes in the elections after 1945 give us a number of clues to an understanding of the processes at work.

Table 1.2 tells us a great deal about differences in the conditions of electoral mobilization: the figures in this table are for the national election of 1957 but the same basic patterns come out in all the elections we have studied.

We find a marked contrast between the most urbanized communes and the sparsely populated communes along the coast. The turnout levels in

Table 1.2. *Differences in Turnout in 1957 between Communes of Different Structure*

Standard typology	Accessibility score		Total communes	Over-all turnout 1957	Distributions by commune of percentage point discrepancy in Men-Women turnout 1957		
			No.	Electorate	Q_1	Md	Q_3
Fisheries	Low:	5+6	62	86,204	64.9	5.1	8.8	13.9
	Medium:	4	60	103,573	66.7	3.5	7.5	11.3
	High:	1+2+3	48	94,684	68.8	3.5	6.6	11.6
Low density	Low:	5+6	46	40,129	72.4	5.4	8.8	12.4
– agriculture,	Medium:	4	110	132,725	75.8	5.1	8.8	12.1
forestry	High:	1+2+3	69	133,098	77.6	5.4	8.3	10.4
Low density	Low:	4+5+6	81	119,920	73.7	5.4	9.3	12.1
– mixed and	Medium:	3	63	161,408	77.2	1.0	5.1	9.1
industrial	High:	1+2	79	281,174	79.5	1.4	4.6	7.7
Urbanized								
– mixed			15	51,416	77.3	0.7	3.5	5.8
– industrial			21	82,093	80.5	1.6	4.3	8.8
Suburbs			26	226,495	80.2	1.0	2.4	5.4

the urbanized communes and in the suburbs comes closest to those of the cities (see *Table 1.1*), about 15 percentage points above the levels for the coastal communes classified as 'low-accessibility' ones in our analysis. We also find a corresponding contrast in the discrepancy of the rates for men and women: least in the suburbs, most marked in the 'low-accessibility' areas. The simplest explanation of the persistency of such differences is a purely physical one: it is plainly not so easy to get to the polling stations in the mountainous coastal areas with few or no roads between the scattered farmsteads and fishing villages. When we tried to work out an index for the average 'accessibility' of the polling stations in each commune we first sought to assemble data on the road networks and other transport facilities, but this proved technically very cumbersome: our current index is an *indirect* measure based on a) the per cent of the resident population living in 'house clusters' according to the census of 1950,[134] b) the per cent of children of school age who could not attend day school in their neighbourhood but had to go to one of the boarding schools provided for sparsely populated areas, c) the per cent of school children attending schools too small to be divided into more than one or two age classes.

Classifying the 680 rural communes on the basis of this composite index we get marked correlations with the turnout levels in all the elections after World War II. We have not yet applied the classification to the elections in the crucial mobilization phase from 1900 to 1937, but all the information we have suggests that the correlations will prove marked throughout the history of elections under manhood suffrage. We know from official statistics that the three Northern provinces have ranked lowest in turnout in most of the national elections ever since 1859, the first year for which such data are available, and we also know that the only other provinces at this low level have been the two West Coast provinces of Hordaland and Sogn and Fjordane: both characterized by a fragmented geography and consequent difficulties of communication even within communes. These five provinces had the lowest average turnout in the national elections from 1921 to 1957. The average aggregate turnout for their rural districts ranged from 64.4 % to 70.0 % as against more than 79 % for such central provinces as Akershus and Buskerud, and this difference was even more marked for the women: 56–62 % for the five 'low' provinces as against 75 % in the two central ones.

Table 1.3. *Turnout Levels in Peripheral Communes: by Region*

Region	Periphery score	No. of comm.	Total elect.	Overall turnout 1957 nat. el.	Commune-by-commune differences in turnout levels:								
					Local el. 1955			Storting el. 1957			Diff. 1957–55		
					Q₁	Md	Q₃	Q₁	Md	Q₃	Q₁	Md	Q₃
East	Not periphery	176	651,786	80.2	70.3	74.1	77.6	78.1	80.6	88.5	4.3	6.1	8.3
	Mod. "	12	13,176	77.1	69.4	73.7	75.4	72.1	74.4	82.8	–3.4	4.1	6.0
	Extr. "	1	978	71.4		63.9			71.4			7.5	
South	Not periphery	45	69,337	75.9	63.1	66.9	71.7	73.4	78.0	80.8	6.3	10.1	12.1
	Mod. "	16	8,286	77.0	67.4	68.7	76.4	73.8	78.5	82.9	4.7	9.2	11.3
	Extr. "	7	2,953	77.8	62.3	66.6	70.3	76.8	78.1	79.5	7.0	12.1	16.7
West	Not periphery	163	343,285	73.7	57.3	64.0	68.4	69.4	74.2	76.8	6.3	10.4	13.6
	Mod. "	33	34,859	70.5	56.7	63.5	68.0	68.9	71.6	74.5	3.4	7.5	14.1
	Extr. "	11	11,417	65.6	32.7	61.0	67.6	56.6	65.2	72.0	–3.7	6.3	9.0
Middle	Not periphery	69	187,978	78.0	65.5	69.4	73.9	74.8	78.3	79.1	4.9	7.9	9.9
	Mod. "	14	11.237	72.8	63.3	67.4	73.5	69.4	73.8	76.8	1.9	6.7	12.4
	Extr. "	11	10.980	67.2	58.7	61.5	65.8	52.4	66.9	72.0	2.8	5.3	10.7
North	Not periphery	49	125,478	68.7	56.5	61.5	65.8	65.2	68.9	73.5	5.4	7.9	10.6
	Mod. "	36	53,766	65.3	56.1	63.1	68.0	52.4	67.3	71.4	–0.1	3.7	9.2
	Extr. "	31	37,459	60.8	49.8	59.0	63.3	52.7	60.4	66.3	–7.1	4.4	9.6

Table 1.3 tells us more about this persistent regional contrast in Norwegian politics. The rural communes in each of the six standard regions have here been classified on the basis of an index of 'peripherality'. This index was originally worked out in an analysis of regional differences in Norwegian agriculture (Thormodsæter, 1960, pp. 141–48), but has proved of

considerable interest in our work with electoral data. Six criteria were used to identify the peripheral communes of Norway:

a) more than 60 % of the economically active in the primary sector;
b) reduction in population size of 4 % for 1950–56 or 7 % for 1946–56;
c) less than one quarter of the farms (over 20 decars) exceeding 50 decares in size;
d) income per capita or per taxpayer under specified minima;
e) least favourable tax rates (because of the low proportion of above-subsistence incomes); and
f) relative isolation in terms of the existing transport networks.

The 61 communes found to qualify on every one of these criteria were classified as 'extreme periphery' and the 111 communes found to meet five of the six criteria were classified as 'moderately peripheral'. It is easy to see from the marginals where the peripheral communes are located: of the 172 communes singled out in the index, 67 are in the North, 44 in the West, and only 13 in the East.

Looking at the figures for the national election we see that the peripheral communes had a markedly lower turnout than the others in the North, in the Middle region and in the West. The differences are less pronounced in the East and disappear in the South: in these regions practically all the communes classified as peripheral are in the uplands and the mountain valleys and not on the coast, and this seems to make for a crucial difference in the conditions of electoral mobilization. In fact, the geographically determined difficulties of access do not constitute the only barrier in the coastal areas: perhaps even more important are the *occupational* handicaps of the fishermen and seamen in these communes, who so often have to be away from their home communities for extended periods of time. The table shows that for each of the three classes of communes the lowest turnout levels are found in the North: the average for the Northern communes in the top stratum in fact barely exceeds the levels for the extreme periphery in the Middle and the Western regions. Our analysis indicates that most of the difference reflects higher proportions of economically active in fisheries and shipping in the North, but this is not the whole story, however. The coastal geographical conditions not only create *barriers* to electoral participation but also set the stage for patterns of *political stimulation* different from those prevailing in the central, urbanized and industrialized communes.

This is where the contrast between local and national elections comes in. We saw in *Table 1.1* that the turnout levels have generally been higher in elections for the *Storting* than in elections of municipal councils. Comparing pairs of elections since 1900 we get a pattern with few exceptions:

Election years National (N)	Local (L)	Cities Tot.	M	W	Rural communes Tot.	M	W
1900	1901	+ 9.5	+ 6.9	–	+ 21.5	+ 14.4	–
1906	1907	+ 3.6	+ 3.3	–	+ 20.4	+ 8.0	–
1909	1910	+ 6.2	÷ 0.6	+ 11.6	+ 18.6	+ 10.6	+ 20.6
1912	1913	+ 3.8	÷ 2.6	+ 9.0	+ 17.4	+ 9.8	+ 19.6
1915	1916	+ 5.6	+ 6.7	+ 4.9	+ 12.5	+ 12.1	+ 13.0
1918	1919	+ 8.7	+ 8.1	+ 9.1	+ 6.8	+ 8.0	+ 5.5
1921	1922	+ 6.0	+ 6.2	+ 5.9	+ 12.6	+ 12.2	+ 13.6
1924	1925	+ 2.5	+ 1.9	+ 3.1	+ 10.4	+ 8.5	+ 10.5
1927	1928	÷ 2.7	÷ 1.9	÷ 3.1	+ 4.9	+ 5.4	+ 4.5
1930	1931	+ 4.6	+ 2.3	+ 6.4	+ 14.6	+ 10.7	+ 18.6
1933	1934	+ 2.0	+ 2.3	+ 1.8	+ 7.3	+ 6.2	+ 8.6
1936	1937	+ 8.0	+ 8.0	+ 8.1	+ 14.6	+ 12.8	+ 17.1
1945	1945	+ 10.5	+ 8.2	+ 12.3	+ 9.1	+ 6.9	+ 11.3
1949	1951	+ 6.2	+ 6.8	+ 5.7	+ 10.4	+ 10.3	+ 10.4
1953	1955	+ 6.8	+ 7.5	+ 6.2	+ 8.3	+ 8.9	+ 7.8
1957	1959	+ 5.3	+ 5.4	+ 5.1	+ 5.7	+ 6.0	+ 5.2

These discrepancy rates are based on the time series in *Table 1.1*. The time series are not fully comparable, but the biases in the two series are such as to make the actual discrepancies even more striking.[135] We have compared each national election with the ensuing local one. During the peak periods of 'politicization' this would have increased the likelihood of a higher turnout in the local contest, but it will be seen that this only occurred in 1928 and then only in the cities. The regular drop in turnout from the national to the local election was, with two exceptions, 1918 to 1919 and 1945, more marked in the countryside than in the cities. There is evidence of wide variations in such turnout drops between rural communes of different socio-economic structure. We have not yet been able to document this in detail for the period up to World War II, but our analyses of the elections since 1945 certainly show up marked variations (cf. Hjellum, 1967).

The determinants of the 'discrepancy levels' are of course manifold and we cannot exhaust the analysis possibilities in this one article. *Table 1.3* shows one source of variation: *there is less difference in turnout in the two types of elections in the peripheral communes than in the more accessible ones at a higher level of socio-economic development.* The tendency is particularly marked in the North, but is also present in the Middle, and in the West. The simplest type of explanation would be in terms of a theory of political stratification: you can always count on some 'hard core' of stable voters to turn up at every type of election and in the peripheral communes it simply is not possible to mobilize any sizeable number of citizens beyond this core. There is no doubt something to this theory but our data will not allow us to test its implications directly. In any case such a theory will not help much to explain the cases where *more people were mobilized in the local contest than in the national elections.* It will be seen that both in the West and in the North the lower quartiles of the distribution for peripheral communes had *negative* discrepancies. In fact we find that *practically all* the communes mobilizing more of its citizens for local than for national contests are either peripheral ones by our classification or situated along the Western and Northern coast. The reverse, of course, does not hold true: the majority of the peripheral and/or fisheries communes do *not* show negative discrepancies. Our problem is to pin down variables in the *local political set-up* which might help to account for such differences among these communes at the edge of the territory. This brings us straight to the question of the character of the local contests for office and, quite particularly, of the tie-in between the local conflicts and the broader, 'standardized' oppositions between the nation-wide parties in the elections for the *Storting.*

II. *The Politicization of Local Elections*
We have so far discussed trends in mobilization without considering the development of the mobilizing agencies themselves: the local party organizations and their cores of active campaign workers. It is not possible to assemble historical statistics on the growth of the party organizations in each locality, but the official records of the elections of communal councillors at least allow us to trace changes over time in the *number and character of the lists presented at such local contests* and this makes it possible for us to gauge the spread of party organizations from the central areas to the periphery. Until 1896 the regulations for local elections directly discouraged partisan politics: the contests were set between candidates and were decided by plurality, and the voting was, at least in the countryside, oral and public. The new law of 1896 enforced written ballots and made it possible, upon the initiative of a specified number of enfranchised citizens, to demand that elections be decided by proportional representation between lists of nominees. These competing lists often had a territorial rather than a functional basis, but the transition from plurality to PR elections generally heralded the entry of national party politics into local life. The PR provisions made it possible for the national parties to find stable local allies and to keep up a core staff of active workers between elections. *Table 2.1* gives the figures for the spread of the PR system from 1901 to 1959.[136] The official records do not give information on the system of representation for the same territorial units throughout the period: until 1951 figures were given for *sogn* (parishes) but after that only for *herreder* (rural communes), whether co-terminous with one *sogn* or divided into several such units. The trend is nevertheless remarkably clear. The process of politicization was almost immediate in the cities, but very gradual in the countryside. By 1910, practically all the urban units of any

size had gone over to PR but only one-third of the rural ones. The politicization of the countryside proceeded very rapidly until 1922 and then slowed down until it was again given a spurt during the crisis years of the thirties. By 1937 only 31 communes were left and even this hard core of 'prepolitical' units has been gradually reduced since World War II.

A crucial factor in this rapid 'nationalization' of party conflict was the competitive pressure to develop a broader mass basis for each organization and to ensure greater continuity and stability in the local agencies.

The Labour party took a lead in this development and was the first to establish a broad mass organization not only in the central areas and the industrial enclaves in the countryside but also in the great majority of other rural communes. Systematic efforts were made from the twenties onwards to establish local organizations throughout the territory and to encourage all such organizations to entrench themselves as distinct groups in the local councils. By 1937 the party had been able to present its own lists of candidates in all but one small town and in 92 % of the rural communes. In the local elections since World War II the party has not been able to proceed much further in 'nationalizing' its network: in 1955 and in 1959 it presented its own lists in all the cities and market towns and in about 90 % of the rural units.

The opposition parties were at first much less concerned to enter local politics as distinct units. At least in the countryside, they operated through groups of local *Honoratioren,* community leaders, teachers, officials of farmers' organizations, and these were generally not very strongly motivated to encourage strict party divisions in local politics. Until far into the fifties the normal strategy of the opponents of Labour was to present competing local or non-partisan lists or to establish joint 'bourgeois' lists, *Borgerlige felleslister.* By 1937, the year the Labour party reached its maximum of 'nationalization' so far, none of the non-socialist parties had as yet reached the halfway mark: the Agrarians had their own separate lists in 40 % of the rural communes, the Liberals in 37 % and the Conservatives, a predominantly urban party, only in 15 %. From 1945 onwards the pressure of the competition from Labour as well as among the opposition parties themselves prompted increased efforts to organize separate local agencies and to commit them to continuous activity in communal politics. This policy was pursued with particular vigour by the Conservative party: its list coverage rose from 10 % of the rural communes in 1945 to 47 % in 1959. The trends for the other parties were similar, but not so pronounced: the Liberal party expanded its coverage from 37 % to 52 %, its split-off wing, the Christian People's party, entered its own lists in 29 % of the rural communes in 1945 and had reached 51 % in 1959, and the Agrarians finally expanded from 27 % to 57 %. The total effect of all these developments was to spread party politics further and further into the periphery and to intensify the efforts of mobilization even in local contests.

Table 2.1. *The Process of 'Politicization' in Norway: the Decline in the Proportion of Parishes and Communes Maintaining Non-partisan Plurality Elections 1901–1959*

Election	Cities and towns			Parishes (sogn)			Rural communes (herreder)			
	Total	Plurality el. No.	P.c.	Total	Plurality el. No.	P.c.	Total	Plurality elections Entire communes No.	P.c.	Separate sogn No.
1901	60	14	23.3	893	674	75.5	551	429	77.9	–
1907	61	10	16.3	908	no data		853	393	67.4	–
1910	61	6	9.8	913	584	63.9	600	369	61.5	42
1913	62	7	11.3	916	490	53.5	612	307	50.2	51
1916	62	6	9.7	918	453	49.3	628	291	46.3	52
1919	62	6	9.7	918	283	30.8	637	No data		
1922	65	5	7.7	921	239	25.9	647	"	"	
1925	65	4	6.2	930	235	25.3	664	"	"	
1928	65	4	6.2	937	203	21.7	675	"	"	
1931	65	4	6.2	942	166	17.6	682	"	"	
1934	65	1	1.5	943	110	11.7	682	"	"	
1937	65	1	1.5	944	63	6.7	682	31	4.5	21
1945	64	0		940	71	7.6	680	32	4.7	27
1947	64	0		934	70	7.5	680	34	5.0	29
1951	64	0		733	44	6.0	680	29	4.3	13
1955	64	0					680	19	2.8	15
1959	62	0					670	16	2.4	

Sources: Norges Officielle Statistikk V. 61 (1907) and subsequent volumes. The reporting practices have varied considerably: this accounts for the gaps in the table. It is not possible to establish further details on the parish statistics without recourse to archival data.

The last communes to be reached by this wave of politicization were generally small and sparsely populated units in the periphery. Most of them were in the South, the West and the North and they were practically all geographically isolated units at a low level of economic differentiation and development.

Our first question about the effects of politicization obviously concerns the *turnout* levels. *Table 2.2* reviews the historical evidence: it gives the aggregate turnout percentage for plurality units vs. PR units from 1913 to 1945 and from 1945 to 1959. It will be seen that the 'prepolitical' units have invariably mobilized 10 to 20 percentage points fewer of their citizens than the politicized ones. The apparent exception for 1945 is easily explained. This was the first election after World War II and in some normally politicized communes only the Labour party was ready to present a list and the election was therefore decided by the plurality procedure: in the largest of these communes the turnout was actually as high as 84.3 %.

If we disregard such exceptional cases the pattern of differences have remained the same as for pre-war elections. The medians and quartiles for the turnout in the plurality communes after the war were as follows:

	N	Q_1	Md	Q_3
1945	32	51.4	58.9	65.5
1947	34	43.9	52.2	57.8
1951	29	41.3	46.1	56.5
1955	19	44.2	52.1	63.4
1959	16	46.4	53.1	62.1

Table 2.2. *Differences in Turnout between Parishes with Non-partisan Plurality Elections and Parishes with PR Elections between Party Lists*

Election	Parishes with plurality el.		Parishes with PR	
	Electorate % of rural total	Turnout %	Electorate % of rural total	Turnout %
1913	38.5	33.1	61.5	50.4
1916	33.4	26.5	66.6	50.3
1919	19.1	32.9	80.9	53.3
1922	16.2	31.4	83.8	55.2
1925	14.6	36.0	85.4	59.4
1928	10.6	42.0	89.4	62.0
1931	8.6	39.8	91.4	63.1
1934	5.2	47.7	94.8	67.5
1937	2.3	49.7	97.7	68.0

For the elections after World War II the official statistics do not provide figures for parishes, but it is possible to calculate turnout differences between *communes* according to the mode of election: the separate parishes still using the plurality procedure within a PR commune are then disregarded.

	Communes with plurality el.		Communes with PR	
	Electorate % of rural total	Turnout %	Electorate % of rural total	Turnout %
1945	2.0	64.0	98.0	62.4
1947	1.9	54.0	98.1	67.0
1951	1.3	49.7	98.7	68.9
1955	0.7	49.8	99.4	68.7
1959	0.5	53.3	99.5	70.7

Table 2.3. Differences in Turnout Levels between Less 'Politicized' and more 'Politicized' Communes: by Region

Region	National party lists in local el. 1955	No. of communes	Total electorate	Over-all turnout 1957	Differences in turnout levels by commune								
					Local el. 1955			Storting el. 1957			Diff. 1957-55		
					Q1	Md	Q3	Q1	Md	Q3	Q1	Md	Q3
East/ Middle	No lists	2	1,153	60.5	–	54.4	–	–	64.4	–	–	+10.2	–
	One list, mostly non-political votes	3	2,984	70.9	–	73.5	–	–	72.6	–	–	+ 1.5	–
	One list, fewer non-political	5	2,843	78.3	65.6	68.4	71.6	79.2	80.2	81.5	+6.7	+ 9.5	+13.1
	Two or more, some non-political	51	103,670	77.2	65.6	71.1	75.0	72.7	77.6	80.4	+2.8	+ 5.6	+ 8.1
	Two or more, no non-political	228	715,499	79.9	68.5	73.2	77.1	76.7	80.2	82.6	+4.4	+ 6.5	+ 9.2
South/ West	No lists	46	43,684	70.2	49.8	60.2	67.6	69.1	71.6	74.8	+6.2	+12.2	+22.8
	One list, mostly non-political	21	35,834	71.7	63.1	66.0	69.1	68.9	74.6	77.0	+3.3	+ 8.0	+ 9.7
	One list, fewer non-political	15	18,330	71.0	52.1	61.5	66.4	62.4	72.6	76.2	+4.5	+10.8	+12.8
	Two or more, some non-political	81	161,295	73.2	60.7	65.8	70.0	69.7	74.4	77.6	+3.6	+ 9.1	+12.0
	Two or more, no non-political	112	210,994	75.4	60.5	65.5	69.7	72.1	76.3	80.2	+7.4	+10.2	+13.7
North	No lists	10	10,889	60.8	45.4	60.2	64.0	46.0	64.4	67.6	-2.1	+ 3.2	+ 9.5
	One list, mostly non-political	3	2,807	60.0	–	61.5	–	–	60.4	–	–	+ 1.6	–
	One list, fewer non-political	11	13,784	64.9	56.7	62.3	64.6	58.5	66.5	69.7	-1.1	+ 7.0	+10.7
	Two or more, some non-political	64	128,521	66.7	57.3	61.8	66.4	60.4	67.3	70.8	+0.8	+ 5.1	+ 9.0
	Two or more, no non-political	28	60,702	67.7	45.4	57.8	65.1	60.4	67.3	71.4	+6.4	+ 9.3	+13.3

We have so far compared the turnout in the units at the one extreme with the aggregated turnout for all the other units. Politicization, however, is a matter of degree and it must be of interest to establish a graduated index and to analyze differences in turnout from one level on such an index to the next. This is what we have tried to do for the elections after 1945. Our index simply combines information on the *number of party lists* registered at local elections with data on the *size of the vote for local lists* without any explicit party affiliation. In *Table 2.3* we have grouped all the rural communes by a simple version of this index and given, for each group, the distributions of turnout percentages at two elections: the local contest of 1955 and the national one of 1957.[137]

The table groups the rural communes both by region and by the level of politicization as measured by this index. The marginals immediately inform us of marked differences in the spread of party polities between the three principal regions. In the Eastern region and in the Trøndelag we find the great majority of communes completely politicized: only 2 communes had no party lists and only one commune in five had non-partisan lists competing with party lists in the local contests for office. In the South and West we find one out of six communes at the lowest level of politicization and we find roughly half of the other communes caught in direct fights between partisan and non-partisan lists. In the North the parties had entered the local arena in all but 10 of the 116 communes but in three out of four cases the local party affiliates had to contend with non-partisan competition for office. These differences correspond to those we have observed earlier for turnout levels: higher in the plains and the valleys of the East and the Trøndelag, lower along the coast and, particularly, in the North. The same geographical conditions tend to determine the activities of potential party organizers no less than they influence the behaviour of ordinary citizens. The difficulties of access from the central areas limit the flow of pressures on the periphery and the difficulties of internal communication make it more important for community leaders within each administrative unit to ensure adequate territorial representation than to ally themselves on one side or another in the conflicts between the national parties.

There are important differences, however, between the South/West and the North in the character of peripheral politics. In the South and the West the Socialist parties have had only minimal success in their efforts to entrench themselves in the countryside outside the isolated industrial enclaves. The peripheral communes in these regions are heavily dominated by the Middle parties, quite particularly the Christian People's party. The least politicized communes in fact almost always give most of their votes to one of the Middle Parties at national elections: the community leaders have little or no competition to fear in the local elections but throw in their lot with the parties defending the rural cultural values in national contests.

In the North the Labour party has always found its primary basis of support among smallholders and fishermen and has been able to entrench itself in most of the peripheral communes. Even in the communes where no formal organizational ties have been established with the provincial Labour party, it can count on substantial support among the voters in national elections. Some of the leaders presenting non-partisan lists at local elections will in fact work for Labour at the provincial level. In general, local politics in the North is characterized by territorial conflicts between leaders with loose and irregular ties with the central organizations. The Labour party or its loosely affiliated groups are invariably opposed by other local interests but these very often prefer to present themselves as non-partisan rather than as affiliates of particular nationwide parties. By contrast to the South and the West, the Middle parties are relatively weak in the North: in fact the non-socialist party attracting most votes in the peripheral fisheries communes of the North is the *Conservative,* a party which elsewhere mobilizes most of the votes in the urbanized areas and the cities.

These contrasts reflect fundamental differences in regional political traditions. We have presented detailed analyses of the background of these differences elsewhere (Rokkan, 1964: 2): here we must limit ourselves to a simple statement of the implications for the analysis of the process of politicization. In the South and the West, the local contests are as a rule likely to be of lesser importance in the least politicized communes and this no doubt primarily reflects the basic fact that the Labour party has not established itself as a real threat to the *status quo.* In the North, there is a greater frequency of genuine conflict at the local level and this results in intensified efforts of mobilization.

We find these differences in party-political constellation reflected in the figures for turnout levels in *Table 2.3.* In the South/West there is a clear increase in turnout from the least to the most politicized communes and this holds both for the local and the *Storting* election. In the North there is no clear pattern of differences for the local election but a trend in the expected direction in the national contest. If we look at the distribution of discrepancy points between the two elections we find a clear pattern: in the South/West hardly any difference from one level of politicization to another, in the North quite a marked contrast. In the areas dominated by the Middle parties there seems to be much less interest in the local than in the national election, while in the areas of Labour strength there is much more concern to mobilize the electorate for the local contests as well.

This interpretation is given further confirmation in *Table 2.4.* We have here distinguished three levels of politicization and within each of these grouped the communes according to the strength of the Socialist parties. The pattern for the least politicized communes is remarkably clear: the 7 Socialist communes, all of them in the North, actually mobilized more of

Table 2.4. *Differences in Turnout between the Local Election of 1955 and the National One of 1957: by the Level of 'Politicization' and the Relative Strength of the Socialist Parties*

Local election of 1955: no. of national party lists	National election of 1957: combined strength of CP + Lab.	Percentage points difference in turnout 1955–1957			
		Total comm.	Q_1	Md	Q_3
No party list (58) or one non-soc. (6)					
	Soc. dom. (1 + 2)	7	− 6.9	− 1.6	+ 3.6
	Close fight (3 + 4)	10	+ 1.6	+ 6.7	+ 9.5
	Non-soc. dom. (5)	11	+ 5.2	+ 9.5	+ 13.9
	(6)	36	+ 7.4	+ 13.8	+ 25.9
One Soc. list (agst. non-pol. lists)					
	Soc. dom. (1 + 2)	14	− 1.6	+ 7.4	+ 10.7
	Close fight (3 + 4)	17	+ 2.5	+ 8.8	+ 10.8
	Non-soc. (5 + 6)	21	+ 3.2	+ 8.1	+ 10.6
Several party lists (1) communes with *less than 1.3 %* in *fisheries/shipping*	Soc. dom. (1 + 2)	97	+ 4.1	+ 6.2	+ 8.3
	Close fight (3 + 4)	75	+ 3.7	+ 6.3	+ 10.4
	Non-soc. dom. (5 + 6)	18	+ 2.6	+ 6.0	+ 14.3
(2) communes with *more than 16.2 %* in *fisheries/shipping*	Soc. dom. (1 + 2)	65	+ 2.1	+ 6.3	+ 9.7
	Close fight (3 + 4)	55	+ 2.9	+ 7.0	+ 10.8
	Non-soc. dom. (5 + 6)	17	+ 7.4	+ 10.7	+ 14.3

their electorate in the local contest than in the national one while the 36 dominated by the Middle parties, all of them in the South (4) or West (32), mobilized many more at the national than at the local election. This pattern is not found at the next level: for the communes where the Labour party (or, in one commune, the Communist party) was the only one to present a list locally. In this type of situation the leaders of the opposition to the Labour party appear much more frequently motivated to mobilize larger groups of citizens in the local contest. By contrast the Labour leaders seem less likely to mobilize all their potential if they are relatively certain of the outcome. The result should be a reduction in the difference in discrepancy scores between Socialist and Middle-party communes.

We get an even clearer picture of these contrasts if we group the communes according to the party which received the largest share of the votes in the Storting election:

Largest party 1957	N = 100 %	L > N	N > L diff. under 10.2 %	over 10.2 %
No national party list				
Lab.	16	31 %	56	13
Lib./Chr.	27	4 %	41	56
Agr.	15	7 %	20	73
One party list				
Lab.	30	17 %	53	30
Lib./Chr.	19	11 %	58	32
Agr./Cons. (1)	9	22 %	55	22

These findings raise interesting problems of interpretation. Essentially we are faced with data on differences in the choice of mobilization strategies in different electoral settings. The marginal utility of the mobilized votes obviously differs enormously in the two cases: in a safe local election there is very little incentive to mobilize towards the maximum but in the national election the mobilized votes serve as 'counters' in bargains for positions and for favours at the provincial level.[138] The situation is different when the local contest is no longer 'safe': in the periphery, this occurs most frequently when the Labour party has established its affiliates and been able to demonstrate some measure of electoral strength.

Our analysis has been limited to data on one single sequence of elections, 1955–1957. It is possible that our results would be radically different if we undertook a similar analysis for sequences of local-national elections in the earlier phases of mobilization, but this will require a great deal of archival and computational work and will not be possible for some time yet. We find the same over-all pattern for all the elections after 1945 and we consider this significant enough to justify publication at this juncture.

III. *Party Membership Figures for Central vs. Peripheral Areas*
We have so far concentrated our discussion on variations in turnout as officially recorded in published statistics and have tried to interpret such variations in terms of differences in the *cost* of such participation as well in the *incentives* offered and the *pressures* exerted to overcome such cost barriers. Essentially we have tried to relate the behaviours of the citizens constituting the electorate to the character of the *alternatives* before them on election day: we first looked into indicators of *ecologically determined* differences in the cost of participation (distance from polling station, difficulties of access, likelihood of absence from home community) and then reviewed data on the *politically* determined differences in a) the ranges of electoral alternatives (the number of separate lists of candidates, the partisan differentiation of the lists) and b) the uncertainty of the electoral outcome and the consequent marginal value of mobilized votes.

In these analyses we have limited our attention to two values of the dependent variable: either the citizen stays home or he votes. This is all we can do with the officially recorded data. But this is only a beginning. We must find ways of going beyond the simple fact of voting to an analysis of the *meaning of the vote* to *the individual citizen:* was he simply mobilized by others just at the time of the election or had he in one way or another entered long-term commitments and taken a socially visible stand among alternatives? The basic instrument for studying these further differentiations in the intensity of participation is the *sample survey*.[139] We undertook two surveys of the rank-and-file electorate in 1957, one of a nationwide sample and one in four communes in the South-West, and we have gained considerable insights into the recruitment of active participants in Norwegian politics through analyses of these data (Rokkan, 1960: 2; Campbell, 1961). Surveys of the usual sample sizes do not, however, readily lend themselves to the type of centre-periphery analysis which concerns us in this article and we therefore made efforts to obtain for our ecological archive *commune-by-commune information* on one important indicator of participation beyond the simple act of voting: *registered membership in a political party*.

Through the courtesy of the national secretariats we were able to assemble for the year 1957–58 near-complete information on memberships by commune for the two largest parties: *Labour* and the *Conservatives*. We also tried to assemble the same information from the three Middle parties, but here we had less success: the Liberals could supply no details by commune and the Christian and the Agrarian parties had to leave out some provinces in their breakdowns. We nevertheless think ourselves justified in reporting our analyses of these data. Not only is this the first time any such analysis has been carried out for Norway: we in fact do not know of any similar ecological study in any country.[140]

It is much to be regretted, of course, that this analysis refers to only one single point in time. There are various time series for the *total* national membership of some of the parties, but these statistics have so far never been broken down in any way which would be of use in our analysis. We are stuck with the data for 1957–58 and we can only hope that the differences we have found between central and peripheral, politicized and 'prepolitical' communes have not been affected by short-term fluctuations but reflect stable relationships.

Table 3.1 gives the votes cast and the membership reported for each party both for the country as a whole and for each of the six regions usually distinguished in our electoral analyses.[141] The differences in the proportions of members to voters are quite marked. The *Agrarian* party, based as it is on a strong network of farmers' associations, has the largest percentage of members. Next comes the *Conservative* party, which has made particularly great efforts to enlist members during the years since

World War II. The membership figures for the Christian People's party and the Liberals are less certain but are clearly well below those for the other two non-socialist parties. The *Christian People's* party is closely tied in with a number of religious layman's organizations and mission societies and can count on support from such circles without strenuous efforts of membership recruitment. The *Liberal* party is the least organized of the five major parties and relies more on personal community leadership than on systematic organizational work.

The figures for the *Labour* party are of particular interest. This is the only party based on two distinct types of membership: individual card-carrying membership and collective affiliation through trade unions. Such indirect memberships are not, as in Great Britain, channelled through nation-wide federations but are decided on by majority vote within each local union. Individual members of affiliated unions can 'contract out' and are in fact required to stay out if they are members of other parties. In practice this does not mean much since there is no individual levy to finance party activities: the union supports the party from its general funds without specifying names of contributors. In fact, many unions do not register all their members in the party, but simply state a round number indicating the extent of its willingness to support the party financially. This makes the meaning of this type of membership for the individual citizen highly problematical: he may often be unaware of the affiliation and in any case need not be more immediately committed to the party than the rank-and-file voter.

Against the background of the electoral strength of the party, the Labour membership figures appear remarkably low. It is true that the figures we have used in the table refer to paid-up, centrally registered membership (see Note 2 under *Table 3.1*). The party secretariat suggests that the 'true' figure would be nearer 175,000, but this would include a) a number of double memberships for members of youth and women's branches, b) some youth movement members under voting age. Even if we included all local members we would therefore not get a proportion of individual members higher than 9 %: this would still be considerably lower than the estimates for the non-socialist parties. It should also be noted that the total member-ship registered through trade unions is very low in relation to the vast potential: the 90,000 affiliations only made up 17 % of the total member-ship of the National Federation of Labour, the *Landsorganisasjon* in 1957.

The Labour party can clearly count on a large body of loyal voters out-side the local organizations: people who feel they belong in the party for economic and social reasons but have not taken steps to register as mem-bers. Our survey data suggests that a greater number of Labour voters consider themselves 'members' than indicated by the central registrations.

In *Table 3.2* we have compared the membership proportions derived from the party data with the proportions found in the 1957 survey of the

Table 3.1. *Votes Cast and Membership Reported for Each Major Party in 1957*

	National totals				East: Oslofj.		East: Inland		South:		West:		Middle:		North:	
	Votes	p.c. of elect.	Members	p.c. of votes	Votes p.c. of elect.	Memb. p.c. of votes	Votes p.c. of elect.	Memb. p.c. of votes	Votes p.c. of elect.	Memb. p.c. of votes	Votes p.c. of elect.	Memb. p.c. of votes	Votes p.c. of elect.	Memb. p.c. of votes	Votes p.c. of elect.	Memb. p.c. of votes
Communist party	60,060	2.6	6,000 [1]	10.0	2.8		4.0		0.9		1.3		2.6		3.5	
Labour party	865,675	37.7	153,981 [2]	17.8	40.4	28.1	45.6	13.5	29.6	12.1	29.2	11.0	38.7	17.3	37.8	9.4
– individ. members			64,073	7.4		5.6		9.3		9.8		5.1		12.1		7.9
– collectively affiliated			89,908	10.4		22.5		4.2		2.3		5.9		5.2		1.5
Liberal party	172,824 [3]	7.5	28,000 [4]	16.2	5.0		4.0		16.5		13.0		6.7		5.2	
Christian people's party	183,243	8.0	29,000 [5]	15.8	5.8	(16.0)	5.5	(16.5)	10.5	(13.4)	13.1	(14.0)	7.8	(16.5)	6.3	(14.5)
Agrarian party	166,806 [3]	7.3	64,000 [6]	38.4	3.7	49.8	10.7	36.5	8.9		8.2	(19.9)	11.6	(40.5)	5.1	
Conservative party	339,293 [3]	14.7	95,976	28.3	24.6	28.1	10.0	32.7	10.9	35.7	10.5	25.8	10.2	27.4	10.0	24.6

national electorate. It will be seen that the survey estimates are slightly *lower* than the party figures for the Liberals, the Agrarians and the Conservatives, but significantly *higher* in the case of the Christians and the Labour party.

A complete fit between the two series of percentages could clearly not be expected. The party figures are likely to include some members under voting age and also some double memberships resulting from affiliations in two or more types of local clubs (the only figures we know to have been corrected on these points are those for the Conservative party). The survey was undertaken of a sample of all registered citizens over 21 and every membership reported counted only once. This should explain the *lower* membership estimates for some of the parties. But what about the *higher* estimates for the Christian people's party and for Labour?

Here it is possible that the actual wording of the question in the survey did not differentiate the categories clearly enough. The question did not probe into the regularity of dues payments and some respondents, particu-

NOTES TO TABLE 3.1:

[1] The Communist party has not made available any figures for its total membership in the fifties. A 1958 report to the Ministry of Education gives a total of 4700 members in the Communist Youth Movement, but there are good reasons for considering this figure much too high (*Innstilling om offentlig støtte til ungdomsorganisasjonene.* Oslo, Kirke og Undervisningsdepartementet, 1959, p. 10.) The estimate of the total party membership given in Table 3.1 is that of 'informed observers', cf. the estimate of 5000 for the end of 1958 in: U. S. Dept., of State, Office of Intelligence Research and Analysis. *World Strength Communist Party Organisations* (Intell. Rep. No. 4489 R–11) Washington, D. C., Bureau of Intelligence Research and Analysis, Jan. 1959.

[2] The figures given for the Labour party are for *the centrally registered, paid-up membership* in 1957. The higher figures published in the Annual Reports of the Party (cf. Torgersen, 1962) also take into account an estimate of locally affiliated members whose dues have not been registered centrally. They also include the *total* of the membership of the *AUF*, the Labour Youth Movement, currently estimated at 12,000. It is not possible to get any estimate of the proportion of these members who are of voting age. We have operated with an estimate of *163,000* members of voting age, but we have no way of ascertaining how accurate this would be.

[3] Votes cast for joint lists have been distributed in proportion to each party's share of the vote in 1953.

[4] The Liberal party could not provide a commune-by-commune breakdown of its membership.

[5] The regional figures for the Christian People's party have been given in parentheses because information is lacking for a number of communes, primarily in the West (19 out of 218 communes). The total membership in the communes for which we have information was 27,846, but it is estimated that the over-all total would have been between 29,000 and 30,000.

[6] Regional breakdowns for the Agrarian party are missing for the South and the North. The figures for the other regions have been given in parentheses because information has not been available for a few communes: 3 in the West, 4 in the Middle region.

Table 3.2. *Differences in Estimates of Party Membership in Norway: Organizational Data vs. Sample Survey Distributions for 1957*

	Proportion of party members in total electorate				Proportion of members in each party total			
	Party estimates N = 2,298,376		Survey N = 1546		Party estimates N = 100 %		Survey N = 100 %	
CP		0.3 %		0.3 %	60,060	10.0 %	19	26.3 %
Labour					865,675		618	
indivi- dual	2.8		(7.6)			7.4 %	(18.9)	
collec- tive	3.9		(3.2)			10.4 %	(7.9)	
total		6.7 %		10.7 %		17.8 %		26.9 %
Liberals		1.2 %		0.6 %	172,824	16.2 %	88	10.2 %
Christians		1.3 %		1.7 %	183,243	15.8 %	106	25.5 %
Agrarians		2.8 %		2.1 %	166,806	38.4 %	104	31.7 %
Conserva- tives		4.1 %		3.2 %	339,293	28.3 %	188	26.6 %
All non- Soc.		9.4 %		7.6 %	862,166	25.2 %	520[1]	22.9 %
All parties					1,787,901[2]		1157	
indiv.	12.6		15.6			16.1 %		20.8
coll.	3.9		3.2			5.0 %		4.2
total		*16.5 %*		*18.8 %*		*21.1 %*		*25.1 %*

NOTES:

[1] Includes 34 respondents intending to vote for joint Non-soc. lists or vacillating between two Non-soc. parties.

[2] Minor parties not included.

larly workers and women, may have said they were members when in fact they only wanted to express an established commitment to their party. The great majority of the voters for the Christian People's party are devoted members of religious associations and some of them may have confused membership in the one with membership in the other. Something similar holds for the Labour party but here there is the added complication of the two categories of membership. The interviewers were asked to note any references to collective rather than individual affiliation and about one out of every three of those who reported membership in the party specified that it was via a trade union. The party statistics suggest quite a different proportion: three out of every five members should have been collectively affiliated. To analyze the origins of this discrepancy we broke down our respondents by union membership. Among those who stated that they were members of a LO union, altogether 33 % said they were members of the Labour party: 14 % specified that their membership was collective and 19 % failed to indicate the category. The 14 % estimate is only slightly below the proportion expected from party statistics but 19 % is probably much too high an estimate for individually affiliated members. We cannot prove this directly but internal evidence suggests that this must be so. Our ecological analyses suggest (see below) that the Labour party recruits a great number of its individual members *outside* the unions and also shows that where the numbers of collectively affiliated is high the numbers of individual numbers is relatively low. It appears that most of the discrepancy between the survey figures and the party estimates must have been brought about through overreporting by trade union members highly indentified with the party but formally not registered as members. In fact union members who specified that they were collectively affiliated were less likely to be loyal to the party than those who failed to specify the type of membership. A summary tabulation of our survey data shows clear differences between the two groups:

INTENDED VOTE 1957:

	N	CP	Lab.	Middle	Cons.	Uncertain, not voting
Respondent member of LO-union						
Reports Labour party membership, *unspecified*	66	–	91 %	1.5	–	7.5
Reports *collective* membership	48	2 %	79	6	4	8
Not a member	234	4 %	59	9	6	22
Spouse LO-member						
Reports Labour membership, *unspecified*	8	–	(87 %)	–	–	(13)
Not a member	173	–	64 %	9	5	22
Not LO-member						
Reports Labour membership, *unspecified*	43	–	91 %	2	–	7
Not a member	974	1 %	24	26	20	29

These notes on the problems of interpreting statistics on membership should caution us against rash conclusions from our ecological analysis. We think we are fully aware of the limitations in our data, but we still find the results of sufficient interest and consistency to justify this report.

Table 3.1 gives a *regional* breakdown of he member-voter ratio. The most marked variations occur in the Labour party: its collective membership is heavily concentrated in Oslo and the Oslofjord area but is of much less importance in the rest of the country. In fact, as we shall see, collective membership hardly ever occurs outside the central areas and the industrial enclaves. The variations for the other parties are very small: the highest member proportions are generally found in the East, but there are several lacunae in the data for the other regions and comparisons are therefore difficult.

Our primary concern, however, is not with regional differences but with differences between communes of different structure and at different distances from the central points.

Table 3.3 gives our findings for *local party organizations*. Adding up the total number of party organizations in each commune we get a clear

Table 3.3. *Differences between Peripheral and Central Communes in the Number of Local Party Organizations*

Type of commune	No. of communes	Average no. of party org.	Average no. of parties with women's org.	Labour party: p. c. with				
				No org.	One org.	Two org.	Women's org.	Youth org.
Fisheries,								
extr. periphery	42	2.8	0.3	26.2	52.4	21.4	26.2	14.3
mod. periphery	42	3.0	0.5	21.4	16.7	61.9	23.8	16.7
not periphery	86	3.8	0.7	31.4	40.7	27.9	24.4	12.8
Low density, agriculture, forestry,								
extr. periphery	19	2.9	0.3	26.3	57.9	15.8	15.8	–
mod. periphery	62	3.5	0.2	25.8	48.4	25.8	19.4	8.1
not periphery	144	4.6	0.8	11.1	41.0	47.2	48.6	20.1
Low density, mixed, industrial								
periphery	7	3.9	0.1	28.6	71.4	–	14.3	–
not periphery	216	5.9	1.2	6.9	36.6	56.5	19.9	38.9
Urbanized,								
mixed	15	7.7	1.7	–	46.7	53.3	66.7	66.7
industrial	21	7.1	1.9	–	33.3	66.7	90.5	57.1
Suburbs	26	7.9	2.1	3.8	23.1	73.1	92.3	42.3
Cities and market towns	64	8.7	2.9	1.6	62.5	35.9	87.5	59.4

picture: fewest in the peripheral communes, whatever their structure, most
in the industrialized and urbanized areas. There is an interesting exception,
however, for the Labour party in the *fisheries communes:* here we find no
consistent difference between the most peripheral and the least peripheral
units. This is the case both for the regular party organizations and for

Table 3.4.1: *Party Membership by Region and Type of Commune:*
Labour and the Conservatives in 1957

		No. of communes	Total elec- torate	Per cent votes for		Party membership					
						in per cent of electorate			in per cent of party vote		
				Labour	Conser- vatives	Lab. ind.	Lab. coll.	Cons.	Lab. ind.	Lab. coll.	Cons.
East/	Fisheries	21	28,162	30.7	8.7	2.7	0.1	2.7	8.7	0.3	31.6
Middle	Low density, agric., forestry[1]	119	204,518	39.2	5.4	5.4	0.2	1.7	13.8	0.1	32.1
	Low density, mixed	115	361,157	43.2	10.4	4.3	1.8	3.8	9.9	4.1	31.5
	Urbanized	16	68,111	48.3	10.9	4.1	6.2	2.8	8.5	12.9	25.2
	Suburbs	18	164,201	42.6	20.4	2.4	2.6	5.8	5.7	6.2	28.2
	Cities, market towns[2]	32	203,874	46.0	21.4	2.4	5.4	7.3	5.2	11.8	34.3
	Oslo	1	336,336	38.5	31.6	1.7	15.3	8.2	4.5	39.8	25.8
South/	Fisheries	64	105,347	20.2	6.6	0.8	–	1.6	4.1	0.1	24.2
West	Low density, agric., forestry	94	83,918	18.1	5.0	1.6	–	1.3	9.1	0.2	26.2
	Low density, mixed	94	168,933	27.9	6.6	2.5	0.3	1.7	8.9	1.1	26.2
	Urbanized	17	53,584	36.6	7.5	3.7	1.2	1.6	10.2	3.4	21.6
	Surburbs	7	58,355	33.0	15.6	1.0	0.7	3.1	3.0	2.2	19.8
	Cities, market towns	19	122,989	36.5	16.9	1.6	4.5	6.7	4.5	12.5	39.4
	Bergen	1	79,120	37.1	19.1	0.8	4.0	3.9	2.2	10.6	20.5
North	Fisheries[3]	85	150,952	35.5	9.1	2.2	0.2	1.8	6.3	0.5	20.3
Norway	Low density, agric., forestry	12	17,586	33.7	6.8	2.8	–	1.6	8.4	–	23.9
	Low density, mixed	14	32,412	42.5	6.0	4.7	0.2	1.5	11.1	0.5	24.3
	Urbanized	5	15,753	41.3	12.6	4.3	0.1	2.8	10.5	0.1	22.1
	Cities, market towns	11	43,068	42.5	16.8	3.8	2.5	5.6	9.0	6.0	33.5

NOTES: Data on membership in the Conservative party were not available for:
[1]) one agricultural commune with electorate 1110, [2]) one market town with electorate
378, [3]) one fisheries commune with 1529.

Table 3.4.2. *Membership in the Christian and the Agrarian Parties in 1957 in the East, Middle and West Regions by Type of Commune*

(membership data incomplete: South and North not included)

Region	Type of comm.	Total		Christian People's party					Agrarian party				
				Memb. data for		Party vote	Members		Memb. data for		Party vote	Members	
		no. of comm.	electorate	no. of comm.	electorate in these	in 1957 p. c. of elect.	p. c. of elect.	p. c. of vote	no. of comm.	electorate	1957 p. c.	p. c. of elect.	p. c. of vote
East/ Middle	Fisheries	21	28,162	20	27,091	11.3	1.5	13.7	19	24,442	11.5	2.7	23.7
	Low density – agric., forestry	119	204,518	118	202,572	6.8	1.4	20.6	119	204,518	18.9	7.4	39.0
	– mixed	115	361,157	114	357,892	6.4	1.5	23.4	115	361,157	12.7	5.7	44.7
	Urbanized	16	68,111	16	68,111	6.1	1.1	18.1	14	64,259	5.1	2.2	44.1
	Suburbs	18	164,201	18	164,201	6.4	1.2	19.3	18	164,201	3.1	1.4	43.5
	Cities, towns (excl. Oslo)	32	203,874	32	203,874	6.1	1.1	18.7	32	203,874	0.8	0.1	9.7
West	Fisheries	57	97,391	52	89,287	21.5	2.6	12.2	57	97,391	6.0	0.8	13.5
	Low density – agric., forestry	67	69,415	61	63,579	16.6	2.6	15.7	67	69,415	23.3	4.6	19.8
	– mixed	67	131,881	62	120,824	14.6	2.8	18.9	64	126,766	13.6	3.0	22.3
	Urbanized	11	36,255	10	33,025	12.8	2.8	22.2	11	36,255	8.1	1.8	22.4
	Suburbs	5	54,619	5	54,619	8.9	1.2	13.2	5	54,619	4.2	1.0	24.1
	Cities, towns (excl. Bergen)	10	85,688	9	84,330	8.5	1.5	17.6	10	85,688	0.3	–	–

affiliated women's and youth groups. Within this category of coastal communes there is relatively little difference in geographical conditions between more peripheral and less peripheral units: other circumstances determine whether the party gets a footing in the locality.

In *Tables 3.4.1 and 3.4.2* we have followed up this analysis of differences between types of communes and given, for each region, the aggregate votes and memberships for each of the four parties for which we have had access to detailed data on both counts.

The tables give substance to our earlier discussion of the regional differences in the politics of the periphery. In the East, the Middle and the North Labour is the dominant party in the fisheries communes and in the low-density agriculture and forestry areas. In the South and the West the Liberals and the Christians dominate the least urbanized and least industrialized areas and are joined by the Agrarians in the agricultural communes: in these areas Labour is weaker than anywhere else in the country. The Conservative party is everywhere weakest in the agricultural communes and strongest in the suburbs and the cities. In the coastal communes, however, there is an interesting regional difference: in the West the Conservatives are particularly weak in such areas while in the East and the North it mobilizes more votes than any other opposition party in the same type of commune.

The frequencies of party membership vary even more from one type of commune to another. For the *Labour party* we find, as already indicated, a marked decline in the proportion of collectively affiliated members as we move from the central, industrialized areas to the periphery. What is interesting is that we find considerably lower frequencies of *individual* memberships in the centre than in part of the periphery. This is very striking in the East and the Trøndelag: compare the 5.4 % for the agriculture and forestry communes with the 1.7 % for Oslo. In the South and West the highest densities of individual memberships are found in the industrial enclaves, the lowest in the fisheries districts and in the cities. In the North there is also very little formal registration in the periphery and considerably more in the industrialized communes and the cities. If we look further to the figures for the *Conservative party* we find clear periphery-centre differences in the South, West and North but no distinct pattern in the East and the Trøndelag. It is of interest to note that the member-voter proportions are everywhere highest in the smaller cities and considerably lower in Oslo and Bergen.

The figures for the *Christian People's* party again shows that this is basically a party for the defence of the periphery: the member frequencies are higher in the fisheries communes and in the low-density communes than in the suburbs and the cities. The *Agrarian* party is naturally low in memberships in the coastal areas, but otherwise the trend is the same as for the Christians.

Table 3.5.1. *Party Membership in the Peripheral Communes: Differences for Labour and the Conservative Party according to the Level of 'Politicization' of Local Contests*

	Total communes		Vote 1957		Membership 1957					
					P. c. of electorate			P. c. of party vote		
	No.	Electorate	Labour	Cons.	Labour		Cons.	Labour		Cons.
					ind.	coll.		ind.	coll.	
Peripheral communes:										
Total	172	185,125	29.5	7.1	2.4	0.1	1.7	8.2	0.4	24.4
No lists 1955	26	19,288	21.9	8.0	0.8	0	2.0	3.6	0	25.2
One list 1955 – mostly non-pol. votes	10	12,771	18.4	8.9	1.2	0	1.6	6.5	0	18.3
– fewer	12	11,106	29.4	7.9	3.9	0	1.4	13.3	0	17.4
Two or more										
– some non-pol. votes	62	80,131	32.1	7.4	2.0	0.3	1.8	6.3	0.8	24.3
– none	62	61,829	30.7	5.9	3.4	0	1.7	11.2	0.2	27.9
Other rural communes:										
Total	508	1,327,864	37.3	10.0	3.4	1.3	2.8	9.0	3.5	27.4
No lists 1955	32	36,438	15.4	4.9	0.1	0	1.1	0.7	0	21.8
One list – mostly non-pol.	17	28,854	18.9	6.2	0.3	0	1.1	1.4	0	18.0
– fewer	19	23,851	30.6	5.3	2.3	0.1	0.9	7.5	0.3	17.4
Two or more										
– some non-pol.	134	313,355	33.6	7.8	2.9	0.5	1.9	8.7	1.3	24.8
– none	306	925,366	40.1	11.2	3.8	1.7	3.2	9.4	4.2	28.6

In *Table 3.5.1 and 3.5.2* we have gone further in this analysis of periphery vs. centre and grouped all the rural communes first by the *Thormodsæter* index and then by our simplified 'politicization' score. Labour, the Conservatives and the Agrarians all have lower members frequencies in the periphery than elsewhere. The Christians, by contrast, have slightly more members per 100 electorate in the periphery than in the rest of the rural territory. The effects of politicization on membership frequencies are again very marked for the Labour party but not quite

Table 3.5.2. *Party Membership in the Peripheral Communes: Differences for the Christian and Agrarian Parties according to the Level of 'Politicization' of Local Contests*

	Christian and Agrarian: East, West and Middle regions							
	Total comm.		Vote 1957		Membership 1957			
					P. c. of elect.		P. c. of vote	
	No.	Elect.	Chr.	Agr.	Chr.	Agr.	Chr.	Agr.
Peripheral communes:								
Total	81	82,661	13.0	16.8	2.0	3.1	14.9	17.8
No lists 1955	13	7,326	18.9	20.0	2.7	2.5	13.5	12.6
One list 1955 – mostly non-pol. votes	7	10,898	15.8	16.6	1.9	1.6	12.2	9.4
– fewer	6	4,573	14.8	12.5	2.6	0	14.6	0
Two or more – some non-pol.	20	24,515	14.2	18.2	1.8	2.7	12.2	14.5
– none	35	35,349	9.8	15.8	2.0	4.5	20.2	26.3
Other rural communes:								
Total	414	1,132,049	9.4	11.2	1.7	4.2	18.6	36.9
No lists 1955	31	34,448	23.3	13.0	2.5	1.2	10.8	9.6
One list – mostly non-pol.	15	26,975	22.2	11.4	2.8	2.7	12.5	24.0
– fewer	14	16,600	14.7	11.0	2.8	2.3	18.0	21.4
Two or more – some non-pol.	100	228,979	12.8	11.6	2.4	3.2	18.1	27.4
– none	254	825,047	7.0	11.1	1.4	4.6	20.6	41.7

so consistent for the non-socialist parties. The Agrarian party shows roughly the same trend as Labour, but the figures for the peripheral communes are more irregular. The Conservative party registers fairly high membership frequencies in the 'no lists' communes in the periphery but follows the basic pattern quite consistently in the rest of the territory. The trend for the Christian People's party again goes in the opposite direction: in the periphery the party has most members in the 'no lists' communes and in the other areas there is a particularly high concentration of members in the 'one-list' communes. By contrast to the other parties the member frequency is lowest in the most politicized of the central and the intermediate communes.

So far we have only considered membership rates per 100 electorate and disregarded the actual vote for each party. If we analyze *member-voter* proportions we get very interesting differences between the parties, but the interpretation of these differences is not always straightforward. A low member-voter proportion would normally suggest a low level of organizational efforts in the local community, but it is obvious that it also indicates a greater *number of mobilized voters per member*. In communities with an established political leadership and no serious competition there is little motive to recruit a mass membership: each member can be counted on to ensure a sizeable number of votes from his kin, his friends and others who trust him. In complex urban communities it may be found essential to recruit a mass membership but such members are not themselves likely to be able to mobilize any appreciable number of rank-and-file voters: here the crucial mobilization agencies would be such organizations as trade unions and business associations.

We find the clearest differences in member-voter proportions in the tables for the *Christians* and the *Agrarians:* for both these parties we find markedly lower proportions in the periphery and in the least politicized communes. There is much less difference for the *Conservatives:* in fact for this party we find remarkably high proportions in the 'no lists' communes, particularly in the periphery. The highest proportions, however, are clearly found in the most politicized communes. The figures for *Labour* are more complex. If we look back at *Table 3.4.1* we are struck by the low proportion of individual members per 100 voters in the cities and the suburbs: the proportions are markedly higher in the industrial enclaves and, in the East, the Middle and the South-West, also in the agriculture and forestry communes. This tells us something important about the character of the support for the party. In the countryside, if not in the coastal periphery, the party must rely heavily on active individual members and their mobilization efforts but in the urban areas the trade unions are the crucial agencies of mass support: this is the case whether the unions actually decide to support the party through collective membership – or fails to do so. If we look further to *Table 3.5.1* we find this confirmed in the comparison between the periphery and the other communes: the member-voter proportions are higher in the most politicized of the peripheral communes than in any other category. In the least politicized communes we find, as expected, very few Labour members, both absolutely and in relation to the vote: this again confirms what we said above about the character of the local Labour organizations in the coastal areas. Particularly in the North, we find a number of local leaders mobilizing support for the Labour party in national elections without actually establishing formally affiliated organizations and registering any memberships with the central secretariats.

We have analyzed these differences from another angle in *Table 3.6*. Here we have grouped the communes in the three major regions on a score for *discrepancy between the proportion of Socialist votes and the propor-*

Table 3.6. Membership in the Labour Party: Differences in Member Percentages According to the Occupational Basis of the Party (Rural Communes only)

Region	Index CP + Lab. — Ind.	Total communes		Labour party 1957			No Labour party org. in		
		No.	Electorate	vote in p.c. of elect.	members in p.c. of vote ind.	coll.	no. of comm.	electorate	Labour vote 1957
East/Middle	Under 0	34	151,580	44.3	7.5	9.1	0	0	–
	0—+12.8	100	326,523	38.7	8.1	5.4	7	7,116	29.8
	+12.8 and over	154	348,046	44.2	12.1	1.7	1	1.001	37.6
South/West	Under 0	169	358,618	25.6	6.0	1.8	53	60,675	14.7
	0—+12.8	81	90,607	25.3	11.0	0.1	22	24,389	18.1
	+12.8 and over	25	20,912	41.9	11.5	0.4	3	510	25.5
North	Under 0	6	13,529	36.5	12.6	0.0	1	1,007	18.3
	0—+12.8	21	53,287	35.3	8.4	1.2	2	2,859	24.0
	+12.8 and over	89	149,887	37.4	7.0	0.2	14	17,998	36.5

tion of economically active in industry, construction and mining. This discrepancy score gives us a very clear picture of the regional differences in the occupational basis of the Socialist parties. If we look at the marginals we see immediately that in the South and in the West only one commune in twelve has scores of + 12.8 or more; the obvious explanation is that in these regions the Socialists are only rarely able to mobilize voters outside industry and related occupations. By contrast we find in the East and in the Trøndelag that more than half of the communes score at this high level: here the Socialist parties base much of their support on forestry workers and smallholders. Finally in the North we find an even greater surplus: here there are hardly any negative scores since the parties get most of their support from smallholders and fishermen.

If we look further to the membership proportions at each level of discrepancy we again find striking regional differences. In the East/Middle and the South/West regions we find a confirmation of the trend we noted above: the Labour party relies primarily on its union channels in the areas where most of its vote comes from workers in industry, construction and mining, but has activated greater proportions of members in the agriculture and forestry communes where it mobilizes sizeable bodies of voters outside the reach of the unions. In the North, however, the tendency is in the opposite direction: the member proportions are *lowest* in the communes where the party gets the largest share of its vote outside industry and related occupations. Most of these are peripheral fisheries communes where the party finds it easy to obtain support in national elections but where it has proved difficult to establish stable local organizations and to recruit any sizeable membership. In these communes it is in fact very difficult to pin down any structural factors which might account for the presence or absence of local party organizations (see our comments on *Table 3.3* above): much seems to depend on personalities and within-commune factions. To get some control for this factor of local organization we have added in *Table 3.6* information on the number and size of communes without any local Labour party organizations. The greatest numbers of communes without such organizations are, characteristically, found *in the 'negative-discrepancy' periphery of the South/West and the 'positive-discrepancy' periphery of the North.* In the South/West the communes without local organizations have a markedly lower Labour vote than the others: 14.7 % vs. 27.8 % for the communes scoring negatively. In the North, by contrast, the absence or presence of local organizations hardly make any difference: we get 36.5 % vs. 37.5 % for the communes scoring highest on the discrepancy index.

This review of differences in organizational activation in the periphery throws light on the structure of the Norwegian party system.

We may schematically describe the system as the resultant of three major conflicts in the political community:

– first a *capital-provinces* and a *centre-periphery conflict,* originally expressed in the opposition of the 'Left' against the 'Right', later reflected in the consistent defence of the moral and cultural values of the periphery by the Christian People's party;

– secondly, and closely related to the first opposition, an *urban-rural conflict,* primarily expressed in the development of a distinct Agrarian party but also reflected in the strains between the urban and the rural wings of Labour and the old 'Left', the Liberals.

– and thirdly, a *class conflict* between industrial workers and the rural proletariat on the one side and the business community on the other.

These conflicts have been superimposed on each other over time and have generated complex processes of accommodation both within party organizations and in the alignments of voters. This 'criss-crossing' of conflict lines in the system has become a central theme in our studies of Norwegian politics and we hope in subsequent publications to be able to give further details on the processes at work. The data on local party organizations and memberships have opened up new avenues of analysis and added important information on the conditions for the maintenance of territorial opposition and the emergence of functional and economic party conflicts.

IV. *The Recruitment of Candidates and the Election of Representatives*
We have so far discussed data on local differences in the distribution of the electorate on *three* strata:
– non-voters,
– rank-and-file voters,
– party members.

We shall now review briefly a set of data on local differences in the rates of recruitment to the *top strata* in the political hierarchy: the *candidates* for office and the elected *representatives.*

We shall focus this discussion on differences between central and peripheral areas in the recruitment of political personnel among *women:* the last category of citizens to be fully enfranchised in the system.

Women became eligible for local office in 1901 and were allowed to enter the competition for the *Storting* in 1909.

The statistics for local elections do not allow us to analyze recruitment rates for *candidates,* but we get a reliable index progress in the activation of women from the figures for *alternates* and *representatives* on local councils from 1901 to 1959 in the Table on p. 216.

These time series tell us a great deal about conditions for the activation of women politics. We saw in *Table 1.1* that it did not take very long to mobilize the women in the cities for electoral action and that even in the countryside the turnout for women has slowly approached the level of the men. The contrast with the figures for the recruitment to local councils is

	Alternates on local councils				Representatives			
	Rural communes		Urban communes		Rural		Urban	
	Totals	Women per 1000	Totals	Women per 1000	Totals	Women per 1000	Totals	Women per 1000
1901	9,496	6	1,129	93	10,476	1	1,952	43
1907	9,823	10	1,535	89	10,876	2	1,980	60
1910	10,318	17	1,777	113	11,136	4	1,980	80
1913	10,484	12	1,888	113	11,393	3	2,064	76
1916	10,512	11	1,793	116	11,683	2	2,064	80
1919	10,447	9	1,917	91	11,908	3	2,084	60
1922	10,929	8	2,134	82	12,192	1	2,252	57
1925	14,971	9	2,612	76	12,402	3	2,252	54
1928	15,346	10	2,518	92	12,547	5	2,252	57
1931	16,212	13	2,583	75	12,672	4	2,260	56
1934	17,311	19	2,627	80	12,715	7	2,260	63
1937	17,614	32	2,605	117	12,788	14	2,268	91
1945	18,225	53	2,754	133	12,822	22	2,256	103
1947	18,472	61	2,818	147	12,830	34	2,272	130
1951	17,766	86	2,780	169	12,896	45	2,336	133
1955	19,360	119	2,808	179	14,014	52	2,404	138
1959	19,125	113	2,789	179	13,978	50	2,370	120

indeed striking: there was very little progress from 1901 until 1937 and the maximum reached in the fifties was one woman for every seventh representative in the cities and one woman for every twentieth in the countryside.

This contrast between rates of mobilization and rates of activation into politics reflects basic differences in the *cost of the alternatives* in the two cases. Electoral turnout is a matter of co-operation, an act of compliance: the participation of one citizen does not exclude that of another. Nominations and elections are *competitive* and it took a long time before women could be motivated to break with established cultural norms and face such public ordeals. Women were traditionally socialized to roles within the household or within such extensions of the household as the family firm. The head of the household represented it in the public affairs of the community and this norm was only superficially affected by the introduction of universal suffrage for women on a par with men. The movement for women's rights had urban and secular roots and it took a long time before it gained a footing in the countryside. Women tended to channel most of their civic activities through voluntary associations and community service organizations rather than into the competitive struggles for political office. Our figures show that a few women entered local councils immediately after the introduction of universal suffrage but this was only of numerical importance in the cities. It is significant that it took practically a generation before there was any sizeable increase in these early recruitment rates. There was no important change until 1937 and the elections immediately after the War: then the rates rose very rapidly for several years, more rapidly, in fact, in the countryside than in the cities. This rise in recruitment rates reflected the increasing importance of women's organizations and the determined efforts of the parties to broaden their mass basis. The cultural barriers against participation were gradually breaking down but there were still only very few who actually crossed the barriers to face the strains of public life.

Recruitment rates may be analyzed from two angles: they clearly reflect the *supply* of politically alert and articulate participants from the given category of citizens but the range of variation is also limited by the *number of structurally set openings for formal participation*. Survey analyses have given us clues to the sources of *supply:* women are more likely to be organizationally active in politics if they have some education beyond the primary school and if they themselves or their husbands are engaged in non-manual work. We also know that there are marked differences between local communities: the percentage of active women is markedly higher in the urbanized and the industrialized communes than in the agricultural and other primary-economy areas (Rokkan, 1960: 2).

Sample surveys of the ordinary size do not, however, allow us to carry out any detailed tests of the effects of the structural conditions on the rate of recruitment. Here our ecological archive adds important elements of information but a definitive analysis of the interaction of supply and opportunities in determining the actual recruitment rates is not possible at the present juncture: this would require sample surveys in a set of communes systematically selected to represent significant differences in political structure.

The numbers of seats on local councils vary with the size of the commune but even so the number of openings per 100 electorate is markedly higher in smaller communes than in larger ones. Theoretically this should make for *less* competition for office in the small communes in the periphery and therefore increase the chances of recruitment from among women. The actual figures, however, go consistently in the opposite direction.

The extremely small numbers of women in elective offices makes any commune-by-commune analysis of little interest before 1945. The analyses we can report all refer to elections after that year.

Lisbeth Broch [142] has classified the local units by the *size of their councils* and found very marked differences in the per cent women recruited at different levels of each political hierarchy in 1951.

What is interesting here is that the differences between the smallest and the largest units increase so markedly as we move from one level to another. There are in every commune a great many openings for participation on boards and committees dealing with specified policy sectors and to these

| | Small councils: under 20 repr. | | Intermediate: 20–40. | | Large: over 40. | |
	Rural	Urban	Rural	Urban	Rural	Urban
Per cent women of all members of						
– local *boards* and *committees*	11.9	–	11.8	17.5	13.5	18.4
– local *councils*	3.2	–	5.2	10.3	11.8	15.7
– local *executives* (formannskap)	0.8	–	2.4	4.5	8.5	15.2

we find a high rate of recruitment from among women even in the smallest rural communes. By contrast, we find a very marked difference at the level of the communal executive: in the smallest rural communes we hardly find one woman for every hundredth member while in the larger cities the ratio is 1:7. The actual chances of representation are in fact much larger in the smallest communes than in the cities, but the social, educational and cultural barriers are so much stronger in the traditional environments of the rural periphery and make for decisively lower supplies of potential recruits.

We have been able to throw further light on these differences through a classification of the results for 1955 by the standard typology of communes used by the Central Bureau of Statistics:

	Alternates: [143] per cent women	*Representatives:* per cent women
Low density		
primary economy	7.6	3.6
mixed	11.7	5.6
industrial	11.8	6.2
Urbanized		
mixed	12.4	6.8
industrial	16.9	8.5
suburban	17.3	9.8
Cities and market towns	17.9	13.8

We find the lowest recruitment ratio in the primary-economy communes: in the communes where cultural traditions and economic necessities still combine to keep women tied to their household chores and severely limit their possibilities of community activity. The ratio increases markedly with the extent of industrialization and urbanization. This fits in with our findings for mobilization: we find the same ecological differences at the highest as well as the lowest level of participation. What we cannot determine from these data is whether the increase in recruitment is exclusively due to the greater number of women with some education and with non-primary and non-manual occupations or whether there are differences in the cultural environment which increase the chances of participation within all or most categories of women. We hope that further controls by the per cent educated beyond primary school will enable us to settle questions of this kind.

We also looked into centre-periphery differences in the *recruitment of candidates at elections to the Storting*.

A woman was for the first time elected to the *Storting* in 1921. Since then the recruitment rates have progressed as follows:

	Candidates		Alternates		Representatives	
Year	Total	Per cent women	Total	Per cent women	Total	Per cent women
1921	1264	4.1	150	3.3	150	0.7
1924	1601	4.6	239	4.2	150	0.0
1927	1306	5.1	236	5.5	150	0.7
1930	1378	6.5	239	5.0	150	1.5
1933	1811	6.5	237	5.9	150	2.0
1936	1756	9.7	236	8.9	150	0.7
1948	1518	13.2	240	13.8	150	4.7
1949	1704	16.4	230	18.7	150	4.7
1953	1518	19.2	298	22.5	150	4.7
1957	1620	17.7	298	22.8	150	4.7

Again we find very little change in the rates until the mid-thirties. A clear upward trend got under way in 1936 and continued from 1945 onwards. The increase was particularly marked for the recruitment to positions *just below* the top of hierarchy: for the *alternates* to those regularly elected. Women were increasingly nominated to high positions on the party lists but had normally to take 'second place' behind the male leaders in each party. Such rankings may often have resulted from deliberate strategies of vote mobilization but cultural norms have clearly also influenced the decisions of the nominating bodies.

We have inquired further into questions of differential rank-ordering in a detailed analysis of the nominations of 1957 (Valen, 1967). Classifying all candidates by their commune of residence we find the same over-all differences for nominations to national elections as we established for the recruitment to local councils: fewer women than men from the primary-economy areas, many more from the urbanized areas and the cities. But this *does not hold for nominations to positions just below those of the elected:* to these, women are recruited at roughly the same rate whatever the structure of the commune. The only consistent differences between types of communes appear in the recruitment to *lower* positions on each list: here, we may conjecture, the nominating bodies are less concerned with mobilization strategy and more with establishing some rough representation of the active and articulate leadership in each area within the constituency (Valen, 1958).

Standard typology	All candidates [144]			Lower-placed			First and second alternates			Regular representatives		
	M	W	Ratio	M	W	Ratio	M	W	Ratio	M	W	Ratio
Low density												
– primary economy	341	42	8.1	279	35	8.0	27	7	3.9	25	0	–
– mixed, industrial	414	77	5.4	318	63	5.0	41	9	4.6	42	4	10.5
Urbanized												
– mixed, industrial	115	30	3.8	92	29	3.2	7	1	7.0	13	0	–
– suburban	98	24	4.1	79	21	3.8	7	2	3.5	8	1	8.0
Cities, towns	343	112	3.1	260	92	2.8	30	12	2.5	41	5	8.2

Given the tendency to rank women second behind the top leadership one might suspect that the difference between primary-economy communes and cities simply results from differences in size. A small commune will either have no or at most one candidate on the constituency list for a given party while a town or a city is likely to have two or more: this would make the odds against the nomination of a woman from a small commune much higher than against the inclusion of a woman from a city. It is true that the size of electorates count in the nomination process and that small peripheral communes are less likely to recruit any candidates than larger ones: for details see *Table 4.1.* But if we control for this factor by restricting our comparison to communes which recruited a maximum of one candidate per party list, we still get a clear difference in the sex ratios: highest in the fisheries communes, middling, but with marked local variations, in the low density agriculture and forestry areas, and lowest in the urbanized communes and the cities.

The same over-all pattern is found for all the parties but there are a number of fluctuations resulting from differences in the clustering of adjacent communes within each constituency. With minor exceptions, the lowest sex ratios occur within the urbanized communes and the cities and within these again we find the higher ratios in the lists of the working-class

Table 4.1. *Nominations of Lower-placed Candidates by Sex 1957: Control of the Number of Candidates per Commune*

Type of commune	Periphery score	Communes classif. by max. no. of candidates per party list[1]						M-W ratios of nomination to lower places:							
		No cand.		Max. one cand.		Two or more		Max. one cand. per list				Two or more cand.			
		Per cent of		Per cent of		Per cent of									
		all comm.	total elect.	all comm.	total elect.	all comm.	total elect.	Total	Soc.	Middle	Cons.	Total	Soc.	Middle	Cons.
Fisheries	Not periphery	33.7	21.2	58.1	56.3	8.1	22.5	7.2	(18:0)	4.7	4.5	10.5	(7:0)	(9:0)	4.0
	Mod. "	30.9	25.9	66.7	71.8	2.4	2.3	5.2	(10:0)	5.7	1.3	1.0	–	1.0	–
	Extr. "	35.7	31.3	64.3	68.7	0.0	0.0	11.7	3.5	19.0	(7:0)	–	–	–	–
Low density,															
– agric., for.	Not periphery	35.4	23.1	60.4	69.6	4.2	7.3	4.2	6.0	5.2	2.0	8.0	(6:0)	5.0	(2:0)
	Mod. "	43.5	32.7	56.5	67.3	0.0	0.0	20.5	7.0	26.0	(7:0)	–	–	–	–
	Extr. "	47.4	47.6	52.6	52.4	0.0	0.0	2.3	1.0	2.5	(1:0)	–	–	–	–
– mixed, ind.[2]	High access.	15.2	6.7	68.3	66.6	16.5	26.7	4.2	5.2	3.3	5.3	3.1	6.5	2.2	4.0
	Med. "	17.5	9.4	71.4	68.0	11.1	22.6	4.0	3.5	3.6	6.0	3.5	1.7	4.5	2.0
	Low "	37.0	24.1	60.5	65.1	2.5	10.8	4.1	4.0	5.3	2.5	(6:0)	(3:0)	(2:0)	(1:0)
Urbanized															
– mixed		0.0	0.0	73.3	62.9	26.7	37.1	2.5	1.7	2.8	3.0	2.8	(4:0)	2.0	2.0
– industrial		14.1	0.0	71.4	71.2	28.6	28.8	2.7	5.5	1.7	3.0	5.0	6.0	(3:0)	(0:1)
– suburbs		0.0	0.0	50.0	35.0	50.0	65.0	6.2	(12:0)	3.5	2.0	2.5	3.5	2.1	1.6
Cities, towns		0.0	0.9	45.3	11.2	40.6	87.9	2.9	4.3	2.6	1.8	2.4	3.4	1.9	1.6

NOTES: [1] Here all candidates (also 'higher-placed') are included.
[2] Since only 7 communes qualify as 'peripheral' among communes of this type we have here subdivided by the 'accessibility score' used in *Table 1.2.*

Table 4.2. *Differences in the Sex Ratios in Nominations according to the 'Politicization' of the Commune: Only for Rural Communes with Maximum one Candidate per List in 1957*

	Total communes		No candidates		One or more cand.		Lower placed candidates: only communes with max. one per list.											
							Total			Soc.			Middle			Cons.		
	No.	Electorate	P.c. of comm.	P.c. of elect.	P.c. of comm.	P.c. of elect.	M	W	Ratio	M	W	Ratio	M	W	Ratio	M	W	Ratio
Peripheral communes																		
No party lists (loc. el. 1955)	22	23,877	36.4	37.2	63.6	36.0	10	0		2	0		5	0		2	0	
One list	26	19,288	69.2	64.0	30.8	62.8	14	4	3.5	0	1		10	3	3.3	4	0	
Several lists																		
− non-pol. votes	62	80,131	25.8	19.2	74.2	80.8	49	9	5.6	15	2	7.5	27	4	6.8	7	3	2.3
− no non-pol.	62	61,829	38.7	32.5	61.3	67.5	46	1	46.0	8	1	8.0	30	0		6	0	
Other rural communes																		
No party lists	32	36,438	53.1	50.7	46.9	49.3	11	1	11.0	1	0		8	1	8.0	2	0	
One	36	52,705	44.5	33.7	55.5	66.3	18	5	3.6	7	1	7.0	9	4	2.3	2	0	
Several																		
− non-pol. votes	134	313,355	20.1	9.6	79.9	90.4	132	20	6.6	36	4	9.0	67	13	5.1	21	2	10.5
− no non-pol.	306	925,366	23.2	9.7	76.8	90.3	288	81	3.6	78	16	4.9	161	46	3.5	36	17	2.1

parties and the lowest in the lists of the Conservative party: this clearly reflects differences in the levels of supply of politically active women in different strata of the electorate.[145]

We have introduced a breakdown by the *level of politicization* to check whether the increasing mobilization under party competition has led to any change in the traditional distributions of political roles. In *Table 4.2* we have classified the peripheral and the other communes according to the number of party lists presented and the size of the vote cast for non-partisan lists at the preceding local election. The over-all sex-ratio for candidates from the periphery is of course high: 8.5 as against 3.9 for other rural areas. But there is no straight pattern of differences by level of politicization. Within the non-socialist parties women seem to rate more of a chance to get nominated from peripheral communes if the parties have *not* entrenched themselves locally: women well known through their community services may not be so easily opposed in the nominating bodies at the *fylke* level if there are no fully authorized party spokesmen from the local commune. This, of course, is an interpretation which will need to be further documented.

Our findings again demonstrate the importance of a multivariate approach. The nomination decision is the resultant of a number of pressures within a pre-set framework leaving few degrees of freedom: the supply of visibly active party workers is one factor, the marginal utility of extra votes from women is another, the established geographical balance within each constituency is a third.

It is not possible within the confines of this chapter to discuss all these sources of variation. Our primary concern has been to throw light on the lags in the activation of the last entrants into the political arena, the women, and we think we have gone far enough in this context to demonstrate the consistency of the differences in recruitment rates between central and peripheral areas of the national territory. Some, but not all, the differences highlighted in this chapter might have been more fully accounted for if we had been able to get access to data on the educational and the occupational background of each participant at each of the levels distinguished, but whatever we could do in that direction would not affect the basic ecological design: the institutions of mass suffrage have to function in geographically, culturally and economically very different conditions and these conditions tend to affect both the *range* of alternatives open to the enfranchised citizens and the *cost* of each alternative. We hope in subsequent publications to spell this out further: here we have been primarily concerned to review descriptively the basic bodies of information at our disposal.

NOTES

[128] Details on the programme will be found in (Rokkan, 1960: 5).

[129] For general discussions, see (Tingsten, 1937) and (Lipset, 1960; Ch. VI). U. S. data are discussed in (Lane, 1959) pp. 46–52 and pp. 265–269.

[130] This breakdown is based on a detailed analysis of tax records for 1876, *Statistiske Oplysninger om de fremsatte Stemmerettsforslags Virkning*. Christiania, Statistisk Centralbureau C. No. 14., 1877, pp. 340–341; for further details see (Rokkan, 1967).

[131] See *Norges Officielle Statistik* III, 306. Kristiania 1898, p. 8.

[132] Sources: (Hartwig, 1928; Hartwig, 1931). For 1953: 'Repräsentativstatistik der Bundestagswahl 1953 (Ohne Bayern und Rheinland-Pfalz)', *Stat. der Bundesrep. Deutschland* 100 (2) 1955: 39. Maurice Duverger (Duverger, 1955: 1) had access to some of these data for his work, but does not discuss them in developmental terms, cf. also (Bremme, 1956: pp. 45–50).

[133] It is of interest to note that in a country such as *Italy*, where the Catholic Church could exert a great deal of electoral pressure, women were mobilized as rapidly in the countryside as in the cities as soon as they were given the vote, cf. (Arcari, 1949), especially Table VII–VIII: these give data for the first election under universal suffrage (1946) broken down by size of community. Similar findings have been established for a number of countries characterized either by strongly entrenched Catholic churches or large-scale land holdings.

[134] This classification in the census tabulations has since been criticized and revised, cf. (Myklebost, 1960: pp. 23–48). For our limited purposes it seemed justified to retain the old classification, but much more precise differentiations can no doubt be established once the 1960 census data have been classified according to the new criteria.

[135] The figures for elections before 1915 are of course affected by the differences in the timing of suffrage extensions for the two types of elections: see above. The total electorate was until 1937 regularly lower in local elections than in national ones because of the two-year residence requirement. Given the well-established tendency for movers to stay away at the polls, the turnout might therefore have been expected to be higher in local than in national elections: the figures, however, go in the opposite direction.

[136] The figures are to some extent affected by changes in the electoral law over this period. The provision for citizen initiative was abolished in 1919: from then on PR was automatic as soon as two or more lists had been presented to the electoral authorities. From 1910 to 1955 it was possible for separate *sogn* (parishes) within a commune to opt for plurality elections even though PR had been established for the remainder of the commune. The motive for such separate arrangements was invariably to ensure territorial representation of isolated areas within the commune. Another solution to the demand for territorial representation was the division of communes into smaller administrative units: the table shows an increase in the number of communes by close to one-fourth from 1901 to 1937. With the improvement of communications and the pressure for administrative rationalization since 1945, the trend has been reversed: a number of mergers are currently under way and these can in most cases be expected to accelerate 'politicization' (Hjellum, 1967: 1 and 2).

[137] In this version of the index we have, for simplicity's sake, grouped together at the lowest level of politicization the 19 communes which stuck to plurality elections in 1955 (cf. the entry in *Table 2*.1) and 39 others where there were PR elections between two or more local lists, but *no lists* tied in with the nationally registered parties. The median turnout in this second group was considerably higher than in the first.

[138] Cf. an interesting parallel in the United States: the analysis of 'local vote delivery' in a community in New York State in (Vidich, 1960: Ch. 8).

[139] For a general discussion of the use of official statistics vs. sample surveys in the study of participation see (Rokkan, 1962: 2).

[140] In Sweden, it should be relatively easy to carry out such studies since the parties report their membership regularly to the authorities, cf. (Sköld, 1958, pp. 20, 84–88, 141, 204, 270) and Statistiska Centralbyrån. *Riksdagsmannavalen åren 1959–60:* II. Stockholm 1961, pp. 66–67.

[141] Earlier information on party membership published under our programme was misleading on one important point. We had erroneously assumed a total of 163,000 Labour members *plus* the collectively affiliated, but these were in fact included in the total, cf. S. Rokkan. 'Electoral activity, party membership and organizational influence'. *Acta Sociol.* 4, 1959: 25–37, especially Table 1, and S. Rokkan and A. Campbell *op. cit.* p. 73, H. Valen and D. Katz. 'An Electoral Contest in a Norwegian Province', in M. Janowitz *ed. Community Political Systems,* Glencoe, Free Press, 1961, p. 217. These figures were corrected in later printings, cf. Chapter 11 below.

[142] (Broch, 1953: pp. 49–56, Tables pp. 35–45). The data on the boards and the executives are based on questionnaire returns from 60 out of 64 urban communes and 596 out of 680 rural ones.

[143] Calculated on the basis of the number of representatives and the number of lists presented. Direct data by commune are not available in official statistics.

[144] Includes 46 top candidates on lists which did not attract the necessary minimum of votes required for representation. Excludes 24 candidates resident outside the *fylke* in which they were nominated.

[145] For other evidence of the high level of participation by women in this party, see Chapter 12 below.

SEVEN

Electoral Mobilization, Party Competition, and National Integration

The histories of the Western European polities since the French Revolution have a number of traits in common: all extended the right of political participation to wider and wider circles of their citizens and finally, with few exceptions, introduced universal and equal suffrage for women as well as for men; all developed, some of them quite early, others much more slowly and erratically, nationwide party organizations based on mass memberships; and all have experienced, largely as a result of the universalization of suffrage and the growth of mass parties, a decline in strictly territorial politics and an increasing emphasis on functional cleavages cutting across the traditional divisions into localities and provinces.

For most countries of the West these trends can be documented statistically, from official electoral counts, from party records, from local newspapers. The introduction of universal suffrage, the standardization of electoral procedures and the equalization of votes led to the production of enormous masses of data for analysis and eventually stimulated the development of a discipline of political statistics. Most of the analyses carried out within this field have limited themselves to single elections and to particular localities and constituencies, but there have been indications in recent years of greater interest in long-term analyses of processes of electoral change and in systematic studies of variations in sequences of change within given nations.[146] The increasing interest in the development of data archives and in the use of electronic computers in processing historical information can be expected to accelerate the production of diachronic as

Origin: This chapter was originally written for a volume published under the auspices of the Committee on Comparative Politics: *Political Parties and Political Development,* eds. J. LaPalombara and M. Weiner (Princeton University Press, 1966; Princeton Paperback, 1969).
I am indebted to Joseph LaPalombara for his critical reading of an earlier version of this chapter. I have also benefited from comments by W. J. M. Mackenzie, Richard Rose and Agne Gustafsson.

well as synchronic analyses of political data [147] and the findings of such analyses can again be expected to have a profound impact on current conceptualization and theorizing in the field of comparative politics.

In this chapter I shall describe a few promising lines of developmental analysis and suggest some possible tasks for systematic comparisons across polities. I shall first summarize the result of the studies we have so far been able to carry out on developments in Norway and shall then discuss a few possibilities of systematic comparisons of rates and directions of change after the breakdown of traditional and absolutist systems of rule in the nineteenth century.

I. Four Steps of Change

Our attempt to piece together a statistical history of Norwegian politics is based on data and analyses bearing on four distinct steps in a complex process of change: the formal *incorporation* of strata and categories of residents kept out of the system under the original criteria; the *mobilization* of these enfranchised citizens in electoral contests; their *activation* into direct participation in public life; the breakdown of the traditional systems of local rule through the entry of nationally organized parties into municipal elections, what we call the process of *politicization*.

For each of these steps we have tried to formulate a series of questions and done some initial work on the sifting of potential data.

One set of questions concerns the process of formal incorporation: What were the original criteria of political citizenship and through what sequences of initiatives, delaying tactics, and compromises were they transformed into universalistic rules of participation? What were the economic, educational, social, and organizational characteristics of the adult residents kept out of the system under the original criteria and what were the characteristics of those first admitted and those last admitted in the subsequent process of universalization? Did the rules affect all communities of the nation in roughly the same way, or did differences in socio-economic structure affect the local balance between the enfranchised and the politically underprivileged?

Another set of questions concerns the electoral mobilization and activation of the last to be enfranchised: How far had they already been organizationally mobilized before they were given the right to vote? How long did it take to mobilize them for electoral participation once they had the vote; and how quickly were citizens from these lately underprivileged strata recruited into organizational work in the political parties, into candidacies and public offices? Did this process of mobilization and activation move forward at roughly the same rate throughout the national territory, or were there marked differences in the rate of change between the central, economically advanced localities and the geographical and economic peripheries?

And a final set of questions concerns the process of politicization after the establishment of mass suffrage: How long did it take the political parties to establish themselves as mass organizations through the recruitment of dues-paying members and to entrench themselves in each locality of the nation, whether through the operation of affiliated branches or through direct participation in contests for municipal offices? How far did the peripheries of the nation lag behind its central areas in this process of politicization? To what extent was this politicization of the periphery accelerated through the development of polarized conflicts between established and underprivileged strata and to what extent was it slowed down through the persistence of local and regional traditions of territorial and cultural defence against the expanding urban centres?

Our analyses are based on six types of sources:

1. Published records of debates, deliberations, and decisions on changes in electoral laws and regulations.

2. Official statistical data, some published, others archived, from elections, referenda, censuses, and other enumerations.

3. Biographical data, from a variety of published and unpublished sources, on the background of candidates and elected representatives at the local as well as the national level.

4. Data from the party press and the party secretariats on the establishment of local branches and the sizes of local memberships.

5. Data from organizations and associations on their local branches and their memberships.

6. Data from sample surveys, some nationwide, others confined to selected localities.

The initial analyses of long-term trends simply consisted of rearrangements and recomputations of the officially established statistics for elections. We are currently at work on the development of an historical archive of ecological data on Norwegian politics (Rokkan, 1968: 6) and hope in this way to be able to pursue much more detailed analyses of variations between localities in the rates and directions of change. This punched-card archive was originally built up to allow multivariate analyses of local variations in turnout and party strength for the elections from 1945 onward, but efforts are now under way to extend the time series for each local unit. We are also making efforts to extend the range of data for each unit: we have so far punched on decks for each commune not only data from local and national elections but also data from censuses, from educational, agricultural, industrial, and fiscal statistics, data from a church attendance count, data on local party organizations and memberships as well as on nominees to party lists for parliament. We have found such data archiving an essential tool in our cooperative research work, and we hope in the years to come to expand the scope of our archive both backward to the earliest partisan contests and forward to the oncoming local and national elections. We think our experiences justify us in recommending that similarly conceived archives be set up in other countries of the West, and we are convinced that the greater control of the data masses achieved through such archiving will facilitate systematic comparisons of rates of development in different countries.

II. A Statistical History of Norwegian Politics

Our analysis of the process of political development in Norway concentrates on three phases:

1. The period of initial mobilization from 1879, the first partisan election, to 1900, the first election under manhood suffrage.

2. The period of politicization and polarization from 1900 to 1935, the year the Labour party came to power.

3. The period after 1945, a period of ideological *détente* at the centre and continued mobilization and politicization in the periphery.

This is not the place to give details of the findings so far established on each of these points: for further information the reader is referred to a number of articles and reports published under our program of electoral research.[148] Much remains to be done to map the variations within the national territory over all the elections since the beginning of competitive politics, but some results already stand out as significant, whether judged within the context of the history of the one nation or judged in the framework of a comparative analysis of similar time sequences across a variety of nations.

The Process of Formal Incorporation

The Constitution of 1814 gave Norway the most democratic system of representation in Europe. All the freehold peasants and most of the lease-holders were given the right to vote. In an overwhelmingly rural nation of small holdings this meant that practically half of all men over 25 were enfranchised.[149] It took decades, however, before the peasants were mobilized to make effective use of their electoral power: they tended to vote for their betters, the King's officials and the local lawyers and teachers, and they were for a long time, in fact up to the 1870's, content to leave the affairs of the nation in the hands of the educated administrators of the realm and the privileged burghers of the chartered cities. There were many signs of incipient mobilization, however: first through religious revival movements against the established state church, subsequently through a variety of cultural movements, not least through the development of a rural 'counter-language' against the standard imposed by the urban centres, and, finally, through a general process of monetization and urbanization, a gradual breakdown of the isolated pockets of subsistence communities in the countryside, and the growth of complex systems of cross-local exchange and interdependence. The conditions for rapid and effective political mobilization were there: a literate peasantry, a growing network of voluntary associations, increasing facilities for cross-local communication through the mails and the press, a steady increase in the spread of urban commodities and ideas toward the periphery, a growing flow of migrants at all levels of the social hierarchy from the rural areas to the cities. The decisive thrust toward power came in the 1870's: an alliance of urban radicals and mobilized peasantry challenged the supremacy of the King's officials and finally won out in 1884.

The decisive thrust toward universal democracy came in the years from 1876 to 1882: the turnout level rose from 55 percent to 83 percent in the cities and from 41 percent to 70 percent in the countryside (Rokkan, 1967: Tab. 1.1; Danielsen, 1964: pp. 47–77). This spurt of mobilization produced the first extension of the suffrage: taxable income was added as a new criterion. While the old rules of 1814 had tended to favour the owners of land and real estate in a primary economy, the new criterion reflected the increasing importance of liquid money in a growing economy: the result was that more than half of the working class men in the largest cities were enfranchised as against only a quarter of the landless proletariat in the rural areas.[150] The electoral reform of 1884 eased the most mobilized of the workers into the political system and left the majority of the under-privileged in the countryside still disfranchised. This was a decision of great importance for the subsequent history of electoral mobilization and alignment in Norway.

There was a brief lull in the process of mobilization after the first extension of the suffrage in 1884, but the new entrants soon made use of their rights: by 1894 the turnout level was at an all-time peak of 91 percent in the cities and 83 percent in the rural areas. This second thrust of mobilization again led to an extension of the suffrage: a reform voted in 1898 introduced near-universal suffrage for all male citizens aged 25 and over.

The Lag in Rural Mobilization

The first result of the introduction of manhood suffrage was a distinct drop in the over-all turnout levels: 63 percent in the cities and 52 percent in the rural areas. The statistics do not allow direct calculations of the turnout for the new entrants but it can be estimated that the differences between the entrants and the established electorate were of the order indicated in *Table 1*.

The rural proletariat clearly lagged behind in the process of mobiliza-tion: the over-all urban-rural difference for the men stayed over 10 percentage points until 1909 and remained at the 5 to 10 point level until 1930. The rural lag was further accentuated through the enfranchisement of women. When women were first given the vote, in the local elections of 1901, only 9.5 percent of them actually voted in the rural areas. When

Table 1. *Estimated Differences in Turnout between old Electorate and new Entrants, by Cities and Rural Areas, 1900–1903*

	Cities			Rural Areas		
	1897 %	1900 %	1903 %	1897 %	1900 %	1903 %
The established electorate						
actual (1897) and estimated (1900–1903)	78	78	78	68	68	68
New entrants (automatically registered)						
estimated turnout	—	44	52	—	33	28

women first entered national politics, in 1909 under an income criterion and in 1915 under the same rules as the men, the rural lag persisted. The discrepancies in turnout levels between cities and country districts stayed at around 20 percentage points for fully two decades and the decisive breakthrough in rural mobilization did not come until the election of 1930, a contest fought largely over issues of fundamentalism and secularism. Even in the elections after World War II the turnout of rural women has remained 8 to 11 percentage points lower than for the women in the cities. Ecological analyses of differences between communes show persistent differences in turnout between central and peripheral communes in the countryside: the over-all turnout is highest in the suburban and the industrialized communes and some 15 to 20 percentage points lower in the primary economy communes along the coast and in the mountainous fjords. The gap in turnout levels between men and women has practically disappeared in the cities and the urbanized countryside but is still very marked in the peripheral areas.

A number of factors account for the persistence of such differences in the Norwegian system: the fragmented geography, the dispersed population and the difficulties of physical access to the schoolhouses and the other places of voting, the occupational handicaps of the fishermen and the seasonal workers, the strong rural traditions of male dominance in community roles (Cf. Chapter 6, above, pp. 183–191). Our analyses indicate marked territorial differences in the economic and the social costs of political participation but also suggest concomitant differences in the incentives offered and the pressures exerted to overcome such cost barriers. The turnout in the peripheral areas is low not only because it takes more effort from the average resident to cast his vote but also because the local political leaders, being less directly tied in with the provincial and the national party organizations, will only rarely assign a high marginal value to the last mobilized vote (Ch. 6 above, pp. 191–199). We cannot study the time lags in the process of mobilization without a detailed mapping of the local entrenchment of party organizations: When were the first members recruited? When was a regular branch set up? When did the party first appear as a distinct unit in the election of local councillors?

The Process of Politicization

Our study of the spread of partisan competitiveness from the central to the peripheral localities has not yet taken us very far toward complete coverage, but even our early findings appear to be of great interest in a comparative perspective.

We have not yet been able to assemble records of the growth of party organizations and party memberships by locality, but the official statistical publications at least allow us to trace changes over time in the number and character of the lists presented at local elections. Under the system in force in Norway after 1896 the first sign of incipient politicization would be a change from the traditional single-list plurality vote to the modern system of competitive lists and proportional representation. This meant that local leaders were no longer certain of their traditional clientèle and had to organize in politically distinct groups to maintain control of municipal affairs. Three-quarters of the cities had reached this initial level of politicization at the very first election under universal suffrage, but only one quarter of the rural districts. By 1910 practically all the urban units of any size had changed to PR but only one-third of the rural ones. There was then a period of rapid rural politicization. The industrialization of a number of isolated localities in the countryside, the sudden increases in the monetization of the primary economy as a result of the war, the spread of socialist and syndicalist ideas into the recently mobilized rural proletariat – all these developments intensified the conflicts within the communes and made it impossible to retain the traditional system of single-list voting. The splits in the working-class movement in the 1920's seem to have halted the process of rural politicization for a while but the gigantic thrust of the Labour party in the crisis years of the 1930's finally reduced the number of traditionally organized communes to a mere handful. By 1937 only 31 out of a total of 682 communes were still in this 'prepolitical' state, by 1945, 32; by 1951, 29; and by 1963, 10.

This, however, was only a first step toward full politicization: A commune might have introduced competitive PR elections and still maintain purely territorial contests between lists for its constituent districts. The next step would normally be the introduction of *one* list identified with a nationally registered party, the next again *two* such lists and the final step a completely partisan contest solely between such national lists. A classification of the rural communes *(Table 2)* for four local elections after the Second World War will demonstrate how far this process of politicization has gone in Norway:

The process of politicization seems to have reached a plateau in the years from 1945 to 1955. Roughly one-sixth of the communes were still at a very low level of partisan competition, well over a quarter of them were at an intermediate level, and just over half of them were fully politicized. From 1959 onward a new wave of change set in: under the pressure of

Table 2. *Electoral List Alternatives in Local Elections in Rural Communes, 1947–1963*

	1947	1955	1959	1963
Total no. of communes = 100 %	680	680	670	476
One list, plurality election	5.0%	2.8%	2.5%	2.1%
Several lists, all non-partisan	4.9	5.7	6.0	5.2
One party list, one or more non-partisan	9.3	8.5	8.7	5.7
Two or more party lists, one or more non-partisan	26.1	29.0	23.2	31.3
Only party lists	54.7	54.0	59.6	55.7

increasing demands for administrative efficiency in the operation of communal services a number of rural units were merged into larger ones and these territorial reorganizations set the stage for further changes in the local cleavage systems.

Our analyses of the geographical, cultural, and socio-economic conditions of politicization suggest these conclusions:

a. the communes in the central provinces of the East were first to reach a high level of politicization.

b. the peripheral primary-economy communes of the outer provinces, most markedly the fisheries communities along the western and the northern coast, were the last to reach even the first stage of politicization and the majority of them were still at the first or intermediate stage in the 1950's.

c. the industrializing and urbanizing communes of the outer provinces differ markedly in their levels of politicization from one region to another. In the West, a region of strong traditions of territorial and cultural opposition to the national centre, politicization still tends to be low in such communes, while in the North, a region of marked class polarization, it tends to be considerably higher.

The contrast between the West and the North *(Table 3)* is indeed intriguing. More than half of the coastal communes of the West were in 1955 still at only the first stage of politicization. In the North only a quarter of these communes were at this level and more than half at the next level. The same differences emerge from the analysis of the inland communes: in the West only about one-third had reached the highest level of politicization as against two-thirds in the northern provinces.

These differences reflect a basic contrast in Norwegian politics: (Rokkan, 1964: 2, sect. III). The emphasis on territorial representation and cultural defence in the West, and the emphasis on functional representation and class cleavage in the North. The territorial-cultural emphasis sets limits to the possibilities of party conflict within localities and tends to reduce politics to questions of external representation. The functional-economic

Table 3. *Numbers of Nationally Registered Parties in Local Elections*
Data for 1955, by Type of Commune

| | | No. of Communes = 100 % | Nationally Registered Parties | | |
| | | | None or only one | Two or more, also non-partisan | Only party lists |
			%	%	%
Coastal communes:					
16 % or more in fisheries					
Peripheral communes [151]	West	16	50	31	19
	North	72	26	51	22
Other communes	West	55	58	27	15
	North	33	18	73	9
Inland communes:					
less than 16 % in fisheries					
Peripheral communes	West	28	39	25	36
	North	20	20	35	45
Other communes	West	108	23	40	37
	North	91	5	27	67

emphasis reflects active alliances across local geographical units, tends to undermine the established leadership structure, and introduces elements of direct interest conflict into community politics.

Comparing the results of local and national elections in communes at different levels of politicization we find marked contrasts between the two regions: in the West the parties in the middle of the political spectrum are strongest in the least politicized communes and considerably weaker in the fully politicized ones; in the North even the least politicized of the communes will be strongly polarized between Socialists and Conservatives.

These differences are also reflected in the data for levels of electoral mobilization. In the least politicized communes of the West the turnout at local elections tends to be markedly lower than the turnout at national elections, while in the North the communes at the same level of politicization tend to mobilize as many or more voters at local than at national elections (see above pp. 197–199). This finding requires detailed checking through case studies in selected communities, but the interpretation closest at hand is that it reflects a basic difference in the strategies of mobilization of the local leaders. In a safe local election the marginal utility of mobilized votes is very small, but in the national election each vote delivered to the provincial total serves as a 'counter' in bargains for positions and for favours at the next level of the system. In an increasingly polarized community the leaders will be as concerned to mobilize their maximum in local as in national elections. This is typically the case in the peripheral communes of the North where the Labour party is on the verge of establishing firm local allies but has not yet organized itself for direct participation in municipal contests.

The Two Peripheries: the 'Counter-central' and the 'Polarized'

The original lines of cleavage in the Norwegian system were territorial and cultural: the provinces opposed the capital, the peasantry fought the officials of the King's administration, the defenders of the rural cultural traditions spoke against the steady spread of urban secularism and rationalism.

Three developments brought about a decisive change in the cleavage system during the first two decades after the establishment of universal suffrage. First, the entry of the bulk of the peasantry into the national money and credit economy and the concomitant shift from an attitude of negative resistance against the tax-collecting state towards a positive emphasis on the role of the national government in meeting the claims of the rural population.[152] Second, the emergence of a nation-wide movement of working-class protest, not only in the cities and the industrializing countryside but also in the forestry and fisheries communities of the eastern, the middle, and the northern provinces. Third, the transformation of the original Right from an organization for the defence of the established administration of the state to a party essentially defending the claims of the urban middle class and the emerging business community against the encroaching apparatus of the national government.

These functional-economic lines of conflict cut across the earlier territorial-cultural cleavage and produced a complex system of alliances and oppositions. In the cities and the industrializing communities in the countryside the electorates were increasingly polarized between a Socialist left and a Conservative right. In the highly stratified forestry and fisheries communities of the East, the Trøndelag, and the North there was a similar, although slower, process of polarization, even in the extreme peripheries of the outlying provinces. In the more equalitarian primary economy communities of the South and the West the forces of territorial defence remained strong and vigorous and resisted effectively the pressures toward a polarization of local political life.

Our ecological analyses show that these regional differences in the levels of class polarization are most pronounced in the peripheral, economically backward communes and tend to disappear with urbanization and economic growth: this is shown in *Table 4*.

The striking difference between the southwestern and the northern peripheries essentially reflects a difference in the timing of the crucial waves of mobilization: in the South and the West the breakthrough came during the second half of the nineteenth century and found expression in a number of religious and cultural movements of resistance against the centralizing urban forces; in the North the breakthrough came with the introduction of manhood suffrage and took the form of a movement of violent social and economic protest, not primarily against the centre of the nation but against the local property owners and employers.

Table 4. *Polarization Scores by Region and Type of Communes*

	Polarization Scores 1957[a]
East and Trøndelag	
Principal cities	.88
Other cities	.85
Central rural[b]	.82
Peripheral	.68
South and West	
Principal cities	.75
Other cities	.68
Central rural[b]	.61
Peripheral	.45
North	
Cities	.84
Central rural[b]	.85
Peripheral	.80

[a] This score simply indicates the relative strength of the 'class' parties vs. the 'territorial-cultural' parties: the higher the score, the greater the preponderance of the Socialists (CP + Labour) and the Conservatives in the locality; the lower the score, the stronger two offshoots of the old Left, the Liberals and the Christians. A third offshoot of the old Left, the Agrarians, has been disregarded in this context since its contribution to within-community polarization varies considerably from region to region.

[b] This classification is based on a score for 'accessibility,' an alternative measure of 'centrality-peripherality.' See the explanation in Chapter 6, above pp. 187.

In the South and the West the struggle centred on the symbols of community identification: the religious creed and the language. The mobilized peasantry fought the lukewarm liberalism of the state church and rejected the standard urban language brought into their communities by the clergymen, the officials, the teachers, and the traders. The rural counter-language, the *landsmål,* became the rallying symbol for a broad movement of cultural defence, not only in the South and the West but also in the old peasant communities of the eastern valleys. In the other regions of the country the movement never rallied such decisive community support; in these regions the functional cleavage lines soon emerged as the dominant ones and the earlier territorial contrasts lost in importance.

In the northern periphery there was much less of a basis for such counter-cultural movements of territorial defence. The communities tended to be culturally fragmented and socially hierarchized; the privileged merchant families stood far apart from the crofters and the landless fishermen, and after the introduction of manhood suffrage even very small and peripheral communes soon found themselves politically divided. The smallholders and the fishermen had for centuries depended for their living on the owners of port facilities who bought their produce and controlled their credit. The introduction of manhood suffrage coincided with a number of changes in the primary economy, the installation of processing plants, the motorization of the fishing fleet and the consequent increase in the need for credit. The result was an explosive mobilization of protest against the owners and the controllers. The Labour party had built its initial organizational strength in the metropolitan areas of the East, but the decisive political breakthrough came in the extreme periphery of the North; the first socialist representatives to enter the *Storting* were elected by the fishermen of the North in 1903, at the second election after the introduction of manhood suffrage. This alliance between the rural proletariat and the urban working class proved of the greatest importance in Norwegian politics: it accelerated the development of a national party system and halted the tendencies toward an accentuation of centre-periphery contrasts.[153]

III. Implications for Developmental Comparisons

I have summarized the principal findings of our current studies of the process of mobilization, politicization, and polarization in Norway. Some of these analyses are primarily of interest to one-nation historians; some of them, I hope, may provide possible paradigms for detailed developmental comparisons across a number of different political systems.

At a high level of abstraction what we have been concerned to study in our programme of developmental analyses is the propagation of waves of political innovation from the centres of the national territory to its peripheries.[154] We have studied the spread of the idea that everybody, whatever his or her status in the community, is entitled to a vote and should make use of it; we have tried to map the diffusion of party memberships and organizations; and we have described the steps in the spread of polarized party politics throughout the localities of the nation.

Our initial concern with the mobilization of the latest subjects to enter the national political arena led us step by step to a wider concern with the latest communities to enter nationalized party politics: why were some communities politicized and polarized so quickly after the introduction of mass democracy while others remained largely unchanged in their community structure for decades after the decisive extension of the suffrage?

Ecological analyses of the conditions of competitive community politics have been attempted in the United States [155] and could easily be repeated in a number of countries. Such *synchronic* analyses of the relationships between levels of economic growth, politicization and polarization must eventually be fitted into a broader context of *diachronic* studies of sequences of change in communities of different structure.

Two tasks must be clearly distinguished in any such attempt at developmental analysis: the sifting of information on variations in the *initial structural conditions* in the locality, quite particularly in the stratification of the population, the concentration of economic power and the extent of social, cultural and religious cleavages; and the collection of data on the *processes of external and internal change* and their consequences for the equilibrium of forces within each community.

Hans Daalder has persuasively argued the importance of research on the inherited structures of urban and rural societies for an understanding of divergencies and convergencies in the development of European party systems. Our own work on Norwegian developments adds further evidence of the importance of such research not only for an understanding of regional variations but also for comparative 'typing' of the resultant national party systems. The contrasts in electoral alignments between East and West, West and North reflect fundamental differences in inherited socioeconomic structure, and the complex crosscutting of cleavage lines in the national system can be understood only against this background.

This, however, is only half the story. The initial structure conditions the process of change toward competitive mass democracy but does not determine its course. Our Norwegian analyses leave no doubt that industrialization and urbanization affected political life in all regions irrespective of inherited traditions: the regional differences have remained in the typical primary-economy communes but tend to disappear in the suburbs and the cities. To study these processes of community change we shall clearly need standardized time series data for as many as possible of the distinct localities. On this point a comparative perspective on processes of nation-building may help us to generate fruitful models for an understanding of our own system. Daniel Lerner (Lerner, 1957) and Karl Deutsch (Deutsch, 1961) have each in his way pointed to important variables in the study of sequences of community mobilization and integration into the national political system.

To account for differences in the rates of political change under conditions of mass democracy it will prove of great interest to collect for each community developmental data for a broad range of cross-local transaction flows:

a. the monetization of exchanges and the consequent entry into a wider network of economic relations;

b. the entry into the credit market and the consequent increase in the defence of the peripheral units on the central ones;

c. the spread of urban commodities, skills, and technologies and the consequent changes in the structure of the local labour force;

d. the mobility of workers from the primary sector into the secondary and the tertiary and from the peripheral areas to the central;

e. the development of cross-local contacts through the schools, the armed forces, the administrative services, and the dominant church;

f. the growth of a membership market for voluntary associations and the establishment of local branches of regional and national organizations;

g. the entry into a wider market of information exchange within the nation, partly as an indirect result of the opening up of other channels of exchange, partly through the diffusion of such personal media as the mails, the telegraph, and the telephone, and partly through the spread of locally, regionally, and nationally based mass media.

If time-series data could be established for each of these channels of exchange for large samples of localities, it should be possible to establish with some precision the average thresholds of economic and social mobilization required to trigger processes off within-community polarization and cross-local party development. We are very far from this goal in our developmental studies in Norway, and the many gaps in the sources of historical and statistical information will force us to resort to a variety of short-cuts in the analysis. We hope, however, that as we continue to accumulate such time-series data we shall be able to differentiate our analysis and our conclusions and to develop more complex models of the processes of change.

A theory of political change can never be built on data for a single country, however. What we need to gain further insight and perspective is a series of parallel analyses of developmental sequences in countries of different social and political structure and with different histories of suffrage extensions.

The official records of elections in the countries of the West contain staggering amounts of information for such comparative time series analyses.[156] With the increasing accessibility of large-scale computers it is no longer an impossible task to collate such political data with demographic, socio-economic, and cultural data from censuses and other official statistics and carry out the appropriate analyses of sequences of change. It is true that conditions for such data collection will vary very much between highly centralized nation-states and loosely organized federations. It is vastly easier to assemble such data in a country with a long history of centralized book-keeping such as Sweden than in such federations as the United States and Australia. In general, countries emphasizing territorial representation tend to have poorer electoral statistics than countries with stronger traditions of estate representation and PR. The British statistics for national elections allow analyses only at the constituency level, and the statistics for local elections have never been centralized. In Australia and New Zealand research workers such as R. M. Chapman and R. S. Parker have not only had to dig their way through local archives and newspapers but also had to draw up boundaries for the territorial counting units they found data for.[157] Uncertainties and changes in the delimitation of the data units do indeed create headaches in ecological research, but in most cases it will be possible to carry out analyses for several shorter periods of relative stability even if it is not possible to cover the total history of the country's electoral politics within one data sequence.[158] An archive organized by periods of comparable data is vastly better than no archive. Replications of similarly designed analyses at different points in time can often reveal a great deal about factors at work in the process of change even in the absence of continuous time series data.

Once such archives are in operation for two or more countries it should be possible to match localities by their economic structure and the level of social mobilization and to study similarities and differences between political cultures in the character of local political divisions and in the extent of turnout at local and national elections.[159]

Several strategies of comparative analysis suggest themselves. My own inclination would be to focus the initial analyses on the lags in rural political change. Our Norwegian analyses have already demonstrated the importance of a concentration on the politics of the rural periphery for an understanding of regional contrasts within the polity. The differences between the equalitarian South and West and the hierarchically stratified East and North underscore the importance of detailed attention to land tenure systems and rural organization. In a cross-national perspective this concentration on rural politics appears equally promising. Differences in rural social structure not only make for difference in the levels of mobilization and politicization in the countryside but also influence the character of the rural-urban alliances and alignments in the party system and consequently the over-all balance in the polity.

Differences in systems of land tenure and rural stratification were of crucial importance in the early history of suffrage extensions in Europe in the nineteenth century.[160] The First Reform Bill had strengthened the power of the aristocracy and the gentry in the counties in England (Moore, 1961; Thompson, 1963) and the introduction of manhood suffrage had also tended to consolidate the positions of the *Gutsbesitzer* of rural Prussia (Nipperdey, 1961: Ch. V) and the *notables* of rural France.[161] Clearly in many of these rural structures the ingrained hierarchical traditions and the sheer force of economic dependence made voting more frequently an expression of loyal deference than of political protest. By contrast, in Scandinavia the decisive thrust toward democracy and parliamentary rule was brought about through the associational mobilization of the freehold peasantry.[162] Their grievances against the established regimes were not exclusively economic: their rejection of the centralizing nation-state and the dominance of the officials and the patricians in the cities was cultural as well. Such counter-movements against the central culture can be documented in all ethnically divided polities: the opposition of the 'Celtic fringe' to the dominance of the Tory culture of England is an obvious example. The rapidly increasing strength of the Liberals in the Welsh countryside paralleled the emergence of the Nordic 'Left': what counted were not just the grievances against the absentee English landlords but also the cultural and religious mobilization against the influences they represented (Morgan, 1963). What distinguished the Nordic developments was the initial polarization of politics along an urban-rural axis: the central culture was predominantly urban and the movements of cultural protest appealed to essentially rural values. In Britain the central culture had its roots in the English landed estates and the movements of opposition were partly recruited from the non-conformists in the growing cities, partly from the subject peasantry of the Celtic peripheries.

Such contrasts in rural-urban relations have had profound effects not only on the rate and direction of mobilization but also on the level of politicization and the development of cross-local party organizations and the integration of the local leadership into the national network.

In Scandinavia the conflict between urban dominance and rural claims was at the heart of the early struggle over constitutional reform and parliamentary power. The basic dimension of cleavage was territorial, and the internal politics of the peripheral units remained largely unchanged. The move toward nationalized politics was essentially a consequence of the spread of the Social Democrats from the cities to the rural areas and the alliance of the industrial working class and the rural proletariat. Wherever the rural lower class could be mobilized the local elections were increasingly politicized and the local leaders found it essential to establish close cross-local alliances within the provincial and national party organizations.

In England the crucial change from constituency to national politics came after 1885 with the entry of the Conservatives into the boroughs and the gradual merger of the landed interests with the urban and suburban business interests (Cornford, 1963). While in Scandinavia the drive toward nationwide class polarization came from the working class, in England it was the Conservatives who brought about the decisive change from the tradition of cross-class territorial representation to the emphasis on cross-constituency class representation. In Scandinavia the rural and the urban establishments were never able to merge into one major party of opposition against the Social Democrats; in Britain the alliance of the aristocracy, the gentry, and the urban middle class eventually produced a strong national party destined to govern the polity for decades.

The consequent contrasts between the over-all levels of rural politicization in Scandinavia and Britain are well-known: in Scandinavia on the whole markedly competitive rural politics and high turnout levels in local elections, in England much lower levels of politicization in the primary economy areas and often very low rates of participation in local elections.[163] Obviously the frequency of contested elections and the level of the turnout are to some extent direct functions of the system of representation: the Scandinavian PR systems encourage general participation, the British plurality system discourages minorities. But as we saw in our account of developments in Norway, the transition from plurality representation to PR was in itself a first sign of increasing politicization. The triumph of PR in the Scandinavian polities reflects the strength of the pressures for representation from below; the persistence of the plurality system indicates higher levels of local consensus and a stronger tradition of rural territorial representation.

It is interesting to reflect on the similarities and dissimilarities between the rural Southwest of Norway and the rural areas of England: in both cases we find low levels of politicization and polarization, but in the deviant Norwegian regions the rural units are typically equalitarian communities of small freeholders, while in England they tend to be dominated by highly stratified structures inherited from a manorial and feudal past. The paternal rule of the aristocracy and the gentry offered as effective a barrier against class politics as the equalitarian structure of the Norwegian communities but the consequences for rural-urban integration were very different in the two cases. In England the rural leaders could ally themselves to a strong national party of prestige and wealth; in Norway the equalitarian Southwest became the stronghold of a rural counter-culture alienated from the society and the politics of the urban centres of the nation (Rokkan, 1964: 2; Rokkan, 1966: 5).

Similar analyses of contrasts in rural-urban cleavage structures can be multiplied for country after country. To get beyond the stage of vague speculation and impressionistic generalization so characteristic of much of the current work in comparative history and comparative politics it is essential to get down to detailed analyses of ranges of variations within countries, both at the initial stage of mobilization and in the current phase of development. Only through such efforts of massive data-gathering and analysis can we avoid the Scylla of hasty overgeneralization and the Charybdis of myopic attention to local and national peculiarities.

NOTES

[146] These are a few of the recent efforts of quantitative historical analyses of electoral data:

Denmark. Erik Høgh is completing an extensive study of elections before and after the introduction of secret voting in 1901 (Høgh, 1968) Paul Meyer and associates have carried out detailed analyses of turnout levels in different types of communities (Jeppesen, 1964). Jan Stehouwer is currently following up these analyses through an historical analysis of the demography of the vote in Denmark (Stehouwer, 1967).

Finland. Erik Allardt has carried out extensive correlation analyses of data on the strength of the Finnish Communists and Social Democrats and made imaginative use of data on local political traditions since 1906; see especially (Allardt, 1964; Allardt, 1967). O. Rantala is engaged in an even more extensive data processing operation for Finnish electoral data and will carry out shortly a number of multivariate regression analyses to pin down factors of change in alignments (Rantala, 1967).

France. The Siegfried school of electoral cartographers has produced thousands of historical electoral maps but has so far rarely engaged in detailed computations of factors making for change. The recent work by statisticians such as J. Klatzmann, J. Desabie and G. Vangrevelinghe (Klatzmann, 1958; Desabie, 1959; Vangrevelinghe, 1961) has paved the way for the application of computers to the processing of electoral data. Mattei Dogan's extensive work on data on recent elections in France and Italy has stimulated increasing attention to the possibilities of detailed ecological analysis, cf. (Dogan, 1965, 1966, 1967).

Germany. A good introductory presentation of trends in German elections since manhood suffrage can be found in (Faul, 1960); Faul's discussion of 'mobilization,' pp. 156–163, is of particular relevance. No nation-wide trend analyses have as yet been attempted. The basic data for the *Reichstag* elections can be related to social and religious divisions; thus (Specht, 1907) give the degree of urbanization and percent of Evangelical and Catholic for each *Wahlkreis.* Analyses such as (Klöcker, 1913), a pioneering study of the religious factor in German elections, could easily be extended by adding further variables and by tracing trends over time.

Sweden. Swedish official statistics are more detailed than any others in Europe and allow a great variety of analyses. Among recent historical analyses are (Wallin, 1961). Of particular interest for their high level of methodological sophistication are the analyses by the statistician C.-G. Janson (Janson, 1961) and the sociologist Gösta Carlsson (Carlsson, 1963). The historian Jörgen Weibull is currently completing a statistical analysis of the occupational bases of party strength for the elections from 1911 to 1920 (Weibull, 1964).

United Kingdom. The poll books and the returns of the elections of the Victorian era have recently been subject to increasingly sophisticated analyses. See especially (Gash, 1953; Moore, 1961; Hanham, 1959; Cornford, 1963). Cornford's work represents a great advance on earlier work in its insightful use of ecological statistics. The possibilities of ecological research in Britain are amply demonstrated in (Moser, 1961); this is essentially an exercise in factor analysis but happens to include, in addition to a great number of demographis, socioeconomic, and health variables, a few basic electoral data for each town. The zero-order correlations calculated between the socio-economic and the political variables prove remarkably interesting but, curiously enough, were left unanalyzed and uninterpreted: here is clearly a task for secondary analysis. A very interesting attempt at developmental analysis at the local level has been made by J. M. Lee (Lee, 1963). This study focuses on changes in the recruitment of elected personnel and seeks to determine the conditions for a 'take off' (p. 215) from the traditional politics of the 'county society' ruled by part-time amateurs recruited from the local social elite to the modern politics of full-time professionals recruited through training and service rather than through family status. If statistical studies of such changes in recruitment could be done systematically for a variety of local units we should know much more about the conditions of changes in political style in mass-suffrage democracies.

United States. Historians such as Lee Benson (Benson, 1961) and sociologists such as Seymour Martin Lipset (Lipset, 1960: Ch. II) have for years called attention to the rich opportunities for diachronic electoral analysis in the United States. The Social Science Research Council has recently taken an important step in helping this movement forward by giving a grant to Walter Dean Burnham for a detailed inventory of the archival sources for early electoral statistics state by state, cf. (Burnham, forthc.). A great advance in historical analysis could be brought about through arrangements for central processing of all such data. The Survey Research Center at the University of Michigan has recently taken steps to build up a county-by-county archive of census and election data: this will be based in part on Burnham's work, in part on the collations of electoral statistics established by Richard H. Scammon and his staff. Cf. (Benson, 1965).

[147] The International Social Science Council and the International Committee on Social Sciences Documentation, both supported by funds from UNESCO, have since 1962 organized several conferences on problems of data archiving in the social sciences, see (Rokkan, 1964: 1). For further developments see (Rokkan, 1965: 1 and 1966: 3).

[148] For a general account of the Norwegian programme of electoral research see (Rokkan, 1960: 5). These publications deal specifically with analyses of long-term change: (Rokkan, 1964: 2; 1966: 5; 1967; as well as Chapter 6 above). A student working within the programme has recently completed a thesis on the politicization of local elections in the rural areas of the Western region from 1900 to 1963: (Hjellum, 1967: 1 and 2).

[149] The standard treatment of the history of the franchise in Norway gives the figures for registered and for qualified citizens in percent of the total resident population in each election year; cf. most recently (Kaartvedt, 1964: p. 113). By this reckoning 6.7 % of the population was registered in 1815 and 7.6 % of the population was qualified at the first election for which such calculations became officially available, that of 1859. Such indexes of democratization are highly questionable because of changes in demographic structure over time. A better indicator for the 19th century would be the percent qualified of all men of 25 and over. Exact figures of the totals qualified for the vote in 1814–15 are not available but estimates based on censuses suggest that 40–50 % of all men over 25 qualified. Cf. (Rokkan, 1967). By comparison, about one out of seven adult males was enfranchised in England and Wales before 1832, about one out of five after the First Reform, one out of three after the Second, and two out of three after the Third. Cf. (Butler, 1968).

[150] (Rokkan, 1967: sect. 1. 3). These estimates are based on a tax census for 1876.

[151] 'Peripherality' is here measured by a six-item score originally developed by the Norwegian geographer A. Thormodsæter. For details see Chapter 6 above.

[152] Knut Dahl Jacobsen has described the first phase of this process of change (Jacobsen, 1964: esp. pp. 172–96). Details about further developments will be available in the forthcoming history of the central administration in Norway 1814–1964.

[153] For further details on the implications of this urban-rural alliance, see (Rokkan, 1966: 5).

[154] This is the central theme of research in the flourishing school of geography at the University of Lund, see particularly (Hägerstrand, 1951). Attempts to apply this technique to the spread of political affiliations and commitments are still very few. Cf. (Lägnert, 1952) and the recent article by G. Carlsson (Carlsson, 1963); see also (Carlsson, 1965).

[155] (Cutright, 1963) presents an analysis of the influence of urbanization, industrialization, and religious divisions on competitiveness in the counties of ten states.

[156] The International Committee on Social Sciences Documentation has taken steps to facilitate comparisons of such data through the preparation in two or more volumes of an *International Guide to Electoral Statistics.* The first volume, edited by S. Rokkan and J. Meyriat, will be published in 1969; it will cover 15 countries of Western Europe (cf. Ch. 5 above).

[157] (Chapman, 1962: particularly Chs. 11–12; Parker, forthc.). I am indebted to Robert Chapman for information on the methodological problems of ecological research in New Zealand and Australia.

[158] W. D. Burnham (Burnham, forthc.) has studied the available data for 19th-century U.S. elections and reports that analyses at the county level will present very few problems of this kind; the major difficulties occur in the analysis of data for congressional districts and city wards.

[159] To give readers some concrete indications of the types of analysis suggested, I shall include here a few tables comparable to the Norwegian ones. The abundant Swedish statistics have not yet been analyzed along the same lines as the Norwegian but preliminary checks indicate largely similar patterns of development:

Table 1. *The Lag in Rural Mobilization*

Election	Turnout in % of electorate			
	Men		Women	
	Urban	Rural	Urban	Rural
1866	40.5	15–16		
1881	45.2	19.5		
1887 (I)	62.9	48.1		
1908	70.0	57.4		
1909 manhood suffrage				
1911	63.0	55.5		
1921 universal suffrage	62.2	61.9	50.5	45.5
1932	74.0	72.7	65.6	60.6
1948	85.7	84.2	82.8	78.7
1956	82.4	80.8	80.0	76.2

Herbert Tingsten, in his pioneering volume on *Political Behaviour* (Tingsten, 1937) was the first to call attention to the early lags and the gradual equalization of turnout discrepancies. He found roughly the same patterns in Denmark and Iceland as in Norway and Sweden: gradual decreases both in the rural-urban and in the men-women discrepancies. In Finland the rural population was mobilized as early as the urban in the national elections, but the same basic pattern of change was found for municipal elections and for the men-women discrepancies.

A review of Swedish statistics for local elections indicates the following sequence of change:

Table 2. *The Politicization of Local Elections*

Election	Party divisions in rural communes		Turnout in local elections			
	Competitive	Not competitive	Competitive		Not competitive	
			M	W	M	W
1920	69.4 %	30.6 %	62.4	56.9	27.9	20.1
1930	75.6 %	14.4 %	59.9	47.2	24.5	12.0
1934	91.8 %	8.2 %	65.7	53.9	29.3	16.7

	Level of politicization			Turnout in local elections					
	I	II	III	I		II		III	
	Political parties only	Several non-political	Only list one	M	W	M	W	M	W
1938	79.3	6.6	14.1	69.7	59.3	62.9	49.3	43.2	27.2
1946	88.5	1.7	9.8	73.9	66.8	63.2	51.8	49.8	34.6
1950 all communes except 6 fully politicized									
1954 all communes except 2 fully politicized									

A breakdown for 1938 indicates the structural conditions for low politicization*:

	Group I	Group II	Group III
Communes with 75 % or more in agriculture	66.7	10.3	23.0
Communes with 50–75 % in agriculture	81.7	6.6	11.7
Other communes, not urbanized	92.8	1.0	6.2
Urbanized communes	94.1	2.5	3.4

* Sveriges off. stat. Alm. val., *Kommunala valen år 1938*, Stockholm, 1939, p. 59.

The rapid politicization of local elections in Sweden can to some extent be explained in ecological and socio-economic terms but the institutional links between local and national elections clearly added decisively to the rate of change: representation in the Upper House is based on elections within the provincial and the city councils and there is accordingly a direct incentive to encourage partisanship at the local level. A report on developments toward local politicization in Sweden was published in 1964 (*Rapport och arbetsmaterial från arbetsgruppen för det kommunala sambandet*, Stockholm: S. O. U., 1964, p. 39).

[160] Cursory comparisons of sequences of suffrage extension are given in Chapter 1 above, cf. (Rokkan, 1961; Bendix & Rokkan, 1964).

[161] For the West of France the basic text on rural politics is André Siegfried's classic (Siegfried, 1913: esp. Ch. 23). For a follow-up analysis of elections under the Fourth Republic see (Fauvet, 1958).

[162] Summaries of historical information on the developments of the Scandinavian party systems have recently been published *(Framveksten, 1964)*.

[163] J. M. Lee has developed a typology of the counties in England and Wales in an effort to study the conditions for local politicization. His essential finding is that the counties least affected by urbanization and industrialization have the lowest numbers of contested elections both at the level of the district councils and at the level of county councils. This of course is in general conformity with results for Norway and Sweden but the over-all level of competitiveness is much lower. Lee's tables for the average politicization of elections from 1946 to 1958 reveal a great deal about patterns of regional variations in England and Wales. The calculations in the following table are adapted from (Lee, 1963: App. D).

Region	Average % contested seats 1946–58		Range of within-region variation			
	County Councils	Rural D.C.s	County Councils		Rural D.C.s	
			Max. % contested	Min. % contested	Max. % contested	Min. % contested
	(% of pop. in R.D.C.s)		(% in parentheses: pop. in R.D.C.s in the county)			
1. Home Counties	72 (19)	41	88 (11)	51 (51)	53 (10 & 30)	26 (32)
2. North & North Midlands	56 (18)	36	74 (14)	43 (20)	47 (14)	27 (20)
3. Midlands	44 (31)	31	52 (33)	37 (33)	47 (33)	22 (22 & 48)
4. Southwest	34 (37)	28	45 (52)	21 (45)	40 (52)	14 (39)
5. Eastern England	33 (43)	27	65 (55)	19 (56)	47 (38)	13 (56)
6. Border Countries	39 (33)	22	46 (13)	26 (55)	36 (45)	10 (55)
7. Wales & Monmouth	27 (32)	36	42 (18)	13 (59 & 67)	66 (18)	9 (59)

The differences at the regional level are quite clear-cut but they tend to cover up important variations among counties within the regions. In regions such as the Midlands, the Southwest, and Eastern England there is in fact no clear relationship between the levels of urbanization and the levels of competitiveness. To account for variations county by county it would be necessary to develop a multivariate analysis design and to take into consideration such factors as the size distribution of land holdings, the strength of agricultural unions and farmer's organizations, the strength of the Liberals during the early phases of competitive politics. The work currently undertaken by Michael Steed at Manchester on partisanship in English local politics may provide important data for such analysis.

III

Citizen Reactions in fully - fledged Party Systems

EIGHT

Cross-National Survey Analysis: Historical, Analytical and Substantive Contexts

The crucial characteristics of the sample survey are easily identified:

– you define, for a given territory of residence or activity, a *population of units,* be they individuals, households, dwelling units, farms, shops, factories, organizations, agencies;

– you want to establish propositions about the distributions of attributes within this population but cannot afford the cost of collecting information about such attributes for *all* the units;

– you therefore proceed by *sampling:* you select a *smaller* set of units for the data gathering operation and make sure to select them in such a way that *statements about distributions in this smaller set can be translated, with known margins of error, into statements about the total set;*

– having established a *target sample* you then proceed to contact these selected sources of information (in the typical case these 'target respondents' will at the same time constitute units of the populations under study, but there will also be cases where the 'sender of data' is not identical with the unit of description or analysis, but e.g., a member of, or an informant about, that unit), and subject them, typically by way of oral interview, but also by use of written questionnaires, check lists or tests, to *standardized series of questions or other response-eliciting stimuli.*

The great majority of the reports produced on the basis of such data-

Origin: This text was originally prepared as an introduction to S. Rokkan, S. Verba, J. Viet and Elina Almasy, *Comparative Survey Analysis,* (The Hague, Mouton: 1969). The 'Bibliography' referred to in the text is the one printed in that volume.

gathering operations have limited themselves to analyses of *one* sample of *one* given population: they may of course include introductory discussions of, or footnote references to, similar studies carried out on the same, or similar, populations in the past or to parallel studies on other populations, in other localities or in other countries, but the bulk of the reports limit themselves to the one sample. The trend, however, is toward an increase in the number of cross-sample, cross-population analyses. More and more social scientists have become dissatisfied with the typical 'one-shot' survey operation: they want to check the stability of findings across a larger number of studies; they want to study the sources of variation over time; they want to explore the possibilities of systematic analysis of the impact of variation in socio-cultural-political *contexts* on the structuring of behaviours, attitudes, values and opinions. This 'trend report' seeks to place *one* of these movements in a broader historical and methodological perspective: the efforts to make use of survey techniques and survey data in the study of similarities and differences *across distinct national populations*. This is a movement of great potential importance for the future of the social sciences: the 'transport revolution', the steady increases in the economic resources for social science research, the rising demand for information about conditions and processes in other countries than one's own, the development of strong supra-national bureaucracies, all these processes are bound to lead almost automatically to a multiplication of investments of time and personnel in the organization of comparative surveys and in the development of facilities for the accumulation and retrieval of survey data across many countries. But this very increase in the opportunities for cross-national data gathering and data organization will add significantly to the intellectual responsibilities of social scientists. The proliferation of survey operations to more and more countries of the world and the continual amassing of more data from so many different socio-cultural and political context raise a series of difficult problems of methodology, of research strategy, of organizational policy: questions about the conditions for the use of different methods of data gathering, issues of comparability and equivalence in the measurement of similarities or differences among distinct populations, difficulties in the logic of multi-level analysis of the type required in comparisons across complex social systems. In this introductory statement an effort will be made to trace a quick map of this frontier of research: to place the methodological developments in their historical and technological contexts, and to review some of the attempts made at coping with the many difficulties encountered in this type of cross-national, cross-cultural study.

I. *The Sevenfold Origins of the Sample Survey*

The practice of subjecting samples of populations to systematic questioning can be traced back to several distinct historical roots.

Three conditions appear to be crucial for the emergence of *any* system of standardized questioning and response registration:

first, some minimal level of *centralization and bureaucratization,* whether in the form of imperial or national territorial administrations, in the form of cross-local church organizations or educational systems, or in the form of private corporations such as banks or merchant networks;

secondly, there must be a sufficient level of *literacy* in the population to make it possible to recruit the required minimum of officials or administrators for the tasks of questioning and information transmission;

and thirdly, there must be enough cross-local *mobility* in the population to make it worthwhile for the central decision-makers to invest in information-gathering of this formal type rather than through the traditional channels of oral communication from person to person.

In these three senses the practice of standardized questioning and data registration is a typical characteristic of *modernizing* polities and organizational networks: the development of such formalization and systematization in the modes of communication can be interpreted as part of the overall transition from the primordial kinship-centred, 'oral' communities of earlier ages to the differentiated mass-bureaucratic polities of the present.

This is a point of basic importance in the discussion of the crosscultural 'reach' of social science techniques: the sample survey grew out of a variety of administrative practices in bureaucratic organizations in countries at a high level of literacy and will for that very reason prove much more problematic as a data-gathering device in pre-literate societies and in traditionally oriented communities within modernizing polities.[164]

Six of the devices developed for the management of the large-scale territorial bureaucracies of the modern world may be singled out as particularly important in the history of this technique of data-gathering:

1. *the administrative questionnaire*
2. *the registration form*
3. *the census*
4. *the election*
5. *the referendum*
6. *the examination.*

The first three are essential devices of information channelling and control within organizations too large to be adequately managed through the traditional networks of person-to-person oral communication: to guard against 'noise' and distortion in the information channels specific questions are formulated for large numbers of 'source-persons' and specific categories are offered for the recording of the data.[165]

Of the three the census represented the greatest advance in systematization. The census was essentially an instrument of control and of resource planning: it helped to define the politically important categories of the territorial population and it allowed estimates of the resources in manpower and mobilizable wealth. Three features of the population census were to prove crucial in the later development of the sample survey:

a) the emphasis on the coverage of the *total range of units* in the population, whatever their status, whatever their circumstances;

b) the insistence on *clear-cut, easily codable categories* of information for subsequent tabulation and analysis;

c) the minimization of interest in information about distinct individuals and the concentration of interest in *aggregated totals*.

The early sample surveys [166] stuck closely to this model:

a) they were administrative devices of immediate utility in the planning of public services, the allocation of manpower, the provision of various types of assistance;

b) they were cheaper and could be administered with greater frequency than the census;

c) they made it possible to cover a broader range of variables and they allowed more detailed coding than the total counts;

d) they divorced the information about individual units of the population completely from the aggregated totals: the individual households or respondents were not contacted and questioned as concrete units but as statistical representatives of all units sharing their socio-economic and areal characteristics.

This programmatic separation of the *individual intelligence* objective from the objective of *statistical aggregation and analysis* is of crucial importance in empirical social research. Official data collection agencies very early established strict rules of secrecy to ensure the protection of individual records against misuse by outsiders: the recent controversy over the plans to link up a variety of individual files within a *Federal Data Center* in the United States has rubbed in the importance of this distinction between intelligence and statistics (Dunn, 1967).

The sample survey pushes the distinction to a further extreme: the data are collected through the questioning of individuals but the respondents are not sought out as potential targets of intelligence operations, but as randomly chosen units for statistical aggregation and analysis.[167]

This characteristic of the sample survey was even further reinforced under the impact of the other major models of data generation: the *election* and the *referendum*.

For the burgeoning social sciences the election and the referendum represented fascinating approximations to the *mass experiment*. But there was one decisive limitation: the individual decisions were conscientiously *registered* but they were *counted as anonymous acts cut off from their origins*.[168] The imposition of secrecy had important consequences for the character of the democratic process of persuasion and counter-persuasion: it allowed the passive rank-and-file to keep out of the socially visible alignments pro or con given candidates, parties or issues and set them clearly off from the politically identifiable party members, militants and campaign workers.

The political survey grew out of the uncertainties created through this stratification of the citizenry: the extension of the suffrage to large masses of inarticulate members of the community and the introduction of safeguards against bribery and intimidation had made the outcomes of elections much more a matter of chance and it soon became increasingly tempting to develop devices for the prediction of the outcomes through 'soundings' and 'straw votes'.

It is highly significant that the earliest ventures into the prediction of electoral outcomes came in the country with the longest continuous history of the wide-suffrage politics: the United States of America. The history of the institution of *straw votes* goes back to the early decades of the nineteenth century (Robinson, 1937). In a highly mobile, egalitarian population with few official restraints on the expression of political opinions, this was a very natural development: the rapid changes in the composition of the local electorates made for uncertainty about the outcomes of political contests and the easy openness of discussions within most sectors of the populations made it very tempting to collect data about preferences before the officials events through the organization of 'straw ballots'. This point is of central significance in the discussion of the 'exportability' of the interview survey as a method of social science research: the United States went through the same development toward the standardization of secret voting as other competitive democracies [170] but *the open partisanship of the primaries kept political identities much more visible and made for much less resistance to questioning about preferences about candidates and policies.* A variety of foreign observers of the rising nation were impressed by the easy informality of personal contacts, the trust in strangers, the willingness to communicate with others, even newcomers, about public and political affairs of all kinds. This political culture offered the ideal climate for the growth of the new technique of social science data gathering: rapid changes in the conditions of electioneering increased in demand for such 'opinion soundings' and the ease and openness of social communication made it very tempting to meet this demand through systematic interviewing across the major segments of the population.

The history of large scale mass questioning begins in 1916 with the *Literacy Digest* polls (Robinson, 1937; Link, 1947; Stephan, 1957): these were 'elections in miniature', administered to millions of citizens through the circulation of very simple ballots or lists of referendum-type questions. These 'mail polls' had their heyday in the 1920s, during the prohibition era, and come to a sad and dramatic end with Roosevelt's victory in 1936: the *Digest* predicted he would only collect 40 per cent of the votes while in fact he got 60 per cent.

This gave the new generation of social scientists their great chance.

George Gallup and Elmo Roper had set up organizations for regular sampling and interviewing the year before this disaster and were given an extraordinary opportunity to demonstrate the soundness of their two operating principles:

– first you must make sure to draw a *sample closely mirroring the structure of the population* you want to predict for;

– secondly, once you have set up your sample you must make *direct personal contacts* with all the target respondents to get as many as possible of them to indicate their preference or their opinion.

The *Literary Digest* had proceeded on the naive assumption that there was 'safety in numbers' and had sinned grievously against these canons:

– the ballots had been indiscriminately sent to all households listed in telephone directories or registers of car owners without any check on the representativeness of these populations (in fact they were heavily middle-class and consequently produced a Republic bias in 1936);

– there was no procedure for checking the extent of bias produced through *differential returns* of mailed ballots (in fact the Republicans most likely to be motivated to mail back their responses tended to be convinced opponents of the New Deal).

What Gallup, Roper and their colleagues were able to demonstrate was that mass questioning of the type indulged in by *Literary Digest* was not only misleading but also wasteful: much more precise estimates of the distributions of political preferences could be established at vastly lower cost through careful sampling of the electorate and through direct interviewing by local staffs (Gallup, 1938; Roper, 1935; Katz, 1937).

This marked the beginning of one important tradition of survey research: the tradition of the commercial *poll* and the market study.

The late 'thirties saw a great mushrooming of private organizations for the conduct of interviews within samples of national populations: first in the United States, then in Britain and even in France. This movement continued in an accelerated tempo during the years immediately after the end of the hostilities in 1944–45: by 1950 all the economically advanced countries of the West, and even some 'Third World' countries, had seen the establishment of at least one polling organization in its territory. Most of these were brought into one or the other of the two world networks of polling agencies, *Gallup Affiliates* and the initially Roper-linked *International Research Associated Associates,* INRA. These two networks served crucial functions in the internationalization of the polling profession: they spread techniques and standards from country to country; they accumulated experiences in the use of equivalent question formulations or measurement techniques across different countries; they offered facilities for the conduct of comparative surveys by governmental agencies, by business corporations, and even by academic scholars. A great number of comparative surveys were made possible as a result of this important effort of international organization: without these American initiatives the movement towards the internationalization of these new methods of social science data gathering would have been vastly slower and more erratic.

But this was only the first of three distinctive developments in this field of data gathering: more and more *governmental* agencies developed staffs for the conduct of sample surveys, and a number of *academic* institutions were able to set up field organizations of some sort, whether separately or through various joint arrangements.

To get some perspective on these developments we shall have to go back to our listing of 'models of data-gathering.'

The commercial survey was essentially modelled on the election and the referendum: the very name used to described field operations of this type, *polls*, rubbed in these origins in attempts at a miniaturization of officially established consultations of the 'people'. The great breakthrough in 1936 was the result of a successful attempt to simulate *elections* ahead of time: there was enough isomorphy between the situation in the interview and the situation in the polling booth to make it safe to infer predictions of official results from the established frequencies of responses to the interviewers. But the crucial development occurred afterwards: *the commercial surveyors shifted from the election model to the model of the referendum* and claimed to be able to take the 'people's pulse' not only in matters of party strength or candidate choice, but even in matters of public policy. The model of the referendum of the plebiscite was to have a profound impact on the style of work in the commercial agencies, not only in their reports to newspapers and radio networks on issues of public policy, but also in their studies in the consumption market, of mass preferences among products.

In the early phase of commercial polling and market research the typical report simply gave for each question the percent of all interviewed responding one way or the other: so many X, so many Y, so many Z, so many Don't Know. The underlying model of the public was plebiscitarian and equalitarian. The 'pollsters' started out from the basic premise of full suffrage democracy: 'one citizen, one vote, one value.' They equated votes and other expressions of opinion and gave the same numerical value to every such expression, whether actively articulated independently of any interview, or elicited only in the interview situation. The sum total of such unit expressions was presented as an estimate of 'public opinion' on the given issue. The aim was clearly not just elicitation, classification, and enumeration; the essential aim was to establish the 'will of the people' through sample interviews instead of through elections and referenda. To such pioneers as George Gallup and Elmo Roper, the 'poll' was essentially a new technique of democratic control: the interviews helped to bring out the will of the 'inarticulate, unorganized majority of the people' as a countervailing power against the persuasive pressure of the many minority interests.[171]

For years to come this emphasis on the plebiscite as a model set the commercial practitioners in opposition to the governmental and the academic survey professionals.

A number of *government agencies* set up survey organizations from the late 1930's onwards to ensure quicker and cheaper data collection in areas thus far poorly covered under the traditional systems of administrative bookkeeping: the best known and most far-ranging of these was probably the Social set up under the Central Office of Information in London. The survey operations of these governmental agencies was essentially modelled on the census: they were used to get inexpensive estimates of distributions within given populations and they were geared to eminently practical tasks of policy guidance.

The *academic* survey organization also stuck close to the census model but added two further elements;

– the fixed-category *test battery,*
– the *informal reportorial conversation.*

Historically, the test battery grew out of the *standardized scholastic examination:* by contrast to the single-question approach of the plebiscite-modelled poll, the test-type interview elicited responses to a wide range of items within the same fields of variation and offered the basis for a variety of summary measures of tendencies, orientations, attitudes, personality syndromes. The techniques of test administration had initially been developed in the classroom and in the study of other 'found' groups of subjects but was, after some experimentation, adjusted to the requirements of the 'doorstep' interview. This development opened up a number of opportunities for innovation, not only in the range and depth of data gathering, but also in the style of statistical refinement. The commercial polls had typically limited themselves to elementary statistical treatments of their data: most of the findings were presented in simple percentage tables. With the introduction of multi-item test batteries, there was a marked increase in the statistical sophistication of survey analysis: the responses collected through interview surveys were not only subject to the typical correlation and factor analytical treatments of the type known from the earlier phase of differential and educational psychology, but also offered opportunities for the development of powerful new techniques, better adapted to the qualitative character of the data, such as Guttman scaling, Lazarsfeld's latent structure analysis, and various forms of attribute space analysis.

A number of academic institutions contributed to the acceleration of such efforts but one of them stands out as particularly important for the development of higher-level techniques of sampling, survey design and multivariate statistical analysis: the Survey Research Center at the University of Michigan.

This institution has a curious history, a history which holds an important lesson for the further efforts to internationalize the survey profession. Just about the time George Gallup and Elmo Roper set up their commercial interview organizations, Rensis Likert was able to persuade the United States Department of Agriculture to develop a regular agency for the conduct of surveys among farmers. During World War II this organization was given a broader definition and was able to carry out a variety of studies. Just after the end of the War, Likert and his associates took up negotiations to transfer these survey operations to an academic site and succeeded in persuading the University of Michigan to offer a home for this novel type of facility for social science research. The result was a mushrooming of significant innovations in the collection and analysis of empirical data about human behaviour and organizational structures, first within American society, later, through flexible institutional arrangements with national scholars, within a number of other advanced societies: Norway, France, Britain, Australia, Japan. Extensive programmes of research were developed in a wide variety of fields: studies of worker satisfaction in industrial and bureaucratic organizations; studies of consumer finances, purchasing behaviour, economic expectations; electoral research; studies of attitudes on issues of public concern; studies of leisure and participation; studies of adjustment and maladjustment within the younger generation . . . This extraordinary proliferation of studies was made possible through hardheaded concentration on the *infrastructure needs* for cooperative social science research: the need for a constantly renewed, constantly supervised *network of interviewers* across the country, the need for *a well-trained professional staff* of sampling experts, field administrators and data processors, and the need for *continuous interaction in the sharing of experiences* at all stages of the research operations. Other academic institutions were able to develop *some* of these infrastructure facilities but none succeeded in maintaining such an even flow of operations and in servicing such a broad range of interests, both in the academic community and in the circles of potential clients for such research.

A major characteristic of the full-blown academic survey operation is its extreme flexibility: it allows the combination of elements from all the six models of 'bureaucratic' data gathering and adds a seventh, perhaps still more important model, the *informal conversation among strangers*. The Survey Research Center at Michigan made a pioneering contribution to the development of the informal, 'open-ended' interview as a tool of data-gathering: there was an increasing realization of the artificiality of many of the response categories in the fixed-alternative questions inherited from the census model and, even more pronouncedly, from the plebiscite, and more and more elaborate attempts were made to approximate the flow of informal colloquial conversation without jeopardizing the imperative controls of cross-interview comparability. This linked up with a number of parallel developments in the 'case-oriented' behavioural sciences: the *therapeutic conversation* inherited from the religious practice of the confession and perfected in the various schools of psychoanalysis, the *counselling interview* developed within the social work tradition and in educational psychology, the *personnel interview* developed within management psychology, the informal *questioning of informants* practised for decades by cultural and social anthropologists in their studies of preliterate and traditional communities. These movements on the data elicitation front had been reinforced by concomitant developments on the data categorization – dataprocessing front: the efforts made within linguistics, folklore and communications research to elaborate techniques for the statistical analysis of the style and contents of oral or textual messages helped the survey analysts to find ways of coping with 'open-ended' responses and to develop techniques for the extraction of significant dimensions of variation in the flow of messages recorded by the interviewers.

II. *The Internationalization of the Sample Survey: Opportunities and Barriers*

The rapid expansion of the networks of polling agencies and market research organizations in the immediate wake of World War II generated a great deal of internationalist ferment: enthusiasts talked about 'world surveying' (Dodd, 1946–47), about global 'demoscopic services' on the model of the meteorological services. The numbers of cross-national polls and surveys did indeed increase rapidly in those years: this can easily be read out of our extensive Bibliography. But the early enthusiasts for world surveying were soon disappointed: it proved difficult to spread the new techniques beyond the confines of the advanced Western countries, and even when organizations could be set up in typically 'developing countries' the sampling and the interviewing proved very difficult to organize beyond the boundaries of the larger urban settlements. More and more social scientists became suspicious of the claims for the universal applicability of the new technique and began to speculate about the limiting factors, the barriers against further diffusion. The critiques of social and cultural anthropologists further reinforced this attitude of suspicious scepticism: the sample survey was essentially a technique for the study of the 'alphabetized', mobile, individualistic and market-oriented societies of the West and could not be expected to produce meaningful data for the analysis of preliterate cultures minimally affected by such processes of modernization as monetization, mobilization and politicization.

The literature on this question has grown voluminous over the years. The 53 items of section I.1 of our Bibliography represent only a selection of the most *explicit* discussions of the conditions for the spread of the survey technique: if we were to cover the *indirect, ad hoc* discussions of the pros and cons of sample surveys *vs.* anthropological observation in particular cases, our list would have been vastly longer. The fundamental reason for the perpetuation of this debate is of course the process of

Westernization itself: with the continuing spread of the Western type of market economy, of the mass media and of the concomitant phenomena of urban mass culture, the developing societies tend to lend themselves less and less to the traditional techniques of the cultural or social anthropologist, but do not, therefore, become obvious territories for the standardized sample survey. The 'transitional' status of large areas of the 'Third World' has increased the uncertainties about methods of data gathering and has added new fire to the old controversies over the boundaries of the disciplines.

To move further ahead in this debate we clearly have to abandon the unitary concept of the sample survey: a variety of elements, inherited from widely differing traditions of data gathering, go into any particular field operation and the balance among the elements have shifted over time and varied across schools of practitioners. Clearly *some* elements in this congeries of data-gathering devices may work in developing communities even if the others do not. There is no basis for a blanket acceptance or rejection of the survey method as such but there is very often definite need for *methodological experiments* before deciding which mode of field operation and which style of questioning will produce valid data in which context and for what purposes of analysis. What is woefully lacking in the literature on the diffusion of survey techniques to developing countries is systematic methodological research of the type carried out in the advanced countries on modes of contacting target respondents, on styles of interviewing, on the effects of variations in question formulations and question sequences, on the consequences of interviewer-respondent differences in sex, age, status, dialect, level of articulation.[172] This is high-priority area of research in the developing countries: with the spread of literacy, the uprooting of traditional cultures and the development of new structures of organization the established methods of anthropological data collection will no longer be adequate and will have to be supplemented, if not replaced, by various forms of standardized questioning of samples of the territorial populations.

One important reason for the failures of the new style of data-gathering in traditional and developing communities was the overconcentration of the plebiscitarian model. This was the most culture-bound of all the seven paradigms of questioning: it was based on the assumption that *all* adults, women as well as men, heads of households as well as other members, were faced with alternatives of choice and had the resources to make meaningful decisions. This was a model eminently suited to the market culture: in the economy as well as in the polity, the monetized/enfranchised citizen was faced with distinct alternatives (products/candidates/policy options) and had the resources (discretionary funds/votes) required to make effective choices among them.

This model worked in the competitive economies which were at the same time competitive polities: the units to be sampled might not be the same in studies of the markets for products (for minor routine products: housewives; for durables: the head of the household or both spouses) as in studies of the markets for candidates, parties or policies (all the enfranchised citizens) but the basic structure of the information-gathering style was the same. The model was also introduced in countries where the markets for *products* were competitive but where the *political* market was heavily monopolistic: this tended to produce acceptable data for the economic clients but much more questionable data for the political analysts. The opposite imbalance has been observed in studies of competitive polities with backward economies; election pools will make sense but consumer preference questions produce data of low validity in communities at a low level of monetization. The fourth cell in this fourfold scheme produces least trouble methodologically: polling organizations are not very likely to move into territories where both the economic and the political motives for the conduct of interview studies are missing. The difficulties occur in the cells off the diagonal:

		Polity	
		Competitive	Monolithic, traditional
Economy	Competitive	Political and economic polls effective	Questionable data on *political* choices (e. g., polls in Southern Italy, Spain, Mexico)
	Monopolistic, traditional	Questionable data on *economic* choices (e. g., polls in remote Indian villages)	Polling not likely to occur

The dilemmas 'off the diagonal' are often solved through geographical concentration: market research forms in the dual economies of the Third World generally find it most profitable to limit their field work to the major cities, to the segments of the population most likely to *have* some effective choice in economic matters (in India, the commercial pollsters opted for another compromise: they interviewed in the cities and in the *nearest* of the villages!)

In the thoroughly monetized nations of Europe and the West, the purchasers of data generally frowned on such restrictions: they wanted to know about their chances in the expanding rural markets as well. But in many of these countries the conditions for *economic* market research were much more favourable than for *political:* the nation might be economically integrated through the spread of the same brands of consumer products and the same ideals of modern living, but there would still be bitter conflicts over cultural, religious and political identity.

In such segmented polities the pollsters attempting to add political questions to their lists of consumer preference items often encountered a great deal of resistance and obstruction. In countries such as Belgium, France, Switzerland, Austria, and Italy, not to speak of Greece and Spain, the refusal rates for political questions tended to be very high and the significance of the responses recorded was often subject to doubt.[173]

Questions about politics may be rejected as impertinent or embarrassing even in the most homogeneous of countries (the refusal rates for party preference questions *are* at their very lowest in Sweden and the United States) but the percentages of such 'lost' responses tend to be so small that they do not affect decisively the possibilities of meaningful analysis. In countries torn by deep-seated conflicts between the central elite and the peripheral communities, between secular and religious camps, between Communist and bourgeois establishments, it will clearly be much more difficult to establish the needed *rapport* with the target respondents and to elicit sincere answers to political questions.

There may be ways of reducing the risk of rejection and increasing the chances of obtaining valid data but the national polling organizations have generally found such devices too expensive. They may establish scores for the likelihood of refusals by type of local community and then oversample the most recalcitrant ones, they may even develop culturally and politically distinctive interviewer teams and assign matching samples of respondents to each of them, but all such tricks will be to little avail as long as the interview organizations adhere so closely to the plebiscitarian model of fixed-alternative questioning: this model may generate useful data in cultural and political contexts where *the costs to the person of reporting a choice or an identity is at a minimum* but will rarely work in contexts where the reporting of such information is seen as potentially disruptive.

This is a source of variation rarely considered in the design of samples and in the planning of interview schedules: the strength of the local cultural and political pressures to *keep information from strangers*. The more severe the strains between the centres of political power and the peripheral communities in a system, the less likely is information to flow freely from respondents to interviewer: conversations with strangers tend to be brief and guarded and the typical fixed-alternative question will be received with great suspicion if not outright scorn. Anthropologists and sociologists have described a large number of such tight-knit local communities within larger nation-states: Julian Pitt-River's work on a village of the Spanish Sierra is a particularly vivid example (Pitt-Rivers, 1954). In such situations anthropological techniques of observation and conversation with informants may be the only appropriate ones but in larger communities of this kind the numbers of households and segments may be so large as to call for some form of sampling: in such cases the census model of questioning may prove the most effective but it may also prove possible to get closer to some mapping of social, cultural and political identifications through the use of test batteries and loosely structured reportorial interviews. But whatever the technique of questioning the crucial condition of success is the estab-lishment of friendly and confident *rapport:* if the interviewer is received as a potential spy, as an agent of the police or of the tax collector, the data he can collect will not be worth much. Survey organizations are 'nationaliz-ing' agencies: they spread questions, requests for information, from the centre to the peripheries of each nation. But by contrast to the army, the police, and the fiscal administration they have no way of forcing their subjects to give information: they depend for their survival on the simple fact of social life that people are willing to communicate freely with stran-gers once a few minimum requirements of confidence have been estab-lished.[174] In thoroughly mobile national communities such as the United States, even 'out-of-towners' may quickly establish this minimal level of confidence, but in countries with many isolated, tradition-tied communities hostile to influences from the power centres, it may be essential to work from inside to establish local contacts and to use local interviewers. *Teachers,* particularly women teachers, may often prove useful in this role: they will generally have established themselves as persons worthy of trust, at least in part of the community, and their contacts with agencies at the national centre will not so easily be viewed with suspicion.

There are well-known limits to any such efforts, however. In countries and territories divided by international power conflicts *any* effort of data-gathering, however innocuous, runs the risk of politicization: the inter-viewer tends to be treated as a potential spy and the survey organization tends to be labelled an agency of foreign dominance. The Camelot scandal over the allocation of Defence Department funds for surveys and other studies in Latin America (Horowitz, 1963) has recently reminded the social science community of these dangers and has prompted a great deal of soul-searching among the strategists of cross-national research: many of them have come to the conclusion that the UN and its agencies might have a useful role to play in the sponsorship of scholarly studies in sensitive areas of the world.

III. *Styles of Cross-national Survey Research: Three Case Studies*
Whatever the difficulties in the way of the diffusion of the survey method a number of countries of the world have for two decades or more been subjected to regular sampling and questioning by private and public or-ganizations. A great number of the questions asked have been similar in structure from country to country to country and have generated potentially comparable data for analysis.

Some of these potentially comparable categories of data bear on essential background characteristics needed in most efforts of analysis: sex, age, status in the household (head, dependent), economic activity status (employer, employed, housewife, retired, unemployed), occupation, type of community, region. The international networks of polling organizations have tried their best to develop uniform styles of questioning and coding for such variables and have to some extent been guided in this work by efforts of statistical standardization pursued by the UN Statistical office, the ILO, the OECD and other agencies.

Many of the attitude-opinion questions have been repeated in similar form in country after country through agreements within the international networks (e.g., Roper, 1948; Démocratie, 1947) or through the intervention of some major international client (e.g., Time, 1948; Wallace, 1948–49; Woodward, 1948; Stern, 1949; Reader's Digest, 1964: 1; Reader's Digest, 1964: 2). Other questions just happened to be formulated in roughly similar ways because they dealt with events, fashions, fads, issues of an international nature: there was no deliberate effort to establish cross-national comparability but the data generated happened to be similar enough to warrant reanalysis in an international perspective. The existence of a great variety of such 'haphazard products of internationalization' is *one* reason for the development of archives of raw data from sample surveys: the literature on this movement is already extensive (Bisco, 1964; Campbell, 1960; Converse, 1964 and 1966: 1; Datum, 1965; Deutsch, 1966: 1; Deutsch, 1966: 2; Gardin, 1960; Hastings, 1961; Hastings, 1963; Hastings, 1964; Lefcowitz, 1963; Lucci, 1957; Merritt, 1965; Miller, 1964; Miller, 1966: 1; Mitchell, 1964: 1; Mitchell, 1964: 2; Mitchell, 1965; Murdock, 1961; Rokkan, 1957 and 1966: 3; 1964: 1; Russett, 1966; Scheuch, 1964; 't Hart, 1964).

Only a small minority of the total number of questions asked in similar fashion across two or more countries have been part of *deliberately designed cross-national surveys*. Such studies are still a rarity: they are costly, they require a great deal of organization, they are not surefire investments. But they are methodologically and strategically much more important than the other studies: they offer a much better basis for serious and systematic consideration of comparability and equivalence issues, of questions about the logic of cross-national and cross-culture research designs, and of the organizational options in such undertakings. It would be impossible, within the confines of this brief introduction to a Bibliography, to review all such attempts at deliberate cross-national data gathering. Instead, I have chosen to report in some detail on three cases:

– the 1948 UNESCO nine-country survey reported in the well-known volume *How Nations See Each Other* (Buchanan, 1953)

– the seven-country survey of primary and secondary school teachers carried out in 1953 by the *Organization for Comparative Social Research* (OCSR, 1954; Rokkan, 1955: 1; Aubert, 1954; Rokkan, 1955: 2)

– the five-country survey of active *vs.* passive citizens reported on by Almond and Verba in their work *The Civic Culture* (Almond, 1963).

3.1. *The UNESCO Nine-country Survey*

The UNESCO survey was part of a broader programme of research on 'tensions' among nations, races and ethnic groups (Klineberg, 1950). The objective was to map variations in 'common ideas about foreign peoples' and in 'attitudes affecting international understanding.' The study was carried out in altogether nine countries. Eight of the countries were economically advanced and could be covered by well-equipped private polling organizations: Australia, France, Germany, Italy, the Netherlands, Norway, the United Kingdom and the United States of America. The ninth country was a 'dual economy' country with very limited elements of pluralist competition in its political system: Mexico. In this country there was no question of establishing a nation-wide cross-section: the sample simply covered the 23 cities where the organization had trained interviewers. The choice of countries was not guided by any considerations of theory, and did not reflect any deliberate research design: the countries were simply chosen in terms of the availability of polling organizations and the convenience of cooperation.

The 1948 study proceeded in a series of steps:

a) elaboration of first draft questionnaire;
b) selection of countries for study and of survey organizations to undertake the field work;
c) preliminary field tests and revision of questionnaire;
d) preparation of final questionnaire in its *English* and *French* 'master versions';
e) transmission to each organization of
    (aa) master questionnaire in English and French;
    (bb) instructions for translations of questionnaire;
    (cc) instructions for sampling (1,000 respondents, cross-sectional quota sample);
    (dd) instructions for coding and tabulation of responses;
f) field work in each country (June 1948–January 1949);
g) coding, punching and tabulating in each country;
h) presentation to UNESCO by each country organization of operational reports and response tabulations in accordance with instructions;
i) central analysis of tabulations;
j) preparations of reports.

In reviewing these operational steps the authors of the principal report emphasize the importance of further coordination and centralization in controlling the levels of comparability and in ensuring fuller exploration of cross-national analysis possibilities. Quite particularly they call attention to the need for such coordination on two points:

'1. Pre-testing the ballot with several hundred interviews in each country, to get a leverage on the translation problems and to standardize the coding.

2. Central coding and tabulation of results from ballots which show as precisely as possible the background information on each respondent.' (Buchanan, 1953: p. 113).

In addition, mention was made of the need for more 'open-ended' questions in such cross-national surveys. The prohibitive cost of central coding of verbatim protocols of free response was, however, found to argue decisively against any substantial change in the proportion of 'check-box' to 'open-ended' questions.

The design of the comparative study was very straightforward. Five general areas of opinion-perception can be said to have been explored through the 1948 study:

1. The individual's estimate of his own position in the class structure of his country, and its relation to his view of other people at home and abroad (Q. 9–10).
2. His feeling of personal security in matters unrelated to international affairs, and his satisfaction with life in his own country (Q. 5–8).
3. The peoples toward whom he feels friendly or unfriendly (Q. 11–12).
4. The stereotypes he carries in his head of his own and certain foreign peoples (Q. 13).
5. His ideas about human nature, peace, world government, and national character (Q. 1–4).

In addition, the design included (6) an item relating to the general political orientation of the respondent (Q. 14), (7) five standard items of information on the basic social characteristics of each respondent (sex, age, education, socio-economic status, occupation).

The study was from the outset presented as a descriptive and exploratory one. The interview instrument was not designed to test any articulate social science theory or its derivations but was organized as it was to allow analyses of empirical relationships between responses in systematically selected problem areas. There were, however, some general and some specific expectations of probable distributions and relationships, and these expectations seem to some extent to have guided the preparation of the instructions for tabulations and the plan of analysis. It can only be said to be unfortunate that in such an exploratory study the actual analysis had to be limited to the relatively few cross-tabulations which had been decided on before the data had been collected and the response distributions for each country were known (Buchanan, 1953: p. 109).

It is of some interest to observe how these pioneers of the comparative survey went about their *analysis* of the data from the nine countries. In the introductory chapter of their report (p. 8) they state:

'Two complementary systems of analysis are employed to reduce this mass of data, not all of which is equally valuable, to workable dimensions:

1. Percentages on a single question or group of questions in all nine nations are juxtaposed, and *similarities* between all or most of the nations are examined.
2. Each national survey is treated as a unit, and examined in the light of what was known about that country, with *differences* receiving major attention'.

They further imply that three types of procedures of analysis may usefully be applied in exploring such similarities or differences (simplified summary of the list p. 9):

Type I.   Direct between-country comparisons of response distributions for single questions;

Type II.   Between-country comparisons of the direction and statistical significance of relationships between responses to one question and some other attribute or variable, whether another response or some 'background' characteristic;

Type III. Ranking of countries on the basis of percentage distributions on one or more questions and cross-national analysis of relationships between several rank orders between different countries.

A fourth type of procedure is considered but is not recommended: 'Percentages, indices, or differences for the nine countries may be added or averaged, but this is avoided where possible, since it serves to obscure national variations from the pattern'.

The actual analysis was severely limited by the 'freezing' of the list of required tabulations ahead of the inspection of the actual data: excerpts of this a *priori* tabulating instructions are given in Appendix C (Buchanan, 1953: pp. 121–24).

Most of the tabulations requested were of Type I or Type II; mostly straightforward comparisons of the marginal distributions question by question, or simple controls for one background characteristic at a time, primarily sex, age, education and interviewer-rated socio-economic status, in a few cases a crude classification by the occupation of the head of the household.

Most of the Type III tabulations bear exclusively on data generated by the survey itself: countries are ranked on single questions or on various summary scores on the basis of the degree of correlation among responses and the correlations of such rank orders are presented. Only in two cases do we find attempts at analyses of the variations in the survey data through the specification of what we now call the *macro*-contexts of the national responses: on p. 25 the countries are grouped by the politics of their current government to account for variations in attitudes to its ideological position ('too much to the right', 'too much to the left') and on p. 34 some

GNP figures are brought in to account for the variations in the national rank orders on the 'satisfaction' and 'security' scores.

The analysis stays practically entirely at the *micro* level: true to the tradition of plebiscitarian polling the analysts treat each respondent as an isolated unit cut out of the day-to-day contexts of historically and culturally channelled interaction in his society. There is some reluctance to merging all units indiscriminately into one set irrespective of the country of residence (Type IV in the scheme above) but the rationale for this reluctance is not developed. The analysts feel intuitively that the data *have to* be grouped and analyzed by country but this classification remains completely nominal in their treatment: beyond the very elementary classification by the party in power and the level of economic development, there is no attempt to identify any analytical dimensions of the national contexts of the variations in recorded responses.

In the further development of cross-national survey research, these questions of *macro-micro* design took on central importance. The crucial analytical distinctions were initially worked out on bodies of single-nation data (Lazarsfeld, 1955; Suchman, 1955) but were obviously of critical importance in comparisons across different political systems.

The essential scheme of distinction can be set out in three steps:

Primary Personal Characteristics:	Examples	Derived Unit Characteristics
An attribute or variable characterizing an *individual qua individual*.	Sex Weight Pigmentation Incidence of some disease.	A rate, an average, a parameter of some distribution within the unit.
An attribute or variable characterizing an *individual qua member of some group of social category*.	Level of education reached, occupation, organizational role, etc.	A rate, an average, a parameter.
Relational Characteristics:		
An attribute or variable characterizing a *relationship of one individual to other individuals*.	Frequency of communication between A and B, sociometric choice.	A rate, an average, a parameter, or a derived structural attribute of the unit (e. g., 'cohesion').
Contextual Characteristics		*Primary Unit Characteristics*
An attribute or variable characterizing an individual through the characteristics of the unit he is part of or is exposed to.	*Unit* datum: a national political community highly dependent on foreign trade *Personal* datum: a citizen of such a nation.	An attribute or variable *characteristic of the unit qua unit,* not derivable from the characteristics of its individual members.

This scheme posits only two levels of variation: the individual and the next-level unit. In cross-national research it will often prove necessary to link up variations at *three or more* levels: at the level of the individual, at the level of his local community (e. g., degree of urbanization), at the level of the geographical region (e. g., peripheral or near the national centre) and at the level of the nation itself (e. g. neutral or committed in Cold War).

The potentialities of such multi-level reasoning is exemplified in the paradigm proposed in Chapter 1 (above pp. 21–22) for the analysis of cross-national variations in the extent of political participation. Such schemes could be multiplied for variable after variable. Perhaps the clearest illustration of a multi-level, cross-national research design is the one presented in the report on the *International Study of Achievement in Mathematics* (Husén, 1967). In this twelve-country study the dependent micro-variations, the scores on a mathematics test, are analyzed as functions of variables in at least five levels, at the level of the *pupil* (B and R in Fig. 1 in Chapter 1), the *family* (parents' occupation and education: a C-type variable in Fig. 1), the *school* (also a C-type variable), the *locality* (urban-rural, size: L in Fig. 1) and the *national educational system* (N in Fig. 1: *global* attributes such as the number of years of compulsory schooling, *aggregate* variables such as the proportion of 16- or 20-year olds attending school). There is no great difficulty in developing the logic of such paradigms: the real challenge of cross-national research lies in the difficulties of linking up theory and data level by level. *Some* progress has been made in the years since UNESCO organized the nine-country survey, but as will be apparent from the Bibliography, the great bulk of the cross-national studies have remained at the level of simple replications without any attempt at a specification of the macro-conditions for the co-variations established at the micro-level.

3.2. *The OCSR Seven-Country Teacher Survey*

The sample survey of *teachers* carried out during 1953 in seven countries of Western Europe offers a good example of the difficulties of developing a strict 'macro-micro' design in comparative research.

The Organization for Comparative Social Research grew out of an initiative taken by the Institute for Social Research in Oslo in 1951 (see Duijker, 1954; Rokkan, 1955: 1). The Institute organized an International Seminar on Comparative Social Research (Christiansen, 1951) and invited younger sociologists and social psychologists from research centres in seven Western European countries to take part in its deliberations. As spelled out at the time, the aims of this Seminar were twofold: a) to ensure detailed discussion and effective agreement on a plan for the conduct of a set of comparative enquiries to be carried out by national teams within some cooperative framework; b) to provide specialized training in behavioural science methodologies through such discussion and planning, and to ensure effective research training on the national level through participation in the actual enquiries to be carried out. The organizers deliberately refrained from assigning any definite priority to one or the other of these objectives. In fact, the two were inextricably entangled: getting comparable data from the different countries inevitably involved some training of personnel, and such training could be accelerated and intensified through the pressure to understand, adapt and implement a joint plan of operation in each country. In terms of the striking unevenness of sociological and social psychological developments, training, and research facilities in the countries of Western Europe at the time, it was relatively easy to justify the Seminar as a training device. Participation in the planning, designing and conduct of comparative enquiries in a number of countries would not only provide opportunities for the training of local researchers and students, but also afford an excellent means for the testing of research standards and the improvement of research facilities.

By contrast, it was much more difficult to agree on a convincing rationale for comparative research *as such,* for the co-ordinated planning of cross-national studies. This problem was considered at some length during the first sessions of the Seminar. Herbert Hyman, of Columbia University, directed the first sessions and took particular interest in this problem of research strategy. He and his Norwegian collaborators prepared a memorandum on 'The Conditions Warranting Cross-National Social Research'. This forms part of a mimeographed volume on *Cross-national Social Research* (Hyman, 1951: 1; Hyman, 1951: 2), a collection of papers on various aspects of comparative research on intergroup conflict and aggression. The memorandum specifies four types of gains that might be derived from comparative research across national populations:

1. gains in training, scientific competence and organizational facilities for international cooperation among intellectuals of different countries;
2. applied social science gains through the accumulation, collation and dissemination of comparative information on a number of different national populations;
3. methodological gains to be achieved through the systematic validation and reliability testing of social science research instruments in different language communities and cultural settings;
4. fundamental social science gains achieved through the development and verification of specifically cross-national or cross-cultural propositions.

This fourth point is of particular importance in any discussion of alternative plans for comparative research. It is an argument *against* the mere replication of conceptually identical experiments or measurement operations in different national populations, and is an argument *for* the development of specifically cross-national designs: these would relate overall system variations or aggregate population differences of one sort or another to dependent variables of a sociological or social-psychological character. The argument against simple replications goes like this: the repetition of an experiment or of a set of measurements in different national populations can only lead to determinate findings if the results are *alike* for all countries; but since this is highly unlikely to happen for most of the relationships of interest to the sociologist or the social psychologist, replications are practically always bound to raise more questions than they settle. This is so because there is no way of deciding conclusively between the many alternative interpretations that can plausibly be advanced in cases of between-country differences: they may be operational or experimental artifacts, they may reflect differences in the stimulus situations through the translation process, they may constitute genuine evidence against the variables operating in *one* country and *not* in others. If this is the case, any comparative research plan focused on the simple replication of one data gathering operation in one or more countries would be fraught with considerable risk. As a consequence it is argued that any comparative research design should include, not only a set of core hypotheses to be tested in all the countries in question, but also another set of *specific hypotheses about possible determinants of differences among the countries.* To quote Hyman: 'To undertake comparative research, without incorporating into the theory just such hypotheses about the possible different findings, and merely to hope that a general or universal law will be established, is a most hazardous undertaking. All past knowledge would suggest that social psychological phenomena would vary in different settings. And merely to establish different phenomena in the different countries without being able to explain them to some degree, would be a most abortive finding.'

The emphasis, then, in this early analysis was on the need to *expect differences* among countries or among cultures, and to develop theories and hypotheses for testing that might account for such differences. This emphasis led logically to the principal contention in the analysis: the contention that the only *theoretical* justification for comparative research lies in the unique opportunities it can provide for the testing of the effects of variations that cannot be established *within* any one national or cultural unit, but only *among* a number of such units. To quote the memorandum:

'What differentiates these hypotheses – the uniquely cross-national or cross-cultural hypotheses – from hypotheses testable within one national boundary? . . . . Obviously not the nature of the dependent variables in the design, since dependent variables of every psychological kind might well be affected by factors present in one nation and not in another. There is no basis for *excluding* phenomena of any type from comparative research . . . .

. . . 'It is on the side of the *independent* variables that the basis for exclusion from comparative research occurs. To establish the influence of an independent variable on some phenomenon, different values of it must be available. If particular values of a given variable cannot be found within a given nation, but *can* be found in contrasting conditions of two or more countries, this provides the instance in which comparative national research serves a unique scientific function. Unless there is at least one independent variable of this type in the schema, the project cannot be justified on the grounds of gains in fundamental knowledge.'

Such a conception of cross-national research clearly implies the need for a *combination of methodologies* to assemble the data that would be required to test the hypotheses: some of the variables might pertain to *individual* characteristics, others to *group* characteristics, and others again to *global* or *aggregate* characteristics of the entire units to be compared. It will be evident from Hyman's specification of the criteria for comparative research that the independent variables in the designs will in most cases be at the macro-level: there will in most cases be sufficient variability in individual or group characteristics to allow the testing of relationships *within* one single nation or culture, but it is by definition impossible to establish any variability in global or aggregate characteristics without comparing and ordering a number of national or cultural units. This is a crucial point in discussions of comparative research: it raises the problems of the rationale for the selection of units of comparison, and the problem of the identification of theoretically significant system-level differences.

It was altogether quite interesting to observe how, in the face of such difficulties, the ideal requirements set forth at the opening of the Seminar were gradually lost sight of, as the members struggled to reach agreement on the design of a common set of inquiries, and the specifications of a common set of research instruments. The crucial point of course was the initial selection of countries to be covered. Ideally, as the original memorandum had stated, countries should be picked that are clearly contrasted with respect to at least one of the variables to be examined. The Seminar, however, was not set up with this purpose in mind: the original idea was simply to get social scientists from a number of countries in the Western European area to sit together and discuss the possibilities of their conducting equivalent enquiries on each of their populations within some joint cooperative framework. There was no deliberate selection of countries for study because there was no advance identification of the system variables that might warrant comparative research. There was no imposition of a design already established, or of a set of procedures already used: the cross-national research programme was to be the *joint responsibility* of the Seminar members, and the research design was accordingly a function of the interests and orientations predominant in the group. In a democratic set-up of this kind it was obviously impossible to uphold the ideal requirements of an experimental design: the research coverage was simply determined by the availability of personnel rather than by theoretical considerations of contrasting values of system-level country variables.

This was not only an organizational matter. There were also important methodological reasons for such departures from the ideal requirements of cross-national social research. Given the limited geographic coverage of the studies that could be undertaken, there was no possibility of getting a sufficient number of national units for each of the cells that would be required for the testing of relationships between system-level variables on the one hand, and group or individual variables on the other. The studies would have to be limited to the testing of the existence or non-existence of differences among the several countries in the direction of within-country relationships. In any case, there were only scanty and unreliable data available for any systematic ordering of the countries in terms of the general relationships on which the Seminar wished to conduct research.

The Seminar members found, after lengthy discussion, that they could agree on a basic research design relating variations in the level of 'threat' experienced by persons or units, to variations in 'pressures for conformity'. (Aubert, 1954; Rokkan, 1955: 2, cf. Chapters 9 and 10 below). This relationship was to be tested on two levels of interaction: through social psychological *experiments at the face-to-face group level,* and through *sample surveys at the national level.*

At the face-to-face group level it was clearly possible to vary the threat variables experimentally in such a way that the functional relationships to the different 'pressures for conformity' variables could be examined, at least for some part of the total range of variability.

At the national level, the ideal procedure would naturally have been to rank order a set of countries according to some criterion for intensity of external threat, and then to select contrasting areas for extensive study. This, however, was clearly out of the question. The study was, for organizational and financial reasons, confined to Western Europe, and it would have made little sense to establish differences between regions along any dimension of *actual* threat. This meant that the studies had to be squarely focused on differences in the ways threats on the national level were *received* and *responded* to by the subjects: what features of the international situation were they most worried about, what developments in world affairs did they consider most likely, what forces did they see at work in these developments?

There were no *a priori* hypotheses as to the directions of differences between the response distributions for the seven countries to be studied, but the designers of the study certainly expected wide discrepancies. Consider not only the marked contrasts in the learning processes of each of these peoples during the preceding couple of decades, but even more, the differences in their current political and strategic positions: of the seven countries, four – Belgium, the Netherlands, Norway, and the United Kingdom – had joined the North Atlantic Treaty Organization and found strong support for NATO policies in public opinion; a fifth country – France – had also joined NATO, but was profoundly split over its policies; a sixth – Western Germany – had at that time no foreign policy of its own, but was preparing to join the Western alliance; while the seventh country – Sweden – had decided to stay neutral in the East-West power conflict, despite active advocacy of NATO-oriented policies in Liberal and Conservative circles. These marked foreign policy differences could obviously be expected to be reflected in the response distributions for each of the national samples, and to modify in one way or another the hypothesized relationships between threat perception responses and policy conformity responses. It should be emphasized however, that expectations of such between-country differences did not form any explicit part of the original study design. Despite the warnings in the initial design memorandum, the Seminar did decide to stick to a replication design for the comparative studies, not only for the group experiment, but even for the attitude survey.

The reasons for these decisions were simple enough. The design was very much a function of the composition of the planning group. There were representatives of research institutions from seven countries, and there was great interest in getting the studies done in each of these countries. It would obviously have been difficult to decide to exclude any one country or add another on grounds of design: not only for psychological and financial reasons, but even more because there were no consistent theories nor any valid factual data to justify any aggregate ordering of countries in terms of design.

In the *small group experiments,* there was also some justifiable expectation that the hypothesized relationships would show up in the findings – that the replications were really worth the risk. There was no *a priori* theorizing about social or cultural determinants of possible between-country differences, but the most elaborate precautions were taken to ensure that any differences that *were* found would not be artifacts of the experimental situation or of behavioural measurement procedures. The findings were on the whole positive: the hypothesized relationships did show up in one way or another in the countries where the controls indicated that the experimental manipulations could be taken to have been conceptually equivalent. The data did, however, in some cases confront the analyst with some harassing dilemmas of interpretation (Rommetveit, 1954; Schachter, 1954: 2).

The *comparative attitude studies* were also designed essentially as replications of the same research procedures in seven different populations. They differed radically from the group experiments, however, in a number of ways: not only were they correlational studies of response distributions in different population samples, but they also had their principal frame of reference in the *nation,* the national political community. This made a considerable difference from the point of view of comparative analysis. When the OCSR field workers asked the teachers, in their different languages, about their country and their government, they did not respond to any generic stimulus, but had in mind the very concrete reality of the national power structure, the policies pursued, the group identifications involved. This obviously made for a more complex data gathering operation and a more intricate comparative analysis.

Formally the attitude surveys were cross-national replications, but the multiplicity of factual, situational and attitudinal data obtained from the respondents made it possible not only to test the same hypotheses across the seven countries, but also to explore the possible determinants of between-country differences in the relationships under study.

The methodologically most interesting findings of the comparative survey analysis can be summarized in the simple table on the facing page.

Some of the cross-national differences in the outcomes of the 'micro-micro' tests are easily accounted for: the fact that Sweden differed in its foreign policy from the other six clearly had to have an influence on the direction of relationships among attitude items bearing on international issues, and the fact that Norway, as well as Sweden, was governed by a working-class party would have equally obvious consequences for the structuring of domestic attitudes. The other deviations are much harder to account for. Further analysis suggests that the *composition of the teaching corps* in each nation should have been much more systematically taken into account in the design of the samples and the organization of the interviews (Albinski, 1959). Some of the most striking differences in attitude structuring were found *across educational subcultures* in the same nation: in Belgium, England, France, Germany and the Netherlands the teachers in the denominational schools scored consistently higher than the state school teachers on the 'F-scale' for authoritarianism (for other studies of this dimension see Albinski, 1959; Brengelmann, 1960; Cohn, 1954; Coladarci, 1959; Gaier, 1959; Institut, 1960; Kanwar, 1958; Kassof, 1958; Kennedy, 1958; Melikian, 1956; Melikian, 1959; Prothro, 1953; Siegman, 1958; Siegman, 1962) but their position on that score was not so clearly related to the political items as for other teachers. Unfortunately the samples were not stratified to allow detailed analysis of such sources of within-nation variance in the cultural contexts of attitude formation. The designers of the seven-country surveys *might* have become aware of this source of variance if they had familiarized themselves more thoroughly with the literature on comparative educational institutions and had access to earlier studies of differences in attitudes and personality characteristics across the different teaching corps, but the project was too one-sidedly operation-oriented to allow any lengthy period of 'contextual immersion' ahead of the actual design of the study. Intellectually, this is perhaps the greatest challenge of comparative survey analysis: the achievement of some

	Variables correlated	Same finding all seven countries	Differences found across countries — I. By foreign policy posture: NATO countries; II. By the party in government			
			Conservatives	Mixed/ Christians	Labour	Sweden
Intensity of 'war-threatenedness'	Intensity of 'enemy-threatenedness'	Negative correlation throughout				
"	Attitude to military preparedness	Neg. corr.				
"	Attitude to national foreign policy		Neg.	Neg.	Neg.	Pos.
"	Attitude to own government's domestic policy		Neg.	Neg.	Pos.	Pos.
"	Intolerance of deviance		Neg.	Not clear	Neg.	Neg.
Authoritarianism score (Rokkan, 1956: 3)	Intensity of 'war-threatenedness'		Neg.	Neg. except in Netherlands	Neg.	Not clear
"	Attitude to world government	Neg.				
"	Support for working class parties (CP + Soc.)	Neg.				
"	Intolerance of deviants	Neg.				

effective balance between the search for detailed understanding of historical-cultural-political contexts and the search for invariances in the structuring of analytical dimensions across the same contexts. *Within* the nation the sample survey in fact forces the analyst to concentrate on the search for invariances: the anonymity of the punched card and the technical difficulties of finding out more about each person than what has already been recorded forces the analyst to squeeze as much as he can out of the data at hand. In comparisons across nations the situation may be very different: if the national units compared are very many and very remote (such as in the analyses of materials in the Yale Data Program presented in Russett, 1964; Merritt, 1966: 1; cf. Retzlaff, 1965) the 'anonymization' effect may be strong enough to favour 'survey-type' analysis, but in narrower comparisons of fewer nations there is bound to be constant oscillation between the 'knowledge by description' and the 'knowledge by acquaintance' poles of the continuum, between analytical precision and contextual intuition.[175] Judging from the literature recorded in our Bibliography it is very unlikely that an effective balance between the two orientations can ever be achieved in *any single project:* this will only be possible through a continuous process of cumulation, through systematic reanalysis and reinterpretation of studies already done, and through the deliberate design of fresh data-gathering operations to settle hypotheses left in doubt by earlier ones.

3.3. *The Almond-Verba Five-Country Study*
An important step in this direction was taken in 1958 in the planning of a comparative survey study of the 'meaning of citizenship.'[176]

Gabriel Almond and Sidney Verba set a landmark in the history of comparative politics through this study. *The Civic Culture* (Almond, 1963) represents an innovation in the literature of comparative politics: it opens up new perspectives on the theory of democratic politics; it demonstrates the potentialities of a new method of data gathering and analysis; it points to a series of problems for further research and theorizing on the sources of national differences in the character of the relationships between government and the governed. It is a great book and it is a measure of its greatness that it raises as many queries and objections as it produces insights and confirmations.

In bare outline, the study reported in this volume seems simple enough: Gabriel Almond and Sidney Verba wanted to find out what sorts of people were active, articulate and 'responsive' and what sorts of people were passive, inarticulate and unconcerned in a number of full-suffrage democracies, and they wanted to study similarities and differences in the backgrounds, the orientations and the motivations of actives and passives in such polities. Indeed, what is surprising is that it took so long before any one did just that. We have had full-suffrage democracies in the West for decades, and the contrasts between the active few and the passive but mobilized mass have been endlessly discussed, and sometimes even in-vestigated, in country after country. A few scattered attempts were made in the twenties and the thirties to assemble some of the statistics and to com-pare them across a few countries, but these attempts stayed at a very low level of theoretical sophistication, (Rokkan, 1960: 1; Rokkan, 1962: 1; Rokkan, 1962: 2). The advent of the poll and the sample survey opened up new possibilities for comparative political statistics, but these possibilities were first seen by sociologists such as Lazarsfeld, Lerner (Lerner, 1958) and Lipset (Lipset, 1960) and only much later by scholars reared in the traditional disciplines of political theory and institutional analysis. It is indeed significant that the most comprehensive of all anthologies of con-tributions to the study of comparative politics, the Eckstein-Apter reader includes only a single example of systematic cross-national analysis of poll or survey data.[177]

Almond and Verba broke new ground: they introduced into the study of comparative politics methods so far primarily developed by social psy-chologists and sociologists and they demonstrated that these methods can yield results of relevance not only in the description of differences and similarities between polities but also in the exploration of central hypotheses in a theory of political development.

The Civic Culture is indeed not just another compilation of comparative statistics. We have travelled a long distance from the crude empirical tabu-lations assembled by Gosnell and Tingsten in their pioneering works of the twenties and thirties. Almond and Verba designed their five-country survey to explore, if not to test, some of the empirical implications of the general theoretical formulations developed within the Committee on Comparative Politics set up by the Social Science Research Council. The key terms in the vocabulary of this group of scholars are 'political development,' 'politi-cal culture,' 'political inputs' and 'political outputs.' The choice of countries to be studied reflects their central concern with processes of change from traditional to modern modes of politics: on the one hand two still heavily traditionbound but rapidly modernizing polities, *Mexico* and *Italy,* on the other hand three advanced but still very different systems, the *German Federal Republic,* the *United Kingdom* and the *United States.* Each of these five has its distinctive 'political cultures,' its particular mix of domi-nant orientations to the objects of politics in the different strata and sectors of its population. To map out such variations in dominant modes of orientation Almond and Verba introduce an intriguing typology: they distinguish the 'parochial' mode of the inhabitants psychologically most remote from the administrative apparatus of the nation-state, the 'subject' mode of the obedient or only passively recalcitrant followers of the orders and regulations of the field bureaucracy, and the 'participant' mode of the citizens who are not only aware of the 'outputs' of the governmental machinery, but also are ready to contribute to the 'inputs' of pressures on those who control the machinery. The five countries chosen for study were taken to represent so many distinctive mixes of such modes of orientation to politics and government: Mexico still largely 'parochial' but with strong participant aspirations, Italy also heavily 'parochial' but essentially distinguished by the high level of alienation in its 'subject' orientations, Germany a more positive 'subject' culture but with only minimal emphasis on participation, and the United Kingdom and the United States finally exhibiting flexible equilibria between 'subject' and 'participant' orientations, the British tending to tilt heavier toward deferential subject roles, the Americans more likely to emphasize the virtues of activity than the duties of civic obedience.

This conceptualization of types of relationships between the governed and their government was fundamental in the study: it decided the priorities of the survey design, it was reflected in the actual sequences of questions in the interview schedule, it also governed the procedures of analysis.

The focus is on the individual adult and his interaction with constituted governmental authorities: how much does he know about them? how does he feel toward them? how far does he trust them? how competent does he feel in dealing with them? what does he actually do to counteract or influence them? The questions used to map out these interrelations and interactions are admirably conceived and the interpretation of the resulting response distributions is often illuminating. Yet one may well ask whether this plebiscitarian concentration on the direct links between individual and nation has not tended to distort the maps given us of the five polities and their differences. There is very little analysis of the sources of cleavage and dissension within each polity: regional differences, even in the very obvious cases of Italy and the United States, are not discussed, differences among denominations and between the religiously active and passive are only touched on, and differences between social classes are largely ignored. The authors offer a perceptive introductory note on the need to consider political subcultures but their data do not go far toward a description of variations in the strength of such alternative foci of political identification as the regional culture, the church, the class, the union, the political party. The five-country study was deliberately centred on one of many axes in the political system and the design was parsimoniously organized to produce data and analysis possibilities in this one direction. The authors state this very clearly (pp. 378–9 and 401) and I can only admire their stubbornness in resisting temptations to broaden the design to offer analysis possibilities in alternative directions. In a first attempt at systematic comparative data gathering my own preference would have been for a multifocused design, fewer questions in each area of variation and a larger number of respondents in each country. This is not just cautious eclecticism: given the fact that we still lack even the simplest comparative compilation of political survey statistics for these countries it would seem to me preferable to start out with a broad mapping of sources of within-nation variation before proceeding to refined analyses along one single axis.

The strong nation-orientation of the survey design is also reflected in the analysis procedures and the tabulations in the report. Of the 127 tables and graphs scattered through the volume, I count as many as 52 presenting straight comparisons between total national cross-sections without any structural differentiations. This is essentially an expository device but it does raise problems when contrasting such differently designed samples as the Italian and the Mexican: in the one case all communities of the nation, even the smallest rural ones, had a chance to be selected, but in the other only the cities of 10,000 or more inhabitants. The reader is reminded of the necessity to take this into account in a footnote (p. 90), but there is only a single graph setting out differences by size of community (p. 235). In general, given the contrasts in geographic and socio-economic structure among countries at such different levels of economic growth, it would have seemed an elementary precaution to alert the reader at every major point in the presentation to the need for such basic controls for within-nation variation. The great majority of the controls used in the tables and graphs presented are for formal education. This is an essential control in any analysis of elicited expressions of opinion or attitudes: we have moved far away from the straightforward plebiscitarianism of the early pollsters. Formal education proves an excellent predictor both of awareness of government outputs and of willingness to take action to influence authorities. This message comes through with great clarity from all the countries and reminds us of a basic problem for all full-suffrage democracies: votes may be equal, but opinions are only likely to be articulated and pressures only likely to be initiated by small minorities. That these minorities tend to be better educated than the average voters is a finding confirmed by political statisticians in country after country, but this does not mean that there are not other, and sometimes as important, channels of recruitment (see Chapter 12 below). Politics may be taught in the family, in youth movements, in unions and clubs, and for citizens with only a minimum of formal schooling such stimulations and experiences may prove decisive. The samples of such citizens were very large in all the countries and further differentiations by the most likely sources of early political stimulation might easily have been introduced: 35 % in the U. S., the most educated of the nations, 63 % in the U. K., 84 % in Germany, 70 % in Italy and 88 % in Mexico. These least educated categories must of necessity be highly heterogeneous: they will include farmers, tenants and labourers in the primary economy as well as unemployed, wage earners and some artisans and shopkeepers in the urbanized communities. Such further differentiations might not only help to map out in detail the typical channels for the recruitment of active citizens but also open up the way for analyses of the *direction* of their activity.

This, perhaps, is the point where the sociologist is most likely to object to the Almond-Verba analysis. There are a variety of ingenious indexes of levels of activity, but there is hardly any direct analysis of the political *context* and the policy *direction* of the activity: is it directed against or in support of the local or the national authorities, is it essentially an expression of *party commitment* or is it an outflow of *community position?* Historically this is one of the crucial questions to be asked in any comparative discussion of the consequences of full-suffrage democracy: were the lower-class citizens brought into each system through the extension of the franchise mostly mobilized by the existing parties and powerholders or did they organize parties and power centres of their own in opposition to the inherited system? There is very little discussion of the genesis of the five national party systems in the book and hardly a word about the socioeconomic, cultural and religious conditions for the continued maintenance of the parties. This may be in full conformity with the deliberate decision to focus on the direct ties between citizen and nation, but it seems legitimate to ask whether this disregard for the political direction of citizen activity has not reduced the utility of the study as an empirical description of differences between countries.

The chapter on 'Patterns of Partisanship' is no doubt the most disappointing to the political sociologist. There is an ingenious analysis of expressions of affect between voters for opposing parties in each country, but no consideration of the socio-cultural factors making for higher or lower levels of polarization between parties or of alienation from the national system: the data collected would have allowed a great deal of analysis in this direction and other studies could have been drawn on to round off the presentation of each party system.

The treatment of *Italy* is particularly problematic. The difficulties of conducting interview studies in a country with a high proportion of Communist voters are well-known: the Milan organization working for Almond and Verba could only register 4.5 % PCI voters and 5.5 % PSI voters in the sample as against 22.7 % and 14.2 % in the election of 1958. Most of the Communists and Nenni Socialists clearly refused either to be interviewed or to report their votes to the interviewers. Almond and Verba discuss the abnormally high refusal rate for Italy on pp. 116–118, but curiously do not relate it directly to the discrepancy for the PCI and the PSI. Other studies carried out in Italy also report marked discrepancies, but none that I have seen report as low per cents for the two parties of the left as Almond and Verba.[178] This discrepancy raises general problems of strategy of research in politically divided countries, problems which ought to receive much greater attention than they have, both among political analysts and among the technicians of the survey profession.[179] Dogan's current work on the stratification of the left vote in France and Italy and Allardt's work on the Communist vote in Finland may point the way toward complex combinations of ecological analyses of local variations with pinpointed survey research which will yield much more than the straightforward cross-sectional sampling procedures so far applied.

I hope I shall not be accused of carping at details in this well-written report on a pioneering study. My concern has been less with details of design and analysis than with the general problem of strategies for cumulative comparative research on political processes. Many of the additional analyses I have suggested can still be done: the authors have generously bequeathed the IBM cards of their five-country study to the Inter-University Consortium for Political Research and I have myself supervised the work of several students at Yale with these decks. What is needed beyond this, however, is a cumulation of efforts to fit this body of data into a wider context of information on elections, parties, local administrations and interest organizations, first in the countries studied in such detail, later for a number of other countries. Almond and Verba have on the whole confined themselves to a presentation of their theory, their method and their basic findings. The community of political analysts must now seek to incorporate these data and these findings into a broader cumulative effort to improve the bases for cross-national comparisons. We still lack even the most elementary compilations of evaluated political statistics for the countries of the West. Experts on comparative economic growth can base their analyses on vast efforts of data collation and compilation by the UN and its agencies. Experts on comparative political development have no such basis for their work.

IV. *The Organization of Comparative Survey Research: the Conditions for Cumulative Development*

The Almond-Verba volume represented a great step forward in the comparative study of styles of political behaviour but was by no means a unique achievement within the social sciences: from the midfifties onwards there was a continuous ferment of plans, designs and schemes for cross-cultural and cross-national data gathering and data analysis and a great many of these generated important bodies of data and led to interesting analytical innovations. The great majority of the centrally coordinated projects were American in origin: until well into the 'sixties it was only possible to raise funds for such costly research enterprises from U. S. agencies and foundations. Any priority listing of these American projects will of necessity be arbitrary but these seem to me to be most important examples of academically oriented data-gathering operations across three or more countries since the early 'fifties:

The earliest of all co-ordinated survey studies in developing countries, the study initiated by Lazarsfeld at the Columbia Bureau of Applied Social Research in six Middle Eastern countries during 1949–51, was at first only presented in a few internal reports but was later analyzed within a broader theoretical framework by Daniel Lerner (Lerner, 1958). Parallel efforts of survey research in the developing countries were pursued by Hadley Cantril, the great pioneer of cross-national polling. He set up an Institute for International Social Research at Princeton, N. J., and organized with his colleague, Lloyd Free, a great number of studies of mass and elite attitudes across the world (Cantril, 1963; Cantril, 1965; Cantril, 1958; Divo, 1958; Free, 1958; Free, 1960; Free, 1959; Free, 1961): the most important of these (Cantril, 1965) reports in detail on the administration of his 'Self-Anchoring Striving Scale' in a wide variety of countries on four continents, four highly developed countries (U. S., W. Germany, Israel and Japan), three very different sorts of Socialist polities (Poland, Yugoslavia and, interestingly, Castroite Cuba) and seven typically 'developing' countries (Panama, the Philippines, the Dominican Republic, Brazil, Egypt, Nigeria and India).[180]

A number of comparative studies have centred on factors of change and modernization in the developing countries. David McClelland (McClelland, 1961) was able to replicate his 'n-Achievement' test on different samples in Brazil, Germany, India, Italy, Japan, Poland and Turkey and developed an intriguing theory of the personality syndromes most likely to produce entrepreneurial talents in developing countries. Alex Inkeles administered a 119-item test of 'attitudinal modernity' to matched 'common man' samples in Argentina, Chile, India, Pakistan, Israel and Nigeria (Inkeles, 1966), and Sidney Verba (Verba, 1965: 2) was able to finance a study of attitudes to social and political changes in the two of these countries, India and Nigeria, for a comparative analysis with corresponding data for Japan and the United States (Mexico had been included in the original scheme but had to be dropped in the wake of project Camelot). A major comparative study of attitudes to economic growth is currently (1969) at the planning stage at the Massachusetts Institute of Technology: this will be directed by Frederick Frey.

A number of psychologists found it tempting to replicate their tests and their techniques in foreign countries. A pioneer in the field of psychological measurement, Charles Osgood, succeeded in persuading colleagues in close to twenty language communities to use his Sematic Differential Technique. The Andersons (Anderson, 1956; 1959; 1961; 1962) were able to replicate their 'Incomplete Story' test in some ten countries to explore differences in student-teacher relations in democratic *vs.* authoritarian environments, and Lambert and Klineberg (Lambert, 1959; 1966) sampled children of different ages in nine countries to test hypotheses about the growth of stereotypes of foreign peoples.

Among anthropologists the Whitings took the lead in the development of standardized schedules for the recording of information about childrearing practices (Whiting, 1966), and organized an important six-culture data gathering operation much on the same lines of the typical cross-national survey (Whiting, 1963).

The Almond-Verba study for some time threatened to remain the only example of a deliberately organized cross-national mass survey of political behaviour variables. Comparative political sociologists such as Seymour Martin Lipset, (Lipset, 1954; 1960; Lipset-Linz, 1956), William Kornhauser (Kornhauser, 1960) and Robert Alford (Alford, 1963) relied on data from independently conducted commercial polls and surveys from many countries and tried to place the findings in broader perspectives of history and theory. Daniel Lerner (Lerner, 1960; cf. Gorden, 1965) and Karl Deutsch (Deutsch, 1965: 1) organized extensive studies of elite attitudes in Western Europe and sought to link up evidence from such top-level interviews with secondary evidence from mass surveys (Merritt, 1966: 2). The active team of electoral analysts at the Survey Research Center moved into Europe country by country and organized local as well as nationwide surveys on lines comparable to the very successful ones carried out in the United States (Campbell, 1961; Converse, 1962: 1; Converse, 1962: 2; Rokkan, 1960:2, cf. Chapter 12 below). Finally, Philip and Betty Jacob were able to finance the organization of an elaborate four-nation study of 'values in local government': this project covers the U. S., Poland, Yugoslavia and India and has generated an impressive array of memoranda conference reports and initial analyses (International Study, 1962–66).

Each of these projects may have proved costly in funds, personnel and intellectual energy, but they still represent only a very small percentage of the total social science effort in the United States during the last fifteen years.

The current generation of social scientists has, at least in the nations of the West, been caught in cross-fire of two conflicting sets of demands: on the one hand they have felt impelled to concentrate their efforts of data-gathering and analysis in the many neglected fields of inquiry within their own nation; on the other hand they have felt increasingly aware of the limitations of single-site studies and increasingly convinced of the methodological rationale and the theoretical pay-off cross-community, cross-national and cross cultural research. The market conditions for decisions in the one direction or in the other have varied enormously from region to region. In the United States the resources of funds and personnel have been large enough to allow a small but expanding phalanx of comparatists to concentrate their work on cross-national and cross-cultural studies. In Latin America the national resources have been meagre and the decisive thrust toward the establishment of regular research services have come from abroad, through the organization of cross-national studies.[181] In Europe there has been a continuous increase in the flow of funds for social science research but a marked concentration on distinctly national tasks. Europe offers a remarkable range of opportunities for detailed cross-national research: there is a wealth of data still to be tapped, there are broad bodies of national experts to draw on for advice, there is increasing interest among policy-makers in studies cutting across the national and regional units (OECD, 1966: esp. pp. 79–80). Curiously little has as yet been done to make use of these opportunities. Significantly, some of the first initiatives came from American scholars and were backed by American funds. Europe-initiated and Europe-financed studies have so far been few and far between. Perhaps the happiest example of a jointly financed and cooperatively planned international study is the twelve-country survey of achievement in mathematics (Husen, 1967): this was planned at the UNESCO Institute of Education in Hamburg, and financed by the U. S. Office of Education (for the international costs of the project) and by national funding agencies in the twelve countries (for the field operations). This project constitutes a model of international academic cooperation: it shows that it *is* possible to achieve solid results through the sharing of responsibilities across many national teams and it shows how UNESCO and other international bodies can perform an important brokerage function in linking up American and European initiatives.

The Research Committees set up by the International Sociological Association have prepared the ground for a similar linking of initiatives but so far the plans for concerted action can be counted on one hand. The Committee on Social Stratification and Social Mobility pioneered the organization of a series of cross-national replications and has offered a fruitful forum of methodological and substantive discussions (Miller, 1960; Glass, 1961): the current three-country project *Metropolit* is a direct outcome of discussions within the Committee (Janson, 1965). Europe is clearly ripe for a variety of cross-national initiatives: what has been lacking has been an organizational focus, a concrete institutional basis for concerted action. Alexander Szalai's spectacular success in getting research workers in a dozen countries interested in joining the cross-national time budget study must be understood against this background (Szalai, 1966: 1; Szalai, 1966: 2): The UNESCO decision to set up a European Co-ordination Centre at Vienna came just at the right moment: communications between sociologists in the East and the West had reached a point where cooperation on concrete tasks of empirical research were possible, and the regional organizations of the West had concentrated their efforts on purely economic studies and failed to offer a minimum of infrastructure for cross-national research in central fields of sociology.

The successes of the Vienna Centre and the UNESCO Institute of Education in Hamburg hold important lessons for the future: cross-national research requires an institutional framework, an organizational basis. Great plans and important pilot studies can result from haphazard encounters of enthusiasts but a cumulative tradition of cross-national research can only develop within a clear-cut organizational setting.

The demographers, the economists and to some extent the educational scientists, have been able to build up broad international professions within the frameworks of large-scale intergovernmental organizations: the UN, the Regional Commissions, the World Bank, the OECD, the EEC and the UNESCO Departments of Education all offer continuous opportunities for experiences in the handling and evaluation of data masses from wide ranges of countries and help to develop genuine cross-national expertise.

There is no such firm basis for cross-national endeavours in the other social sciences: in anthropology, in sociology, in political science. There is some movement in the fields closest to demography, economics and education. It is interesting to observe that the two Research Committees under the International Association which have come closest to the development of a cumulative programme of cross-national studies are those focused on the Family and on Mobility: both of them centring on variables closer to the concerns of demographers and both relying heavily on data from enumerations or from surveys close to the model of the census. It is also significant that the ISA has so far been unable to mount an active Research Committee for the Sociology of Education: there is already a basis for cooperative work on educational statistics in UNESCO and the OECD and there is therefore not the same need for an institutionalization of personal communication networks.

In other fields of sociology it has proved much more difficult to develop continuous programmes: there have been no institutional frameworks for long-term commitments to cross-national inquiries and, still worse, hardly anything has been done to evaluate or to standardize the production of data across any two or more nations.

Take the case of political sociology. Enormous masses of data for analysis are produced in every nation every year: election statistics, polls and surveys, information on elite characteristics. But no international agency has seen any need to train any sizeable body of experts in the handling of such data: the data gathering and the analysis are almost invariably done *within* each nation and there is no organizational framework for continuous planning and promotion of research *across* nations.

In the face of these difficulties a number of strategies have been tried out, some with significant intellectual payoffs, but none of them as yet with assured cumulative effects.

I shall confine myself, largely for purposes of illustration, to three such strategies:

1) the Tingsten-Duverger-Lasswell line, the collation and comparison of 'process-produced' political statistics, be they electoral counts, organizational bookkeeping data or regularly assembled information on key personnel (Tingsten, 1937; Duverger, 1951; Lasswell, 1952);

2) the Dogan-Lipset line, the assembly, evaluation and analysis of raw data from independently conducted field operations, primarily from polls

and surveys (Dogan, 1956; 1959; 1960; Lipset, 1954; 1956, 1960; 1957: 2; Alford, 1963);

3) the Almond-Verba line, the design and execution of explicitly comparative sample surveys across a number of distinct national populations.

Each of these lines of inquiry has produced worthwhile results but it has proved remarkably difficult to ensure cumulative continuity in the systematization of the evidence across countries. No one has yet tried to 'do a Tingsten' for post-war elections.[182] No one has as yet tried to assemble a comparative compendium of historical and statistical information on political parties to fill in the many lacunae in Duverger's work. Lasswell's and Lipset's efforts generated longer-term programmes of research but enormous masses of data on elite recruitment and mass politics are still waiting to be systematically collated, evaluated and analyzed in a comparative context. There has been a tendency to 'skim the cream' off the most accessible batches of comparative data and to pass on to new tasks at the first signs of routinization. This would be unthinkable in economics and in demography: the professions are broad enough to encourage a division of labour between the theorists concerned to test out new models and new methods, and the empiricists concerned to gain some measure of control over the onrushing masses of information.

The current movement towards the development of *computer archiving of data* must be understood in this perspective: the data banks will have to be built up by hard-headed and down-to-earth empiricists but will leave the theorists a number of degrees freer to explore new hypotheses and new analytical notions (Rokkan, 1965: 1; Rokkan, 1963: 3; Converse, 1966: 1; Bisco, 1966). But however international they might be in their coverage the data banks cannot in themselves create the intellectual environments for effective advances in comparative research: there is no easy substitute for the intensive interaction of individual experts within organized networks of the type built up in economics and in demography. In fact the rush to feed computers with unevaluated data from a variety of different countries may produce a great deal of numerological nonsense: it will be essential to build in safeguards through close contacts with local informants and experts. Kingsley Davis has recently issued strong warnings against the 'ready-data' schemes: there is the risk of 'progressive diffusion of misinformation' and the danger of serious mis-interpretation of analysis findings through ignorance of variations in the cultural, social and political contexts.[183] This, obviously is not an argument against the archiving of data but a plea for the development of broader cross-national analysis centres: it is not enough to make the data computer readable; they have to make empirical and analytical sense and they have to be evaluated in the light of thorough contextual knowledge. The strict evaluation procedures established for the data archive of the Inter-University Consortium at Ann Arbor, Michigan, suggest a model for operations in other countries: the object is not the accumulation of *any* prima facie comparable data but the organization of a systematic file of information likely to offer *clear analytical payoffs.*

Data archives of this type seem destined to serve an important function in the planning of fresh *field operations:* archives of time series data for localities have already proved useful in the design of nation-wide sample surveys (Rokkan, 1966: 1) and backlog data from earlier surveys are increasingly used in calculations of alternative strategies of further data-gathering.[184]

Erwin Scheuch, in a recent paper (Scheuch, 1967), reported that a Latin American social scientist had reacted to a plan for a survey by saying that it implied a 'know-nothing' approach to the population under investigation, a studied posture of ignorance of social-structural facts already known. The sample survey inherited this studied ignorance from the full-suffrage election and the referendum: the early polls were deliberately modelled on these political institutions and even very sophisticated survey practitioners are still heavily influenced by this heritage. Under the old *régime censitaire* elections reflected the social structure of the national population: through the universalization of the suffrage and the introduction of secrecy, the act of voting was isolated from the social structure.

The poll and the survey start out from the same equalitarian postulates: every adult is given the same chance to express himself or herself, irrespective of position in the social hierarchy, of level of education, of level of articulateness. This procedure is obviously justified in the study of elections: each adult has formally equal weight and has the same chance of influencing the fate of the Government. But what about studies of other areas of behaviour, processes of communication, attitudes to issues in the community, the spread of social, cultural and political innovations?

The argument generally heard for cross-section surveys in such areas is that one first has to establish the facts of the structure before moving on to the pinpointed surveys of strategic sectors of the population. But there is still a tendency to stick to the old cross-sectional model even after large quantities of information have been established. This seems to me to be a *basic rationale for the developments of archives of secondary analysis:* the more we know about the results of earlier studies the easier it will be to design new studies and particularly to decide on strategic groups requiring further study.

This is one point on which the procedure of the already classic Almond-Verba study might have been decisively improved. Such costly research enterprises should be preceded by detailed scrutiny of the data already at hand for each country. In some cases such scrutiny may of course still lead the researcher to decide on a cross-sectional approach in each country. It may well be that the Almond-Verba decision to carry out cross-sectional surveys in the United States, the United Kingdom, Germany and Italy, was based on such analyses of existent data, but the decision to exclude the

rural communities of Mexico was clearly based on quite different considerations of fieldwork conditions. It seems to me that it would have been
better to limit *all* the samples to populations at the same level of urbanization. This would not only have increased the overall comparability of the
five samples but also allowed much more detailed analysis for the same
investment of research dollars. Obviously, to make such a decision it would
have been essential to carry out detailed analysis of rural-urban differences
in the existing bodies of survey data. With the development of data archives
this type of preparatory analysis should become possible for more and
more countries and in the future it ought to become a matter of standard
practice to fit new efforts of data gathering into the broader corpus of
cumulating evidence for each country.

There is an obvious danger, to quote Mattei Dogan, that data archive
may degenerate into *cimetières de cartes perdues,* but it seems to me very
difficult to limit their size through priority rankings of topics of research.
The best criteria are probably the range of variables covered in each study
and the variety of analysis possibilities it allows: the more varied the possibilities the more useful will the archive be for future research workers
planning fresh data-gathering enterprises.

But all such efforts only make sense within interlocking programmes of
active cooperation among social scientists intimately familiar with conditions in the countries under study: 'instant comparisons' through computer manipulations are bound to boomerang. The traditional exchanges
of papers at international conferences may still help to bring together
'opposite numbers' but the decisive confrontations must come *before* the
papers: at the stage of data gathering data evaluation and comparative
analysis. The demographers and the economists have built up the infrastructure for such confrontations: the other social scientists are still groping for
solutions. UNESCO and the International Social Science Council have seen
the need for active exploration of new strategies in the advancement of
cross-national comparisons and have tried to draw up a long-term programme to this end (Rokkan, 1965: 2; Rokkan, 1968: 3). The fate of this
programme is still uncertain. We know from bitter experience that isolated
cross-national projects tend to have very little cumulative payoff but we
still have not been able to set up any international machinery to ensure
project-to-project linkages over time. The powerful funding agencies in the
United States are taking steps in this direction and may in fact be able to
achieve some useful coordination of data-gathering operations organized
under their auspices, but this still leaves the problem of *international*
coordination unsolved. The Vienna Centre may point the way to a solution
within Europe but is still too weak to take on these broader functions. A
decisive move in this direction could only be made through an arrangement
among the principal funding agencies for the social sciences in Europe, but
this will still remain to be worked out.

Meanwhile, there is no way of stopping the flow of new projects. Many of them will still proceed in blithe ignorance of contextual factors affecting the outcome of cross-national replications. Many of them will still rush into fresh field operations without detailed reanalysis of data and experiences from earlier studies. Many of them will remain at the 'safari' level of cultural immersion: the studies will be designed and the questions will be formulated without detailed consultation of scholars steeped in contextual knowledge of each of the societies to be covered. None of this can be changed overnight: we can only hope that the *proportions,* if not the absolute numbers, of such poorly designed studies will be reduced over the next couple of decades. The further development of data archives will no doubt facilitate this process of study-to-study and study-to-context linkage. So will the current efforts to inventorize surveys question by question and population by population to allow effective retrieval of all the information required in the design of new studies.[185] And so will bibliographies such as the one presented in the volume *Comparative Survey Analysis:* especially if it can be transformed in due time into a computer readable record of the coded characteristics of all available reports on past attempts at cross-national analysis of data from sample surveys.

NOTES

[164] Jack Goody and Ian Watt have forcefully argued the decisive importance of *alphabetization,* not only for the structuring of societies, but also for the *strategies of data gathering and the formulation of analytical concepts* in the social sciences: 'Looked at in the perspective of time, man's biological evolution shades into prehistory when he becomes a language-using animal; add writing, and history proper begins. Looked at in a temporal perspective, man as animal is studied primarily by the zoologist, *man as talking animal primarily by the anthropologist, and man as talking and writing animal by the sociologist*' (Goody, 1963: p. 304) my italics.

[165] For examples of particular relevance for the later development of the survey see (Diamond, 1963).

[166] For reviews of these developments see the introduction to (Eaton, 1930) and (Stephan, 1948). For German developments see (Oberschall, 1965).

[167] Large-scale sample surveys *may,* of course, serve purposes of individual intelligence or camouflage attempts at personal persuasion: the best known case of this is probably the Colin Hurry survey in Britain, see (Rose, 1966: p. 138).

[168] For analyses of the functions of secrecy in mass voting see Chapters 1, 4 and 5 above.

[169] The most important work of this type has been done by J. R. Vincent at Cambridge (Vincent, 1966).

[170] For accounts of the development of standardized voting procedures in the United States see (Wigmore, 1889; Evans, 1917).

[171] The plebiscitarian assumptions of commercial polling have been analyzed with great critical skill by the German philosopher Wilhelm Hennis (Hennis, 1957). This work is of particular interest as an attempt to bridge the gap between the political theory of representation and democracy and the current controversies about the assumptions underlying the practice of mass interviews. This theme is discussed in a broader perspective of historical sociology (Habermas, 1961). The

position of the 'pollsters' has been ably defended by G. Schmidtchen (Schmidtchen, 1959) and Manfred Kuhn (Kuhn, 1959).

[172] Among the major contributions to research on such questions are: (Riesman, 1948; Hyman, 1954; Benney, 1957; Kahn, 1957; Mayer, 1964; Richardson, 1965).

[173] For a general discussion of alternatives to the survey methods in politically divided countries, see (Linz, 1969).

[174] The contrast between the survey interviewer and the judge or lawyer in the elicitation of *legal testimony* has been analyzed with great insight in (Richardson, 1965: Ch. 7). In backward communities with some history of tolerant connivance of acts against the central authorities there is a real danger that the less educated will unconsciously identify any outside interviewer as a police inquisitor, a judge or an attorney. This points to an important task of methodological research: how much internal differentiation, how much exposure to the outside world is required before a local community can be effectively incorporated as a sampling point in nation-wide study?

[175] This point has been brilliantly brought out in Sidney Verba's review, in *World Politics* 20(1) Oct. 1967 of (Dahl, 1966).

[176] The ensuing section is adapted from a review written for *Amer. Pol. Sci. Rev.* 58(3) 1964: 676–679.

[177] (Eckstein, 1963). The example included is a chapter from (Kornhauser, 1959).

[178] See specifically the studies reported on in (Spreafico, 1963).

[179] See above pp. 260–264.

[180] The sampling report appended to the Cantril volume adds further evidence of the difficulties of interviewing in the rural areas of dual-economy territories: in Cuba, it was only possible to interview in Havana and some other cities ('... the name of the organization that did the work, long since disbanded and out of the country, must remain anonymous'), in Egypt only 82 rural interviews could be collected and had to be weighted nine times to match the urban sample, in India only 10 per cent of the women could be interviewed because of local taboos.

[181] For details see (Germani, 1965).

[182] A first step in this direction: (Rokkan, 1969:4).

[183] (Davis, 1964), cf. the argument *for* the archiving of cross-country data in (Russett, 1964; Alker, 1967).

[184] For a remarkable example of the use of past data in determining on optimal strategies of new data gathering see (Mayer, 1964).

[185] Marten Brouwer of the Steinmetz Stichting of the University of Amsterdam in April, 1967 completed an inventory of surveys stored in European archives (Cf. Bisco, 1966). Similar efforts of 'study description' are under way for all U. S. archives under the auspices of the Council for Social Science Data Archives. Frederick Frey at M. I. T. has developed a computer readable register of questions asked and responses recorded in surveys conducted in developing countries. In the future it should be possible to retrieve quickly and effectively information about all surveys covering a given variable for a given country: see (Bisco, 1965; Levy, 1966; Scheuch, 1964: 1; Scheuch, 1966: 2).

NINE

Party Preferences and Opinion Patterns in Western Europe

This chapter will present a set of findings from a cooperative study undertaken in seven countries of Western Europe by members of the Organization for Comparative Social Research.[186] Altogether 2,758 teachers in the primary and secondary schools of Belgium, England, France, the Netherlands, Norway, Sweden, and Western Germany were interviewed with equivalent schedules during January – April 1953, to explore their opinions and attitudes on a number of educational, social, and political issues. The field work was undertaken by national teams at research institutions in each of the seven countries and was coordinated from a Central Office at the Institute for Social Research in Oslo.[187] Each team coded its national data according to an agreed scheme and punched them on IBM cards for statistical processing. Duplicates of all the national punch cards were assembled at the Oslo Institute and have provided the basis for the comparative analysis work to be reported.[188]

The findings to be presented in this chapter all relate to the teachers' reported affiliations or sympathies with the political parties of their respective countries. The study was not specifically designed as an inquiry into

Origin: This analysis report was written at the Center for International Studies at M. I. T. in 1955: a large part of it was published by the UNESCO *International Social Science Journal*, Vol. VII, No 4, 1955 (Rokkan 1955: 3). Some of the tables have been corrected.

the determinants and correlates of party identification,[189] but the analysis work that has been undertaken gives very clear indications of the central importance of this variable for an understanding of relationships in the opinion and attitude data. The study did not include any specific checks on the reliability of the teachers' reports on their party identifications nor did it inquire into the stability and intensity of identification or into the extent of participation in political processes. Nevertheless, the cross-tabulations that have been made against the distributions for party identification lend considerable credence to the teachers' reports on this point and seem to provide adequate justification for detailed analysis, at least across five of the seven countries studied.[190] The data on party identification for the French and the Western German teachers are less complete than the data for the other countries and have therefore not been subject to the same amount of comparative analysis: the tabulations for these countries are included primarily for expository purposes.

Characteristics of the Study

Any study of the determinants and correlates of different types and degrees of party identification must of necessity take into account a wide range of factors interacting in complex networks of relationships. Any *comparative* study of such determinants and correlates across a number of national political systems is faced with a multi-variate complexity of relationships that seems to defy any attempt at hypothesis testing and generalization. Any effort to explore the critical sources of variance across a set of political systems would involve analyses of the phenomena of individual party identification in at least six more or less overlapping empirical and conceptual contexts:

the *'legal'* context – the framework of legal norms establishing suffrage rights, voting procedures, systems of representation; [191]

the *'political'* context – the party systems, the patterns of opposition, coalition, and compromise, the internal organization of the parties, the distribution of leadership roles, the categories of membership, the policies of recruitment (Duverger, 1951);

the *'socio-economic'* contexts – the ties of kinship, friendship, neighbourhood and community, the implications of education, occupation, status, group membership; [192]

the *'communication'* contexts – the distribution of information on party programmes and policies, the ideological pressures exerted, differences in exposure and receptivity, individual reflections and responses, predominant formulations of issues and arguments bearing on party identification (Katz, 1955);

the *'cognitive'* context – the individuals' images of the situation and the alternatives, of the parties, the goals, the issues, the policies and their interrelations, of the divisions of opinions, the forces making for unity or disunity;[193]

the *'personality'* context – the dimensions of individual development, the motivational tendencies and the general trait syndromes that may account for differences in party identification.[194]

No comparative study of political behaviour has yet attempted to cover the full range of factors affecting party identification. The Western European interview study undertaken by the OCSR can mainly help to throw light on relationships in three of the analytical contexts distinguished: a) the study included a number of questions centred on occupation, role and status, and thus allowed some analysis of the socio-economic contexts of party preferences; b) the primary focus, however, was on the 'cognitive' contexts: the study was designed to elicit data for an understanding of cross-national regularities in the patterning of perceptions, opinions and judgements on issues of national and international policy; c) the study included a couple of simple attitude tests intended to provide indices of general ideological orientations: these data might prove to be of some indirect relevance to an examination of the 'personality' contexts of party and policy preference.[195]

By implication, the study also offered some basis for an understanding of the 'communication' contexts of party allegiances: the reflections in individual response relationship of the predominant patterns of exposition, appeal and argumentation in organizational and mass-directed communication within and across each of the national political communities. The study did not provide any data of direct relevance to an understanding of political communication processes as such, but it did allow some analysis of differential receptivity to predominant patterns of mass-directed communication on some major issues of national and international policy.[196]

In the 'socio-economic' context of analysis, the OCSR study data offer some unique opportunities for comparisons across as well as within countries. The original intention was to cover cross-sectional samples of each of the national populations, but limitations in time, funds, and facilities restricted the study to functionally defined sub-groups within each country. The study was therefore deliberately limited to *two occupational categories:* primary school teachers and secondary school teachers. In this respect it differed markedly from previous studies of party identification and electoral behaviour. Whatever the methodologies, most inquiries in this area have been more concerned with comparisons between broad status categories or income levels than with differentiations between specific occupations. The importance of increasing our knowledge of the political predispositions of some of the strategic groups in the upper half of the occupational structure can hardly be doubted, but so far very little has been done to get any reliable estimates of the distributions of party allegiances in different countries for such important categories as civil servants, officers, lawyers, physicians, scientists, clergymen, and other members of the free or salaried professions. The difficulties to be faced in any such inquiries on the national as well as the cross-national level are obvious. The best data for such study are probably still of the traditional historical kind, but analyses from such sources will be mostly limited to the leadership roles. Ecological analyses of election statistics have offered important insights into some of the broad features of the socio-economic contexts of party support, but have for obvious reasons provided very limited possibilities for occupational differentiations (Tingsten, 1937; Nilson, 1950; Heberle, 1951; Eldersveld, 1951; Dupeux, 1955). Sample inquiries by interviews or paper-and-pencil questionnaires in this field have practically always cut across the gamut of occupations and have only allowed differentiations by broad categories of function, status, or income: this has been the case with community studies (Lazarsfeld, 1944; Berelson, 1954) as well as with nation-wide and region-wide surveys (Campbell, 1954). Oversampling or special sampling of leadership categories has yielded illuminating results in the few cases it has been attempted (Stouffer, 1955). Secondary analyses of cumulated data from successive surveys of the same populations have also allowed further differentiations by occupational categories (Bonham, 1954). Only a small handful of studies, however, have been directly focused on any one set of occupational categories.[198] To our knowledge, the OCSR study is the only one thus far to have centred exclusively on the *teacher* category for purposes of political participation analysis.

This approach had some important advantages but also implied some definite limitations. Concentrating on the two categories of teachers instead of cutting across all occupational sections obviously reduced one central source of variance and allowed the testing of relationships that could not possibly be explored in nation-wide samples of the same size. Given the need to keep each country sample as small as possible and still allow some scope for valid statistical analysis within each of them, it was considered essential to concentrate on one small occupational subgrouping of each national population. The decision to sample the *teachers* was prompted by a number of considerations. There were some telling technical advantages in choosing teachers for such an initial study on comparative lines: they were an easily identifiable group of citizens, readily sampled from available lists of names or school classes. The main reasons, however, were substantive and theoretical:

first, there was considerable interest in the teacher as an important link in social and political communication processes in the national community: as a transmitter of information and an actual or potential moulder of opinions;

second, there was some interest in the professional problems of the teacher in the different countries, in his adjustment within the national educational system, his problems of status and community relations, his attitudes to pedagogical practice and child rearing in general.

These interests combined in determining the choice of teachers as the focus of the study, but could not be equally well met within the limits of one interviewing operation. The major focus of the study was on the teacher as a citizen: on the teacher in his role as a member of the national community and not as much on the teacher in his particular occupational role. The analysis was originally conceived just in these terms, but the tabulations that were made gave very clear indications of the importance of differences between national educational systems in accounting for differences in opinion patterning among the teachers. The analysis has provided evidence of the dependence of the 'citizen' role on the 'teacher' role, and made it imperative, at least in four of the countries, to take the major divisions of the school system into account in discussing the available data on opinions and attitudes.

The teaching profession functions in a highly 'politicized' sector of the social structure. Conflicts over the control of education have divided public opinion throughout Western Europe and have been of central importance in the development of the party systems of such countries as France and Germany, Belgium and the Netherlands. The story of this controversy goes back to the emergence of the nation-state: the conflict between Church and State over education has been a central one in European politics at least since the French Revolution.[199] From the *Kulturkampf* of the seventies and the fight over the Ferry Laws of 1882 to the *guerre scolaire* of the 'fifties in Belgium, the teacher has been in the centre of public controversy and has had to find his place and take his stand in a deep-rooted struggle over educational policy. The organizational solutions that were reached through these conflicts have profoundly affected the recruitment and composition of the teacher *corps,* their general ideological orientations, and their political allegiances. In at least four of the countries covered by the OCSR study, it would therefore appear essential to explore the relationships between party identification and the teacher's place in the educational system of his country.

This raises important problems of methodology: to what extent are the teacher samples comparable and with what limits will they allow cross-national comparisons of the relationships between party identification and the various opinion and attitude responses?

To clarify these questions it will be necessary, first, to summarize the sampling procedures and the sample characteristics by country; second, to consider the basic distributions for reported party identification in their relations to major divisions within the national school systems.

The Samples

The agreement reached among the seven participating research teams called for 400 teacher interviews in each country.[200] The populations to be sampled in each country were two:

a) full-time teachers in regular primary schools (nursery schools, special schools, and continuation schools excluded);
b) full-time teachers teaching 'major subjects' in secondary schools leading to University entrance examinations.

Three hundred teachers were to be sampled from the primary school population and 100 from the secondary school population in each country: this proportion was to be maintained regardless of the actual national ratio between the two populations. Some difficulties were encountered in equating 'secondary school' teachers across the seven educational systems: thus, for England and Wales, the 'primary' sample includes teachers from the secondary modern schools as well as from the junior and all-age primary schools. Such differences, however, have not affected the comparability of the samples as much as *the divisions within the national school systems:* public vs. private schools, state system schools vs. confessional or denominational schools. The decision on this point was to include in the national samples teachers from both sectors *in all countries where this division was of major importance.* Unfortunately it was not found practicable to sample the English 'public school' teachers: the sample had to be confined to the state system teachers. In the other countries, the major educational divisions could be taken into account in the sampling. This gave seven national samples composed as shown on the facing page.[201]

In terms of school systems, the seven samples can therefore be grouped in three sets: 1) the English, Norwegian, Swedish ones, confined to the state system teachers only, 2) the Belgian and French ones, including public and Catholic school teachers, and 3) the Dutch and West German ones, including teachers from three different school systems, the public, the Catholic, and the Protestant. These divisions have obvious implications for the analysis of party identification among the teachers.

The comparability of the samples was also limited by the necessary clustering of the interviews in major population areas. As is seen from the above summary, the Norwegian and Swedish samples were limited to central geographical areas of the countries. To reduce field cost, similar clustering procedures were in fact adopted in all the countries: the samples can be said to be primarily representative of the teacher populations in the larger cities and the rural areas within 50–100 kilometres distance. For Belgium and the Netherlands this of course still yields samples that are fully representative of the total teacher populations, but in the other coun-

	Primary school teachers	Secondary school teachers
BELGIUM		
State system	148 out of 17,377	55 out of 8,627
Catholic	152 out of 18,424	45 out of 7,128
ENGLAND & WALES		
State system only	300 out of 155,291 (Junior, all-age, secondary modern schools)	100 out of 27,375 (Grammar schools)
FRANCE		
State system	229 out of 160,000	47 out of 24,000
Catholic	43 out of 35,000	31 out of 24,000
NETHERLANDS		
Public	80 out of 9,801	53 out of 2,297
Catholic	130 out of 14,967	31 out of 1,378
Protestant	85 out of 9,874	16 out of 827
Private secular	5 out of 747	
NORWAY		
State system only (Northern Norway excluded)	300 out of 9,725	100 out of 1,375
SWEDEN		
State system only (cluster areas around 4 major cities only)	324 out of 6,345	119 out of 1,950
WEST GERMANY		
Gemeinschaftsschulen	150⎫	95⎫
Kath. Bekenntnisschulen	77⎬ out of 130,000	5⎬ out of 29,000
Evang. Bekenntnisschulen	38⎭	–⎭

tries there is a definite under-representation of teachers in rural areas distant from larger cities.

Within the geographical limits thus set, the potential respondents were selected on a basis of stratified probability sampling from available rosters of names or classrooms. Interviewers were instructed to contact only those thus selected. In the case of not-at-homes, refusals, and other kinds of sample loss, replacements were designated for the interviewers by matching and random selection. In no instance were interviewers given any responsibility for the ultimate selection of respondents. Sample loss was particularly heavy in France and West Germany: it will be seen that the total of obtained interviews do not add up to 400 for these countries.

The teacher samples obtained in the seven countries do not readily allow any comparative estimate of the parameters of any distribution for the total teacher populations of the different countries. The samples do not justify any conclusions about differences between 'the Belgian teacher,' 'the English teacher,' 'the French teacher,' etc., on some single opinion question. What the samples do allow, are *analyses of relationships between responses, and comparisons of the directions of such relationships across the countries.* The comparative tables to be presented for analysis are all cross-tabulations of two or more response distributions: the characteristics to be compared are the directions and degrees of association between the items tabulated, not the marginal distributions for each item. It is particularly important to keep this in mind in considering the opinion responses since there may be considerable between-country differences in coding.

Basic Distributions for Reported Party Identification

Table 1 gives the distributions of reported party allegiances or sympathies for each of the national samples. It will be seen that the *percentages of non-response* vary considerably between countries, from 4 per cent in Sweden to 18 per cent in France and 19 per cent in Germany. The percentages of teachers reporting *no party identification* vary even more strikingly. Only one teacher in Sweden said he sympathized with no particular party while as many as 25 per cent of the French and 31 per cent of the German teachers gave this response. It is difficult to assess to what extent these variations are due to genuine differences in political involvement or only reflect differences in the teachers' willingness to give any information on such a question. The very high percentages of negative responses in the French and West German samples were clearly affected by the difficulties of field work in these countries. Overall refusal rates were higher in these countries than in any of the others and there was a marked reluctance to give full data on individual political preferences. There is little justification for subjecting these samples to detailed comparative analysis on this particular point. Most of the comparative analysis to follow will be confined to the data for the other five countries.

The party systems of the different countries differ markedly in various respects. The parties do not arrange themselves neatly along any definite 'left-right' dimension. They come nearest to this in England and Sweden, but in the other countries the left-right dimension cuts across other dimensions of political conflict. For purposes of comparative analysis, the parties can perhaps be best grouped along two dimensions: 1) religious orientation, and 2) socio-economic recruitment basis.

In five of the countries studied, specifically 'Christian' parties of one variety or another were active: in Belgium (the Social Christians), France (the MRP), the Netherlands (the two Catholic parties, and the two Calvinist ones, the Anti-Revolutionaries and the Christian Historical Union), Norway (the Christian People's Party), and Western Germany (the Christian Democrats and the Christian Social Union). It will be seen that among our teachers, these parties were particularly well represented in Belgium, the Netherlands, and West Germany. This, of course, reflects the divisions within the educational systems in these countries. *Table 2* provides dramatic evidence of the close connection between school organization and party identification. In Belgium and the Netherlands it is clearly only within the state system schools that we find any diversity of political orientation: in the confessional schools there is almost complete uniformity of identification among those who give positive responses – and the proportions of negative responses are clearly lower than in the public schools. This, of course, reflects the very direct relationship in these countries between national politics and educational policies: the Christian parties in fact came into existence and gained most of their support in the struggle to ensure

Table 1. *Party Identifications in the National Teacher Samples Compared to National Vote Distributions*

Parties		OCSR Teacher Samples						National Elections		
	Tot.	Primary			Secondary			Date	Per cent of	
		Tot.	M	F	Tot.	M	F		Votes cast	Elec-torate
BELGIUM	N = 400	300	132	168	100	64	36	1954		
	%	%	%	%	%	%	%			
Soc. Chr.	53	51.7	46	56	58	55	64		41.4	36.5
Liberals	6.5	6	6	6	8	8	8		12.1	10.5
Socialists	10	11	13	9.4	7	9	3		37.3	33
Communists	0.5	0.7	0.8	0.6	–	–	–		3.5	3
Other	–	–	–	–	–	–	–		5.7	5
No party	14	13.6	18.2	10	16	16	16	} Not voting 12[1]		
No answer	16	17	16	18	11	12	9			
ENGLAND	N = 400	300	114	186	100	52	48	1951		
	%	%	%	%	%	%	%			
Conservatives	37.75	39.3	32	44	33	25	42		47.8	39.7
Liberals	16.5	15.3	15	15.5	20	19	21		2.6	2.2
Labour	19	19	28	13	19	21	17		49.5	41
Communists	0.25	0.3	–	0.5	–	–	–		0.04	–
Other	–	–	–	–	–	–	–		0.16	–
No party	13.25	12	12	12	17	21	12	} Not voting 17		
No answer	13.25	14	13	15	11	14	8			
FRANCE	N = 350	272	113	159	78	48	30	1951		
	%	%	%	%	%	%	%			
Gaullists	} 7	6	6	6	13	10	17	{	21.7	17.1
Ind. right								{	13.1	10.3
MRP	11	10	10	10	17	21	10		12.3	9.6
Radicals	15	16	15	16	12	10	13		11.5	9
Socialists (SFIO)	21	23	35	16	9	6	13		14.5	11.3
Communists (PCF)	3	4	4	4	2	4	–		26.5	20.6
No party	25	25	12	33	24	27	20	} Not voting 22		
No answer	18	16	18	15	33	21	27			

| Parties | OCSR Teacher Samples | | | | | | | National Elections | | |
| | Tot. | Primary | | | Secondary | | | Date | Per cent of | |
		Tot.	M	F	Tot.	M	F		Votes cast	Elec- torate
NETHERLANDS N = 400	*400*	*300*	*163*	*137*	*100*	*82*	*18*	*1952*		
	%	%	%	%	%	%	%			
Liberals (VVD)	8	5	5	5	19	14	39		8.8	8.1
Calvinists										
CHU, SGP	8	9	9	9	3	4	–		11.3	10.4
AR	14	16	20	10	10	10	11		11.3	10.3
Catholic										
KNP	3	3	3	3	5	6	–		2.7	2.5
KVP	35	39	38	42	22	24	11		28.7	26.5
Labour (PvdA)	19	17	18	16	25	27	17		29.0	26.7
No party	5	4	3	5	7	7	11	Not voting 8.0[1]		
No answer	8	7	4	10	19	8	11			
NORWAY N = 400	*400*	*300*	*161*	*139*	*100*	*89*	*11*	*1953*		
	%	%	%	%	%	%	%			
Agrarians	2	2	2	2	–	–	–		8.8	7
Conservatives	13	11	5	18	17	16	(27)		18.4	14.9
Chr. Peoples' party	8	11	10	12	1	1	–		10.5	8.3
Liberals	36	39	45	32	27	28	(18)		10.0	8
Labour	18	14	17	10	30	32	(18)		46.7	37.3
Communists	0.25	–	–	–	1	1			5.1	4.1
No party	8	7	8	5	14	13	(18)	Not voting 20.7		
No answer	14.75	16	13	20	10	9	(18)			
SWEDEN N = 443	*443*	*324*	*96*	*228*	*119*	*62*	*57*	*1952*		
	%	%	%	%	%	%	%			
Agrarians	–	–	–	–	–	–	–		10.7	8.5
Conservatives	44.1	38	25	44	60	55	67		14.4	11.4
Liberals	41.1	45	51	43	29	29	30		24.4	19.4
Soc. Dems.	10.5	12	21	7	8	13	1.5		46.1	36.5
Communists	–	–	–	–	–	–	–		4.3	3.4
No party	0.2	–	–	–	1	1.5	–	Not voting 20.9		
No answer	4.1	5	3	6	2	1.5	1.5			
W. GERMANY N = 365	*365*	*265*	*171*	*94*	*100*	*75*	*25*	*1953*		
	%	%	%	%	%	%	%			
DP, other right wing	3	4	4	3	–	–	–		5.5	3.2
FDP/DVP	10	9	8	11	14	15	12		9.5	7.8
BP, GB-BHE	2	2	1	2	2	3	–		7.6	6.5
CDU/CSU	26	21	16	32	35	29	52		45.2	37
SPD	9	12	16	4	3	4	–		28.8	23.5
KPD	–	–	–	–	–	–	–		2.2	1.8
No party	31	32	33	29	29	30	24	Not voting 14		
No answer	19	20	21	19	17	19	12			

Note: N = Number of persons questioned in the particular category. Percentages are in parentheses when N is too small.

[1] Estimated.

Table 2. *Party Identifications Compared by School Systems: Belgium, France, Germany, Netherlands*

Primary schools only

| | | Tot. Public (govt., munic.) schools | | | Private/confessional schools | | | | | | |
| | | | | | Tot. | Catholic | | | Protestant | | |
		Tot.	M	F		Tot.	M	F	Tot.	M	F
BELGIUM	N = 300	148	86	62	152	152	46	106	–	–	–
	%	%	%	%	%	%	%	%	%	%	%
Soc. Chr.	51.7	25.7	35	16	76.7	76.7	72	79			
Liberals	6	11.6	9	15	0.7	0.7	–	1			
Socialists	11	21	19	24	1.5	1.5	2	1			
Communists	0.7	0.7	–	2	0.7	0.7	2	–			
No party	13.6	21	17	24	6.6	6.6	11	5			
No answer	17	20	22	19	13.8	13.8	13	14			
FRANCE	N = 272	229	97	132	43	43	16	7	–	–	–
	%	%	%	%	%	%	%	%	%	%	%
Gaullists, etc.	6	1	–	2	33	33	(44)	26			
MRP	10	7	8	7	23	23	(19)	26			
Radicaux	16	16	13.5	18	14	14	(2.5)	7			
Socialists, etc.	23	28	41	18	2	2	–	4			
Communists	4	4	4	4	–	–	–	–			
No party	25	26	13.5	34	21	21	(6)	30			
No answer	16	18	20	17	7	7	(6)	7			
NETHERLANDS	N = 300	80	45	35	220	130	65	65	90[1]	53	37
	%	%	%	%	%	%	%	%	%	%	%
Liberals (VVD)	5	19	18	20	–	–	–	–	–	–	–
CHU, SGP	9	1	–	3	12	–	–	–	30	30	30
AR	16	1	21	–	21	–	–	–	51	60	38
KNP	3	–	–	–	4	5	6	5	1	–	2
Kath. Volksp.	39	4	4.5	3	52	89	91	86	–	–	–
Labour (PVDA)	17	56	60	51	3	–	–	–	7	4	11
No party	4	9	4	14	2	1	1.5	–	5	4	5
No answer	7	10	11	9	6	5	1.5	9	6	2	14
W. GERMANY	N = 265	150	100	50	115	79	48	31	36	23	13
	%	%	%	%	%	%	%	%	%	%	%
DP, etc.	4	3.3	3	4	4	3	4	–	8	8.5	(8)
FDP/DVP	9	11.3	9	16	6	4	4	3	11	13	(8)
BP/GP-BHE	2	2	3.2	2	1	1	–	3	–	–	–
CDU/CSU	21	14	10	22	32	39	33	49	17	8.5	(30)
SPD	12	14	18	6	9	5	8	–	17	22	(8)
No party	32	31.3	30	34	32	33	40	22.5	30	35	(23)
No answer	20	24	28	16	16	15	10	22.5	17	13	(23)

[1] Includes 5 teachers in 'private secular' schools.

Table 3. *Party Identification and Religious Affiliation*

Note: balance to 100 % for each party is 'No answer' on question of religion.

	Primary school teachers						Secondary school teachers					
	N	Cath. %	Prot.[1] %	Nonconformist (England) %	Oth. %	No relig. %	N	Cath. %	Prot.[1] %	Nonconformist (England) %	Oth. %	No relig. %
BELGIUM												
Soc. Chr.	155	99	–	–	–	1	58	98	2	–	–	–
Lib.	18	56	–	–	–	44	15	40	7	–	–	47
Soc.	33	42	–	–	–	55						
No party	41	76	–	–	–	14	27	63	7	–	–	19
No answer	51	71	–	–	–	19						
ENGLAND												
Cons.	118	14	66	17	1	1	33	6	67	15	–	12
Lib.	46	9	39	50	–	–	20	–	40	45	–	15
Labour	58	7	59	24	2	8	19	5	31	41	–	15
No party	36	8	56	25	–	11	28	–	57	21	–	7
No answer	42	13	41	18	3	–						
FRANCE												
Gaullists	16	100	–	–	–	–	10	90	10	–	–	–
MRP	27	74	–	–	–	22	13	85	–	–	–	15
Radicaux	43	67	5	–	2	26	9	(67)	(11)	–	–	(22)
Soc. & Comm.	75	43	1	–	1	53	9	(11)	(32)	–	(11)	(44)
No party	67	61	4	–	3	27	19	63	5	–	–	21
No answer	44	48	7	–	–	32	18	55	–	–	–	39
NETHERLANDS												
Lib.	15	–	93	–	–	7	19	–	63	–	–	37
CHU, AR	75	–	100	–	–	–	13	–	100	–	–	–
KNP, KVP	126	99	1	–	–	–	27	100	–	–	–	–
Labour	51	–	53	–	10	37	25	–	52	–	–	48
No party	12	17	75	–	–	8	16	38	25	–	6	31
No answer	21	33	33	–	5	29						
NORWAY												
Cons. & Agr.	39	–	97	–	–	–	17	–	77	–	6	–
Chr.	34	–	100	–	–	–	1	–	–	–	–	–
Lib.	117	–	97	–	1	–	27	–	78	–	4	11
Lab.	41	–	85	–	7	5	31	–	55	–	10	22
No party	20	–	85	–	–	–	24	4	50	–	4	21
No answer	49	–	69	–	4	–						
SWEDEN												
Cons.	124	–	100	–	–	–	72	–	96	–	1	1
Lib.	147	–	91	1	7	–	35	–	97	–	–	3
Soc. Dem.	37	–	92	–	5	3	9	–	–	–	–	–
No answer	16	–	100	–	–	–	3	–	–	–	–	–

	N	Primary school teachers					N	Secondary school teachers				
		Cath. %	Prot.[1] %	Nonconformist (England) %	Oth. %	No relig. %		Cath. %	Prot.[1] %	Nonconformist (England) %	Oth. %	No relig. %
WEST GERMANY												
Cons. & Lib.	38	26	74	–	–	–	16	19	75	–	–	6
CDU/CSU	58	76	22	–	–	2	35	69	31	–	–	–
SPD	31	10	87	–	3	–	3	–	–	–	–	–
No party	84	42	54	–	2	2	29	31	69	–	–	–
No answer	54	46	52	–	–	2	17	23	71	–	6	–

[1] 'Protestant' includes Church of England, Lutheran-Evangelical (in W. Germany), Calvinist (*Hervormd* and *Gereformeerd* in the Netherlands), the State Churches in Norway and Sweden.

the independence of the confessional schools. *Table 3* provides some further evidence on this point.

A grouping of the parties by their socio-economic recruitment basis is equally essential to an understanding of the comparative distributions in *Table 1*. The peculiarities of the social position of the teacher have been the subject of much literature and have also given rise to some comparative research across a number of societies.[202] Teachers are normally assigned some place 'in the middle of the middle classes.' Functionally they will in most cases be classed among the professional groups, but economically they rank lower than all the independent professions and, in some countries, earn less than some skilled worker categories (Hammer, 1953). This contrast between functional importance and economic reward clearly affects the prestige and status accorded to teachers. The Hall-Jones findings indicate consensus in Britain on grading the primary school teacher in the neighbourhood of the 'news reporter,' the 'jobbing master builder,' and the 'commercial traveller,' i. e., somewhere below the independent professions and the industrial managers, and above the minor members of the business community and the typical white collar worker (Hall, 1950; cf. Glass, 1954). Comparative studies of prestige ranking seem to indicate that the position of the primary school teacher is much the same in all industrialized societies.[203] The position of secondary school teachers seems to vary somewhat as between countries, mainly, it appears, as a function of differences in educational qualifications required. The secondary school teachers have higher incomes than the primary teachers in all the countries studied, but their status concerns may be even more pronounced because they earn so much less than members of professions that do not require

Table 4. *Party Identification and Attitudes to Government*

Attitudes expressed on:

	N	Govt. domestic policies				Defence policy			Foreign policy			Idea of world govt.			
		for	agst.	DK	NA	for strong-er def.	for same or less	NA	full sup-port	reser-vations	NA	for	agst.	DK	NA
BELGIUM	*400*	71	18	6	5	36	34	30	63	26	11	47	43	5	5
Soc. Chr.	*213*	82	9	6	3	39	27	34	70	25	5	43	51	3	3
Lib.	*26*	54	31	7.5	7.5	31	54	15	54	35	4	65	27	4	4
Soc.	*42*	50	37	11	3	26	62	12	53	28	19	64	26	5	5
No party	*57*	65	25	8	2	42	39	19	56	28	16	44	42	8	8
No answer	*62*	63	19	3	15	31	22	47	53	26	21	42	37	11	10
ENGLAND	*400*	66	24	2	8	28	42	30	71	22	7	45	43	2	10
Cons.	*151*	79	14	2	5	35	38	27	86	11	3	34	55	1	10
Lib.	*66*	56	30	6	8	26	47	27	66	23	11	61	30	4.5	4.5
Lab.	*77*	49	46	1	4	22	54	23	46	52	2	64	30	1	5
No party	*53*	73	15	2	10	24	44	32	79	15	6	38	40	5	17
No answer	*53*	58	19	2	21	23	32	45	66	15	19	42	41	–	17
FRANCE	*350*	48	34	10	8	29	54	17	43	46	11	50	42	4	4
Gaullists	*26*	62	26	12	–	84	12	4	61	27	12	42	54	4	–
MRP	*40*	63	27	3	7	55	30	15	52	43	5	53	42	5	–
Radicaux	*52*	48	44	4	4	31	57	12	48	48	4	57	43	–	–
Soc. & Comm.	*84*	38	56	5	1	7	88	5	24	74	2	53	41	4	2
No party	*86*	43	21	21	15	23	44	33	45	35	20	45	42	6	7
No answer	*62*	50	20	11	19	23	51	26	48	29	23	49	40	3	8

	N														
NETHERLANDS	400	67	28	4	1	56	29	15	52	45	3	62	35	3	1
Liberals	34	47	44	6	3	41	32	27	50	47	3	71	23	3	3
CHU, SGP	31	62	32	6	–	65	16	19	52	45	3	42	55	3	3
AR	57	58	40	–	2	65	21	14	49	48	3	49	48	3	–
KNP	13	15	69	8	8	69	23	8	31	69	–	54	46	–	–
KVP	140	72	21	7	–	61	26	13	61	36	3	57	39	3	1
Labour	76	86	12	2	–	42	42	16	50	46	4	83	16	1	–
No party	19	69	26	5	–	58	31	11	42	53	5	69	26	–	5
No answer	30	67	30	–	3	37	43	20	40	60	–	60	30	7	3
NORWAY	400	51	42	2	5	59	28	13	84	13	3	52	42	3	3
Cons./Agr.	56	35	60	2	4	68	23	9	87	9	4	52	48	–	–
Christian	35	43	45	6	6	54	26	20	86	12	2	43	48	6	3
Lib.	144	49	45	1	5	65	27	8	89	10	1	53	42	2	3
Lab.	72	81	18	–	1	51	34	15	83	17	–	68	25	4	3
No party	34	38	52	3	7	56	32	12	76	15	9	50	47	3	–
No answer	59	48	37	7	8	49	27	24	71	19	10	39	46	5	10
SWEDEN	443	39	58	2	1	48	37	15	34	61	5	55	39	6	–
Cons.	196	30	67	2	1	60	24	16	34	61	5	47	44	8	1
Lib.	182	37	61	1	1	40	45	15	35	61	4	52	35	3	–
Soc. Dem.	46	87	13	–	–	28	63	9	39	61	–	66	28	6	–
No answer	18	28	61	11	–	50	22	28	21	68	11	39	55	6	–
W. GERMANY	365	60	33	5	2	49	44	7	64	30	6	68	23	5	4
Cons. & Lib.	54	63	33	4	–	57	39	4	65	31	4	67	28	5	–
CDU/CSU	93	81	17	1	1	56	38	6	80	17	3	66	26	4	4
SPD	34	27	68	7	5	21	76	3	53	47	–	94	3	–	3
No party	113	52	39	7	2	50	42	8	50	41	9	63	29	4	4
No answer	71	59	30	7	4	48	41	11	70	21	9	67	20	8	5

any more training than theirs. All these factors may play some part in determining political orientations and party preferences.

Looking first at the parties that have a primary basis in the working class populations, we find in all countries a lower proportion of identifiers among teachers than in the electorate at large. The numbers of teachers who indicate identification with Communist parties are much too small to allow any analysis. The percentage of teachers reporting sympathies with Labour parties, Socialists, or Social Democrats varies from 9 per cent in Germany to 21 per cent in France. These teachers constitute political minorities in the educational systems and deserve special analysis as 'deviant cases': unfortunately the sizes of our samples set severe limits to the amount of cross-tabulation that can be undertaken.

The secondary school teachers tend to be less pro-Labour than the primary school teachers in all the countries *except the Netherlands and Norway*. This difference is of considerable interest. In the Netherlands this discrepancy mainly reflects the divisions within the educational system: there are proportionately more state system teachers than confessional school teachers in the secondary schools, and consequently, as is evident from *Table 2*, a higher probability of Labour identifiers among the teachers at that level. In Norway, the primary-secondary difference can probably best be explained in terms of the contrast between normal school and University education, a contrast which is probably more marked in Norway than in the other countries.

Looking further to the parties that have their primary basis in the middle class populations, we find in England, Norway, and Sweden a markedly higher proportion of identifiers with such parties among the teachers than in the national electorates. The relationship between Conservatives and Liberals is of particular interest. In England and Norway the percentage of Liberals is strikingly high. It will be seen that as many as 20 per cent of the secondary teachers identify with the Liberal party in England despite the fact that this party has practically disappeared as a force in national politics.[204] In Norway the Liberals *(Venstre)* are clearly the strongest party among the teachers: this has its historical explanation in the central role of the teaching profession in bringing this party to power at the end of the nineteenth century. In Sweden, the teachers who are not Social Democrats are evenly split between the Conservatives *(Högern)* and the Liberals *(Folkpartiet):* the Liberals, however, are the stronger in the primary school, while the Conservatives can count on 60 per cent of the secondary school teachers in the areas sampled.

The differences between the male teachers and the female teachers in their political orientation are quite marked. It will be seen that in all countries except the Netherlands the female teachers tend to identify *more* frequently with the Conservative or Christian parties and *less* frequently with the Labour or Socialist parties than the male teachers.[205] This, of course, is in general conformity with regularities observed in numerous countries (Lipset, 1954: pp. 1134 seq.; Duverger, 1955: 1). In the Netherlands, the divisions within the school system, as shown in Table II, seem to be a more important determinant of political orientation than the sex of the teachers.

The marital status of the teacher does not seem to affect political preferences except in so far as particular school systems are apt to employ single teachers rather than married ones. In Belgium, for instance, we find 77 per cent of the single female teachers identifying with the Social Christian party and only 1 per cent with the Socialists, while the corresponding figures for the married females are 28 per cent and 21 per cent: this simply reflects the fact that the teachers in the Catholic schools are mostly single.

This summary of salient characteristics of the basic distributions for party identification would seem to indicate that of our seven teacher samples, the English, Norwegian, and Swedish are the most readily comparable for the present purposes; that the Belgian and the Dutch samples allow extensive comparison if broken down by the major divisions of the school systems; and that the French and West German samples present additional difficulties for comparative analysis. In the ensuing presentation of findings, these limitations should be kept in mind. The small sizes of the samples have not allowed as detailed breakdowns and as extensive cross-tabulations as would be desirable to test the relative importance of the different factors that may affect the relationships. A number of the findings must therefore remain suggestive rather than conclusive. This, of course, is a hazard that must be faced in any effort to test the generality of cross-national relationships on the basis of sample data.

Party Identification and Opinions on Government Policies
Table 1 establishes that in all the seven countries the teachers who identify with the working class parties make up minorities within their professions. In the wider national contexts, however, the position of these minorities differed markedly: in some countries their party identification would entail opposition to the government in power, in other countries, support of the government. In three of the countries the Labour parties played major roles in the national government: in the Netherlands, the Labour party held one-third of the Cabinet posts, in Sweden there was a coalition of the Social Democrats and the Agrarians, in Norway there was an all-Labour government. In Belgium the Catholics were in power at the time the interviews were taken, but the Liberal-Socialist coalition was to regain power a year later. In Great Britain, on the other hand, there was a Conservative government, but the Labour party had been in power until some eighteen months before the interviews were taken. In France and Germany, finally, the working class parties made up the core of the opposition to the current governments. These differences between the countries would obviously be

expected to be reflected in the opinion correlates of party identification. As will be seen in *Table 4,* there is a clear-cut difference between the countries in the direction of the relationship between party identification and opinions expressed on the domestic policies of the government. The main question used to elicit such opinions focused directly on the class and interest divisions within the national community: *'Would you say that this country's government's policy serves the interests of all people equally or does it tend to favour certain groups unduly?'* In the three countries that had Labour-oriented governments, those who identified with the working class parties were significantly *more* likely than the 'bourgeois' identifiers to say that their government served the general interests of all people rather than any one group or set of groups. In the other countries the relationship went in the opposite direction: those who identified with working class parties were *less* likely to say that the government served the general interests of all people equally. This finding is in itself mainly of interest as a check on the reliability of the teachers' reports on their party identifications, but it also raises some important problems of interpretation: what are the factors that make for differences among identifiers with the same party in their opinions of their government? An exhaustive study of these differences cannot be undertaken with samples of this size. It is clear that in countries like Belgium and the Netherlands the teacher's position in the school system would make a difference: within each party, the teacher in the state system school will be less prone to criticize the government than the teacher in the confessional school. The *sex* of the teacher also seems to make considerable differences in this respect. If we analyze the relationships separately for male teachers and female teachers, we find that within *opposition parties* – whether 'bourgeois' or Labour – the females are more critical of their government's domestic policies than the men. There are several possible interpretations of this finding: the female teachers may have given more reliable reports on their party identification, the male teachers may be more reluctant to express any criticism of the government in power, the question may have been interpreted differently. It is of particular interest that a similar finding seems to emerge from an analysis of within-party differences on other issues: this will be discussed in detail in a subsequent section.

Different patterns of cross-national relationships emerge from an analysis of the party distributions for opinion expressions bearing on external policies: defence, efforts for world peace, the problem of world government.

Opinions on the defence policies of the governments are related to party identification in much the same way across all the seven samples: the 'left' identifiers are *most,* and the 'right' and 'Christian' identifiers are *least* likely to express opposition to increases in the budgets for military preparedness. This, of course, is a traditional ideological contrast: what is interesting is that the 'left-right' difference is as pronounced in the three countries where the governments were Labour-oriented – despite the strong emphasis given to the needs for strengthened national defence in the programs and policies of the Labour parties of these countries.

Another traditional contrast appears in the cross-tabulation of party identification and expressed opinions on the idea of world government.[206] In all the countries the 'left' identifiers are clearly more favourable to this idea than the 'right' identifiers. These differences would seem to relate to the degree of 'nationalist' emphasis in the party ideologies. It should be noticed that the 'middle-class' parties are not uniformly more 'nationalist' in this sense than the working class parties: the Conservative or Christian party identifiers are everywhere the most 'nationalist' but the 'Liberal' party identifiers differ in their response across the countries. In Belgium, England, and France, there is no difference between the 'Liberals' and the 'Labour' identifiers on this score, while in Norway and Sweden the 'Liberals' are closer to the position of the Conservative or Christian party identifiers. This finding simply serves to illustrate the difficulties of equating and ordering ideological groupings across political communities.

A more complex pattern of cross-national differences will appear in the cross-tabulation of party identification and opinions expressed on the foreign policy of the national government. The main question used in this area was an indirect one: *'Do you feel that our government is doing all it possibly can to maintain peace in the world?' Table 4* indicates:

a) that in three of the countries there is a clear-cut difference between identifiers with the government parties and identifiers with the opposition parties on the 'left': this is the case in Belgium, England, and France;

b) that in two countries, the Netherlands and West Germany, there is a higher frequency of critical reservations both to the 'right' and to the 'left' of the 'centre' party: the Catholic people's party and the Christian Democrats;

c) that in Norway and Sweden, finally, there is no clear difference between any of the party identifiers on this score.

These differences among the countries must obviously be interpreted in the light of the actual policies pursued by each national government. Five of the countries were members of the North Atlantic Treaty Organization; a sixth country, Western Germany, still had no foreign policy of its own, but its government was preparing to join the Western alliance system; the seventh country, Sweden, had decided to stay neutral in the current power conflict and had not committed itself to any alliance. In all the seven countries there were considerable divisions of opinion over the national policies thus set. The split was particularly marked in France and West Germany. In the other countries, there was a large measure of agreement

Table 5. Party Identification and Orientations to International Problems

Measures:

HS – high salience of worries about international situation, spontaneous reference to dangers of war, international tension.

LS – low salience, no spontaneous reference.

HE – highly enemy-threatened, spontaneous attribution of primary responsibility for any new world war to East bloc.

LE – low on enemy-threatenedness, no spontaneous attribution of primary responsibility to East.

HW – highly enemy-threatened: ranks 'World War' as 'least good' alternative (worse than Soviet predominance) and cannot conceive of any circumstances that would make a world war the 'lesser of two evils'.

LW – low on war-threatenedness': – only one or neither of the two 'high' responses.

Party:	N	Salience			Enemy-thr.			War-thr.			N	Combined index		
		HS %	LS %	NA %	HE %	LE %	NA %	HW %	LW %	NA %		HELW %	HEHW and LELW %	LEHW %
BELGIUM														
Soc. Chr.	213	20	73	7	59	29	12	16	83	1	176	47	42	11
Lib.	26	46	50	4	50	46	4	27	73	–	25	32	40	28
Soc.	42	36	54	10	24	60	16	52	31	17	34	15	26	59
No party	57	37	56	7	28	56	16	34	61	5	47	23	39	38
No answer	62	24	68	8	40	44	16	37	61	2	47	21	34	45
ENGLAND														
Cons.	151	34	63	3	47	29	24	22	75	3	111	45	42	13
Lib.	66	42	54	3	37	39	24	29	58	13	47	36	38	26
Lab.	77	42	53	5	32	47	21	39	60	1	58	21	38	41
No party	53	34	60	6	29	47	24	17	72	11	39	23	31	46
No answer	53	30	49	21	25	26	49	28	70	2	25	35	43	22
FRANCE														
Gaullist	26	23	70	7	77	8	15	31	69	–	22	59	36	5
MRP	40	20	80	–	23	37	40	45	35	20	23	13	52	35

Rad.	*52*	37	63	—	29	39	32	60	40	—	*33*	18	36	46
Soc. & Comm.	*84*	52	47	1	11	72	17	64	32	4	*64*	3	25	72
No party	*86*	26	67	7	14	48	38	51	39	4	*52*	10	18	72
No answer	*62*	42	51	7	11	50	39	49	46	5	*37*	—	33	67
NETHS.														
Liberals	*34*	47	47	6	50	35	15	29	65	6	*24*	42	29	29
CHU, SGP	*31*	52	48	—	62	22	16	3	94	3	*23*	61	30	9
AR	*57*	35	65	—	74	17.5	8.5	9	91	—	*50*	76	20	4
KNP	*13*	38	54	8	69	31	—	—	100	1	*13*	69	23	8
KVP	*140*	28	71	1	75	18	7	6	93	1	*127*	73	22	5
Labour	*76*	58	42	—	55	29	16	25	74	—	*61*	42.5	42.5	15
No party	*19*	37	58	5	48	42	10	25	74	3	*17*	41	35	24
NA	*30*	33	64	3	43	37	20	10	82	3	*22*	41	45	14
NORWAY														
Cons. & Agr.	*56*	48	47	5	63	14	23	21	77	2	*40*	60	35	5
Chr.	*35*	40	57	3	49	17	34	9	91	—	*21*	71	24	5
Lib.	*144*	54	46	—	54	20	26	16	84	—	*99*	61	25	14
Lab.	*72*	50	49	—	36	37	27	35	65	—	*50*	42	28	30
No party	*34*	44	56	—	41	24	35	18	79	3	*18*	61	17	22
No answer	*59*	58	40	2	30	31	39	29	66	5	*33*	37	30	33
SWEDEN														
Cons.	*196*	53	45	2	75	18	7	14	84	2	*170*	59	33	8
Lib.	*182*	48	41	1	75	22	3	21	79	—	*169*	54	34	12
Soc. Dem.	*46*	63	37	—	61	35	4	22	78	—	*39*	41	36	23
No. answer	*18*	55	39	6	50	39	11	22	72	6	*16*	44	31	25
W. GERMANY														
Cons./Lib.	*54*	61	39	—	32	48	20	43	57	—	*43*	16	40	44
CDU	*93*	47	51	2	55	28	17	20	78	2	*75*	47	38	15
SPD	*38*	47	53	—	38	47	15	50	50	—	*29*	28	38	34
No party	*113*	40	59	1	25	47	28	42	55	3	*78*	17	44	39
No answer	*71*	53	47	—	20	40	40	35	59	6	*40*	20	40	40

on basic policy among the leaders of all the parties except the Communist, but there were still important divisions of opinion within some of the major parties. In the NATO countries there were misgivings about the effects and implications of the alliance policy in some segments of the Labour parties: these doubts became explicit and articulate during the controversies over the hydrogen bomb, German rearmament, and the EDC-WEU agreements in 1954 and 1955. In Sweden, the pattern was reversed: the policy of neutrality had its strongest supporters among the Social Democrats and was opposed in some segments of the Conservative and the Liberal parties.

These divisions of opinion are reflected in the teachers' responses to the question focused on their government's efforts for world peace. The question was deliberately vague and 'projective' and the responses must be fitted into a wider pattern of relationships. The interpretation of the question as well as the direction of the response would very much hinge on the teachers' general views of the international situation, the forces opposing each other, the alternatives to be considered, the possible and probable outcomes. Data on the teachers' orientations to world affairs may help to account for the within-party differences in the appraisal of national policy.

The findings for Norway and Sweden seem to call for special analysis. Both countries had Labour-oriented governments, but Norway had joined NATO while Sweden had stayed uncommitted. It will be seen that there was nevertheless no difference between the two countries in the relationship between party identification and opinions on foreign policy: in Norway the Labour identifiers were as likely as 'bourgeois' identifiers to express support of the alliance policy, while in Sweden there was no difference between the parties in the proportions of supporters of the policy of neutrality. It turns out, however, that the relationships are quite different if the male teachers and the female teachers are considered apart. Both in Norway and Sweden, the male teachers who identify with the 'left' are significantly *more critical* of their government's foreign policy than the males who report 'bourgeois' identifications. For the female teachers, the relationships tend to go in the *opposite* direction, in Norway not very clearly, but in Sweden quite markedly. Unfortunately, the groups get too small for further analysis of this difference, but it can no doubt be accounted for to a considerable extent in terms of contrasting orientations to the international situation. This will be discussed in our next section.

Party Identification and Orientations to International Conflict
A central aim of the OCSR study was to explore the predominant patternings of perceptions, judgements, and attitudes that underlay the contrasting orientations to world politics in the current situation. As formulated in the original design agreed upon among the research teams, the study objective was to identify major dimensions of *individual orientations to potential threats* in international politics (Aubert, 1954: pp. 26–31). Four major

aspects of threat orientation were tentatively distinguished in the construction of the interview schedule:

a) the *salience* of the respondent's worries about world affairs;
b) the relative *probability,* as respondent saw it, of the occurrence of alternative developments in Western Europe;
c) the *valence,* the relative acceptability or unacceptability to the respondents of these alternative developments; and
d) the *principal sources of dangerous developments* and the consequent *attribution of responsibility and blame* for developments that may take place.

These abstract formulations were translated into concrete issues in a series of open-ended questions and a couple of tests requiring the ranking of alternative developments in terms of probability and valence. No attempt has been made to explore the possibilities of 'scaling' the responses along one or more dimensions but some indexes have been set up and have proved useful in differentiating response patterns in the different countries.

The first index provides a basis for ordering the respondents according to the *salience* of their worries about international conflict and war. The measure is based on content analyses of responses to an initial question designated to explore what problems were 'foremost in the mind' of the respondent. The question came immediately after some discussion of educational problems and was simply: *'What, in your opinion, are the two or three most important problems that demand urgent attention these days?'* The index simply differentiates between 1) those who immediately mentioned problems of war and international tensions, 2) those who mentioned such problems in the second or third instance, and 3) those who did not refer to any such problems at all. *Table 5* gives the distributions for this salience index by categories of party identification. It will be seen that there are considerable differences between the parties in all countries: the 'left' and 'Liberal' identifiers are more likely to be 'high' on salience than the Conservatives or the Christian party identifiers in all countries except West Germany, where the socialists and the Christian Democrats are the least likely to be 'high' and the German party – Free Democrat group the most. The differences between the Labour parties and the Liberal parties are less easy to interpret: it will be seen that the Liberals in Belgium express more worry than the Socialists, that the Liberals in England and Norway do not differ much from the Labour identifiers in this respect, while in Sweden the Liberals are slightly lower than the Conservatives on salience.

The index for *probability* was derived from a test requiring the teachers to rank five possible developments from the most to the least likely: another World War, American dominance in Western Europe without war, Soviet dominance without war, 'cold war' continued indefinitely, development of 'really peaceful' conditions. These alternatives were of course not unambiguously exclusive of each other but they were intended to yield some data about the prevalent expectations. The measure does not seem to have served this purpose reliably in all the countries. The cross-tabulations that have been made against other response distributions bearing on the probability of war do not indicate any high degree of consistency. The relationships to reported party identification are not very clear but indicate a general tendency for those on the 'right,' the Conservatives and the Christian party identifiers, to be the most pessimistic: this comes out particularly clearly in their ranking of the possibility of a development toward 'really peaceful conditions.' [207] There are exceptions, however: in England, the Labour identifiers are the most pessimistic and the Liberals the least; in Norway there is no difference between the Conservatives, the Liberals, and the Labourites, while the Christians are significantly more pessimistic; in West Germany there is no difference between CDU and SPD while the FDP group is clearly the most pessimistic.

Two further indexes of threat orientation proved particularly useful in the analysis: an index of *'war-threatenedness'* and an index of *'enemy-threatenedness.'*

These indexes are closely related to each other conceptually as well as empirically. They reflect the relative emphasis given in the responses to the two major sets of factors that must be weighed against each other in the solution of international conflict: the effects of war *per se* and the implications of the advances of the potential enemy. Very few people, probably, have articulate sets of conceptions of the considerations that count *pro* or *contra* particular decisions, but it still seems possible to order people by the relative predominance of the fear of war as such vs. the fear of the aggressive actions of the potential enemy. The measures that were developed in the OCSR study were very crude and provisional, but they seem to have served a useful function in providing a basis for meaningful differentiations between ideological orientations.

The index of *'war-threatenedness'* was based on two responses: a) the ranking of the five alternative developments (see above) from 'would result in the *best* situation for us if it should happen' to 'would result in the *least good* situation for us,' and b) responses to the question *'Under what circumstances would you look upon a world war as an alternative that would be the lesser of two evils.'* It will be evident from *Table 5* that these responses were closely associated with party identification in all countries *except Sweden:* the Labour identifiers and the Socialists are significantly more likely to give consistently 'high' responses than the identifiers to the right. In Sweden there is a slight difference between the Conservatives and the two other parties, but this may be due to chance variation. It is of interest to note that there are considerable differences on this index among those who do not identify with Labour or Socialist parties: the Christian party identifiers are everywhere the least 'war-threatened,' but the 'Liberal' party identifiers are not always an intermediate group as might be expected. In France, the Radicals do not differ much from the Socialists on this index; in Norway the Liberals are *less* 'war-threatened' than the Conservatives; in West Germany the FDP identifiers are closer to the Socialists than to the CDU identifiers.

The measure of 'enemy-threatenedness' was based on content analyses of responses to open-ended questions such as: *'In your judgement what developments in international affairs constitute a danger?'* and *'If a world war were to occur, do you think any one nation or group of nations would be most to blame?'* As would be expected, this measure is negatively associated with the 'war-threatenedness' index in all the teacher samples: those who are less prone to express fear of war as such are more likely to see the major source of danger in the Soviet bloc, while those who express fear of war are more likely to stress the general features of the bipolar power struggle, or, in a few cases, the responsibility of the Western powers. The association of the two measures differs somewhat according to the sex of the teacher, thus there is only a slight tendency in the negative direction for the men teachers in the Netherlands and the women teachers in Sweden. There are also some important differences for the different categories of party identification.

Table 5 shows significant relationships between 'enemy-threatenedness' and party identification: in all the countries without exception there is a higher proportion of teachers expressing fear of the Soviet Union as a primary source of danger among the Christian or Conservative party identifiers than among the 'left' identifiers. This, of course, is in conformity with well-known ideological patterns. It is again of interest to see how the FDP group in West Germany deviates from the pattern in the other countries: the proportion of 'Soviet-blamers' in this group is actually *lower* than among the Socialist party identifiers.

A further index was constructed to differentiate the teachers who were 'pattern-consistent' from those who were 'inconsistent' in their responses to the measures of 'threatenedness.' In *Table 5* three groups are distinguished on the basis of the combined index:

a) 'high enemy – low war': those who express fear of the aggressive intentions of the enemy and at the same time express no explicit fear of war as such;
b) 'low enemy – high war': those who express no explicit fear of any enemy and at the same time express fear of war as such;
c) the rest of the respondents who gave codable responses to the questions.

It will be seen that this combined index yields clear relationships to party identification in all the countries studied. The relationships are most consistent if the 'high enemy – low war' group is considered as against the remainder of each sample. There is more variation in the relationship for the 'low enemy – high war' group: this relationship is not very clear for the Netherlands, mainly because of the high proportion of pattern-inconsistent responses among the Labour identifiers.

Party Identification, Threat Orientations, and Attitudes to the National Government

Table 4 indicated considerable within-party differences in all countries in the opinions expressed on central government policies. These differences raise some interesting problems of ideological analysis: what are the factors that account for homogeneity or heterogeneity of opinion within the membership or followership of a given political party, what are the organizational limits of dissension, under what conditions is a basic division of opinion likely to bring about a division of loyalties and identifications? The controversy over the proposed expulsion of Bevan from the British Labour party is an interesting case in point. The division of opinion in the Labour party was perhaps primarily based on contrasting orientations to the international situation: the problems of the hydrogen bomb, German rearmament, American policy in Asia. It would probably not be very incorrect to assume that the division corresponded to our contrast between high and low 'enemy-threatenedness' and between high and low 'war-threatenedness.' There is no direct way of checking this, but it would probably be a good guess that the proportion of Bevanites would be highest among the 41 % of the Labour identifiers who were found to respond in the 'low enemy-high war' category.[208]

Hypotheses:	Findings:	BELGIUM		ENGLAND		NETHERLANDS			NORWAY		SWEDEN	
		Soc. Chr.	Lib. & Soc.	Cons.	Lib. & Lab.	Calv. & Lib.	Cath.	Lab.	'Bourgeois'	Lab.	Cons. & Lib.	Soc. Dem.
A. Those *high on* 'enemy-threatenedness' are more likely than those *low* to												
1. express *approval* of the govt's. *domestic policies*		0	*Pos*	Pos	*Pos*	*Pos*	Pos	0	0	0	*Pos*	neg

Hypotheses:	*Findings:* BELGIUM		ENGLAND		NETHERLANDS			NORWAY		SWEDEN	
	Soc. Chr.	Lib. & Soc.	Cons.	Lib. & Lab.	Calv. & Lib.	Cath.	Lab.	'Bour-geois'	Lab.	Cons. & Lib.	Soc. Dem.
2. *favour* increases in the *defence budget*	0	*Pos*	0	*Pos*	0	0	*Pos*	*Pos*	*Pos*	0	Pos
3. express *full support* of the govt's. *foreign pol.*	0	Pos	*Pos*	*Pos*	*Pos*	*Pos*	*Pos*	0	0	0	0
4. express *disapproval* of the idea of a *world govt.*	0	0	0	*Pos*	0	*Neg*	*Neg*	*Neg*	0	0	0
B. Those *high on* 'war-threaten-edness' are more likely than those *low* to											
1. express *disapproval* of the govt's. *domestic policies*	0	0	0	*Pos*	*Pos*	0	0	0	0	0	0
2. *be against* increases in the *defence budget*	*Pos*	*Pos*	*Pos*	Pos	0	0	*Pos*	*Pos*	*Pos*	0	0
3. *have reservations* about the govt's. *foreign policy*	0	*Pos*	0	*Pos*	*Pos*	0	0	0	0	0	Neg
4. express *approval* of the idea of a *world govt.*	neg	0	0	*Pos*	*Pos*	0	0	0	0	0	0

Note: 'Pos' means tendency in direction of the specified hypothesis; '*Pos*' means significant relationship in this direction; '0' no clear relationship; 'Neg' indicates tendency and '*Neg*' significant relationship in the direction *opposite* to the one specified in the hypothesis.

To find out to what extent these contrasts in orientation to world affairs might affect within-party differences in opinion expressed on government policies, a series of multiple tabulations were made for all the seven samples. Unfortunately the samples were too small and the distributions too skewed to allow any comparisons for all the party identification categories: some parties had to be combined and some of the variance was no doubt lost in this way. *Table 6* gives the results for five of the countries. The relevant relationships can be summarized as shown in the table on pp. 318–19.

There is no straightforward interpretation of these cross-national differences in within-party relationships. Some of the relationships seem to be highly random, others seem to fit more or less into plausible patterns. The 'enemy-threat' measure seems on the whole to provide a better basis for differentiation: the 'war-threat' index is mainly effective in accounting for some of the differences of opinion on defence matters.

The most striking regularity would seem to be the one for the acceptance of the national government's domestic policies. Here the interpretation seems to suggest itself that *'enemy-threatenedness' primarily tends to make a difference to the acceptance of domestic policies among those who identify with the opposition parties* – both in the countries where Conservatives or Christian parties were in power *and* in the countries that had Labour-oriented governments. In Belgium and England there is a clear 'high enemy – low enemy' difference among those who identify with the Liberal or the Labour parties, while in Sweden the difference holds for the bourgeois opposition. The Dutch sample also fits into this pattern, despite the complication caused by the multi-party coalition in power: the 'high enemy – low enemy' difference is only significant for the teachers who identify with the party grouping most critical of the government's foreign policy, the Calvinist and the Liberal parties. The Norwegian findings do not fit this pattern: this may simply be due to the heterogeneity of the parties which for statistical reasons had to be grouped together in one 'bourgeois' category. The findings for France and West Germany are not conclusive: the French data do not seem to fit the pattern, while the West German data show 'high enemy – low enemy' differences both for the DP-FDP group on the right and for the SPD group on the left, but none for the CDU/CSU group in the middle.

Looking further to the opinions expressed on the national government's policy of military preparedness, it will be seen that 'enemy-threatenedness' primarily tends to make a difference on this scale for the 'left' identifiers in all the countries. There are exceptions for France, where the index makes a difference within the 'right' and 'centre' groups, as well as for the Netherlands and West Germany, where the differences are significant within all the party groupings. Opinions on defence are also markedly affected by the level of 'war-threatenedness,' but there is no distinctive

Abbreviations: see Table 5.

Attitudes expressed on:		N	Govt. domestic policy			Defence policy			Foreign policy			Idea of world govt.		
Party:			for %	agst. %	DK NA %	for stronger def. %	for same or less %	NA %	full support %	reservations %	NA %	for %	agst. %	DK NA %
BELGIUM														
Soc. Chr.	HE	126	82	11	7	41	23	36	75	24	1	44	52	4
	LE	63	84	6	10	38	37	25	64	26	10	46	52	2
	HW	34	79	18	3	27	41	32	76	18	6	29	59	18
	LW	176	82	9	9	42	26	33	69	26	5	45	50	5
Lib. & Soc.	HE	23	70	21	9	39	52	9	61	39	–	65	30	5
	LE	37	48	41	11	22	68	10	51	30	19	67	24	9
	HW	29	59	31	10	17	69	14	41	35	24	59	31	10
	LW	39	46	36	18	36	51	13	62	31	7	69	23	8
ENGLAND														
Cons.	HE	71	83	9	8	32	41	27	92	8	–	32	59	9
	LE	43	74	26	–	34	33	33	79	19	2	40	51	9
	HW	34	82	15	3	27	50	23	88	12	–	38	50	12
	LW	112	80	14	6	37	36	27	86	11	3	33	58	9
Lib. & Lab.	HE	49	61	33	6	31	42	27	71	23	6	47	45	8
	LE	62	45	47	8	18	53	29	41	53	6	74	18	8
	HW	49	41	49	10	20.5	59	20.5	45	51	4	74	22	4
	LW	91	60	33	7	26	47	26	61	33	6	55	36	9
NETHERLANDS														
Calv. & Lib.	HE	85	60	35	5	66	22	12	59	40	1	56	44	–
	LE	34	44	50	6	59	20.5	20.5	29	68	3	50	44	6
	HW	70	47	47	6	60	23	17	43	57	–	59	38	3
	LW	61	61	36	3	60	24	16	53	42	5	50	48	2
Cath. P. P.	HE	105	76	21	3	62	27	11	65	35	–	62	35	3
	LE	25	60	28	12	56	28	16	48	44	8	48	48	4
	HW	54	70	26	4	63	30	7	59	39	2	57	41	2
	L W	85	73	20	7	62	22	16	62	34	4	58	39	3

Table 6 (cont.)

Attitudes expressed on: Party:	N	Govt. domestic policy			Defence policy			Foreign policy			Idea of world govt.		
		for %	agst. %	DK NA %	for stronger def. %	for same or less %	NA %	full support %	reservations %	NA %	for %	agst. %	DK NA %
Labour													
HE	*41*	90	10	–	46	39	15	54	41	5	92	8	–
LE	*24*	87	8	5	34	54	12	38	58	4	71	25	4
HW	*56*	86	12	2	32	52	16	50	48	2	84	16	–
LW	*19*	95	5	–	64	20	16	42	47	11	74	22	4
NORWAY													
'Bourgeois' parties													
HE	*130*	44	50	6	74	18	8	87	11	2	57	38	5
LE	*43*	47	49	4	55	40	5	91	9	–	42	54	4
HW	*38*	47	42	11	50	37	13	82	16	2	58	42	–
LW	*196*	44	50	6	63	27	10	89	9	2	50	44	6
Labour													
HE	*26*	85	11	4	73	15	12	88	12	–	61	27	12
LE	*26*	81	19	–	42	46	12	81	19	–	69	31	–
HW	*24*	83	17	–	42	46	12	83	17	–	67	29	4
LW	*47*	81	17	2	57	26	17	85	15	–	66	24	10
SWEDEN													
Cons. & Lib.													
HE	*284*	35	62	3	51	34	15	35	60	5	53	41	6
LE	*76*	24	75	1	50	32	18	36	63	1	54	37	9
HW	*192*	34	63	3	51	37	12	35	60	5	54	38	8
LW	*182*	33	65	1	50	31	19	33	64	3	55	40	5
Soc. Dem.													
HE	*28*	82	18	–	32	64	4	39	61	–	64	32	4
LE	*18*	94	6	–	25	56	19	44	56	–	68	19	13
HW	*26*	85	15	–	27	65	8	46	54	–	65	31	4
LW	*20*	90	10	–	30	60	10	30	70	–	65	25	10

cross-national patterning of the kind suggested for 'war-threatenedness.'

This analysis of the relationships between threat orientation and policy acceptance by categories of party identification is not very conclusive, but it does suggest that sensitivity to external danger may affect conformity to national policy for those who express traditional allegiance to parties currently in the opposition. In the original research design, the hypothesis was advanced that within certain limits of variation increased perception of potential enemy threat would increase conformity to national policies.[209] This psychological hypothesis could obviously only be tested within concrete political structures and at given levels of traditional allegiance to the central government. The analysis that has been undertaken does seem to suggest that the hypothesis can be maintained for individuals identifying with parties in opposition to those in power. Further analysis of these relationships are fraught with many difficulties. Additional data would be required to explore the extent to which increased fear of enemy aggression has increased not only policy acceptance, but also shifts in allegiances and votes toward the parties in power. The OCSR study was limited to one point of time and did not provide any data on the genesis and stability of party identification. In view of the tendencies emerging from this cross-national analysis, it must be said to have been most unfortunate that no provisions were made for the collection of data that might throw further light on these processes.

Party Identification, Threat Orientation and Opinions on National Unity and Dissent

The difficulties of accounting for cross-national differences in the data of a limited sample survey are even more in evidence in the analysis of the measures used to gauge opinions on national unity, consensus, and deviance. *Tables 7, 8* and *9* will indicate the complexities of the relationships across the countries between party identification, threat orientation and the responses given to the questions that could be included to tap the teachers' perceptions of conflict and dissent within the nation, their feelings about national disagreements and their attitudes to deviants from majority policy.

The questions used were very crude and general and do not seem to have produced highly reliable responses across the countries. This was very much an outcome of the difficulties involved in getting agreement among the research teams on a set of concrete cases to question the teachers about. If it had been possible to work into the interview schedule a series of concrete examples of controversial issues and modes of deviance,[210] it would no doubt have been easier to analyse the crucial between-country and between-party differences in this important area. As it is, the study can only offer some very limited data for tentative analysis and interpretation.

21 *

Table 7. *Party Identification and Opinions on National Unity and Dissent*

	N	Fundamental conflicts in country			Consensus on defence policy			Difference of opinion on defence		
		sees imp. confl. %	sees no imp. confl. %	DK NA %	sees wide con-sensus %	sees little con-sensus %	DK NA %	good to have diffs. %	not good %	DK NA %
BELGIUM										
Soc. Chr.	213	52	38	10	47	38	15	33	61	6
Lib.	26	38	54	8	46	46	8	35	54	11
Soc.	42	38	55	7	38	55	7	33	62	5
No party	57	40	55	5	41	44	15	33	59	8
No answer	62	23	57	20	42	33	25	26	52	22
ENGLAND										
Cons.	151	51	37	12	52	25	23	45.5	44.5	10
Lib.	66	54	38	8	53	17	30	55	42	3
Lab.	77	51	38	11	44	26	30	59	35	6
No party	53	43	41	15	48	31	21	50	39	11
No answer	53	32	42	26	32	17	51	36	38	26
FRANCE										
Gaullists	26	50	50	–	38	15	47	39	61	–
MRP	40	37	60	3	50	30	20	58	42	–
Radicaux	52	46	48	6	35	42	23	69	31	–
Soc. & Comm.	84	61	36	3	20	66	14	74	24	2
No party	86	35	55	10	16	23	61	63	34	3
No answer	62	42	48	10	23	23	54	65	25	10
NETHERLANDS										
Lib.	34	62	26	12	59	18	23	35	62	3
CHU, SGP	31	65	29	6	56	23	19	19	78	3
AR	57	65	30	5	51	30	19	19	77	4
KNP	13	69	23	8	69	23	8	38	62	–
KVP	140	62	22	16	61	26	13	24	76	–
Lab.	76	63	32	5	65	22	13	42	57	1
No party	19	53	31	16	68	21	11	26	69	8
No answer	30	50	33	17	57	33	10	40	60	–
NORWAY										
Cons. & Agr.	56	31	58	11	43	35	22	32	65	3
Chr.	35	52	45	3	49	32	19	46	54	–
Lib.	144	37	58	5	61	29	10	45	54	1
Lab.	72	31	67	2	61	23		50	46	4
No party	34	29	65	6	62	20	18	53	38	9
No answer	59	31	56	13	43	25	32	46	36	18
SWEDEN										
Cons.	196	50	46	4	63	23	14	50	47	3
Lib.	182	49	48	3	70	20	10	64	34	2
Soc.	46	37	59	4	78	11	11	65	35	–
No answer	18				66	17	17	66	28	6

	N	Fundamental conflicts in country			Consensus on defence policy			Difference of opinion on defence		
		sees imp. confl. %	sees no imp. confl. %	DK NA %	sees wide con- sensus %	sees little con- sensus %	DK NA %	good to have diffs. %	not good %	DK NA %
W. GERMANY										
Cons. & Lib.	*54*	61	35	4	28	61	11	70	30	–
CDU/CSU	*93*	62	33	5	27	62	11	59	33	8
SPD	*34*	64	36	–	15	82	3	68	29	3
No party	*113*	53	41	6	21	62	17	77	20	3
No answer	*71*	65	27	8	20	58	22	70	24	6

The measures that have been found of some use in this analysis were the following:

for perception of basic within-nation cleavages – '*Are there any conflicts between opposing groups in this country that create fundamental problems?*'

for judgements of the extent of consensus on defence policies – '*In your judgement, about what proportion (of your countrymen) agree with the government on this issue?*' [211]

for feelings about national disagreements – '*Do you think it is good or bad to have fundamental differences of opinion, within a country, on such matters as military preparedness?*'

for attitudes to deviants – '*In general, what do you think should be done with people who have different opinions from those of the majority in times of war?*' [212]

The responses to these four items are not systematically related to each other across the countries. This might perhaps have been expected between the two items bearing on perceptions of the national situation, since the first focuses on the gravity of whatever internal conflicts are seen to exist while the second asks for estimates of the opinion split on the specific issue of defence. The two items bearing on disagreement and dissent, however, were expected to be closely associated in all the countries, but this did not turn out to be the case, partly, it would seem, because of difficulties of translation equivalence: there are highly significant relationships in two countries only, less definite in three, and no association at all in the Belgian and the English samples.

Looking first to the perception items, we find some interesting relationships to political party identification. In Belgium and Norway the Christian party identifiers were clearly the most likely to see fundamental conflicts within their nation. In Sweden, the Conservatives and the Liberals were significantly more conflict oriented than the Social Democrats, while in

France the 'right-left' relationship went in the opposite direction. A very definite pattern appears in the relationships between party identification and perception of national unity on the defence issue. In all the seven

Table 8. *Threat Orientations and Opinions on National Unity and Dissent*
Abbreviations: see Table 5.

	N	Fundamental conflicts in country			Consensus on defence policy			Difference of opinion on defence		
		sees imp. confl. %	sees no imp. confl. %	DK NA %	sees wide con- sensus %	sees little con- sensus %	DK NA %	good to have diffs. %	not good %	DK NA %
BELGIUM										
HE	190	49	41	10	48	36	16	30	63	7
LE	159	40	53	7	43	45	12	36	58	6
HW	105	31	62	7	46	44	10	37	55	8
LW	288	49	41	10	45	40	15	31	61	8
HELW	117	52	37	11	50	33	17	32	63	5
HEHW &										
LELW	127	47	58	5	43	51	6	32	64	4
LEHW	85	30	64	6	46	39	15	39	53	8
ENGLAND										
HE	149	55	34	11	52	23	25	46	46	8
LE	144	52	37	11	49	26	25	50	44	6
HW	107	48	44	8	48	30	22	47	49	4
LW	279	49	38	13	47	23	30	50	40	10
HELW	98	55	33	12	53	19	28	45	46	9
HEHW &										
LELW	108	54	37	9	47	30	23	52	43	5
LEHW	74	50	38	12	48	27	25	49	47	4
FRANCE										
HE	71	51	46	3	38	30	32	53	45	2
LE	167	48	48	4	24	48	28	72	27	1
HW	190	45	51	4	27	43	30	66	32	2
LW	150	48	47	5	29	29	42	63	35	2
HELW	29	52	45	3	37	21	42	58	42	–
HEHW &										
LELW	69	52	47	1	33	41	26	55	42	3
LEHW	133	47	49	4	24	48	28	73	26	1
NETHS.										
HE	256	63	27	10	68	21	11	26	73	1
LE	99	60	31	9	49	32	19	33	64	3
HW	52	52	35	13	60	30	10	33	61	6
LW	342	63	27	10	61	25	14	29	70	1
HELW	205	62	28	10	66	22	12	27	73	–
HEHW &										
LELW	98	71	21	8	60	28	12	28	69	3
LEHW	34	35	47	18	50	30	20	41	59	–

	N	Fundamental conflicts in country			Consensus on defence policy			Difference of opinion on defence		
		sees imp. confl. %	sees no imp. confl. %	DK NA %	sees wide con-sensus %	sees little con-sensus %	DK NA %	good to have diffs. %	not good %	DK NA %
NORWAY										
HE	188	34	60	6	60	27	13	43	56	1
	96	36	58	6	53	29	18	49	45	·
HW	86	28	67	5	46	34	20	51	43	6
LW	309	37	57	6	57	27	16	31	64	5
HELW	143	35	61	4	64	25	11	41	58	1
HEHW &										
LELW	71	44	46	10	47	32	21	54	45	1
LEHW	47	19	77	4	55	32	13	42	47	11
SWEDEN										
HE	322	47	49	4	70	20	10	56	42	2
LE	99	50	48	2	65	19	16	66	31	3
HW	81	56	40	4	68	18	14	79	19	2
LW	357	46	51	3	68	21	11	53	45	2
HELW	216	44	54	2	68	21	11	55	44	1
HEHW &										
LELW	133	53	44	3	67	20	13	62	38	–
LEHW	46	48	50	2	74	13	13	68	26	6
W. GERMANY										
HE	124	70	27	3	28	59	13	65	31	4
LE	149	57	39	4	19	69	12	72	25	3
HW	131	58	36	6	21	65	14	72	24	4
LW	225	63	33	4	24	64	12	67	29	4
HELW	75	73	27	–	26	67	7	59	36	5
HEHW &										
LELW	103	64	31	5	29	54	17	74	24	2
LEHW	87	54	41	5	15	74	11	73	25	2

countries there are tendencies for those who identify with the opposition to give lower estimates of national consensus than those who identify with the party or parties in power. This finding is of considerable interest since it cuts across any 'left-right' dimensions: the differentiating factor is not ideology as such but the actual power position of the political movement.

An examination of the relationships between threat orientations and the responses to the two perception items indicates some interesting differences: conflict perception seems to be most affected by the 'war-threat responses' while consensus perception on the defence issue is most directly affected by 'enemy-threat.' None of these relationships cut across all the countries, however. It will be seen that the 'war-threat' index affects the conflict perception responses differently in Sweden than in the other

Table 9. *Party Identification, Threat Orientation and Opinions on National Unity and Dissent*

Abbreviations: see Table 5.

		N %	*Fundamental conflicts in country*			*Consensus on defence policy*			*Difference of opinion on defence*		
			sees imp. confl. %	sees no imp. confl. %	DK NA %	sees wide con-sensus %	sees little con-sensus %	DK NA %	good to have diffs. %	not good %	DK NA %
BELGIUM											
Soc. Chr.	HE	126	56	34	10	48	35	17	32	64	4
	LE	63	48	44	8	41	51	8	38	57	5
	HW	34	50	50	–	53	47	–	29	68	3
	LW	176	54	36	10	47	38	15	35	57	6
Lib. & Soc.	HE	23	39	52	9	48	52	–	30	61	9
	LE	37	35	60	5	43	46	11	38	60	2
	HW	29	28	58	14	30	53	17	45	49	6
	LW	39	46	51	3	49	49	2	26	66	8
ENGLAND											
Cons.	HE	71	54	35	11	45	25	30	41	52	7
	LE	43	51	39	10	63	28	9	54	42	4
	HW	34	47	47	6	47	35	18	53	47	–
	LW	112	53	35	12	54	22	24	44	46	10
Lib. & Lab.	HE	49	57	35	8	65	14	21	60	38	2
	LE	62	56	37	7	40	27	33	52	42	6
	HW	49	53	39	8	47	29	24	51	43	6
	LW	91	53	38	9	49	19	32	60	37	3
NETHS.											
Calv. & Lib.	HE	85	62	32	6	66	22	12	22	77	1
	LE	34	65	29	6	53	23.5	23.5	26	74	–
	HW	70	66	30	4	53	28	19	24	73	3
	LW	62	63	29	8	63	21	16	27	73	–
Cath. P. P.	HE	105	63	23	14	64	23	13	25	74	1
	LE	25	60	24	16	52	36	12	16	80	4
	HW	54	72	19	9	61	26	13	17	81	2
	LW	85	58	25	18	64	24	12	28	72	–
Lab.	HE	41	71	27	2	76	17	7	39	61	–
	LE	24	54	38	8	42	38	20	46	50	4
	HW	56	61	34	5	64	27	9	41	59	–
	LW	19	68	27	5	68	16	16	42	53	5
NORWAY											
'Bourgeois'	HE	130	35	60	5	59	27	14	41	58	1
	LE	43	46.5	46.5	7	49	32	19	47	51	2
	HW	38	37	58	5	40	45	15	56	42	2
	LW	196	38	56	6	58	28	14	40	59	1
Labour	HE	26	42	54	4	66	19	15	42	58	–
	LE	26	19	77	4	61	31	8	50	50	–
	HW	24	17	79	4	58	29	13	38	54	8
	LW	47	36	62	2	64	19	17	58	42	–

		N %	sees imp. confl. %	sees no imp. confl. %	DK NA %	sees wide con- sensus %	sees little con- sensus %	DK NA %	good to have diffs. %	not good %	DK NA %
			Fundamental conflicts in country			**Consensus on defence policy**			**Difference of opinion on defence**		
SWEDEN											
Cons. & Lib.	HE	284	48	49	3	69	21	10	55	43	2
	LE	76	54	45	1	63	22	15	68	29	3
	HW	192	52	45	3	69	19	12	63	34	3
	LW	182	48	50	2	60	23	17	51	47	2
Labour	HE	28	39	54	7	86	11	3	64	36	–
	LE	16	31	69	–	62.5	12.5	25	63	37	–
	HW	26	42	54	4	76	8	16	73	27	–
	LW	20	30	65	5	80	15	5	55	45	–

countries: in the Swedish sample those who express explicit fear of war rather than of the enemy are the most likely to perceive deep-seated internal conflicts in the nation; in the other samples the opposite tends to be the case. This difference would primarily seem to reflect the Swedish position of neutrality and the consequent opinion divisions within the country. The responses on the consensus perception item are not so clearly related to threat orientations as they are to party identification. The English data are of particular interest in this connection. It will be seen that 'enemy-threat' seems to affect the consensus estimates in opposite directions according to party identification: among the Conservatives those who are high on 'enemy-fear' see *less* consensus than those low, while among the Liberals and the Labourites, those high see *more* consensus than those low. This might well be explained as a reflection of deviant positions to the right as well as to the left of the current policy of the government in power.

Looking further to the responses bearing on attitudes to dissent and deviance, we again find some interesting relationships to party identification. In all the countries except Belgium, there are clear tendencies for the 'left' identifiers to express more frequent approval of differences of opinion than those identifying with Conservative or major Christian parties. It should be noted, however, that the 'Liberal' groups in most cases come very close to the Socialist and Social Democrat groups on this score. This is even clearer in the cross-tabulations between party identification and the code for 'tolerance' in the treatment of deviants. Again, there is no party difference in the Belgian sample, but quite significant relationships in the other samples. The Conservative or Christian party identifiers have lower 'tolerance' responses than the Liberals and the Labour identifiers in France, the Netherlands, Norway, and West Germany. In England, however, the Liberals are significantly more 'tolerant' than both the Conservatives and the Labourites, while in Sweden the Social Democrats score lower than either the Conservatives or the Liberals.

A central hypothesis in the original study design related increases in 'external threat' to increases in 'pressures for conformity (Aubert, 1954; Schachter, 1954: 1). One of the more specific tests of this abstract hypothesis was seen to lie in the relationship to be observed between expressed 'enemy-threatenedness' and 'attitudes on dissent and toward deviants'. If we look at the cross-tabulations made between the 'enemy-threat' responses and the responses to the question about differences of opinion on matters of preparedness, we find some confirmation of the hypothesis: in all the countries, the percentage differences between 'high-enemy' and 'low-enemy' go in the hypothesized direction.[213] The percentage differences are not very striking, however: if we consider the country samples separately, we find significant relationships in France and Sweden only. It is of interest to note that the relationship is distinctly affected by party preferences in some of the countries: thus in England the relationship is significant among the Conservatives, in Norway and West Germany among the Labourites.

The findings for 'tolerance of deviants' are in much the same direction. The threat orientation indexes make differences in England, France, Norway, and Sweden: those who express most concern with the danger of Soviet aggression are more likely to give 'intolerant' responses than those who express less worry about enemy intentions. This, in a sense, yields some confirmation of the original hypothesis, but the relationships differ by categories of party identification and need to be tested on larger samples allowing more extensive breakdowns. The exceptions for Belgium, the Netherlands, and West Germany are particularly interesting and require further analysis. Clearly a major factor affecting these differences is the split in the school systems: the three samples that do not fit the pattern are the only ones that include a substantial proportion of confessional school teachers. It is therefore particularly significant that the response patterns for the Catholic-Christian parties in these countries differ so markedly from the patterns found in the other countries: thus among the Catholic party identifiers in the Netherlands and the CDU identifiers in Germany there is a definite tendency for the 'high-enemy' group to give more tolerant responses than the 'low-enemy' group. The extent to which this difference in response patterns can be accounted for in terms of personality characteristics or in terms of the occupational environment cannot be estimated on the basis of the data thus far analysed. It is hoped that the detailed country analyses to be undertaken will throw further light on these relationships.[214] Any such analysis will of necessity be limited by the size of the samples and the scope and quality of the interview materials available.

Concluding Remarks
The set of findings discussed in this paper do not go very far towards

establishing any framework of propositions for the comparative study of party preference and party support. At best, this exercise in cross-national analysis may have proved suggestive of hypotheses for future study and thrown some light on the concrete and practical difficulties that lie in the way of any substantial progress along this line of research. Much can still be done through systematic collation, classification, and comparison of existing data in each country: election statistics, party records, communication materials. A particularly important source to be exploited for comparative analyses of this kind is constituted by the records of public opinion surveys already undertaken in the different countries. Such data have only rarely been subject to the kind of multivariate analysis that would be required to sort out the factors that account for party preferences, party allegiances, and, even more, for within-party differences over policy preferences. Secondary analysis of such data through the cumulation of punched card records from a series of surveys may produce important bodies of information and allow opportunities for the testing of hypotheses about factors affecting party preference. The difficulties involved in any such venture need no emphasis: problems of sampling, interviewing and coding practices, problems of opinion coverage, problems of cross-national comparability. Nevertheless, there can be little doubt that this source of data is well worth full exploration before any extensive collection of fresh comparative data is undertaken.

John Bonham's study of the middle-class vote in England indicates some of the potentialities of this approach; similar procedures could probably be used in a number of countries to explore cross-national similarities and differences in the recruitment of party support.[215] Comparative analysis of the occupational bases of party identification may prove particularly important to an understanding of the over-all ideological contexts of political choice: What are the factors that make for a closer 'fit' between occupation and vote? What are the factors that favour recruitment across a wider range of occupational categories? Systematic analysis of survey records from a number of countries may provide some important clues for such research and help to focus the designs of new data-gathering operations on particularly promising hypotheses. The OCSR study was limited to one occupational category across seven countries and thus provided an opportunity for a closer examination of cognitive and ideological factors that might affect party support. Quite particularly, the OCSR analysis affords some insight into the problems of within-party difference in policy preferences as well as in general orientation; further exploration of such factors is essential to the understanding of political change. It is hoped that it will be possible to pursue researches of this kind along comparative lines for a wider range of occupational categories: quite a few findings of relevance may no doubt emerge from secondary analysis of existing public opinion data, but at some point it will clearly be necessary to resort to some amount of coordinated field work in a number of countries to ensure adequate data for comparative analysis.

NOTES

[186] The research projects undertaken by this organization are described in (OCSR, 1954) and in (Rokkan, 1955: 1).

[187] The composition of the national teams is given in (OCSR, 1954) pp. 2–3. The team directors were: for Belgium, Dr. Claire LePlae, Institut de Recherches Economiques et Sociales, University of Louvain; for England, Dr. Hilde T. Himmelweit, London School of Economics; for France, M. Paul Maucorps, Centre d'Etudes Sociologiques, and M. Marcel Brichler, Institut National de la Statistique et des Etudes Economiques, Paris; for the Netherlands, Professor A. Oldendorff, Carolus Magnus University, Nijmegen; for Norway, Dr. Vilhelm Aubert, Institute for Social Research, Oslo; for Sweden, Mr. Eskil Björklund, University of Stockholm; and for Western Germany, Dr. Ulrich Jetter, Institut für Demoskopie, Allensbach. The field work was coordinated by Dr. Eugene Jacobson of the Survey Research Center of the University of Michigan, at that time resident as Fulbright research scholar at the Oslo Institute. For further organizational details see Chapter 8 above.

[188] The analysis work was directed first by Dr. Jacobson and later by Professor Burton R. Fisher of the University of Wisconsin during his term of residence as Fulbright research scholar at the Oslo Institute.

[189] For a description of the central design and a preliminary review of the over-all findings of the study, see (Aubert, 1954).

[190] The question used was: '*What political party do you belong to or are you most in sympathy with?*' or its equivalent in the languages of the respondents. The respondents entered their answers themselves on the personal data sheet submitted for completion at the end of the interviews. In France no direct question was asked to this effect: the categorizations were based on interviewer judgements. This obviously limits the value of any direct comparison with the French data on this particular point.

[191] Cf. among comparative studies (Tingsten, 1932; Hermens, 1941; Duverger, 1950).

[192] For a comparative summary of research evidence, see (Lipset, 1954); cf. the discussion of French data (Duverger, 1955: 2).

[193] A comparative study of some relevance in this context is (Buchanan, 1953).

[194] A recent summary with some comparative research evidence is (Eysenck, 1954).

[195] The principal test was based on the F. H. Sanford 'authoritarianism-equalitarianism' scale, a development of one section of the California 'F-scale' A special analysis of these test data is presented in Chapter 10 below.

[196] See the general discussion of the study design in (Aubert, 1954, pp. 26–31).

[198] An interesting example is Edmund Dahlström's Swedish study of the political attitudes of white collar employees, foremen, and manual workers (Dahlström, 1954; cf. Rokkan, 1955: 4).

[199] See (Reisner, 1927; Kandel, 1933: Ch. III; Hans, 1949). Information for a great number of countries and regions is assembled in *The Year Book of Education 1951,* cf. also (Hylla, 1953).

[200] Details on sampling procedures are given in (Jacobsen, 1954).

[201] The figures given for the teacher populations are those used by the national research teams in setting up their samples. The figures were based on the most recent statistics available. For a useful compilation of data on the school systems and the teacher populations at that time see (Hylla, 1953).

[202] A comparative survey of 'The Social Position of Teachers' is given by Robert King Hall, Nicholas Hans, and J. A. Lauwerys in the Introduction to *The Year*

Book of Education 1953, a volume devoted to reports on the status of teachers in a number of countries and areas of the world. A particularly important national study is (Tropp, 1953).

[203] Data for five countries are analyzed by Alex Inkeles and Peter H. Rossi (Inkeles, 1956).

[204] It is regrettable that Bonham (Bonham, 1954) does not give any details on Liberal party identification in the British surveys. His estimates on p. 134 for the 'lower professional group' are: 45 per cent Conservative, 25 per cent Labour, 30 per cent 'Neither,' i. e., Liberal plus Independent plus no vote. He indicates that the primary school teachers do not deviate markedly from this pattern. Our study seems to provide confirmation on this point, although further analysis would be required for the 30 per cent who did not identify with the major parties.

[205] The French data are less clear on this point because of the high proportion of negative responses.

[206] The question was: *'Do you think it would be a good idea for this country to give up some of its sovereignty to become part of a United World Government?'*

[207] The same tendency is evidenced in a cross-tabulation against the responses to an item in the Sanford 'A–E scale:' *'Human nature being what it is, there must always be war and conflict';* cf. Chapter 10 below.

[208] BIPO in March 1952 asked: *'Bevan says that war is more likely to come from the economic conditions of the world than from Soviet military ambitions: which do you think?'* Among the Conservatives, 33 % would stress the economic conditions, 47 % Soviet ambitions; among Labour voters, the figures were 47 % and 31 % (Release S–295, 13 March, 1952). The BIPO figures for the proportion of Bevan followers among Labour voters has varied between 26 % and 34 % in surveys from 1952 to 1954.

[209] Some related experiments on threat and policy acceptance are discussed by I. L. Janis (Janis, 1953; cf. Janis, 1954).

[210] Cf. the tolerance index constructed in (Stouffer, 1955).

[211] The question used in England was – *'How great would you say is the agreement among people in this country on this issue?'* This version does not seem to have been equivalent to the ones used in other countries.

[212] The French and West German versions of this question were markedly different in content from the common items used in the other countries.

[213] Assuming, as a null hypothesis, that a positive difference was as likely as a negative difference, the probability of getting all the seven differences in the same direction by chance variation is less than 1 per cent.

[214] A special analysis of Flemish-Walloon differences in the Belgian sample was made by Dr. Claire Leplae; cf. (Leplae, 1955).

[215] A comparison between Bonham's findings for England (1951) and Barton's findings for Norway (1949) suggests an interesting topic for closer investigation: in England, the Conservative party got as much as 49 per cent of its vote from the manual working class, while in Norway the 'bourgeois' parties got only around 19 per cent of their combined votes from this class, (cf. Barton, 1954: Ch. VI). The data for this analysis were gathered by the FAKTA agency under a programme of studies sponsored by the Institute for Social Research in Oslo. For further details see (Rokkan, 1960: 5 and 1967).

TEN

Ideological Consistency and Party Preference: Findings from a Seven-Country Survey

Discussions of the social psychology of political participation have since the early fifties focused attention on the problem of the *comparability of ideological dimensions* across different political systems. Historians of political ideas have debated problems of this type more or less directly for generations, but these analyses were of necessity limited to the level of *elite communications*. Of much more recent origin are the attempts by psychologists and sociologists to analyze dimensions in *mass reactions* to politics. Systematic research into the problem of comparability will of necessity require a combination of methodologies: it will be as important to study syndromes of consistency in mass-directed communications as to analyze the response of samples of the populations to series of test and interview items. Historians of ideas have gradually become aware of this convergence of approaches. In his history of *La Droite en France*, René Rémond concludes his account with a general discussion of the problem of the comparability of ideological dimensions: he sets out to determine in what sense and to what extent the 'left-right' polarity is a *phénomène national* and in what sense and to what extent it refers to a *catégorie universelle*.[216] Historically, of course, this topographical terminology was distinctly a *phénomène national;* it dates from the famous session in the French Assembly on September 11, 1789. But as the ideas of the Revolution spread through the countries of the world it proved surprisingly easy to apply this pair of opposites to contrasts of political tempers and orientations in a vast variety of contexts and systems. Is there a universal content to these polarities or do they only reflect the peculiarities of local and time-limited conflicts and ideologies? The French historian tends to see a transcultural category in the left-right dimension and finds his primary evidence for this not in the vocabularies and arguments of official ideological documents,

Origin: This chapter was originally prepared for a Conference of the World Association of Public Opinion Research in 1956. It was the result of further analysis of the OCSR data reported on in chapters 8 and 9 and was prepared in close cooperation with Daniel Levinson, one of the co-authors of *The Authoritarian Personality* (Adorno, 1950).

but surprisingly enough in a work of this kind, through an analysis of a test for 'conservatism-radicalism' developed by H. J. Eysenck for the English population (Eysenck, 1950). René Rémond goes over each statement in this test to check how far they would measure the some dimension if administered to a *French* population. He finds between the two sets of reactions 'des ressemblances si poussées qu'elles feraient douter du fossé qui sépare l'histoire des deux pays . . .' It is not concluded, however, that comparable tests for 'conservatism-radicalism' could be constructed for use within all political systems, even in the West. So very much of the content of the test reflects the deep-seated ideological conflicts over the principles of the French Revolution: 'La distinction droite-gauche a une raison d'être pour toutes les sociétés politiques où les problèmes d'organisation se posent dans la perspective ouverte par la Révolution française . . .' The French historian finds the contrast less pronounced and harder to describe in the countries that were least affected in the course of their politics by the events of 1789: he sees in this circumstance a possible explanation for the absence of a clear-cut tradition of right-left polarization in the United States. The universality of the polarity is thus a relative one: dependent on the diffusion of a particular wave of ideas and the similarity of their inter-action with political, social, and economic forces at work in the different countries.

Historians of René Rémond's inclination have so far had very little help from political psychologists. A great number of tests have been developed since the thirties to measure propensities to 'conservatism,' 'radicalism,' 'fascism,' etc., but the vast majority of these instruments were too nation-specific, too culture-bound, to provide any basis for comparative research across different political systems. With the expansion of international re-search contacts after World War II, a scattering of attempts were made at systematic comparisons of the patterning of test responses for different national populations. The Eysenck test was indeed not only used on English subjects: it was also administered to samples in Germany and Sweden (Eysenck, 1953). Perhaps the most extensive efforts of comparative data gathering and analysis in this field might have been expected to follow on the development in the United States of a series of diagnostic tests for ethnocentric and authoritarian traits. The researches reported in *The Authoritarian Personality* reflected distinctly European concerns with the practice of politics and the theory of human motivation and thinking (Adorno, 1950): nothing would have seemed more natural than to under-take the same types of studies on samples of different European popula-tions and thus to provide some basis for a systematic analysis of the inter-action between individual reaction patterns, structural contexts and histori-cal conditions. A number of local studies were indeed inspired by the work of the California research team, but so far no investigations have been suf-ficiently coordinated across several countries of Western Europe to allow detailed comparison with the U. S. findings.[217] This chapter will report briefly on the findings of a seven-nation study of teachers' reactions to a set of statements derived from one of the California tests: the 'F' scale.

The Organization for Comparative Social Research completed in 1953 a set of sample surveys of teachers' attitudes in seven countries of Western Europe: Belgium, England, France, the Netherlands, Norway, Sweden, and West Germany. Details on the samples, the field procedures, the analysis arrangements have been published elsewhere (see Chapters 8 and 9). The interview schedule included toward the end a 15-item list of statements designed to provide a measure of the teacher's orientation toward authority and discipline. Only four of these items were direct adaptations of statements in the California 'Fascism' test, the others were from the related 'Authoritarianism-Equalitarianism' scale developed by F. H. Sanford (Sanford, 1950) and from various European studies of attitudes to problems of child rearing and education.

The items were:
1. Human nature being what it is, there must always be war and conflict.
2. The most important thing a child should learn is obedience to his parents.
3. A few strong leaders could make this country better than all the laws and talk.
4. Most people who don't get ahead just don't have enough will power.
5. Women should stay out of politics.
6. People can be trusted.
7. Our national life suffers from lack of discipline.
8. Parents these days allow their children too much freedom.
9. Children would rather look up to a teacher than treat him as an equal.
10. Modern education is effective in preparing children for the hazards of the world.
11. Honesty and hard work are not sufficiently rewarded these days.
12. Only the person who has been taught strict discipline can fully appreciate freedom.
13. Once a problem child, always a problem child.
14. Only too often the home undoes the work of the school.
15. These days too much attention is being paid to the difficult child at the expense of normal children.

The statement list was not meant to provide a single composite measure of 'authoritarianism-equalitarianism' or any conceptually related dimension: rather it was intended to allow exploration of a variety of possible relationships between general ideological responses of this sort and specific responses on issues of current politics. After some initial exploration by Vilhelm Aubert *et al.* (Aubert, 1956) a plan to derive an 'F-type' score from these response data was developed in cooperation with Daniel J. Levinson and Arthur Couch at Harvard University. On the following pages a brief account will be given of the more salient findings: this might serve as a basis for a discussion of various possibilities of further advance in this area of comparative research as ideological syndromes.

Ten of the fifteen items in the list were found to correlate at .35 or better with the list total in all the seven countries. These items were: (1), (2), (3), (4), (5), (7), (8), (12), (13), (15). Using the same scoring system as in *The Authoritarian Personality,* total 'F' scores were added up for each respondent: these ranged from a maximum high of 70 for those who checked 'agree very much' on all items, to a minimum low of 10 for those who checked 'disagree very much' on all items.

The mean total scores and SDs for each country sample were found to be:

	Mean	*SD*	*N*
Belgium	50.1	9.4	400
England	40.9	10.1	392
France	46.7	9.5	344
Germany (W)	50.4	8.9	363
Netherlands	44.5	9.5	397
Norway	37.1	10.7	398
Sweden	43.3	10.6	439

Differences in sampling procedures, rates of sample loss, etc. make it difficult to undertake any direct comparisons between sample means for each country. The analysis has been focused on the mapping of *consistencies* in the relationships between individual total scores and a series of background variables, various opinion responses, and some indexes for attitudes on political issues.

I shall first give a summary of the findings for the relationships between the total score and a series of indications of *basic orientations to national politics:* analyses of this type may throw some light on the validity of the test. The first finding of importance is that *there is a consistently significant difference in total scores across all the seven countries between those who report preferences for 'working class parties' and those who report preferences for 'middle class parties':* in all countries, the teachers who said they preferred Conservative, Christian centre, or Liberal parties scored higher on the test than those who said they preferred Social Democratic, Labour, or Communist parties *(Table 1).* The data thus clearly corroborate findings already registered for the United States and Britain.

The classification of parties across the seven countries obviously entailed some difficulty (see Chapter 9 above). It was hard to attach any definite

Table 1. *Differences in Total 10-Item Score Between Major Party Preference Groupings: Teachers in Seven West European Countries*

	Mean	SD	N
BELGIUM			
Social Christians	51.2	8.6	213
Liberals	49.7	12.2	26
Socialists (40) and	44.9	11.2	42
Communists (2)			
No Party	50.4	9.5	57
ENGLAND			
Conservatives	43.0	9.0	150
Liberals	40.3	10.2	66
Labour (76) and	35.6	10.9	77
Communists (1)			
No Party	41.8	9.1	51
FRANCE			
Right wing (26) and	50.5	8.5	66
MRP (40)			
Radicals	49.5	8.3	51
Socialists (71) and	41.8	10.1	83
PCF (12)			
No Party	47.7	8.4	83
GERMANY			
Various right wing (16) and	53.0	10.0	54
FDP (38)			
CDU/CSU	52.2	7.0	91
SPD	42.6	10.5	34
No Party	51.2	8.1	113
NETHERLANDS			
Protestant (88),	47.1	8.6	134
Catholic right wing (12),			
Liberals (34)			
Catholic People's Party	45.5	9.3	140
Labour	39.1	9.0	75
No Party	45.1	10.3	14
NORWAY			
Conservative (50),	41.0	9.6	91
Christian (35), and			
Agrarian (6)			
Liberal	37.3	10.5	144
Labour	31.8	11.1	71
No Party	39.5	12.2	34
SWEDEN			
Conservatives	45.5	9.7	195
Liberals	42.4	10.0	181
Social Democrats	37.1	13.6	45
No Party	–	–	1

meaning to a right-centre-left classification of parties in all the countries: particularly so in the countries where religious party contrasts cut across economic party contrasts.

Such difficulties did not, however, seem to affect the possibility of comparing the scores for the identifiers with 'working class' parties with the scores for those who identified with other parties: these differences were indeed consistently significant across all the seven countries. It is of interest to note, however, that while the 'left' identifiers had clearly the lowest *mean scores* in all countries, the *standard deviations* for these groups were nevertheless higher than for the others in all countries except Belgium and the Netherlands. Our analysis seems to indicate that this wide spread of scores among the 'leftists' is related to contrasts in their outlook on world affairs: on this point the data seem to provide some corroboration of the Rokeach finding of an F-score difference between Attlee Socialists and Bevan Socialists in Britain (Rokeach, 1960, Table XIV). Unfortunately, the samples did not allow any testing of the Eysenck hypothesis [219] of a significant difference between Socialists and Communists on tests of this type: the numbers of teachers reporting preference for the national CP were much too small to allow statistical analysis.

The differences between Conservatives and Liberals are significant in England, Norway, and Sweden: in the other countries the party systems do not so easily allow any equivalent 'right'-'centre' contrast.

The OCSR data thus point to the existence of stable syndromes of response consistency in the general area covered by this 'F-type' score. These syndromes differentiate clearly among party preference groups on the right, in the centre, and on the left in all the countries characterized by predominantly unidimensional party systems. In the countries with complex party systems, the response syndromes serve primarily to set off the party sympathizers on the left from all the rest. This finding may give us some perspective on the general problem raised by René Rémond and other historians of political movements: to what extent do the same ideological differentiations apply in all multiparty political systems and how are such differentiations reflected in and influenced by the structure of party constellations in each system?

One important set of differentiations bears on *international policy options*. Our analysis of 'F' correlates in the area of international politics reveals a number of consistent relationships across several countries.

High scorers have been found to be

a) *less* likely than low scorers to express spontaneous worry about the possibility of a new world war (not clear for France, Netherlands), but

b) *more* likely to think that a world war will occur in the not too distant future (not clear for Belgium, Netherlands);

c) *less* likely to consider war the worst that could happen to their country (not so for the Netherlands and Sweden), and

Table 2. *The Relation between 'F' score and the Attitude towards Increasing Military Strength***

Country		Standing on 'F' scale			t-tests*
		HIGH	MIDDLE	LOW	t_{HL}
BELGIUM	Mean	2.7	2.8	2.9	1.0
	Var	1.3	1.2	1.3	
	N	149	84	46	
ENGLAND	Mean	3.0	3.4	3.5	2.4
	Var	1.1	1.3	1.4	
	N	42	117	121	
FRANCE	Mean	3.3	3.8	4.4	5.8
	Var	1.7	1.3	1.0	
	N	108	113	65	
GERMANY	Mean	2.5	2.8	3.2	4.1
	Var	0.9	1.2	1.3	
	N	188	106	43	
NETHERLANDS	Mean	1.8	2.9	2.9	3.6
	Var	2.7	1.2	1.0	
	N	99	136	36	
NORWAY	Mean	2.8	2.9	3.1	1.4
	Var	1.1	1.0	1.0	
	N	37	105	204	
SWEDEN	Mean	2.2	2.5	2.7	3.3
	Var	1.0	1.0	1.4	
	N	102	153	118	

* t_{HL} = the t ratio between High vs Low 'F' score groups. 5 % significance t = 1.96; 1 % significance t = 2.58.
** This attitude was measured by an over-all rating based on answers to several questions concerning military strength and preparation. A low score indicates a strong approval of increasing military strength; a high score indicates strong disapproval of increasing military strength. The scale was from 1 to 5.

    d) *more* likely to impute all the blame for any new war on the enemy – the Eastern powers (not so for Germany and the Netherlands),

    e) *more* likely to favour a strengthening of national defence efforts (not clear for Belgium and Norway) *(Table 2)*, and

    f) *less* likely to favour any transfer of national sovereignty to a world government (significant differences in all countries: *Table 3*).[220]

    These cross-national data thus seem to corroborate previous findings for the political correlates of 'authoritarianism': stronger identification with the

Table 3. *The Relation between 'F' Score and the Attitude towards Giving up Some Sovereignty for World Government***

Country		Standing on 'F' scale			t-tests*
		HIGH	MIDDLE	LOW	t_{HL}
BELGIUM	Mean	2.8	2.6	2.4	1.9
	Var	1.9	1.8	1.7	
	N	182	121	58	
ENGLAND	Mean	3.7	3.5	2.7	3.8
	Var	2.1	2.5	2.4	
	N	55	139	146	
FRANCE	Mean	3.0	2.6	2.6	2.4
	Var	1.8	1.5	1.6	
	N	121	126	73	
GERMANY	Mean	2.3	1.9	1.7	3.2
	Var	1.2	1.0	0.5	
	N	176	107	39	
NETHERLANDS	Mean	2.8	2.4	2.2	3.5
	Var	1.4	1.3	1.1	
	N	111	157	117	
NORWAY	Mean	2.9	2.8	2.5	2.0
	Var	1.1	1.1	1.0	
	N	44	113	216	
SWEDEN	Mean	3.1	2.7	2.3	4.5
	Var	1.9	1.9	1.5	
	N	110	159	143	

* t_{HL} = t ratio between High vs Low 'F' score groups. 5 % significance t = 1.96; 1 % significance t = 2.58.

** The actual item was: 'Do you think it would be a good idea for our country to give up some of its sovereignty to become part of a united world government?' (IV 43). A low score indicates strong approval; a high score indicates strong disapproval. The scale goes from 1 to 5.

nation, sharper in-group/out-group differentiation, more express power-orientation, more emphasis on the need for 'toughness'. Further corroboration is found in an analysis of the relationship between the 'F' score and some measures of *intolerance of national deviance on policy issues*. Significant differences were found in all the seven countries on this point: the high scorers were more likely to express disapproval of differences of opinion and to suggest severe sanctions against deviants *(Table 4–9)*.

The analysis of the OCSR teacher data thus offers provisional evidence

Table 4. *The Relation between 'F' Score and Attitude towards Differences of Opinion within a Country***

Country		Standing on 'F' scale			t-tests*
		HIGH	MIDDLE	LOW	t_{HL}
BELGIUM	Mean	3.2	3.1	2.8	1.5
	Var	2.7	2.6	3.2	
	N	185	121	85	
ENGLAND	Mean	2.9	2.8	2.4	1.9
	Var	2.6	2.3	2.0	
	N	55	140	159	
FRANCE	Mean	2.9	2.6	2.6	1.8
	Var	2.1	2.2	2.1	
	N	128	132	74	
GERMANY	Mean	2.3	2.2	2.1	1.0
	Var	2.1	2.0	1.8	
	N	191	115	42	
NETHERLANDS	Mean	3.6	3.4	3.0	2.8
	Var	2.3	2.5	2.9	
	N	113	159	118	
NORWAY	Mean	3.9	3.3	3.3	2.1
	Var	3.1	3.3	3.4	
	N	41	115	222	
SWEDEN	Mean	4.2	3.9	3.8	2.4
	Var	1.3	1.6	1.8	
	N	116	169	144	

* t_{HL} = the t ratio between High vs Low 'F' groups. 5 % significance t = 1.96; 10 % significance t = 1.66.

** The actual item was: 'Do you think it is good or bad to have fundamental differences of opinion within a country on such matters as military preparedness?' (V 32). Responses were scored 1 = Very good, 2 = Somewhat good, 3 = Both good and bad, 4 = Somewhat bad, and 5 = Very bad.

of the existence of stable syndromes of response consistency on issues of authority and discipline, national unity and defence, in-group/out-group relations. The first question to be tackled in attempting an interpretation of this set of findings is this: to what extent are these syndromes peculiar to the teaching profession and equivalent middle class groupings and to what extent can they be expected to manifest themselves in cross-sectional samples of national populations?

We have only very scanty data in Western Europe to help us decide on

Table 5. *The Relation between 'F' Score and the General Level of Tolerance for Deviants***

Country		Standing on 'F' scale			t-tests*
		HIGH	MIDDLE	LOW	t_{HL}
BELGIUM	Mean	3.1	3.0	2.8	1.4
	Var	2.0	2.0	1.8	
	N	177	114	55	
ENGLAND	Mean	2.3	2.1	1.8	2.6
	Var	1.9	1.5	1.1	
	N	57	146	157	
FRANCE	Mean	3.3	2.7	2.6	2.8
	Var	2.1	2.2	2.2	
	N	126	128	73	
GERMANY	Mean	3.2	2.7	2.3	4.1
	Var	1.6	1.5	0.8	
	N	193	111	39	
NETHERLANDS	Mean	3.2	3.2	3.1	1.0
	Var	0.8	1.0	0.8	
	N	112	152	113	
NORWAY	Mean	3.1	2.9	2.8	1.8
	Var	1.0	0.8	0.8	
	N	40	114	209	
SWEDEN	Mean	2.6	2.6	2.6	0.0
	Var	1.3	1.3	1.4	
	N	102	142	128	

* The t_{HL} = the ratio between High vs Low 'F' score Groups. 5 % significance t = 1.96; 10 % significance t = 1.66.

** The general tolerance level was coded from responses to the question: 'In general, what do you think should be done with people who have different opinions from those of the majority in times of war?' (Q 36, col. V 75). A low score represents a tolerant position; a high score represents intolerance. The scale goes from 1 to 5.

The French and German questions were not strictly comparable, see CO/55 p. 81.

this problem. There are quite a few considerations that seem to favour the hypothesis that these syndromes are more pronounced in the teacher samples than they would be for cross-sectional samples of the national population:

a) Teachers are likely to be more articulate and coherent in their arguing and they would also seem less likely to be 'acquiescence-prone' than less educated groups. They make their living by talking and they are used to saying 'no'.

Table 6. *Means and Variances of Political Attitude Scales*

Country	'Nationalism' Scale N	Mean	Variance
BELGIUM	365	4.2	2.6
ENGLAND	362	4.3	3.0
FRANCE	330	3.4	4.0
GERMANY	342	4.1	2.7
NETHERLANDS	389	4.1	2.7
NORWAY	382	4.2	2.2
SWEDEN	430	5.0	3.2

Country	'Political Intolerance' Scale N	Mean	Variance
BELGIUM	365	4.7	6.9
ENGLAND	362	3.1	6.1
FRANCE	330	4.1	7.4
GERMANY	342	3.6	5.9
NETHERLANDS	389	5.1	5.6
NORWAY	382	4.9	7.7
SWEDEN	430	5.4	3.9

The 'Nationalism' Scale:
This scale contains three items scored in such a way that a high score represents agreement with a 'nationalistic' political attitude. The items are:
1. 'Do you think it would be a good idea for our country to give up some of its sovereignty to become part of a united world government?' (disagreement given high score) (Q.26, IV 43).
2. 'Now with regard to national defence; what are your views on the proportion of the budget spent on military preparedness – should it be kept at the same level, be reduced, or should it be increased?' (Q.31, V 12) (agreement with increase given high score).
3. Attitude towards increasing military strength. This attitude was measured by an over-all rating based on answers to several questions concerning military strength and preparation (agreement with increasing military strength given high score) (Q.31–34, V 27). SR: item 3. as an over-all rating also took into account response to question 31; index should therefore be revised.

The 'Political Intolerance' Scale:
This scale contains two items scored in such a way that a high score represents agreement with an *'intolerant'* attitude towards political deviancy. The items are:
1. 'In general, what do you think should be done with people who have different opinions from those of the majority in times of war?' (Q.36, V 75) The general tolerance level was coded from responses to this question: (agreement with an intolerant position given high score. NB: French and German question wordings markedly different.
2. 'Do you think it is good or bad to have fundamental differences of opinion within a country on such matters as military preparedness?' (Q.35, V 32) Responses were scored: 1 = Very good, 2 = Somewhat good, 3 = Both good and bad, 4 = Somewhat bad, and 5 = Very bad.

Scoring:
Each item in the scales had a range from 1 to 5. The items were added together in each scale to form a total score, which was algebraically adjusted to have a range of 0 to 9.

Table 7. *The Relation between Political Party Membership and the Score on the 'Nationalism' Scale*

Country		Political Grouping			t-tests*
		LEFT	CENTRE	RIGHT	t_{LR}
BELGIUM	Mean	3.1	4.5	3.9	1.9
	Var	3.5	2.3	1.6	
	N	40	200	25	
ENGLAND	Mean	3.5	3.8	4.9	5.8
	Var	3.3	2.6	2.4	
	N	74	62	141	
FRANCE	Mean	2.2	3.4	4.7	7.7
	Var	3.2	3.2	4.0	
	N	72	51	64	
GERMANY	Mean	2.6	4.5	3.9	1.9
	Var	2.7	2.1	7.7	
	N	34	123	10	
NETHERLANDS	Mean	3.1	4.4	4.5	6.3
	Var	2.7	2.2	2.1	
	N	75	135	131	
NORWAY	Mean	3.6	4.2	4.7	3.8
	Var	2.4	2.2	1.9	
	N	66	177	50	
SWEDEN	Mean	3.7	4.7	5.6	6.5
	Var	3.1	2.4	3.3	
	N	43	179	190	

* t_{LR} = the t ratio between Left vs Right Political Groupings. 5 % significance t = 1.96; 1 % significance t = 2.58.

Explanatory Note to Table 7

Country	Party Groupings		
	'Right'	'Centre'	'Left'
BELGIUM	Liberals	Social Christian	Socialists Comm. (2)
ENGLAND	Conservatives	Liberals	Labour Comm. (1)
FRANCE	Gaullists Mod. M.R.P.	Radicaux	S.F.I.O. P.C.F. (12) Other left (10)
GERMANY	D.P. (10) FDP/DVP (38) BP (3) GB-BHE (3)	CDU/CSU	SPD

Explanatory Note to Table 7 (con't.)

| | Party Groupings | | |
Country	'Right'	'Centre'	'Left'
NETHERLANDS	CHU, SGP, AR (all Prot.) (88) VVD (Liberal) (34) KNP (right-wing Cath.) (13)	KVP (Cath. Peoples p.)	P.v.d.A. (Lab.)
NORWAY	Agr. (6) Cons. (50) Chr. (35)	Liberal	Labour (71) Comm. (1)
SWEDEN	Conservatives	Liberal	Soc. Dem.

Table 8. *The Relation between 'F' Score and the Score on the 'Nationalism' Scale*

Country		Standing on 'F' scale			t-tests*
		HIGH	MIDDLE	LOW	t_{HL}
BELGIUM	Mean	4.4	4.0	3.9	2.3
	Var	2.6	2.4	2.6	
	N	185	121	59	
ENGLAND	Mean	5.0	4.7	3.8	4.5
	Var	2.4	2.6	3.0	
	N	58	148	156	
FRANCE	Mean	4.2	3.4	2.4	6.3
	Var	3.8	3.5	3.2	
	N	126	129	75	
GERMANY	Mean	4.4	3.8	3.1	4.8
	Var	2.3	2.6	3.2	
	N	186	115	41	
NETHERLANDS	Mean	4.4	4.2	3.7	3.3
	Var	2.3	2.5	3.1	
	N	113	159	117	
NORWAY	Mean	4.5	4.4	4.0	2.2
	Var	1.9	1.9	2.3	
	N	43	118	221	
SWEDEN	Mean	5.7	5.0	4.5	5.3
	Var	3.2	2.7	3.3	
	N	116	168	146	

* t_{HL} = the t ratio between High vs Low 'F' groups. 5 % significance t = 1.96; 1 % significance t = 2.58.

Table 9. *The Relation between the 'Political Intolerance' Score and 'F' Score within Various Political Party Groupings in Seven Western European Countries*

	'F' Score	LEFT			CENTRE			RIGHT			Left	Centre	Right
		Low	Middle	High	Low	Middle	High	Low	Middle	High	t_{LH}	t_{LH}	t_{LH}
BELGIUM	Mean	4.1	5.5	5.1	4.6	4.5	4.9	2.9	4.2	6.0	0.9	0.7	2.5
	Var	7.6	6.3	5.2	8.2	6.0	6.7	7.2	5.1	5.6			
	N	19	12	9	44	80	76	9	6	10			
ENGLAND	Mean	2.1	3.5	2.8	3.0	1.7	3.2	2.3	3.7	3.5	1.1	0.3	2.2
	Var	4.4	9.3	5.7	3.6	2.2	3.9	4.5	6.4	7.0			
	N	38	20	16	22	18	22	29	55	57			
FRANCE	Mean	3.2	3.5	3.2	4.1	3.8	3.7	4.2	6.1	6.1	0.1	0.4	2.1
	Var	5.6	7.1	4.0	12.5	6.4	5.7	5.7	5.6	6.0			
	N	34	27	11	10	17	24	11	21	32			
GERMANY	Mean	2.7	2.0	4.9	3.0	4.2	4.4	1.0	5.0	6.8	2.1	2.0	3.6
	Var	4.1	0.9	8.1	5.1	5.4	6.2	1.5	4.0	6.2			
	N	20	7	7	22	56	45	4	2	4			
NETHERLANDS	Mean	3.9	4.5	4.9	5.9	5.6	5.4	4.5	5.4	5.6	1.3	1.0	2.2
	Var	5.8	6.2	4.8	4.6	3.9	5.0	5.7	5.6	4.0			
	N	39	23	13	38	51	46	24	54	53			
NORWAY	Mean	4.2	4.9	5.3	4.6	4.9	5.3	5.5	5.2	6.1	1.1	1.2	0.7
	Var	9.2	5.4	7.2	7.1	8.0	7.1	7.7	7.7	4.9			
	N	33	19	14	43	82	52	11	17	22			
SWEDEN	Mean	5.4	5.5	6.7	4.8	5.1	5.5	5.4	5.6	5.6	1.5	1.7	0.6
	Var	7.0	1.7	0.8	4.7	4.5	4.3	4.2	3.2	2.7			
	N	21	12	10	54	68	57	30	90	70			

* t_{LH} = the t ratio between Low vs High 'F' score groups.
Note: For explanation of party groupings, see note to Table 7.

Table 10. *Differences in 'F' Score Between Primary and Secondary Teacher Groups in Seven Western European Countries*

Country		Teacher Group		t-test*
		Primary	Secondary	t$_{PS}$
BELGIUM	Mean	50.5	48.9	1.5
	SD	9.4	9.0	
	N	300	100	
ENGLAND	Mean	41.5	38.2	2.9
	SD	9.9	10.2	
	N	295	97	
FRANCE	Mean	46.6	47.3	0.5
	SD	9.4	10.1	
	N	268	76	
GERMANY	Mean	50.8	49.5	1.2
	SD	8.8	9.2	
	N	264	99	
NETHERLANDS	Mean	45.3	42.4	2.6
	SD	9.5	9.3	
	N	300	97	
NORWAY	Mean	38.1	34.3	3.1
	SD	10.3	11.4	
	N	299	99	
SWEDEN	Mean	44.1	41.6	2.1
	SD	9.9	12.1	
	N	321	118	

* t$_{PS}$ = The t-ratio between Primary and Secondary teachers.
The N's for the t-test in each case vary. However, for most purposes the 5 % level of significance would be a t of 1.96. The 1 % level would be a t of 2.58.

b) The teacher role gives central focus to problems of authority and discipline.

c) The teacher's community position puts him under unusual pressure to produce consistent answers to such problems of authority and discipline, not only in the family and the school situation, but also in the local and national setting.

d) In all countries, except possibly France, teachers expressing preferences for 'working class' parties are clearly in a minority. These deviant groups would be expected to manifest a high degree of consistency in their rejection of statements identified as characteristic of the majority ideology.

These are matters of speculation: we need cross-sectional survey data from a number of countries to test out such notions. Further work on these problems will require extensive cooperation between survey organizations

Table 11. *The Relation between 'F' Score and Religious Affiliation**

Country		Catholic	Protestant	Minor Protestant	None
				Religious Affiliation	
BELGIUM	Mean	50.4	47.3		47.9
	Var	83.3	177.7		102.8
	N	326	4		55
ENGLAND	Mean	43.0	41.2	40.5	37.5
	Var	78.9	90.3	105.6	142.1
	N	36	213	103	22
FRANCE	Mean	48.8	45.7		43.4
	Var	76.1	162.0		91.5
	N	204	14		106
GERMANY	Mean	51.8	50.0		41.0
	Var	58.5	88.0		87.7
	N	156	197		6
NETHERLANDS	Mean	46.0	45.1		39.0
	Var	83.2	84.3		96.9
	N	167	174		48
NORWAY	Mean		37.9	34.4	28.5
	Var		109.1	83.4	155.0
	N		336	10	5
SWEDEN	Mean		43.5	44.9	27.0
	Var		109.9	79.0	0.7
	N		418	13	3

* Other categories not included here are: No answer, Don't Know, and religious affiliations of very small frequency. In general, these showed no striking relationship to 'F' score.

in different parts of the world. As a minimum, 5 or 6 of the more discriminating items in such 'authoritarianism-equalitarianism' tests should be included in a number of the routine political polls to be undertaken in countries of Western Europe over the next few years. In this way we might not only be able to develop reliable instruments for comparative analyses of ideological dimensions, but also to add significantly to our knowledge of factors affecting political participation and electoral behaviour in different structural contexts.[221]

A great deal of theorizing has been published on determinants of authoritarian attitude patterns, but so far only very little has been done to test out on comparative lines even the more obvious of the hypotheses. The OCSR studies unfortunately do not bring us much further toward an understanding of the forces at work in forming these response consistencies. Cross-

Table 12. *The Relation Between 'F' Score and Age*

Country		Age					
		0–25	26–30	31–40	41–50	51–60	61–70
BELGIUM	Mean	46.3	47.3	49.1	51.4	53.9	57.6
	Var	84.7	85.2	81.8	78.8	80.0	72.7
	N	31	60	119	112	60	9
ENGLAND	Mean	38.5	41.3	39.5	41.5	41.2	51.2
	Var	102.2	86.3	84.3	103.8	109.5	37.3
	N	53	56	91	93	62	13
FRANCE	Mean	46.3	46.1	45.4	46.4	49.0	54.9
	Var	116.8	91.1	96.4	76.8	84.0	72.8
	N	26	40	104	104	58	9
GERMANY	Mean	46.1	50.5	47.8	50.1	51.8	54.5
	Var	155.2	57.7	100.9	66.9	77.6	51.3
	N	7	49	67	96	106	35
NETHERLANDS	Mean	43.3	44.3	43.9	45.8	44.6	47.9
	Var	59.1	97.0	79.7	91.7	116.1	117.8
	N	64	51	97	97	71	15
NORWAY	Mean	33.8	34.7	33.6	36.8	40.6	38.8
	Var	105.3	82.9	116.2	119.7	118.2	66.7
	N	16	38	70	123	103	46
SWEDEN	Mean	39.6	40.4	40.5	45.1	45.4	46.2
	Var	126.7	83.9	154.9	96.4	87.0	112.9
	N	36	50	78	123	117	34
TOTAL	Mean	41.8	43.8	43.4	45.1	46.4	47.6
	N	233	344	626	748	577	161

tabulations against the usual background classifications corroborate the available evidence on the relationship between educational level and F score total (Christie, 1954: 2; pp. 91–94; Christie, 1955: pp. 169–75; Mackinnon, 1956). The secondary school teachers are thus significantly lower on the score in England, the Netherlands, Norway, and Sweden, while there is a tendency in the same direction in Belgium and Germany. *(Table 10)*. This seems to be primarily related to 'exposure to modern ideas.' Thus the score tends to be higher among teachers in confessional or denominational schools than in state schools, higher among those who report definite religious affiliations than among those who report none *(Table 11)*. There is also a consistent tendency in most countries for *women* to score higher than *men,* but this relationship is only significant in the Netherlands and probably reflects other differences. Of particular interest is the relationship to *age:* in all countries there is a clear tendency for those *under* 40 to score lower than those *over* 40 *(Table 12)*.[222] Here again it would seem that an *exposure* factor is at work. The age difference might simply reflect a general historical trend in the liberalization of normal school teaching and the diffusion of modern ideas about child rearing, discipline, and the role of authority. Situational factors may of course also be of importance in this relationship. The typical succession of *life cycle roles* may affect orientations to authority problems in personal as well as national contexts. Multivariate analyses of the relationships between age, marital status, and total score on the ten items have been tried out to throw some light on this question. Given the very small samples the findings must of necessity remain inconclusive, but they may point to possibilities for further advance through systematic data gathering on comparative lines. The OCSR data have produced encouraging evidence of the existence of comparable patterns of attitudes and orientations across countries of very different history and political structure, but the findings will only make sense in a wider framework of continued international research.

NOTES

[216] (Rémond, 1955: pp. 253–56), cf. also Aron, 1955: Ch. I and the interesting issue of *Les Temps Modernes* on 'La Gauche', nos. 112–113, 1956: this includes an IFOP study 'A la recherche de la 'Gauche' ', pp. 1576–1625.

[217] On 'subcultural' variations see esp. (Christie, 1954: 1). The F-scale was administered to various *British* samples by T. Coulter, see (Eysenck, 1954: pp. 152–53), further by M. Rokeach, cf. (Rokeach, 1960). For *Germany*, cf. (Cohn, 1954). N. Christie used the F-scale on ex-Nazi prison guards in Norway. Tests similar to the F-scale have been administered in France (Perlmutter), Norway (Bay, Gullvåg, Ofstad, Tønnessen) and in Sweden (Björklund and Israel). For a fuller bibliography see (Rokkan, 1969: 3).

[219] (Eysenck, 1954: ch. 5). Eysenck reports a higher mean F-score in a sample of Communists than in a sample of 'non-Communists' and 'non-Fascists'. This finding has been challenged by M. Rokeach & C. Hanley (Rokeach, 1956) and R. Christie (Christie, 1955).

[220] For details on these opinion measures, see Chapter 9.

[221] Of particular importance here are of course analyses of the interaction between 'personality' and socio-economic position in determining political behaviour, cf. (Eysenck, 1954) and (Lipset, 1955), also Lipset's chapter on 'working-class authoritarianism' in *Political Man* (Lipset, 1960).

[222] Cf. the life-cycle curve found by MacKinnon & Centers (MacKinnon, 1956).

ELEVEN

Electoral Activity, Party Membership and Organizational Influence

The Norwegian programme of empirical investigations and statistical analyses of *electoral processes* seeks to combine four major approaches to the study of the political and social processes during elections:

the tradition of *cartographic description* and *ecological analysis* of the data produced by the election process itself (cf. Chapters 6 and 7 above);
the tradition of *campaign observation* and *content analysis* of the speeches, the party literature, and the political press *(e. g.* Høyer, 1960; Torgersen 1962);
the tradition of *community surveys* focusing on the exploration of the impact of informal pressure, organizational efforts, and the mass media campaign on the attitudes and decisions of local voters (Valen, 1964);
and finally the tradition of the *national cross-sectional survey* typified in the intensive interviewing operations of the *Survey Research Center* at the University of Michigan (Rokkan, 1960: 4; 1966: 5).

The statistical analyses [224] and the campaign descriptions [225] cut across several elections and aim at the exploration of trends. The first community studies and the first nationwide survey, however, were directly focused on one point in time: *the election of representatives to the Storting on 7 October, 1957*.[226]

Two major data-gathering operations were carried out during the campaign and immediately after the election: 1) a set of parallel interviews with party leaders and rank-and-file voters in four communes in Rogaland in the Southwest of Norway, and 2) a set of before-and-after interviews with a cross-sectional sample of the national electorate. The data collected in these operations have been analyzed in great detail elsewhere

Origin: This chapter represents the first report on the nationwide election survey carried out in Norway in September-October, 1957. The chapter reproduces, except for a few minor amendments, a paper first presented at the Rome Congress of the International Political Science Association, September, 1958.

(cf. Rokkan, 1966: 7): this chapter will focus on one set of early findings only.

The community studies and the nation-wide survey shared two basic objectives:

1) they were designed to explore the *political effects of the ongoing process of economic and social change* in Norway: the effects of industrialization, bureaucratization, and the over-all rise in the levels of living;
2) they sought to throw light on the *functioning of the democratic system* in Norway: the amount of participation in the political process, the recruitment of activists, the role of the party organizations, the changes brought about through the continuous growth of the network of interest organizations.

The first analyses were exclusively concerned with problems and findings in this *second* sector: we tried to throw some light on the ways in which our political parties, through their leaders and their membership, were embedded in the wider framework of national and local organizations and associations.

Daniel Katz and Henry Valen have reported on analysis results from the community studies in the Southwest. They have focused on comparisons of data for the local party leaders with corresponding data for the rank-and-file electorate. They are primarily concerned with an analysis of the *parties as organizational units* (Valen, 1961, 1964). In this paper, a first series of tabulations and comparisons will be presented from the *nationwide survey*. Our analysis will be exclusively concerned with *individual differences in the intensity of participation* in political and community life: we shall seek to throw light on relationships between *electoral activity, party membership on the one hand* and *participation in interest organizations and voluntary associations on the other*.

In planning our studies of the political process in Norway we considered it of crucial importance to come to grips with this *basic contrast in the modes of participation in decision-making:* participation in the anonymous citizen role in elections versus participation in responsive member roles in organizations seeking to influence policies in the community or the nation.

An analysis of this contrast seemed to us essential in any effort to reach some understanding of the operation of pluralist political systems: how do one man, one vote systems of electoral decision-making fit into the increasingly complex systems of bargaining relationships between corporate units?

This is not the place to develop the details of a theoretical scheme; we shall confine ourselves to crude formulations of what we consider crucial differences:

equality vs. *hierarchy* – in elections each citizen counts as one unit of influence, irrespective of the amount of influence he may wield in his actual organizational roles;

anonymity vs. *visibility of preference* – in elections unit of influence is anonymous, it is divorced from the person and the roles of the participating citizen;

privacy vs. *responsibility* – in elections there are institutional arrangements for the safeguarding of the privacy of the preference act, leaving it to the individual citizen to decide whether or not to reveal his behaviour and take responsibility for it in his day-to-day role relationships (cf. Ch. 1 and 4).

Formally, elections are instituted to aggregate the *abstract wills* of so many 'unit citizens' divorced from their particular roles in the organizational structure of society. In actual fact, the preferences expressed on polling day will tend to reflect in some way or other *the concrete wills* of organizations as interpreted and mediated through leaders and 'activists' in the system. It is a task for empirical research to reach some assessment of the extent of such organizational influences on voting and to provide a basis for an understanding of the processes at work here: the role of mass-directed vs. informal communications, the functions of the 'activists', their interlocking roles in the political and the socio-economic networks.

Any student of elections must necessarily be struck by the contrast between the high level of participation at the polling stations and the very low level of active involvement in the campaign and in discussions of the alternatives confronting the citizen. In Norway, as in most other countries of W. Europe, turnout figures at national elections oscillate around 80 %. Voting is clearly a culturally accepted norm: there is evidence of considerable reluctance to admit to deviations from this norm. In cross-sectional interview surveys we can normally have a great deal of confidence in what people say about their party preferences: there is much more reason to doubt their statements about their participation at the polls. The proportions of people reporting that they do no intend to or in fact did not vote have almost invariably been found to be lower than the actual per cent of non-voters in the electorate. In our pre-election survey of a national cross-section we had 13.5 % saying they would probably or definitely not vote. In our post-election survey an even smaller proportion, 9.5 %, said they had not voted. The actual per cent of non-voters in 1957 was a high as 22.1 %. Our analyses so far make it unlikely that these differences can be accounted for from sampling errors or biases in the rates of obtained interviews.[227]

Contrast to this high level of turnout the very low level of direct participation in the campaign and the only moderate interest in the electoral efforts of the parties. We find:

barely 2 % taking part personally in campaign work;
7 % attending one or more election meetings;

19 % claiming to have read most of the election editorials in their regular newspaper, and
22 % to have read other election news with some regularity.

Of the mass-directed campaign efforts the radio programmes, all officially controlled and taking the form of debates between leaders of all six parties, clearly reached the widest audience: 42 % claimed to have heard some part of the final debate and 51 % had listened to at least one of the five debates. Other party activities clearly affect much smaller proportions of the electorate: 7 % report that they were visited by a party worker during the campaign, 23 % say they received free newspaper subscriptions from some party for the period of the campaign, 29 % claim to have seen or read the most widely distributed electoral pamphlets.

Our Norwegian data clearly fit in with the general pattern of findings for a number of countries: only a small minority of the electorate take an active interest in the struggle between the parties at election time. To reach any understanding of the electoral process, it is essential to analyze the social and political characteristics of this minority in some detail. Who are these activists? How are they motivated? How are they placed in the organizational structure of society?

Cross-tabulations against sex, age, education, and socio-economic position give fairly consistent indications of the importance of *role expectations in every day life:* the more the citizen is expected to deal independently with matters outside his immediate household or his work group, the more he is likely to take an active interest in politics at election time. We find a significantly lower proportion of women than of men giving evidence of active participation or search for information. We find a higher level of interest among people in middle age than among the young, higher among people educated beyond the primary school than among others. Such factors, however, can only explain one part of the variance. Another very important source of variation is clearly *the degree of long-term commitment* to given political parties and the traditions they stand for.

Election studies in a number of countries have shown that the citizens most likely to expose themselves to the campaign and to take an active interest in the election are those already definitely committed to a party; those who are not so clearly in any particular camp are generally less likely to be reached by the campaign efforts of the parties. In our Norwegian analysis, we have seen it as a central task to explore in detail the conditions making for such a close relationship between party commitment, participation, and exposure to campaign communication.

In our initial analysis we found it convenient to focus on one single index of commitment: *reported party membership.* Outside Scandinavia the proportions of party members in the electorate are in most cases too small to allow analyses within ordinary cross-sectional samples.[228] In Norway, the proportions are large enough to allow systematic comparisons between members and non-members not only across all parties, but also to some extent within groups of parties. This has made it possible to undertake a type of analysis only rarely attempted with cross-sectional survey data.[229]

Duverger (Duverger, 1951: Ch. II) and a number of other students of party organizations have emphasized the multiplicity of meanings attached to the term 'party member'. Our respondents certainly did not all interpret the term exactly the same way, yet there can be little doubt that the positive responses may be taken to express some degree of commitment to the given party – the question is: how strong a commitment? Whatever the psychological significance of the response, the member-voter ratios in our sample do not depart too violently from those estimated from the figures obtained from the party secretariats.[230]

One difficulty here concerns the reports on memberships in trade unions collectively affiliated to the Labour party: here we would expect some respondents to be unaware of such indirect membership, others to confuse individual and collective membership.[231] In our analysis of the effects of party commitment, we have focused exclusively on reported *individual* membership: this may involve some error in the case of the Labour party, but we hope to reduce this to a minimum through further controls.

Analyzing the socio-economic background of party membership we find marked differences between the Labour party and the non-socialist parties in the structure of their recruitment. In the Labour party the member-voter ratio is much higher for men than for women, in the other parties there is a markedly higher proportion of women members. In the Labour party the occupational composition of the membership is remarkably similar to the composition for the entire group of Labour voters: in the other parties, there are disproportionately more members in the higher status groups and disproportionately fewer members among the lower status groups voting for these parties (cf. Ch. 12 below).

In spite of these differences in recruitment basis, we have found it fruitful in our initial analysis to contrast members with non-members *en bloc,* cutting across all party lines. This means that we have taken it for granted that *whichever the party,* reported membership indicates a higher level of commitment than a mere preference in voting. From such evidence as we have, we consider this assumption justified. We have, however, sought to guard against the risk of overinterpretation by introducing a number of *controls:* we have carried out each comparison separately for each sex, for several age groups, for different educational levels, for urban vs. rural respondents. In later analyses, we shall explore in detail the differences between the parties. Here we shall deal with party members *en bloc,* as a strategic group in the total system.

Comparing the behaviour of members and non-members during the campaign, we find marked differences not only, as we might well expect, in the proportions taking direct part in election work, but also in the proportions indicating an active interest in the communications of the parties. It seems clear that the citizens most likely to seek information about the parties and their arguments in the campaign are those already visibly committed, those who are under role pressure to defend one particular line in the debates aroused before election: in this sense, a high proportion of party members can be taken to be 'opinion leaders' of the kind suggested by the Lazarsfeld theory of the 'two-steps flow of communication' (Katz, 1955).[232]

Perhaps the most striking is the finding for attendance at election meetings and rallies. In the rural communes, we find that the *one-sixth* reporting to be party members account for more than *half* of the audience at such meetings.[233] In these circumstances election meetings clearly cannot achieve much with the uncommitted: their major function seems to be to energize those already committed and to give them the arguments they may need in their efforts of informal persuasion in their normal environments. In the cities there is no such tendency: the audience of the election meetings does not include a higher proportion of members than the electorate. This difference requires further analysis: it suggests a different type of communication flow in urban communities.

Table I summarizes the differences between members and non-members on a number of further points. It will be seen that the differences are most

Table 1. *Differences between Party Members and Non-Members in the Extent of Electoral Involvement*

		Took direct part in party campaign work	Attended one or more meetings	Read election editorials regularly	Listened to one or more radio debates	N = 100 % for each item
MEMBERS						
Men	under 45	11.8 %	18.5 %	32.3 %	69.2 %	65
	over 45	11.8 %	25.8 %	48.4 %	72.0 %	93
Women	under 45	3.1 %	3.1 %	9.4 %	40.6 %	32
	over 45	2.2 %	15.2 %	23.9 %	47.8 %	46
All members		9.3 %	18.6 %	33.9 %	62.3 %	236
NON-MEMBERS						
Men	under 45	1.9 %	9.0 %	24.7 %	58.0 %	312
	over 45	1.6 %	6.3 %	31.0 %	59.6 %	255
Women	under 45	1.2 %	2.1 %	5.4 %	41.9 %	334
	over 45	0.6 %	3.7 %	6.5 %	39.8 %	322
All non-members		1.3 %	5.2 %	15.9 %	49.1 %	1223
Total sample		2.6 %	7.3 %	18.8 %	51.3 %	1459

marked for the *men* in the sample, most consistently so for those over 45. For women under 45 membership does not so consistently increase electoral involvement; many wives are members only because their husbands are, and duties in the household often prevent them from taking such an active part in politics. This pattern seems to hold up both at the lower and the higher educational level.

Our analysis has indicated some of the characteristics of the activists in one of our system of decision-making: the electoral. Our next task is to explore the linkage to the other system of decision-making: the organizational.

What we can do at this stage of the analysis is very elementary. We have compared our party members with the rest of our sample on two counts: the number of *memberships* and the number of *offices* held in *non-political organizations* of all sorts. The results are summarized in *Table 2.*

Survey findings for a number of countries indicate that the number of organizational memberships increase with higher socio-economic status (Reigrotzki, 1956: p. 173–76; Wright, 1958). Our findings for Norway go in the same direction. Workers report relatively few memberships beyond their trade unions, while salaried employees, farmers and other independents report a greater variety of non-political memberships. At all these levels, however, we find a definite difference between party members and others. *Party members have a higher number of non-political memberships.* This is seen to be the case both for men and for women.

Table 2. *Differences between Party Members and Non-Members in the Number of Memberships and Offices Held in Non-Political Organizations*

		MEMBERSHIP in two or more organizations	OFFICES in one or more organizations	N = 100 % in each case
PRIMARY SCHOOL ONLY				
Party members	*men*	36.9 %	37.9 %	103
	women	39.5 %	23.3 %	43
Non-members	*men*	24.5 %	21.5 %	404
	women	20.3 %	15.0 %	474
Total lower-educated group		24.4 %	20.2 %	1024
EDUCATED BEYOND PRIMARY				
Party members	*men*	58.2 %	61.8 %	55
	women	54.3 %	25.7 %	35
Non-members	*men*	36.8 %	38.0 %	163
	women	33.5 %	23.1 %	182
Total higher-educated group		39.5 %	33.8 %	435
Total sample		28.9 %	24.3 %	1459

The same pattern emerges from an analysis of offices held in non-political organizations. Whatever the educational level, we find party members more likely than others to have been decision-makers in non-political organizations. This difference is most marked for the *men;* in the case of the women the difference comes out at the *lower* educational level, but not among those educated beyond the primary school.

This type of analysis clearly has its limitations. Counting memberships and offices across such a vast variety of non-political organizations may involve analytical pitfalls. Trade unions, religious organizations, neighbourhood associations and hobby clubs cannot very well be expected to carry the same weight in the decision-making processes in the community. What is so remarkable is that even this crude procedure of counting across all categories of associations should produce such consistent results. Further analysis will allow us to establish differentiations between types of organizations and map out in greater detail the linkage between party memberships and decision-making roles in non-political organizations. At this stage we confine ourselves to a statement of the over-all linkages between party roles and roles in non-political organizations.

The findings of our national survey fits into a broader pattern of research evidence. Daniel Katz and Henry Valen have shown even more marked differences in non-political memberships between party leaders and rank-and-file voters in the communes studied in the Southwest (Valen, 1961: 1). Similar differences have been established for a number of countries.[234]

This does not mean that the overlap between political and socio-economic leadership is anywhere near complete – at least not in pluralist societies. In any macro-comparison of systems, it must clearly be a central task to assess the sources of differences in the degree of such overlap. In micro-analyses of the recruitment of active participants, we must again pay fully as much attention to those who *do not* make up links between parties and organizations as to those who do.

In our further work with the data from our 1957 studies, we shall be concerned with differences in background and orientations between four major groups:

a) those high on political commitment but low on organizational participation,
b) those high on both scores: the 'overlappers',
c) those low on political commitment but high in organizational participation, and, of course,
d) those low on both counts.

A central problem in this analysis is the assessment of the extent of *Entideologisierung* attendant on the growth of the network of interest organizations. It will be of interest to compare the four groups on their attitudes to a number of party-differentiating issues and we shall, quite particularly, seek to assess differences in the extent of *over-all orientations to party conflict:* avoidance vs. acceptance of party struggle. Here we have hopes of finding important clues to an understanding of the crucial differences in the operation of the two systems of decision-making: the electoral vs. the organizational.

In the analysis so far given we have confined ourselves to *one* out of at least *four* major approaches to an understanding of the relationships between these systems: we have started out from the *electorate-at-large.* It goes without saying that we cannot hope to get anywhere near the complete picture before we have explored the other major lines of research: the one starting out from the *parties* and their leadership, the one starting out from the *interest groups* and the *voluntary associations,* and the one starting out from the *central decision-making bodies* themselves. The Norwegian programme of studies has attempted to combine the *three first approaches:* [235] this should allow as to present increasingly more unified interpretations of our findings at the micro-level.

It is our conviction that studies of this kind can be fruitfully undertaken in a wide variety of countries and on increasingly comparative lines. In analyzing our Norwegian data we shall at every possible point be concerned to compare our results with available evidence from other countries and we shall be grateful to all colleagues who will inform us of studies and data of any relevance. But we feel that there is a strong case for going beyond such exchanges of findings which happen to be there: a case for organizing cooperative programmes of data gathering across a variety of countries. Important steps have already been taken in this direction and we hope that the international associations active in the social sciences will be in a position to give further encouragement to such efforts.

NOTES

[224] An ecological analysis of the effects of *industrialization* on voting has been completed by E. Sæter (Sæter, 1959). For further analyses see Chapters 6 and 7 above and (Rokkan, 1964: 2 and 1967).

[225] A content analysis of newspaper editorials during the three Storting elections has been completed by S. Høyer in consultation with U. Torgersen (Høyer, 1960).

[226] For a descriptive account see (Valen, 1964).

[227] Details on sampling procedures and comparisons with known parameters are given in (Rokkan, 1960: 4).

[228] For the U. S., the 1952 survey carried out by the Michigan Survey Research Center found 2 % belonging to political clubs or organizations, see (Campbell, 1954: p. 29). Within W. Europe, there are very considerable differences between countries. For W. Germany, the UNESCO survey indicated only 3 % party members in the electorate, see (Reigrotzki, 1956: p. 59). Party statistics indicate much higher proportions of party members in *Great Britain,* even when collectively affiliated members are discounted (1951: 20 % party members among Conservative voters, 6.5 % individual and 35.5 % trade union affiliated party mem-

bers among Labour voters). For the *Netherlands,* a government-sponsored survey conducted in 1953–54 had as many as 27 % indicating that they were members of some political party (De Nederlandse, 1956: p. 79) this figure, however, is much higher than the figure estimated from party statistics. *op. cit.* p. 89. For *Sweden* E. Håstad estimates that 25 %–30 % of the 1952 electorate were registered party members (Håstad, 1954: p. 41); the sample survey directed by J. Westerståhl in 1956 indicated a lower estimate, however: 18 % of the electorate (20 % of the voters) reported party membership.

[229] The Dutch survey reported on in (De Nederlandse, 1956) allows extensive analyses of relationship between party membership and electoral involvement; the report, however, is limited to a series of two-way cross-tabulations without any controls for party, sex, age or education.

[230] A table comparing the survey findings with the party statistics will be found in Chapter 6 above *(Table 3.1).* In the *Dutch* survey cited above, the discrepancy between the sample proportion and the estimate from party statistics was very high, 27 % vs. 10 %; it is suggested that the question about membership 'was not properly understood' particularly by the women respondents, *op. cit.* p. 89. Cross-tabulations nevertheless suggest that the response can be taken as a valid index of the level of political commitment.

[231] In the detailed sample survey of the *Swedish* electorate before 1956 election, Jörgen Westerståhl found 21 % of the Social Democrat voters reporting membership in that party: this contrasts with party estimates of more than 40 %. The discrepancy is attributed to lack of knowledge about collective affiliation. The analysis of the data from the Southwest survey points to a similar explanation for Norway (Valen, 1964, Ch. 3 pp. 67–70), cf. also Chapter 6 above, pp. 201–205.

[232] Some interesting applications to the situation in Sweden are suggested by Joachim Israel (Israel, 1957).

[233] In the Dutch survey, it was found that 70 % of the audience at election meetings were party members (De Nederlandse, 1956: p. 78).

[234] Reigrotzki (Reigrotzki, 1956: p. 178) finds for W. Germany that a high number of non-political memberships increases the likelihood of party membership. Among men belonging to only *one* organization, he finds no more than 5 % who are party members; among those belonging to *four or more,* he finds 13 % party members. In our Norwegian sample the corresponding percentages are 22.6 % and 46.3 %.

[235] Henry Valen is engaged in a study of the interlinkages between parties and interest organizations and has focused on the analysis of the affiliations of *candidates on party lists,* see (Valen, 1958; 1966; 1967). For an attempt at a synthesis of macro-interpretations and micro-analyses see (Rokkan, 1966: 5).

TWELVE

Citizen Participation in Political Life: a Comparison of Data for Norway and the United States of America

Origin: This chapter was first printed in a special issue on 'Citizen participation' published by UNESCO (Rokkan, 1960: 1). It was subsequently reprinted in J. Meynaud (ed.) *Decisions and Decision-Makers in the Modern State* (Paris: UNESCO, 1966).

We shall present in this article a set of findings from parallel analyses of data from election surveys in two Western democracies: Norway and the United States of America. Our analysis will be concerned with similarities and differences in the recruitment of active participants in electoral contests in these two political systems: What kinds of citizens are most likely to become active in politics and to take a personal interest in public affairs? What are the primary channels of recruitment of such 'activists'? How do the different parties compare in their patterns of recruitment?

In any such confrontation of data on citizen behaviour in different political systems the fundamental problem is to find meaningful ways of relating variations at this 'micro' level of individual reactions and choices to differences in the 'macro' properties of the structures within which they occur: to differences in the range and character of the alternatives set for the citizen by the institutional arrangements and by the constellation of competing forces in his society. In a rigorous analysis design, such macro-properties would have to be varied systematically and related to differences in patterns of citizen reactions and preferences. Such rigour is hardly practicable in the comparison of units differing in such complex ways along a variety of dimensions, but step-by-step approximations should be within the range of the possible.

In the present attempt, the two systems to be compared were not picked out because they fitted any rigorously developed design of analysis. Quite to the contrary we felt tempted to try out a number of parallel analyses for the very simple reason that data had been assembled in fairly similar ways in our two countries within an interval of less than a year and seemed to lend themselves to comparisons on a few points of general theoretical interest. At the present stage of comparative political research, we feel that such focused two-country or three-country comparisons may prove of considerable importance in accumulating findings, in sharpening the tools of analysis and in building up a body of hypotheses for exploration within a wider set of systems.

Differences in the Conditions for Citizen Participation
We felt tempted to set beside each other data from Norway and the United States both because of the basic similarities in political values, and because of the salient differences in the conditions for citizen participation in the two systems: we felt that the two systems were similar enough to make it meaningful to attempt such comparisons at the 'micro' level, yet differing so markedly in the setting of their politics as to open up interesting opportunities for an analysis of factors affecting the levels of citizen participation.

Our two systems have very much in common: they are both within the Western family of economically-advanced pluralist democracies, they have both developed complex networks of organizations and associations actively influencing the process of decision-making, and they are both dominated by political cultures giving strong encouragement to citizen participation in public affairs.

Geography and history have combined, however, to produce markedly different conditions for individual participation in the process of politics in the two systems:

	Norway	United States
Size of principal territory (sq. km)	324,000	7,828,000
Population, 1957	3,478,000	171,229,000
Concentration, 1950		
Population density (in thousands per sq. km.)	9	21
Percentage in 'urban' localities, as administratively defined	32.2	64.0
Percentage in localities of 2,000 or more	44.1	65.1
Structure of labour force, 1950		
Percentage in agriculture, forestry and fisheries	25.9	12.5
Percentage in industry (mining, manufacturing and construction)	36.4	33.7
Percentage salaried employees *(funksjonaerer),* professional, technical, managerial, clerical and sales workers (exclusive of those self-employed)	19.8	31.2
Income (G.N.P.) *per capita, 1957*	$1,130	$2,577
Political system		
Structure	Unitary, parliamentary, unicameral	Federative, presidential, bicameral
Electoral procedures: representatives for national legislatures	PR by lists	Plurality system, single-member constituencies
Party system		
No. of major parties	6	2
Principal party cleavages	Labour (1957: 48 per cent of vote) versus four non-socialist parties (1957: 10 per cent, 10 per cent, 9 per cent and 19 per cent)	Democrats (1956: 51 per cent of vote for Congress) versus Republicans (49 per cent of vote for Congress)
Distinctiveness of party platforms	High	Low
Tie-ins with socio-economic groupings	Strong, stable	Weak, unstable
Party organizations	Centralized	Localized
Party influence over press	Considerable	Insignificant

Whatever the difficulties encountered in establishing exact comparisons on each of these points, these differences clearly point to major contrasts in the conditions for citizen activity in the politics of the two systems: contrasts in the life situations of the citizens, in the ranges of alternatives facing them in the public arena, in the alignments of forces impinging on their behaviour.

Our task is to gain some understanding of the impact of these contrasting conditions on the political activities of the general citizenry in the two systems: Are there any differences in the over-all levels of participation in the two systems? Are there differences in the distributions for the major types of participant behaviour? Are there differences in the recruitment of citizens of different socio-economic background to the ranks of the 'actives' in the two electorates?

Differences in the Over-all Levels of Participation in the two Systems

Estimates from official statistics and from documentation from the parties indicate some differences between the two countries in the proportion of active citizens: the proportion of regular voters and the proportion of registered party members both appear to be markedly higher in the Norwegian electorate than in the United States.

There are a number of intricate questions to be asked about these differences: (a) How far can they be accounted for by differences in the definition of the total electorates and in the procedures of enumeration? (b) How far does it make sense to compare such proportions of individual acts when they occur in systems differing so clearly in the ranges of alternatives set for the citizen? (c) Granting that there are genuine differences between the systems in such over-all proportions, how far can these be explained by the contrasts at the 'macro' levels of the total systems and how far can they only be accounted for by breakdowns within each system?

We cannot deal exhaustively with these problems in this context, but will discuss the questions briefly for each of the two categories of participation: voting and party membership.

Voting

In Norway the average turn-out at the four Storting elections from 1945 to 1957 was 79 per cent (82 per cent for men and 76 for women); the corresponding figure for the four communal elections from 1945 to 1955 was 70 per cent (74 per cent for men and 69 for women).

In the United States the 'raw' participation figures for the three presidential elections from 1948 to 1956 averaged 58 per cent and the corresponding figure for the last four 'off-year' elections has been 41 per cent.

These figures would indicate a substantially higher level of electoral participation in Norway than in the United States. The data, however, cannot be compared without adjustments and qualifications: the two countries differ a great deal in the procedures used for registering and enumerating the electorate and in the availability of accurate statistics for turn-out variations.

In Norway a *manntall* is established by the local authorities about two months before each election: this register will include all resident citizens of age 21 or more who have lived in Norwegian territory for five years or more and only exclude those of the resident inhabitants who have lost their right to the suffrage as the result of judicial action, mainly in cases of mental illness or serious crimes. The officially-published statistics give for each *kommune* the number of men and women entitled to a vote and therefore readily allow calculations of the turn-out levels.

In the United States there is no such uniform system of official registration and enumeration of the electorate. The voting lists will in most states include only the names of those who have gone to the trouble to register: the lists, therefore, do not in any way constitute a census of all those who meet the qualifications for the suffrage as laid down by the laws of each state. There is no way of extracting turn-out percentages directly from the official statistics for elections. The 'raw' turn-out percentages generally given are based on census estimates of the 'civilian population of voting age', [236] but a sizeable proportion of this population would not meet the legal requirements for voting. The most important of these are the varying requirements for minimum length of residence in the state, the county and the voting district; it has been estimated that about 5 per cent of the 'civilian population of voting age' are prevented from voting by the current residence requirements.[237] The literacy tests applied with varying rigour in about one-third of the states, and the poll taxes still retained in five Southern states, further reduce the number of potential voters, but it is hardly possible to draw any line, in these cases, between legal disfranchisement and social discouragement or even intimidation. The low turn-out figures for the one-party South have been analysed in considerable detail by a variety of scholars,[238] but it has proved practically impossible to find any basis for accurate estimates of the sizes of the 'legal' electorates of these states. For these and other reasons, there are very small chances of reaching consensus on the 'correction coefficients' to be used in establishing the 'true' turn-out level for the United States. V. O. Key, who has analyzed the data as thoroughly as anyone, hazards the suggestion that one would have to add 6 to 7 percentage points to the 'raw' proportions for presidential elections to get turn-out figures comparable with those for western European countries (Key, 1959: p. 624; cf. Campbell, 1960: Ch. 5). This would still make the average turn-out in the United States significantly lower than in Norway, but it must be remembered that we are then comparing the total national electorates: the difference would be reduced to half its size if we excluded from consideration the politically very different Southern states.[239]

Party Membership

The difficulties of direct cross-system comparison increase dramatically as we move higher on the political activity scale: they are largely of a technical nature at the level of electoral participation, but raise serious conceptual problems as soon as we try to compare data on the proportions of citizens who in some way or other have joined one of the conflicting parties in each system.

In Norway, all the six parties have provisions for formal affiliation and regular dues-paying: they are, in Duverger's terminology, 'mass parties' (Duverger, 1951: pp. 63–71 in the English ed.). This does not mean that 'party member' is a clear and unambiguous term: there are variations in the procedures for affiliation and in the strictness of the dues requirements; there are also differences between the main party organizations and the auxiliary associations for young people and for women. Barely 10 per cent of the party members are 'militants' in the sense that they are active party workers, but even the less active members differ markedly from the 'rank-and-file voters' in their commitment to the party, in the interest they manifest in political affairs, and in their level of informedness.

The membership figures published or otherwise made available by the central party secretariats are not always based on accurately kept local records, but can be taken to be fair estimates of the situation in the electorate. The total individual memberships reported for the six parties in 1957 was about 280,000:[240] the electorate amounted to 2,298,000. A small, but unknown, proportion of the reported members were not yet of voting age and there are also possibilities of over-reporting because of double affiliations between the main organizations and the auxiliary associations. The percentage of party members in the electorate may therefore be evaluated at a maximum of 13 per cent: this figure does not differ markedly from the proportion reporting individual party membership in the 1957 election survey (cf. Table 3.2 page 204 above).

In the United States the term 'party member' does not have a settled political connotation: it may indicate any degree of commitment to a party, from simple registration at primaries or elections to active campaign work (Berdahl, 1942; Epstein, 1956). The American parties have not built up the mass memberships characteristic of the dominant parties in western Europe: they are, in the Duverger terminology, 'cadre parties' based on localized caucus organizations. There are no nationally established procedures for enrolment and consequently no general register of members and no statistics of such affiliation. Politically active citizens may join local clubs and engage in campaign work in their precincts, but much of this is motivated by loyalty to local candidates rather than to the party as a permanent organization. It is technically difficult to assess the proportions of citizens who thus qualify as 'party members' in the strict sense. The Survey Research Center at the University of Michigan asked questions about membership in 'political clubs or organizations' in the national sample surveys before the presidential elections in 1952 and 1956: the proportions claiming such membership were 2 per cent and 3 per cent. Membership of this kind is clearly much less common in the United States than in Norway, but it would be misleading to take this as the ultimate measure of the over-all difference in political participation in the two countries. Political activity is definitely more widespread in the United States than is indicated by the low proportion of party 'members' in the electorate. The two surveys also included questions about volunteer work and about contributions of funds during the elections, and the results provided evidence of a larger core of active party supporters in the American electorate. In both surveys, 3 per cent of the sample declared that they had been volunteer workers during the campaign and less than half of these were members of political organizations. The proportions reporting active support through contributions of funds were larger: 4 per cent in 1952 and as many as 10 per cent in 1956. The great majority of these supporters were not 'members' in the strict sense, but they were probably about as active for their parties as those who reported party membership in Norway.[241]

The Design of the Comparative Survey Analysis
We have discussed the problems of direct comparisons of over-all levels of political participation for two major activity indicators: voting and party membership. Judging by these two indicators, there is evidence that participation is higher in Norway than in the United States, but it is very difficult to establish such equivalences in the data as would allow exact assessments of the differences and make it possible to explore the factors making for such differences.

This does not mean that all comparative analysis will prove barren of results. Direct comparisons of over-all levels of participation may prove inconclusive because of the difficulties of establishing equivalences, but indirect, 'second order' comparisons of regularities in the differences within the system may still prove of great theoretical interest.

The present analysis focuses on such 'second order' comparisons and for two major reasons:
1. It is clearly easier to establish differences between groups within the same political systems than to compare across entirely different systems: in the one case we have very good reasons for interpreting participation as a response to similar ranges of political alternatives while in the other any such assumptions are problematic.

2. Any between-system differences in over-all levels of participation must be the resultants of the interaction of a variety of factors and these cannot be disentangled without detailed breakdowns by groups within each system.

In this analysis we are no longer concerned with the proportions of active citizens in the total electorates but with the recruitment of such participants from the different groups within each system. We do not compare 'party membership' in Norway with 'party membership' in the United States because it proves so difficult to establish equivalent categories. Instead we choose our 'dependent' variables, our participation indicators, *within* each system and compare the differences in the levels of participation between comparable groups within each of them: differences in participation between men and women, country folk and city dwellers, farmers, manual workers and salaried employees, and so on. This amounts to a comparison of factors making for higher or lower citizen participation in the politics in each system. Our 'dependent' variable, the indicators of individual participation, are system-specific while our 'independent' and 'intervening' variables, the causal factors we seek to identify, are roughly comparable characteristics of groups within each system: sex, rural-urban residence, education, occupation, party preference.

Data from official records cannot readily be broken down for the purposes of such comparisons. The Norwegian turn-out data are given separately for men and women and can be analyzed in terms of the over-all characteristics of the smallest counting unit: the *kommune*. In the United States any such analysis of turn-out data will involve serious technical difficulties. The only practical solution is to resort to data from sample surveys. This is what we have done in the present analysis.

We shall base our analysis on two sets of interview data from cross-sectional surveys: for Norway, a sample of 1,406 citizens drawn by random probability methods from the registers in 99 *kommuner* and interviewed before and after the election for the Storting on 7 October 1957;[242] for the United States, a sample of 1,772 persons interviewed before and after the presidential election on 6 November 1956 (Campbell, 1960).

The analysis will proceed as follows: (a) we shall present, for each country, two indexes of political activity derived from a combination of several indicators in the survey responses; (b) we shall present and discuss comparative tables indicating similarities and differences shown by these indexes between the sexes, between communities at different levels of urbanization, between educational and occupational strata in each electorate; and (c) we shall present and discuss differences in the recruitment patterns for the major party groupings in the two countries.

Two Indexes of Political Activity
Both nation-wide surveys included a number of questions about the politically relevant activities engaged in by the citizens to be interviewed. In comparing the data from the two surveys we tried to summarize this information in two simple indexes: one for organizational participation and another for the attention paid to politics in the mass media. These indexes make it possible to characterize citizens in terms of their relative levels of activity within each system: the indexes cannot be compared directly between the systems but they allow analysis of the differences between the two electorates in the recruitment of the 'actives' in each system, in their demographic and socio-economic background and in their party attachments.

Organizational Participation
The index for organizational participation summarizes information about energy inputs into some organized political framework: from the act of voting to direct campaign work.

The index has a very simple structure, it divides the samples into three groups: the 'non-voters', the 'only-voters' who indicate no other political activity, and the 'organizationally active' who indicate one or more activities beyond voting.

Sample surveys generally fail to produce reliable estimates of the proportion of non-voters in a given electorate. We cannot cite any exception to the rule that the proportions reporting abstention in cross-sectional samples of interviewed citizens will be lower than the officially reported or estimated proportions of non-voters in the total electorate. In the Norwegian survey carried out in 1957, 13 per cent of those interviewed before the election indicated that they were not likely to vote, while barely 8 per cent of those interviewed after the election reported a failure to vote: the officially reported proportion of non-voters in the entire electorate was 22 per cent. In the United States, the carefully designed cross-sectional sample surveys undertaken by the Survey Research Center at the University of Michigan since the 1948 election have regularly had a higher proportion of respondents reporting having cast a vote than would be expected from the raw participation percentages established on the basis of census data on the size of the population of voting age (Campbell, 1952: pp. 4–6; 1954: pp. 4–5; 1956: pp. 7–11; 1960: Ch. 5).

It is not difficult to account for these regular discrepancies between sample proportions and proportions for the total electorates.

First, it must be remembered that the proportions of non-voters in a survey are always given as percentages of the number of obtained interviews: these figures cannot be compared with the official turn-out estimates without controls for the coverage of the sample (does it deliberately exclude or for other reasons fail to cover any identifiable sections of the given electorate?), and the non-response (do those interviewed differ significantly from those not interviewed within the given example?). There is a great deal of evidence indicating that there are substantial differences in the proportions of non-voters between those actually interviewed and those who for one reason or another are not interviewed: people who are never or rarely at their given address, people in transit between addresses, asocial individuals, physically or mentally handicapped people, and so on.[243] The citizens not reached by sample surveys are exactly the citizens least likely to vote: this clearly biases the samples in the direction of higher turn-out levels.

Secondly, there is also some evidence of a culturally determined reluctance to admit a failure to vote: the majority of the citizens contacted in a survey will consider it a definite duty to vote and may not be willing to tell an interviewer that they have been negligent in this duty. Even if it were possible to obtain interviews with all the citizens drawn for the sample, it would accordingly be most unlikely that the survey would produce a proportion of non-voters tallying statistically with the turn-out figures established from the total counts.

It is technically impossible for us to go beyond the recorded interview responses to check the accuracy of the reports on turn-out.[244] We are accordingly not in a position to report with any accuracy how much of the bias was due to non-coverage and non-response and how much must be attributed to over-reporting.[245] It seems clear, however, that both these factors must have been of importance in determining the actual distributions found between reported voters and reported non-voters.

These difficulties do not necessarily jeopardize our analysis. Our index only assumes the validity of the reports on non-voting: these are taken to indicate the lowest level of political participation. The reported voters are subjected to a number of further tests to sort out the 'actives': the remaining group of 'only-voters' may include some actual non-voters but this is not a serious drawback since all the analysis focuses on the differences at the extremes of the distribution.

In the Norwegian survey, the number of respondents who admitted that they had not voted was too small to allow extensive analysis. It was therefore decided to establish a broader category of 'probable non-voters' by taking into account not only the report after the election, but also the expressed intention before the election and the report given on the regularity of turn-out at previous elections: this gives a group of 'low probability voters' with a record of erratic turn-out and chronically low interest in participation. This group was found to make up 21 per cent of the sample: this corresponds very closely to the official turn-out figures, but some of these respondents must clearly have voted in 1957, however poor their previous record.

The next step in the construction of the index was to identify the 'organizationally active' within the groups of reported voters. In the Norwegian survey, the 'actives' were sorted out on the basis of responses to three questions, in the United States on the basis of four questions (see *Table 1*).

The percentages given for each question are for those classified as voters, not for the entire samples. Naturally, only very few of the non-voters report any such activities. The Norwegian percentage for party membership is particularly high: it includes not only those reporting individual membership, but also those who said they were collectively affiliated through their union. Cross-tabulations against other activity indicators showed little difference between these two membership categories: they were therefore grouped together.

Table 1

Norway		United States	
Question	Per cent positive among voters	Question	Per cent positive among voters
Are you a member of any political party?	23	Do you belong to any political club or organization?	4
Were you yourself present at one or more election meetings or political rallies this autumn?	8	Did you go to any political meetings, rallies, dinners, or things like that?	9
(Not asked)		Did you give any money or buy tickets or anything to help the campaign for one	12
Did you yourself take an active part in the election work for any of the parties this autumn?	3	of the parties or candidates? Did you do any other work for one of the parties or candidates?	4

Table 2. *Levels of Organizational Participation in Politics: Men and Women Compared in Norway and the United States*

Percentage of respondents classified as:	Norway			United States		
	Total sample (1 406)	Men (688)	Women (718)	Total sample (1 772)	Men (791)	Women (981)
	%	%	%	%	%	%
'Non-voters'	21	15	26	27	20	33
'Only-voters'	57	55	60	59	64	55
'Organizationally active'	22	30	14	14	16	12
	100	100	100	100	100	100

To simplify the analysis our index of organizational participation assembles in one 'active' category all those who indicated at least one of the activities listed. *Table 2* gives the resulting distribution for the two countries. It will be seen that sizeable proportions of the 'actives' thus defined have reported two or more activities: in Norway, this was the case with 18 per cent of all 'actives', in the United States with as many as 32 per cent. Political activities of these kinds are clearly cumulative:[246] a citizen engaging in one given type of activity is much more likely than other citizens to engage in another type of activity in the sphere of politics.

The table shows that 22 per cent of the Norwegian sample and 14 per cent of the United States sample indicated one such activity beyond voting. The reader is again warned against direct comparisons between such percentages: the categories are clearly relative to each system and to the content of the questions asked in order to identify the 'actives'.

The originally constructed index for the United States data took into account two further categories of political activity: efforts of informal persuasion and visible manifestations of political preference (wearing a campaign button or putting a 'sticker' on one's car). This allowed further differentiation within the group of organizationally passive voters: altogether 20 per cent out of the 59 per cent in the present 'only-voter' category were found to be 'informally active'. This distinction is clearly of great relevance in any analysis of participation, but unfortunately there were no directly comparable questions in the Norwegian survey: our present efforts will therefore have to be concentrated on the comparison of 'organizationally active' and 'non-voters'.

Attention to Politics in the Mass Communication Media
Our second index of activity is different in structure and serves to measure another dimension of participation: the citizen's private efforts to keep abreast of what is happening in local and national politics and to seek information about matters of public concern.

The U. S. index is based on a sequence of four questions in the survey of 1956:

Table 3. Media Attention in the U. S. Sample: 1956

Question	Percentage paying attention to medium
We're interested in this interview in finding out whether people paid much attention to the election this year. Take newspapers for instance – did you read about the campaign in any newspaper?	69
How about radio – did you listen to any speeches or discussions about the campaign on the radio?	45
How about television – did you watch any programmes about the campaign on television?	74
How about magazines – did you read about the campaign in any magazines?	31

A score for the attention paid to the campaign was made up by the simple procedure of counting the number of media in which the campaign was followed: the resulting distribution will be found in *Table 4*.

In the Norwegian survey there was unfortunately no equivalent sequence of questions about the attention given to the campaign in the media, but it was possible to construct an index of similar dimensions by combining the responses to questions about radio listening, newspaper reading and acquaintance with party pamphlets. There were no regular television programmes in Norway in 1957 and there was no point in asking about politics in magazines since these were too unimportant to matter in a cross-sectional survey. The questions were not phrased in the same way as in the United States study and it was difficult to decide on distinctions between those who 'followed the campaign' in the medium and those who simply paid some attention to it. In the case of radio listening, it was decided to include in the 'followed the campaign' category all those who reported that they had listened to one or more of the five election debates staged between the parties before election day: they amounted to 52 per cent of the sample. In the case of newspaper reading, we classified as 'following the campaign' all those who reported that they read the editorials or the campaign news in the newspaper most days of the week: they amounted to 27 per cent of the sample. The party pamphlet item caused the greatest difficulty: 78 per cent of the sample reported that they had received or seen one or more mass distributed items of party literature during the campaign, but the questions asked in this area did not readily allow an analysis of the relative attention paid to this medium of communication. It was decided to classify as 'following the campaign' all those who reported seeing or receiving two or more items, but this procedure can clearly be questioned. In the circumstances, we nevertheless found it worth while to use this index for exploratory purposes. A more reliable scale for 'information-seeking activity' has been developed for the

Table 4. *Levels of Attention to Politics in the Mass Communication Media: Men and Women Compared in Norway and the United States*

Percentage of respondents who report that they follow campaign in:	Norway			United States		
	Total sample (1 406)	Men (688)	Women (718)	Total sample (1 772)	Men (791)	Women (981)
	%	%	%	%	%	%
No media	19	12	26.5	8	6	11
One (N.) or two (U.S.A.)	35	28.5	41	51	48	53
Most (N. two; U.S.A. three)	32	38.5	25.5	28	31	25
All the media inquired into	14	21	7	13	15	11
	100	100	100	100	100	100

Norwegian survey, but the results arrived at differ too much from the United States score to allow comparative analysis within the present framework. We shall therefore confine ourselves to the analysis of group differences on the indexes set beside each other in *Table 5:* the steps in these indexes cannot at all be compared across the countries, but there is a good deal of evidence to show that the indexes produce reliable system-specific measures of the relative attention paid to politics within each electorate.

The Relationships between the two Indexes
The two indexes constructed for the two samples could clearly be expected to be correlated with each other: we should expect the 'organizationally active' citizen to pay more attention to politics in the media than the 'only-voter' and, even more, the non-voter. *Table 5* shows that this is clearly the case. The correlations between the indexes are significant in both countries ($r = 0.18$ for the Norwegian sample, $r = 0.37$ for the United States), but they are far from perfect: we find quite a few 'organizationally active' who pay little attention to the media, and we find substantial proportions of 'only-voters' and 'non-voters' who nevertheless manifest considerable interest in the media. The indexes clearly measure different dimensions of participation: the circumstances and the motives behind a decision to take on an organizational role in politics will differ from those behind decisions about the consumption of mass-directed information. We shall therefore take both the indexes into account in our analysis and pay particular attention to the patterns of differences between groups in the electorates in their scores on the two indexes.

The correlation between the two indexes is lower in Norway than in the United States. This clearly reflects the lower level of urbanization in Norway: the smaller local units and the strong working class organizations make it possible to take on active organizational roles without depending to the same extent as in the United States on the urban system of mass

Table 5. *Relationships between Indexes for Organizational Participation and Attention to Politics in the Media*

Organizational participation	Norway					United States				
	No. of persons	Mass media				No. of persons	Mass media			
		None	One	Two	All		None	One or Two	Three	All
		%	%	%	%		%	%	%	%
'Non-voters'	295	26	42	24	8	481	19	61	16	4
'Only-voters'	804	19	36	32	13	1.044	5	49	31	15
'Organizationally active'	307	13	27	39	21	247		36	40	24

communications. We shall see in our further analysis how this difference comes out again and again in the parallel tabulations for the two indexes.

Differences between Communities

Our two countries differ markedly in the extent of the geographical concentration of the population: Norway is much less urbanized than the United States, whether this be measured in terms of the officially designated local units or in terms of ecological clusters of a given minimum size.

How will this difference be reflected in the levels of political activity within the two systems?

We know from a variety of analyses of electoral statistics that turn-out will regularly be higher in urban areas than in sparsely populated rural districts: this clearly reflects the easier access to the polling stations in the cities and the greater opportunities for exerting pressure through social communication in densely populated areas.[247] On the other hand, we have reason to expect a higher level of active participation in the rural areas than in the cities simply because the smaller units of local government will allow a higher proportion of formal political roles than the larger units. In the Norwegian setting this is clearly a factor of some importance: if we consider the ratio of representatives or alternates on the communal councils to the total electorate, we find for 1955 that there were 22 such openings for direct political participation per 1,000 electorate in the rural areas as against 6 in the cities; if we take into account the local party contests for such openings and consider the number of candidates on the lists at communal elections, we find that there were as many as 37 of these per 1,000 electorate in the rural areas as against 14 in the cities. It is technically very difficult to establish comparable ratios for the United States: there is much less uniformity in the organization of local government and a great deal of overlap in the territorial units. The Bureau of the Census counted 3,000 counties, 17,000 municipalities and 17,000 townships or towns in 1957 and estimated that there was an average of 21 elected officials per county as against about 7 for each municipality and 6 for each township or town. The total number of elected officials within these three categories of local units was 290,000 or about 3 per 1,000 electorate. [248] The difference between Norway and the United States on this score not only reflects the contrast in the degree of urbanization; local government is clearly much more party-dominated and much less managerial in Norway than in the United States. This would best be brought out by tables for the extent of competition for local offices in the two countries, but no nation-wide figures for the numbers of candidates at local elections are at hand for the United States.

Table 6 shows some of the effects of these differences in the conditions for political activity in communities of different size and complexity. In the Norwegian survey it was clearly necessary to cut across the adminis-

Table 6. *Organizational Participation and Media Attention: Differences between Men and Women by Community of Residence*

Norway

Sex	No. of persons	Non-voters %	Actives1 %	Mass media None %	Mass media Most or all1 %
Four largest cities					
M.	180	13	22	8	67
W.	184	16	20	18	34
Other cities and large communes					
M.	98	15	32	12	62
W.	123	24	14	31	36
Rural communes, 40 + per cent in industry					
M.	88	15	30	11	63
W.	107	26	14	34	34
Rural communes, 20–40 per cent in industry					
M.	215	18	35	14	55
W.	192	30	13	27	38
Rural communes, less than 20 per cent in industry					
M.	107	14	34	13	53
W.	112	38	6	28	26

United States

Sex	No. of persons	Non-voters %	Actives1 %	Mass media None %	Mass media Most or all1 %
Metropolitan areas					
M.	189	20	17	6	45
W.	250	30	14	10	34
Other cities					
M.	192	19	20	6	52
W.	238	25	14	11	43
Towns					
M.	171	22	15	4	45
W.	196	34	11	10	41
Rural areas					
M.	239	21	13	7	43
W.	269	39	11	10	32

1 Percentages for each index do not add up to 100 because middle categories have been left out.

trative classifications of localities to establish a sociologically meaningful stratification. The officially 'rural' communes were grouped with the cities when they had more than 12,000 inhabitants and the smaller ones were stratified by the percentage of the population deriving their livelihood from industrial occupations: this classification is closely correlated with the concentration of the population and is highly relevant in analyses of the distributions of the vote. In the United States survey, the classification into 'metropolitan areas', 'cities', 'towns' and 'rural areas' is standard and requires no comment here.

The table shows variations in turn-out very similar to those regularly found in official statistics: highest in the cities and, in Norway, in the larger and industrialized rural communes, lowest in the sparsely populated agricultural and other primary economy areas. It is of particular interest to see that the pattern of differences between men and women is much the same in the two countries: largest in the least industrialized communities (Norway: 14 versus 35 per cent; United States: 21 versus 39 per cent), smaller in the cities (Norway: 13 versus 16 per cent; United States: 19 versus 25 per cent). This fits in with a variety of findings on the impact of urbanization on the roles of women in the wider society outside the household.[249]

The findings for organizational participation go very much in the same direction in Norway but are not so easy to interpret for the United States. In the Norwegian sample we find very little difference between the strata in the total proportion of 'actives' in the electorate, but a dramatic change in the recruitment of 'actives' from the two sexes as we move from the primary economy communes to the cities: at the lowest level of urbanization 34 per cent 'active' men as against 6 per cent women, in the largest cities 22 against 20 per cent. This corresponds closely to the official breakdowns for the elected representatives to local government: in the least industrialized communes only 3.6 per cent of the representatives were women, in the suburban communes 9.8 and in the cities 13.8.[250] These figures clearly reflect differences in the patterns of role relationships in the household: in the primary economy the male head is typically given responsibility for all dealings with the community at large while the women are discouraged from any such activities partly because of the heavy burden of household chores, partly because of the pressure of cultural norms; in the urbanized communities there is much more sharing of responsibility and greater opportunities for women to take part in activities outside the household.

The table for the United States sample indicates some increase in participation with increasing urbanization for both sexes: the gap in the proportion of 'actives' does not tend to disappear with increasing urbanization as it clearly does in Norway but remains roughly the same whatever the size of the community.

The average attention to politics in the mass media also tends to increase as we move from sparsely populated to urban communities. In Norway, this difference comes out clearest for the men, less consistently so for the women. In the United States sample, the metropolitan areas again score lower than the other urban areas: this reflects the higher proportions of culturally separate ethnic minorities of low average educational standing in the largest cities.

Differences between Lower and Higher Educational and Occupational Strata

With the contrast in the degree of urbanization goes a marked difference in the socio-economic structure of the two electorates: Norway lags far behind the United States in economic growth, has a larger proportion of its labour force in the primary economy as farmers, forest workers and fishermen, and has a smaller proportion in the tertiary sector of its economy as salaried employees in 'white collar' occupations.

With this difference in socio-economic structure goes a clear contrast in the character of the cleavages between the political parties: the Norwegian parties correspond much more closely than the United States ones to the major economic divisions in the population and fit much more definitely in with the dominant interest organizations. The Norwegian parties all have their distinctive electoral clientèle: each body of party supporters differs pronouncedly from the total electorate in socio-economic structure, in organizational affiliations.[251] In the United States the two contending political parties are both near the 50 per cent mark: they are highly heterogeneous in the composition of their clientèle and they appeal for support from all major sectors of the electorate.[252]

How would we expect these differences in socio-economic structure and party divisions to be reflected in the levels of political activity within the two systems?

This question gets us into the heart of the problem of identifying the major channels of recruitment to the ranks of the politically active in a system.

It is analytically convenient to distinguish four such channels: (a) the learning of politics in the family; (b) the development of skills for public life through formal education; (c) the strengthening of political commitments through roles in occupational life and through the growth of loyalties in one's economic career; (d) the encouragement of political activity through membership in economic, social and cultural organizations and associations.

Our survey interviews did not seek to trace the entire political life history of each citizen: we can only attempt assessments of the importance of these channels through rough classifications by background factors.

In the Norwegian survey we asked questions about the political activities of the parents and found a distinct relationship between the level of activity in the family of origin and the current participation of the offspring: the 12 per cent who said their fathers had been 'very active' were found to be about twice as likely as the others to be 'organizationally active' themselves. A tabulation from the Survey Research Center study of the 1958 congressional election indicates a similar relationship.

The present analysis will focus on the differences between Norway and the United States in the recruitment of 'actives' through formal education and through higher-status positions in occupational life.

Our hypothesis is that formal education and occupational position will make less of a difference in the level of political activity in a class-distinct party system such as the Norwegian and more of a difference in a system of two socially and economically highly heterogeneous parties such as the American.

In general terms, we might say that we shall seek to use the contrast between the two countries to test a set of hypotheses about the effects of the status distinctiveness of the parties in a system on the recruitment of active participants from the strata of the less educated and of the holders of lower occupational statuses: (a) the greater the distinctiveness of the electorates of each party in the system, the better the opportunities and the stronger the net incentives for active participation within the lower strata; (b) the greater the status heterogeneity of the electorates of the major parties in the system, the greater the importance of formal education and occupational status in the recruitment of active participants in politics.

In the Norwegian setting, workers and farmers get activated for politics through strong economic organizations dominating distinctive parties of their own: the trade unions in the Labour Party and the farmers' associations in the Agrarian Party. Family traditions certainly count in the recruitment of 'actives' among workers and farmers, but the decisive influences are organizational: the unions and the economic associations create incentives for active participation in party politics and open up opportunities for promotion to positions of trust in the party organizations. What counts in the recruitment of militants and leaders in these parties is the learning process in the economic organizations: formal education may of course be a prerequisite for positions in the central party bureaucracies and probably increasingly so as the organization grows in complexity, but education counts very little in the recruitment of local party workers.

In the United States, the workers and the farmers have large and efficient organizations but none of them has achieved any position of dominance in any of the national parties. The trade union leadership has strong influence on the Democratic Party organizations in several states, but there are few open channels of recruitment from the unions to the party. The farmers' organizations have established themselves in a strategic bar-

Table 7. *Organizational Participation and Media Attention: Differences between Men and Women by Level of Education*

Norway

Sex	No. of persons	Non-voters %	Actives[1] %	Mass media None %	Mass media Most or all[1] %
Primary education only					
M.	300	27	28	17	49
W.	399	30	10	31	28
Primary plus vocational					
M.	245	18	33	9	68
W.	165	24	18	22	38
Christian Youth or Folk High School					
M.	43	9	44	14	68
W.	59	27	19	15	32
Secondary					
M.	50	2	22	2	66
W.	72	17	25	21	34
Gymnasium, university					
M.	50	8	26	8	76
W.	23	13	9	17	39

United States

Sex	No. of persons	Non-voters %	Actives[1] %	Mass media None %	Mass media Most or all[1] %
Grade school					
M.	253	30	10	11	31
W.	290	48	7	20	20
High school					
M.	357	19	16	4	45
W.	533	30	11	8	36
College					
M.	178	9	25	2	69
W.	153	12	27	1	68

[1] Percentages for each index do not add up to 100 because middle categories have been left out.

Table 8. Organizational Participation and Media Attention: by Sex and Occupation

Norway

Occupation of head	No. of persons	Non-voters %	Actives¹ %	Mass media None %	Mass media Most or all¹ %
Manual worker	630	21	22	21	44
M.	315	16	34	15	57
W. Act.	65	42	15	34	23
W. Dep.	250	22	10	25	32
Salaried employee	269	15	24	16	55
M.	127	11	25	7	71
W. Act.	44	18	18	39	32
W. Dep.	98	16	24	16	44
Smallholder, fisherman	116	35	16	18	40
M.	53	28	21	9	58
W.	63	40	11	25	24
Farmer	140	19	27	19	46
M.	60	8	43	8	58
W.	80	26	15	28	37
Other self-employed	108	15	25	13	47
M.	61	8	30	8	59
W.	47	23	19	19	32
Pensioner, retired	137	29	15	24	41
M.	70	22	21	14	53
W.	67	36	7	34	28

United States

Occupation of head	No. of persons	Non-voters %	Actives¹ %	Mass media None %	Mass media Most or all¹ %
Manual worker	583	33	11	12	32
M.	270	26	13	8	39
W.	313	39	9	15	26
'White collar'	785	18	21	4	54
M.	359	14	23	3	58
W.	426	22	19	4	52
Farmer	165	28	8	10	37
M.	78	23	12	9	42
W.	87	32	5	10	33
Other	239	28	11	7	40
M.	84	14	12	4	42
W.	185	36	10	9	38

¹ Percentages for each index do not add up to 100 because middle categories have been left out.

gaining position between the two major parties and for this very reason do not tie in with any of them as regular channels for the recruitment of active party workers. The American parties are complex alliances of interest alignments and this very complexity tends to discourage the recruitment of active participants from the strata of the less educated and the lower status-holders.

Tables 7, 8 and 9 present evidence for the differences in the conditions for the recruitment of active participants in the two systems: the first table divides the cross-sectional samples according to the level of formal education, the second according to major categories of occupation and the third according to the party preferred or identified with.

Electoral Turn-out

Tables 7 and 8 show very similar trends in the variations in the proportions of non-voters in the two countries. Electoral turn-out is regularly lowest among citizens with little education beyond the primary level, among manual workers, fishermen and smallholders; it is regularly higher among citizens with higher education, among salaried employees, managers and businessmen.

These survey findings accord very well with regularities found in analyses of official voting registers in a number of countries. (Tingsten, 1937: Ch. 2; Lane, 1959: Ch. 16)

Organizational Activity

Table 7 shows a definite contrast between Norway and the United States in the educational bases for the recruitment of the 'organizationally active'. In the Norwegian sample there is no regular increase in the proportions of 'actives' from one educational level to another. The peak proportions are reached among citizens trained in various vocational courses after the completion of primary school and among citizens moulded by the Folk High Schools and the Christian Youth Schools. Both these groups are made up of citizens who could not continue their formal education beyond the primary school but showed sufficient personal interest in further education to enter such courses and schools. A substantial proportion of the active members of the Labour Party have vocational training of some sort beyond the primary school. The Folk High School Movement and the network of Christian Youth Schools have had a very telling impact on the recruitment of community leaders in the rural areas: they make up important elements in the core groups of the Liberal Party, the Christian People's Party and the Agrarian Party. What is perhaps most interesting in the table for the Norwegian data, however, is the lower proportion of participants among the citizens with higher formal education: this seems to reflect the current trends toward increasing political 'disengagement' within the professional elite.[253]

We may compare with this complex recruitment pattern in Norway, the very straightforward progression in the United States data: for these, the table shows substantial and consistent increases in the proportions of 'actives' from one educational level to the next.

The same contrast appears in *Table 8:* in Norway we find the highest proportions of actives among the male farmers and workers and lower proportions within the middle-class groups: in the United States the trend is the other way, 'white collar' citizens highest in participation, manual workers and farmers lowest.

There are important differences, however, between men and women and between economically active and economically dependent women: these are of sufficient theoretical interest to warrant detailed analysis in a separate section.

Media Attention

There is no similar contrast in the findings for the other index: for the attention to politics in the mass media.

The findings for the Norwegian sample run very much along the same lines as for the United States data: the higher the level of education and the higher the occupational status the greater the average number of media attended to.

There is a clear contrast between the findings for the two indexes of activity in the Norwegian data: the lower strata have a higher proportion of organizationally active but a lower proportion of alert media consumers while the higher strata have a lower proportion of active party supporters and a higher proportion of passive information gatherers.

Data from a variety of sources offer evidence of the limited influence of the mass media on the political motivations of working class citizens: they may be exposed to a continuous flow of stimuli from mass media such as newspapers, magazines, radio and television but the messages they expose themselves to are of little political relevance to them. We know from a study of the readership of the political press in Norway (Chapter 13 below) that about two-thirds of the Labour Party voters read newspapers opposed to or indifferent to their party. Their political loyalty is developed and maintained in the face-to-face environments of the kin group, the workplace and the secondary organizations and is seldom decisively influenced by the mass-directed messages in the press: the organizationally active among them pay more attention to the politics in the newspapers but they are at the same time much more likely to read their own party press. In the middle-class groups, among salaried employees and businessmen, there are clearly much larger proportions of 'political spectators': citizens who follow the media closely for information about current politics and yet are not strongly enough induced to take on active roles in party organizations.

Differences between Men and Women in the Lower and in the Higher Strata

Our analysis of the differences in the levels of political activity in communities of different size and complexity indicated a striking similarity between the two countries in the distributions for the two sexes: the differences between men and women in the proportions of actives tended to even out with increasing urbanization. In Norway, this was found to be the case both for differences in turn-out and for differences in organizational activity. In the United States the trend was found to be the same for turn-out but not for organizational activity.

If we look at *Table 7 and 8* we find evidence of similar trends of narrowing differences in comparisons for educational level and occupational status: the difference between the sexes tends to be largest in the lower strata and tends to disappear in the higher strata. The trends are on the whole similar in the two countries but the data do not coincide completely.

Electoral Turn-out

In Norway, the gap in the proportions of non-voters tends to disappear with higher education and higher occupational status but the trend is not uniform: it is clearly different in communities at different levels of urbanization. The difference in proportions is definitely the most marked among smallholders and fishermen (28 versus 40 per cent) and among farmers (8 versus 26 per cent). It is considerably higher among workers than among salaried employees but this is largely due to the very low turn-out level among women who earn their own living as manual workers: among these are classified domestic workers and these have in a variety of statistics proved to have low turn-out proportions.

In the United States the trend is a marked one by education, but barely significant by occupational level: the 'white collar' category is clearly too heterogeneous for the purposes of this analysis. (Campbell, 1960: Ch. 17).

Organizational Activity

In the Norwegian data, the differences between men and women in the proportions of organizationally active follow much the same trends as for turn-out: the difference is largest in the rural occupations and among the workers, smallest within the higher urban occupations. We find this reflected in the composition of the active cores of the voters for the different parties: this is shown in *Table 9*. The active cores of supporters are predominantly male in the parties with strongholds in the rural districts and in the parties of the working class. In the Conservative Party, on the other hand, we find a completely even distribution between the sexes: this is predominantly a party of the urban middle class of business and professional families and salaried employees and in these strata there is a pronounced trend toward equal participation from men and women.

Table 9. *Organizational Participation and Media Attention: Differences between Men and Women by Party*

| | Norway | | | | | | United States | | | | |
| | | | | Mass media | | | | | | Mass media | |
Intended to vote for	No. of persons	Non-voters (final classif.) %	Actives[1] %	None %	Most or all[1] %	Party identification	No. of persons	Non-voters %	Actives[1] %	None %	Most or all[1] %
Communists	17	(12)	(24)	(6)	(59)						
Labour	573	7	28	18	48	Democratic	770	27	15	8	40
M.	310	4	38	12	60	M.	358	21	19	4	44
W.	263	11	14	25	34	W.	412	32	11	11	37
Liberals	82	1	20	13	61						
M.	42		26	7	67						
W.	40	3	15	20	55						
Christians	97	12	33	22	39	Independent	414	26	10	7	39
M.	42	14	40	10	57	M.	213	21	10	6	46
W.	55	11	27	31	26	W.	201	31	11	8	33
Agrarians	97	12	32	22	48						
M.	45	7	51	11	69						
W.	52	17	15	31	31						
Conservatives[2]	202	9	24	17	46	Republican	514	20	18	7	48
M.	103	9	23	16	54	M.	200	14	20	6	53
W.	99	10	25	19	37	W.	314	25	17	7	45
Uncertain, refuse to say	132	13	11	15	55						
Not decided to vote: first wave	188	100		29	28						

[1] Percentages for each index do not add up to 100 because middle categories have been left out.
[2] Includes voters for joint non-socialist lists.

Table 10. *Organizational Participation and Media Attention: Differences between Men and Women by Educational Level within Major Party Groupings*

Norway

Level of education	No. of persons	Actives¹ %	Mass media None %	Mass media Most or all¹ %
Intended to vote Socialist				
Primary only	357	25	21	41
M.	172	36	14	53
W.	185	15	28	30
Further education	233	33	12	59
M.	151	40	10	68
W.	82	12	16	44
Non-socialist				
Primary only	166	14	27	38
M.	69	21	23	42
W.	97	8	30	36
Further education	312	34	14	52
M.	163	36	7	68
W.	149	31	21	37

United States

Level of education	No. of persons	Non-voters %	Actives¹ %	Mass media None %	Mass media Most or all¹ %
Identification: Democrat					
Grade school	229	39	11	14	26
M.	119	32	13	8	31
W.	110	47	9	20	22
High school	415	23	15	7	40
M.	172	17	20	3	44
W.	243	28	11	10	36
College	122	15	19		69
M.	64	11	25		79
W.	58	19	12		69
Republican					
Grade school	166	30	9	13	31
M.	71	23	8	11	38
W.	95	36	9	15	25
High school	220	20	14	5	47
M.	73	11	19	4	52
W.	147	14	12	6	44
College	125	7	36	1	72
M.	56	5	34	2	73
W.	69	9	37		71

¹ Percentages for each index do not add up to 100 because some categories have been left out.

In the United States data, the trends for organizational activity are not very easy to interpret in the direct tabulations. Our further analysis will show that a clear trend emerges in the sex differences as soon as we classify by education or by occupation within party identification groups: *Tables 9 and 10* indicate that the difference between men and women in the proportion of actives tends to disappear within the higher strata of the Republican identifiers. This finding is of considerable theoretical importance: it will be dealt with in a wider context in a subsequent section.

Media Attention

In the Norwegian sample the differences between men and women in the proportions following politics in the media are marked at all levels of education and in all the occupational groups: there is no trend toward a narrowing of the gap in the proportions.

In the United States sample, on the contrary, there is again a clear trend in this direction: there are practically as many women as men following politics in several media in the higher socio-economic strata.

The Recruitment of Active Participants within the Major Party Groupings

We have found evidence of marked differences between our two countries in the recruitment of active participants in politics from the lower and from the higher socio-economic strata and we have formulated a set of general hypotheses about the conditions making for such differences: these hypotheses focused on the degree of class distinctiveness of the party systems and the consequent differences in the character of the alternatives facing citizens af similar socio-economic levels in systems differing in the average class distinctiveness of their parties.

We have so far formulated these hypotheses for comparisons between the entire samples of the electorates and in fact stayed at this level in our discussion of the evidence: *Tables 7 and 8* give the variations on our indexes within the entire samples by sex and education and sex and occupation.

Our analysis so far has offered some evidence that the hypotheses hold at this over-all system level but also underscored the need for detailed breakdowns by the major party preference alignments within each system.

At this level it is possible to specify our initial hypotheses in terms of comparisons, not between systems, but between parties: (a) the more a party is dominated by lower-stratum economic organizations the less the importance of formal education and occupational position in the recruitment of active participants among its voters; (b) the less a party is dominated by lower-stratum economic organizations the greater the importance of formal education and occupational position in the recruitment of actives among its voters.

It was technically impossible, as a means of testing these hypotheses on

Table 11. Organizational Participation and Media Attention: Differences between Men and Women by Occupational Level within Major Party Groupings

Norway

Occupation of head	No. of persons	Actives[1] %	Mass media None %	Mass media Most or all[1] %
Intended to vote Socialist				
Manual worker[2]	363	30	17	49
M.	194	43	13	61
W.	169	16	22	36
Salaried, self-employed[2]	105	20	16	49
M.	56	25	7	63
W.	49	14	27	32
Non-socialist				
Manual[2]	98	21	23	43
M.	44	27	20	53
W.	54	17	20	36
Salaried, self-employed[2]	214	30	14	53
M.	110	32	9	63
W.	104	28	18	43

United States

Occupation of head	No. of persons	Non-voters %	Actives[1] %	Mass media None %	Mass media Most or all[1] %
Identification: Democrat					
Manual worker	358	29	14	11	32
M.	170	28	18	6	32
W.	188	31	11	16	25
'White collar'	232	19	19	3	54
M.	106	11	25	2	50
W.	126	25	14	3	52
Republican					
Manual	197	29	10	10	39
M.	84	19	9	6	42
W.	113	37	10	13	37
'White collar'	186	10	30	3	61
M.	74	12	31	3	66
W.	112	14	29	3	57

[1] Percentages for each index do not add up to 100 because some categories are left out.
[2] Outside agriculture and fisheries.

the data for Norway and the United States, to compare each of the six parties in the one country with the two in the other: the size of the Norwegian sample would have had to be several times larger for that to be possible. Instead we found it justifiable to divide the Norwegian parties into Socialist and non-socialist and to compare the intended voters for these two party groups with the potential voters for the Democratic and the Republican parties.

The non-socialist voter group established in the Norwegian sample is highly heterogeneous. It can be readily seen from *Table 9* that the four parties grouped together in this way differ considerably in the proportions of active participants and, what is very important in the analysis, quite particularly in the sex composition of these nuclei of supporters: the two older parties, the Liberals and the Conservatives, have a relatively low ratio of activists to voters while the newer 'interest group parties', the Christians and the Agrarians, have higher proportions of actives: these parties are the political expression of important networks of associations and recruit their actives directly through such organizational channels. In this they resemble the 'lower stratum' Socialist parties: formal education is not a very important factor in the recruitment of actives in these parties. The Agrarian Party also comes close to the Socialist parties in the sex composition of its active core: half of the men intending to vote for the party reported organizational activities as against only 15 per cent of the women. We nevertheless decided to contrast Socialist and non-socialist voters in a first approximation to a test of our hypotheses: we have since endeavoured to guard ourselves against over-interpretation by checking our findings against alternative procedures of tabulations. *Table 10* divides each voter group according to the level of education and includes all the intended voters, while *Table 11*, dividing according to occupational status, excludes all citizens in the primary economy: this should make for a purer test of our hypotheses since the status contrast comes out so much more clearly outside agriculture, forestry and fisheries.

Theoretically, the party dichotomies in the two national samples give us six possibilities of paired comparisons, but only three of these are of direct relevance in the testing of the hypotheses: (a) Socialist voters versus non-socialist voters in Norway; (b) Democrats versus Republican identifiers in the United States; (c) Socialists in Norway versus Democrats in the United States.

Comparisons (a) and (b) simply serve to test the two hypotheses by replication in two different systems. In both cases the contrast is in terms of the relative dominance of lower-stratum organizations within the parties: the expectation is that the status differentials will be more marked the stronger the predominance of middle-class organizations in the parties.

This is borne out quite clearly by *Tables 10 and 11*.

For education we find in Norway a 25–33 per cent differential among the Socialist voters, but 14–34 per cent among the non-socialist: this compares to a 11–19 per cent differential for the Democrats against a 9–36 per cent differential for the Republicans.

For occupation we find for the Socialists in Norway a higher proportion of actives among workers than among middle-class voters and a difference in the opposite direction for the non-socialist voters: this compares to a 14–19 per cent differential for the Democrats as against a marked 10–30 per cent differential for the Republicans.

Comparison (c) cuts across the systems and serves to test the hypotheses for different degrees of lower-stratum dominance within the parties: very strong in the case of the Socialist parties in Norway, only moderate in the case of the Democratic Party in the United States. Our expectation would be that the status differentials would be even less marked among the Socialists than among the Democrats.

This is again borne out by the tables, not very clearly for education but remarkably clearly for occupation: among the Socialists there is actually a higher proportion of actives among the workers than among the middle-class voters, while among the Democrats there is a tendency in the opposite direction.

Perhaps the most interesting feature of these tables is the contrast they show in the status differentials for the women: in the lower-stratum parties status makes very little difference in the proportions of organizationally active among the women while in the middle-class parties the status differentials for women tend to be more marked than for men.

We have already seen from *Tables 7 and 8* that the differences between men and women in the proportions of actives tend to disappear in the higher status groups and we find this reflected again in the figures for the proportions within party groups in *Table 9:* in the typical middle-class parties, the Conservatives in Norway and the Republicans in the United States, the differences between men and women in the proportions of actives are clearly smaller than in the 'lower-stratum' parties. *Tables 10 and 11* make it possible for us to clarify these findings further.

The tables show very clearly that it is only in the non-socialist and Republican parties that the higher-status women reach near-equality with the men in the proportions of actives: in the Socialist and the Democratic parties women at a higher educational or occupational level still differ markedly from men at the same level in the proportions of actives.

Women are definitely more 'status sensitive' than men in their political orientations: higher education and higher economic status is only likely to make a significant difference in their motivation for participation in parties dominated by middle-class voters, in the 'parties of respectability'. A variety of experiences and environmental forces may make them feel at home in and vote for 'lower-stratum' parties but their organizational participation in such parties will stay relatively low whatever their level of education or their economic status. Within the middle-class parties, on the other hand, women at the higher levels of education and economic position are markedly more likely to approach positions of leadership; the lower status women voting for such parties definitely do not feel stimulated to participate actively themselves.

What we have said so far only applies to variations in organizational activity as measured by our simple indexes. There is little evidence of corresponding patterns of differences in the index for attention paid to politics in the mass media: the major factors influencing variations in this dimension tend to be sex, education and the size of the community, not to any extent the party preferred or identified with. These variations need to be analyzed in further detail: we cannot do this here but hope to find an opportunity to present such an analysis in another context.

The Need for Further Comparative Analysis

Tingsten's classical comparisons of official turn-out statistics focused on the few conditioning factors covered in such records: sex, age, marital status, occupation, income, the size and character of the local community. (Tingsten, 1937).

In this two-country comparison we have concentrated on a new source of data, sample surveys, and broadened our analysis to cover further dimensions of political participation: we have not only been concerned with variations in turn-out in elections, but even more with variations in organizational activity and in information seeking.

We have broadened the range of dependent variables, but in this first set of analyses we have not gone much beyond Tingsten in our coverage of independent, explanatory variables: we have dealt with similarly crude indicators of the citizen's environment and his role and place in this environment.

Tingsten could not have gone much further than he did because of the scantiness of the information about citizens on the electoral rolls and because of the limitations of ecological analysis procedures.[254] Using sample surveys as a source of data we can go much further: not only in our coverage of different dimensions of participation but even more in our analysis of the factors making for differences in the extent and character of political activity. In this article we have only made a first step toward the systematic use of sample surveys in cross-system comparisons: we have only considered the best-documented structural factors within each electorate and have not touched on data on the wider ranges of social influences impinging on the citizen and on his or her motivation or orientation to issues in the given political community.

We have already at hand a set of data which could help us to gain greater insight into the processes behind the distributions we have found:

1. We have more detailed data about the life career and the current situation of each respondent.
2. We have some data on other types of community activities, memberships in social organizations, offices held. (cf. Valen, 1964: Chs. 9–10).
3. We have various data, not always easy to compare, on attitudes to politics, feelings about political conflicts, sense of efficacy in community affairs.
4. We have a considerable amount of data on the character of the respondents' opinions about political issues, their orientations to policy differences, their images of the contending forces.[255]

We hope at some future occasion to present further comparative analyses of these and related data. In this chapter we have only wanted to illustrate some of the opportunities opened up by the accumulation of sample survey data for countries of different political structures. Any such venture will encounter grave difficulties of comparability and standardization, but the very necessity to grapple with such problems of equivalence is bound to increase our insight into the peculiarities of the institutional solutions found in our separate systems.

Perhaps the most important problem in further work with sample survey data in the comparative study of politics is this: How can we single out crucial differences between systems in the way they set the alternatives for their citizens and how can we order such 'system variables' in accounting for differing processes of individual decision-making?

This is the problem of the design of 'macro-micro' comparisons. Most cross-national analyses of survey data have so far dealt exclusively with 'micro-micro' comparisons: the exploration of similarities between countries in the relationships between individual characteristics and individual reactions. (cf. Chapters 1 and 8 above).

The majority of the findings reported in our article are based on 'micro-micro' comparisons. We find in both countries that the following considerations make a great deal of difference to a citizen's turn-out at election and his attention to politics in the mass media: (a) what his or her role is in the household; (b) whether he or she lives in an urbanized or a sparsely populated area; (c) whether he or she has had any education beyond the elementary school; and (d) whether he or she or the head of the household has a lower-status or a higher-status occupation.

Tingsten demonstrated the consistency of these sorts of relationship with respect to turnout; we have shown that they also hold for attention to politics in two otherwise very different political systems.

What changed the nature of our analysis was our finding that these basic relationships did not hold for organizational activities in the case of Norway: the proportion of actives in the electorate did not appear to be higher in the urbanized areas, among the better educated, and among citizens in higher-status occupations.

We interpreted this to reflect important contrasts in the institutional settings for citizen decisions about politics in our two countries. We thus become concerned with 'macro' comparisons.

In discussing the finding concerning the effect of urbanization we pointed to the organization of local government as a potentially important 'system' variable: the greater number of structurally given openings for participation in the rural communes of Norway might account for the high level of participation in these areas.

Our principal concern, however, was with the findings concerning the impact of education and occupational status on political participation. Why was there such a difference between Norway and the United States? We ventured to interpret the difference to reflect a major contrast between the two régimes in the character of their party systems: in the one case a highly class-distinct, 'status-polarized' party system, in the other much less correspondence between socio-economic cleavage and political conflict. In the highly polarized setting, citizens of little formal education and in lower-status occupations would be under a minimum of cross-pressure and would feel much less discouraged from taking on active roles in the political organizations to which they would give their vote. In a less class-distinct party system, on the other hand, citizens of lower status would be under conflicting pressures and be more likely to be discouraged from active participation in any of the political organizations open to them.

We do not rule out other interpretations of the difference we found between the two countries but we feel convinced that 'macro-micro' comparisons of this kind will prove to be of major importance in the development of systematic theorizing about the processes of politics. Our hypotheses will clearly have to be tried out for more countries; we have, after all, only studied the effects of status polarization at two different points of a conjectured continuum. Such comparisons would not just serve the interests of academic research: they would be of direct relevance in practical discussions of trends in pluralist democracies. The focus of such analysis would be on changes in the reactions of the working-class electorates in the on-going processes of increasing national integration. With continued economic growth, the conflict lines in national political systems tend increasingly to cut across each other, rather than to coincide; as Simmel intimated, such 'criss-crossing' of the lines of cleavages tends to strengthen and stabilize the total structure, to integrate the systems.[256] The problem for empirical research is this: how far can this process of integration go on before it brings about a dangerously high level of apathy and even alienation among the masses of the less educated in lower-status positions? Political theorists have speculated extensively about this process and its implications,[257] but we need much more extensive comparative research on systems at different levels of polarization to reach any understanding of the forces at work.

NOTES

[236] For the 1920 to 1956 elections, see United States Bureau of Census, *Statistical Abstracts of the United States, 1952*, Washington, D.C., United States Government Printing Office, 1957, Table 425.

[237] This estimate was made for the 1954 election: (Goldman, 1956: pp. 6–9, 46).

[238] The best analysis of these data is in (Key, 1956: Chs. 23–30). The problems of legal and factual exclusions from the vote in the South is dealt with in detail in the *Report of the U.S. Commission on Civil Rights*, Washington, D.C., United States Government Printing Office, 1959: the commission estimates that only 25 per cent of the Negroes of voting age are registered on the electoral rolls in the South, as against 60 per cent of the whites.

[239] For the three presidential elections from 1948 to 1956 the average 'raw' participation was 32.6 per cent for the 11 Southern states as against 65.5 per cent for the other states in the Union.

[240] The Communist Party membership has been estimated at around 6,000; the Labour Party recorded 163,000 (of which some 93,000 affiliated via local trade unions); the Liberals indicated 28,000 members, the Christians 30,000 (approximate figure), the Agrarians 64,000 and the Conservatives 96,000. For a detailed evaluation of these statistics, see Chapter 6 above.

[241] Woodward and Roper found as many as 11 per cent of their sample reporting activity over the 'last four years' (1944–48); see (Woodward, 1950). Some of the 11 per cent might not have been equally active in all the elections covered, cf. (Lane, 1959: p. 54).

[242] For a general presentation of this sample survey, see (Rokkan, 1960:5) Details of the sampling procedures are given in (Rokkan, 1960:4).

[243] In some cases it has been possible to provide evidence of such differences by checking the voting records for all the persons selected for interviewing. In the meticulously conducted survey of the Swedish electorate in 1957, it was found that 53 per cent of those not interviewed in the sample of names drawn were non-voters according to the voting registers: see (Särlvik, 1959: p. 23).

[244] This was done in the nation-wide surveys carried out in Sweden in 1956 and in 1957: see (Westerståhl, 1957; Särlvik, 1959).

[245] A tentative analysis of the factors making for higher turn-out estimates from sample surveys in the United States is given in (Campbell, 1960: Ch. 5). The 12 per cent difference found in 1956 is allocated as follows: non-coverage of total civilian population of voting age (sample only covers the dwelling unit population, not those in institutions), 6 per cent; voted, but ballot invalidated, 2 per cent; higher voting rate for those interviewed than for those refusing or not at home, 1 per cent; unexplained, but probably mostly over-reporting, 3 per cent.

[246] This characteristic of community activities is discussed in some detail by Erik Allardt (Allardt, 1958).

[247] For a detailed analysis of 'centre-periphery' differences in turn-out in Norway, see chapter 6 above.

[248] Computed from United States Bureau of the Census, *1957 Census of Governments*, Vol. 1, Part. 4, Washington, D.C., United States Government Printing Office, 1958, p. 3.

[249] For a more detailed analysis of United States data, see (Campbell, 1960: Ch. 17).

[250] Calculated from *Norges offisielle Statistikk*, XI, 252, Kommunevalgene og ordförervalgene, 1955, Oslo, Statistisk Sentralbyrå, 1957.

[251] In the Norwegian 1957 survey, 48 per cent of the heads of all the households interviewed were classified as manual workers: the corresponding proportion for Socialist (Communist and Labour) voters was 70 per cent, for Liberal voters, 30, Christians, 30, Agrarians, 14, and for Conservatives, 21.

252 In the United States presidential election survey in 1956, 44 per cent of the nation-wide sample were classified as belonging to 'blue collar' households: of those who identified with the Democrats there were 47 per cent in this blue collar category and of those identifying with the Republicans, 38 per cent. The deviations from the national average were thus markedly smaller in the United States than in Norway. There is evidence of significant changes in the degree of 'status polarization' of United States politics, see (Converse, 1958; Campbell, 1960: Ch. 13). A detailed analysis of the contrast between Norway and the United States has been undertaken by Angus Campbell and Henry Valen: (Campbell, 1961).

253 V. Aubert, *Norsk Sakförerblad,* 26, 1959, p. 73–82, has analyzed data on publicly-recorded political participation among lawyers in Norway and has found a decrease in the proportions of politically active from 17 per cent in 1932 to 7.5 per cent in 1950.

254 Stein Rokkan and Henry Valen have undertaken a detailed multivariate analysis of factors in turn-out for the entire electorate of the city of Stavanger: the possibilities of analysis were, however, very much limited since the municipal statistical office only had information about each citizen's sex, age, marital status, occupation and place of residence. For details see (Rokkan, 1964:3).

255 The reader will find the United States data analyses in great detail in (Campbell, 1960).

256 Simmel's notions are discussed in (Coser, 1956: Ch. 4). For further developments see: (Parsons, 1959:2 Lipset, 1959; Lipset, 1960).

257 See the discussion in (Berelson, 1954: pp. 314–17) and the counter-arguments in (Lane, 1959: pp. 340–48). For a highly provocative extrapolation from current trends, see (Young, 1958).

THIRTEEN

The Voter, the Reader
and the Party Press

The Norwegian programme of electoral studies has focused on a series of major themes: the political consequences of social-structural change, the structuring of the pluralist channels of participation, the impact of the new media of mass stimulation and mass persuasion. Whatever the theme, the emphasis has throughout the enterprise been on the *joint use of many methodologies,* on the merging of many approaches.

In the study of *functions of the mass media in the political process* this is an absolute imperative: we cannot get anywhere through isolated analyses; we have to work toward the development of a common framework for *studies of institutional structure, analyses of communication content* and *inquiries into the characteristics, the conditions, motivations and reactions of the audience.*

In the present article we shall be concerned with the functions of only *one* of the mass media in Norway: we shall deal with *the press,* its ties with the parties, its readers and the way they behave at elections.

Origin: This chapter reproduces one of the early analyses within the Norwegian programme of electoral research. It was first published in German in the *Kölner Zeitschrift* (Rokkan, 1960: 6) and shortly thereafter in English in *Gazette.* A fuller analysis has for some time been available in a stencilled report in Norwegian: Per Torsvik & Stein Rokkan *Velgeren, leseren og partipressen,* Oslo, Institutt for presseforskning, 1964.

The analysis derives its data from two sources:

First, from the circulation statistics assembled by *Avisenes Informasjonskontor* and supplemented by special inquiries by the Norwegian Press Research Institute.

Secondly, from the nationwide survey carried out before and after the election of representatives to the *Storting* in October, 1957.

Voting Strength vs. Circulation: A Major Contrast

The analysis focuses on one major problem in the study of the political functions of the press in party systems divided along status lines: the contrast between the voting strength of the 'lower-stratum' parties and the dominance of the press of the 'higher stratum' parties in the national readership.

Very little has so far been done to analyze this contrast systematically. Herbert Tingsten has called attention to the problem and has assembled some overall statistics for several countries (Tingsten, 1958). Jörgen Westerståhl and Carl-Gunnar Janson have completed a detailed ecological correlation study on the basis of Swedish circulation statistics and also analyzed the readership of the party newspapers on the basis of several cross-sectional surveys (Westerståhl, 1959). Our Norwegian analysis seeks to provide a basis for comparisons with the Swedish findings and to explore the possibilities of testing similar hypotheses about factors making for contrasts between citizens' preferences at the polls and citizen' choices of newspapers for regular reading.

Table 1 gives a rough picture of the vote-circulation contrasts in the two countries. The contrasts are very marked in both countries. In Sweden the Social Democrats polled 44.6 % of the votes cast in 1956, but their press had only 16.2 % of the total newspaper circulation. In Norway, the Labour party came close to a majority of votes cast in 1957, but its press accounted for less than a quarter of the circulation in the country. In both countries, the older 'bourgeois' parties, the Liberals and the Conservatives, had markedly smaller shares of the votes than of the total press readership. In Sweden, the Liberal party had less than a quarter of the votes but more than half of the circulation. In Norway, no single party press held such a position of dominance, but the total contrast was nevertheless a very marked one: the four non-socialist opposition parties together polled about the same number of votes as the Labour party, but the non-socialist newspapers, whether directly party affiliated or independent, sold more than three times as many copies as the Labour press. These overall figures set the problem for our Norwegian analysis: why such a discrepancy? why do so many citizens vote Labour without reading the party's press and why do so many citizens read non-socialist newspapers and yet fail to vote for any of the non-socialist parties?

Table 1. Voting Strength and Party Press Circulation: Swedish and Norwegian Data

Party:	Comm.	Soc. Dem./ Lab.	Lib.	Chr. (in Norway only)	Agr.	Cons.	Joint non-soc. (Norway)	Other	N
Sweden 1956[1]									
Votes	5.0 %	44.6	23.8		9.4	17.1		0.1	3,902,114
Circulation	0.9 %	16.2	50.8		4.1	23.3		4.1	3,727,300
Norway 1957[2]									
Votes	3.4 %	48.3	9.6	10.2	8.6	16.8	2.9	0.2	1,791,128
Circulation	No info.[3]	23.9 %	23.6	2.4	4.2	30.2	2.4	13.2	1,551,557

Notes: [1] *Source*: (Westerståhl, 1959: Tab. 1, p. 15). The circulation figures are for *dailies* only.
[2] These circulation figures cover 139 newspapers accounted for in *Norsk Aviskatalog*, 12. utg. 1958 plus 33 other units for which information was obtained directly by the Norwegian Press Research Institute. Some 30 minor newspapers are not covered in these statistics.
[3] Neither of the two Communist papers provide data on circulation: an unofficial estimate is 10,000.

A full analysis of this contrast would call for the combination of a variety of research approaches:

an *historical and institutional* study of the growth and organization of the press, the patterns of ownerships and control, the ties between party, owners and editorial staff, the production and marketing procedures;

an analysis of trends and regularities in the *content emphases* for the different categories of newspapers, particularly in the proportion of *attention given to politics* by newspapers differing in party affiliation, size and community coverage;

and finally, an analysis of the *readership* for each party's press, its socio-economic background, its political orientations, its motivations for subscribing and reading, the attention given to the different categories of newspaper content.

Our current analysis focuses on the characteristics of the *readership:* what we can say about the growth and the organization of the Norwegian newspaper industry is not based on original research and what we can say about the political content of the papers is largely based on unsystematic acquaintance and on a minor analysis of the largest papers.

Our analysis focuses on the *Socialist* voters and *the workers* in the electorate: how do the 'party loyal' newspaper readers among them differ from the 'party indifferent'? In the cross-sectional survey carried out during 1957 we found both categories well represented in two groups: of those intending to vote Communist (very few) or Labour we found only 27 % keeping exclusively Socialist papers in their household as against 28 % reading nothing but non-socialist or unaffiliated newspapers; for the working class households the corresponding proportions were 25 % and 44 %. Our task in the analysis is to identify factors which may account for such variations in partisanship and class loyalty in newspaper attention.

A citizen might be 'party indifferent' in his choice of newspapers for a variety of motives:

1) *The local choice situation*
   The party of his preference might not have a paper readily accessible in his community: the choice between a paper exclusively kept for its politics and a paper kept for its services to him as a member of community would then be highly unequal.
2) *The party ties and the political content of the paper.*
   The paper of his choice may be indifferent to his own party but in fact gives very little emphasis to politics and instead devotes the bulk of its space to news and general information of interest to him as a member of the local community.
3) *The personal relevance of the choice.*
   Whatever the content emphasis, the citizen may keep the paper purely as a community service, may not read any of the politics in it, and may

consider the choice of newspaper politically irrelevant since his party preference primarily reflects attitudes and opinions in his immediate face-to-face environment, in his neighbourhood, at his workplace.

We shall first review briefly the evidence on the local choice situations and the tie-ins between parties and newspapers in Norway. We shall then proceed to the core of our analysis and present a set of data from our nation-wide survey on differences between 'party loyal' and 'party indifferent' newspaper readers.

Newspapers in Norway: Number, Circulation, Distribution by Localities
The official newspaper catalogue tells us that there were 173 newspaper units in Norway in 1957 and estimates their total circulation at around 1,600,000.[263] These statistics only cover newspapers in the Newspaper Publishers' Association. There are another 30-odd minor papers outside this Association but these hardly matter in a nationwide analysis. Of the 173 papers, only 82 were dailies: with a few exceptions, the rest were two- and three-a-week papers.

By European standards, none of the papers had a very large circulation. Only five of the papers had more than 50,000 circulation and another 18 had between 15,000 and 50,000.

Norway has a very high number of organizationally separate newspapers in proportion to its population. This is due to geographical barriers and to the low concentration of the population. A great number of local papers grew up during the 19th and early 20th century, frequently two or three papers in each district. The circulation was in most cases very small and the outlook highly parochial. As the communication system improved, a number of these local papers folded up but there is still a sizable core of

Table 2. *The Choice of Newspapers in the Trade Districts: Numbers and Political Affiliation* [1]

No. of papers	No. of districts	No. of households in districts[2]	Socialist (CP or Labour)	Non-soc.	Non-affiliated	Total no. of papers
None	36	141,185				
One	26	117,920	2	10	14	26
Two	32	271,968	16	31	17	64
Three	18	136,049	16	35	3	54
Four or more	7	322,612	9	21	10	40
Totals	119	1,016,734	43	97	44	184

[1] The table covers 173 units classified in *Norsk Aviskatalog* plus 11 others; newspapers appearing only once a week have been excluded.
[2] Computation on the basis of 1950 census data and later increases in total population by district.

26 Citizens

well established community papers in the countryside and the smaller cities.

The larger cities all have several newspapers, but nearly all of them have one dominant paper covering anywhere from 70 % to 95 % of the households in the city and the area around. The dominant papers in Oslo, Bergen, Trondheim and Stavanger reach particularly large areas but none of them are 'national' papers in the sense that they will have any significant circulation outside their own region of the country.

In the majority of the ecological centres the citizen seeking information about events will have direct access to several local newspapers. *Table 2* gives a breakdown of the 119 officially delimited trade districts, by the number of papers published locally. It will be seen that close to half of the districts have more than one newspaper. This means that 75 % of the households in the country will have access to at least two newspapers, edited and issued within their own district. One third of the districts, with 13 % of the households, live in districts without any local newspaper in this sense. Most of these districts, however, are within manageable distances from localities where newspapers are published.

The Parties, their Voters and the Readers of their Press

Districts differ, however, in the *politics* of their dominant press. In some areas the supporter of a particular party will be able to receive a paper speaking for this party through direct distribution. In other areas he can only get a paper of his own party through the mail. In some areas his own paper may be the dominant community paper, serving a number of important social and economical functions in addition to the political ones, in other areas his paper may be a minority one, read almost exclusively for political reasons.

Tables 3 and 4 tell us a great deal about the importance of the *initial conditions of establishment* for the growth of community dominant newspapers. The Conservative and the Liberal papers are the oldest and consequently the most likely to dominate their community. They developed a broad community readership at the time when the Conservatives and the Liberals were the major political protagonists and they generally kept up and expanded their readership even after the newer parties, Labour and the Agrarians, developed a sizeable press of their own. It is clear from the tables that a high proportion of the readers of the Conservative and the Liberal papers no longer vote for these parties: other forces pulled them over politically but they stayed with the papers established in their community.

The regional split in Norwegian politics is very clearly reflected in the circulation figures for the press. *Table 3* gives a breakdown for the rela-

Table 3. Voting Strength vs. Party Press Circulation by Region

Region:	Party:	Labour	Liberal	Christian	Agrarian	Conservative	Joint non-soc.	Not affiliated	N
East Central (Oslofjord area)	Votes	49.0 %	6.1	7.0	3.4	25.5	5.6	–	594,633
	Circ.	24.0 %	15.4	2.3	3.5	41.1	–	13.6	524,802
East Inland	Votes	57.2 %	4.7	6.8	11.9	10.5	3.8	–	377,554
	Circ.	32.2 %	9.6	2.4	8.3	24.1	8.3	15.3	259,705
South	Votes	39.1 %	20.1	14.2	11.1	12.8	1.5	–	110,101
	Circ.	13.2 %	43.4	1.8	4.7	26.9	–	10.5	104,179
West	Votes	38.0 %	18.1	16.9	10.3	14.9	–	–	357,449
	Circ.	15.3 %	51.3	4.8	4.3	15.6	–	8.7	293,264
Middle	Votes	49.5 %	9.0	11.8	14.7	11.8	0.2	–	244,918
	Circ.	27.3 %	16.4	0.6	3.3	33.6	6.8	12.1	159,436
North	Votes	55.4 %	7.0	9.3	6.4	12.4	4.4	–	146,473
	Circ.	36.2 %	10.5	0.6	0.4	32.5	–	19.8	111,718

Note: The circulation totals for the six regions do not add to the country total given in Table 1: for 98,819 copies there was no information available about distribution. The data for the Communist party have not been included: see Table 1.

Table 4. Newspaper Coverage vs. Votes by the Party Dominance in the Local Press

Trade areas dominated by	No. of areas	Total households	Total electorate	Labour newspaper coverage	Labour votes in p.c. of electorate	Non-soc. newspaper coverage	Non-soc. votes in p.c. of electorate
Conservative or independent Non-Soc. press	10	601,267	1,345,171	33.8	40.9	99.2	35.9
Liberal press	9	285,568	644,568	20.3	29.0	110.2	45.5
Labour press	5	129,899	308,637	50.1	42.6	72.4	27.5
All areas	25	1,016,734	2,298,376	32.0	37.8	98.9	37.5

Note: Areas are classified according to the one of the three major presses with the highest percentage of copies sold within the given total of households. With the Conservative press are here grouped 'Bourgeois' and Independent Non-Socialist newspapers. Newspapers affiliated with the Communist, the Christian and the Agrarian parties are disregarded in this classification.

tionships between voting strength and circulation by six major regions.

The Conservative press has its major strength in the Oslo area, around Trondheim and in the North, while the Liberal press is markedly dominant in the South and the West: these are the traditional strongholds of the Liberal party and still the regions where the three middle parties come closest to a majority position. The Liberal press in these areas is most markedly community dominant and is read by large proportions of the voters for all other parties. The Labour press is clearly at its weakest in these areas and covers the smallest proportion of its voters. The Labour press is markedly stronger in the areas where the party gets near or above the 50 % mark at the polls: in the East Inland region, the Middle region and the North. There is a clear correlation between the strength of the party and the strength of its press, but it is difficult to get exact measures of this correlation since the distribution data are not available for small enough units. A crude impression of the relationship between circulation and votes for the Labour party can be gained from *Fig. 1*.

The scattergram is based on estimates for the 25 'trade areas' of the country: the percentages for each area refer to 1957 estimates for the household coverage of the Labour press and to the proportion of the

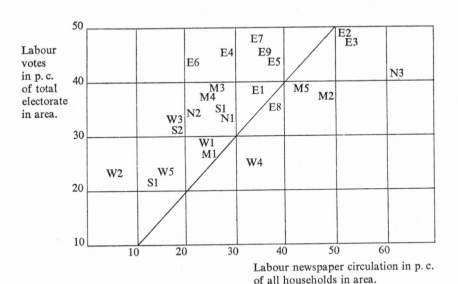

Fig. 1. Scattergram for the 25 trade areas delimited by the Central Bureau of Statistics: points indicate the Labour newspaper circulation in per cent of all households and the Labour votes in per cent of the total electorate. The trade areas are grouped by regions: *E*ast, *S*outh, *W*est, *M*iddle, *N*orth.

electorate who cast a vote for the party at the election that year. The product-moment correlation between the two percentages for the 25 units is 0.66. The correlation is clearly not linear, however: the percentage of Labour votes increases less as the Labour press gets stronger and the gap between the two percentages tends to disappear in the areas where the Labour party is dominant.[264] We get a similar result when we group the areas by the party of the *dominant press in the area:* we see in *Table 4* that there is a discrepancy in the *opposite* direction in the five areas where the Labour press is the dominant one. There is a marked difference between the areas where the Labour papers are minority papers and the areas where they are close to community dominance. In the 'minority areas' a considerable proportion of Socialist voters will choose their papers as community members rather than as party supporters; in the 'dominance areas' this is not likely to be a dilemma.

Table 4 adds an important correction to the contrast presented in Tables 1 and 3: by calculating in terms of *household coverage* instead of in terms of the total circulation we can show that the contrast is not so much the effect of an *under*-representation of the Labour press as of an *over*-representation of the opposition press. Calculating from the total number of households and the total electorate makes it possible to assess the effects of *multiple subscriptions* and, more indirectly, of the extent of *non-voting* on the total contrast between circulation and vote: these factors are disregarded in the percentages given in Tables 1 and 3. Table 4 indicates that in the areas dominated by opposition papers the Labour newspapers will in most cases be kept as one among several papers in the household, while in the five areas dominated by the Labour press, papers of this persuasion are more likely to be found in one-paper households. The aggregate circulation statistics do not allow any direct inference about the newspaper choices of the 22 %, who *did not vote* in the election. The marked over-representation of the Non-Socialist press in all the 25 areas, even in the five where Labour has the highest coverage percentage, suggests, however, that the non-voters will preponderantly keep opposition papers in their households: we shall see that this hypothesis is confirmed by our analysis of the sample survey data.

By contrast to the non-Socialist press, the Labour press is only found to be markedly over-represented in *two* of the 25 areas: in the other three 'dominance areas' the two percentages differ very little. Only in these two areas, representing only 5 % of the electorate, do Labour papers attract a wide readership outside the households of the party's voters: only here are the reader's interests as a community member likely to coincide with his interests as a party supporter.

Our analysis of the circulation statistics made it clear that we could not tabulate our cross-section survey data for the entire sample without regional breakdowns: we had to find ways of differentiating according to the *local choice situation* for the voter/reader and to classify our primary sampling units in terms of 'party press dominance' and 'party press accessibility'. The size of the sample did not allow us to go very far in this direction, but our tables will show that even crude trichotomies make for marked differentiations.

The Parties and the Political Content of the Newspapers

Norwegian newspapers have traditionally been highly concerned with politics. Most papers manifest a marked political tendency and present their party affiliation much in the same way as they print the name of the editor. Readers generally take it for granted that their papers should be slanted one way or the other politically: this also goes for the papers preferring to be labelled 'independent'. Of the 44 newspapers classified as 'non-affiliated' in the statistics a majority manifest definite political preferences – always on the non-socialist side.

The entire Norwegian press is privately owned. There are three types of such ownership: *party owned* papers, *family owned* papers, and papers organized as *stock-holding companies*. One important point needs to be stressed here: there has never been a tendency to form *cartels* among newspapers in Norway. There are very few cases where one newspaper company is in a position to control other newspapers editorially. The kind of cooperation that may be found is nearly always of a technical nature, although in a few cases a smaller daily has been taken over or backed financially by a larger one in the same area. Newspaper 'chains' have never existed, and the kind of dual ownership mentioned never constituted any choice problem for the consumer in the area.

There are only two *party* owned papers: the principal organ of the Communist party, *Friheten,* and the central organ of the Labour party, *Arbeiderbladet.* In both cases, the party controls the paper financially, but there is no continuous control of editorial policy: this is in the hands of an editor-in-chief elected for limited periods of tenure.

The *'family newspapers'* are among the largest and best established ones. They have their traditional party labels, Conservative or Liberal, but are not tied in organizationally with the parties. The papers are normally operated and managed by the family, but not necessarily edited by family members.

The remainder of the newspapers are organized as stock-holding companies or private business enterprises. The non-socialist papers in this category do not differ fundamentally from the family papers in control structure. The Labour press has a different organization. We have noted that *Arbeiderbladet* is owned directly by the party; the other 40 papers are organized as joint stock companies with the shares divided among party locals and trade unions. All these units are organized in a national co-operative and run a joint press bureau for the distribution of news and features.

The non-socialist parties also run their own press bureaux and offer similar services to the affiliated papers. The relationships between the political organization and the editorial staffs are much more personal and informal in these parties than in the Labour party: they are consequently much more difficult to assess. There is clearly less central control of editorial policy and greater dependence on local interests within the non-socialist papers. No systematic study of these relationships has as yet been undertaken, but there is no doubt that an analysis would provide evidence of marked local differences. One important approach would be by way of an analysis of the role of newspaper personnel in local politics and party work. It is well known that the non-socialist parties will make frequent use of the personnel of their newspapers in their campaigns, in the preparation of the pamphlets and programmes and in local government.

How will these differences in the ties between parties and the editorial staff affect the content of the papers, their emphasis on political information and argument? We have not undertaken a general analysis of content frequencies for the different categories of papers but there is a great deal of evidence indicating that community dominant papers generally tend to give much less emphasis to politics than papers addressing themselves to narrower groups of readers. In a content analysis of the party press in the four largest cities during three election campaigns, Svennik Høyer (Høyer, 1960) found a marked difference in the emphasis on politics between community dominant organs and lower-circulation papers both on the extreme left and on the right. To use terms introduced by Westerståhl and Janson in their analysis of Swedish data, the *'narrow-coverage'* press tends to be much more distinct in its politics than the *'wide-coverage'* press addressing itself to a highly heterogeneous public (Westerståhl, 1959: pp. 50, 84–87). The Communist press and to a large extent also the Labour press in Norway are clearly 'narrow-coverage' presses: their papers are very little read outside the circles of party voters. The Liberal and the Conservative papers, on the other hand, are in the majority of cases community dominant and are, therefore, more likely to reach voters of very different political persuasions. This means that a great number of the papers officially classified as anti-socialist in fact concentrate on general community services and give very little emphasis to their political differences with Labour. For the majority of citizens, therefore, the choice of newspaper for regular subscription is not a choice between clearly contrasted organs of political opinion: it is more likely to be a choice between a politically committed minority paper on the one hand and a generally read community paper without distinct political colouring on the other. The gap between the proportions of votes and the strength of the party press must clearly reflect such differences in the *political content* of the newspaper: in the statistics each copy sold or subscribed to counts as *one unit* although in fact they vary markedly in the character of their messages to the readers and in their potential influence on their political orientations and behaviours.

The Personal Relevance of the Choice

This brings us to our third factor: the *relevance of the choice* of a newspaper *to the reader* in his given social, economic and political roles: what does it mean to him to take one newspaper rather than another, what are its functions in his daily life, what information does he seek in it and what information does he disregard? In the official statistics, it is not only assumed that *each newspaper copy* has equal weight: it is also assumed that *each reader* equals one unit of potential influence just in the way electoral law postulates *each voter* to count as one equal unit of actual influence. (Westerståhl, 1959: pp. 8. 49–50) To get beyond these assumptions and to reach greater insight into the functions of the press in the political process we must go directly to each newspaper and to samples of individual readers and collect data on the actual flow of information from the one to the other. This is a complex and challenging task for empirical research: with the data we now have at hand we can only take up one among a number of possible lines of analysis and focus on one major hypothesis.

Our hypothesis is that newspapers have different functions for the *politically active* than for the *passive* and that the vote-circulation discrepancies in the statistics reflect differences in the *attention given to the politics of the papers* by active vs. passive readers. Westerståhl and Janson found ample evidence for this in data from Swedish sample surveys of newspaper readers: they established that the readers of the *'narrow-coverage'* press paid markedly more attention to political editorials in their papers and expressed greater confidence in their political judgment than the readers of the *'wide coverage'* press did in theirs. The 'narrow-coverage' press has a politically homogeneous readership and is primarily read for its *political* content by the active supporters of the given party while the 'wide-coverage' press is primarily read for its *'community service'* content by actives and passives alike, whichever their party. In Sweden this contrast could be analyzed across the entire party system: the two categories of 'narrow-coverage' press, the Social Democrat press generally and the Conservative press in the metropolitan areas, were found to differ markedly from the two categories of 'wide-coverage' press, the Liberal press generally and the Conservative press in the rest of the country (Westerståhl, 1959: Ch. II). In Norway we did not find it possible to undertake such a differentiated analysis: we could only contrast the readers of the *Socialist* press, whether Communist (very few) or Labour, with the readers of all other papers.

Analysis Procedures

The data for this analysis were collected through a *nation-wide cross-sectional interview survey* conducted in two waves in 1957, the one immediately before the October election, the other during the month after the election.[265] The interview schedule elicited, in addition to a variety of details on family background and occupational career, information about past and present voting, current political views and activities, exposure to party campaign efforts and interest in the political messages of the mass media. The schedule included a question about the newspapers regularly kept in the household and inquired into the frequency of attention to election editorials and news stories about the election. There were, unfortunately, no direct questions about the reasons for keeping each given paper and about the attention given to contents other than the political. Given these limitations, the findings of our analysis cannot in any way claim to be conclusive: we report them here because they fit into a broader context of theoretical work on political communication and because they point to important possibilities for systematic comparative research.

Table 5 gives the basic breakdown of the voters by the party ties of the newspapers in their household. This table gives a breakdown for the entire national cross-section and does not differentiate according to local dominance situations. A comparison with the corresponding figures from the Swedish surveys (Westerståhl, 1959, Tab. 34, p. 80) is of considerable interest:

	Respondents voting for:				
	Soc./Soc. Dem	*Lib.*	*Chr.*	*Agr.*	*Cons.*
Norway:					
Have Soc. paper(s) in household	68 %	18 %	11 %	11 %	21 %
Have non-Soc. paper(s)	69 %	98 %	92 %	98 %	97 %
Sweden:					
Read Soc. Dem. paper(s)	59 %	13 %	–	6 %	18 %
Read Liberal paper(s)	51 %	83 %	–	53 %	63 %
Read Agrarian paper(s)	5 %	4 %	–	44 %	15 %
Read Cons. paper(s)	24 %	28 %	–	34 %	69 %

The percentages are not exactly comparable but the findings for party loyalty vs. party indifference in the choice of newspaper go much in the same direction: between one-third and two-fifths of the Socialist voters in the two countries do not read papers of their own parties while practically all the non-Socialist voters keep one or more papers of the same general persuasion in their households.

In the Swedish analysis of differences between party loyal vs. party indifferent readers, the primary focus was on differences in the attention to the political opinions expressed in the editorials.

Table 5. *Newspapers Regularly Bought or Subscribed to in Household:*
Relationship between Political Affiliation of Newspaper and Own Party
Preference for Entire Cross-sectional Sample (irrespective of Local Press
Dominance)

Intended Vote:	N	No Socialist paper in household	One or more Socialist papers, no others	One or more Soc. papers plus non-soc. papers	No papers at all, N.A.
Socialist (CP or Labour)	637	28 %	27	41	4
Liberal	88	81 %	1	17	1
Christian	106	83 %	2	9	6
Agrarian	104	88 %	1	10	1
Conservative	221	77 %	1	20	2
Uncertain, refuses to say	161	61 %	8	28	3
Not decided to vote	208	55 %	16	21	8
Total sample	1515	53 %	15	28	4

In our Norwegian analysis we tried out a multivariate design using information from official circulation statistics as well as data from the sample survey:

a) we ordered the primary sampling units in the survey according to the per cent of households taking Socialist newspapers and grouped the respondents correspondingly according to the *accessibility of Socialist papers* in the local community;
b) we analyzed, at each accessibility level, the party ties of the respondent's regular newspapers and sought to account for this choice against the background of the given occupational role, the degree of commitment to the party, the level of interest shown in political information and the extent of active participation in politics.

In the present chapter, we can only give a selection of the tables so far produced in this analysis: a more detailed report has been prepared in Norwegian.

Findings
Table 6 presents our data on variations in newspaper choice between major occupational groupings. Within each group the per cent taking Socialist papers is given for three 'accessibility' levels: areas where the Labour press covers less than 20 % of the households, areas with coverage between 20 % and 30 %, areas with more than 30 %. The figures indicate that the industrial workers are the least 'dominance sensitive' of

Table 6. *Newspaper Preferences by Occupation of Head of Household:*
Differences According to Local Coverage of Socialist Press

Occupation of head	Accessibility of Socialist papers	Tot. N =	No Socialist paper in household	One or more Socialist papers	No papers at all or N.A.
Worker in industry		285	33 %	62	5
	Low	122	48 %	48	3
	Medium	129	26 %	68	6
	High	34	9 %	88	3
Worker, other, outside		359	46 %	48	6
primary economy	Low	187	56 %	39	5
	Medium	120	47 %	47	6
	High	52	6 %	84	10
Agricultural worker,		236	55 %	41	4
smallholder, fisherman	Low	113	69 %	25	6
	Medium	71	56 %	41	3
	High	52	21 %	75	4
Farmer		171	83 %	15	2
	Low	89	90 %	9	1
	Medium	70	84 %	13	3
	High	12			
Salaried		319	60 %	37	3
	Low	159	68 %	31	1
	Medium	124	60 %	35	5
	High	36	22 %	72	6
Self-employed outside primary		139	58 %	40	2
economy	Low	78	73 %	24	3
	Medium	42	45 %	55	–
	High	19	26 %	74	–

the group: they show the highest proportion of Socialist press readers at
the low and the middle level of accessibility. The increase from the
middle to the high level of accessibility is much more marked for the
other worker groups: they are more likely to take a Socialist paper if this
is a wide-community choice. These groups have a lower proportion of
firmly committed Socialist voters and are accordingly more likely to
choose their newspapers as community members rather than as party supporters.

Table 7 indicates a similar pattern: the least committed are most likely
to conform to the dominant community choice. For this table we grouped
the workers and the rest of the sample on the basis of a comparison of the
party preferences expressed in the interview before and the interview
after the election. This gave us a division into five groups: *Stable Socialists* (same preferences both interviews), *Unstable Socialists* (wavering
between a Socialist and a non-socialist preference or indicating uncer-

Table 7. *Newspaper Choice related to Stability of Pro- or Anti-socialist Preference: Differences between Workers and Non-workers by Level of Local Accessibility of Socialist Newspapers*

Stability of preference:	Occupational group	Low accessibility areas			High accessibility areas		
		N	None of papers in household Socialist	No papers in household N.A.¹	N	None of papers Socialist	No papers, N.A.¹
1. Stable Socialist	Worker²	140	41 %	2	327	20 %	5
	Non-w.	114	39 %	3	255	19 %	4
		26	46 %	–	72	25 %	6
2. Unstable Socialist³	Worker	63	64 %	5	90	34 %	7
	Non-w.	45	62 %	7	53	28 %	6
		18	67 %	–	37	43 %	8
3. Uncertain, not decided to vote	Worker	50	78 %	8	71	42 %	6
	Non-w.	31	81 %	13	41	39 %	10
		19	74 %	–	30	47 %	–
4. Unstable non-socialist⁴	Worker	47	85 %	6	56	71 %	2
	Non-w.	27	81 %	4	23	65 %	4
		20	90 %	10	33	76 %	–
5. Stable non-socialist	Worker	158	90 %	1	180	73 %	4
	Non-w.	59	93 %	2	54	76 %	6
		99	88 %	1	126	71 %	3

¹ Percentages do not add up 100 % since category 'One or more Soc. papers' left out.
² 'Worker' includes agricultural workers, smallholders and fishermen.
³ Includes those indicating Socialist preference in one interview, non-socialist in the other.
⁴ Excludes those already in group 3.

tainty or unwillingness to be committed in one of the interviews), *Uncommitted* (no commitment in either interview), *Unstable non-socialist* (indicating a non-socialist preference in one interview, no commitment in the other), *Stable non-socialists* (this preference both interviews). The table makes it patently clear that occupation matters very little in the choice of newspaper: the differences between workers and others are generally very small within each preference group. What is of greater importance, however, is that *Stable* citizens are much less 'dominance-sensitive' than the *Unstable* and the *Uncommitted:* if we compare the lowest accessibility (less than 20 % coverage and a maximum of 2 Socialist papers in the area) with the middle and the high accessibility areas we shall see that the differences in percentage points for 'No Socialist papers' are 20 to 17 in the two Stable worker groups, 34 in the Unstable Socialist group and 42 in the Uncommitted group. The non-voters and the consistently apolitical clearly tend to take whatever paper is dominant in their local area: they do not read papers for their political content but for such services as they render to them as members of their community.

Table 8 presents corresponding findings for *attitudes on government policy:* this was measured on the basis of seven questions about the policies of the Labour government in such fields as taxation, the control of inflation, investments, the regulation of business, and housing. Comparing within the group of 'potential Socialists', we find a marked difference in the low accessibility areas between those articulating a highly pro-Labour orientation and those who are either negative or do not take a stand: the core group of supporters are markedly more likely to have a Socialist paper in their household. The difference does not come out so clearly in the areas where Socialist papers are easily accessible. Our data do

Table 8. *Newspaper Choice and Attitudes on Major Political Issues: Differences among 'Potential Socialists' (Preference Indicated in one of Interviews or Both)*

	N	None of papers Socialist	One or more Soc.	No papers at all, N.A.
Low accessibility areas:				
0–2 pro-Labour resp.	50	70 %	28	2
3–4 resp.	59	46 %	52	2
5 or more	90	38 %	59	3
Higher accessibility:				
0–2 pro-Labour resp.	56	41 %	54	5
3–4 resp.	126	21 %	72	7
5 or more	232	20 %	75	5

not allow us to draw definitive conclusions as to the *causal* relations between attitude structure and newspaper choice. There is clearly a process
of two-way enforcement: a pronounced pro-Labour orientation will make
for a strong motivation to keep Socialist papers in the household, even
where this is minority choice, but the regular reading of such papers will in
itself provide arguments for maintaining the orientation and strengthen
the commitment to the party.

Table 9 presents a breakdown of our data for the 'potential Socialists'
by three indicators of political activity and information seeking: to simplify the table, the data have only been given for the areas where the
Socialist press covers less than 20 % of the households.

Table 9. *Newspaper Choice related to Indicators of Political Activity and
Information Seeking: Differences among 'Potential Socialists' in Low
Accessibility Areas*

	N	No Socialist papers in household	One or more Soc.	No papers at all, N. A.
Attention to politics in newspapers				
Reads regularly	46	35 %	63	2
Rarely, never	153	52 %	45	3
General index of information seeking (Newspapers, radio)				
High	49	37 %	61	2
Medium	74	47 %	50	3
Low	80	55 %	41	4
Organizational participation:				
Active (membership, attendance meetings, campaign work)	43	42 %	56	2
'Only-voter'	117	48 %	49	3
Probable non-voter	43	53 %	42	4

There are clear and marked relationships between information seeking
and newspaper choice: the Socialists who regularly read the political news
and editorials in their papers and follow election debates and election
news on the radio are much more likely to be 'party loyal' in their choice
of newspaper. Our analysis thus confirms the hypothesis tested on Swedish survey data by Westerståhl and Janson.[266] The relationship is clearly
a two-way one: the politically alert voters are more likely to choose papers
supporting their orientation while the voters keeping papers from other
parties tend to disregard the politics and to keep them exclusively for
their community services.

The index of *'organizational participation'* divides the 'potential' Socialists in four groups:
- the *'probable non-voters'*
- the *'only-voters'*
- those reporting *one party activity* beyond voting (membership, attendance at meetings, campaign work)
- those reporting *two activities* beyond voting.[267]

The non-voters tend, as already shown in Table 7, to be the least 'party-loyal' in their choice of newspaper. There is very little difference, however, between the 'only-voters' and those reporting one activity beyond voting. The difference indicated in the table is almost entirely due to the 10 respondents reporting *two or three* activities in the party: 8 of these 10 had Socialist papers in their households as against 16 out of the 33 with one activity. The sample is unfortunately not large enough for a reliable analysis of this core of party workers in the low accessibility areas, but there is little reason to doubt that these are genuine 'opinion leaders' in Lazarsfeld's sense (Katz, 1955), and that it is organizationally essential for such people to keep regularly abreast of the news, the debates and the arguments in the papers of their own party. These active supporters hold strategic roles in the communication network: they spread the messages in the party press to wider circles of potential voters who do not keep such papers in their households. It is only through such processes that it is possible for a party to maintain its hold on such large bodies of voters without reaching them through its press.

Further Work
The analysis reported in this chapter is the first in a series of studies of the role of the mass media in Norwegian politics.

We hope through these studies to throw light on a central problem in the sociology of politics: the problem of the integration of conflicting movements and organizations in a viable and effective national system. Simmel's notions of the integrative functions of criss-crossing conflict lines in the system [268] are of the highest relevance in any such analysis: the conflict lines between the voter groups cut across the divisions between readers of newspapers of different political tendencies and this places a considerable proportion of the electorate in a situation of cross-pressure, not so much between opposing political demands as between loyalties to their local communities and loyalties to national party grouping. Robert A. Dahl (Dahl, 1956), Talcott Parsons (Parsons, 1959:2), and Seymour M. Lipset (Lipset, 1959; Lipset, 1960) have recently given us penetrating analyses of such balancing processes in political systems. In the Norwegian situation there is an interesting two-way process of mutual restraints: on the one hand a majority of the Socialist voters are regularly exposed to newspaper messages from the opposition parties, on the other hand the non-socialist papers, just because they in so many cases dominate their community and address themselves to a variety of politically heterogeneous groups, are found to exercise a great deal of restraint in the expression of conflicting opinions and to devote most of their content to 'service' information of little political relevance.

This 'equilibrating' process cannot be analyzed in sufficient details on the basis of the data now at hand. We need to go further in combining the techniques of mass communications research with the procedures of political sociology: quite particularly to combine content analyses of a sample of local newspapers with detailed interviews with samples of readers. We also see a great need for the confrontation of evidence from a variety of political systems and we look forward to opportunities to explore with colleagues in other countries the possibilities of concerted comparative research on the functions of the mass media in maintaining and in cutting across political conflict lines.

NOTES

[263] *Norsk Aviskatalog.* Oslo, Avisenes Informasjonskontor, 1958, 12. utg. p. 8.
[264] This was also found to be the case in Sweden. (Westerståhl, 1959: pp. 21, 122).
[265] Details on sampling procedures, non-response and basic distributions are found in (Rokkan, 1960: 4).
[266] (Westerståhl, 1959) Ch. 10, particularly the table for *The reading of editorials* p. 80.
[267] For details on this index see Chapter 12 above.
[268] See the discussion in (Coser, 1956: Ch. IV).

FOURTEEN

Readers, Viewers, Voters

This autumn more than one hundred million citizens on the two sides of
the Atlantic will exert their sovereign wills in the voting booths and help
to determine the fate of the two leading English-speaking democracies:
more than seventy million in the United States, not far from thirty million
in the United Kingdom.

How do all these millions of citizens make up their minds about the
choices they have before them? How much information do they absorb
about the alternatives and how far does such information actually affect
their decisions? How many of them are stuck in their convictions and
need no further information to make up their minds and how many are
actually affected in one way or another by the news, the arguments and
the imagery showered on them through the local grapevine, through their
organizations and associations, through the press, through the radio and
through television? How many depend essentially on the gentle promptings or the implicit intimidations within their immediate environment and
how many pay serious attention to what they read about politics in their
magazines or their newspapers or are told about the alternatives through
the electronic mass media?

These are the sorts of questions I want to consider this evening: they
are central in the study of mass politics and they suggest important tasks
for research on human communication.

I shall try not to bore you with detailed statistical estimates: in fact I
have nothing to report for the current campaigns. What I propose to give
you is a general map of this territory of research: I want to familiarize
you with the methodological background and trace some of the principal
lines of theorizing and empirical analysis. I shall not restrict myself to the
two English-speaking democracies, but concern myself with general problems in the analysis of political campaigns in Western systems of government. I shall certainly cite British and American studies whenever I find
them of particular interest, but the bulk of my empirical examples will be
taken from my home base in Scandinavia.

Any research on mass politics in full-suffrage democracies must start

Origin: This chapter reproduces my *Granada* lecture (London, McGibbon & Kee,
1964) given in Guildhall, London, in October, 1964: this explains the reference to
the two elections that autumn, the British (which brought Labour back to power)
and the American (which confirmed Johnson).

out from a consideration of the very act repeated so many millions of times in the gigantic data-gathering operations we call elections: the act of voting.

The vote is a datum of human behaviour but it is an *anonymous* datum. Most Western democracies introduced strict provisions for secrecy either before or immediately after the promulgation of general manhood suffrage: the act was severed from the person and was only registered and counted as a contribution to an aggregate. This very anonymity set new tasks of inquiry and analysis, first for the practical intelligence workers in the parties, later for the academic social scientists: the official returns gave totals for the district or the constituency only, and much ingenuity had to be exerted in efforts to find out who voted for whom. In the tight-knit rural communities the task was generally very simple: political allegiances were socially visible and very easily mapped. In the urban agglomerations it took greater organizational efforts to trace the sources of the votes for the competing parties: the agents and the campaign managers had to build up complex network of local informants, they had to enlist volunteers to canvass each area and they had to build up extensive files not only for regular supporters but also for a variety of potential targets of persuasion, pressure or sheer physical mobilization. These are the indispensable tools of mass politics: none of the later refinements of data gathering or statistical analysis has made them any less indispensable.

The commercial poll was essentially modelled on the canvass: citizens were sought out in their homes or at their workplaces in an effort to gauge the strengths of the competing parties and to map their sources of support and their possible campaign targets. The polling organizations proceeded much more systematically than the pragmatic party workers and, at least in the English-speaking and the Northwestern democracies, found it surprisingly easy to get the majority of the citizens to reveal what the electoral system allowed them to keep secret: their past and their present choices among the political alternatives open to them. But the poll is no shortcut to the complete canvass: the data may have been elicited from individual respondents but the individuals do not speak for themselves but for categories within the sampled electorate. The vote in the election booth and the response to the interviewer are equally anonymous: they are acts divorced from the citizen in his unique concreteness. In both cases the acts are registered and counted by categories: in the case of votes the primary category is that of the territorial unit of residence, in the case of poll responses, there is a wide range of primary categories and virtually no end to the possibilities of detailed cross-classification. But the campaign managers cannot rest content with information about categories: the anonymous tables may help them to evaluate their tactics and to develop new lines of electioneering but in their day-to-day efforts to mobilize votes they depend much less on such abstract information and much more on their concrete knowledge of individual constituents and the amount of support they can mobilize for the party on the day of reckoning. Those of you who have read Eugene Burdick's recent diatribe against electronic electioneering, his novel *The 480,* will know how far it is possible to push the categorization of poll respondents for purposes of political analysis. Computers have been fed with data from dozens of polls and have ground out information on the electoral proclivities of such strategic targets as the White Protestant Primary-Educated Working Class Housewives over 45 in Home-Owning Households in Suburban Areas of the American North-East. The academic social scientist confronted with information on hundreds of such categories of the United States electorate may well find ways of identifying underlying tendencies and regularities, but what can the campaign manager do with it all? He may, of course, find that his party ought to pitch different lines of appeal to different categories of potential voters, but how can he be sure that such differentiated propaganda, *e.g.* to Klansmen and to the Negro middle class, will not backfire? Differentiated appeals require differentiated channels: the mass media address themselves indiscriminately to a generalized public and the only safe channels for pinpointed electoral appeals are the organizational and the personal. If the polls tell the campaign strategist that there is a potential pay-off in differentiated appeals he has in fact only two alternatives: he can spread his messages through existing associational networks or he can resort to old-fashioned door-to-door canvassing in designated target areas. In either case the poll will only have served to call attention to a problem or a possibility: the actual electioneering operation must rely on concrete information about identifiable individuals and their connections, not on abstract data for category after category.

These are not idle methodological considerations: they bear on a central point in the study of elections. In the early systems of representative government the enfranchised citizen expressed his will openly and publicly: he was identified with his act and there was a direct link between his role in every day life and his role as a voter choosing his representative. With the institutionalization of universal, equal and secret elections all this changed: the vote remained an act of communication from the government to his authorities but it was abstracted from its context, taken out of the pulsating flow of interactions in the community.

In one sense, the vote was no longer a *responsible* act: the citizen could no longer be taken to account for what he had done, neither by his superiors nor by his peers. The vote was, so to speak, taken out of the currency of everyday life: it could not be used to placate an irascible landlord, it could not be sold for a consideration, it could not serve as a token to manifest one's allegiance and solidarity. Elections became rituals of separation: in the voting booth one citizen was equal to any other in his constituency and was free to choose as he pleased; as soon as he left it he was back in a hierarchical community imposing a variety of restraints on his behaviour. Our legal systems are shot through with such provisions for the separation of the person from his roles and offices, but elections offer a larger stock of data on the operation of such devices than perhaps any other institution.

Our complex society assigns a wide range of distinguishable roles to their members: roles in the family and the household, roles in kinship and friendship networks, roles at the workplace and in the economy, roles in churches, sects and associations, roles in the cultural, the linguistic and the ethnic community, roles in the communication process, roles in the public affairs of the locality and the nation. In each of these roles the citizen learns something about the issues and the alternatives in his system and in most of them he is exposed to experiences, pressures and rewards which help to determine the stand he will take in the contests between competing parties in elections. Which of these multiple influences weigh the heaviest with him in the solitude of the voting booth? What is his conception of his social self as he reaches his decision? How did he arrive at his political identity and which of his life-time roles counted most in the process?

These are the central questions in the sociology of elections. Commercial polls and academic surveys have produced a wealth of data for country after country on the regional, socio-economic, religious and cultural backgrounds of political diversities. Curiously little has been done as yet to evaluate and to compare these statistics systematically, but the evidence at hand suggests complex variations from one type of party system to another. The extension of the franchise to the underprivileged strata of society did not automatically produce a polarization of politics by class: roles in the local community, the church, the sect or the ethnic association often proved as important as roles at the work place or in the economy. In religiously divided countries, denomination and church attendance generally offer a better basis for predictions of votes than occupation or income. Even in the religiously most homogeneous of political systems we never find a complete fit between class and party. You will all have heard about the Tory working-men: at least one-third of the working-class electors in Britain tend to vote with the middle-class parties. In Scandinavia the great political statistician Herbert Tingsten used to say that elections were becoming increasingly difficult to distinguish from censuses: the citizens would register their party choice at the polling station with the same calm and the same indifference as they recorded their job to the census taker. It is, of course, easy to be overwhelmed by the high level of class voting in the Scandinavian countries: our Norwegian surveys suggest that some 80 per cent of the voters from working-class households will side with the Socialists and the official estimate for Sweden, reported by the way as a matter of course by the Central Bureau of Statistics, is roughly the same. This, however, does not mean that the Socialist parties in these countries recruit their clientele exclusively among manual workers and the members of their households. On the contrary, the surveys show that the two Social Democrat parties have strong middle-class wings: the Norwegian party counts some 20 per cent from the households of salaried employees, officials and members of the professions and the business community, and the Swedish party has acquired an even stronger middle class wing. Detailed questioning of these deviants from straight class voting suggests that the sequences of life-time roles and experiences count as much as the current economic position in the decisions between the parties: the occupation and the politics of the father proves as good a predictor of the vote as the job held at the time of election. This accounts for much of the middle-class strength of the Social Democrats: with continuing economic growth, with the expansion of the public services and with the entry of the working-class representatives into positions of control in the local and the central administrations, an increasing number of workers' sons and daughters were recruited into middle-class positions. These upward movements in the social hierarchy did not bring about appreciable losses for the Labour party: the majority of the recruits to the middle class stayed loyal to the politics of their working-class father. The Labour party did not lose in the electoral strength but its very success created new pressures on its policies and brought it closer to the middle range of the political system: our analyses do indeed suggest a direct relationship between victory at the polls, 'bourgeoisification' and 'depoliticization'.

Does all this mean that campaigns are of no avail, that all efforts of mass persuasion are doomed to failure? If the great majority of citizens did in fact establish their political identities before they left their parental household or at least as soon as they had completed their formal schooling and found their place in the economic system, whatever difference will it make to the results whether the parties wage their campaigns or not?

Sociological studies of the origins of electoral decisions have indeed often provided arguments for sceptical and defeatist attacks on the propaganda and public relations machineries of the parties. In differentiated party systems, such as the Scandinavian and the Dutch, there is as a matter of empirical fact very little leeway for campaign efforts: a 2 or 3 per cent swing tends to be looked upon as a landslide. In the cruder party systems of the English-speaking countries there is, of course, a much greater margin of indeterminacy and a case is much easier to make for concerted campaign efforts.

But the net changes in party strength from election to election do not tell us much about the possibilities of influence through systematic party campaigns. There is in fact no way of drawing direct conclusions from analyses of the social or cultural origins of electoral decisions to estimates of the potential scope for campaign efforts. Experiences in socio-economic and cultural roles do not translate themselves into electoral decisions just like that: on the contrary the entire process could not have got under way without the organizational efforts of the parties and their *militants,* without their educational and promotional activities and without their tireless drives to mobilize more and more of their clientèle. The close fit between social class and political identity in some countries does not reflect an automatic process of polarization brought about through the extension of the suffrage to all accountable adults: it is the result of decades of mobilization efforts on each side of the line of conflict in the system. The current level of polarization simply represents the net outcome of a series of competitive efforts to mobilize new voters on each side.

In the first couple of decades after extension of the franchise to all adult men and women, the parties in most countries of the West were indeed engaged in a giant scramble for additional support, and efforts on one side of the line were countered by equal or greater efforts on the other. As more and more of the enfranchised citizens were brought to the polls the scope for further mobilization was reduced and the parties entered what has been termed the stage of trench warfare: they could no longer hold hopes of great conquests but they could not dismantle their defences for fear of potential raids from the other side. Party managers, of course, have to be optimistic to keep their jobs and will not easily accept evidence that they have mobilized their clientèle to the maximum, but even if they were to become convinced that there was nothing further to gain they would still have to keep their campaign apparatus in full trim: there may be a stalemate but there is a very little temptation to give up the deterrent unilaterally! The success of the different mobilization efforts may to a greater or lesser extent be explained through a sociological analysis of the structural conditions in the national community, but the electorate is not likely to stay mobilized unless the parties keep up their competitive efforts. The lesson to be drawn from the analyses of the sociologists is not that campaigns have lost their point but that strategies of defence will become more important than strategies of mass persuasion as the mobilization levels reach their maximum.

It is exactly on this question of the effectiveness of different lines of party strategy that we face the most challenging tasks for empirical analysis in the field of political communication research. I cannot cite any examples of controlled experimentation to test the effects of different lines of campaign strategy, but there is a quite considerable body of studies of the social conditions for the success of alternative techniques of electioneering: as you might expect, the majority of these studies have been carried out in the United States, but quite a few have also been completed in Britain, in Germany and in Scandinavia. I shall not try to review the evidence for all the different campaign techniques but focus my discussion on one central dilemma of party planning: how much of the total campaign investment should be allocated to work through the *organizational channels* and how much should be allocated to messages and appeal through the *mass media?*

In every political party of some size there is a latent conflict between 'organizers' and 'public relations men': the organizers want to spend the party funds on the recruitment, training and indoctrination of party workers and party members while the public relations men want to spend as much as possible on the spread of information, appeals and image-building materials to the general public through the use of posters, mass-distributed pamphlets, advertisements, films, radio and television programmes. The strength of the one or the other faction will depend on a variety of factors: the amounts of discretionary funds available to the party, the character of the party organization and its ties to a wider network of associations, the opportunities for exerting control over the different mass media and their contents. In the fluid and poorly integrated party organizations of the United States, there is a natural tendency to use the bulk of the available funds for general mass appeal. The situation is very different in the European countries where the parties have been able to build up large membership organizations: in these countries there is much more pressure to channel the party funds into the organizational networks and greater resistance to the use of indiscriminate mass appeal. There is a curious paradox here, however: much of the research evidence used in the defence of the organizational approach has been collected in America, but the conditions for the success of this strategy are vastly more favourable within the socially and politically more homogeneous parties of Western Europe. Let me illustrate this through an example from Sweden.

In the tight political situation after the governmental losses in the election of 1956 the *Riksdag* decided to call a consultative referendum on the most divisive of the current issues of Swedish politics: the conflict over the Social Democrats' proposal to introduce a general governmental scheme for income-graded service pensions for all private as well as public wage-earners and employees. This was in itself an interesting departure in Swedish politics but what made it of particular concern to social scientists was the decision to give equal grants of public funds to each of the three sides in the controversy to allow them to finance their efforts to inform the electorate about their position. This placed before the managers of the party machineries very difficult problems of strategy: they knew they had so much money to spend on the campaign but they had very little evidence to guide them in deciding how to use the funds. They all wanted to maximize the returns for each *krona* spent on the campaign but how could they know whether the one strategy would pay off better than another? The Social Democrats had staked much of their future as the governing party on the pensions issue and decided to consult a group of social scientists on the choice of campaign strategy. The polls taken before the start of the campaign indicated that the party would fare much worse at the referendum than it had at the election the year before: a substantial number of the regular Social Democrat voters simply did not know that their party was behind the compulsory pensions scheme and some of them had clearly been swayed by the arguments of the Agrarian, Liberal or Conservative opponents. The question put to the social scientists was a straightforward one: how could the party get all its established voters to choose its alternative in the referendum and how could it influence a large enough number of the less committed citizens to add further to the total? The advice given by the social psychologists, sociologists and political scientists consulted was equally straightforward: public rallies, posters, leaflets, advertisements, even radio programmes would make little impact unless backed by a massive effort to contact, to inform and to stimulate the trusted party workers in each locality, the spokesmen and the active officers of each union, the more articulate members of the secondary associations tied in with the labour movement and the unions. The messages spread through the mass media simply would not reach the passive and the less articulate of the voters unless they were reinforced through informal discussions and efforts of persuasions in the immediate environments of the work place, the union, the association or the neighbourhood (Israel, 1957).

It is not quite clear how far the Social Democrats actually followed this advice, but there is no doubt that they improved their position substantially during the last weeks of the campaign and the evidence available suggests that the late changers were much less influenced by the mass media than by promptings within their immediate environment. Whether this would have been the case even if the party had neglected the advice of the social scientists and spent all the funds on generalized mass appeals is of course impossible to say with any certainty: after all the organizational apparatus was there in any case and would have provided a basis for personal contacts and pressures even without any extra efforts to train and stimulate the officers and the active influentials. This line of reasoning might prove valid for routine elections: then there are few problems of identification and choice even for the least articulate and the least committed of the party supporters. But in any situation where the alternatives are novel and unfamiliar it will be essential to reactivate and direct the latent political identifications of the rank-and-file and to bring this about, pressures through the immediate personal environments seem most likely to be effective.

Interestingly enough the advice given by the Swedish social scientists was not primarily based on research done in their own country: they worked with a model of the communication process developed in a series of local studies in the United States. The Viennese-American sociologist Paul Lazarsfeld had pioneered the study of the impact of the new mass media on public taste and opinion in the late thirties, and in 1940 launched the first systematic inquiry into the communication process in an electoral campaign.

His findings suggested a general model of the transmission of political messages through the electorate: the two-step model of communication flow. The mass media, at that time essentially the press and the radio, might well reach the bulk of the electorate but the contents of their political messages had very little impact on the rank-and-file of passive, inarticulate and uncommitted citizens: they paid very little attention to messages that did not fit in with their established orientations, and if they were at all affected by the campaign this was less likely to be due to direct exposure to mass appeals and more likely to result from the intensification of informal discussions in their immediate environments. The mass media exerted their influence in two steps: a small stratum of active and interested citizens paid close attention to the political messages and would, if sufficiently stimulated, spread them further among friends, acquaintances, workmates and neighbours who trusted them and sought their advice in matters of general concern in the community. This model was subsequently tested in a series of American studies, not only of election campaigns but of a variety of other processes of mass dissemination: the spread of new fashions, the popularity of new films, the acceptance of technical innovation. The model has proved a useful source of hypotheses for research not only in the United States but in a number of European countries. The two-step model has, of course, proved too crude for detailed analyses of communication process, but such refinements have not affected the basic logic of the underlying theory: there is a differentiated hierarchy of publics within any mass audience, and messages will rarely have any widespread impact unless relayed and reinforced within the innumerable face-to-face environments in each community.

Models of this type have proved of particular importance in analyses of the impact of the *press* on the political divisions in mass electorates. The popular press emerged as a major political factor during the nineteenth-century struggles for democracy and parliamentary rule. The newspapers became the major organs of public debate and provided important links of communication within the emerging parties. Very few of the daily papers became completely politicized, however: they were generally tied in with a party or a diffuse elite group, but the bulk of the contents served broader interests in the local, regional or national community. As a result many newspapers acquired great economic power and were able to establish themselves as an indispensable service for a wide cross-section of the population in their territory. To these well-entrenched newspapers, the

growth of mass literacy and the introduction of mass suffrage was anything but a threat: in fact mass democracy brought about a marked
strengthening of their position. To the rising working-class movement this
set a considerable barrier: it was very difficult to find a market for distinctly Socialist newspapers and as a consequence a large proportion of
the Socialist voters were regularly exposed to counter-arguments in the
dominant Liberal or Conservative newspapers. This was true even in the
countries with the strongest working-class movements: in Norway and
Sweden the Social Democrat Labour parties poll between 45 and 50 per
cent of the votes but their party newspapers reach less than a quarter of
households. Surveys carried out in the two countries indicate that roughly
one third of the Socialist voters are exclusively exposed to 'bourgeois'
newspapers, another third to papers from both camps, and the final third
exclusively to papers of their own party. This sets an intriguing problem
for research on political communication: how can so many Socialists
expose themselves regularly to the counter-arguments in the Liberal or
the Conservative press and still remain unaffected in their behaviour as
voters? A great deal of analysis has been devoted to this problem in Norway and Sweden and the evidence assembled tells us a great deal about
the limitations of the mass media as channels of political influence. Our
principal findings can be summarized in three points:

First of all the Socialists, however ardent in their ideology, are also
members of their local community and depend in this role on the dominant newspaper in the territory, whatever its particular party ties.

Secondly the rank-and-file Socialists will generally pay little attention
to the political appeals in these dominant papers and mainly read them
for news, advertisements and announcements.

Finally, and most significantly, the more committed, the more active
and the more informed among the Socialists will also manifest greater
loyalty to the party in their choice of newspaper.

These findings seem to fit the 'two-step' model very well: the minority
of active and alert voters serve as transmitters of messages, appeals and
arguments from the party press to the wider circles of passive and indifferent followers. The party press does not reach them directly, but in two
steps: the crucial links in the system are provided by the face-to-face
communication in the immediate environments of the rank-and-file.

The practitioners of the arts of persuasion have been surprisingly slow
to work out the implications of this body of research for their strategies
of promotion. True enough, an increasing number of marketing organizations have seen the light and have begun to concentrate attention on
potential 'taste leaders' in each community: as far as I can ascertain, most
countries of Western Europe have by now been thoroughly exposed
to one variety of such 'two-step' promotion campaigns, the organized
commissioning of private coffee parties for friends and friends' friends to

spread information about new goods and even to ensure direct sales. Political parties in fact use the same technique when they base their drives
for new members on the existing networks of friendship and acquaintance.
Whether the technique can be used with equal success in electoral campaigns is much more in debate. The line advocated by the 'organizers' is
essentially a strategy of defence. In effect they say: 'We have established
this network of contacts and we know they have access to so many others
through face-to-face interaction – let us make the fullest possible use of
this network and encourage every one of the contacts to exert himself
to a maximum.' There is an element of resignation in this approach: the
party is urged to accept as final and unalterable the social basis it had
already established and to concentrate its efforts on the consolidation of
this base rather than on offensive moves beyond the entrenchments. There
is also an element of risk: the party leaders and the party managers may
not want to rely on the networks of *militants* and members if this limits
the possibilities of central control and increases the opportunities for
splinter movements. This is why the mass media offer such tempting
alternative channels: they do make it possible to spread the party messages
beyond the limits of the established personal networks and they do allow
the leaders and the managers to maintain a greater measure of central
control. This, of course, does not mean that a strategy of attack will necessarily pay off. In the Swedish case, the Liberals and the Conservatives
relied heavily on mass appeals, but this did not help them much: they did
not do too badly in the referendum but they suffered substantial losses in
the elections that followed. The Social Democrats had hit on an issue of
great potentiality: the pensions proposal brought out a conflict of interest
between employees and owners and this conflict proved highly divisive
within both of the opposition parties. It is quite possible that this conflict
could not have been tempered by any amount of internal communication
within the two parties: that the losses were inevitable whatever the campaign strategy. But the Swedish case again underscores the importance of
the organizational infrastructure for the success of a campaign: the Social
Democrats did not only use their established networks within the party
and the working-class movement but they were also able to make extensive use of their contacts in the middle-class unions of the salaried and
the professions.

But, I shall be asked: has not *television* broken down these barriers in
the system of social interaction and made the parties much less dependent
on any such infrastructure of organized networks? It is true that the
Lazarsfeld model was developed and tested before television had made
such a decisive impact on American public life. It is also true that the
Swedish attempt to apply the 'two-step' strategy in a nationwide campaign
occurred on the very eve of the television era. The data at hand for a
variety of countries suggests a distinct increase in the exposure of the

population to national politics with the spread of the new medium. The first Swedish television election took place in 1960. 40 per cent of the households had by that time acquired sets, but as many as 60 per cent of the electorate saw at least one election programme on television. There was a substantial increase in the turnout, quite particularly among manual workers and among housewives, and most of these new votes were mobilized by the Social Democrats. The concentration of the campaign on the pension issue again paid off, but the television programmes helped to dramatize the conflict over welfare policy and no doubt added to the impact of the mobilization efforts at the organizational level. A curiously similar sequence of events took place in Norway in the summer of 1963: Labour staked its future as a governing party on a radical programme of welfare measures and made full use both of its established organizational machinery and of the new opportunities offered by television. The result was again a marked increase in electoral turnout and a substantial gain for the Labour party.

How can one disentangle the effects of the old-fashioned techniques of organizational mobilization from the effects of the new mass medium as such? How sure can one be that television appeals have greater impact than such long established media as the press and sound broadcasting? It has always been said that television is bound to be the most effective medium because of its directness of appeal: you are not just talked at but looked at and you are much more likely to react to the diffuse appeals of the strong personality than to the contents of the actual argument. That great hater of typographical civilization, Marshal McLuhan, has hailed television as the herald of the return to the oral community of our forbears. But do people actually react to the television speaker as if he were a member of a face-to-face group? Very much, of course, depends on the *mystique* of the political personality and on the amount of competition he has to suffer. For General de Gaulle television is clearly *the* medium: it establishes the direct line of communication between citizen and state which the Jacobins advocated and de Tocqueville feared. We know of the dangers of this kind of electronic plebiscitarianism in the emerging nations of Africa and Asia, but are there really any such prospects in Western countries with stronger traditions of corporate pluralism? This is a challenging field for concerted comparative research. There is a scattering of attempts to gather systematic information on the influence of television exposure on orientations to political issues, parties and leaders, but the data are often difficult to get hold of and are rarely organized in ways which will allow meaningful comparisons. In the United States there are still curiously few studies of the political impact of television. The early studies found very little evidence of any impact. The Kennedy-Nixon debates in 1960 reached a very large nation-wide audience, but polls taken before and after suggest only minor effects on the actual behaviours of the voters. We shall know much more about this when details from the large-scale study carried out by the Survey Research Centre at Michigan become available. In Britain, Granada Television has given generous encouragement to systematic research on the impact of television during election campaigns, but these studies have so far been confined to local contexts. The extensive nation-wide panel survey organized by Nuffield College will, of course, offer a variety of opportunities for detailed analysis and the report will be eagerly awaited by political analysts everywhere. The only nation-wide surveys of television effects in an election so far reported on in the literature were carried out in Sweden in 1960: the one was done by the official statistical authorities as part of their routine operations, the other was done by a commercial organization on behalf of the Swedish Broadcasting Corporation. There are a couple of very interesting parallels in the findings of the Granada study carried out in Leeds in 1959 and the findings of the Swedish 1960 surveys, and I want to conclude my review of trends in the study of political communication with a discussion on these parallels.

Both the British and the Swedish studies focus attention on the manifest party change: those who said they would vote for one party in the interview earlier in the campaign but reported a vote for a different party in the final interview. In the Leeds study this group made up 8 per cent of the total sample, in the Swedish sample only 6 per cent. In both cases the party change turned out to be highly interested in political information and not at all ignorant of the alternatives they were to choose among: they scored as high or even slightly higher than the consistent one-party voters and contrasted quite markedly with the uncertain and uncommitted citizens who could not be pinned down to any party or did not vote. The British study concludes that these 8 per cent of the sample 'represent the small fringe who do in fact weigh up the relative merits of the parties': their behaviour does indeed come surprisingly close to the rational-utilitarian ideal of the democratic citizen. Unfortunately there is very little discussion in the British report of the social and political contexts of this behaviour. The Swedish report is not very complete either, but at least gives us a few clues to the background of this important group of party changers. It turns out that they are better than average educated but are less active than the stable voters both in voluntary associations and in informal discussions of politics. They also rely less on newspapers for their political information and distinctly more on television: this is particularly marked for those of them who did not return to the party they had voted for earlier but actually made a decision for a different party. The cross-tabulations so far published do not allow any precise test, but I think my interpretation would hold up in further analysis. The typical party changer was caught in long-term cross-pressures between contrasting social and political environments and had not committed himself openly and clearly to one side or the other. He was sufficiently educated to feel that he ought to be able to reach a decision and was searching for new arguments, new clues. The televised debates between the party leaders offered a new source of information and stimulation and he was anxious to make the most of it. Exposure to television did not make him change his party: on the contrary his eagerness to follow the television programmes reflected a basic uncertainty of commitment and identification.

I believe that this interpretation would fit the British data as well as the Swedish. What makes me particularly confident in my interpretation is the information at hand on the earlier votes of the party changers and the alternatives they were faced with. In Leeds 40 per cent of them had been Liberals but were without a candidate of their own and another 25 per cent wavered between the Liberals and one of the two major parties. In Sweden a great majority of the party changers had voted either Conservative or Liberal at the previous election and had clearly lost their political bearings under impact of the pensions issue. In both countries the bulk of the party changers seem to have come from the intermediate strata between the established bourgeoisie and the trade union movement: their day-to-day environments gave them too many conflicting cues and they looked to the new electronic medium for the decisive arguments and assurances they had been unable to find in face-to-face interaction.

But are these 6–8 per cent of the electorate the only ones affected in any way by television? Clearly the impact of a medium cannot be gauged exclusively by the amount of change it produces in manifest behaviour. Changes in attitudes to the parties, in the strength of convictions, in the intensity of identifications should also be taken into account. Our studies of newspaper reading and party preference in Norway show that the Socialists who are regularly exposed to Liberal or Conservative appeals through the press differ markedly from the loyal readers of the party press in their attitudes on a number of issues: exposure to the opposition press may not have prompted them to change their political identity but has certainly made them more critical of their own party. Television might conceivably have a similar effect on the opinions and attitudes of the viewers, but so far the research evidence is very meagre. Trenaman and McQuail in their study of Leeds found that exposure to television added significantly to the political knowledge of the viewers but saw little or no evidence of any effect on attitudes. It is, of course, possible that the very balancing of party programmes on television neutralizes its impact. By contrast to the press, television acts as a great 'equalizer' of the flow of political stimulation: the press established itself before the extension of the suffrage, television is very much a child of the age of mass democracy. If each party could have its own pay-as-you-go television station it might be able to produce a much heavier impact on its potential clientèle, but this happily is not on the cards. We know very little about this equalizing function of television and its implications for our political life. It may make for greater tolerance across party lines, it may help to stabilize the balance of forces in the electorate and it may add further to the powers of the central party leaders and their staff over the local branches and the party workers. To gain further understanding of these processes of change in Western mass democracies we shall have to undertake much more detailed research than we have been able to so far. We need to know more not only about the changes underway in each country but also about similarities and differences across countries of different political structure. This autumn millions of viewers on both sides of the Atlantic will follow the drama and the ritual of two giant elections. It is time the social sciences tried to keep up with these developments.

Bibliography

Adorno, 1950.

Akzin, 1960.

Albinski, 1959.

Alford, 1963.

Alker, 1965.

Alker, 1968.

Allardt, 1956:1.

Allardt, 1956:2.

Allardt, 1958.

Allardt, 1962.

Allardt, 1964.

Allardt, 1966:1.

Allardt, 1966:2.

Allardt, 1967.

Almond, 1960.

Adorno, T. W. *et al.*, *The authoritarian personality* (N. Y.: Harper, 1950).
Akzin, B., 'Election and appointment'. *Am. Pol. Sci. Rev.* 54, 1960: 705–13.
Albinski, M., *De onderwijzer en de cultur-overdracht* (Assen: van Gorcum, 1959).
Alford, R., *Party and society (Chicago:* Rand McNally, 1963).
Alker, H. R., *Mathematics and politics* (N. Y.: Macmillan, 1965).
Alker, H. Jr., 'The comparison of aggregate political and social data: Potentialities and problems', in S. Rokkan (ed.) *Comparative research across cultures and nations* (Paris: Mouton, 1968).
Allardt, E. & K. Bruun, 'Characteristics of the Finnish non-voter', *Trans. Westermarck Soc.* 3, 1956: 55–76.
Allardt, E., *Social struktur och politisk aktivitet* (Helsinki: Söderström, 1956).
Allardt, E., *et al.*, 'On the cumulative nature of leisure time activities', *Acta Sociol.* 3 (1) 1958: 165–72.
Allardt, E., 'Community activity, leisure use and social structure', in S. Rokkan (ed.) *Approaches to the study of political participation* (Bergen: Chr. Michelsen Inst., 1962), revised version in E. Allardt & S. Rokkan (eds.) *Mass Politics* (New York: Free Press, 1969).
Allardt, E., 'Patterns of class conflict and working class consciousness in Finnish politics', pp. 97–131 in E. Allardt & Y. Littunen (eds.) *Cleavages, ideologies and party systems* (Helsinki: Westermarck Soc., 1964) Revised version in E. Allardt & S. Rokkan (eds.) *Mass Politics* (New York: Free Press, 1969).
Allardt, E. & O. Riihinen, 'Files for aggregate data by territorial units in Finland', pp. 128–35 in S. Rokkan (ed.) *Data archives for the social sciences* (Paris: Mouton, 1966).
Allardt, E., 'Implications of within-nation variations and regional imbalances for cross-national research', pp. 337–48 in R. L. Merritt & S. Rokkan (eds.) *Comparing nations* (New Haven: Yale Univ. Press, 1966).
Allardt, E. & P. Pesonen, 'Structural and non-structural cleavages in Finnish politics', in S. M. Lipset & S. Rokkan (eds.) *Party systems and voter alignments* (N. Y.: Free Press, 1967).
Almond, G. A. & J. S. Coleman (eds.) *The politics of developing areas* (Princeton Univ. Press, 1960).

Almond, 1963.

Almond, G. & S. Verba, *The civic culture* (Princeton: Princeton Univ. Press, 1963) Cf. the review article by Stein Rokkan, *Amer. Pol. Sci. Rev.* 58 (3) Sept. 1964: 676–679.

Almond, 1966.

Almond, G. & G. B. Powell, Jr., *Comparative politics: a developmental approach* (Boston: Little, Brown, 1966).

Anderson, B., 1959.

Anderson, B. & C. O. Mélén, 'Lazarsfeld's two-step hypothesis: Data from Swedish surveys', *Acta Sociol.* 4, 1959: 20–23.

Anderson, H. H., 1956.

Anderson, H. H. & G. L. Anderson, 'Cultural reactions to conflict: a study of adolescent children in seven countries', pp. 27–32 in G. M. Gilbert (ed.) *Psychological approaches to intergroup and international understanding* (Austin, Texas: Hogg Foundation for Mental Hygiene, Univ. of Texas, 1956).

Anderson, H. H., 1959.

Anderson, H. H. *et al.*, 'Image of the teacher by adolescent children in four countries: Germany, England, Mexico, and the United States', *J. of Soc. Psy. 50 (1) 1959: 47–55.*

Anderson, H. H., 1961.

Anderson, H. H. & G. L. Anderson, 'Image of the teacher by adolescent children in seven countries', *Am. J. of Orthopsychiatry* July 1961: 481–92.

Anderson, H. H., 1962.

Anderson, H. H. & G. L. Anderson, 'Social values of teachers in Rio de Janeiro, Mexico City, and Los Angeles County, California: a comparative study of teachers and children', *J. of Soc. Psy.* 58 (2) 1962: 207–26.

Andrae, 1926.

Andrae, P. G., *Andrae and his invention: the proportional representation method* (Cph.: Privately publ., 1926).

Andrae, 1968.

Andrae, C. G. 'The popular movements and the process of mobilization in Sweden', Paper, UNESCO Symposium, Gothenburg, 1968, printed in *Soc. Sci. Info.*, 8 (1) 1969: 65–79.

Arcari, 1957.

Arcari, P. M., 'Le rôle des femmes dans la vie politique', in *Studi Economico-Guiridici* (Fac. of Law, Univ. of Cagliari, Padua: Cedam, 1957).

Aron, 1955.

Aron, R., *L'opium des intellectuels* (Paris: Calmann, Lévy, 1955).

Arrow, 1963.

Arrow, K. J., *Social choice and individual values* (N. Y.: Wiley, 1951, 2nd ed. 1963).

Aubert, 1954.

Aubert, V. *et al.*, 'A comparative study of teachers' attitudes to international problems and policies', *J. of Soc. Iss.* 10 (4) 1954: 25–39.

Aubert, 1956.

Aubert, V. *et al.*, *Lærernes holdning til yrkesrollen og oppdragelsesspørsmål* (Oslo: Inst. for Social Research, 1956) repr. from *Norsk Pedagogisk Årbok 1956.*

Aubert, 1960.

Aubert, V., U. Torgersen *et al.*, 'Akademikerne i norsk samfunnsstruktur 1720–1955', *Ts. f. samfunnsforskn.* 1, 1960: 185–204.

Augst, 1916.

Augst, E. R., *Bismarcks Stellung zum parlamentarischen Wahlrecht*, Diss., Leipzig, 1916.

Banks & Textor, 1963. Banks, A. & R. Textor, *A cross-polity survey* (Cambr.: M. I. T. Press, 1963).

Barton, 1954. Barton, A. H., *Sociological and psychological problems of economic planning in Norway*, Ph. D. diss., Columbia Univ., 1954.

Bastid, 1948. Bastid, P., *L'avènement du suffrage universel* (Paris: Presses Universitaires de France, 1948).

Bateman, 1883. Bateman, J., *The great landowners of Great Britain and Ireland* (London, 1883).

Becarud, 1962. Becarud, J., *La Deuxième République espagnole* (Paris: Centre d'Etude des Relations Internationales, 1962) mimeo.

Belknap, 1951–52. Belknap, G. & A. Campbell, 'Political party identification and attitudes toward foreign policy', *Publ. Op. Quar.* 13, 1951–52: 601–23.

Bendix, 1957. Bendix, R. & S. M. Lipset, 'Political sociology', *Curr. Sociol.* 6 (2) 1957: 79–169.

Bendix, 1964. Bendix, R., *Nation-building and citizenship* (N. Y.: Wiley, 1964).

Bendix – Rokkan, 1964. Bendix, R. & S. Rokkan, 'The extension of national citizenship to the lower classes', pp. 74–100 in R. Bendix, *Nation-building and citizenship* (N. Y.: Wiley, 1964).

Benney, 1957. Benney, M. *et al.*, 'Sex and age in the interview', *Am. J. of Sociol.* 62, 1957: 143–52.

Benoist, 1896. Benoist, C., *La crise de l'état moderne: de l'organisation du suffrage universel* (Paris: Didot, 1896).

Benson, 1961. Benson, L., *The concept of Jacksonian democracy* (Princeton: Princeton Univ. Press, 1961).

Benson, 1965. Benson, L., 'The comparative analysis of historical change', Paper, Conf. on Comp. Research organized by the International Social Science Council, April 1965. Later printed in S. Rokkan (ed.) *Comparative research across cultures and nations* (Paris: Mouton, 1968).

Berdahl, 1942. Berdahl, C., 'Party membership in the United States', *Am. Pol. Sci. Rev.* 36, 1942.

Berelson, 1952. Berelson, B., 'Democratic theory and public opinion', *Publ. Op. Quart.* 16, 1952: 313–30.

Berelson, 1954. Berelson, B. *et al.*, *Voting* (Chicago: Univ. of Chicago Press, 1954).

Berry, 1966. Berry, B. J. L., 'By what categories may a state be characterized?', *Econ. Devel. and Cult. Change* 15 (1) 1966: 91–94.

Binder, 1969. Binder, L. *et al.*, *Crises in political development* (Princeton: Princeton Univ. Press, 1969).

Birch, 1964. Birch, A. H., *Representative and responsible government* (Lond.: Allen & Unwin, 1964).

Birke, 1961. Birke, W., *European elections by direct suffrage* (Leyden: Sijthoff, 1961).

Bisco, 1964. Bisco, R. L., 'Information retrieval from data archives: the ICPR System' *Am. Behav. Sci.* 7 (10) 1964: 45–47.

Bisco, 1965. Bisco, R. L., 'Social science data archives: technical considerations', *Soc. Sci. Info.* 4 (3) 1965: 129–50.

Bisco, 1966.   Bisco, R., 'Social science data archives: a review of recent developments', *Am. Pol. Sci. Rev.* 60 (1) 1966: 93–109.

Bisco, 1967.   Bisco, R., 'Social science data archives. Progress and prospects', *Soc. Sci. Info.* 6 (1) 1967: 39–74.

Black, 1958.   Black, D., *The theory of committees and elections* (Cambr.: Cambr. Univ. Press, 1958).

Blank 1904–05.   Blank, R., 'Die soziale Zusammensetzung der sozialdemokratischen Wählerschaft Deutschlands', *Arch. f. Soz.wiss. u. Soz.pol.* 20, 1904–05: 507–50.

Bock, 1919.   Bock, E., *Wahlstatistik. Ein Beitrag zur politischen Statistik* (Halle a. d. Saale, 1919).

Bonham, 1954.   Bonham, J., *The middle class vote* (Lond.: Faber, 1954).

Borg, 1966.   Borg, O., 'Basic dimensions of Finnish party ideologies', *Scand. Pol. Stud.* I, 1966: 94–120.

Boudon, 1963.   Boudon, R., 'Proprietés individuelles et proprietés collectives', *R. franç. sociol.* 4, 1963: 275–99.

Bracher, 1960.   Bracher, K., *Die Auflösung der Weimarer Republik* (3rd ed. Villingen: Ring, 1960).

Bracher, 1968.   Bracher, K. D., 'Staatsbegriff und Demokratie in Deutschland', *Pol. Vierteljahresschr.* 9 (1) 1968: 2–27.

Braun, 1903.   Braun, A., 'Die Reichtagswahlen von 1898 und 1903', *Archiv f. Soz.wiss. u. Soz.pol.* 18. 1903: 539–63.

Braunias, 1932.   Braunias, K., *Das parlamentarische Wahlrecht* (Berlin: de Gruyter, 1932).

Bremme, 1956.   Bremme, G., *Die politische Rolle der Frau in Deutschland* (Göttingen: Vandenhoeck, 1956).

Brenan, 1943.   Brenan, G., *The Spanish labyrinth* (Lond.: Cambr. Univ. Press, 1943, 2nd ed. 1950, paperback 1960).

Brengelmann, 1960.   Brengelmann, J. C. & L. Brengelmann, 'Deutsche Validierung von Fragebogen dogmatischer und intoleranter Haltungen', *Zeitschr. f. experimentelle u. angewandte Psychologie* 7, 1960: 451–71.

Broch, 1953.   Broch, L., *Political interests and activity of women in Norway,* Report to the International Political Science Association, 1953.

Bryce, 1921.   Bryce, J., *Modern democracies* (Lond.: Macmillan, 1921).

Buchanan, 1953.   Buchanan, W. & H. Cantril, *How nations see each other* (Urbana: Univ. of Illinois Press, 1953).

Buchanan, 1962.   Buchanan, J. M. & G. Tullock, *The calculus of consent: Logical foundations of constitutional democracy* (Ann Arbor: Univ. of Michigan Press, 1962).

Bull, 1922.   Bull, E., 'Die Entwicklung der Arbeiterbewegung in den drei skandinavischen Ländern', *Arch. f. Geschichte des Sozialismus* 10, 1922: 329–61.

Burnham, forthc.   Burnham, W. D., 'The United States of America 1789–1920', prepared for S. Rokkan & J. Meyriat (eds.) *International guide to electoral statistics,* vol. II, forthcoming.

Butler, 1958.   Butler, D. E., *The study of political behaviour* (Lond.: Hutchinson, 1958).

Butler, 1963.   Butler, D. E., *The electoral system in Britain since 1918* (Enl. ed. Oxf.: Clarendon, 1963).

Butler, 1968.   Butler, D. E. & J. Cornford, 'Britain', in S. Rokkan & J. Meyriat (eds.) *International guide to electoral statistics* (The Hague: Mouton, 1969).

Campbell, 1952.   Campbell, A. & R. L. Kahn, *The people elect a President* (Ann Arbor: Survey Research Center, 1952).

Campbell, 1954.   Campbell, A. *et al.*, *The voter decides* (Evanston: Row, Peterson, 1954).

Campbell, 1956.   Campbell, A. & H. C. Cooper, *Group differences in attitudes and votes* (Ann Arbor: Survey Research Center, 1956).

Campbell, 1957.   Campbell, A. & W. Miller, 'The motivational basis of straight and split ticket voting', *Am. Pol. Sci. Rev.* 51, 1957: 273–312.

Campbell, 1958.   Campbell, P., *French electoral systems and elections: 1789–1957* (N. Y.: Praeger, 1958).

Campbell, 1960:1.   Campbell, A. *et al.*, *The American voter* (N. Y.: Wiley, 1960).

Campbell, 1960:2.   Campbell, A., 'The archival resources of the Survey Research Center', *Publ. Opin. Quar.* 24 (4) 1960: 686–88.

Campbell, 1961.   Campbell, A. & H. Valen, 'Party identification in Norway and the United States', *Publ. Op. Quar.* 25 (4) 1961: 505–45.

Campbell, 1966.   Campbell, A. *et al.*, *Elections and the political order* (N. Y.: Wiley, 1966).

Canton, 1968.   Canton, Dario. *Materiales para una sociologia politica de la Argentina.* Introd. by S. Rokkan. (Buenos Aires: Inst. di Tella, 1968).

Cantril, 1958.   Cantril, H., *The politics of despair* (N. Y.: Basic Books, 1958).

Cantril, 1962.   Cantril, H. & L. A. Free, 'Hopes and fears for self and country', *Am. Behav. Scient.* 6 (2) Suppl. 1962.

Cantril, 1963.   Cantril, H., 'A study of aspirations', *Scientific American* 208 (2) 1963: 41...

Cantril, 1965.   Cantril, H., *The pattern of human concerns* (New Brunswick: Rutgers Univ. Press, 1965).

Carlsson, 1963.   Carlsson, G., 'Partiförskjutningar som tillväkstprocesser', *Statsv. ts.* 66 (2–3) 1963: 172–213.

Carlsson, 1965.   Carlsson, G., 'Time and continuity in mass attitude change', *Publ. Opin. Quar.* 29 (1) 1965: 1–15.

Carr, 1966.   Carr, R., *Spain, 1908–1939* (Oxf.: Clarendon, 1966).

Carson, 1955.   Carson, G. B. jr., *Electoral practices in the U.S.S.R.* (N. Y.: Praeger, 1955).

Chapman, 1962.   Chapman, R. M. *et al.*, *New Zealand politics in action* (Lond.: Oxf. Univ. Press, 1962).

Charnay, 1964.   Charnay, J. P., *Societé militaire et suffrage politique en France* (Paris: S. E. V. P. E. N., 1964).

Charnay, 1965.   Charnay, J. P., *Le suffrage politique en France* (Paris: Mouton, 1965).

Christiansen, 1951.   Christiansen, B. & S. Rokkan (eds.) *International seminar on comparative social research. Proceedings 1–5* (Oslo: Institute for Social Research, 1951) mimeo.

Christie, 1954.   Christie, R., 'Authoritarianism re-examined', pp. 123–96 in R. Christie & M. Jahoda, *Studies in the scope and method of 'The Authoritarian Personality'* (Glencoe: Free Press, 1954).

Christie, 1955.   Christie, R., 'Eysenck and the Communist personality: some critical remarks', MS, 1955.

Clapham, 1921.   Clapham, J. H., *The economic development of France and Germany* (Cambr.: Cambr. Univ. Press, 1921).

Clark, 1962.   Clark, G. K., *The making of Victorian England* (Lond.: Methuen, 1962).

Clarke, 1936.   Clarke, M. V., *Medieval representation and consent: a study of early Parliaments in England and Ireland, with special reference to the 'Modus tenendi parliamentum'* (N. Y.: Russell, 1936, 2nd ed. 1964).

Cohn, 1954.   Cohn, T. S. & H. Carsch, 'Administration of the F-scale to a sample of Germans', *J. of Abn. and Soc. Psy.* 49 (3) 1954: 471.

Coladarci, 1959.   Coladarci, A. P., 'The measurement of authoritarianism in Japanese education', *California J. of Educ. Res.* 10, 1959: 137–41.

Coleman, 1965:1.   Coleman, J. S., 'The development syndrome', draft Jan. 1965, cf. Binder, 1969.

Coleman, 1965:2.   Coleman, J. S. (ed.) *Education and political development* (Princeton: Princeton Univ. Press, 1965).

Converse, 1958.   Converse, P. E., 'The shifting role of class in political attitudes and behavior', pp. 388–99 in E. Maccoby *et al., Readings in social psychology* (N. Y.: Holt. 1958).

Converse, 1962:1.   Converse, P. E. & G. Dupeux, 'De Gaulle and Eisenhower: the public image of the victorious general', Paper, IPSA Congress, Paris, 1962, French version *Rev. Franç. de Sci. Pol.* 12 (1) 1962: 54–92.

Converse, 1962:2.   Converse, P. E. & G. Dupeux, 'Politization of the electorate in France and the United States', *Publ. Opin. Quar.* 26 (1) 1962: 1–23.

Converse, 1964.   Converse, P. E., 'A network of data archives for the behavioral sciences', *Pub. Opin. Quar.* 28 (2) 1964: 273–86.

Converse, 1966:1.   Converse, P. E., 'The availability and quality of sample survey data in archives within the United States', pp. 419–40 in R. L. Merritt & S. Rokkan (eds.) *Comparing nations* (London-New Haven: Yale Univ. Press. 1966).

Converse, 1966:2.   Converse, P., 'The problem of party distances in models of voting change', pp. 175–207 in K. Jennings & H. Zeigler (eds.) *The electoral process* (Englewood Cliffs: Prentice Hall, 1966).

Conze, 1962.   Conze, W. (ed.) *Staat und Gesellschaft im deutschen Vormärz 1815–1848* (Stuttgart: Klett, 1962).

Cornblit, 1968.   Cornblit, O. *et al.*, 'A model for political change in Latin America', *Soc. Sci. Info.* 7 (2) 1968: 13–48.

Cornford, 1963.   Cornford, J., 'The transformation of Conservatism in the late 19th century', *Vict. Stud.* 7, 1963: 35–66.

438   *Bibliography*

Coser, 1956.   Coser, L. A., *The functions of social conflict* (Lond.:
                        Routledge, 1956).
Costa, 1902.   Costa, J. (ed.) *Oligarquia y caciquismo como el forma
                        actual de gobierno en España* (Madrid: Hernández,
                        1902).
Cotteret, 1960.   Cotteret, J. M. *et al., Lois électorales et inégalités de
                        réprésentation en France, 1836–1960* (Paris: Colin,
                        1960).
Cox, 1966.   Cox, K. R., *Regional anomalies in the voting behavior
                        of the population of England and Wales: 1921–1951*,
                        diss. Univ. of Illinois, 1966, summary published in
                        E. Allardt & S. Rokkan (eds.) *Mass Politics* (New
                        York: Free Press, 1969).
Crutti, 1951.   Crutti, M. *et al., Profilo storico degli ordinamenti
                        elettorali* (Empoli, Italy: Caparrini, 1951).
Cutright, 1958.   Cutright, P. & P. H. Rossi, 'Grass roots politicians
                        and the vote', *Am. Sociol. Rev.* 23 (2) 1958: 171–79.
Cutright, 1963.   Cutright, P., 'Urbanization and competitive party
                        politics', *J. of Pol.* 25 (3) 1963: 552–64.
Daalder, 1955.   Daalder, H., 'Parties and politics in the Netherlands',
                        Pol. Stud. 3, 1955: 1–16.
Daalder, 1958.   Daalder, H., 'Nederland: het politieke stelsel', pp.
                        213–38 in L. van der Land (ed.) *Repertorium van de
                        Sociale Wetenschappen* I (Amst.: Elsevier, 1958).
Daalder, 1966:1.   Daalder, H., 'The Netherlands: Opposition in a
                        segmented society', pp. 188–236 in R. A. Dahl (ed.)
                        Political opposition in Western democracies (New
                        Haven & Lond.: Yale Univ. Press, 1966).
Daalder, 1966:2.   Daalder, H., 'Parties and elites in Western Europe',
                        pp. 43–77 in J. LaPalombara & M. Weiner. *Political
                        parties and political development* (Princeton: Prince-
                        ton Univ. Press, 1966).
Dahl, 1956.   Dahl, R. A., *A preface to democratic theory* (Chicago:
                        Univ. of Chicago Press, 1956).
Dahl, 1958.   Dahl, R. A., 'A critique of the Ruling Elite Model',
                        Am. Pol. Sci. Rev. 52, 1958: 463–69.
Dahl, 1966.   Dahl, R. A. (ed.) *Political oppositions in Western
                        democracies* (New Haven: Yale Univ. Press, 1966).
Dahl, 1967.   Dahl, R. A. & E. R. Tufte, 'Size and democracy',
                        Paper, Center for Advanced Study in the Behavioral
                        Sciences, Stanford, 1967.
Dahlström, 1954.   Dahlström, E., *Tjänstemännen, näringslivet och sam-
                        hället* (Sth.: SNS, 1954).
Dahlström, 1968.   Dahlström, E., 'The Project Scandinavian Social Struc-
                        ture', Paper, UNESCO Symposium, Gothenburg, Aug.
                        1968.
Dahrendorf, 1965.   Dahrendorf, R., *Gesellschaft und Demokratie in
                        Deutschland* (Munich: Piper, 1965).
Danielsen, 1964.   Danielsen, R., *Det Norske Storting gjennom 150 år*,
                        vol. II. (Oslo: Gyldendal, 1964).
DATUM, 1965.   DATUM, *Erster Bericht über DATUM* (Bad Godes-
                        berg: DATUM, 1965) mimeo.

David, 1961–62.

David, P. T. & R. Eisenberg, *Devaluation of the urban and sub-urban vote* I–II (Charlottesville: Univ. of Virginia, Bureau of Publ. Adm., 1961–62).

Davis, 1964.

Davis, K., 'Problems and solution in international comparison for social science purposes', Paper, International Conference on Comparative Social Research in Developing Countries, Buenos Aires, Sept. 1964.

de Grazia, 1963.

de Grazia, A., *Essay on apportionment and representative government* (Wash.: American Enterprise Institute for Public Policy Research, 1963).

de Jong, 1956.

de Jong, J. J., *Overheid en onderdaan* (Wageningen Zomer & Keunings, 1956).

Démocratie, 1947.

'Démocratie dans la monde. Une enquête internationale', *Sondages* 8, 1947: 83–86.

Desabie, 1959.

Desabie, J., 'Le réferendum. Essai d'étude statistique' *J. soc. statist. Paris* 100 (7–8–9) 1959: 166–180.

Deutsch, 1953.

Deutsch, K., *Nationalism and social communication* (N.Y.: Wiley, 1953, 2d ed. Cambr.: M.I.T. Press, 1966).

Deutsch, 1956.

Deutsch, K. W., *An interdisciplinary bibliography on nationalism. 1935–1953* (Cambr.: M.I.T. Press 1956).

Deutsch, 1961.

Deutsch, K., 'Social mobilization and political development' *Am. Pol. Sci. Rev.* 55 (3) 1961: 493–514.

Deutsch, 1965:1.

Deutsch, K. W. & R. L. Merritt, 'Effects of events on national and international images', pp. 132–87 in H. C. Kelman (ed.) *International behaviour* (N.Y.: Holt, 1965).

Deutsch, 1965:2.

Deutsch, K. W. & H. Weilenmann, 'The Swiss City Canton: a political invention' *Comp. Stud. Soc. Hist.* 7 (4) 1965: 393–408.

Deutsch, 1966:1.

Deutsch, K. W., 'The theoretical basis of data programs', pp. 27–56 in R. L. Merritt & S. Rokkan (eds.) *Comparing nations* (Lond.–New Haven: Yale Univ. Press, 1966).

Deutsch, 1966:2.

Deutsch, K. W. *et al.*, 'The Yale political date program', pp. 81–94 in R. L. Merritt & S. Rokkan (eds.) *Comparing nations* (Lond.–New Haven: Yale Univ. Press, 1966).

Deutsch, 1969.

Deutsch, K. W. & R. L. Merritt, *Nationalism: An interdisciplinary bibliography 1935–1966* (Cambr.: M.I.T. Press, 1969).

Deutsch, forthc.

Deutsch, K. W. & H. Weilenmann, *United for diversity: The political integration of Switzerland* (forthcoming).

d'Hondt, 1878.

d'Hondt, V. *La représentation proportionelle des partis* (Ghent, 1878).

d'Hondt, 1882.

Westdeutscher Verl., 1965).
sentation proportionelle (Brussels: Muquardt, 1882).

Diamond, 1963.

Diamond, S., 'Some early uses of the questionnaire', *Publ. Op. Quar.* 27 (4) 1963: 528–42.

Diederich, 1965.

Diederich, N., *Empirische Wahlforschung* (Cologne: Westdeutscher Verl., 1965).

DIVO, 1958.   DIVO, *Was denken die Volksvertreter. Ergebnisse aus*
                             einer internationalen Untersuchung politischer Füh-
                             rungsschichten in 7 Ländern (Frankfurt am Main:
                             DIVO, 1958) mimeo.

Dodd, 1946–47.   Dodd, S. C., 'Toward world surveying', *Publ. Opin*
                             Quar. 10 (4) 1946–47: 470–83.

Dogan, 1955.   Dogan, M. & J. Narbonne, *Les françaises face à la*
                             politique (Paris: Colin, 1955).

Dogan, 1956.   Dogan, M., 'Le comportement politique des femmes
                             dans les pays de l'Europe occidentale', in *La condition*
                             sociale de la femme (Brussels: Institut de Sociologie
                             Solvay, 1956).

Dogan, 1959.   Dogan, M., 'Il voto delle donne in Italia e in altre
                             democrazie', *Tempi Moderni* 2 (11)–12) 1959: 621–44.

Dogan, 1960.   Dogan, M., 'Le vote ouvrier en Europe occidentale',
                             Rev. Franç, de Sociol. 1 (1) 1960: 25–44.

Dogan, 1963.   Dogan, M., 'La stratificazione sociale dei suffragi', pp.
                             407–74 in A. Spreafico & J. LaPalombara (eds.) *Ele-*
                             zioni e comportamento politico in Italia (Milan: Ed.
                             di Communita, 1963).

Dogan, 1965.   Dogan, M., 'Le vote ouvrier en France. Analyse
                             écologique des élections de 1962', *R. franç. de sociol.*
                             6 (4) 1965: 435–71.

Dogan, 1966.   Dogan, M.,'Les contextes politiques en France'. Paper,
                             Symposium on Quantitative Ecological Analysis,
                             Evian, Sept. 1966.

Dogan, 1967.   Dogan, M., 'Political cleavage and social stratification
                             in France and Italy', pp. 129–196 in S. M. Lipset &
                             S. Rokkan (eds.) *Party systems and voter alignments*
                             (N. Y.: Free Press, 1967).

Dogan & Rokkan, 1969.   Dokan, M. & S. Rokkan (eds.) *Quantitative Ecological*
                             Analysis in the Social Sciences (Cambr.: M.I.T. Press,
                             1969).

Dovring, 1960.   Dovring, F., *Land and labour in Europe 1900–1950*
                             (2d. ed. The Hague: Nijhoff, 1960).

Downs, 1957.   Downs, A., *An economic theory of democracy* (N. Y.:
                             Harper, 1957).

Droop, 1968.   Droop, H. R., *On methods of electing representatives*
                             (Lond.: Macmillan, 1968).

Duijker & Rokkan, 1964.   Duijker, H. C. J. & S. Rokkan, 'Organizational aspects
                             of cross-national social research', *J. of Soc. Iss.* 10 (4)
                             1964: 8–24.

Dunn, 1967.   Dunn, E. S. D. Jr., 'The idea of a national data center
                             and the issue of personal privacy', *The Am. Statisti-*
                             cian 21 (1) 1967: 21–27.

Dupeux, 1954–55.   Dupeux, G., 'Le comportement électoral', *Curr. Sociol.*
                             3 (4) 1954–55, 281–344.

Dupeux, 1959.   Dupeux, G., *Le front populaire et les élections de*
                             1936 (Paris: Colin, 1959).

Duverger, 1950.   Duverger, M. *et al.*, *L'influence des système electoraux*
                             sur la vie politique (Paris: Colin, 1950).

Duverger, 1951.   Duverger, M., *Les partis politiques* (Paris: Colin,
                             1951). Engl. transl. (Lond.: Methuen, 1954).

Duverger, 1955:1.   Duverger, M., *La participation des femmes à la vie politique* (Paris: UNESCO, 1955).

Duverger, 1955:2.   Duverger, M. (ed.) *Partis politiques et classes sociales en France* (Paris: Colin, 1955).

Easton, 1957.   Easton, D., 'An approach to the analysis of political systems' *World Pol.* 9 (3) 1957: 383–400.

Eaton, 1930.   Eaton, A. & S. M. Harrison, *A bibliography of social surveys* (N. Y.: 1930).

Eckstein, 1963.   Eckstein, H. & D. Apter, (eds.) *Comparative politics. A reader.* (N. Y.: Free Press, 1963).

Eldersveld, 1951.   Eldersveld, S. J., 'Theory and methods in voting behaviour research', *J. of Pol.* 13, 1951: 70–87.

Élections eur., 1960.   *Les élections européennes au suffrage universel direct* (Brussels: Inst. de Sociologie Solvay, 1960).

Engelmann, 1966.   Engelmann, F. C., 'Austria: The pooling of opposition', pp. 260–83 in R. A. Dahl (ed.) *Political oppositions in Western Democracies* (Lond.: Yale Univ. Press, 1966).

Epstein, 1956.   Epstein, L. D., 'British mass parties in comparison with American parties', *Pol. Sci. Quart.* 71 (1) 1956: 97–125.

Epstein, 1964.   Epstein, L. D., 'A comparative study of Canadian parties', *Am. Pol. Sci. Rev.* 58, 1964: 46–59, cf. also *Political Parties in Western Democracies* (N. Y.: Praeger, 1967).

Evans, 1917.   Evans, E. D., *A history of the Australian Ballot System in The United States* (Chicago: Univ. of Chicago Press, 1917).

Eyck, 1945.   Eyck, E., *Bismarck* (Erlenbach-Zürich: Rentsch, 1945).

Eysenck, 1950.   Eysenck, H. J., 'Social attitude and social class', *Brit. J. Sociol.* 1 (1) 1950: 55–66.

Eysenck, 1953.   Eysenck, H. J., 'Primary social attitudes. II. A comparison of attitude patterns in England, Germany and Sweden', *J. Abn. Soc. Ps.* 48, 1953: 563–68.

Eysenck, 1954.   Eysenck, H. J., *The psychology of politics* (Lond.: Routledge & Kegan Paul, 1954).

Faul, 1960.   Faul, E. (ed.) *Wahlen und Wähler in Westdeutschland* (Villingen: Ring-Verl., 1960).

Fauvet, 1958.   Fauvet, J. & H. Mendras (eds.) *Les paysans et la politique* (Paris: Colin, 1958).

Fivelsdal, 1964.   Fivesdal, E., *Funksjonærenes syn på faglige og politiske spørsmål* (Oslo: Univ. forl., 1964).

Fogarty, 1957.   Fogarty, M. P., *Christian democracy in Western Europe* (Notre Dame: Univ. of Notre Dame Press, 1957).

Fraenkel, 1958.   Fraenkel, E., 'Parlament und öffentliche Meinung', in *Zur Geschichte und Problematik der Demokratie. Festgabe für H. Herzfeld* (Berlin: Duncker & Humblot, 1958).

Framveksten, 1964.   'Framveksten av de politiske partier i de nordiske land på 1800-tallet', *Problemer i nordisk historieforskning II* (Oslo: Univ. forl., 1964).

Free, 1958.   Free, L. A., 'Polling decision-makers: an experiment in political psychology', *Publ. Opin Quar.* 22 (2) 1958: 184–86.

Free, 1959.   Free, L. A., *Six allies and a neutral* (Glencoe: Press, 1959).

Free, 1960.   Free, L. A., *A compilation of attitudes of Philippine legislators* (Princeton: Inst. for International Social Research, 1960).

Free, 1961.   Free, L. A., *Some international implications of the political psychology of Brazilians* (Princeton: Inst. for International Social Research, 1961).

Friedrich, 1941.   Friedrich, C. J., 'Introduction', to F. A. Hermens *Democracy or anarchy?* (Notre Dame: Univ. of Notre Dame Press, 1941).

Gagel, 1959.   Gagel, W., *Die Wahlrechtsfrage in der Geschichte der deutschen liberalen Parteien* (Düsseldorf: Droste, 1959).

Gaier, 1959.   Gaier, E. L. & B. M. Bass, 'Regional differences in inter-relations among authoritarianism, acquiescence and ethnocentrism', *J. of Soc. Psy.* 49, 1959: 47–51.

Galbraith, 1925.   Galbraith, G. R., *The constitution of the Dominican order: 1216–1360* (Manchester: Manchester Univ. Press, 1925).

Gallup, 1938.   Gallup, G. & C. Robinson, 'American Institute of Public Opinion Surveys, 1935–38', *Publ. Op. Quart.* 2, 1938: 373–99.

Gardin, 1960.   Gardin, J. C., 'Les 'Human Relations Area Files' et la mécanographie dans la documentation ethnographique', *Cahiers d'études africains* 3, 1960: 150–52.

Gash, 1953.   Gash, N., *Politics in the Age of Peel* (Lond.: 1953).

Geertz, 1963.   Geertz, C., 'The integrative revolution', pp. 105–57 in C. Geertz (ed.) *Old societies and new states* (N. Y.: Free Press, 1963).

Geismann, 1964.   Geismann, G., *Politische Struktur und Regierungssystem in den Niederlanden* (Frankfurt am Main: Athenaum, 1964).

Germani, 1965.   Germani, G., 'Report on the ISSC Conference in Buenos Aires in 1964', *Soc. Sci. Info.* 4 (2) 1965: 150–72.

Gerschenkron, 1943.   Gerschenkron, A., *Bread and democracy in Germany* (Berkeley: Univ. of California Press, 1943).

Gilissen, 1958.   Gilissen, J., *Le régime représentatif en Belgique depuis 1790* (Brussels: Renaissance du Livre, 1958).

Girod, 1964.   Girod, R., 'Geography of the Swiss party system', pp. 132–61 in E. Allardt & Y. Littunen (eds.) *Cleavages, ideologies and party systems* (Helsinki: Westermarck Soc. 1964).

Glaser, 1966.   Glaser, W. & R. Bisco, 'Plans for the Council of Social Science Data Archives', *Soc. Sci. Info.* 5 (4) 1966: 71–96.

Glass, 1954.   Glass, D. V. (ed.) *Social mobility in Britain* (Lond.: Routledge & Kegan Paul, 1954).

Glass, 1961.   Glass, D. V. & R. König (eds.) *Sociale Schichtung und Mobilität* (Cologne: Westdeutscher Verl., 1961).

Glass, 1965.

Glass, D. V. & D. E. C. Eversley (eds.) *Population in history. Essays in historical demography.* (Lond.: Arnold, 1965).

Goldman, 1956.

Goldman, R. M., 'Move – lose your vote', *Nat. Municipal Rev.* 45, 1956.

Gollwitzer, 1952.

Gollwitzer, H., 'Der Cäsarismus Napoleons III im Widerhall der öffentlichen Meinung Deutschlands', *Hist. Zs.* 173 (1) 1952: 23–76.

Goodman, 1959.

Goodman, L., 'Some alternatives to ecological correlation', *Am. J. Sociol.* 64, 1959: 610–25.

Goody, 1963.

Goody, J. & I. Watt, 'The consequences of literacy', *Comp. Stud. Soc. Hist.* 5 (3) 1963: 304–45.

Gorden, 1965.

Gorden, M. & D. Lerner, 'The setting of European arms control: political and strategic choices of European elites', *J. of Confl. Res.* 9 (4) 1965: 419–33.

Gosnell, 1930.

Gosnell, H., *Why Europe votes* (Chicago: Univ. of Chicago Press, 1930).

Gravier, 1958.

Gravier, J.-F., *Paris et le désert français* (2d ed. Paris: Flammarion, 1958).

Gruijters, 1967.

Gruijters, H. *et al., Experimenten in demokratie* (Amst:. de Bezige Bij, 1967).

Grumm, 1958.

Grumm, J. G., 'Theories of electoral systems', *Midw. J. of Pol. Sci.* 2, 1958: 357–76.

Gruner, 1966.

Gruner, E. & K. Frei, *Schweizerische Bundesversammlung 1848–1920,* I–II (Bern: Francke, 1966).

Guttsman, 1963.

Guttsman, W. L., *The British political elite* (Lond.: McGibbon & Kee, 1963).

Habakkuk, 1962.

Habakkuk, H. J., *American and British technology in the 19th Century* (Cambr.: Cambr. Univ. Press, 1962).

Habermas, 1961.

Habermas, J., *Strukturwandel der Öffentlichkeit* (Neuwied: Luchterhand, 1961).

Hägerstrand, 1951.

Hägerstrand, T., *Innovationsförloppet ur korologiskt synspunkt* (Lund: Gleerup, 1951).

Hall, 1950.

Hall, J. & D. C. Jones, 'The social grading of occupations', *Brit. J. of Soc.* 1 (1) 1950: 31–55.

Hall, 1953.

Hall, R. K. *et al.,* 'The social position of teachers', *Yearbook of Education,* 1953.

Hammer, 1953.

Hammer, E. L., 'Salaries of teachers', *Yearbook of Education,* 1953: 102–8.

Hanham, 1959.

Hanham, H. J., *Elections and party management: Politics in the time of Disraeli and Gladstone* (Lond.: Longmans, 1959).

Hans, 1949.

Hans, N., *Comparative education* (Lond.: Routledge, 1949).

Hansen, 1899.

Hansen, A., *Norsk folkepsykologi* (Kristiania: Dybwad, 1899).

Hare, 1857.

Hare, T., *The machinery of representation* (Lond.: Maxwell, 1857).

Hartung, 1955.

Hartung, F. & R. Mousnier, 'Quelques problèmes concernant la monarchie absolue', *Relazioni X Congr. Int. Sci. Storiche* IV (Florence: 1955).

Hartwig, 1928.

Hartwig, R., 'Wie die Frauen im deutschen Reich von ihren politischen Wahlrecht Gebrauch machen', *Allg. Statist. Archiv* 17, 1928.

Hartwig, 1931. Hartwig, R., 'Das Frauenwahlrecht in der Statistik', *Allg. Statist.* Archiv 21, 1931.

Håstad, 1954. Håstad, E., *Det moderna partiväsendets organisation* (Sth.: Bonniers, 1954).

Hastings, 1961. Hastings, P. K., 'The Roper Public Opinion Research Center: a review of its first three years of operation', *Pub. Opin. Quar.* 25 (1) 1961: 120–26.

Hastings, 1964. Hastings, P. K., 'International Survey Library Association of the Roper Public Opinion Research Center', *Publ. Opin. Quar.* 28 (2) 1964: 331–33.

Heberle, 1945. Heberle, R., *From democracy to Nazism* (Baton Rouge: Louisiana State Univ., 1945). Publ. in German: *Landbevölkerung und Nationalsozialismus* (Stuttgart: Deutsche Verlags-Anstalt, 1963).

Heberle, 1951. Heberle, R., *Social movements* (N. Y.: Appleton, 1951).

Heckscher, 1957. Heckscher, G., *The study of comparative government and politics* (Lond.: Allen & Unwin, 1957).

Hennis, 1957. Hennis, W., *Meinungsforschung und repräsentative Demokratie* (Tübingen: Mohr, 1957).

Hermens, 1941. Hermens, F. A., *Democracy or anarchy?* (Notre Dame: Univ of Notre Dame Press, 1941). New ed. *Europe between democracy and anarchy* (Notre Dame: Univ. of Notre Dames Press, 1951).

Hermens, 1958. Hermens, F. A., *The representative republic* (Notre Dame: Univ. of Notre Dame Press, 1958).

Herz, 1932. Herz, H., *Über Wesen und Aufgaben der politischen Statistik* (Leipzig: Gräfe, 1932).

Heuss, 1957. Heuss, T., *Friedrich Naumann* (Stuttgart: Deutsche Verlagsanstalt, 1957).

Himmelstand, 1960. Himmelstand, Ulf, *Social pressures, attitudes and democratic processes* (Sth.: Almquist & Wiksell, 1960).

Himmelstrand, 1962. Himmelstrand, U., 'A theoretical and empirical approach to depolitization and political involvement', in *S. Rokkan (ed.) Approaches to the study of political participation* (Bergen: Chr. Michelsen Inst., 1962), revised version publ. in E. Allardt & S. Rokkan (eds.) *Mass Politics* (New York: Free Press, 1969).

Hintze, 1930. Hintze, O., 'Typologie der ständischen Verfassung des Abendlandes', *Hist. Zs.* 141, 1930: 229–48.

Hintze, 1962. Hintze, O., *Staat und Verfassung: Gesammelte Abhandlungen zur allgemeinen Verfassungsgeschichte* (2d enl. ed. Göttingen: Vandenhoeck & Ruprecht, 1962).

Hjellum, 1967:1. Hjellum, T., *Partiene i lokalpolitikken* (Oslo: Gyldndal, 1967).

Hjellum, 1967:2. Hjellum, T., 'The politicization of local government in Norway', *Scand. Pol. Stud.* II, 1967: 69–93.

Hoag, 1926. Hoag, C. G. & G. H. Hallett, *Proportional representation* (N. Y.: Macmillan, 1926).

Hodgson, 1966. Hodgson, J. H., *Communism in Finland* (Princeton: Princeton Univ. Press, 1966).

Högh, 1968. Högh, E., *Den danske velger,* manuscript 1968.

Höyer, 1960.

Höyer, S., *Enkelte stiltrekk i avisenes lederartikler foran tre stortingsvalg* (Oslo: Institutt for Samfunnsforskning, 1960) stencilled.

Hogan, 1945.

Hogan, J., *Election and representation* (Cork: Cork Univ. Press, 1945).

Holt, 1966.

Holt, R. & J. Turner, *The political basis of economic development* (Princeton: Van Nostrand, 1966).

Horowitz, 1963.

Horowitz, I. L., 'The life and death of Project Camelot', *Transaction* 3 (1) 1963: 3–7 and 44–47.

Hovde, 1948.

Hovde, B. J., *The Scandinavian countries 1720–1865* (Ithaca: Cornell Univ. Press, 1948).

HRAF, n.d.

Human Relations Area Files, *A laboratory for the study of man, 1949–1959,* (New Haven, HRAF, no date).

Hunter, 1953.

Hunter, F., *Community power structure* (Chapel Hill: Univ. of North Carolina Press, 1953).

Huntington, 1965.

Huntington, S. P., 'Political development and political decay', *World Pol.* 17 (3) 1965: 386–430.

Huntington, 1966.

Huntington, S. P., 'Political modernization: America vs. Europe', *World Pol.* 18 (3) 1966: 378–414.

Huntington, 1968.

Huntington, S. P., *Political order in changing societies* (New Haven: Yale Univ. Press, 1968).

Husén, 1967.

Husén, T., *International study of achievement in mathematics. A comparison of twelve countries* (Sth.: Almquist & Wicksel, 1967, N. Y.: Wiley, 1967).

Hylla, 1953.

Hylla, E. & W. L. Wrinkle, *Die Schulen in Westeuropa* (Bad Nauheim: Christian-Verl., 1953).

Hyman, 1951:1.

Hyman, H., 'The conditions warranting cross-national research', pp. 3–8 in B. Christiansen, H. Hyman & R. Rommetveit, *Cross-national social research* I (Oslo: Institute for Social Research, 1951).

Hyman, 1951:2.

Hyman, H., 'The modification of a personality-centred conceptual system when the project is translated from a national to a crossnational study', in B. Christiansen, H. Hyman & R. Rommetveit, *Cross-national social research* I (Oslo: Institut for Social Research, 1951).

Hyman, 1954.

Hyman, H. *et al., Interviewing in Social Research* (Chicago: Univ. of Chicago Press, 1954).

Inkeles, 1956.

Inkeles, A. & P. H. Rossi, 'National comparisons of occupational prestige', *Am. J. of Soc.* 61, 1956: 329–39.

Inkeles, 1966.

Inkeles, A., 'The modernization of man', in M. Weiner (ed.) *Modernization: the dynamics of growth* (N. Y.: Basic Books, 1966).

Inst. Sozialf. 1936.

Institut für Sozialforschung. *Studien über Authorität und Familie* (Paris: Alcan, 1936).

Inst. Electoral Res., 1960.

Institute of Electoral Research, *A review of elections 1954–58, ... 1959, ... 1960, ... 1961–62,* (Lond.: the Institute, 1960 et sqq.).

Inst. Electoral Res., 1962.

Institute of Electoral Research, *Parliaments and electorat systems: A world handbook* (Lowestoft, England: Scorpion, 1962).

Israel, 1957.

Israel, J., 'Propagandan kring folkomröstningen' *Tiden* 40 (9) 1957: 534–541.

446   *Bibliography*

Jacob, 1962–66.
International studies of values in politics, *Reports 1962–66* (Philadelphia) mimeo.

Jacobson, 1954:1.
Jacobson, E. & S. Schachter (eds.) 'Cross-national research: a case study', *J. of Soc. Iss.* 10 (4) 1954: 1–68.

Jacobson, 1954: 2.
Jacobson, E., 'Methods used for producing comparable data in the O.C.S.R. Seven-Nation Attitude Study', *J. of Soc. Iss.* 10 (4) 1954: 40–51.

Jacobsen, 1964.
Jacobsen, K. Dahl, *Teknisk hjelp og politisk struktur* (Oslo: Univ. forl., 1964).

Janis, 1953.
Janis, I. L., 'Fear-arousing appeals', pp. 56–98 in Carl I. Hovland *et al.*, *Communication and persuasion* (New Haven: Yale Univ. Press, 1953).

Janis, 1954.
Janis, I. L., 'Problems of theory in the analysis of stress behavior', *J. of Soc. Iss.* 10 (3) 1954: 12–25.

Janson, 1961.
Janson, C.-G., *Mandattilldelning och regional röstfördelning* (Sth.: Idun, 1961.)

Janson, 1965.
Janson, C.-C., 'Project Metropolit', *Acta Sociol.* 9 (1–2) 1965: 110–15.

Jennings, 1960.
Jennings, Sir Ivor, *Party politics I: Appeal to the people* (Cambr.: Cambr. Univ. Press, 1960).

Jeppesen, 1964.
Jeppesen, J. & P. Meyer, *Sofavelgerne* (Aarhus: Institut for Statskundskap, Aarhus Univ., 1964).

John, 1884.
John, V., *Geschichte der Statistik* (Stuttgart: Enke, 1884).

Jutikkala, 1960.
Jutikkala, E., 'Political parties in the elections of deputies to the Estate of Burgesses and the Estate of Farmers', *Sitzungsber, der finn. Akad. Wiss.*, 1960: 167–184.

Kaartvedt, 1964.
Kaartvedt, A., *Fra Riksforsamlingen til 1869*, Vol. 1 of *Det Norske Storting gjennom 150 år* (Oslo: Gyldendal, 1964).

Kahn, 1957.
Kahn, R. L. & C. Cannell, *The dynamics of interviewing* (N. Y.: Wiley, 1957).

Kandel, 1933.
Kandel, I. L., *Comparative education* (Boston: Houghton Mifflin, 1933).

Kanwar, 1958.
Kanwar, U., 'Social structure in authoritarian and non-authoritarian personality', *Education and Psychology*, 5, 1958: 15–23.

Kassof, 1958.
Kassof, A., 'The prejudiced personality: a cross-cultural test', *Social Problems* 6, 1958: 59–67.

Katz, 1937.
Katz, D. & H. Cantril, 'Public opinion polls', *Socio-Metry* I, 1937: 155–79.

Katz, 1961.
Katz, D. & S. J. Eldersveld, 'The impact of local party activity upon the electorate', *Publ. Opin. Quar.* 25 (1) 1961: 1–24.

Katz, 1955.
Katz, E. & P. L. Lazarsfeld, *Personal influence* (Glencoe: Free Press, 1955).

Kennedy, 1958.
Kennedy, J. L. & H. D. Lasswell, 'A cross-cultural test of self-image', *Human Organization* 17 (1) 1958: 41–43.

Kesselman, 1966.
Kesselman, M., 'French local government: a statistical examination of grass roots consensus', *Am. Pol. Sci. Rev.* 60, 1966: 963–73.

Key, 1950.
Key, V. O., *Southern politics* (N. Y.: Knopf, 1950).

Key, 1959.   Key, V. O. Jr., *Politics, parties and pressure groups* (N. Y.: Crowell, 1959, 1964).

Kindleberger, 1964.   Kindleberger, C. P., *Economic growth in France and Britain 1851–1950* (Cambr.: Harvard Univ. Press, 1964).

Kirchheimer, 1957.   Kirchheimer, O., 'The waning of opposition in parliamentary regimes', *Soc. Res.* 24, 1957: 127–156.

Kitzinger, 1964.   Kitzinger, U., *Britain, Europe and beyond. Essays in European politics* (Leiden: Sijthoff, 1964).

Klatzmann, 1957.   Klatzmann, J., 'Comportement électoral et classe sociale', pp. 254–85 in M. Duverger *et al., Les élections du 2 janvier 1956* (Paris: Colin, 1957).

Klatzmann, 1958.   Klatzmann, J., 'Géographie électorale de l'agriculture française', pp. 39–67 in J. Fauvet & H. Mendras (eds.) *Les paysans et la politique* (Paris: Colin, 1958).

Klineberg, 1950.   Klineberg, O., *Tensions affecting international understanding* (N. Y.: Social Sciences Research Council, 1950).

Klöcker, 1913.   Klöcker, A., *Die Konfession der sozialdemokratischen Wählerschaft 1907* (M. Gladbach: Volksverein-Verl., 1913).

Kornhauser, 1959.   Kornhauser, W., *The politics of mass society* (Glencoe: Free Press, 1959).

Kraditor, 1965.   Kraditor, A. S., *The ideas of the woman suffrage movement 1890–1920* (N. Y.: Columbia Univ. Press, 1965).

Kruijt, 1959.   Kruijt, J. P., *et al., Verzuiling* (Zaandijk: Heijnis, 1959).

Kruijt, 1962.   Kruijt, J. P. & W. Goddijn, 'Verzuiling en ontzuiling als sociologisch proces', pp. 227–63 in A. J. den Hollander *et al.* (eds.) *Drift en Koers* (Assen: Van Gorcum, 1962).

Kuhn, 1959.   Kuhn, M., *Umfragen und Demokratie* (Allensbach: Verl. für Demoskopie, 1959).

Labedz, 1962.   Labedz, L. (ed.) *Revisionism* (N. Y.: Praeger, 1962).

Lachapelle, 1934.   Lachapelle, G., *Les régimes électoraux* (Paris: Colin, 1934).

Lägnert, 1952.   Lägnert, F., *Valmanskåren på Skånes landsbygd 1911–1948* (Lund: Gleerup, 1952).

Lakeman, 1955.   Lakeman, E. & J. D. Lambert, *Voting in democracies* (Lond.: Faber, 1955).

Lambert, 1959.   Lambert, W. E. & O. Klineberg, 'Pilot study of the origin and development of national stereotypes', *Int. Soc. Sci. J.* 11 (2) 1959: 221–38.

Lambert, 1966.   Lambert, W. E. & O. Klineberg, *Children's views of foreign peoples: a cross-national study* (N. Y.: Appleton, Century, Crofts, 1966).

Lancelot, 1964.   Lancelot, A. & J. Ranger, 'Développements récents de la recherche électorale en France', *Il Politico* 29 (4) 1964: 763–87.

Lane, 1959.   Lane, R. E., *Political life* (Glencoe: Free Press, 1959).

LaPalombara, 1963.   LaPalombara, J. (ed.) *Bureaucracy and political development* (Princeton: Princeton Univ. Press. 1963).

448   *Bibliography*

LaPalombara, 1966.   LaPalombara, J. & M. Weiner (eds.) *Political parties
                        and political development* (Princeton: Princeton Univ.
                        Press, 1966).
LaPalombara, 1968.   LaPalombara, J., 'Macrotheories and microapplica-
                        tions in comparative politics', *Comp. Pol.* 1 (1) 1968:
                        52–78, revised version to be published in R. Holt (ed.)
                        Essays on comparative methods, in press 1969).
Laqueur, 1962.   Laqueur, W. & L. Labedz, *Polycentrism: The new
                        factor in international communism* (N. Y.: Praeger,
                        1962).
Laslett, 1965.   Laslett, Peter, *The world we have lost* (Lond.: Me-
                        thuen, 1965).
Laslett, 1969.   Laslett, Peter, 'Historical and regional variations in
                        Great Britain', in M. Dogan & S. Rokkan, *Quantitative
                        Ecológical Analysis in the Social Sciences* (Cambr.,
                        Mass.: M.I.T. Press, 1969).
Lasswell, 1952.   Lasswell, H. D. *et al., The comparative study of elites*
                        (Stanford: Stanford Univ. Press, 1952).
Lazarsfeld, 1944.   Lazarsfeld, P. F. *et al., The people's choice* (N. Y.:
                        Duell, 1944).
Lazarsfeld, 1955.   Lazarsfeld, P. & M. Rosenberg (eds.) *The language of
                        social research* (Glencoe: Free Press, 1955).
Lazarsfeld, 1961.   Lazarsfeld, P. F., 'Notes on the history of quantifica-
                        tion in sociology', pp. 147–203 in H. Woolf (ed.)
                        Quantification (Indianapolis: Bobbs-Merrill, 1961).
Lee, 1963.   Lee, J. M., *Social leaders and public persons. A study
                        of county government in Cheshire since 1888* (Oxf.:
                        Clarendon, 1963).
Lefcowitz, 1963.   Lefcowitz, M. J. & R. M. O'Shea, 'A proposal to
                        establish a national archives for social science survey
                        data', *Am. Behav. Sci.* 6 (7) 1963: 27–31.
LeFèvre-Pontalis, 1902. LeFèvre-Pontalis, A., *Les élections en Europe à la fin
                        du XIXe siècle* (Paris: Plon, 1902).
Lehmbruch, 1967.   Lehmbruch, G., *Proporzdeomkratie: Politisches System
                        und politische Kultur in der Schweiz und in Öster-
                        reich* (Tübingen: Mohr, 1967).
Leibholz, 1960.   Leibholz, G., *Das Wesen der Repräsentation und der
                        Gestaltwandel der Demokratie im 20. Jahrhundert*
                        (2d ed. Berlin: Gruyter, 1960).
Lenski, 1954.   Lenski, G. E., 'Status crystallization: a non-vertical
                        dimension of social status', *Am. Sociol. Rev.* 19 (4)
                        1954: 405–413.
Lenski, 1956.   Lenski, G., 'Social participation and status crystalliza-
                        tion', *Am. Sociol. Rev.* 21, 1956: 458–64.
Lenski, 1963.   Lenski, G., *The religious factor* (rev. ed. Garden City:
                        Doubleday Anchor Books, 1963).
LePlae, 1955.   LePlae, C., 'Différences culturelles entre instituteurs
                        d'expression française et flamande', *Bull. Inst. Rech.
                        Econ. et Soc.,* Louvain, 21 (7) 1955: 709–754.
Lerner, 1958.   Lerner, D., *The passing of traditional society* (Glen-
                        coe: Free Press, 1958).
Lerner, 1960.   Lerner, D. & M. Gorden, *European leaders look at
                        world security* (Cambr., Mass.: M.I.T. Center for
                        International Studies, 1960) mimeo.

Levy, 1966.	Levy, F., 'An outline of two systems: SYNTOL and the General Inquirer', pp. 465–98 in R. L. Merritt & S. Rokkan (eds.) *Comparing nations* (New Haven: Yale Univ. Press, 1966).
Lewis, 1956.	Lewis, O., 'Comparisons in Social Anthropology', pp. 259–92 in W. L. Thomas, Jr. (ed.) *Current anthropology* (Chicago: Chicago Univ. Press, 1956).
Lewis, 1965.	Lewis, W. A., *Politics in West Africa* (Lond.: Allen & Unwin, 1965).
Liepelt, 1966.	Liepelt, K., 'Wählerbewegungen in der Bundesrepublik', Paper, Arbeitstagung 21. Juli 1966, Institut für angewandte Sozialforschung, Bad Godesberg.
Lijphart, 1967.	Lijphart, A., 'Typologies of democratic systems', Paper, Seventh World Congress of Political Science, Brussels, 1967, also printed in *Comp. Pol. Stud.* 1 (1) Apr. 1968: 3–44.
Lijphart, 1968.	Lijphart, A., *The politics of accomodation: Pluralism and democracy in the Netherlands* (Berkeley: Univ. of California Press, 1968).
Lindbekk, 1967.	Lindbekk, T., *Mobilitets- og stillingsstrukturer in tre akademiske profesjoner 1910–63* (Oslo: Univ. forl., 1967).
Link, 1947.	Link, H. C., 'Some milestones in public opinion research', *Int. J. Opin. Attit. Res.* 1, 1947: 36–47.
Link, 1964.	Link, W., 'Das Nationalverein für das liberale Deutschland', *Pol. Vierteljahresschr.* 5, 1964: 422–44.
Linz, 1964.	Linz, J., 'Spain: an authoritarian regime', pp. 290–341 in E. Allardt & Y. Littunen (eds.) *Cleavages ideologies and party systems* (Helsinki: Westermarck Soc., 1964), also in E. Allardt & S. Rokkan (eds.) *Mass Politics* (New York: Free Press, 1969).
Linz, 1966.	Linz, J. & A. de Miguel, 'Within-nation differences and comparisons: The eight Spains', pp. 267–319 in R. L. Merritt & S. Rokkan (eds.) *Comparing nations* (New Haven: Yale Univ. Press, 1966).
Linz, 1969.	Linz, J., 'Ecological analysis and survey research', in M. Dogan & S. Rokkan (eds.) *Quantitative ecological analysis in the social sciences* (Cambr. Mass: M.I.T. Press, 1969).
Lipset, 1954.	Lipset, S. M. *et al.*, 'The psychology of voting', pp. 1123–75 in G. Lindzey (ed.) *Handbook of social psychology* (Cambr.: Addison-Wesley, 1954).
Lipset, 1955.	Lipset, S. M., 'The Radical Right', *Brit. J. of Sociol.* 6 (2) 1955: 176–209.
Lipset, 1959.	Lipset, S. M., 'Some social requisites of democracy', *Am. Pol. Sci. Rev.* 53 (1) 1959: 69–105.
Lipset, 1960.	Lipset, S. M., *Political man* (Garden City: Doubleday, 1960).
Lipset, 1963.	Lipset, S. M., *The first new nation* (N.Y.: Basic Books, 1963).
Lipset, 1964:1.	Lipset, S. M., 'The changing class structure and contemporary European politics', *Daedalus* 93, 1964: 271–303.

Lipset, 1964:2.

Lipset, S. M., 'Religion and politics in the American past and present', pp. 69–126 in R. Lee & M. Martin, *Religion and social conflict* (N. Y.: Oxf. Univ. Press, 1964).

Lipset & Linz, 1956.

Lipset, S. M. & J. Linz, *The social bases of political diversity* (Stanford: Center for Advanced Study in the Behavioral Sciences, 1956).

Lipset & Rokkan, 1967.

Lipset, S. M. & S. Rokkan, 'Cleavage structures, party systems and voter alignments: An introduction', pp. 1–64 in S. M. Lipset and S. Rokkan (eds.) *Party systems and voter alignments* (N. Y.: Free Press, 1967).

Little, 1967.

Little, I.M.D., *A critique of welfare economics* (2d ed. Oxf.: Clarendon, 1957).

Lorwin, 1958.

Lorwin, V. R., 'Working class politics and economic development in Western Europe', *Am. Hist. Rev.* 63, 1958: 338–51.

Lorwin, 1966.

Lorwin, V., 'Belgium: Religion, class, and language in national politics', pp. 147–87 in R. A. Dahl (ed.) *Political opposition in Western democracies* (New Haven & Lond.: Yale Univ. Press, 1966).

Lorwin, 1968.

Lorwin, V. R., 'Historians and other social scientists: the comparative study of nation-building in Western societies', in S. Rokkan (ed.) *Comparative research across cultures and nations* (Paris: Mouton, 1968).

Lousse, 1943.

Lousse, E., *La societé d'ancien régime: Organisation et représentation corporatives* (Louvain, Belgium: Bibliothèque de l'Université, 1943).

Lucci & Rokkan, 1957.

Lucci, Y. & S. Rokkan, *A library center of survey research data* (N. Y.: Columbia Univ., School of Library Service, 1957).

Luethy, 1962.

Luethy, H., 'Has Switzerland a future? The dilemma of a small nation', *Encounter* 19, 1962.

McClelland, 1961.

McClelland, D. C., *The achieving society* (N. Y.: Van Nostrand, 1961).

Mackenzie, 1958.

Mackenzie, W. J. M., *Free elections* (Lond.: Allen & Unwin, 1958).

Mackenzie, 1960.

Mackenzie, W. J. M. & K. Robinson, *Five elections in Africa* (Oxf.: Clarendon, 1960).

Mackinnon, 1956.

Mackinnon, W. J. & R. Centers, 'Authoritarianism and urban stratification', *Am. J. of Sociol.* 61 (6) 1956: 610–20.

McPhee, 1962.

McPhee, W. & W. Glaser, *Public opinion and congressional elections* (Glencoe: Free Press, 1962).

Maquet, 1959.

Maquet, J., *Élections en societé féodale: une étude sur l'introduction du vote populaire en Ruanda-Urundi* (Brussels: Académie Royale des Sciences Coloniales, 1959).

Marshall, 1950.

Marshall, T. H., *Citizenship and social class* (Lond.: Cambridge Univ. Press, 1950).

Marwick, 1960.

Marwick, D. (ed.) *Political decision-makers: Recruitment and performance* (Glencoe: Free Press, 1960).

Mathes, 1965.

Mathes, J. (ed.) *Religiöser Pluralismus und Gesellschaftstruktur* (Cologne: Westdeutscher Verl., 1965).

Mayntz, 1959.

Mayntz, R., *Parteiengruppen in der Grosstadt* (Cologne: Westdeutscher Verl., 1959).

Mayr, 1895–1917.

Mayr, G. v., *Statistik und Gesellschaftslehre,* vol. I–III (Freiburg: Mohr, 1895–1917).

Melikian, 1956.

Melikian, L. H., 'Some correlates of authoritarianism in two cultural groups', *J. of Psy.* 42, 1956: 237–48.

Melikian, 1959.

Melikian, L., 'Authoritarianism and its correlate in the Egyptian culture and in the United States', *J. of Soc. Iss.* 15 (3) 1959: 58–69.

Merritt, 1965.

Merritt, R. & R. E. Lane, 'The training functions of a data library', *Soc. Sci. Info.* 4 (3) 1965: 115–26.

Merritt, 1966.

Merritt, R. L. & D. J. Puchala (eds.) *Western European attitudes on arms, control, defense and European unity, 1952–1963* (New Haven: Political Science Research Library, Yale Univ., 1966) mimeo.

Merritt & Rokkan, 1966.

Merritt, R. L. & S. Rokkan (eds.) *Comparing nations* (New Haven: Yale Univ. Press, 1966).

Meyer, 1903.

Meyer, G., *Das parlamentarische Wahlrecht* (Berlin: Haering, 1903).

Michels, 1906.

Michels, R., 'Die deutsche Sozialdemokratie. Parteimitgliedschaft und soziale Zusammensetzung', *Arch. f. Soz. wiss. u. Soz. pol.* 23, 1906: 471–556.

Michels, 1911.

Michels, R., *Zur Soziologie des Parteiwesens in der modernen Demokratie* (Leipzig: 1911, new ed. Stuttgart: Kröner, 1957) Engl. ed. *Political parties* (Chicago: Hearst, 1915, new ed. N. Y.: Collier, 1962).

Miller, 1956.

Miller, W., 'One-party politics and the voter', *Am. Pol. Sci. Rev.* 50 (3) 1956: 707–25.

Miller, 1960.

Miller, S. M., 'Comparative social mobility', *Curr. Sociol.* 9 (1) 1960: 1–89.

Miller, 1964.

Miller, W. E. & P. E. Converse, 'The Inter-University Consortium for Political Research', *Int. Soc. Sci. J.* 16 (1) 1964: 70–76.

Miller, 1966.

Miller, W. E., 'Inter-university Consortium for Political Research: Current data holdings', pp. 95–102 in S. Rokkan (ed.) *Data archives for the social sciences* (Paris: Mouton, 1966).

Miller, forthc.

Miller, W. E. & D. E. Stokes, *Representation in the American Congress* (Englewood Cliffs: Prentice-Hall, forthcoming).

Milne, 1958.

Milne, R. S. & H. C. Mackenzie. *Marginal seat, 1955* (Lond.: Hansard Soc., 1958).

Mitchell, 1962.

Mitchell, W., *The polity* (N. Y.: Free Press, 1962).

Mitchell, 1964:1.

Mitchell, R. E., *The program of the International Data Library and Reference Service Survey Research Center. Univ. of California, Berkeley,* Paper, Conference on Data Archives, International Social Science Council, Sept. 1964.

Mitchell, 1964:2.

Mitchell, R. E., 'The Survey Research Center. University of California, Berkedely', *Int. Soc. Sci. J. 16 (1) 1964: 86–89.*

Mitchell, 1965.

Mitchell, R. E., 'A social science data archive for Asia, Africa, and Latin America', *Soc. Sci. Info.* 4 (3) 1965: 85–103.

Matthias, 1960. Matthias, E. & R. Mosey, *Das Ende der Parteien 1933* (Düsseldorf: Droste, 1960).

Mayer, 1929. Mayer, G., *Bismarck u. Lasalle* (Berlin: Dietz, 1929).

Mayer, 1964. Mayer, C. S., *Interviewing costs in survey research: A computer simulation study* (Ann Arbor: Univ. of Michigan Press, 1964).

Mitchell, 1967. Mitchell, W., *Sociological analysis and politics: The theories of Talcott Parsons* (Englewood Cliffs: Prentice-Hall, 1967).

Moberg, 1961. Moberg, D. O., 'Religion and society in the Netherlands and in America', *Am. Quart.* 13, 1961: 172–78.

Mommsen, 1959. Mommsen, W., *Max Weber und die deutsche Politik 1890–1920* (Tübingen: Mohr, 1959).

Moore, 1966. Moore, D. C., 'The other face of Reform', *Vict. Stud.* 5, 1961: 7–34.

Moore, 1961. Moore, B. Jr., *Social origins and dictatorship and democracy: Lord and peasant in the making of the modern world* (Boston: Beacon Press, 1966).

Morgan, 1963. Morgan, K. O., *Wales in British politics 1868–1922* (Cardiff: Univ. of Wales Press, 1963).

Moser, 1961. Moser, C. & W. Scott, *British towns* (Edinburgh: Oliver and Boyd, 1961).

Moulin, 1953. Moulin, L., 'Les origines religieuses des techniques électorales et délibératives modernes', *Rev. Int. d'Hist. Pol. et Const.,* New Series (3) 1953: 106–48.

Müller, 1959. Müller, P. F., *Das Wahlsystem: Neue Wege der Grundlegung und Gestaltung* (Zürich: Polygraphischer Verl., 1959).

Munger, 1966. Munger, F., 'The legitimacy of opposition: The change of government in Ireland in 1932', Paper, Annual Meeting of the American Political Science Association, 1966.

Murdock, 1961. Murdock, G. P. *et al., Outline of cultural materials* (Rev. ed. New Haven: Human Relations Area Files Inc., 1961).

Myklebost, 1960. Myklebost, H., *Norges tettbygde steder 1875–1950* (Oslo: Univ. forl., 1960).

Namier, 1930. Namier, Sir L., *England in the age of the American revolution* (Lond.: Macmillan, 1930).

Nederlandse, 1956. *De Nederlandse Kiezer* ('s Gravenhagen: Staatsdrukkerij en vitgeverijbedr., 1956).

Nettl, 1968:1. Nettl, J. P. & R. Robertson, *International systems and the modernization of societies* (Lond.: Faber, 1968).

Nettl, 1968:2. Nettl, J. P., 'The State as a conceptual variable', *World Pol.* 20 (4) 1968: 559–92.

Nicholas, 1951. Nicholas, H. G., *The British General Election of 1950* (Lond.: Macmillan, 1951).

Nilson, 1950. Nilson, S. S., *Histoire et science politique* (Bergen: Chr. Michelsen Inst., 1950).

Nipperdey, 1961. Nipperdey, T., *Die Organisation der deutschen Parteien vor 1918* (Düsseldorf: Droste, 1961).

Nuechterlein, 1961. Nuechterlein, D. E., *Iceland: Reluctant ally* (Ithaca: Cornell Univ. Press, 1961).

Oberschall, 1965.   Obershall, A., *Empirical social research in Germany, 1848–1914* (Paris: Mouton, 1965).

OCSR, 1954.   Organisation for Comparative Social Research, 'Cross-national research: a case study', *J. of Soc. Iss.* 10 (4) 1954: 1–68.

OECD, 1966.   OECD, *The social sciences and the policies of government* (Paris: OECD, 1966).

O'Leary, 1961.   O'Leary, C., *The Irish republic and its experiment with proportional representation* (Notre Dame: Univ. of Notre Dame Press, 1961).

Olmsted, 1958.   Olmsted, M. S., 'Communism in Iceland', *Foreign Affairs* 36, 1958: 340–47.

Olsson, 1923.   Olsson, J., 'Den politiske partifördelningen inom de olika sociala klasserna i Sverige', *Statsvet. ts.* 1923: 115–39.

Oncken, 1914.   Oncken, H., *Historisch-politische Aufsätze u. Reden* (Munich: Oldenbourg, 1914).

Ostrogorski, 1902.   Ostrogorski, M., *Democracy and the organization of political parties* (Lond.: Macmillan, 1902, new ed. Garden City: Doubleday, 1964).

Palmer, 1959.   Palmer, R. R., *The age of the Democratic Revolution* (Princeton: Princeton Univ. Press, 1959).

Parker, forthc.   Parker, R. S. (ed.) *Political handbook of Australia 1890–1962*, forthcoming.

Parsons, 1956.   Parsons, T. & N. J. Smelser, *Economy and society* (Lond.: Routledge, 1956).

Parsons, 1959:1.   Parsons, T., 'General theory in sociology', pp. 39–78 in R. K. Merton *et al.*, (eds.) *Sociology today* (N. Y.: Basic Books, 1959).

Parsons, 1959:2.   Parsons, T., 'Voting and the equilibrium of the American political system', pp. 80–120 in E. Burdick and A. Brodbeck (eds.) *American voting behavior* (N. Y.: Free Press, 1959).

Parsons, 1960.   Parsons, T., 'Pattern variables revisited', *Am. Sociol. Rev.* 25, 1960: 467–83.

Parsons, 1963.   Parsons, T., 'On the concept of political power', *Proc. Am. Philos. Soc.* 107, 1963: 232–62.

Parsons, 1964.   Parsons, T., 'Evolutionary universals in society', *Am. Sociol. Rev.* 29, 1964: 339–57.

Pedersen, 1966.   Pedersen, M. N., 'Preferential voting in Denmark', *Scand. Pol. Stud.* I. 1966: 167–87.

Pedersen, 1967.   Pedersen, M. N., 'Consensus and conflict in the Danish Folketing 1945–65', *Scand. Pol. Stud.* II, 1967: 143–66.

Pedersen, 1968.   Pedersen, M. N., 'Rekrutteringen av danske Folketingsmænd', Paper, Nordic Conf. on Pol. Sci., Helsinki, Aug. 1968.

Pinson, 1935.   Pinson, K. S., *A bibliographical introduction to nationalism* (N. Y.: Columbia Univ. Press, 1935).

Pitt-Rivers, 1954.   Pitt-Rivers, J. A., *People of the Sierra* (N. Y.: Criterion, 1954).

Pocock, 1966. Pocock, J. G. A., 'The case of Ireland truly stated: Revolutionary politics in a context of increasing stabilization', Paper, Dept. of History, Washington Univ., St. Louis, 1966).

Polsby, 1963. Polsby, N. W., *Community power and political theory* (New Haven: Yale Univ. Press, 1963).

Porter, 1918. Porter, K. H., *A history of the suffrage in the United States* (Chicago: Univ. of Chicago Press, 1918).

Prothro, 1953. Prothro, E. T. & L. H. Melikian, 'The California public opinion scale in an authoritarian culture', *Publ. Opin. Quar.* 17 (3) 1953: 353–62.

Pye, 1963. Pye, L. W., (ed.) *Communications and political development* (Princeton: Princeton Univ. Press, 1963).

Pye, 1965:1. Pye, L. W., *Aspects of political development* (Boston: Little, Brown, 1965).

Pye, 1965:2. Pye, L. 'Identity and legitimacy: crises of the political culture', draft 1965.

Pye, 1965:3. Pye, L. W. & S. Verba (eds.) *Political culture and political development* (Princeton: Princeton Univ. Press, 1965).

Pye, 1968. Pye, L. W., 'Political systems and political development', pp. 93–101 in S. Rokkan (ed.) *Comparative research across cultures and nations* (Paris: Mouton, 1968).

Pyfferoen, 1903. Pyfferoen, O., *L'électorat politique et administratif en Europe* (Paris: Giard, 1903).

Rama, 1962. Rama, C. A., *La crise espagnole au XXe siècle* (Paris: Fischbacher, 1962).

Ranney, 1962. Ranney, A., (ed.) *Essays on the behavioral study of politics* (Urbana: Univ. Illinois Press, 1962).

Ranney, 1965. Ranney, A., *Pathways to Parliament* (Lond.: Macmillan, 1965).

Rantala, 1956. Rantala, O., *Konservatiivinen puolueyhteisö (The Conservative party community)* (Helsinki: Tammi, 1956).

Rantala, 1967. Rantala, O., 'The political regions of Finland', *Scand. Pol. Stud.* II, 1967: 117–40.

Reader's Digest, 1964. Reader's Digest, *Products and people, The Reader's Digest European Surveys* (Lond.: Reader's Digest Assoc., Ltd., 1964).

Reigrotzki, 1956. Reigrotzki, E., *Soziale Verflechtungen in der Bundesrepublik* (Tübingen: Mohr, 1956).

Reisner, 1927. Reisner, E. H., *Nationalism and education since 1789* (N. Y.: Macmillan, 1927).

Rémond, 1955. Rémond, R., *La droite en France* (Paris: Aubier, 1955, new ed. 1966).

Retzlaff, 1965. Retzlaff, R. M., 'The use of aggregate data in comparative political analysis', *J. of Pol.* 27, 1965: 797–817.

Rice, 1924. Rice, S. A., *Farmers and workers in American politics* (N. Y.: 1924).

Rice, 1928. Rice, S. A., *Quantitative methods in politics* (N. Y.: 1928).

Richardson, 1965.   Richardson, A. *et al.*, *Interviewing. Its forms and functions* (N. Y.: Basic Books, 1965).

Riesman, 1948.   Riesman, D. & N. Glazer, 'The meaning of opinion', *Publ. Opin. Quart.* 12, 1948: 633–48.

Riker, 1961.   Riker, W. H., 'Voting and the summation of preferences: an interpretive-bibliographical review of selected developments during the last decade', *Am. Pol. Sci. Rev.* 55, 1961: 900–911.

Riker, 1962.   Riker, W. H., *The theory of political coalitions* (New Haven: Yale Univ. Press, 1962).

Ritter, 1959.   Ritter, G. A., *Die Arbeiterbewegung im wilhelminischen Reich* (Berlin, Dahlem, Colloquium, 1959).

Robinson, 1937.   Robinson, C. E., *Straw votes* (N. Y.: Columbia Univ. Press, 1937).

Robinson, 1950.   Robinson, W. S., 'Ecological correlations and the behavior of individuals', *Am. Sociol. Rev.* 15, 1950: 351–57.

Rokeach, 1956.   Rokeach, M. & C. Hanley, 'Eysenck's tender-mindedness dimension: a critic', *Ps. Bull.* 53 (2) 1956: 169–176.

Rokeach, 1956:2.   Rokeach, M., 'Political and religious dogmatism: an alternative to the authoritarian personality', *Psych. Monogr.* 70, no. 18, 1950.

Rokeach, 1960.   *The open and the closed mind* (N. Y.: Basic Books, 1960).

Rokkan, 1955:1.   Rokkan, S.: 'An experiment in cross-national research cooperation', *Int. Soc. Sci. Bull.* 7 (4) 1955: 645–52.

Rokkan, 1955:2.   Rokkan, S., *Party identification and opinions on issues of domestic and international policy* (Cambr., Mass.: Center for International Studies, 1955) mimeo. Partly repr. as Chapter 9 of the present volume.

Rokkan, 1955:3.   Rokkan, S., 'Party preferences and opinion patterns in Western Europe', *Int. Soc. Sci. Bull.* 7 (4) 1955: 575–96. Part of Ch. 9 of the present volume.

Rokkan, 1955:4.   Rokkan, S., 'Eine schwedische Untersuchung über die sozialen und politischen Einstellungen von Angestellten und Arbeitern in der Industrie', *Kölner Zeitschr. f. Soziol.* 7 (2) 1955: 247–252.

Rokkan, 1956:1.   Rokkan, S., 'The case for comparative secondary analysis: an example from political sociology', Paper, ESOMAR Conference, 1956, mimeo.

Rokkan, 1956:2.   Rokkan, S., 'Current sociological research: a note on trends toward international comparability', *Trans. Third World Congr. Sociol.* (Lond.: I.S.A., 1956: vol. VII, 51–60).

Rokkan, 1956:3.   Rokkan, S., *Ideological consistency and party preference: a note on findings from a seven-country survey on teachers' attitudes*, Paper, WAPOR Conf., 1956. Reprinted as Ch. 10 of the present volume.

Rokkan, 1957.   Rokkan, S., 'P. M. om opprettelse av et senter for utforskning av nordisk folkeopinion', *Nordisk råd* 4, session 1956 (Kbh.: Schulz, 1957) pp. 638–46.

Rokkan, 1958:1.   Rokkan, S., *et al.*, 'Les élections norvégiennes du 7 octobre 1957', *Rev. franç. de sci. pol.* 8 (1) 1958: 73–94.

Rokkan, 1958:2.   Rokkan, S., *Sammenlignende politisk sosiologi* (Bergen: Chr. Michelsen Inst., 1958).

Rokkan, 1959.   Rokkan, S., 'Electoral activity, party membership and organizational influence', *Acta Sociol.* 4 (1) 1959: 25–37. Reprinted as Ch. 11 of the present volume.

Rokkan, 1960:1.   Rokkan, S., 'Citizen participation in political life. Introduction', *Int Soc. Sci. J.* 12 (1) 1960: 1–99.

Rokkan, 1960:2.   Rokkan, S. & A. Campbell, 'Citizen perticipation in political life: Norway and the United States of America', *Int. Soc. Sci. J.* 12 (1) 1960: 69–99. Reprinted as Ch. 12 in the present volume.

Rokkan, 1960:3.   Rokkan, S., *National consensus and political perticipation* (Stanford: Center for Advanced Study in the Behavioral Sciences, 1960) mimeo.

Rokkan, 1960:4.   Rokkan, S., *The Nationwide Election Survey 1957: Basic Tables* (Bergen: Chr. Michelsen Inst., 1960).

Rokkan, 1960:5.   Rokkan, S. & H. Valen, 'Parties, elections and political behaviour in the Northern Countries', in O. Stammer (ed.) *Politische Forschung* (Cologne: Westdeutscher Verl., 1960).

Rokkan, 1960:6.   Rokkan, S. & P. Torsvik, 'Der Wähler, der Leser und die Parteipresse', *Kölner Zeitschr. f. Soziol.* 12 (2) 1960: 278–301. English version reprinted as Ch. 13 of the present volume.

Rokkan, 1961.   Rokkan, S., 'Mass suffrage, secret voting and political participation', *Arch. eur. de sociol.* 2 (1) 1961: 132–54.

Rokkan, 1962:1.   Rokkan, S., 'The comparative study of political participation', pp. 47–90 in A. Ranney (ed.) *Essays on the behavioral study of politics* (Urbana: Univ. of Illinois Press, 1962). Reprinted as Ch. 1 of the present volume.

Rokkan, 1962:2.   Rokkan, S. & H. Valen, 'The mobilization of the periphery', in S. Rokkan (ed.) *Approaches to the study of political participation* (Bergen: Chr. Michelsen Inst., 1962). Reprinted as Ch. 6 of the present volume.

Rokkan, 1964:1.   Rokkan, S., 'Data in Comparative Research: Introduction', *Int. Soc. Sci. J.* 16 (1) 1964: 7–18.

Rokkan, 1964:2.   Rokkan, S. & H. Valen, 'Regional contrasts in Norwegian politics', pp. 162–238 in E. Allardt and Y. Littunen (eds.) *Cleavages, ideologies and party systems: Contributions to Comparative political sociology* (Helsinki: Westermarck Soc., 1964), partly reprinted in E. Allardt & S. Rokkan (eds.) *Mass Polities* (New York: Free Press, 1969).

Rokkan, 1964:3.   Rokkan, S., *Valgdeltakelsen blant de yngste* (Bergen: Chr. Michelsen Inst., 1964).

Rokkan, 1965:1.   Rokkan, S., 'Second conference on data archives in the social sciences', *Soc. Sci. Info.* 4 (1) 1965: 67–84.

Rokkan, 1965:2.   Rokkan, S., 'Trends and possibilities in comparative social science', *Soc. Sci. Info.* 4 (4) 1965: 139–65.

Rokkan, 1966:1.   Rokkan, S. & H. Valen, 'Archives for statistical studies on within-nation differences', pp. 122–127 in S. Rokkan (ed.) *Data archives for the social sciences* (Paris: Mouton, 1966). Also printed in R. L. Merritt & S. Rokkan (eds.) *Comparing nations* (New Haven: Yale Univ. Press, 1966).

Rokkan, 1966:2.   Rokkan, S., 'The comparative study of electoral statistics', *Soc. Sci. Info.* 5 (2) 1966: 9–19. Reprinted as Ch. 5 of the present volume.

Rokkan, 1966:3.   Rokkan, S., (ed.) *Data archives for the social sciences* (Paris: Mouton, 1966).

Rokkan, 1966:4.   Rokkan, S., 'Electoral mobilization, party competition and national integration', pp. 241–65 in J. LaPalombara & M. Weiner (eds.) *Political parties and political development* (Princeton: Princeton Univ. Press, 1966). Reprinted as Ch. 7 of the present volume.

Rokkan, 1966:5.   Rokkan, S., 'Norway: Numerical democracy and corporate pluralism', pp. 89–105 in R. A. Dahl (ed.) *Political oppositions in Western democracies* (New Haven: Yale Univ. Press, 1966).

Rokkan, 1966:6.   Rokkan, S. & T. Hjellum, 'Norway: The Storting election of September 1965', *Scand. Pol. Stud.* I, 1966: 237–46.

Rokkan, 1966:7.   Rokkan, S., 'Political research in Norway 1960–65', *Scand. Pol. Stud.* I, 1966: 266–280.

Rokkan, 1967.   Rokkan, S., 'Geography, religion and social class: Crosscutting cleavages in Norwegian politics', in S. M. Lipset & S. Rokkan (eds.) *Party systems and voter alignments* (New York: Free Press, 1967).

Rokkan, 1968:1.   Rokkan, S., 'Electoral systems', vol. V, pp. 6–21 in *International Encyclopedia of the Social Sciences* (N.Y.: Macmillan, 1968). Reprinted as Ch. 4 of the present volume.

Rokkan, 1968:2.   Rokkan, S. & K. Szczerba-Likiernik, 'A programme for the advancement of comparative social science research: The action of the International Social science Council', in S. Rokkan (ed.) *Comparative research across cultures and nations* (Paris: Mouton, 1968).

Rokkan, 1968:3.   Rokkan, S., 'The structuring of mass politics in the smaller European democracies', *Comp. Stud. Soc. Hist.* 10 (2) 1968: 173–210. Partly included in Ch. 3 of the present volume.

Rokkan, 1968:4.   Rokkan, S. & K. Salhus, 'Changes in the channels of recruitment to Parliament: Specimen tables for three countries', Paper, UNESCO Symposium, Gothenburg, 1968.

Rokkan, 1969:1.   'Methods and models in the comparative study of nation-building', Paper, UNESCO Symposium, Gothenburg, 1968. Reprinted as Ch. 2 of the present volume.

Rokkan, 1969:2.   Rokkan, S. & F. Aarebrot, 'The Norwegian archive of historical ecology', Paper, UNESCO Symposium, Gothenburg, 1968. Printed in *Sco. Sci. Info.* 8 (1) 1969.

Rokkan, 1969:3. Rokkan, S., S. Verba, J. Viet, & E. Alnasy *Compara-tive survey analysis: A trend report and bibliography* (Paris: Mouton, 1969).

Rokkan, 1969:4. Rokkan, S. & J. Meyriat (eds.) *International guide to electoral statistics*. Vol. I. W. Europe. (Paris: Mouton: 1969).

Rommetveit, 1954. Rommetveit, R. & J. Israel, 'Notes on the standardiza-tion of experimental manipulations and measurements in cross-national research', *J. of Soc. Iss.* 10 (4) 1954: 61–68.

Rommi, 1964. Rommi, P., 'Finland', pp. 103–30 in *Problemer i nor-disk historieforskning II. Framveksten av de politiske partier i de nordiske land på 1800-tallet* (Bergen: Univ. forl., 1964).

Roper, 1935. Roper, E., 'Fortune quarterly survey', *Fortune,* 1935 and ensuing issues.

Roper, 1948. Roper, E. & J. L. Woodward, 'International polling and international democracy', pp. 384–91 in *Learning and world peace* (N. Y.: Harper, 1948).

Rose, 1954. Rose, A. M., *Theory and method in the social sciences* (Minneapolis: Univ. Minnesota Press, 1954).

Rose, 1966. Rose, R., *Influencing voters* (Lond: Faber, 1966).

Roset, 1964. Roset, I., *Det Norske Arbeiderparti og Hornsruds regjeringsdannelse i 1928* (Oslo: Univ. forl., 1964).

Ross, 1955. Ross, J. F. S., *Elections and electors: Studies in democratic representation* (Lond.: Eyre & Spottis-woode, 1955).

Ross, 1959. Ross, J. F. S., *The Irish Election System: What it is and how it works* (Lond.: Pall Mall, 1959).

Rossi, 1959. Rossi, P., 'Four landmarks in voting research', pp. 5–54 in E. Burdick & A. J. Brodbeck (eds.) *American voting behaviour* (Glencoe: Free Press, 1959).

Rossi, 1960:1. Rossi, P. H. & P. Cutright, 'The political organization of an industrial community', in M. Janowitz (ed.) *Community Power Systems* (Glencoe: Free Press, 1960).

Rossi, 1960:2. Rossi, P. H., 'Power and community structure', *Midw. J. Pol. Sci.* 4 (4) 1960: 390–401.

Rossi, 1960:3. Rossi, P. H., 'Public' and 'Private' leadership in Ame-rica' prep. for The Fund for the Advancement of Education, May, 1960, mimeo.

Rossi, 1960:4. Rossi, P. H., 'Theory and method in the study of power in the local community', Paper, Conf. on Metropolitan Leadership, Northwestern Univ., 1960.

Roth, 1963. Roth, G., *The Social Democrats in Imperial Germany* (Totowa: Bedminster, 1963).

Rumpf, 1959. Rumpf, E., *Nationalismus and Sozialismus in Irland* (Meisenheim: Hain, 1959).

Russett, 1964. Russett, B. *et al., World handbook of political and social indicators* (New Haven: Yale Univ. Press, 1964).

Russett, 1966. Russett, B., 'The Yale political data program: experience and prospects', pp. 95–107 in R. L. Merritt & Rokkan (eds.) *Comparing Nations* (New Haven: Yale Univ. Press, 1966).

Rustow, 1956. Rustow, D. A., *Politics and westernization in the New East* (Princeton: Center of Intern. Stud., 1956).

Ryffel, 1903. Ryffel, H., *Die schweizerischen Landsgemeinden* (Zurich: Schulthess, 1903).

Särlvik, 1959. Särlvik, B., *Opinionsbildningen vid folkomröstningen 1957* (Sth.: Stat. off. utredningar 1959: 10).

Sæter, 1959. Sæter, E., *Industrialisering og stemmegivning: en valgstatistisk analyse* (Oslo: Inst. of Political Science, Univ. of Oslo, 1959) typewritten.

Sainte-Laguë, 1910. Sainte-Laguë, A., 'La représentation proportionelle et la méthode des moindres carrées', Académie des Sciences, Paris, *Comptes rendus hebdomadaires* 151, 1910: 377–78.

Sanford, 1950. Sanford, F. H., *Authoritarianism and leadership* (Philadelphia: Stephenson, 1950).

Sänger & Liepelt, 1965. Sänger, F. & K. Liepelt, *Wahlhandbuch 1965* (Frankfurt: Europäische Verlagsanstalt, 1965).

Sartori, 1963. Sartori, G. (ed.) *Il parlamento italiano 1946–1963* (Rome: Ed. Scientifiche Ital., 1963).

Sartori, 1969. Sartori, G., *Parties and party systems* (N. Y.: Harper, 1969).

Schachter, 1954:1. Schachter, S. *et al.*, 'Cross-cultural experiments on threat and rejection', *Hum. Rel.* 7 (4) 1954: 403–39.

Schachter, 1954:2. Schachter, S., 'Interpretative and methodological problems of replicated research', *J. of Soc. Iss.* 10 (4) 1954: 52–60.

Schepis, 1955. Schepis, G., *I sistemi elettorali* (Empoli, Italy: Caparrini, 1955).

Schepis, 1958. Schepis, G., *Le consultazioni popolari in Italia dal 1848 al 1957: Profilo storico-statistico* (Empoli: Italy: Caparrini, 1958).

Scheuch, 1964:1. Scheuch, E. K. & P. J. Stone, 'The General Inquirer approach to an international retrieval system of survey archives', *Am. Behav. Sci.* 7 (10) 1964: 23–28.

Scheuch, 1964:2. Scheuch, E. K. & J. Bruning, 'The 'Zentralarchiv' at the University of Cologne', *Int. Soc. Sci. J.* 16 (1) 1964: 77–85.

Scheuch, 1965. Scheuch, E. & R. Wildenmann, *Zur Soziologie der Wahl* (Cologne: Westdeutscher Verl., 1965).

Scheuch, 1966:1. Scheuch, E., 'Cross-national comparisons using aggregate data: some substantive and methodological problems', pp. 131–68 in R. L. Merritt & S. Rokkan (eds.) *Comparing nations* (New Haven: Yale Univ. Press, 1966).

Scheuch, 1966:2. Scheuch, E. K. & P. J. Stone, 'Retrieval systems for data archives: the General Inquirer', pp. 441–64 in R. L. Merritt & S. Rokkan (eds.) *Comparing nations* (New Haven: Yale Univ. Press, 1966).

Scheuch, 1968.

Schmidtchen, 1959.

Schramm, 1964.

Schultze, 1958.

Schultze, 1961.

Seip, 1958.

Seppänen, 1965.

Seymour, 1915.

Seymour, 1918.

Shils, 1957.

Siegfried, 1913.

Siegman, 1958.

Siegman, 1962.

Sköld, 1958.

Smith, 1960.

Specht, 1907.

Spreafico, 1963.

Stammer, 1960.

Stammer, 1965.

Stat. Oppl., 1877.

Stehouwer, 1967.

Scheuch, E., 'Progress in the cross-cultural use of sample surveys', in S. Rokkan (ed.) *Comparative research across cultures and nations* (Paris: Mouton, 1968).

Schmidtchen, G., *Die befragte Nation* (Freiburg: Rombach, 1959).

Schramm, W., *Mass media and national development* (Stanford: Stanford Univ. Press, 1964).

Schultze, R. O., 'The role of the economic dominants in community power structure', *Am. Sociol. Rev.* (23 (1) 1958: 3–9.

Schultze, R. O., 'The bifurcation of power in a satelite city', pp. 19–80 in M. Janowitz (ed.) *Community power systems* (Glencoe: Free Press, 1961).

Seip, J. A., *Det opinionsstyrte enevelde* (Oslo: Univ. forl., 1958).

Seppänen, P., 'Changing society', (Finnish) *Sociologica* 2, 1965.

Seymour, C., *Electoral reform in England and Wales* (New Haven: Yale Univ. Press, 1915).

Seymour, C. & D. P. Frary, *How the world votes* (Springfield, Mass.: Nichols, 1918).

Shils, E., 'Primordial, personal, sacred and civil ties', *Brit. J. of Sociol.* 7, 1957: 130–45.

Siegfried, A., *Tableau politique de la France de l'Ouest sous la Troisième République* (Paris: Colin, 1913, 2d ed. 1964).

Siegman, A. W., 'The effect of cultural factors on the relationship between personality, intelligence and ethnocentric attitudes', *J. of Consulting Psychology* 22, 1958: 277–375.

Siegman, A. W., 'A cross-cultural investigation of the relationship between religiosity, ethnic prejudice and authoritarianism', *Psychological Reports* 11 (2) 1962: 419–24.

Sköld, L., *Kandidatnominering vid andrakammarvalen* (Sth.: Statens Off. Utr. 6, 1958).

Smith, T. E., *Elections in developing countries* (Lond.: Macmillan, 1960).

Specht, F. & P. Schwabe, *Die Reichtstagwahlen von 1867 bis 1907* (Berlin: 1907).

Spreafico, A. & J. LaPalombara (eds.) *Elezioni e comportamento politico in Italia* (Milan: Ed. di Comunità, 1963).

Stammer, O. (ed.) *Politische Forschung* (Cologne: Westdeutscher Verl., 1960).

Stammer, O. (ed.) *Max Weber und die Sociologie heute* (Tübingen: Mohr, 1965).

Statistiske Oplysninger om de fremsatte Stemmeretts-forslags Virkning (Christiania: Statistisk Centralbureau, C. No. 14, 1877).

Stehouwer, J., 'Long term ecological analysis of electoral statistics in Denmark', *Scand. Pol. Stud.* II, 1967: 94–116.

Stengers, 1966.   Stengers, J., 'Belgium', in H. Rogger & E. Weber (eds.) *The European Right* (Lond.: Weidenfeld, 1966).

Stephan, 1948.   Stephan, F. F., 'History of the use of modern sampling procedures', *J. Am. Stat. Assn.* 43, 1948: 12–40.

Stephan, 1957.   Stephan, F. F., 'Advances in survey methods and measurement techniques', *Publ. Op. Quar.* 21 (1) 1957: 79–90.

Stern, 1949.   Stern, E., 'On the 'Time' international study (WAPOR Conference)', *Int. J. of Opin. and Attit. Res.* 3 (2) 1949: 329–33.

Sternberger, 1964.   Sternberger, A., *Die grosse Wahlreform: Zeugnisse einer Bemühung* (Cologne: Westdeutscher Verl., 1964).

Stiefbold, 1966.   Stiefbold, R. et al. (eds.) *Wahlen und Parteien in Österreich. Österreichisches Wahlhandbuch* (Vienna: Österreichisches Bundesverl., 1966).

Stokes, 1965.   Stokes, R., 'A variance components model of political effects', in *Mathematical applications in political science* (Dallas: Arnold Found., 1965).

Stouffer, 1955.   Stouffer, S. A., *Communism, conformity and civil liberties* (N. Y.: Doubleday, 1955).

Suchman, 1955.   Suchman, E. A., *The comparative method in social research* (Ithaca, N. Y.: Cornell Univ., 1955) mimeo.

Szalai, 1966:1.   Szalai, A., 'Differential evaluation on the time budgets for comparative purposes', pp. 239–58 in R. L. Merritt & S. Rokkan (eds.) *Comparing nations* (New Haven: Yale Univ. Press, 1966).

Szalai, 1966:2.   Szalai, A., 'Trends in comparative time-budget research', *Am. Behav. Scient.* 9 (9) 1966: 3–8.

Taylor, 1962.   Taylor, C. L., *The emergence of British working class politics,* Ph. D. diss., Yale Univ., 1962.

't Hart, 1964.   't Hart, H., 'The inauguration of the Steinmetz Foundation', *Gazette* 10 (3) 1964: 261–64.

Thompson, 1963.   Thompson, F. M. C., *English landed society in the nineteenth century* (Lond.: Routledge, 1963).

Thormodsæter, 1960.   Thormodsæter, A., *Regionale ulikheter i norsk jordbruk* (Oslo: Norges Landbruksøkonomiske Inst., 1960).

Tilly, 1965.   Tilly, C., *The Vendée* (Lond.: Arnold, 1965).

Time, 1948.   'Plain people – Europe in the Spring', *Time* Apr. 12, 1948.

Tingsten, 1932.   Tingsten, H., *Majoritetsval och proportionalism* (Sth.: 1932).

Tingsten, 1937.   Tingsten, H., *Political behaviour* (Lond.: King. 1937, repr. Totowa: Bedminster, 1963).

Tingsten, 1958.   Tingsten, H., 'The press', pp. 316–328 in J. A. Lauwerys (ed.) *Scandinavian democracy* (Cph.: The Danish Inst., Norwegian Off. of Cult. Rel., and the Swedish Inst., 1958).

Tingsten, 1963.   Tingsten, H., *Mitt liv: Tidningen* (Sth.: Norstedts, 1963).

Tocqueville, 1835.   Tocqueville, A. de, *De la démocratie en Amerique* (Paris: Gosselin, 1835).

Tönnies, 1924.   Tönnies, F., 'Korrelation der Parteien in der Statistik der Kieler Reichstagsvalen', *Jahrb. f. Nat. oekon. u. Stat.,* 122, 1924: 633–72.

Torgersen, 1962.

Torgersen, Ulf., 'The Trend toward Political Consensus the Case of Norway', pp. 159–172 in S. Rokkan (ed.) *Approaches to the Study of Political Participation* (Bergen: Michelsen Inst., 1962).

Torgersen, 1964.

Torgersen, U., 'The structure of urban parties in Norway during the first period of extended suffrage 1884–1898', in E. Allardt & Y. Littunen (eds.) *Cleavages, ideologies and party systems* (Helsinki: Westermarck Soc., 1964).

Torgersen, 1966.

Torgersen, U., *Landsmøtet i norsk partistruktur 1884–1940* (Oslo: Inst. for Social Research, 1966) mimeo.

Tropp, 1953.

Tropp, A., 'The changing status of the teacher in England and Wales', *The Year Book of Education*, 1953: 143–70.

Tynell, 1910.

Tynell, K., 'De olika befolkningsgruppers deltagande i de allmänna valen', *Statsvet. ts.* 1910: 81–96.

Ulich, 1961.

Ulich, R., *The education of nations* (Cambr.: Harvard Univ. Press, 1961).

UNESCO, 1961.

UNESCO, *Freedom of information: Development of information in under-developed countries* (Paris: UNESCO, 1961).

Unkelbach, 1956.

Unkelbach, H., *Grundlagen der Wahlsystematik* (Göttingen: Vandenhoeck, 1956).

Unkelbach, 1961.

Unkelbach, H. & R. Wildenmann, *Grundfragen des Wählens* (Frankfurt a. M.: Athenäum, 1961).

UNRISD, 1968.

United Nations Research Institute for Social Development, *Research Notes*, No. 1: 1–7 (Geneva: UNRISD, June 1968).

Valen, 1958.

Valen, H., 'Factional activities and nominations in political parties', *Acta Sociol.* 3 (4) 1958: 183–199.

Valen, 1959.

Valen, H., *De politiske partier i Norge* (Oslo: Inst. for Samfunnsforskning, 1959) stencilled.

Valen, 1960.

Valen, H., 'Velgerne og den partipolitiske stabilitet' *Tidsskr. for samf. forskn.* 1 (1) 1960.

Valen, 1961.

Valen, H. & D. Katz, 'An electoral contest in a Norwegian province', in M. Janowitz (ed.) *Community power systems* (Glencoe: Free Press, 1961).

Valen, 1964.

Valen, H. & D. Katz, *Political parties in Norway* (Oslo: Univ. forl., 1964).

Valen, 1966.

Valen, H., 'The recruitment of parliamentary nominees in Norway', *Scand. Pol. Stud.* I, 1966: 121–166.

Valen, 1967.
Vangrevelinghe, 1961.

Valen, H., 'Nominasjonene', draft 1967.
Vangrevelinghe, G., 'Étude statistique comparée des résultats des réferendums de 1958 et 1961', *J. soc. statist. Paris* 102 (10–11–12) 1961: 279–294.

Verba, 1965:1.

Verba, S., 'Crises, capabilities and sequences', draft June 1965.

Verba, 1965:2.

Verba, S., *Cross-national program in political and social change* (Stanford: Inst. of political studies, 1965) mimeo.

Verney, 1957.

Verney, D. V., *Parliamentary reform in Sweden, 1866–1921* (Oxf.: Clarendon, 1957).

Vidich, 1960.

Vidich, A. J. & J. Bensman, *Small town in mass society* (Garden City: Doubleday Anchor, 1960).

Villey, 1895.

Vincent, 1966.

Vodopivec, 1961.

Vulpius, 1957.

Wahlrechtskommission, 1955.

Wallace, 1948.

Wallin, 1961.

Wandruszka, 1952.

Ward, 1964.

Webster, 1960.

Weibull, 1964.
Weiner, 1965.

Westerath, 1955.

Westergaard, 1932.

Westerståhl, 1957.

Westerståhl, 1959.

Whiting, 1954.

Whiting, 1963.

Whiting, 1966.

Wigmore, 1889.

Williamson, 1960.

Woodhouse, 1966.

Villey, E., *Législation électorale comparée des principaux pays de l'Europe* (Paris: 1895).
Vincent, J. R., *Poll Books: How Victorians voted 1830–1872* (Cambr.: Cambr. Univ. Press, 1966).
Vodopivec, A., *Wer regiert in Österreich?* (Vienna: Verl. für Geschichte und Politik, 1961).
Vulpius, A., *Die Allparteienregierung* (Frankfurt a.M.: Metzner, 1957).
Germany (Federal Republic), Wahlrechtskommission, *Grundlagen eines deutschen Wahlrechts: Bericht* (Bonn: Bonner Universitäts-Buchdrückerei, 1955).
Wallace, D. *et al.*, 'Experience in the 'Time' international study: a symposium' *Publ. Opin. Quar.* 12 (4) 1948–49: 708–21.
Wallin, G., *Valrörelser och valresultat. Andrakammarvalen i Sverige 1866–1884* (Sth.: Christophers, 1961).
Wandruszka, A., 'Österreichs politische Struktur' in H. Benedikt, *Geschichte der Republik Österreich* (Vienna: Verl. für Geschichte und Politik, 1952).
Ward, R. E. & D. A. Rustow (eds.) *Political modernization of Japan and Turkey* (Princeton: Princeton Univ. Press. 1964).
Webster, R. A., *The cross and the fasces* (Stanford: Stanword Univ. Press, 1960).
Weibull, Jörgen, Unpublished report, 1964.
Weiner, M., 'Participation and integration: crises of the political process', draft 1965.
Westerath, H., *Die Wahlverfahren und ihre Vereinbarkeit mit den demokratischen Anforderungen an das Wahlrecht* (Berlin: Gruyter, 1955).
Westergaard, H., *Contributions to the history of statistics* (Lond.: King, 1932).
Westerståhl, J. & B. Särlvik, *Svensk valrörelse* 1956 (Göteborg: Statsvetenskapliga Institutionen, 1957).
Westerståhl, J. & C.-G. Janson, *Politisk press* (Gothenburg: Political Science Institute, 1959).
Whiting, J. W., 'The cross-cultural method', in G. Lindzey (ed.) *Handbook of social psychology*, vol. I (Cambr.: Cambr. Univ. Press, 1954).
Whiting, B. B. (ed.) *Six cultures: studies in child rearing* (N. Y.: Wiley, 1963).
Whiting, J. W. M. *et al.*, *Field guide for a study of socialization* (N. Y.: Wiley, 1966).
Wigmore, J. H., *The Australian ballot system* (Boston: Boston Book Co., 1889).
Williamson, C., *American suffrage: from property to democracy, 1760–1860* (Princeton: Princeton Univ. Press, 1960).
Woodhouse, C. E. & H. J. Tobias, 'Primordial ties and political process in pre-revolutionary Russia: The case of the Jewish *Bund*', *Comp. Stud. Soc. Hist.* 8, 1966: 331–60.

Woodward, 1948.   Woodward, J. *et al., Where stands freedom? A report
                         of the findings of an international survey of public
                         opinion* (N. Y.: Time Inc., 1948).
Woodward, 1950.   Woodward, J. & E. Roper, 'Political activity of Ame-
                         rican citizens', *Am. Pol. Sci. Rev.* 44, 1950.
Wright, 1958.   Wright, C. R. & H. H. Hyman, 'Voluntary association
                         memberships of American adults', *Am. Sociol. Rev.*
                         23 (3) 1958: 284–94.
Wrigley, 1966.   Wrigley, E. A. (ed.) *An introduction to English
                         historical demography. From the sixteenth to the nine-
                         teenth centuries* (Lond.: Weidenfeld, 1966).
Young, 1958.   Young, M., *The rise of the meritocracy* (Lond.: Tha-
                         mes & Hudson, 1958).
Zapf, 1965.   Zapf, W., *Wandlungen der deutschen Elite* (Munich:
                         Liper, 1965).
Zapf, 1969.   Zapf, W., *Materialen zur Theorie des sozialen Wan-
                         dels* (forthcoming 1969).
Zetterberg, 1960.   Zetterberg, H., 'Voluntary associations and organized
                         power', *Industria International,* 1960.
Zwager, 1958.   Zwager, H. H., *De motivering van het algemeen kies-
                         recht en Europa: Eeen historische studie* (Groningen:
                         Wolters, 1958).

Index

Adorno, T. W., 335
Alford, R., 285
Allardt, Erik, 9, 243
Almond, G. A., 15, 18, 29, 47, 60–67, 70
Almond-Verba five-country study, 278–283, 289–290
Andrae, C.-G., 68
Andrae, P. G., 162
Argentina, 179
Attitudes
– authoritarian, 335–351
– intolerant, 340–344, 347
– nationalist, 344–347
– to international conflict, 314–323
Australia, 153, 163, 171, 240, 245
Austria
– electoral data, 179
– electoral system, 88
– *Lager*, 135, 144
– nation-building, 80, 83
– party system, 92–93, 111, 129, 135–136
– suffrage, 84–87, 150–151
Authoritarianism, 334–335
– F-scale, 276, 336–351
– age differences, 350–351
– differences between parties, 337–339
– religious differences, 349
– working class authoritarianism, 351

Belgium
– electoral system, 88, 157
– nation-building, 81, 124
– party system, 94–95, 121, 125, 135–136
– secret voting, 153
– suffrage, 33, 83–86, 149
Bendix, Reinhood, 48, 52
Bismarck, 31, 150
Britain (see also Scotland, Wales)
– class voting, 331, 333
– electoral data, 171
– electoral research, 243–244
– electoral system, 76, 156, 163, 165, 166–167
– nation-building, 52–60, 80

– parliamentary rule, 91
– party membership, 360–361
– party system, 99–100, 107–108, 115–117, 128, 131, 138, 300
  – compared to Dutch, 117
  – compared to Scandinavian, 106, 120, 240–242
– politicization of local elections, 247
– secret voting (Ballot Act), 34–36, 153
– suffrage, 31–36, 82–86, 149
– television, 429–431
– turnout, 21
Brouwer, Marten, 292
Buchanan, W., 266–267

Camelot scandal, 264
Campbell, Angus, 9, 17, 175
Canadian party system, 91
Cantril, Hadley, 44, 266–267, 284, 292
Celtic fringe, 100, 241
Center for Advanced Study in the Behavioral Sciences, Stanford, 9
China, 50
Citizenship
– equalization, standardization (*unit citizen*) 27, 152–154
– immediacy of State-citizen contact, 28–29, 35
Cleavage model, 57–60, 97–99, 114–116, 130–138
Community power, 40–43
Comparisons: orders of, 21–25
Comparative cross-national research
– aggregate national data, 20–21, 49, 60, 65–68, 176
– ecological data, 20–21
– elite data, 68–69, 71
– institutional data, 49, 60
– statistical standardization, 170
– survey data, 252, 260, 266–292
Condorcet, Marquis de, 162
Converse, Philip, 140
Crises of development, 61–67, 176

Dahl, Robert, 44, 415
Data archives, 48, 68–71, 288–290